BRUCE L. SHELLEY

Revised by R. L. Hatchett

CHURCH HISTORY

IN PLAIN LANGUAGE

UPDATED 4th EDITION

THOMAS NELSON
Since 1798

NASHVILLE   DALLAS   MEXICO CITY   RIO DE JANEIRO

© 2008, 2013 by Bruce L. Shelley

Published in Nashville, Tennessee, by Thomas Nelson. Thomas Nelson is a registered trademark of HarperCollins Christian Publishing, Inc.

Typesetting by Rainbow Graphics, Kingsport, Tennessee.

Thomas Nelson titles may be purchased in bulk for educational, business, fund-raising, or sales promotional use. For information, please e-mail SpecialMarkets@ThomasNelson.com.

ISBN: 978-1-4016-7631-5

The Library of Congress has catalogued the earlier edition of this book as follows:

Library of Congress cataloging-in-publication-data
Shelley, Bruce L. (Bruce Leon), 1927–
Church history in plain language, 3rd edition
Includes bibliographies and index.
ISBN 978-0-7180-2553-3
1. Church history—Popular works. I. Title.

Printed in the United States of America

*To my students in Church History classes who
pressed the question of significance.*

M MONGROO

CONTENTS

FOREWORD

THIS BOOK EXECUTED A noble purpose: to lead evangelical readers to engage their own story and to encounter the larger Christian world. The book is successful because of Bruce Shelley, who brought many gifts to the project. He brought his good character and concern for the church, his historian's training and eye, his vivid prose for both conversation and narrative, and his years of effective classroom experience.

The book is widely and warmly received because of his discipline. He kept his focus on a popular audience, maintaining the straightforward, plain language he promised. He was selective in ways I am sure were painful for a person of his historical training. He did not seek some comprehensive goal but elected to tell representative stories that might still give the reader a sense of the larger whole. For the most part, each of the stories can be read independently. He did not distract his reader with citations. Curious readers or students could find the references in the endnotes for each chapter and general indebtedness in the suggested reading sections at the end of each chapter. I have followed his informal style, adding endnotes and marking my own new recommendations for books with asterisks.

It is an honor to be entrusted with updating the work. There are minor alterations throughout, but I wished to honor Shelley's personal imprint upon every page. I have added information concerning Gnosticism and its ongoing relevance, the theology of the early church and Reformation, and most extensively the rapid global extension and transformation of Christianity since 1900 (in 3 new chapters). Recent history is always vexing, but I have attempted to address the surprising circumstance of Christianity in both the West and Global South. Addressing the new shape of Christianity requires explanation as much as merely retelling its many stories.

A word about numbers and nomenclature is necessary, and perhaps most important for the reader. Descriptions like "Global South" and "majority world" are inevitably problematic. Without intent to offend or make a point, I use common but unsatisfactory terms because better terms have not been commonly accepted. The "West" is North America, England, and Western Europe. The "Global South" refers to the Third World, counting South America, Africa, and Asia, and includes places such as China that are above the equator. Similar frustration exists with the Western point of reference in terms like "Far East" and "Middle East." Perhaps a discerning student will point a better way forward. I hope, however, no reader will miss the point that American evangelicals need a larger frame of reference to participate in the great kingdom work flourishing in the world today. I usually cite modest numbers from established sources but believe these are typically under-reported. I watched my friend, the late Walter Lumpkin, attempt to account for non-denominational church life in Houston, Texas. The experience impressed me that mainline churches count well, but the most vital people to count are the ones we miss altogether.

Several students deserve mention for help in typing or research: Jimmy Parks, Ashley Ashcraft, Karl Russell, and Joel Burdeaux. Jim Denison, Daniel Vestal, Pete Sanchez, and Randy Richards, friends with significant experience in the wider world, have offered fruitful conversation about the project. Thanks to David Capes and Heather McMurray of Thomas Nelson who recruited me to the project, and to Maleah Bell who patiently saw it to completion. Thanks most of all to my wife Debbie. She assisted with some typing, good judgment, and a keen eye. She contributes to anything I do well.

R. L. Hatchett
Professor of Theology and Philosophy
Houston Baptist University

PROLOGUE

FOR YEARS I KEPT a cartoon on my study door. Students who stopped to read it often stepped into my office smiling. It encouraged easy conversation. It was a *Peanuts* strip. Charlie Brown's little sister Sally is writing a theme for school titled, "Church History." Charlie, who is at her side, notices her introduction, "When writing about church history, we have to go back to the very beginning. Our pastor was born in 1930." Charlie can only roll his eyes toward the ceiling.

Many Christians today suffer from historical amnesia. The time between the apostles and their own day is one giant blank. That is hardly what God had in mind. The Old Testament is sprinkled with reminders of God's interest in time. When he established the Passover for the children of Israel, he said, "Tell your son . . . it will be like a sign . . . that the Lord brought us out of Egypt" (Ex. 13:8, 16, NIV). And when he provided the manna in the wilderness, he commanded Moses to keep a jar of it "for the generations to come" (Ex. 16:33, NIV).

As a consequence of our ignorance concerning Christian history, we find believers vulnerable to the appeals of cultists. Some distortion of Christianity is often taken for the real thing. At the same time other Christians reveal a shocking capacity for spiritual pride, *hubris*. Without an adequate base for comparisons they spring to the defense of their way as the best way, their party as the superior party. Finally, many Christians engage in some form of ministry without the advantage of a broader context for their labor. When they want to make the best use of their time or their efforts, they have no basis for sound judgment.

I am not suggesting that one book surveying our Christian past will refute all error, make the reader a humble saint, or plot a strategy for effective ministry. But any introduction to Christian history tends to separate the transient from the permanent, fads from basics. That is my hope for this book among my readers.

The book is designed for laypeople. We all know that term is made of wax; we can twist it to suit our own tastes. After four decades of teaching first-year seminarians, I have concluded that college graduates entering the ministry and an engineer or salesman who reads five books a year are members of the same reading public. For my purposes here, both are *laypeople.*

In preparation for classes a professor digests hundreds of books and accumulates thousands of quotations. In this survey volume I have borrowed freely from the ideas and descriptions of others, while working with a simple aim: keep the story moving. I have tried to corral all of these resources and list the most helpful books at the end of each chapter and my major quotations at the end of the book.

From years of teaching I have also concluded that clarity is the first law of learning. So the divisions of the subject are all here. We call them *ages* because the conditions of the church's life change. Great eras, I know, do not suddenly appear like some unknown comet in the skies. In every age we find residue of the past and germs of the future. But if the reader wants to get the plot of the story, all he or she has to do is to read the paragraphs on the title pages of the major divisions.

This device was important for unity, I felt, because each chapter is arranged in a certain way. Only one issue appears in each. The reader can find it, in the form of a question, after an introduction to the chapter. The introduction is usually some anecdote from the time. This means that each chapter is almost self-contained and could be read in isolation, almost like an encyclopedia article on the subject.

Taking this issues approach admittedly leaves plenty of gaps in the story. Some readers will wonder why certain important people or events are not included. But this approach has the advantage of showing to the layperson the contemporary significance of church history. Many of today's issues are not unique. They have a link with the past.

Finally, some readers may wonder about the amount of biographical material. Why so many personal stories? Again, the answer is communication. Without ignoring ideas, I have tried to wrap thoughts in personalities, because I assume most readers are interested in meeting other people.

Church historians often ask, "Is the church a movement or an institution?" These pages will show that I think it is both. So I have talked about missionary expansion as well as papal politics. Professionals in the field may not be happy with my failure to set limits by a strict definition of the term *church*. But that fuzziness is due to the fact that I believe the people of God in history live in a tension between an ideal—the universal communion of saints—and the specific—the particular people in a definite time and place. The church's mission in time calls for institutions: special rules, special leaders, special places. But when institutions themselves obstruct the spread of the gospel rather than advancing it, then movements of renewal arise to return to the church's basic mission in the world. These pages will illustrate how often that has happened.

For the third edition I had my share of helpers. Daniel Hallock, a student friend and master of the World Wide Web, supplemented my research, especially for chapter 49, with dozens of articles from that mystical realm called *the Internet*. My colleague David Buschart, author of *Exploring Protestant Traditions*, contributed scores of titles for our updated Suggested Reading lists in addition to helpful dialogue about the emerging churches. Finally, Scott Wenig, my colleague and successor, added other new titles to the reading lists, vigorous discussion, and the foreword for this edition. I am deeply grateful for all three.

Bruce L. Shelley

THE AGE OF JESUS AND THE APOSTLES

6 BC–AD 70

Christianity's roots go back into Jewish history long before the birth of Jesus Christ. It was Jesus of Nazareth, however, who attacked established Judaism and brought a renewal movement into history's light early in the first century. After his crucifixion under Pontius Pilate, a Roman official, Jesus' teachings spread throughout the Mediterranean area. An apostle named Paul was especially influential. He stressed God's gift of salvation for all men and thus led in Christianity's emergence from Palestinian Judaism to a position as a universal religion.

The Age of Jesus and the Apostles

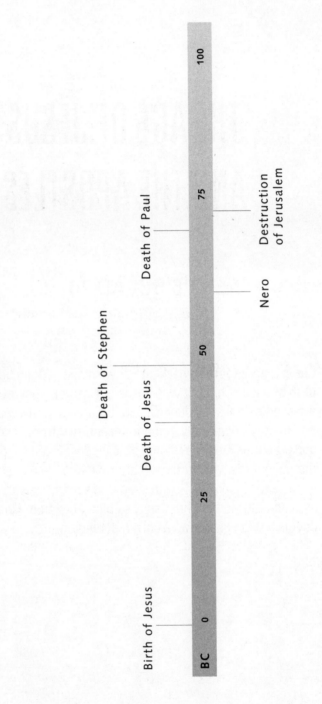

Birth of Jesus

Death of Jesus

Death of Stephen

Death of Paul

Nero

Destruction of Jerusalem

BC

0

25

50

75

100

CHAPTER 1

AWAY WITH THE KING!

The Jesus Movement

Christianity is the only major religion to have as its central event the humiliation of its God.

> "Dear dying Lamb," believers sing,
> "thy precious Blood
> Shall never lose its power,
> Till all the ransomed Church of God
> Be saved to sin no more."

Crucifixion was a barbarous death, reserved for agitators, pirates, and slaves. Jewish law cursed "everyone who hangs on a tree" and the Roman statesman, Cicero, warned, "Let the very name of the cross be far, not only from the body of a Roman citizen, but even from his thoughts, his eyes, his ears."

Part of the victim's punishment was to be whipped and then to carry the heavy crossbeam to the place of his own death. When the cross was raised, a notice was pinned to it giving the culprit's name and crime. In Jesus' case, INRI: *Iesus Nazarenus Rex Iudaeorum* (Jesus of Nazareth, King of the Jews).

Pontius Pilate, Jesus' Roman judge, apparently intended it as a final thrust of malice aimed at the Jews, but, like the cross itself, Jesus' followers found a special meaning in the message.

JESUS AND THE CHURCH

Jesus was a Jew. He came from a Jewish family; he studied the Jewish scriptures; he observed the Jewish religion. Any serious study of

3

his life makes this so clear that many people have asked if Jesus ever intended to create that company of followers we call the church. Albert Schweitzer, the famous missionary to Africa, believed that Jesus was obsessed with a dream of the impending end of the world and died to make the dream come true. Rudolf Bultmann, an influential German theologian, taught that Jesus was a prophet who challenged people to make a radical decision for or against God. Other Christians have held that Jesus' kingdom was a brotherhood of love and forgiveness. If he founded a society at all, they say, it was an invisible one, a moral or spiritual company—not an institution with rites and creeds.

This anti-institutional view of Christianity is so widespread that we had better face the question straightaway. Did Jesus have anything to do with the formation of the Christian church? And if he did, how did he shape its special character?

The gospel writers picture Jesus as retracing the steps of Israel. Reminiscent of Israel, Jesus spent time in Egypt, entered the Jordan (baptism), was tempted in the wilderness, called twelve apostles (like twelve tribes), spoke God's word like Moses (Sermon on the Mount), preached five sermons (compare the Pentateuch) in Matthew, performed mighty deeds of deliverance (signs, wonders, and exorcisms), and confronted imperial powers. Where Israel had failed, Jesus had been a faithful Son. His followers were to take up the task of being God's servant people. He worked with a faithful band of disciples, he taught them about life in what he called "the kingdom of God," and he introduced them to the new covenant that bound them together in forgiveness and love.

Granted, that simple company lacked many of the laws, officials, ceremonies, and beliefs of later Christendom, but it was a society apart. Jesus made a persistent point about the special kind of life that separated the kingdom of God from rival authorities among men. Little by little his disciples came to see that following him meant saying no to the other voices calling for their loyalties. In one sense that was the birth of the Jesus movement. And in that sense, at least, Jesus "founded" the church.

PALESTINE IN JESUS' DAY

During the days of Jesus, Palestine never lacked for loyalties. It was a crossroads of culture and peoples. Its two million or more people, ruled by Rome, were divided by region, religion, and politics. "In a day's journey a man could travel from rural villages where farmers tilled their fields with primitive plows to bustling cities where men enjoyed the comforts of Roman civilization. In the Holy City of Jerusalem, Jewish priests offered sacrifices to the Lord of Israel, while at Sebaste, only thirty miles away, pagan priests held rites in honor of the Roman god Jupiter."

The Jews, who represented only half the population, despised their foreign overlords and deeply resented the signs of pagan culture in their ancient homeland. The Romans were not just another in a long series of alien conquerors. They were representatives of a hated way of life. Their imperial reign brought to Palestine the Hellenistic (Greek) culture that the Syrians had tried to impose forcibly on the Jews over a century before. All the children of Abraham despised their overlords; they simply disagreed about how to resist them.

Centuries earlier the prophets of Israel had promised a day when the Lord would deliver his people from their pagan rulers and establish his kingdom over the whole earth. On that day, they said, he would send an anointed ruler, a messiah, to bring an end to the corrupt world of the present and replace it with an eternal paradise. He would raise the dead and judge their actions in this world. The wicked would be punished, but the righteous would be rewarded with eternal life in the kingdom of God.

According to the book of Daniel and other popular Jewish writings, the Lord's kingdom would be established only after a final cosmic struggle between the forces of evil, led by Satan, and the forces of good, led by the Lord. It would end with the destruction of the existing world order and the creation of a kingdom without end (Dan. 7:13–22). This belief, along with ideas about the resurrection of the dead and the last judgment, was in Jesus' day very much a part of popular Jewish faith.

Out of the distaste for life under the Romans, several factions arose among the Jews, each interpreting the crisis in a different way. The Jesus movement was one of them.

One group, the *Pharisees*, emphasized those Jewish traditions and practices that set them apart from pagan culture. Their name means *separated ones*, and they prided themselves on their strict observance of every detail of the Jewish law and their extreme intolerance of people whom they considered ritually unclean. This piety and patriotism won respect among the people.

On the other hand, some Jews found Roman rule a distinct advantage. Among them were members of Jerusalem's aristocracy. From this small group of wealthy, pedigreed families came the high priest and the lesser priests who controlled the temple. Many of them enjoyed the sophisticated manners and fashions of Greco-Roman culture. Some even took Greek names. Their interests were represented by the conservative political group known as the *Sadducees*. At the time of Jesus, these men still controlled the high Jewish council, or Sanhedrin, but they had less influence among the common people. Another party, · the *Zealots*, were bent on armed resistance to all Romans in the fatherland. They looked back two centuries to the glorious days of the Maccabees when religious zeal combined with a ready sword to overthrow the pagan Greek overlords. Thus the hills of Galilee often concealed a number of guerrilla bands ready to ignite a revolt or destroy some symbol of Roman authority in Palestine.

Finally came the *Essenes*, who had little or no interest in politics or in warfare. Instead, they withdrew in protest to the Judean wilderness, believing the temple of Judaism to be hopelessly compromised. There, in isolated monastic communities, they studied the Scriptures and prepared themselves for the Lord's kingdom, which they believed would dawn at any moment.

Scholars typically identify the Essenes as the occupants of the Quran community who copied ancient manuscripts and wrote commentaries. These documents, called the Dead Sea Scrolls, were discovered in 1946.

Jesus had to call for the loyalty of his followers without confusing the purpose of his mission with the objectives of these other parties among the Jews. It was a tough assignment.

Judaism Now and Then

The Pharisees' version of first-century Judaism has survived and evolved to become the Rabbinic Judaism we know today. The destruction of the temple in AD 70 changed the character of Judaism. The Roman resolve to quash revolutionary movements made the Zealots (a protest seeking political revolution) and the Essenes (a protest seeking purity) impracticable.

The Sadducees were the aristocratic power brokers who operated the temple, and they saw their vision of Judaism vanish with the temple's destruction. The destiny of Judaism was left to the "book people" (the Pharisees), who sought to direct the entirety of their lives by the instructions of the Hebrew Scriptures. The Pharisees' book-oriented version survived once the temple was destroyed and Roman power silenced revolutionary voices.

JESUS' MINISTRY

Jesus chose to begin by recognizing a new movement in the Judean wilderness led by a prophet named John. The ford of the Jordan, just north of the Dead Sea, was one of the busiest parts of the whole region, so John the Baptist got the crowds he wanted to hear him. Wearing a garment of camel's hair, his eyes ablaze, he stood on the riverbank and warned all who passed by to repent of their sins and prepare for the coming day of judgment by receiving baptism in the Jordan. Israel first entered the land by crossing the Jordan; Jesus began his ministry at this pivotal place.

Many thought John was the promised Messiah, but he vehemently denied any such role. He explained his mission in the words of the prophet Isaiah: "The voice of one crying in the wilderness: Prepare the way of the Lord, make his paths straight" (Matt. 3:3). He was, he claimed, only the forerunner of the Messiah. "I baptize you with water" he said, "but . . . he will baptize you with the Holy Spirit and with fire" (Luke 3:16).

John's call to repentance and righteousness drew Jesus to the Jordan. He found in John's message the truth of God, so "to fulfill all righteousness" he submitted to John's baptism and soon afterward began his own mission, proclaiming, "The time is fulfilled, and the kingdom of God is at hand; repent, and believe in the gospel" (Mark 1:15).

Jesus, however, rather than remaining in the desert, chose to begin his missionv in Galilee, a land of gentle hills and warm, green valleys. During those early weeks and months he traveled from village to village throughout Galilee, preaching in synagogues in the evening and on the Sabbath. Carrying a bundle of bread, a wineskin, and a walking stick, he hiked along the dusty highways. He probably dressed as any other traveler, in a rough linen tunic covered by a heavier red or blue mantle.

On a typical day Jesus would set out at dawn and walk mile after mile. Toward sunset he would enter a village and proceed to its synagogue. As one popular history puts it, "There he probably received a warm welcome from the townspeople, who often had no resident rabbi and relied on the services of wandering teachers like Jesus. When the lamps had been lit and the men of the village had taken their places, Jesus would seat himself on the raised central platform" and begin reading a passage from the sacred Scriptures. In a clear, forceful voice he would announce the fulfillment of some prophecy or relate some parable.

The main theme of Jesus' teaching was the kingdom of God. What did he mean by that? Did he believe in a dramatic intervention of God in the history of the world? Or did he mean that the kingdom is already here in some sense? He probably meant both. The two can be reconciled if we recognize that the phrase stands for the sovereignty of a personal and gracious God, not a geographical or local realm.

Jesus taught that the rule of God was already present in saving power in his own person. And he offered proof of the point. His miracles of healing were apparently not just marvels; they were *signs*, the powers of the age to come already manifest in the present age. "But if it is by the finger of God that I cast out demons," he once said, "then the kingdom of God has come upon you" (Luke 11:20). Yet he feared that his cures would be misinterpreted, that people would see him as just another magician, and he often cautioned those he healed to be silent.

Of course, the news spread, and before long people in every town and village in Galilee were talking excitedly of the new wonder-worker who could cure the blind, the lame, and the sick with the power of his voice and the mere touch of his strong carpenter's hands. Soon large crowds gathered wherever he spoke.

Jesus' growing popularity aroused controversy, especially among the Pharisees, who hated to see people following a man who had never studied under their learned scribes. They didn't hesitate to question his credentials openly.

JESUS' MESSAGE

Jesus welcomed their challenge for it gave him a chance to contrast his message of repentance and grace with the self-righteousness of the Pharisees.

On one occasion, probably as pilgrims were on their way to Jerusalem for one of the great feasts, Jesus told about two men who went to the temple to pray. What a striking contrast they made! One was a Pharisee; the other, surprisingly, was a despised tax collector.

With a touch of showmanship, the holy man took his stand and prayed, "God, I thank thee that I am not like other men, extortioners, unjust, adulterers, or even like this tax collector. I fast twice a week, I give tithes of all that I get" (Luke 18:11–12). That, at any rate, is what he prayed to himself, and it was not a hollow boast. Pharisees excelled in those works of righteousness—fasting and tithing—that set them apart from wicked men.

The fault of the prayer was in its spirit of self-righteousness and its cruel contempt for others. The Pharisee alone was righteous, and all his fellow mortals were included under one sweeping condemnation.

The tax collector believed he was religiously compromised. By working to collect taxes for the Romans, he broke faith with his own people. Sensing his own feeble religious standing, he stood at a distance, the very image of contrition. His eyes were downcast, his head bowed in guilt. His prayer was a sob of remorse, a cry for mercy: "God, be merciful to me a sinner!"

"I tell you," said Jesus, "this man went down to his house justified rather than the other" (Luke 18:14). The contrast between the piety of the Pharisees and the attitude of the Jesus movement could hardly be greater. One was based on the observance of the hundreds of religious laws of the Jews; the other rested upon a denial of self-righteousness and a trust in the mercy of God.

Out of his hundreds of followers Jesus called a handful to travel with him full time. They came to be called *apostles*, meaning *sent ones*. At first they were a rather motley group, twelve in all, drawn from fishing boats and tax tables, but their loyalty to Jesus was strong.

So for them Jesus drew the distinction between his kingdom and the kingdoms of the world. His followers, he said, represented another type of society and another type of greatness. In the kingdoms of this world, powerful leaders lord it over others; but God's kingdom is governed in a wholly different way, by love and service.

"Fear not," he told them, "it is your Father's good pleasure to give you the kingdom" (12:32).

The highwater mark of Jesus' popularity came about a year before his arrest in Jerusalem. After he fed over five thousand Passover pilgrims on a grassy hillside in Galilee, many of his disciples tried to proclaim him king. Jesus knew, however, that they had no idea of God's unfolding plan for his life—and death. So he fled to the hills with a committed few.

Jesus knew that he had a unique role in God's plan of redemption, but he feared the traditional titles for a messianic redeemer. Crowds were too likely to misunderstand them. The picture that appears in his teaching of the twelve is along the lines of Isaiah's portrait of the Suffering Servant, "despised and rejected by men . . . with his stripes we are healed" (Isa. 53:3, 5), and the image of Zechariah's predicted king who would be "humble and riding on an ass" (Zech. 9:9).

THE LAST WEEK

Apparently with these prophetic portraits in mind on the Sunday before his last Passover, Jesus rode into Jerusalem on a donkey in fulfillment of Zechariah's prediction. Crowds threw palm branches in his path and shouted, "Hosanna! Blessed is he who comes in the name of the Lord."

This seems to be the only occasion when Jesus openly identified himself with the Messiah of Jewish prophecies. He apparently intended to challenge the Jerusalem authorities to make up their minds: Would they or would they not accept the rule of his kingdom? The Holy City was stirred, asking, "Who is this?"

The next day Jesus led a procession through Jerusalem's teeming, narrow streets, to the temple. There, in an act of protest reminiscent of the Old Testament prophets, he "entered the temple of God and drove out all who sold and bought in the temple, and he overturned the tables of the money-changers, and the seats of those who sold pigeons. He said to them, 'It is written, "My house shall be called a house of prayer"; but you make it a den of robbers' " (Matt. 21:12–13).

News of this dramatic event quickly swept through Jerusalem and people began flocking to the temple, hoping to catch a glimpse of Jesus. Rumors spread of the appearance of the Messiah and the imminent destruction of the temple.

Such talk of a messiah alarmed the temple authorities. What if this Galilean were to ignite another revolt against the Roman government? Yet they were hesitant to arrest him for fear of provoking a riot.

A man like Jesus presented a real danger to the Sadducees, because they held their privileged position with the support of the Roman authorities. Anyone who aroused talk of a messiah undermined the people's allegiance to the established political order and endangered the relationship the Sadducees had with the Romans. Such a man, they concluded, had to be silenced before he sparked an uprising, which the Romans would crush with characteristic brutality. If that happened, the Sadducees stood to lose their privileges.

Thus their common fear of Jesus brought about an unusual alliance between the Sadducees and their rivals, the Pharisees. Jesus, who openly violated the Sabbath laws and questioned the validity of other laws, seemed to be undermining the authority of the Jewish religion. For their separate reasons, both parties saw this self-styled prophet from Galilee as a dangerous enemy, and together they concluded that he should be brought to trial and condemned to death.

The temple authorities found their opportunity among Jesus' closest followers. With the aid of Judas from Iscariot, one of the Twelve, they could arrest Jesus secretly without provoking a riot; so "they paid him thirty pieces of silver," nearly four months' wages for a skilled worker, providing he would lead them to Jesus.

THE NEW COVENANT

"The next day was the first day of the Jewish Passover, and Jesus and his disciples prepared for the ritual dinner that evening. At sundown they gathered secretly at the appointed place. Their mood was solemn as they ate the meal, commemorating the Exodus of the Jews from Egypt. Reclining on couches arranged around a low table, they drank wine and ate the bitter herbs and unleavened bread." Toward the end of the meal, Jesus took a piece of bread, gave thanks to God, broke it, and said, "This is my body which is given for you. Do this in remembrance of me" (Luke 22:19). In the same way he took a cup, saying, "This cup is the new covenant in my blood. Do this, as often as you drink it, in remembrance of me" (1 Cor. 11:25).

What did Jesus mean by this "new covenant"? The background, to be sure, was the Exodus from Egypt and the formation of Israel as a nation at Mount Sinai. But Jesus had in mind more than this reminder of the obvious.

He spoke of the new covenant in his own blood. His words were an echo of the prophet Jeremiah who had promised a day when the covenant on tablets of stone would be replaced by a covenant written on the hearts of men: "This is the covenant which I will make with the house of Israel after those days, says the LORD: I will put my law within them, and I will write it upon their hearts; and I will be their God, and they shall be my people . . . for I will forgive their iniquity, and I will remember their sin no more" (Jer. 31:33–34).

The time of the new covenant, said Jesus, has come. A new people of God, enjoying the forgiveness of sins, is now possible through the shedding of his own blood.

At that moment the disciples were undoubtedly as puzzled by his words as by his actions. But in a matter of weeks they would see all these final hours in a new, revealing light.

After the meal Jesus led the disciples to a familiar meeting place at the foot of the Mount of Olives, an olive grove known as Gethsemane. There was a full moon, and the grove was bathed in soft light. While the disciples slept, Jesus withdrew to pray: "My Father, if it be possible, let this cup pass from me; nevertheless, not as I will, but as thou wilt" (Matt. 26:39).

After renewing his commitment to God in prayer, Jesus aroused his sleeping disciples. "While he was still speaking, Judas came . . . and with him a great crowd with swords and clubs, from the chief priests and the elders" (Matt. 26:47). They seized Jesus and dragged him away to the palace of Caiaphas, the high priest, in the western section of Jerusalem.

THE TRIAL AND DEATH

Inside the splendidly appointed mansion, the Sanhedrin swept aside all tokens of justice and hastily secured two witnesses who testified against Jesus. The court charged him with blasphemy and voted to put him to death, but for that they were forced to turn to a despised Roman.

When the first rays of light appeared, the Jewish authorities led Jesus out of Caiaphas's palace and through the streets to the Antonia, a palace-fortress where the Roman governor, Pontius Pilate, was staying during the Passover. Since the Sanhedrin was not empowered to carry out the death sentence, the members had to present their case against Jesus to Pilate.

"A messenger entered the sumptuous chambers of the Antonia to summon Pilate, while the council members and their prisoner waited below in the paved courtyard of the fortress. A few minutes later the governor appeared. He wore a red toga draped over a white tunic in customary Roman fashion, the distinctive mark of a Roman citizen."

After asking about their purpose, the Roman governor pondered the situation. It seemed to him that the chief priests had approached him to settle a petty religious dispute, and to convict Jesus during the festival could surely spark at least a minor uprising. Yet if he ignored their accusations and this Galilean eventually proved to be a traitor to Rome, his own position would be endangered. Meanwhile a belligerent crowd had gathered outside the Antonia, clamoring for Pilate's decision. Fearful of offending Caesar, Pilate delivered Jesus to his soldiers for crucifixion.

When the execution party reached a hill outside Jerusalem called Golgotha, the soldiers stripped the clothes from Jesus and divided the garments among themselves as the crosses were assembled. "Each prisoner was then placed on his cross. Jesus suffered in silence as the soldiers nailed his wrists to the crosspiece with large iron spikes and drove another spike through both ankles. As they lifted his cross upright, his weight was supported by a peg jutting out from the cross between his legs." Then the soldiers fastened over the cross that sign describing his crime: "Jesus of Nazareth, King of the Jews."

"It was a slow and painful death. Jesus hung there helplessly for long hours as the hot sun beat down on his body and insects buzzed about his limbs. Curious passersby paused to watch his agony and to read the sign. Gradually he weakened, his body tortured by muscle cramps, hunger, and thirst." A small group of his despairing followers watched in silence as his life slipped away, a strange and revealing prelude to the history of Christianity.

As he grew weaker and weaker Jesus cried out, "It is finished," and yielded up his spirit. Within hours a friend, Joseph from Arimathea, carried Jesus' body into his own garden. There he had a tomb hewn out of a large rock. Inside near the rear of the tomb was a couch, also of stone, and Joseph gently placed the corpse upon it. Then he rolled a heavy stone across the entrance and went home.

Suggestions for Further Reading

Blomberg, Craig L. *Jesus and the Gospels: An Introduction and Survey*. Nashville: Broadman and Holman, 1997.

Drane, John. *Jesus and the Four Gospels*. New York: Harper and Row, 1979.

Reader's Digest Association. *Great People of the Bible and How They Lived*. Pleasantville: The Reader's Digest Association, 1974.

*Strauss, Mark. *Four Gospels, One Jesus: A Survey of Jesus and the Gospels*. Grand Rapids: Zondervan, 2007.

*Wright, Christopher. *The Mission of God's People: A Biblical Theology of the Church's Mission*. Grand Rapids: Zondervan, 2010.

Wright, N. T. *The New Testament and the People of God*. Minneapolis: Fortress, 1992.

Wright, N. T. *Jesus and the Victory of God: The Resurrection of the Son of God*. Minneapolis: Fortress, 1996.

CHAPTER 2

WINESKINS: OLD AND NEW

The Gospel to the Gentiles

THE SANHEDRIN HAD AN uprising on their hands and they knew it. They had barely escaped a riot by bringing Stephen, the agitator, before them. But what to do with him—that was the question.

The Jewish Council had little rest since the trial of Jesus. No one knew how to stop the spread of the Nazarene movement. Time and again the council had commanded them to stop their incessant jabbering about Jesus, but each time the Nazarenes grew bolder, even accusing the council of killing the Messiah.

Stephen, however, was a special case. He dared to renounce the law of Moses and attack the temple of God, openly and repeatedly. The angry men felt that Stephen had to be silenced. But how?

All eyes were upon Stephen as he began his defense. He spoke of Jewish history, but he argued that men might worship God apart from the temple. He traced the ways of God with his people from Abraham to Moses and showed that Moses prophesied the coming of Messiah saying, "God will send you a prophet like me from your own people" (Acts 7:37, NIV).

He also told how the Lord gave Moses the pattern of the tabernacle and how Solomon built the temple, but he quoted the prophet Isaiah to prove that the Most High does not dwell in temples made with hands:

Heaven is my throne,
   and the earth is my footstool.

14

Where is the house you will build for me?
Where will my resting place be?
Has not my hand made all these things . . . ? (Isa. 66:1–2, NIV).

The council stirred excitedly. But Stephen moved on boldly to the climax of his speech: "You stiff-necked people!" he cried. "You are just like your fathers: you always resist the Holy Spirit! Was there ever a prophet your fathers did not persecute? They even killed those who predicted the coming of the Righteous One. And now you have betrayed and murdered him—you, who have received the law . . . but have not obeyed it" (Acts 7:51–53, NIV).

Enough! Enough! The council was furious! They covered their ears as a mob rushed at Stephen. They dragged him out, through the streets, beyond the walls and stoned him again and again until all was silent.

CHRISTIANITY AND JUDAISM

That mob scene, including the trial and death of Stephen, the first Christian martyr, holds the answer to the question, how did Christianity emerge from its Jewish roots? How did a Jewish Messiah preaching a Jewish theme (the kingdom of God) to a Jewish following become the Savior of people everywhere?

The answer lies in Stephen's confrontation with the Jewish authorities. It centered upon the interpretation of the Old Testament. The encounter with Jesus prompted the early believers to examine the Old Testament anew. They discovered in the Old Testament documents a greater and comprehensive message for the entire world that Israel had failed to embrace. God had promised Abraham long ago that all the peoples of the world would find their blessing in him (Gen. 12:3). While Jesus appealed to the lost sheep of Israel, his scope was greater.

The experts in the Jewish Scriptures, the Scribes and Pharisees, believed the Old Testament presented the law of God for his special people, the Jews. The law began with the Ten Commandments, but it also provided instruction for every area of life, worship, and piety. Stephen, however, disagreed—and said so. He insisted that the institutions of Jewish life, the law and the temple, were temporary. God intended them to point beyond themselves to the coming Messiah, who would fulfill all righteousness for all people. The Old Testament's central purpose was to promise the Messiah. And he has come, said Stephen. Jesus is his name. We know this because the events surrounding Jesus' crucifixion give clear evidence of the hand of God.

Resurrection Faith

Critics argue that the followers of Jesus were desperate to be with Jesus and were filled with a longing hope; dejected followers worked themselves into a series of hallucinations, some even group hallucinations. Critics reason that resurrection faith or hope of the believers produced the encounters or visions of the risen Jesus. But the first-century evidence points in the opposite direction. Despite all the remarkable things the followers of Jesus had witnessed him do, they concluded that Jesus was one more messiah whom the Romans executed. The disciples were defeated. Not even the empty tomb provoked them to conclude that Jesus was alive; the risen Jesus had to confront them to awaken resurrection faith. Encounters with the risen Jesus prompted resurrection faith, not vice versa.

How could Stephen say that? The crucifixion had sent Jesus' apostles into hiding, confused and fearful. Their hopes for the kingdom in Israel had vanished in the darkness that had enveloped the cross.

Early on Sunday morning some of the women claimed they had seen Jesus alive. And upon checking the grave, several of the disciples had indeed found it empty. Some of the apostles, however, remained skeptical until an encounter with the risen Jesus convinced them all that he was indeed raised from the dead. During one of these appearances in Galilee, Jesus told the disciples to gather in Jerusalem and to wait there until they were baptized with the Holy Spirit a few days later.

PENTECOST

When they returned to the Holy City to join the other pilgrims for the celebration of Pentecost, seven weeks after Jesus' crucifixion, excitement among them was running high. During the festival about 120 disciples were meeting in a home, when suddenly God's Spirit fell upon those gathered there. Some thought that it was a violent wind rushing through the house; others testified to a tongue-like flame of fire resting on each of them.

Swept up in the experience, they rushed into the streets and headed for the temple. Many of the visitors in the city saw them and followed because they heard their native tongue coming from the lips of the disciples.

Tongue Speaking or *Glossolalia*

Christians have disagreed about the nature of tongue speaking. Some say it is an ability to deliver a message in a language without ever having studied or learned the language. This ability is given by the Holy Spirit and provides God's message in the listener's language even though the speaker usually does not understand that language.

Others say that tongue speaking is ecstatic speech. This series of sounds does not represent a spoken human language. If this is the nature of tongue speaking, then the book of Acts would not picture a language miracle (giving the speaker the ability to speak a foreign language) but a hearing miracle (granted to the listeners, enabling them to understand). Although ecstatic speech was being spoken, the listener heard or understood in his or her own language.

Once at the temple Peter, one of Jesus' apostles, stood before the huge crowd and told them that the miracle they were witnessing was a fulfillment of the prophet Joel's promise about the outpouring of God's Spirit in the "last days." The explanation for the marvel, he said, lay in the recent crucifixion of Jesus of Nazareth. God had made him Lord and Messiah by raising him from the dead!

Peter's announcement of the resurrection was an astounding development. How could he ever substantiate such a claim? He appealed to the Jewish Scriptures, which said that the Messiah would not be abandoned in death but would be enthroned at God's right hand until universal victory was his (Ps. 16:10; 110:1).

But what do such Scriptures have to do with Jesus of Nazareth? "He was the Messiah," said Peter. "We know it is so, because God raised him from the dead and we are all witnesses of the fact" (Acts 2:32).

From the beginning, then, the apostles preached the resurrection of Jesus as the fulfillment of God's purpose announced in the Old Testament. The Messiah, once crucified, was exalted above the universe. Apart from that miracle, said the apostles, there is no gospel, no salvation, and no church. But it is true. Therefore, "Repent," Peter told the Pentecost pilgrims, "and be baptized in the name of Jesus and your sins will be forgiven and you too will receive the gift of the Spirit" (Acts 2:38).

Many accepted Peter's invitation. They were baptized and about three thousand were added to the Jesus movement that day. That is how the Christian church started.

It was quite a beginning. Stephen knew the story well and Christians ever since have insisted that the death of Jesus on the cross, his resurrection from the grave, and the empowering mission of the Holy Spirit are the foundational realities of Christianity. The first forty years saw the infant church spread at a phenomenal rate. It sprang up in most of the major cities in the Roman Empire and was transformed from a tiny Jewish sect into a fellowship of many different peoples.

Stephen, of course, never lived to see it. Yet he grasped first of all the special meaning of Jesus' crucifixion, resurrection, and outpouring of the Spirit for biblical history. He sensed deeply that Christianity could never be confined to the rigid boundaries of the Pharisees' laws.

Jesus himself had hinted that a breach would open. Once, when asked why his disciples did not fast like the Pharisees, he said, "Men [do not] pour new wine into old wineskins. If they do, the skins will burst, the wine will run out and the wineskins will be ruined. No, they pour new wine into new wineskins, and both are preserved" (Matt. 9:17, NIV). The most important development in first-century Christianity was the rip in the old wineskins.

THE FIRST COMMUNITY

No one doubted that the first company of believers was Jewish. It included Jesus' mother, Mary, and some other kinsmen, along with the apostles: Peter, James and John, Andrew, Philip, Thomas, Bartholomew, Matthew, James son of Alphaeus, Simon the Zealot, and Judas, son of James. They chose a disciple named Matthias to become the twelfth apostle, replacing Judas Iscariot, who had committed suicide soon after the crucifixion.

Since the whole company was devoutly Jewish, they remained loyal, for a time, to their Jewish law and continued to worship in synagogues and at the temple. In all outward respects their lifestyle resembled any other Jewish sect of the time. The disciples called their new movement "The Way," emphasizing their belief that Jesus would lead his followers to the kingdom of God. Before long, however, the Jerusalem community came to speak of itself by an Old Testament term used to refer to the assembly of Israel. The Greek equivalent was *ekklesia* (or *church* in English) and meant a gathering of people, God's people.

Despite their outward conformity to Jewish religion and their use of the Jewish Scriptures, the disciples sensed that the resurrection of Jesus and the coming of the Spirit at Pentecost had made them something unique—a new wineskin?

Shortly after Pentecost the temple authorities, uneasy about the preaching of Jesus' resurrection, arrested Peter and the other eleven apostles. They futilely threatened the church's leaders not to proclaim Jesus' resurrection. Despite this the followers of Jesus attended temple services regularly and strictly observed Jewish laws and rituals. They showed no signs of rejecting the law of Moses or the authority of the temple. Within two years their ranks had grown to several thousand.

Under the leadership of the apostles, the fledgling movement maintained its unity by two special ceremonies that kept the reality of Jesus' death and resurrection at the center of their fellowship.

The first, baptism, was familiar to them because many of the early disciples had followed the ministry of John the Baptist. But baptism in the apostolic community was different. John's baptism was a way of professing faith in a kingdom yet to come. Baptism in the infant church was what theologians now call *eschatological*. It marked entrance into a spiritual kingdom already proclaimed, though still to be revealed in its fullness.

These first Christians came to believe that the death, burial, and resurrection of Jesus, followed by the coming of the Spirit at Pentecost, were divine events. They inaugurated a new age, and people could enter life in that spiritual kingdom by faith in Jesus as Lord and witness to that faith by baptism.

In a similar way the second ceremony, the Lord's Supper as it was soon called, looked back to Jesus' betrayal and death and found in the events of Calvary and the empty tomb evidence of the new covenant promised by the prophet Jeremiah. Jesus' death and the new life in the Spirit were symbolized and sealed to the congregation of disciples in their drinking from the cup and eating the consecrated bread. This simple meal renewed their covenant with God and with one another.

THE HELLENISTS

Bound together, then, by the teaching of the apostles and the two ceremonies depicting the death and resurrection of their Lord, the infant church spread throughout Judea. This rapid growth, however, aroused new fears in the authorities and created tensions within the church. More and more of the converts were recruited from among Hellenist Jews. These were Jews who had come to Jerusalem from all parts of the Roman Empire to settle in the Holy City. Many of them had come on pilgrimages, then decided to remain permanently. Like immigrants everywhere, they lived in separate communities. They spoke Greek and used a common Greek translation of the Old Testament called the Septuagint.

The Hellenistic Jews were faithful to their religion, but in the world beyond Palestine—Egypt, Asia Minor, Europe—they had long been exposed to Greek culture. They mixed more easily with Gentiles and were more responsive to new ideas than were their Palestinian cousins.

At first the apostles welcomed to the church the Hellenists who believed in Jesus. The spirit of oneness was marred, however, by a growing rivalry between Palestinian and Hellenist members. Some of the Hellenist believers complained that their widows were overlooked in the church welfare program. In an attempt to remove these resentments, the apostles created a council of seven Hellenist disciples, among them Stephen and Philip, to oversee the distributions. These men may have been the first to occupy an office called elsewhere *deacon* (in Greek, *diakonoi*), meaning *servant* or *minister.*

Before long, however, Stephen began preaching in Jerusalem's Hellenist synagogues. That touched off the riot that led to his death. It proved to be only the beginning. Groups of vigilantes began to seize and imprison suspected Nazarenes. One of the vigilante leaders was a zealous Pharisee named Saul of Tarsus.

This first Christian bloodletting, in about AD 36, marked the widening chasm between Judaism and Christianity and turned the young faith into a missionary movement. Though the Hebrew apostles were not molested, the Hellenist disciples were forced to flee Jerusalem. They found refuge in Samaria and in Syria, where they founded Christian communities. Other unnamed Hellenist Christians founded churches at Damascus, Antioch and Tarsus in Syria, on the island of Cyprus, and in Egypt.

News of the churches among the Hellenists filtered back to the Holy City, and the Christian elders in Jerusalem soon sent delegates to establish ties with the new Christian centers. Peter and John went to Samaria to confer with Philip. Barnabas, a Jew from Cyprus who was among the earliest Jerusalem converts, traveled to Antioch in Syria. There unnamed "men of Cyprus and Cyrene" had founded a successful Christian movement by taking the revolutionary step of evangelizing Gentiles.

Antioch was the administrative capital of the Roman province of Syria. With a population of half a million, it was also the third largest city in the empire, after Rome and Alexandria. As a busy cosmopolitan center, its racially mixed population was overwhelmingly Gentile, but there was also a large Jewish community. At Antioch, for the first time, Jesus' followers were called *Christians.* Originally, opponents of the church used the term as a derogatory label for the "devotees of the Anointed One" (in Greek, *Christianoi*). But the believers soon adopted it gladly.

Thus Antioch grew in Christian influence. In time it succeeded Jerusalem as the center of missionary outreach. This was due in large part to the work of Saul of Tarsus, who joined Barnabas there about AD 44.

THE APOSTLE PAUL

No man—other than Jesus, of course—has shaped Christianity more than Saul (or, as Christians came to say, Paul, a name more familiar to the ear of Greek-speaking people). No one did more for the faith, but no one seemed less likely.

When Stephen had crumpled to the ground, bleeding from the stones thrown by his enraged accusers, Saul had stood nearby as leader of the attack upon the Nazarenes. How, he asked, could anyone profess to follow a crucified Messiah? Almost by definition the Messiah is one upon whom the blessing of God rests in a unique way. What fool can believe that crucifixion is a blessing from God?

Saul found the answer to that question when he confronted the Lord one day outside Damascus. He dropped to the ground blinded by a light and he heard a voice: "Saul, Saul, why are you persecuting me?" Soon after Stephen's argument fell into place, and Saul became a believer.

He later explained that the law pronounces a curse on everyone who fails to keep it in its entirety, so all who hope to gain God's favor by keeping the law are exposed to a curse. Fortunately, God provided a way of escape. "Christ redeemed us from the curse of the law by becoming a curse for us," by hanging on a cross (Gal. 3:10–14, NIV).

Stephen, then, was right. The law of God was given for a time to convince men of their inability to fulfill the will of God and to leave them with no option except to embrace the good news of Jesus Christ's death and resurrection.

That was strong medicine for Judaism. The authorities wanted no part of it. So the persecutor of Christians became the persecuted among Christians. He was, however, a leader uniquely qualified to bridge the gap between Jewish and Gentile Christianity. He was a man of three worlds: Jewish, Greek, and Roman.

Though he had been educated in the strictest Jewish tradition and had studied under the famous rabbi Gamaliel in Jerusalem, Paul spoke Greek fluently and was familiar with Greek thought and literature. This meant he could express the doctrines and teachings of Jesus, many of which were based on Old Testament beliefs completely foreign to the Gentiles, in ways that the pagan mind could grasp. In addition, Paul was a Roman citizen, which gave him special freedom of movement, protection in his travels, and access to the higher levels of society.

The title *apostle* or *sent one* was never more appropriate. Paul made a series of trips throughout Asia Minor (today's Turkey) and Greece preaching Jesus as the Christ and planting churches of Gentile believers.

Paul's converts were a mixed lot. A few of them were from honorable backgrounds, but the majority were pagans with sordid pasts. In one of his many letters Paul reminds his readers of their former life: sexually immoral, idolaters, adulterers, male prostitutes, thieves, greedy, drunkards, slanderers, and swindlers. But, says Paul, "You were washed, you were sanctified, you were justified in the name of the Lord Jesus Christ and by the Spirit of our God" (1 Cor. 6:11, NIV).

What was the best way to instill Christian principles of morality in these churches? That question was at the heart of the continuing tensions between Jewish and Gentile believers in first-century Christianity.

The Palestinian Christians, steeped in traditional Judaism, said, "Tell them that unless they submit to the Jewish law, in addition to believing in Jesus, there is no hope for their faith."

Paul, however, found this impossible. His own experience pointed another way. If a person could gain the righteousness of God by obeying the law, said Paul, I would have been the greatest in the kingdom. But righteousness by personal effort can only lead to failure. Man can be accepted as righteous only through God's undeserved mercy. That is grace. And grace always arises from the life, death, and resurrection of Jesus Christ.

Many Christians thought Paul was impossibly optimistic. They were deeply troubled by the decline in Christian morality they felt sure would come in the gentile churches. If you teach justification by faith alone, they argued, people will imagine that once they have accepted Christ by faith it does not really matter how they live.

On the contrary, said Paul, if they really have accepted Christ by faith, they have accepted the way of Christ and the mind of Christ. The man who really loves God can do as he chooses, for if he really loves God he will choose to do the will of God.

This difference between Paul and his Jewish opponents did not pass away with the apostles. It has endured in Christianity to our own day. The legally minded think Paul and his kind are rash and unrealistic; Paul and his followers accuse the legally inclined of treason against the meaning of God's grace.

Paul's itinerant ministry, however, won more and more believers to his convictions. On his first journey he visited the island of Cyprus and the main cities in the province of Galatia in central Asia Minor. On his second journey he revisited the congregations he had founded earlier. Then he traveled across western Asia Minor to Troas, where he decided to carry his mission to Europe. Sailing to Macedonia, he set foot for the first time on European soil. From Philippi in northern Macedonia, Paul traveled to Thessalonica and Berea. Then he visited Athens, the birthplace of Western civilization.

Paul's task of carrying the gospel of Jesus to the Gentiles was difficult but not impossible, for the gentile world was far from irreligious. Aside from allegiance to a pantheon of Greek gods, adopted and renamed by the Romans, a town, village, or family often had an allegiance to one deity. In his travels Paul encountered most major pagan beliefs. In particular, a group of so-called mystery cults had developed in different regions in the empire. They were local cults based on legends of gods who were reborn every spring: Hercules, Dionysius, Isis, Mithras, and others. Although their central beliefs were based on the fertility cycle of nature, the mystery cults embraced a number of sophisticated ideas, including those of immortality, resurrection, and the struggle between good and evil. This superficial similarity to Christian belief was useful to Paul in explaining the message of Jesus to pagans.

From Athens Paul traveled to Corinth, where he founded a sizable Christian community. A year and a half later he returned to Antioch in Syria.

On his third missionary tour, Paul founded a church at Ephesus and preached and taught there for more than two years. When he returned to Jerusalem at the end of his journey, Jewish officials finally arrested and imprisoned him. He spent the next two years under house arrest at Caesarea, the Roman capital of Judea, until he finally exercised his right as a Roman citizen to appeal his case directly to the emperor.

Thus Paul came at last to the capital of the empire, Rome. He spent the final years of his life awaiting trial. Allowed to continue his preaching, he probably won other converts. But after the Emperor Nero's persecution of Christians (AD 64) we never hear from Paul again, though there are traditions claiming he went to Spain.

By that time the breach with traditional Judaism was almost complete. Gentile believers were not circumcised, they neither knew nor practiced Jewish dietary laws, and in most areas the Sabbath (seventh day) observance had given way to worship on the first day of the week, the day on which Jesus rose from the dead.

THE DECLINE OF JERUSALEM

Voices from Jerusalem, not Rome, however, represent the climax of the separation of ways. While Paul was gathering gentile followers throughout the pagan world, the church in Jerusalem continued its strict adherence to Jewish orthodoxy. Persecution still remained a possibility. About AD 41, James, the son of Zebedee, long one of Jesus' closest followers, was murdered by the order of Herod Agrippa I, king of Palestine from 41 to 44. James's brother John, "the beloved disciple," may have then fled Jerusalem. Peter was arrested shortly after James's death, but he escaped and embarked on an extensive missionary journey. He visited Antioch, Corinth, and other cities in Asia Minor. Toward the end of his life he traveled to Rome where he, along with Paul, was caught up in Nero's persecution and martyred.

The leadership of the Jerusalem church rested first in the hands of James, "the brother of the Lord." A devout, law-abiding Jew, he was revered by his followers, but in AD 62 he was murdered by command of the Jewish high priest. His death left the Jerusalem church leaderless and demoralized.

Meanwhile, tensions between the Jews and their Roman overlords were growing ever stronger. The completion of the Jewish temple in AD 64 put thousands of laborers out of work, adding to the general discontent. Finally in AD 66 the Jews revolted, signaling their intent by refusing to perform the daily sacrifice for the emperor.

As one account describes it,

> The tragic, bloody war that followed cost more lives than any previous conflict. The Jews held out against overwhelming odds for four years, but they could not withstand the power of Rome. In AD 70 Emperor Vespasian's forces, led by Titus, broke through the walls of Jerusalem, looted and burned the temple, and carried off the spoils to Rome. The Holy City was totally destroyed. In the reprisals that followed, every synagogue in Palestine was burned to the ground.
>
> At the start of the revolt, the leaders of the Jerusalem church were advised in a vision to flee the city.

Pious Jews considered the Christian flight an act of treason, and it sealed the fate of the church in the Jewish world. With the decision to bar Christian Jews from synagogue services some years later, the break was complete. Any Jew who wished to remain faithful to his religion could not also be a Christian. The new faith had become and would remain a gentile movement. The old wineskin was irreparably torn.

For practical purposes AD 70 and the destruction of Jerusalem mark the end of the apostolic age. Most of the original apostles were dead, and the churches they had founded had passed into new hands. Through their tireless activity a powerful new elixir had spilled out into the Mediterranean world. More lasting and resilient than the forces that opposed it, the message of the apostles would endure persecution and opposition, emerging centuries later as the dominant faith of the Roman Empire.

Suggestions for Further Reading

Barnett, Paul. *Jesus and the Rise of Early Christianity.* Downers Grove, IL: Inter-Varsity, 1999.

Barclay, William, ed. *The Bible and History.* Nashville: Abingdon, 1968.

Blomberg, Craig L. *From Pentecost to Patmos: An Introduction to Acts through Revelation.* Nashville: Broadman & Holman, 2006.

Bruce, F. F. *New Testament History.* London: Nelson, 1969.

*Capes, David, Rodney Reeves, and E. Randolph Richards. *Rediscovering Paul: An Introduction to His World, Letters, and Theology.* Downers Grove, IL: Inter-Varsity Press, 2007.

Wenham, David Paul. *Follower of Jesus or Founder of Christianity?* Grand Rapids: Eerdmans, 1995.

THE AGE OF CATHOLIC CHRISTIANITY

70–312

In this period Christianity spread throughout the Roman Empire and probably east to India. Christians realized that they were a part of a rapidly expanding movement. They called it *catholic*. This suggested that it was universal, in spite of pagan ridicule and Roman persecution, and it was the true faith, in opposition to all perversions of Jesus' teachings. To face the challenges of their times, Christians turned increasingly to their bishops for spiritual leadership. Catholic Christianity, therefore, was marked by a universal vision, by orthodox beliefs, and by episcopal church government.

The Age of Catholic Christianity

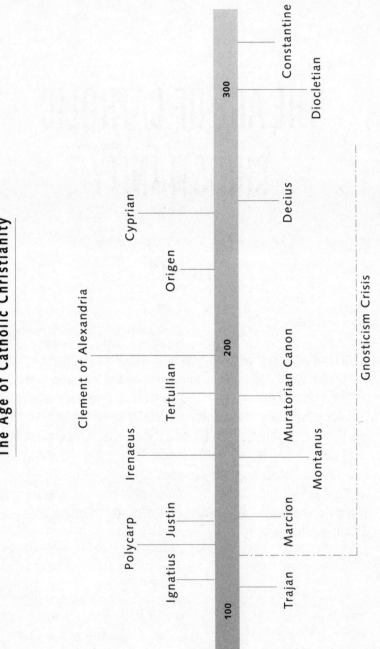

CHAPTER 3

ONLY WORTHLESS PEOPLE

Catholic Christianity

Eusebius, the early Christian historian (c. AD 265–339), records a charming story from the first days of Christianity. Apparently it came from Edessa, a town northeast of Antioch, beyond the border of the Roman Empire. At the time it was the capital of the tiny kingdom of Osrhoene, and, so the story goes, the ruler of the kingdom, Abgar the Black (c. AD 946), sent a letter to Jesus inviting him to come to Edessa. He had heard of Jesus' power to heal, and since he was himself sick, he entreated Jesus "to come to me and heal the affliction that I have."

The Lord Jesus answered the king, explaining that he had to fulfill his destiny in Palestine but after his ascension he would send one of his disciples to heal the king "and give life to you and to those who are with you."

The story is a fascinating bit of legend but an important reminder that early Christians, in their efforts to carry the gospel to all men, did not stop at the borders of the Roman Empire. Osrhoene became the first Christian kingdom and an important link with countries farther east.

First-century Christianity was a spiritual explosion. Ignited by the Event, the presence of Jesus Christ, the church extended in all directions, geographic as well as social. The second and third centuries provided the channel for this power.

This period was an important age for the church; it allowed Christianity to come to terms with time. It laid plans for the long haul and in the process shaped the character of the Christian faith for generations to come.

Today, with the Apostles' Creed, we confess faith in "the holy, catholic church." That is what this period gave us: "catholic" Christianity. It was more than an organization. It was a spiritual vision, a conviction that all Christians should be in one body.

Jesus had commissioned his disciples to go into all the world, and Paul had laid down his life opening the door of the church for the Gentiles. In a sense catholic Christianity was simply a development of Jesus' plans and Paul's efforts.

We call the years between AD 70 and AD 312 the Age of Catholic Christianity because this thought dominates Christian history between the death of the apostles and the rise of the Christian emperors.

Though the universality of Christianity is a common idea in the New Testament, the term *catholic* never appears. Ignatius, bishop of Antioch in the early second century, is apparently the first to use the word. He spoke of the "catholic church," when he said, "Wherever Jesus Christ is, there is the catholic church." By the end of the second century the term *catholic* was widely used of the church in the sense that the catholic church was both universal, in contrast to local congregations, and orthodox, in contrast to heretical groups.

In a later chapter we want to take a close look at the orthodox character of early Christianity, but at this point we must ask, how did the scattered congregations of apostolic times become catholic Christianity?

Any fair answer to that question calls for an overview of the spread of Christianity geographically and some picture of its success socially. It might be helpful to consider one a flying tour of the world of early Christians and the other as a glance at a recently discovered family album.

Did Christianity Grow Miraculously?

The Bible reports that miracles accompanied and encouraged the growth of Christianity; but does that mean that the rate of growth was itself miraculous? Some contemporary theorists, such as Rodney Stark, hold that the numerical expansion of Christianity can be accounted for by a steady growth rate, comparable to Mormonism in the American setting. Christianity's greatest expansion has occurred in the last fifty years.

Christianity, as we have seen, began as a tiny offshoot of Judaism. Three centuries later it became the favored and eventually the official religion of the entire Roman Empire. Despite widespread and determined efforts to eliminate the new faith, it survived and grew. By the reign of Constantine (312–337), the first Christian emperor, there were churches in every large town in the empire and in places as distant from each other as Britain, Carthage, and Persia.

How did that happen? Where, specifically, did Christianity spread and why did it expand so rapidly?

THE SPREAD OF THE FAITH

The apostle Paul told the Roman Christians, "For I am not ashamed of the gospel of Christ: for it is the power of God unto salvation . . . to the Jew first, and also to the Greek" (Rom. 1:16, KJV). The best place to launch a tour of early Christian expansion, it seems, is with the Jew.

The descendants of Abraham were present in large numbers in every part of the Roman Empire. Some authorities tell us that they may have numbered as high as 7 percent of the total population. Their distinctive religious beliefs made them a constant source of attraction and repulsion to their gentile neighbors. In uncertain times many Gentiles (Greeks and Romans) found the teaching of the synagogues a profound and compelling wisdom. At other times they were not so sure.

Some Gentiles submitted to the rite of circumcision, and thereby became a part of the Jewish people. However, the majority of these interested Gentiles remained in the category of *God-fearers*, interested spectators of the synagogue service.

The preaching of the gospel found its most fruitful response from this group. When Christian preachers made it plain to these folk who, without submitting to the rite of circumcision—which both Greeks and Romans considered degrading and repulsive—they could receive all that Judaism offered and more, it was not difficult for them to take one further step and accept Jesus as the Christ.

The presence of this prepared elite makes comparisons of evangelism in the age of the apostles and any later age almost impossible. Most of the "God-fearers" knew the Old Testament well; they understood its theological ideas; they accepted its moral values. Few, if any, other missionary movements in Christian history could look upon such a prepared field for harvesting.

This preparation for the gospel also helps to explain why Christians thought in catholic terms. Like the Jews and their synagogues, Christians had their local assemblies. But from the start they saw themselves as a faithful Israel, a fellowship of believers throughout the world.

The *world* in ancient Rome meant cities. The apostle Paul set the pattern for evangelism in the early centuries of Christianity by settling for a time in one of the great cities of the empire and, through his younger helpers, thrusting out from this center to smaller towns of the region. We may trace the major steps of progress in the spread of the gospel in this way.

After the fall of Jerusalem in AD 70, the center of the Christian movement moved north and eventually west. The second home of the church was Antioch of Syria. Under a succession of notable bishops, the church in this third largest city of the empire took root and exerted widespread influence throughout Syria. By the end of the fourth century, Antioch was a city of half a million people, and half of these were Christians.

Edessa lay beyond the border of the empire, but its ties with Antioch were apparently close. It later claimed that the founder of the church there had been one of the seventy disciples of Jesus, a man named Addai. We know that Serapion, Bishop of Antioch about 200, consecrated an Edessene Christian named Palut to be bishop of the capital.

There is good reason to suppose that from Edessa some unknown Christian continued east until he came to India. So-called *Thomas Christians* in India today believe that the Christian was the apostle Thomas. That may be true. A voyage by Thomas to south India in the first century was well within the realm of possibility. It will probably never be settled beyond historical doubt, but we can say with some certainty that the church in India has existed from very early times.

THE MOVE WEST

The mainstream of early Christian missionary work, however, did not move east of Antioch but west. The apostle Paul had set a course for Italy and Spain, and his work proved to be the path of the future.

Moving west from Antioch, the next city of note would be Ephesus. This seaport and the surrounding regions of Asia Minor (modern Turkey) proved another fruitful field for Christian labor. From the days of Paul, the Greek-speaking city dwellers in this area responded eagerly to the appeals of the gospel.

We also know that the remote and rather rural province of Bithynia in northwest Asia Minor was for a time in the early second century a center of unusual growth. Pliny, the governor of the region, wrote a letter to the Emperor Trajan in the year 112. In it he expressed his dismay over the rapid spread of the Christian faith. He spoke of "many in every period of life, on every level of society, of both sexes . . . in towns and villages and scattered throughout the countryside." What was he to do with them? Pliny was afraid that the shrines of the pagan gods would soon be completely deserted.

We may have here the first mass movement in Christian history. It is rather unusual for rural areas in the ancient world. The general picture suggests that backward areas, inhabited by people who preferred to keep their barbarian speech, were usually more resistant to the encroachments of the gospel. We know at any rate that as late as the sixth century Emperor Justinian was still rallying Christian forces for an assault on paganism in the interior of Asia Minor.

Farther west, Rome, the heart of the vast empire, drew to itself peoples from all regions. Once planted by some unknown believers in the first century, the church grew rapidly. The highly respected German scholar Adolf Harnack calculated that by AD 250 no fewer than thirty thousand Christians lived in Rome! Most of these came from the poorer classes. We know this because for more than a century Christians in Rome spoke Greek, the language of slaves and poor men. True Romans of the upper classes used Latin.

From its beginnings this church in the capital, with its claim to the ministry of the apostles Peter and Paul, gained the respect and admiration of Christians throughout the empire. Once a church took root in the capital, it naturally assumed leadership in Christian affairs, even as large churches in metropolitan areas do in our own time.

Beyond Rome to the west and north, progress of the gospel seems to have been slow. In the southern area of what is now called France (then Gaul) we know a church existed in Lyons in the middle of the second century, for the bishop Irenaeus left us a number of his writings.

By the end of the third century we also hear of churches and bishops in Spain. But the evidence suggests that the western regions of the empire trailed the eastern in the strength of the Christian witness.

We have no firm idea how Christianity first entered Britain. It may have been through some Roman soldier or merchant. All that we know for certain is that three bishops from Britain attended a church council at Arles in southern France in AD 314. Beyond this we have only imagination and hearsay.

NORTH AFRICA

Moving south across the Mediterranean we come to North Africa. Again the witness focuses upon a city, Carthage, which dominated the area we know as Tunisia and Algeria. Christianity in this region was led by bishops. Every town and almost every village had its bishop. It also had its tensions. The writers, martyrs, and bishops we know are nearly all from the Romanized section of the community. In point of fact, North African Christianity produced the first Latin-speaking churches in the world. This means they tended to be of the upper class. Not surprisingly problems of race and language arose in this area, for the Punic language, brought by the early Phoenician settlers, and the Berber language, spoken by the village and desert dwellers, could also be found in and around Carthage. In the great persecutions of the third century these cultural differences spelled trouble for the churches.

Moving east across North Africa we come to Cyrene, just west of Egypt. This territory is mentioned four times in the New Testament. Simon of Cyrene carried the cross of Jesus on the way to Golgotha (Mark 15:21). It is almost certain that Simon became a believer since we later meet his son Rufus in the circle of Christians (Rom. 16:13). Cyrenians were also present on the Day of Pentecost when Peter delivered his rousing message to the throng in Jerusalem (Acts 2:10). Some of them later disputed with Stephen (Acts 6:9). And finally we learn that Cyrenians took part in that decisive step that carried the gospel beyond Israel to the gentile world (Acts 11:20).

Almost certainly such zeal led to the planting of churches in Cyrene itself. We know that by the fifth century a half dozen bishops labored in the area.

Our circle around the Mediterranean brings us at last to Alexandria. The name itself is a reminder of Alexander the Great who founded the city in 332 BC and made it a cultural capital and a center for trade with East and West. As the second largest city in the empire, it had a sizeable Jewish population. Led by the well-known philosopher Philo, a contemporary of the apostle Paul, Jews in Alexandria tried to interpret Judaism in terms of Greek philosophy.

Christians in the city wrestled with the same problem. We know that a famous catechetical school there concentrated on making the gospel intelligible to people immersed in Greek culture.

Early Christians in Alexandria liked to claim John Mark as the founder of their church. How it was established we do not know, but during the third and fourth centuries few churches exerted more influence.

To sum up this flying tour of the early expansion of the church we may say that by the end of the third century, no area of the empire was without some testimony to the gospel. The strength of this witness, however, was uneven. The strongest areas were Syria, Asia Minor,

North Africa, and Egypt, with a few other noteworthy cities such as Rome and Lyons. Less is known about the scope of Christianity in rural regions.

THE SOCIAL IMPACT OF THE GOSPEL

The catholic vision of early Christians, however, was as evident in the social impact of the gospel as in its geographical expansion. Throughout the first three centuries the majority of believers were simple, humble people: slaves, women, traders, and soldiers. Perhaps this is simply due to the fact that most in the population were in this class. At any rate, Celsus, the outspoken critic of Christianity, took note of it: "Far from us, say the Christians, be any man possessed of any culture or wisdom or judgment; their aim is to convince only worthless and contemptible people, idiots, slaves, poor women, and children . . . . These are the only ones whom they manage to turn into believers."

Celsus was right to observe many poor and disadvantaged embraced the message of Jesus' victory. It is to the church's credit that it did not neglect the poor and despised. But by the end of the second century the new faith was on its way to becoming the most forceful and compelling movement within the empire. Many people with the keenest minds of the day were becoming followers of Christ.

To answer critics like Celsus, a number of Christian writers arose to defend the Christian faith against the rumors and railings of the pagans. We call these men *the apologists*. Not because they were sorry for anything: the word comes from Greek and means *defense*, such as a lawyer gives at a trial.

As Professor Ward Gasque says, although most of the writings of these apologists were dedicated to the emperors, their real audience was the educated public of the day. If they could answer the accusations of the enemies of Christianity and point out the weaknesses of paganism, they hoped this would help to change public opinion about Christianity and lead to conversions. Men such as Aristides, Justin Martyr, his disciple Tatian, Athenagoras, Theophilus of Antioch, the unknown author of the *Letter to Diognetus*, and Melito, bishop of Sardis in Asia Minor, all directed their intellectual and spiritual gifts to this cause.

"Toward the end of the second century," says Gasque,

Irenaeus, bishop of Lyons in Gaul, wrote five monumental books against the gnostic heresies of his area, together with a book entitled *Proof of the Apostolic Preaching* . . . . His theology was grounded in the Bible and the church's doctrines and helped provide a steadying, positive influence in the church. He wrote of the cosmic implications of the work of Christ and God's plan in history, and paved the way for the later Christian interpretations of history by writers such as Augustine.

The real intellectual giants, however, were still to come.

Tertullian, the "father of Latin theology," was born in Carthage around AD 150. After his conversion to Christianity, he began writing books to promote the Christian faith. The large number he wrote in Greek are now lost, but thirty-one surviving in Latin are highly significant.

> Tertullian's *Apology* underlined the legal and moral absurdity of the persecution directed against Christians. Some of his other books offered encouragement to those facing martyrdom. He attacked the heretics, explained the Lord's Prayer and the meaning of baptism, and helped develop the orthodox understanding of the Trinity. He was the first person to use the Latin word *trinitas* (trinity) . . . . His intellectual brilliance and literary versatility made him one of the most powerful writers of the time.

While Tertullian was at work in Carthage, Alexandria, to the east, was becoming another key intellectual center for the Christian faith. By about AD 185 a converted Stoic philosopher named Pantaenus was teaching Christians in Alexandria. He probably also traveled to India and was a very able thinker. His pupil Clement carried his work to even greater heights in the closing days of the second century. In spite of periods of intense persecution, the school gained great importance, strengthening the faith of Christians and attracting new converts to the faith.

By the third century the Christian church was beginning to assume the proportions of an empire within the empire. The constant travel between different churches, the synods of bishops, the letters carried by messengers back and forth across the empire, and the loyalty that the Christians showed to their leaders and to one another impressed even the emperors.

REASONS FOR THE GOSPEL'S SPREAD

Why did the Christian faith spread in this extraordinary way? The devout Christian will want to stress the power of the gospel. By ordinary standards nothing could have been less likely to succeed. But believers have always insisted that God was at work in this movement. He went with those early witnesses. There was a divine side to the expansion of the church. But God usually works through human hearts and hands, and there is some value in asking what human factors contributed to the spread of the gospel.

Several prominent factors, however, appear to have contributed to the growth of Christianity. First, and rather obviously, early Christians were moved by a burning conviction. The Event had happened. God had invaded time and Christians were captivated by the creative power of that grand news. They knew that men had been redeemed and they could not keep to themselves the tidings of salvation. That unshakable assurance, in the face of every obstacle including martyrdom itself, helps explain the growth of the church.

Second, the Christian gospel met a widely felt need in the hearts of people. Ancient Stoicism, for example, taught that men achieve tranquility by the suppression of desire for everything that man cannot get and keep. "Before the external disorder of the world and bodily illness, retreat into yourself and find God there." Thus the Stoic soul stood firm in the storms of life by practicing apathy, the discipline of not being attached to people or things. If a person was not emotionally attached to things, he could not be victimized and thus could live in tranquility. Stoics called for the virtue of courage in facing whatever was to come. While Christians were committed to the personal God revealed in Jesus, they could still admire some Stoic convictions, once those convictions were refitted for Christian teaching. For example, Stoics called for facing suffering with courage, independence from the things of this world, and a trust in a greater providence. Many people came to see that what the Stoics aimed for, the Holy Spirit produced in Christians.

Third, the practical expression of Christian love was probably among the most powerful causes of Christian success. Tertullian tells us the pagans remarked, "See how these Christians love one another." The pagans' words were sincere. Christian love found expression in the care of the poor, of widows and orphans; in visits to brethren in prisons or to those condemned to a living death in the mines; and in acts of compassion during a famine, earthquake, or war.

One expression of Christian love had a particularly far-reaching effect. The church often provided burial service for poor brethren. Christians felt that to deprive a person of honorable burial was a terrible thing. Lactantius, the North African scholar (c. 240–320) wrote, "We will not allow the image and creation of God to be thrown out to the wild beasts and the birds as their prey; it must be given back to the earth from which it was taken."

In the second half of the second century, at least in Rome and Carthage, churches began to acquire burial grounds for their members.

One of the oldest of these is south of Rome on the Appian Way at a place named Catacumbas. Thus Christian compassion for bodies of the dead explains how Christians became associated with the catacombs, the underground corridors used for cemeteries in and around Rome.

The impact of this ministry of mercy upon pagans is revealed in the observation of one of Christianity's worst enemies, the apostate Emperor Julian (332–63). In his day Julian was finding it more difficult than he had expected to put new life into the traditional Roman religion. He wanted to set aside Christianity and bring back the ancient faith, but he saw clearly the drawing power of Christian love in practice:

> Atheism [i.e., Christian faith] has been specially advanced through the loving service rendered to strangers, and through their care for the burial of the dead. It is a scandal that there is not a single Jew who is a beggar, and that the godless Galileans care not only for their own poor but for ours as well; while those who belong to us look in vain for the help that we should render them.

Finally, persecution in many instances helped to publicize the Christian faith. Martyrdoms were often witnessed by thousands in the amphitheater. The term *martyr* originally meant "witness," and that is precisely what many Christians were at the moment of death.

The Roman public was hard and cruel, but it was not altogether without compassion; and there is no doubt that the attitude of the martyrs, and particularly of the young women who suffered along with the men, made a deep impression. In instance after instance what we find is cool courage in the face of torment, courtesy toward enemies, and a joyful acceptance of suffering as the way appointed by the Lord to lead to his heavenly kingdom. There are a number of cases of conversion of pagans in the very moment of witnessing the condemnation and death of Christians.

For these and other reasons the Christian churches multiplied until Rome could neither ignore nor suppress the faith. It finally had to come to terms with it.

This period, however, the age of extraordinary expansion before Christianity moved from the catacombs to the imperial courts, serves to remind us that the church is truly catholic only when it is impelled by the gospel to bring all men to living faith in Jesus Christ.

Suggestions for Further Reading

Davidson, Ivor J. *The Birth of the Church: From Jesus to Constantine, AD 30–312, Baker History of the Church.* Vol. 1. Grand Rapids: Baker, 2004.

Davies, J. G. *The Early Christian Church: A History of Its First Five Centuries.* Garden City, NY: Doubleday, 1967.

Dunn, J. D. G. *Jews and Christians: The Parting of the Ways.* Grand Rapids: Eerdmans, 1999.

*Ferguson, Everett. *Church History, Volume 1: From Christ to the Pre-Reformation.* Grand Rapids: Zondervan, 2005.

Green, Michael. *Evangelism in the Early Church.* Grand Rapids: Eerdmans, 1970.

Hurtado, Larry. *How on Earth Did Jesus Become a God? Historical Questions about Earliest Devotion to Jesus.* Grand Rapids: Eerdmans, 2005.

Wagner, W. H. *After the Apostles: Christianity in the Second Century.* Minneapolis: Fortress, 1994.

CHAPTER 4

IF THE TIBER FLOODS

The Persecution of Christians

IN THE POPULAR MIND, the early church was above all else a noble army of martyrs. In many ways it was, and none was nobler than Polycarp, the aged bishop of Smyrna in western Asia Minor.

The authorities brought the highly respected pastor into the crowded arena, prepared to shove him to the lions—but only reluctantly. They much preferred a denial of the charge against him. He was a Christian.

"Simply swear by Caesar," the governor pled.

"I am a Christian," said Polycarp. "If you want to know what that is, set a day and listen."

"Persuade the people," answered the governor. Polycarp said, "I would explain to you, but not to them."

"Then I'll throw you to the beasts."

"Bring on your beasts," said Polycarp.

"If you scorn the beasts, I'll have you burned."

"You try to frighten me with the fire that burns for an hour, and you forget the fire of hell that never goes out."

The governor called to the people, "Polycarp says he is a Christian." Then the mob let loose. "This is the teacher of Asia," they shouted, "the father of the Christians, the destroyer of our gods."

So Polycarp, praying that his death would be an acceptable sacrifice, was burned at the stake.

Yet the picture of defenseless, peaceful Christians standing in their white robes before menacing lions while an amphitheater echoes with the shouts for blood from a Roman throng is largely misleading. Prior to AD 200 Roman attempts to silence Christians were halfhearted at best. Few Roman emperors were bloodthirsty villains.

Why, then, did Rome persecute Christians? Why do we look back to this period as the age of martyrs?

ROME'S POLICY

Let's start with Rome's basic policy. Imperial authorities were remarkably tolerant of religions from those lands overrun by the Roman legions. If the national religions of the conquered countries would add homage to the emperor to their other ceremonies, Rome almost never interfered.

In one notable instance, Rome even dropped the requirement of burning incense to the emperor. The Jews, with their fanatical loyalty to their one true God, and their readiness to turn their homeland into a blood-soaked wilderness before they would acknowledge any other deity, were the exception.

As long as Roman authorities considered Christians as just one more sect of Jews, followers of Jesus enjoyed this same immunity from imperial pressure. But when the Jews made it known in no uncertain terms that they would have nothing to do with the new movement, the situation changed dramatically.

Once the Romans discovered what the Christians were up to, they were confronted by the problem of toleration in a more exasperating form than even the Jews had presented. The Jews, after all, were "a sort of closed corporation, a people set apart from others by the mark of circumcision, who lived and worshiped largely by themselves, and did little active proselyting." The Christians, on the other hand, were always talking about their Jesus. They were out to make Christians of the entire population of the empire, and the rapidity of their spread showed that this was no idle dream. Not only did they, like the Jews, refuse to worship the emperor as a living god, but they were doing their utmost to convince every subject of the emperor to join them in their refusal. From time to time, then, Christians felt the wrath of the empire and its people.

REASONS FOR PERSECUTION

The main cause of the hatred of early Christians in Roman society lies in their distinctive lifestyle. "We have the reputation," said Tertullian in his *Apology*, "of living aloof from crowds."

The word used to describe the Christian in the New Testament is highly significant. It is the term *hagios*, often translated *saints*. It means *holy ones*, but its root suggests *different*. So a holy thing is different from other things. The temple is holy because it is different from other buildings; the Sabbath day is holy because it is different from other days. The Christian, therefore, is a person who is fundamentally different.

Men always view with suspicion people who are different. Conformity, not distinctiveness, is the way to a trouble-free life. So the more early Christians took their faith seriously, the more they were in danger of crowd reaction.

Thus, simply by living according to the teachings of Jesus, the Christian was a constant unspoken condemnation of the pagan way of life. It was not that the Christian went about criticizing and condemning and disapproving, nor was he consciously self-righteous and superior. It was simply that the Christian ethic in itself was a criticism of pagan life.

Fundamental to the Christian lifestyle and the cause of endless hostility was the Christian's rejection of the pagan gods. The Greeks and Romans had deities for every aspect of living: for sowing and reaping, for rain and wind, for volcanoes and rivers, for birth and death. But to the Christians these gods were nothing, and their denial of them marked the followers of Jesus as "enemies of the human race."

One simply could not reject the gods without arousing scorn as a social misfit. For the pagan every meal began with a liquid offering and a prayer to the pagan gods. A Christian could not share in that. Most heathen feasts and social parties were held in the precincts of a temple after sacrifice had been made, and the invitation was usually to dine "at the table" of some god. A Christian could not go to such a feast. Inevitably, when he refused the invitation to some social occasion, the Christian seemed rude, boorish, and discourteous.

Other social events Christians rejected because they found them wrong in themselves. Gladiatorial combats, for example, were to the Christian inhuman. In amphitheaters all across the empire, the Romans forced prisoners of war and slaves to fight with each other to the death, just for the amusement of the crowd. The excitement was seductive. As late as the early fifth century, Augustine tells the story of his friend Alypius, who agreed to attend a spectacle to please a friend, but resolved to keep his eyes shut. When the shouting began, his eyes popped open, and he was yelling above the rest.

The Christian fear of idolatry also led to difficulties in making a living. A mason might be involved in building the walls of a heathen temple, a tailor in making robes for a heathen priest, an incense maker in making incense for the heathen sacrifices. Tertullian even forbade a Christian to be a schoolteacher, because such teaching involved using textbooks that told the ancient stories of the gods and called for observing the religious festivals of the pagan year.

We might think that working with the sick would be a simple act of kindness. But even here early Christians found the pagan hospitals under the protection of the heathen god Aesculapius, and while a sick friend lay in his bed, the priest went down the aisle chanting to the god.

In short, the early Christian was almost bound to divorce himself from the social and economic life of his time if he wanted to be true to his Lord. This meant that everywhere the Christian turned, his life and faith were on display because the gospel introduced a revolutionary new attitude toward human life. It could be seen in Christian views of slaves, children, and sex.

Slavery ate like a canker in Roman society. The slave, whether male or female, was always at the disposal of his master for the most menial tasks. And if he failed to satisfy his owner he could be discarded, even slaughtered like a worthless animal.

In this kind of society, some Christians also held slaves but they treated them kindly and allowed them to have the same rights within the church as anyone else. At least one former slave, Callistus, became the bishop of Rome.

The same value upon human life applied to infants. Unlike his pagan neighbor the Christian refused to take his weak and unwanted children out in the woods and leave them to die or be picked up by robbers. If a Christian woman was married to a pagan and a girl baby was born, the father might say, "Throw her out," but the mother would usually refuse.

Naturally this regard for life applied also to sex and marriage. In modern times the church has often borne the brunt of criticism for its dated views of sex and the sanctity of marriage, but it is unlikely that such a charge would have been voiced in the decaying Roman Empire. Pagan society, through its excesses, teetered on the brink of racial extinction. Christianity, however, represented another way—a new way. The Pauline doctrine that the body is the temple of the Holy Spirit introduced to the ancient world an uncompromising condemnation of unchastity and a sacred calling to family life.

This widespread hatred of Christians helps explain the first persecution from Roman hands. In the year 64, during the reign of Emperor Nero, fire broke out in Rome. For six days and nights the fire burned. The greater part of the city was laid in ashes. The rumor circulated that Nero himself had caused the city to be set on fire. This aroused great hatred among the people of Rome against the emperor.

To turn this hatred away from himself Nero accused the Christians of having set the fire. The accusation certainly was not true, but large numbers of Christians were arrested and a terrible persecution followed. Many Christians were even crucified. Some were sewn up in the skins of wild beasts; then big dogs were let loose upon them, and they were torn to pieces. Women were tied to mad bulls and dragged to death. After nightfall Christians were burned at the stake in Nero's garden. The Roman people who hated the Christians were free to come into the garden, and Nero drove around in his chariot enjoying the horrible spectacle to the full.

It was probably during this persecution that the apostles Peter and Paul suffered martyrdom in Rome. Reports have it that Peter, at his own request, was crucified with his head down. He said he was not worthy to be crucified in the same manner as his Master. Paul, being a Roman citizen, was beheaded.

Such outbursts of bloodshed were not common during the first and second centuries. For long periods Christians were left in peace. But like the sword of Damocles, persecution was always poised above them. It only took a malicious informer, a popular uproar, a governor determined to carry out the letter of the law, and the storm would burst. The fact remained, the Christian as a Christian was legally an outlaw. "Public hatred," says Tertullian, "asks but one thing, not the investigation of the crimes charged, but simply the confession of the Christian name."

SEX AND SLANDER

A second and obviously related cause of persecution of early Christians was the slanders disseminated about them. Once these were started, they could not be halted. The suspicion that the Christian gatherings were sexual orgies and cover for every kind of crime took hold of the popular imagination with a terrible vehemence.

These wild charges probably arose from a characteristic of human nature: secrecy breeds distrust. When the public learned that they were barred from Christian services they simply followed their imaginations from rumor to hatred.

Christians were accused of a host of practices, but most often of sexual sins and cannibalism. The charge of gross immorality came from the fact that one Christian meeting was called the Agape—the Love Feast—and from the custom of the holy kiss of peace the Christians gave to one another. Indeed, in the end the kiss became so susceptible to abuse that the churches almost completely abandoned it.

The charge of cannibalism probably started because the Lord's Supper was practiced in secret. The heathen did not know what happened at these closed meetings, but they heard that somebody was being eaten. Jesus had said at the Last Supper, "This bread is my body. This cup is my blood." The pagans concluded that the Christians must be eating and drinking human flesh and blood.

The mobs thought that people who did such terrible things, if allowed to live, would bring all sorts of trouble on the land. Such wickedness would stir up the gods, who would punish not only the Christians but those who had allowed them to exist.

This secrecy of Christian meetings and the slander of the pagan public created unusual headaches for the usually fair-minded Roman authorities. About AD 112 one governor in Asia Minor, a man named Pliny, wrote to the Emperor Trajan and asked his advice about the best way to deal with followers of Christ:

> I do not know just what to do with the Christians, for I have never been present at one of their trials. Is just being a Christian enough to punish, or must something bad actually have been done? What I have done, in the case of those who admitted they were Christians, was to order them sent to Rome, if citizens; if not, to have them killed. I was sure they deserved to be punished because they were so stubborn.

If the accused person would deny Christ and offer a sacrifice to the gods or the emperor, then the person would be released, even if it were known that he had been a Christian. The emperor responded by generally affirming Pliny's policy: there are too many Christians to attempt to prosecute them; yet if the matter comes before a Roman authority he has to deal with the crime of being a Christian.

Pliny seems to feel that Christians are guilty of something. He isn't sure what it is. But at least he knows that it isn't immorality or cannibalism. These ancient letters offer an explanation as to how the persecution of Christians could be at times sporadic and at times savage—both intermittent and intense.

A third cause of Christian suffering may strike us as strange. Christians were accused of atheism. The charge arose from the fact that many within the empire could not understand an imageless worship. Monotheism held no attraction for such people. As a result they blamed Christians for insulting the gods of the state.

The pagan gods were viewed as patrons who would extend some kindness to a city. As an act of loyalty, citizens of good standing would participate in various civic festivals that showed respect to one of the gods. Good pagans may have been especially loyal to one of the gods but would pay tribute to all of the gods. Christians would not give tribute to the gods and appeared disloyal to their pagan neighbors. The popular notion held that disasters would strike if the gods were neglected. In his *Apology* Tertullian writes, "If the Tiber floods the city, or if the Nile refuses to rise, or if the sky withholds its rain, if there is an earthquake, a famine, a pestilence, at once the cry is raised: 'Christians to the lion.' "

CAESAR IS LORD

The supreme cause of Roman persecution of Christians arose from the tradition of emperor worship. This conflict between Christ and Caesar did not break out overnight. Only gradually did the worship of the emperor assume a central place in the life of the empire.

The roots of the practice lie in the merits of Roman rule. When the Romans took over the government of a country, impartial Roman justice arrived, and men were freed from the capricious authority of unpredictable and often savage and bloodthirsty tyrants. When Roman administration came, the roads were cleared of robbers and the seas of pirates, and a new security entered into life. This was *pax Romana*, the Roman peace.

The result of this was a deep and heartfelt gratitude to the spirit of Rome. It was an easy step for the spirit of Rome to become the goddess Roma, and by the second century BC there were many temples in Asia Minor to the goddess Roma. But the human mind and heart need a symbol; it was a further easy step to see the goddess Roma and the spirit of Rome incarnated in the emperor. He embodied Rome; he was Rome; in him the spirit of Rome resided and had its earthly dwelling. The first temple actually built to the godhead of the emperor was built in 29 BC at Pergamum in Asia Minor.

At first the emperors were hesitant to accept this reverence. Claudius (AD 41–59) refused to have temples erected to him because, as he said, he did not wish to be offensive to his fellowmen. But slowly an idea began to form in the official mind. The problem of the Roman Empire was the problem of unification. The empire stretched from the river Euphrates to the shores of the Irish sea.

It stretched from Germany to North Africa, from Spain to Egypt and Syria. Here were all kinds of peoples and languages and faiths and traditions. How could they be welded into a unity? How could the consciousness of one empire be brought into the lives of such diverse peoples?

There is no unifying force like the force of a common religion, and Caesar worship lay ready at hand. None of the local and ancestral faiths had any hope of ever becoming universal, but Rome was universal. As a result Caesar worship became the keystone of imperial policy. It was deliberately organized in every province in the empire. Everywhere temples to the godhead of the emperor appeared.

Little by little people within the empire came to believe that any allegiance in conflict with loyalty to the emperor, and therefore to the empire, could only lead to the disintegration of order. Worship of another Lord could only open the floodgates of chaos.

Emperor Decius (249–251) took another important step in persecution. Caesar worship was made universal and compulsory for every race and nation within the empire with the single exception of the Jews. On a certain day in the year every Roman citizen had to come to the Temple of Caesar and had to burn a pinch of incense there, and say "Caesar is Lord." When he had done that, he was given a certificate to guarantee that he had done so. After a man had burned his pinch of incense and had acknowledged Caesar as Lord, he could go away and worship any god he liked, so long as the worship did not affect public decency and order.

Thus we see that Caesar worship was primarily a test of political loyalty; it was a test of whether a man was a good citizen. If a man refused to carry out the ceremony of acknowledging Caesar, he was automatically branded as a traitor and a revolutionary. Exaltation of the emperor, then, created a problem for the Christians. They had not failed to pray for the emperor in their meetings, but they would not pray to him in private or in public.

Scholars have studied Roman coins and have found a striking similarity between the praises Christians offered in worship of Christ and the adulation Roman citizens directed to the reigning emperor. The coins, usually celebrating the blessings each successive emperor was to bring to a waiting world, announce his reign with, "Hail, Lord of the Earth, Invincible, Power, Glory, Honor, Blessed, Great, Worthy art Thou to inherit the kingdom."

Any tourist visiting Rome in the third century could find the same language used in the forum for the advent of the emperor and in the catacombs for the celebration of the appearance of Christ. How could a Christian compromise with this?

Who was worthy to ascend the throne of the universe and direct the course of history—Caesar or Christ?

Thus, Christian worship and Caesar worship met head-on. The one thing that no Christian would ever say was "Caesar is Lord." For the Christian, Jesus Christ and he alone was Lord. To the Roman the Christian seemed utterly intolerant and insanely stubborn; worse, he was a self-confessed disloyal citizen. Had the Christians been willing to burn that pinch of incense and to say formally, "Caesar is Lord," they could have gone on worshiping Christ to their heart's content; but the Christians would not compromise. That is why Rome regarded them as a band of potential revolutionaries threatening the very existence of the empire.

In one sense Rome was right because many Christians considered this conflict of loyalties a cosmic struggle. The Revelation of John in the New Testament reflects the Christian response to the imperial cult in Asia Minor toward the end of the first century. John traces the oppression of believers to the devil himself, to the great red dragon, who wages war against the saints through two agents, the beasts of Revelation 13. The first is the beast from the sea (or abyss), the imperial power. The second is the beast from the land (the false prophet), or the imperial worship.

And what was the Christian defense against this attack from Rome? They conquered the dragon, John says, "by the blood of the Lamb and by the word of their testimony, for they loved not their lives even unto death" (Rev. 12:11).

Suggestions for Further Reading

Davidson, Ivor J. *The Birth of the Church: From Jesus to Constantine, AD 30–312,* Baker History of the Church. Vol. 1. Grand Rapids: Baker, 2004.

*Ferguson, Everett. *Church History, Volume 1: From Christ to the Pre-Reformation.* Grand Rapids: Zondervan, 2005.

Frend, W. H. C. *Martyrdom and Persecution in the Early Church.* New York: New York University Press, 1967.

Grant, Robert M. *Augustus to Constantine.* New York: Harper and Row, 1970.

———. *The Sword and the Cross.* New York: Macmillan, 1955.

Middleton, Paul. *Radical Martyrdom and Cosmic Conflict in Early Christianity.* London: T & T Clark, 2006.

CHAPTER 5

ARGUING ABOUT THE EVENT

The Rise of Orthodoxy

Mahatma Gandhi, the revered leader of India's independence, once said, "I have never been interested in a historical Jesus. I should not care if it were proved by someone that the man Jesus never lived, and that what was narrated in the Gospels were a figment of the writer's imagination. For the Sermon on the Mount would still be true for me."

Gandhi was a great man. But he was not—and never claimed to be—a Christian. Many people who profess to be Christians, however, approach Christianity just as Gandhi did. They try to separate *what* Jesus said from *who* Jesus was. They want to set aside the doctrine of a supernatural Jesus and exalt his ethical teachings. They find the beliefs of historic Christianity an embarrassment. They prefer to stress Christian behavior.

Early believers considered that move a betrayal of the faith. The gospel, they said, was good news about the Event. So beliefs were basic. Questions of behavior always followed confession of Christ as Lord and Savior. The early churches saw this so clearly that they made belief in who Jesus was a test of true Christianity.

Most Christians came to see that while Christianity had deadly external enemies—as the conflict with emperor worship demonstrated—a subtler and no less critical danger came from within, from the realm of ideas. If the Christian faith could be undermined by "another gospel" then its living power would be lost.

Catholic Christianity was both universal, in contrast to local, and orthodox, in contrast to heretical. We have traced the expansion of the Christian faith throughout the Roman Empire and beyond. And we have discovered why imperial authorities persecuted Christian believers. Now we want to take a closer look at the meaning of *orthodox*. What did the early Christians believe? And why did they insist that only these beliefs were orthodox?

FAITH AND THEOLOGY

Many modern Christians would rather not discuss the central teachings of Christianity. They are not sure that ideas about religion or theology are all that important. "I love flowers," a minister once said, "but I hate botany; I love religion, but I hate theology." This widespread attitude often springs from good reasons. Theology can be dull, or much worse, it can be ruthless. In Christianity, however, the answer to bad theology can never be no theology. It must be good theology. God gave us minds, and he surely expects us to use them in thinking about his truth.

Theology comes from two Greek words: *theos*, meaning God, and *logos*, meaning word or rational thought. So theology is rational thought about God. It is not identical with religion. Religion is our belief in God and our effort to live by that belief. Theology is the attempt to give a rational explanation of our belief: it is thinking about religion.

When we err in our thinking we call it heresy or bad theology. Heresy is not necessarily bad religion, but like all wrong thinking it may lead to bad religion.

Heretics, in fact, served the church in an unintended way. Their pioneering attempts to state the truth forced the church to shape good theology: a rounded, well-organized statement of biblical revelation.

Good theology we call *orthodox*, a term that always seems to stir emotions. It is that form of Christianity that won the support of the overwhelming majority of Christians and that is expressed by most of the official proclamations or creeds of the church. So catholic Christianity is orthodox.

Orthodoxy and *Heresy*

Confusion abounds concerning these terms. The term "orthodox" can mean one of the three branches or confessions that compose most of the Christian family: Roman Catholic, Eastern Orthodox, and Protestant. Orthodoxy also means right belief or practice. But orthodoxy also refers to the right belief that is officially embraced by the church. The work of early church-wide councils is thought to recognize language that rightly speaks of Jesus' identity. People who cannot affirm what orthodox theologians say is necessary for right belief are called heretics. Thus Arius is branded a heretic because he cannot affirm what the Council of Nicaea claimed was right belief (orthodox), that Jesus is fully divine. Here orthodoxy and heresy refer to affirming or rejecting officially sanctioned doctrine. Confusion continues when we understand that what was held as officially sanctioned doctrine varied among Christians. Also much of what we hold as officially sanctioned was actually only widely embraced by the larger church much later. For example, Nicaean verdicts are widely embraced by the church today but were hotly disputed in their day.

Most importantly, one must remember that there was functional orthodoxy held by consensus among the earliest Christians. Early Christians agreed on much of the basic outline and content of early Christian teaching. One can see this in what several early theologians call the *rule of faith*. The rule of faith was a short statement of the essential Christian story. While not a fixed creed, it shows consensus on some early essentials. This functional, early orthodoxy is important because of a common misconception drawn from this maxim: "there can be no heresy if there is no orthodoxy." The statement rightly acknowledges that doctrine has to be articulated or stipulated as orthodoxy before one can be guilty of breaking with official church teaching. It would be anachronistic to charge second-century people as being guilty of rejecting teaching that was only spelled out in the fourth century. Some, however, wrongly conclude that since classic orthodoxy was not spelled out by the church councils until the fourth and fifth centuries that there were no heretics before this. Yet there were teachings that the church rejected before the councils. For example, the church rejected Marcion, who held Jesus had nothing to do with the Old Testament God or his people. Early Christians also ruled out a Trinitarian theory called modalism (seeing Father, Son, and Holy Spirit as only modes or roles played by the genuine God). The church has some convictions that were widely held that compose an early functional orthodoxy. People like Marcion were kicked out of churches and their teaching rejected prior to official orthodoxy of the fourth century.

Church history shows us that Christian theology is not primarily a philosophical system invented by men in the quiet of an academic study. Doctrines were hammered out by men who were on the work crew of the church. Much of orthodoxy was articulated because some heresy had arisen that threatened to change the nature of Christianity and to destroy its central faith.

Since orthodoxy arose from the conflict of the gospel with error, we speak of its development. The idea of development in Christian doctrine may seem strange to those who believe firmly in God's revelation of himself through Christ, given once and for all. But theology, don't forget, is not synonymous with God's revelation itself; rather, theology is the human understanding of revelation and the effort to express it clearly in teaching and preaching. Theology is using our own language and our own way of thinking to explain God's truth. And we know that people belonging to different times and cultures simply think and speak in different ways.

Spelling out the true teaching of the faith was complicated, in part because early Christianity included people from a variety of different cultures and outlooks. Scholars frequently note the clash between Hebrew and Hellenistic cultures, even though these had been in dialogue since before the time of Jesus. The Hebrews rooted their thinking in the framework of their covenant with the Creator God. This God chose the Hebrews to carry forward his purposes. He revealed himself among the concrete realities of history. Hellenists would bring their own strategies for reasoning to reflect upon the distinctive Hebrew story. Some Greeks would only respect the Hebrew's stories if they could demonstrate their truth by logical argumentation. The church wisely avoided this trap. Christians believed these things about God because he had revealed himself. Ironically, the Greeks' reasoning depended upon their own stories, and where reason failed them they filled in the blanks with their own foundational stories.

Since the first Christians were all Jews, they presented their message about Jesus in terms of the promised Savior of God's people: "Jesus is the Messiah (Christ)." In their preaching to Jews, the apostles emphasized the resurrection of Jesus more than his death because it demonstrated that the man executed as a criminal was nevertheless God's Messiah.

Following guidelines laid down by Jesus himself, the apostles pointed to Old Testament passages that had been fulfilled in his career and in the beginnings of the church. "This is what was prophesied" was frequently on their lips. In describing Jesus they used Old Testament images. He was the Passover Lamb, the second Adam, the Son of David. He was the stone the builders rejected, but God chose him to be the cornerstone in the construction of his church.

FALSE GOSPELS

While relying almost completely on the language and concepts of the Jewish Scriptures, the apostles nevertheless drew sharp lines between true and false versions of the Christian message. They condemned rival gospels outright. In Galatians, Paul curses those who add Jewish legal requirements to the gospel. First John establishes this point: Christians must believe that Christ came "in the flesh." And 1 Corinthians fixes belief in the historical resurrection of Jesus as the indispensable basis of salvation.

During the apostolic period, church members encountered the central truths of the faith in a number of ways. Although at first converts were often baptized in the name of Jesus alone, baptism in the name of the Trinity soon became standard practice. The gospel of Matthew shows that baptism "in the name of the Father and of the Son and of the Holy Spirit" was practiced in his day (Matt. 28:17–20). By Justin's time, the middle of the second century, converts at Rome were baptized as they answered questions about their belief in "God, the Father and Lord of the universe, Jesus Christ who was crucified under Pontius Pilate, and the Holy Spirit who through the prophets foretold all things about Jesus."

Scholars have discovered summaries of the teaching of the apostles—1 Corinthians 15:3–4 and Ephesians 4:4–6 are examples—that indicate the first-century Christians formulated their beliefs and had a basis for resisting the errors they encountered.

They also sang their beliefs. From time to time the New Testament quotes one of these hymns. First Timothy 3:16 (NIV) is likely an example:

> He [Christ] appeared in a body,
>   was vindicated by the Spirit,
> was seen by angels,
>   was preached among the nations,
> was believed on in the world,
>   was taken up in glory.

Since the worship of Jesus was central, first-century Christians drew the line of irreconcilable difference through the doctrine of Christ. When we read the Fourth Gospel carefully we recognize that the author is fighting on two fronts. One set of readers he has in view are not convinced that Jesus was in the full sense God. To them he points out that the life of Jesus can only be explained by the fact that in Christ the eternal Word of God has become incarnate. Toward the end of his gospel he explains his purpose in writing: "that you may believe that Jesus is the Christ, the Son of God, and that by believing you may have life in his name" (John 20:31, NIV). In other words, he has to persuade some readers of Christ's deity.

John had other readers, however, who had to be persuaded of Christ's full humanity. They evidently thought of Christ as an appearance of God on earth in human form but without actual flesh and blood. Against these John points out how at the crucifixion of Jesus real blood and water flowed from his pierced side. Thus John fights on two fronts, against those who thought Jesus was a mere man and against those who believed him to be a heavenly ghost.

We know from other sources that both of these heresies existed in the first and second centuries. The first position was held by a Jewish-Christian sect known as the Ebionites. They taught that Jesus was a mere man who by his scrupulous obedience to the Law was "justified" and became the Messiah.

The opposite position was called *Docetism*. The word comes from a Greek verb, *to seem*. Some bright theologian has suggested we call it *Seemism*. The title comes from their teaching that Christ was not really a man: he was a spectral appearance. He only seemed to suffer for man's sins since we all know divine phantoms are incapable of dying.

The Event—God in flesh—has always struck man as religious nonsense. History shows how tirelessly man schemes, searching for some substitute explanation. One of his most popular devices is to lift the story out of time and present it as an "eternal" truth, some mystery of the universe, a myth that explains the way things really are.

MEN WHO KNEW

In the early church the most ambitious attempt to reshape the gospel along these "spiritual" lines was Gnosticism. The term Gnosticism is an umbrella term used to identify a variety of movements, each one offering some way of enlightenment prescribed by a guru, a philosopher who possessed the *gnosis* or knowledge of the way of life. This special knowledge of the spiritual world posed a major threat to apostolic Christianity.

Strong feelings often flared between orthodox Christians and the Gnostics. On one occasion, according to Polycarp, a student of John the disciple, the apostle was entering the baths at Ephesus. Inside he saw Cerinthus, a well-known Gnostic, preparing to bathe. John, presumably garbed in a towel and a sour expression, rushed outside without taking a bath.

"Let's flee," he said, "before the baths fall in. Cerinthus the enemy of the truth is inside."

Along with apostolic Christianity they accepted the idea of salvation, the idea of a supreme deity, and the idea of heavenly beings at work in the universe. Such common beliefs help explain why Gnostics lingered around the edges of the church during the second century and why many of them found their way in. In entering, however, Gnostics intended to purify these basic ideas from what they considered the low and crude interpretations that a "materialistic" Christianity had somehow introduced.

What Gnostics Believe

The origin and sources for Gnosticism are disputed, but common elements taught by the major Gnostic teachers of the second century give a good window into their mysterious perspective. These Gnostic teachers were refuted by major theologians such as Irenaeus, Tertullian, and Origen.

Common Elements for Second Century Gnosticism

1. Most of the Gnostic schools held to a moral and metaphysical dualism (theory picturing two kinds of real things); there were spiritual things that were regarded as inherently pure, while they regarded material things as intrinsically evil.
2. The supreme reality or god is not the creator. The material world must result from a primeval disorder, or the ignorance or mischief of an inferior deity: a demiurge, the Old Testament God, or Jesus (a lower being for Gnostics).
3. Gnostics believed that there is a spiritual or divine element in mankind or the chosen among mankind; the spiritual element is the true identity of persons who are aliens in the material world and body (which the Gnostics regarded as inherently evil).
4. They pictured a series of mediators in successive aeons or heavens to help people escape the evil world of matter.
5. Salvation involves the genuine person or spirit being liberated from the evil physical world through knowledge.

The basic belief of the Gnostics was what we call *dualism*, that is, they believed that the world is ultimately divided between two cosmic forces, good and evil. In line with much Greek philosophy, they identified evil with matter. Because of this they regarded any Creator God as wicked. Creation by a deity, they felt, was not so much impossible as it was indecent. Their own Supreme Being was far removed from any such tendency to "evil."

Since the ultimate deity could have no contact with the material world, the Gnostic explained creation by a series of emanations. If we think of God as a kind of sun, these emanations would be sunbeams, extensions of his own nature, yet distinct. These supernatural powers, however, were capable of producing other inferior powers until they had fashioned, as Charles Bigg, the Oxford scholar, once said, "a long chain of divine creatures, each weaker than its parent," and came at last "to one who, while powerful enough to create is silly enough not to see that creation is wrong." This was the God of this world, the God of the Jews.

The exact relationships of the series of emanations differed in the different Gnostic schools. But they agreed that somehow the pure light of heaven in the soul of man had become involved in this unpleasant business of matter and had to be redeemed.

The Gospel of Thomas

Gnostic versions of Jesus' life are typically late compared to the Gospels of the Christian canon; most date from the late second to fifth centuries, with *The Gospel of Thomas* being a possible exception. It was uncovered in Egypt in 1945. A copy in the Coptic language dates from the fourth century. Several fragments found in Greek date from the third century, with one as early as AD 200. The gospel was likely written in Syriac and translated into Greek and Coptic, though it is commonly assumed to be written in Greek. Many date this gospel's composition in the second century, with a few scholars dating it in the first century. Recent assessments are placing the gospel much later, however, because of its familiarity with Syriac traditions. A more likely date for *The Gospel of Thomas* is AD 150–200, with AD 175–200 being most likely. It is important to note that an early date would change little concerning the early church's response to the Gnostic challenge. The early church is pictured as actively working to maintain the genuine memory of Jesus and his teaching.

Gnostics created their own versions of Christian literary works. Generally Gnostics took Jesus to be one of the many lesser deities lacking the purity and potency of the supreme reality or god. It was only such a lesser being who would engage the evil material world at all. Even so, they predictably picture a Jesus who was unconnected to the environment he came from and the movement he left behind. He rejected his Jewish orientation, the Torah, and Jewish titles like Son of God. He is not pictured as performing miracles or defeating death in resurrection. This was an otherworldly Jesus who passed on knowledge by what he said. Scholars differ concerning what the "Gnostic Jesus" actually taught. Often readers reconstruct a Jesus from these sayings who looks like the readers themselves. It is fashionable to picture a Jesus who is tolerant and inclusive of people who claim intuitive, prophetically given insights (typically suppressed by the controlling bishops). This Gnostic Jesus supposedly supported women, despite a misogynist declaration about women not being included in heaven at the close of the most famous of the Gnostic documents, *The Gospel of Thomas.*

The church seems to have known of these Gnostic gospels and rejected them. The documents may actually include some things that Jesus said, but they were rejected because they leave the wrong overall impression of Jesus.

Other Gnostics used different arguments to escape from the dilemma of a human Savior. One group insisted that Jesus did not really have a body at all; it was a clever hallucination—the same heavenly ghost idea we saw in Docetism. In any case Gnostics agreed that the Christ could not be human.

Thus we have what a modern Christian must think a striking surprise. The first major test to faith in the Event was not denial of Jesus Christ's deity; it was rejection of his humanity!

Compared with apostolic Christianity, Gnosticism was full of surprises, not the least of which was a strange doctrine of "predestination," for lack of a better term. Many Gnostics recognized a kind of proletariat and bourgeoisie of heaven. The lower spiritual class lived by faith and the upper class, the illuminated or the perfect, lived by knowledge. Still a third group, the spiritually disadvantaged, were not capable of *gnosis* under any circumstances. Some capricious deity had created them without the capacity to "see" even under the best guru.

Politics and Interpretation

Interpretation occurs in politically charged contexts, and that is especially so when trying to understand Jesus. One interpretive strategy assumed that history's winners survived to leave a written record or history, while the losers are written out of the story. In the case of Jesus, according to this strategy, a bishop-led and doctrinally tedious version of Christianity survived; the winning version won by oppressing and suppressing the other versions that were practically eclipsed or dismissed as deviant. *The Gospel of Thomas* was thought to give an earlier window into one of these alternative versions.

The discovery of *The Gospel of Thomas* gave an important boost to another interpretive strategy where researchers suspect that a counterfeit Christianity has replaced a genuine form. Within this framework, the version of Christianity that is well-known is not catholic (universal) after all; instead, traditional Christianity offers an untrue version of Jesus. Even Thomas Jefferson employs this strategy. He believed that Matthew, Mark, Luke, and John passed on a corrupt version of Jesus, but an enlightened mind could remove the layers of crude religion and discover the teaching of the genuine Jesus.

With *The Gospel of Thomas*, the stage was set for these strategies to converge. Scholars could reconstruct the Gnostic Christianity which had been oppressed by the winning but untrue traditional view of Jesus. *The Da Vinci Code* presents a popular, non-scholarly version of these strategies, which implausibly fixes the move to traditional Christianity in the fourth century after Jesus.

THE DANGERS OF KNOWING

Gnosticism holds an important lesson for all Christians who try to disentangle the gospel from its involvement with "barbaric and outmoded" Jewish notions about God and history. It speaks to all who try to raise Christianity from the level of faith to a higher realm of intelligent knowledge and so increase its attractiveness to important people.

In his effort to reconcile Christ and the gospel with the science and philosophy of his day, the Gnostic denied the Event and lost the gospel. He interpreted the Savior in light of the fascinating ideas of the enlightened men of his day. But the attempt to tie the gospel to the latest theories of men is self-defeating. Nothing is as fleeting in history as the latest theories that flourish among the enlightened, and nothing can be more quickly dismissed by later generations.

If the Gnostics had triumphed, Christians would have surrendered their priceless heritage from Judaism. The robust message of Christianity to all men would have shriveled to a discussion by a chosen few, and Christ would have ceased to be the model human, the second Adam. He would have been lost among the many gods of the mystery religions.

Orthodox Christians found the Gnostics very difficult to combat. Gnostics claimed that they had some secret information. Jesus, they said, had passed on this information to the gnostic teachers of his time and had hidden it from the materially blinded Jews who founded the church. If this line of argument failed, Gnostics would appeal to a special revelation from heaven to prove their point.

Yet Christians rose up to cast out the gnostic heresy, and in doing so they clarified their own orthodox convictions. The best summary of early Christian beliefs is what we call the Apostle's Creed, to this day repeated every Sunday in many churches. It was not written by the apostles, in spite of its title, but appeared first as a baptismal confession

An Overview of Gnosticism

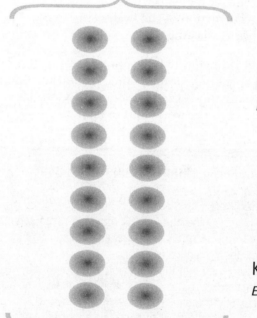

UNNAMED FATHER
[Spiritual & Good]

Pleroma
Fullness

Aeons
*Emanations
or Mediators*

Kenoma
Emptiness

WORLD
[Material & Evil]

in second-century Rome. Scholars call the early version of it the Old Roman Creed:

> I believe in God Almighty
> And in Christ Jesus, his only Son, our Lord
> Who was born of the Holy Spirit and the Virgin Mary
> Who was crucified under Pontius Pilate and was buried
> And the third day rose from the dead
> Who ascended into heaven
> And sits on the right hand of the Father
> Whence he comes to judge the living and the dead.
> And in the Holy Ghost
> The holy church
> The remission of sins
> The resurrection of the flesh
> The life everlasting.

The Creed is obviously built upon belief in the Trinity. Yet it does not, strictly speaking, develop the Trinitarian doctrine. It nowhere seeks to explain the three-in-oneness of God. Its central concern is how God relates to the world and to men.

Answers to Gnosticism

Responding to Gnostic Challenges (Ancient or Contemporary)

The ancient church points the way for us today, responding to the Gnostics and other efforts to revise or distort Christian thinking with three basic responses drawing from clergy, creed, and canon.

By clergy we mean that the leadership of the early church had direct connections with the men whom Jesus had called to himself to be his inner circle; it was a matter of custody: the ones whom Jesus had traveled with and taught for three years had passed on the message and left a written witness to their encounter with Jesus. Identifying with these witnesses is the sure way forward.

By creed we mean the early condensing of the basic Christian story and message in a simple narrative summary. While they come from different places with substantially different emphases, the summaries of Tertullian (from North Africa), Irenaeus (from Turkey), and Origen (from Alexandria) are amazingly similar: the basic message of Christianity involved the Father sending his Son to the world to recall, reclaim, and restore it through the death and resurrection of the Son and the ongoing work of the Spirit. This consistent and publicly accessible message is sure.

By canon we mean the four New Testament Gospels, which were firmly embraced by the great body of the church within the second century. Early fathers knew of other renderings of who Jesus was and rejected them; instead they held to these four gospels as giving the right overall impression of Jesus. (Even good fragments are not enough alone; they must be organized to make a whole story.) Trusting the gospels of Jesus' companions is the sure way ahead.

First, the Creed affirms belief in "God Almighty." A later version adds "Maker of heaven and earth." Thus it repudiates the gnostic idea that the created world is evil or the work of an evil god. This material world is good and worthy to be used and enjoyed by man.

"There is no good trying to be more spiritual than God," is the way C. S. Lewis, the widely read Cambridge professor, put it in his *Mere Christianity.* "God never meant man to be a purely spiritual creature. That is why He uses material things like bread and wine to put the new life into us. We may think this rather crude and unspiritual. God does not: He invented eating. He likes matter. He invented it."

Next, the Creed affirms belief in "Jesus Christ his only Son our Lord: who was born of the Holy Spirit and the Virgin Mary, crucified under Pontius Pilate and was buried."

Many a modern man has been stopped by the phrase "born of the Virgin Mary." He cannot believe in the virgin birth. But ironically, to the early Gnostics, the problem was not *Virgin*: it was *born*. Modern man sees a red flag because he hears "born of the *Virgin* Mary"; the Gnostic saw a red flag because he heard "*born* of the Virgin Mary." This phrase, however, together with the ones about crucifixion and burial, was the church's way of underscoring its belief in the complete humanity of Jesus.

In orthodox Christianity redemption came not by some secret knowledge of spiritual realms but by God's action in history. The Son of God entered time, was born of a virgin, was crucified under Pontius Pilate, and was buried. That is not *gnosis;* that is Event.

Finally, the phrase in the Creed, "the resurrection of the flesh" is aimed at the Gnostic. It stressed that man is a whole; he is not divided, as the Gnostic taught, into a good soul and an evil body. The body, said orthodox Christians, is no burden to be discarded. It is God's gift to man for life on earth and for the life to come.

Man needs salvation not because he is imprisoned in a body but because he willfully chooses his own way rather than God's way. Man's evil is not in his body; it is in his affections. He loves the wrong things.

This affliction is so deep, so basic to man's life on earth, that only a special Savior can free him from himself. That is why catholic Christianity insists that Gandhi and all who agree with him are wrong. Man does not need a teacher. He needs a Savior.

Understanding Gnosticism Today

Two analogies or comparisons may help us assess Gnostic claims about Jesus. The first is about historical proximity. The church's gospels are written about thirty to sixty-five years after Jesus' life. This span of time would be comparable to the relationship of a fifty-five-year-old professor in the year 2010 to the Vietnam War or the Korean Conflict, which occurred in his lifetime. This professor can assess what he reads about these conflicts with his own living memory and that of his eyewitness contemporaries. By contrast, the earliest Gnostic gospel is probably written 140 years after Jesus' life (and much later for all except *The Gospel of Thomas*). This span of time would be comparable to our professor's relationship to the Civil War. Our professor would have no living memory of or connection to these events. Fortunately, the Civil War is remarkably well-documented. Without its many eyewitness accounts readers would be left to depend upon retellings by people with no memory of the events they report.

Another comparison centers upon the difficulty of offering historical reconstructions of events and persons. There have been a great many books and movies that reconstruct the life and work of Abraham Lincoln. These typically share some general consensus about the outline of his basic life story, family, and service, but they still vary about his motives, religion, and person. But a very different reconstructing of his life emerges from the vampire mania of contemporary culture. This carnivorous cultural phenomenon offers a variety of interpretations of a seemingly endless variety of topics. Its reconstruction of Lincoln replaces some of the consensus story and supplements the surviving elements of the story. Intriguing elements take on new significance: for example, Lincoln was prone to long sleepless nights, and he could handle an axe, two facts that take on sinister implications in the vampire mythology. Even the overall reconstruction yields an interesting insight: slavery, like vampire wars, was draining the life force from slaves and the nation for the sake of money (see the numerous reviews). The book picturing Abraham Lincoln as a vampire hunter is typically understood as fantasy; but on the issues of proximity and methodology, it is an illuminating comparison to the Gnostic versions of Jesus. The old narrative is replaced or supplemented to make a substantially different story.

Suggestions for Further Reading

Davidson, Ivor J. *The Birth of the Church: From Jesus to Constantine, AD 30–312, Baker History of the Church.* Vol. 1. Grand Rapids: Baker, 2004.

Hall, Christopher A. *Learning Theology with the Church Fathers.* Downers Grove, IL: InterVarsity, 2002.

Hurtado, Larry, W. *Lord Jesus Christ: Devotion to Jesus in Earliest Christianity.* Grand Rapids: Eerdmans, 2003.

*Litfin, Bryan *M. Getting to Know the Future: An Evangelical Introduction.* Grand Rapids: Brazos Press, 2007.

Kelly, J. N. D. *Early Christian Doctrine,* 5th ed. New York: Harper, 1978; London: Continuum, 2000.

Martin, Ralph P. *Worship in the Early Church.* Grand Rapids: Eerdmans, 1964.

Wand, J. W. C. *The Four Great Heresies.* London: A. R. Mowbray, 1955.

CHAPTER 6

THE RULE OF BOOKS

The Formation of the Bible

DURING THE LAST GREAT persecution of Christians in the Roman Empire, early in the fourth century, a believer in Sicily was brought before the governor. He was charged with possessing a copy of the Gospels.

"Where did these come from?" asked the judge, pointing to the books. "Did you bring them from your home?"

"I have no home," replied the prisoner, "as my Lord Jesus knows."

Once again pointing to the Gospels, the judge said, "Read them!"

The Christian opened the Gospels and read, "Blessed are those who are persecuted for righteousness' sake: for theirs is the kingdom of heaven."

He turned to another place and read again, "If any man will come after me, let him deny himself, and take up his cross, and follow me."

That was too much. The judge ordered his prisoner away—to death.

Roman officials came to see that the suppression of Christianity demanded the destruction of the Scriptures. So the last great persecution of Christians included the burning of the Scriptures.

To this day we find it almost impossible to think of the Christian faith without the Bible. It is the foundation of Christianity's evangelism, its teaching, its worship, and its morality. When we look back over Christian history, we find few if any decisions more basic than those made during the first three centuries surrounding the formation of the Bible. The Scriptures served not only as the inspiration for believers facing martyrdom, but as the supreme standard for the churches threatened by heresy. If catholic Christianity was orthodox, the Bible made it so, for the constant test of any teaching was, what do the Scriptures say?

We need to ask, then, how did we get the Bible?

THE BASICS OF THE BIBLE

The name itself—*Bible*—suggests that Christians consider these writings special. Jerome, the fourth-century translator, called them "the Divine Library." He wanted to stress that the many books were, in fact, one. Greek-speaking believers made the same point when they shifted from the early plural form *Biblia,* meaning *The Books,* to *The Bible,* meaning *The Book.*

Long before, Jews had faced the same problem when they spoke of *The Scriptures* and *Scripture.* That explains how, in time, the *Bible* and *Scripture* came to mean the same thing in Christian circles, the sixty-six books that Christians consider the written Word of God.

Today, we find the Scriptures grouped under *Old Testament* (or Covenant) and *New Testament.* In the ancient world a *testament,* or more often a *covenant,* was the term for a special relationship between two parties. Occasionally we still speak of the *marriage covenant,* which binds husband and wife to each other.

Used in the Bible, the term stands for the special relationship between God and man, initiated and sustained by the grace of the Lord God. The old covenant was first between the Lord and Abraham, then between God and Abraham's descendants, the children of Israel. Later years knew them as Jews. So the Old Testament contains the books that tell the story of the Jews and their ancient worship of God.

Early Christians believed that Jesus of Nazareth was God's promised Messiah, who established a new covenant with his new people, the church. So the New Testament stands for the books telling the story of Jesus Christ and the birth of the church.

The Bible contains two portions: the Old Testament, which the early Christians claimed along with the Jews, and the New Testament, which the early Christians produced in spite of the Jews. The Old Testament promised; the New Testament fulfilled.

The word for the special place these books occupy in Christianity is *canon.* The term from the Greek language originally meant *a measuring rod* or, as we might say, *a ruler.* Eventually the word was applied to the Scriptures: the books or listing of books that the church discerned were authoritative or inspired by God. Since the first Christians were all Jews, Christianity was never without a *canon,* or, as we say, *Scripture.* Jesus himself clearly accepted the Old Testament as God's word to man. "Scripture cannot be broken," he said. "Everything written about me in the law of Moses and the prophets and the psalms must be fulfilled" (John 10:35; Luke 24:44).

Jesus believed the statements of Scripture, endorsed its teaching, obeyed its commands, and set himself to fulfill the pattern of redemption it laid down. Early Christians were simply heirs of this attitude. Had not the hopes and plans of the old covenant come true in Jesus? Had not the promised messianic age dawned in him?

Christians, almost without exception, embraced the Old Testament as their own. Early Christians, both Jews and Gentiles, believed that Jesus was the fulfillment of the promises running through the Old Testament. Christians also inherited strategies for interpreting from Jesus. Jews in Alexandria had read much of the Bible as allegory. They sought a deeper spiritual or intellectual message beyond the literal meaning. Still others employed a method called typology. The reader discerns a pattern (type) or correspondence between two images or stories. Thus, the story of Jesus may be read with an awareness that he is like an Old Testament sacrifice or an Old Testament deliverer such as Moses.

By the third century the church had sophisticated scholars who could defend the Christian claim to the Old Testament by the use of allegory. The most influential was a teacher at Alexandria named Origen, who spoke of the different levels of Scripture:

> The Scriptures were composed through the Spirit of God, and have both a meaning which is obvious, and another which is hidden from most readers . . . . The whole law is spiritual, but the inspired meaning is not recognized by all—only by those who are gifted with the grace of the Holy Spirit in the word of wisdom and knowledge.

Christian appeals to allegory infuriated pagan critics of the faith because their case depended on their taking the Old Testament at face value. The move remained popular, however, since it enabled Origen and other believers to find the Christian message just beneath the surface of the Old Testament.

THE QUESTION OF THE APOCRYPHA

When Christians retained the Old Testament for their own use, they did not settle completely just which books this included. To this day Christians differ over the inclusion or rejection of the so-called Apocrypha in the Old Testament list of books. The term stands for twelve or fifteen books, depending upon how you group them, that Roman Catholics and Eastern Orthodox accept as canonical and most Protestants reject.

Some Jews embrace a canon that includes the typical Protestant canon for the Old Testament of thirty-nine books. Scholars often picture this being more typical for the Jews in Palestine. They numbered these books in clusters and organized them by a three-fold division of

Law, Prophets, and Writings. The three-fold structure of this emerging canon may explain Jesus referring to the Law of Moses, the prophets, and the Psalms (the first book in the Writings, Luke 24:44). Most scholars believe Jesus quoted only from this smaller canon, which is frequently but perhaps deceptively called the "Palestinian Canon."

The Greek translations of the Old Testament included the books of the Hebrew canon, with additional books as well. Protestants routinely call these additional books the Apocrypha, or more generically the Deuterocanonical books. The Greek translations, the chief of these being the Septuagint, were influential in making the books of the Apocrypha more popularly circulated. Greek translations of the Old Testament were made in the City of Alexandria. This larger canon, consisting of the Hebrew canon and the Apocrypha, is called the "Alexandrian Canon."

Early Christians differed over the question of the Apocrypha. In the West the influential Augustine, the well-known bishop of Hippo, embraced the Apocrypha as part of the canon of Scripture. During the sixteenth-century Reformation most Protestants rejected the Apocrypha as canonical. The Roman Catholic Church, following Augustine, accepted the books. And that is how the churches differ to this day.

From the beginning, however, Christians had more than the Old Covenant as their rule for faith. During Jesus' life on earth they had the Word made flesh, and after Jesus' departure they had the living leadership of the apostles. The reverence for the apostles' message, whether oral or written, as the authentic channel to the will of the Lord Jesus, is reflected throughout early Christian literature.

During the days of the apostles, congregations often read letters from the companions of the Lord. Some of these letters were obviously intended to be read in public worship, probably alongside some portion of the Old Testament or with some sermon.

Churches also relied on accounts about the life of the Lord Jesus. The first gospels were not written before AD 60 or 70, but their contents were partly available in written form before this. Luke tells us that many had undertaken some account of the events of the life of Jesus.

The question is, out of this growing body of Christian literature, how did the twenty-seven books we know as the New Testament come to be set apart as Scripture? How and when did they cross the line between books regarded as important and even authoritative, and books regarded as holy and the Word of God? To put it in one word, how did they become canonical?

Several factors were at work in this process. Some were internal characteristics of the developing life of the churches; others were external, threats to the gospel arising from historical events and pagan influences.

First, the books that are Scripture and are truly the Word of God have about them a self-evidencing quality. They carry their uniqueness on their face. They have always exercised, and still exercise, a transforming power upon the lives of men.

For example, as a young man Justin Martyr searched energetically for truth in a variety of philosophical schools: first as a Stoic, then a Pythagorean, then a Platonist. But none of them satisfied him. One day, while meditating alone by the seashore, perhaps at Ephesus, he met an old man. During their conversation the stranger exposed the weaknesses of Justin's thinking and urged him to turn to the Jewish prophets. By reading Scripture, Justin became a Christian. Scores of other men and women in the early days of the church had a similar experience: Tatian, Theophilus, Hilary, Victorinus, Augustine.

One of the primary reasons, then, behind the adoption of the New Testament books as Holy Scripture was this self-authenticating quality.

Second, certain Christian books were added to Scripture because they were used in Christian worship. Even in the New Testament itself there are signs that the reading of Scripture was very much a part of Christian congregational life. The apostle Paul urged the Colossians, "After this letter has been read to you, see that it is also read in the church of the Laodiceans and that you in turn read the letter from Laodicea" (Col. 4:16, NIV).

Justin Martyr, writing in the middle of the second century, gives us the first description of a Christian service:

> On the day called the Day of the Sun all who live in cities or in the country gather together to one place, and the memoirs of the apostles or the writings of the prophets are read, as long as time permits; then, when the reader has ceased, the president verbally instructs, and exhorts to the imitation of these good things. Then we all rise together and pray.

Thus we see by Justin's time *The Memoirs of the Apostles*, which was his title for the Gospels, were a central part of Christian worship.

The mere act of reading a book in Christian worship did not assure the writing an eventual place in the canon. We know, for example, that Clement, Bishop of Rome, wrote a letter to the church at Corinth about AD 96 and eighty years later it was still the custom in Corinth to read Clement's letter at public worship. Yet Clement's letter was never added to the canon. Books read at the worship of the church had a special position and had started on the road that led to entrance into the canon of Scripture—but some did not make it.

Third, and perhaps the fundamental factor behind a Christian book's acceptance into the New Testament, was its ties to an apostle. This was the test of a book's validity: was it written by an apostle, or at least by a man who had direct contact with the circle of the apostles?

In the early church the apostles held a place that other men simply could not fill. Early believers always regarded them as men who had a unique relationship with the Lord. Did not Jesus say, "He who receives you receives me" (Matt. 10:40)?

Clement of Rome reflects this general attitude of Christians when he writes, "The apostles were made evangelists to us by the Lord Christ; Jesus Christ was sent by God. Thus Christ is from God, and the apostles from Christ . . . . The Church is built on them as a foundation" (1 Clement 42). Any gospel or letter, therefore, that could make a strong claim to apostolic authorship stood a good chance of acceptance as Scripture.

A LIST OF CHRISTIAN BOOKS

Given enough time the churches, under the influence of these factors, and perhaps others, probably would have drawn up a list of canonical Christian writings. But certain events forced the hand of the churches.

About AD 140 a wealthy and much-traveled ship owner from Sinope on the Black Sea came to Rome. His name was Marcion. Although the son of a bishop, Marcion fell under the spell of the gnostic teacher Cerdo, who believed that the God of the Old Testament was different from the God and Father of the Lord Jesus Christ. The God of the Old Testament, he said, was unknowable; the Christian God had been revealed. The Old Testament God was sheer justice; whereas the God of the New Covenant was loving and gracious.

Marcion developed Cerdo's distinction. He held that the Old Testament God was full of wrath and the author of evil. This God, he said, was only concerned for the Jewish people. He was prepared to destroy all other people. In contrast, the Christian's God was a God of grace and love for all, who disclosed himself in Jesus Christ, his Son.

Because he believed that the God of the Old Testament loved the Jews exclusively, Marcion rejected the entire Old Testament and also those New Covenant writings that he thought favored Jewish readers—for example Matthew, Mark, Acts, and Hebrews. He also rejected other Christian writings that appeared to him to compromise his own views, including the Pastoral Letters (1 and 2 Timothy and Titus). So he was left with only a mutilated version of Luke's gospel (we suppose he omitted the nativity stories) and ten letters of Paul. The Apostle to the Gentiles, it seems, was the only apostle who did not corrupt the gospel of Jesus.

Marcion's garbled Christian views were firmly repudiated by the church in Rome, and Marcion was excommunicated from the church in AD 144. Before long, however, Marcionite churches appeared, modeled on orthodox congregations. They had their own ministers and rituals. For example, they did not use wine at communion, as a result of the ascetic emphasis of their teaching. Some of the Marcionite beliefs spilled over into the various gnostic sects, and Marcionites were themselves affected by gnostic views. Their ideas spread, however, throughout Italy and as far afield as Arabia, Armenia, and Egypt. In the East they exercised a considerable influence for many decades. A number of Marcionite villages existed near Damascus as late as the fourth century.

Most importantly, however, Marcion presented the orthodox churches with a twofold problem: his list of New Testament books, shaped in the image of Paul, and his rejection of the Old Testament.

Marcion's worship of Paul was little short of idolatry. As he saw it, Paul was the great enemy of the law and the great spokesman for the gospel. He was in fact the supreme figure in the church. Marcion believed Christ had descended from heaven twice, once to suffer and to die, and once to call Paul and to reveal to Paul the true significance of his death. In heaven, said Marcion, Paul sits at the right hand of Christ, who sits at the right hand of God.

As the North African lawyer Tertullian put it, Paul had become the apostle embraced by the heretics! Of course, Marcion had to misinterpret Paul to make the apostle fit his beliefs, but that didn't make the churches' problem any less real: how could they accept Paul's letters as God's word without endorsing Marcionite teaching?

In the end Paul meant too much to the church to dismiss him because of Marcion's extreme views. The apostle's letters were too well known and too widely used to discard them. The church chose, instead, to restore the Pastorals and the letters of the other apostles and to link all the letters to four gospels by using the book of Acts as the bridge. While the church treasured the grace of God preached by Paul, it realized that jettisoning the Old Testament was suicidal. Does the New Covenant make sense without the Old?

By retaining the Old Testament the church scored two important points. First, it insisted that faith for the Christian would identify the idea of the creating God with the idea of the redeeming God. Marcion's message was too easy. Marcion had not only misread the Old Testament; he also broke the unity seen in the entire Christian Scriptures: the same God who made the world also chose Israel; that God sought to reclaim his creation by Jesus, who fulfills Israel's destiny. Second, by retaining the Old Testament the church underscored the importance of history for the Christian faith. Christianity is a historical religion, not just in the sense that it comes from the past or that it is associated with a historical character named Jesus. It is historical because it stems from the belief that within history itself, in a particular place, at a particular time, God himself took a hand in human affairs. And that means that living by faith for the Christian includes facing the puzzles of human existence—all of the "why, Lord?"s of life—and still believing that God has some good in mind.

If Marcion, a heretic, nudged the churches into thinking about forming a New Testament, another troublemaker, Montanus, forced the churches into thinking about closing it.

FRESH VOICES FROM GOD

Christianity has always been a religion of the Spirit. According to the Fourth Gospel Jesus had promised to his people the Paraclete, the Spirit of Truth, to guide them (John 16:13–15). How, then, did there ever come a time when the church declared that all the inspired books that could be written had been written, and that nothing more could ever be added to the written word of God? How did it come about that, as Tertullian bitterly put it, "the Holy Spirit was chased into a book"?

In the second half of the second century a change was coming over the church. The days of enthusiasm were passing and the days of ecclesiasticism were arriving. The church was no longer a place where the Spirit of prophecy could be heard. More and more people were joining the churches, but the distinction between church and world was fading. The church was becoming secularized; it was coming to terms with heathen thought and culture and philosophy. The way of the cross was no longer rough and steep.

Into this situation, sometime between AD 156 and 172, Montanus appeared, a voice in the wilderness of Asia Minor. He came with a demand for a higher standard and a greater discipline and sharper separation of the church from the world. Had he halted there, he could have done little but good, but he went much further. He and his two prophetesses, Prisca and Maximilla, went about prophesying in the name of the Spirit, and foretelling the speedy second coming of Christ. That in itself was not extraordinary. But these new prophets, in contrast to prophets in biblical times, spoke in a state of ecstasy, as though their personalities were suspended while the Paraclete spoke in them. Montanus was convinced that he and his prophetesses were the God-given instruments of revelation, the lyres across which the Spirit swept to play a new song. With that Montanus's super spirituality went too far.

Clearly the church had to act. One problem was simply disorder. Montanus as a herald of a new spiritual vitality and a new challenge to holiness was one thing; but when Montanists insisted that opposition to the new prophecy was blasphemy against the Holy Spirit, many churches split over the question.

Montanus argued that the new age of the Spirit had displaced the previous ages. The Old Testament age, with its ten commands or law, had been surpassed by the age of the Son with its more demanding Sermon on the Mount. The age of the Spirit would call for even greater rigorous obedience, as well as surpassing revelations. In the name of the Spirit, Montanus denied that God's decisive and normative revelation had occurred in Jesus Christ.

In the face of this challenge how could the church keep the gospel central? It had to make all later Christian worship, teaching, and life center in Christ and the apostolic witness. Free utterances of the Spirit would not guarantee that; Montanism was making this clear. The best way to make the original apostolic gospel basic was to set apart the apostolic writings as uniquely authoritative. This would require all later faith and action to be judged in the light of that central message.

It was not that the church had ceased to believe in the power of the Holy Spirit. The difference was that in the first days the Holy Spirit had enabled men to write the sacred books of the Christian faith; in the later days the Holy Spirit enabled men to understand, to interpret, and to apply what had been written.

One of the reasons we know that the church assumed this position lies in the appearance of lists of New Testament books. One of the first is a document written about AD 190. We call it the Muratorian Canon, from its discoverer L. A. Muratori, who first published it in 1740. The document is damaged at the beginning, and actually begins with Luke, but its list of books is as follows: Matthew, Mark, Luke, John, Acts, 1 and 2 Corinthians, Ephesians, Philippians, Colossians, Galatians, 1 and 2 Thessalonians, Romans, Philemon, Titus, 1 and 2 Timothy, Jude, 1 and 2 John, the Apocalypse of John (that is, the Revelation), the Apocalypse of Peter, and The Wisdom of Solomon. The last two, we know, did not remain on the approved list. But by AD 190 the churches clearly accepted the idea of Christian Scriptures alongside Jewish Scriptures, one fulfilling what the other promises.

By the early third century only a handful of books continued to create any question. Hebrews faced some opposition in the western regions of the empire and Revelation was unpopular in the east. At the outset of the fourth century, Eusebius, the church historian, summed up the situation and indicated that James, 2 Peter, 2 and 3 John, and

The New Testament as It Gained Acceptance by the Early Church

100	200	250	300	400
Different parts of our New Testament were written by this time, but not collected and defined as "Scripture." Early Christian writers (for example Polycarp and Ignatius) quote from the Gospels and Paul's letters, as well as from other Christian writing and oral sources. Paul's letters were collected late in the first century. Matthew, Mark, and Luke were brought together by 150.	**New Testament used in the church at Rome (the "Muratorian Canon")** Four Gospels Acts Paul's letters: Romans 1 & 2 Corinthians Galatians Ephesians Philippians Colossians 1 & 2 Thessalonians 1 & 2 Timothy Titus Philemon James 1 & 2 John Jude Revelation of John Revelation of Peter Wisdom of Solomon **To be used in private, but not public, worship** The Shepherd of Hermas	**New Testament used by Origen** Four Gospels Acts Paul's letters: Romans 1 & 2 Corinthians Galatians Ephesians Philippians Colossians 1 & 2 Thessalonians 1 & 2 Timothy Titus Philemon 1 Peter 1 John Revelation of John **Disputed** Hebrews James 2 Peter 2 & 3 John Jude The Shepherd of Hermas Letter of Barnabas Teaching of Twelve Apostles Gospel of the Hebrews	**New Testament used by Eusebius** Four Gospels Acts Paul's letters: Romans 1 & 2 Corinthians Galatians Ephesians Philippians Colossians 1 & 2 Thessalonians 1 & 2 Timothy Titus Philemon 1 Peter 1 John Revelation of John (authorship in doubt) **Disputed but well known** James 2 Peter 2 & 3 John Jude	**New Testament fixed for the West by the Council of Carthage** Four Gospels Acts Paul's letters: Romans 1 & 2 Corinthians Galatians Ephesians Philippians Colossians 1 & 2 Thessalonians 1 & 2 Timothy Titus Philemon Hebrews James 1 & 2 Peter 1, 2, & 3 John Jude Revelation of John **To be excluded** The Shepherd of Hermas Letter of Barnabas Gospel of the Hebrews Revelation of Peter Acts of Peter Didache

Jude were the only books spoken against by some while recognized by others. Revelation, however, continued to bewilder him.

The first complete list of books, as we have them today, came in an Easter letter written in 367 by Bishop Athanasius from Alexandria. Shortly thereafter councils in North Africa at Hippo (393) and at Carthage (397) published the same list.

The Logic of the Canon

Everett Ferguson has expounded the process and progress of canonical thinking. First, believers come to recognize that there are books that carry divine authority, and once the concept of "sacred writings" is embraced, the process of canonical thinking is underway. Second, one begins to think of a boundary for the canon. Sacred writings are different from other writings, and one might even think there is a limited number. Third, believers might move to a closed canon, an explicit listing of all the sacred writings. Finally, a consensus emerges around this common listing of sacred books.

In one sense, of course, Christians created the canon. Their decisions concerning the books were a part of history. In another sense, however, they were only recognizing those writings that had made their authority felt in the churches. The shape of the New Testament shows that the early churches' primary aim was to submit fully to the teachings of the apostles. In that purpose they shaped the character of Christianity for all time. The faith remained catholic precisely because it was apostolic.

Suggestions for Further Reading

Blackman, E. C. *Marcion and His Influence.* London: S.P.C.K., 1948.

Bruce, F. F. *The Canon of Scripture.* Downers Grove, IL: InterVarsity, 1988.

Campenhausen, Hans von. *The Formation of the Christian Bible.* Philadelphia: Fortress Press, 1968.

Filson, Floyd Vivian. *Which Books Belong in the Bible? A Study of the Canon.* Philadelphia: Westminster, 1957.

Grant, Robert M. *The Bible in the Church.* New York: Macmillan, 1948.

Metzger, B. M. *The Canon of the New Testament.* Oxford: Oxford University Press, 1987.

*McDonald, Lee Martin. *Formation of the Bible: The Story of the Church's Canon.* Peabody, MA: Hendrickson, 2012.

CHAPTER 7

THE SCHOOL
FOR SINNERS

The Power of Bishops

"THE WIND BLOWS WHEREVER it pleases," Jesus had said to Nicodemus. "You may hear its sound, but you can't tell where it comes from or where it is going. So it is with everyone born of the Spirit" (John 3:8). And so it seemed during the age of the apostles. The Spirit swept freely through the churches empowering believers, inspiring prophets, exorcising devils.

The first Christians believed that the new birth by the Spirit was the indispensable mark of the Christian. "If anyone does not have the Spirit of Christ," Paul told the Roman believers, "he does not belong to Christ." Baptism in water was the sign. When asked by his listeners on the Day of Pentecost, what shall we do? Peter replied, "Repent and be baptized . . . in the name of Jesus Christ for the forgiveness of your sins. And you will receive the gift of the Holy Spirit" (Acts 2:38, NIV).

But what if a Christian sins seriously after receiving the Spirit and submitting to baptism? Are there sins after baptism for which there is no forgiveness?

Such questions troubled Christians deeply in the second and third centuries, especially after Montanus "began to rave in a kind of ecstatic trance," accusing the churches of sins against the Spirit. The rejection of Montanism with its prophesying and moralizing disclosed the church as an institution more clearly than at any other moment. The church preached to the nations and revealed its universality; it confronted heretics and articulated its orthodoxy; it struggled with sin and developed its episcopacy. When the churches granted to bishops the power to forgive sins, catholic Christianity was complete.

75

Episcopacy (from the Greek word *episcopos*, bishops), the power and prestige of the bishops, developed slowly. The apostles, as we have seen, were the unchallenged leaders of first-century churches. They had walked with Jesus; they were witnesses of his resurrection. Yet the Spirit moved as he pleased. Prophets and teachers and miracle workers and healers could also claim the Spirit's power. Even in the face of the Corinthian confusion created by rivalries over spiritual gifts, Paul refused to deny the manifestations of the Spirit. "In the church," he wrote, "God has appointed first of all apostles, second prophets, third teachers. . . . The . . . Spirit . . . gives them to [the church] just as he determines" (1 Cor. 12:28, 11, NIV).

LEADERS FOR THE CHURCHES

Paul made sure, however, that the churches planted in the path of his missionary journeys had pastoral leaders to care for the spiritual needs of believers in a given place. These local leaders were of two sorts. One group was called *elders* or *presbyters* (from the Greek for elders). These same men were also known as *bishops* (overseers) or *pastors* (shepherds). The other group of leaders was called *deacons.*

The duties of these leaders varied from place to place, but generally speaking the presbyters taught new converts, led in public worship, and maintained discipline. The deacons assisted the presbyters in every way except perhaps presiding at the Lord's Supper. Thus the apostolic age knew both a traveling group of Spirit-empowered leaders and a resident group caring for the needs of established congregations.

This general picture, however, soon changed. After the turn of the century, Ignatius, the pastor of the church at Antioch, wrote a series of letters. In these he speaks habitually of a single bishop (or pastor) in each church, a body of presbyters, and a company of deacons. God's grace and the Spirit's power, he teaches, flow to the flock through this united ministry.

No one seems to know just how the single pastor, assisted by the elders and deacons, became the widespread pattern within the churches, but we know it did. Several factors probably influenced the trend. Apparently one of the presbyters emerged to correspond with other churches, to handle the funds for the poor, to preach the true faith in the conflicts with heretical teachers, and to administer the Lord's Supper (or Eucharist).

It took some years before Ignatius's threefold ministry was adopted everywhere. We know, for example, that Alexandria had no single bishop until about AD 180.

And when the churches accepted the pattern, not all administered affairs in the same way. Numerous small churches in Asia Minor and Africa had their own bishops. But elsewhere, for example in Gaul, the bishop of a large town would supervise congregations in surrounding areas by assigning presbyters to them.

By the late second century, however, the unchallenged leader in church affairs was the bishop. His hands were gently strengthened by the conflict with the Gnostics, who appealed to a succession of teachers traced back to the apostles. Jesus, so the Gnostics argued, had entrusted a secret wisdom to certain teachers before he ascended. These teachers, in turn, passed on this special truth to other teachers. And they, in turn, to others. So the gnostic teachers, rather than the Catholic churches, had the true philosophy.

Catholic Christians countered this argument by stressing the public teaching of the churches, the rule of faith, and the bishops in the churches established by the apostles. This argument was outlined first by Hegesippus, a historian who traveled from Palestine to Rome in the mid-second century. He associated with numerous bishops along the way and heard the same teaching from all. Catholic (or orthodox) teaching was public, available to anyone. "In every succession and city," he said, "what the law and the prophets and the Lord preached is faithfully followed." To support his point he drew up succession lists of bishops, going back to the apostles, at least for Corinth and Rome.

Later in the century Irenaeus in Gaul and Tertullian in North Africa followed in this anti-gnostic path mapped out by Hegesippus. They pointed to the succession of bishops in the Catholic churches stemming from the apostles and argued that this guaranteed the unbroken tradition of the apostles' doctrine within the Catholic churches. Gnostics were wrong; Catholics were right.

These changes in the structure and functioning of the church, especially the role of bishops, raise crucial and controversial questions. Christians of nearly every denomination admit that these changes took place. The question is, what do the changes mean, and what authority, if any, do they have for the church of later times, especially our own?

WHAT TO MAKE OF BISHOPS

Three quite different answers to this question are possible:

1. Some Christians argue that the men who guided the destiny of the early church willfully and sinfully departed from a divinely authorized pattern, so that the changes they made should be repudiated and reversed.

This is the assumption of most attempts to "restore primitive Christianity." We sometimes call them "back-to-the-Bible" movements. It is the common characteristic of most reforming movements in the history of the church. Such movements always face the troublesome task of deciding how much of what the apostolic church did was intended to be part of the permanent pattern that churches of all ages should follow. If, for example, we accept the office of elder as a norm for our times, shall we also insist that women remain silent in the church?

2. Other Christians contend that the church and its leaders were exercising the liberty they had in the absence of any divinely authorized pattern. The government they developed may have served a good purpose in their time, but it is open to change to meet the needs of later generations, including our own.

This position is usually held by those impressed with the church as a social institution immersed in the stream of historical development. It is the position of "progressives" who want the church to adapt to the times. Such Christians suffer the disadvantage of being unable to identify any faith or pattern of church government that has the seal of God's approval. In its extremes it is Christianity without ultimates and absolutes. Everything is up for grabs.

3. Still other Christians argue that the Holy Spirit so dwelt in the church and guided its decisions that the developments of the early centuries in doctrine and church structure were the work not of men but of God. They are, therefore, permanently binding for the church.

This third answer, advanced by most Catholic Christians, makes much of what its spokesmen call the witness of history. But if the changes made in the second, third, and fourth centuries are attributed to the Holy Spirit, why not the eighteenth, nineteenth, and twentieth? Why must we stop with the so-called catholic centuries?

Our question—what authority does the rise of the episcopal (or bishop's) office have for Christians?—suffers not from silence but from conflicting responses. Our disagreements explain, in part, our denominational differences to this day. However, even in the third century many felt that the coming of episcopacy meant the departure of the Spirit.

In the first and second centuries, Christians looked for proof of the Spirit's power, not in an office, but in the lives of believers. They saw the Paraclete in terms of moral energy.

The apostle Paul had led the way in this. He described the Spirit's work in terms of the edification of the entire church. This edification means growth in all that is good. "The fruit of the Spirit," he said, "is love, joy, peace, patience, kindness, goodness, faithfulness, gentleness, and self-control" (Gal. 5:22–23, NIV). Spiritual regeneration and the moral life were not merely one side of Christianity to Paul but its very fruit and goal on earth.

In the generations after the apostles, Paul's emphasis continued. Throughout the writings of the early church fathers and the apologists you find the ethical demands occupying the front rank. Beyond all question, these Christian communities tried to regulate their common life by principles of the strictest morality, tolerating no unholy members in their midst. Gross sinners were ejected from the church.

One early Christian put the matter bluntly: "There is a distinction between death and death. For this reason the disciples of Christ die daily, torturing their desires and mortifying them according to the divine scriptures; for we have no part at all in shameless desires, or scenes impure, or glances lewd, or ears attentive to evil, lest our souls thereby be wounded."

The high level of morality evident in the Christian congregations was, in fact, a primary argument for the truth of Christianity. In his *Apology*, Justin devotes lengthy sections to a statement of the moral principles in Christianity and to a proof that these are observed by Christians. What the apologist wants to prove is that goodness among Christians is not an impotent claim or a pale ideal but a power developed on all sides and actually exercised in life.

Athenagoras, a Christian philosopher at Athens, put it this way: "Among us are uneducated folk, artisans, and old women who are utterly unable to describe the value of our doctrines in words, but who attest them by their deeds."

But Christians were not alone in testifying that they had been lifted into a new world of moral power and holiness: even their opponents witnessed to their exemplary lives. Pliny told the Emperor Trajan that during his examination of Christians he had been unable to find anything criminal or vicious in them. Justin confessed that the steadfastness of Christians convinced him of their purity, and that these impressions proved decisive in bringing him over to the faith. We frequently read in the accounts of the martyrs that the courage and loyalty of Christians made an overwhelming impact on those who witnessed their trial or execution, so much so that some of these spectators suddenly decided to become Christians themselves.

At the beginning of the third century, however, something significant happened. The extraordinary moral fiber in the church weakened. Montanus was not entirely wrong. By the year 220 it was evident
that the Christian churches, together with their bishops and clergy,
were no longer what they had been.

WHAT ABOUT UNFORGIVABLE SINS?

During the first two centuries most Christians believed that baptism
canceled all sins committed up to that moment in the believer's life.
Serious postbaptismal lapses called for special treatment. Three sins
in particular—sexual immorality, murder, and the denial of the faith
(apostasy)—were considered forgivable by God, but never by the
church. The penalty for any one of these was exclusion from the fellowship of the church and deprivation of the Lord's Supper. Since the
Communion, most believed, was a special channel of divine grace,
withholding it placed a person's salvation in peril. Ignatius had called
it "the medicine of immortality and the antidote of death."

The first half of the third century was a long period of calm for
the church; few were called before Roman officials to renounce their
faith. Some felt spiritual warfare was a thing of the past; disciplines and
moral standards were relaxed. The first to accept repentant sinners as
a matter of policy was the bishop of Rome. Callistus (217–222) readmitted penitent members who had committed adultery and abortion. He
argued that the church is like Noah's ark. In it unclean as well as clean
beasts can be found. Then he defended his actions by insisting that the
bishop of Rome was "close to Peter" and the Lord had given keys to
Peter to bind and to loose the sins of men. This marks the first time a
bishop of Rome claimed this special authority.

Tertullian, living in North Africa at the time, was horrified. "We
do not forgive apostates," he cried, "and shall we forgive adulterers?"
It was a voice from the past. The future rested with Callistus. If those
guilty of adultery could be readmitted to the church, why not apostates? By midcentury many were asking that very question.

In AD 250 the most violent persecution the church had yet faced
was instigated by the Emperor Decius (249–251). A general from the
Danubian frontier, Decius was determined to have no nonsense from
Christians. In his eyes, they were enemies of the empire. Their atheism was responsible for the many troubles in the realm. Thus Decius
commanded all citizens of the empire to sacrifice to the traditional
Roman gods. Those who did so were given certificates (*libelli*, in Latin)
as evidence that they had obeyed the order. Those who refused to obey

and were unable (or unwilling) to obtain false *libelli* from sympathetic or corrupt officials faced death.

To save their lives many Christians complied. Others were able to obtain certificates without having actually sacrificed. But an unknown number of Christians were imprisoned or executed, among them the bishops of Rome, Antioch, and Jerusalem.

Those who were killed were called "martyrs," that is, "witnesses." Decius, however, was not out to make heroes. He wanted to discredit Christianity, so many Christians were tortured until they denied Christ by saying "Caesar is Lord." If a Christian endured this persecution without denying Christ he was called a "confessor." If a believer under torture did what the Romans demanded, he was classed among the "lapsed," the fallen ones. The fury ended, at least for a season, in AD 251, when Decius, deserted by his gods, was killed in a battle with the barbarian Goths.

Then the question of readmission to the church arose with striking intensity. Many believers were guilty of apostasy, sometimes as many as three-quarters of a congregation. Without adequate spiritual preparation they had bowed to imperial pressure. Like Peter in the courtyard of the high priest, they had denied their Lord and now they wept bitterly.

The implications of their exclusion from the church were now clearer than ever. Bishop Cyprian of Carthage said flatly, "Outside the church there is no salvation." And many agreed with him. Thus a clamor arose for readmission.

But how could the church receive those who had denied the faith? Wasn't this the "sin against the Holy Spirit" for which there was no forgiveness? What evil could be worse than to deny, from fear or pain, the only way to salvation? If this is pardoned, anything can be pardoned!

THE BIRTH OF SAINTS

The awe and admiration of the martyrs and confessors was enormous. Martyrdom, the baptism of blood, represented the utmost glory that a Christian could attain. The names of the martyrs were carefully kept in the records of the churches and their "birthdays" into eternal life were remembered by annual celebrations at their tombs. The "saints" were coming!

In Carthage, Cyprian confronted those who held that the confessors by their unusual courage had achieved a special power from God. The Holy Spirit had ordained them extraordinarily so that they had the power to absolve men of their sins. They could "cover with their merits the demerits of the lapsed." Many urged Cyprian to announce such a blanket pardon.

Cyprian declined, however, in favor of a system of readmission based on the degrees of seriousness of the sins. Leniency, he said, should be extended to those who had sacrificed only after excruciating torture and who well might plead that their bodies, not their spirits, had given way. Those, however, who had gone willingly to make sacrifices must receive the severest punishment.

His argument won general approval, so to deal with these degrees of guilt, the church created a graded system of penance. Only after varied periods of sorrow for sin (penance) were the sinners allowed to return to the Lord's Supper. The bishop extended forgiveness to the fallen, provided they proved their sorrow by coming before the congregation in sackcloth and with ashes on their heads. After this confession and act of humility the bishop laid his hands upon the penitent as a symbol of restoration to the church.

The proposal from the North African confessors, however, was only temporarily defeated; it did not die. It reappeared years later in the Roman Catholic doctrine of the Treasury of Merit and the practice of indulgences. In these, too, the church transferred the merits of the unusually spiritual (the saints) to needy sinners.

The most prominent voice for the traditional strict policy came from Rome. A presbyter and highly respected theologian, Novatian, argued that the church had no power to grant forgiveness to those guilty of murder, adultery, and apostasy. It could only intercede for God's mercy at the Last Judgment.

Novatian met the stiff opposition of another presbyter named Cornelius, who held that the bishop could forgive even grave sins. The church was split over the matter, the past arrayed against the future. The primitive concept defended by Novatian considered the church as a society of saints; the new view advocated by Cornelius saw the church as a school for sinners.

Cornelius's view was popular enough to get him elected bishop of Rome by a majority. Novatian received the backing of a minority. Soon Novatianists built up a network of small congregations and considered the catholic churches polluted as a result of their lenient attitude toward sinners. They may have been right, for the catholic churches now offered unlimited forgiveness to all who sinned.

Along with baptism, and ever after it, catholics had a second sacrament; it was still without form, but they relied upon it as a thing that had form, and considered themselves justified in applying it in almost every case: it was the sacrament of penance.

Suggestions for Further Reading

Chadwick, Henry. *The Early Church*. Middlesex: Penguin, 1967.

Davidson, Ivor J. *The Birth of the Church: From Jesus to Constantine, AD 30–312, Baker History of the Church*. Vol. 1. Grand Rapids: Baker, 2004.

Davies, J. G. *The Early Christian Church*. Garden City, NY: Doubleday, 1967.

Greenslade, S. L., ed. *Early Latin Theology*. Philadelphia: The Westminster Press, 1976.

Prestige, G. L. *Fathers and Heretics*. London: S.P.C.K., 1963.

CHAPTER 8

APOSTLES TO INTELLECTUALS

The Alexandrians

JEROME, BEST KNOWN FOR his translation of the Bible into the Latin Vulgate version, was a rigid monk. Once, however, about 374, while still a novice in the life of self-denial, he fell ill during Lent and in a nightmare he dreamed that he was standing before the great judgment seat. From somewhere came a voice, strong and terrifying: "You, Jerome, are a Ciceronian, not a Christian."

It was the voice of conscience, no doubt. Jerome loved the Lord but he also knew and loved the works of the classical authors: Cicero, Sallust, Lucretius, Virgil, Horace, and Juvenal. His nightmare is typical of the struggle of soul the early church had over pagan literature and philosophy. It is a struggle without end. What fellowship has Christ with Belial? What has the Psalter to do with Horace, the Gospels with Nietzsche, or Paul with Hemingway?

As the Christian message spread, believers faced the spiritual and intellectual challenge of teaching people with differing philosophical outlooks. Many of these outlooks belonged under the umbrella term Hellenism—the period of Greek culture and thinking from Aristotle until the emergence of the Romans. New arguments and criticisms prompted Christian thinkers to give a more complete account of Christian teaching.

In the third century Christianity was no longer a minor Jewish sect. It was fast emerging as the dominant rival to the old ways of Rome. Men of culture and power were asking the big questions: what is Christianity's role in the affairs of men and empires?

LIGHT IN THE WORLD

The church always stands in a dual relationship to human affairs. Jesus summarized the role best when he spoke of his disciples: "not of the world" but "sent into the world" (John 17:16, 18). This suggests that in God's plan the church feels the rhythm of detachment and involvement: detachment because the gospel and eternal life are not from men but from God, yet involvement because God sends the church into the world to shine as light and to lead men to the truth.

Thus the church moves through history to a special beat: separation from the world yet confrontation of the world. This means struggle, because Christians often differ with each other over the boundaries of withdrawal and engagement. Witness to some is compromise to others.

Predictably, then, some Christians resisted the efforts of orthodox scholars to reconcile the Christian faith with Greek philosophy. Withdrawal, they argued, was the way of the apostles.

John had warned his "little children" not to love the world. "If anyone loves the world," he wrote, "the love of the Father is not in him." And the apostle Paul, who likely received a Greek education, discerned that the message of the cross appeared as mere foolishness to Greeks. What fellowship does light have with darkness?

In the third century the most violent opponent of Christian reconciliation with Hellenic philosophy was Tertullian. Heresies, he shouted, are prompted by philosophy. Valentinus was a Platonist! Marcion was a Stoic! "What do Athens and Jerusalem have in common? Away with all attempts to produce a mottled Christianity of Stoic, Platonic, and dialectic composition! We have no need of curiosity reaching beyond Christ Jesus. When we believe, we need nothing further than to believe. Search that you may believe; then stop!"

Considering the church's life-and-death struggle with Gnosticism, Christians could ill afford to dismiss Tertullian's attitude as the narrow-minded reaction of some religious bigot. The gnostic Valentinus had in fact trained his philosophical guns on incorporating the gospel and had left many a Christian camp in confusion. Gnosticism created a version of Christianity drastically recast to fit several trendy and extreme convictions common in the ancient Mediterranean culture.

But once the Gnostic had been identified for what he was, an enemy within the ranks, could Christians continue to resist Hellenic philosophy as a foreign spy or could it be recruited as an ally?

During the third century when Christians were struggling to retain their faith under the persecuting policies of the emperors, they were also discovering ways to present the gospel in terms of Hellenic thought.

Eventually the emperor accepted the gospel, and Rome became Christian. But the path to that reconciliation was paved by those Christian teachers who demonstrated that faith and philosophy could live in harmony when both bowed before Christ.

Leadership in this union arose in Alexandria at the so-called catechetical school led by Clement and Origen. They were the first of a succession of Christian scholars thoroughly familiar with the wisdom of Greece and enthusiastic for its philosophy, yet loyal to the teaching of Christ. They tried to blend into Christianity all that was best in the culture of the Hellenic world, especially in the Platonic and Stoic philosophers. "The way of truth," Clement said, "is one. But into it as into a perennial river, streams flow from all sides."

Historians still debate whether the school arose from within the church at Alexandria or whether it was at first independent of the church. The evidence, it seems to me, points to an independent beginning. We know that individual philosophers—Stoic, cynic, and gnostic—opened schools in major cities and drew students to their lectures. Christians followed this practice. When Justin stood trial in Rome, his pagan judge asked about his activities. According to the official transcript, Justin answered, "I live on the second floor of the house of a certain Martin near the bath of Timotheus. There I have been staying since I have come to Rome a second time. I know of no other meeting place. All of those who visited me there I have instructed in the doctrine of truth. Yes, I am a Christian."

Apparently around 180 a Sicilian Christian named Pantaenus established a similar school of Christian Gnosticism in Alexandria and lectured there on Christianity as the true philosophy. He aimed to enter the thought world of pagans to show the superiority of the catholic faith. The teaching was *gnostic* (literally, knowledge) because it asked the big questions of meaning; but it was *Christian Gnosticism* because it retained orthodox answers. Pantaenus appealed to all who hungered for knowledge, not only to Christians but also to pagans seeking truth. By his thorough and inspiring expositions, he won many a pagan for Christianity and lifted many Christians with him to the theological heavens.

A PASTOR TO PHILOSOPHERS

Pantaenus's reputation drew Clement to Alexandria. There he remained for twenty years first as Pantaenus's pupil, then as his successor as head of the school. We know Clement primarily through his surviving writings. His most revealing works form a possible trilogy: the *Exhortation to the Heathen*, the *Instructor*, and the *Miscellanies*, which he never completed.

His contemporaries, however, knew him not so much as an author, but as a "messenger of Christianity in philosopher's garb." The philosopher's garb was the sign of one taking up a distinctive life and community in pursuit of genuine knowledge. Clement gave witness to the truth and knowledge found in following Christ against the backdrop of Alexandria, an intellectual center for searching after the truth.

Clement, "the first Christian scholar," was versed not only in the Holy Scriptures but also in the knowledge of his time, including Greek philosophy and classical literature. He understood the questions and problems of the young people who came from such educational centers as Rome, Athens, and Antioch. They were just as dissatisfied with their instruction as he had been and now sought and found the last and highest wisdom in the Christian revelation. Many of the students, no doubt, had encountered Christianity before in the form of some heretical gnostic theory. Clement had to enter their world, disentangle their conceptions, and lead them slowly from error to the true knowledge of Christianity. He lived and taught like a philosopher and used the forms and the language of the Gnostics of his time.

Clement's purpose was clear. He seized not only the external garb and forms of expression of the contemporary pagan philosophers but also their problems. If, for example, he discussed the universe and its meaning (cosmology), so loved by Gnostics, he did not do it with the intention of proving these ideas wrong offhandedly and then discarding them quickly, but instead he pointed out how the fundamental religious questions about the creation of the world, the existence of evil in this life, and the salvation through the Word, Jesus Christ, found their last and deepest answer in Christian revelation. He wanted to be an apostle to the Hellenistic intellectual world. His purpose was not purely or even primarily theological, but pastoral. His greater purpose was not to win arguments, but men to Christ, and lead them to salvation.

It was a risky venture, especially in Alexandria where the influence of Valentinian Gnosticism was in the air. The church had reason to be afraid of Greek philosophy and pagan literature. Pagan religion permeated classical literature, and this simultaneously religious and philosophical framework tended to distort key Christian convictions. Poorly informed Christian converts often faced a choice between clever, eloquently defended heresy or a modest orthodoxy. Any informed Christian in a modern secular school would recognize the problem. Clement was determined to offer a third possibility.

Like the heretical Gnostics, the Alexandrian scholars aimed to bring Christianity into touch with the thought of the times. This called for some positive role for philosophy. Clement argued that it was preparation for Christianity. "Before the advent of Christianity," he says in the opening chapter of his *Miscellanies*, "philosophy was needful to the Greeks for righteousness. Now it is useful to piety for those who attain faith through demonstration. Philosophy was a schoolmaster to the Greeks, as the law was to the Hebrews, preparing the way for those who are perfected by Christ."

The methods of Clement and Origen, however, were sharply opposed to those of the heretical Gnostics. In building their philosophical case for Christianity, the Gnostics left the apostolic gospel in shambles. But Clement and Origen remained thoroughly loyal to the essential message of Peter and Paul even as they explored its implications.

Clement and Origen differ from the Gnostics in another important respect: Christian behavior. Many gnostic heretics believed that acquiring knowledge was unrelated to the training of character, since matter and body were inherently evil and corrupt. But Clement insists that spiritual insight comes to the pure in heart, to those humble enough to walk with God as a child with his father, to those whose motive for ethical behavior goes far beyond fear of punishment or hope of reward to a love of the good for its own sake. It is an ascent from faith through knowledge to the beatific vision beyond this life, when the redeemed are one with God. The basis for this possibility of mystical union is the image of God implanted by creation.

Thus we come to the fundamental conflict between Clement and the heretical Gnostic. The Valentinians had rejected creation as the product of some evil deity, but Clement makes creation central. God, he believed, had implanted the good seeds of truth in all his rational creatures. The Christian can learn from the Greeks because all truth and goodness, wherever found, come from the Creator.

Clement's ministry, then, marked an important juncture in the progress of Christian doctrine. After him, Greek thinking united with Christian thought. In the great saints and theologians of later Eastern Christianity this bond was secured. Without it the staggering theological achievements of the first church councils would have been impossible. Origen's genius was dedicated to building on the foundation of this union.

ORIGEN AND THE THIRST FOR TRUTH

Shortly after the turn of the third century a persecution against Christians broke out in Alexandria. Clement was forced to flee the city, but as he had learned from Plato, "necessity is the mother of invention."

He surrendered leadership in the school to a remarkably gifted eighteen-year-old.

Even at that tender age Origen proved a worthy successor to Clement. He shared his master's enthusiasm for philosophy. He, too, traced man's thirst for knowledge to the work of God:

> If we see some admirable work of human art, we are at once eager to investigate the nature, the manner, the end of its production; and the contemplation of the works of God stirs us with an incomparably greater longing to learn the principles, the method, the purpose of creation. This desire, this passion, has without doubt been implanted in us by God. And as the eye seeks light, as our body craves food, so our mind is impressed with the . . . natural desire to know the truth of God and the causes of what we observe.

Origen (185–254), the great Alexandrian teacher, always considered the exposition of Scripture his primary task.

Only Christianity holds this knowledge, and Origen aimed to bring all truth into God's plan of salvation provided by Christ.

Origen came from a Christian home. His father Leonides had, in fact, suffered martyrdom in the same persecution that drove Clement from Alexandria. To support his family Origen sold his secular books and began his extraordinary career as teacher and scholar.

Unfortunately, the scholar was often in trouble with his bishop, Demetrius. He thought Demetrius a power-hungry church official, consumed with his own self-importance. For his part, Demetrius found

Origen uncooperative in his efforts to organize the church in Egypt. In the ancient church the bishop directed the ministry of people under his care. Origen's opportunities for ministry were restricted by his bishop.

About 229 Origen was invited to Athens, and on his way to Greece he passed through Palestine where he had many admirers. At Caesarea he accepted ordination to the ministry. Demetrius considered this crass insubordination and led in a public condemnation of Origen. Thereafter, Origen made his home at Caesarea. Thus the great scholar's career is divided between his years at Alexandria (202–230) and those at Caesarea (230–254).

In any city, however, Origen was a magnetic teacher. He accepted invitations to travel from many quarters. Students from hundreds of miles came to capture something of his wisdom as the Queen of Sheba came to Solomon. Among the earliest was a young prospective law student from Asia Minor named Gregory, later nicknamed the Wonderworker, because of his unusually successful missionary labors among his own people.

After five years under Origen's instruction, Gregory wrote a book praising his teacher. According to Gregory, from the first Origen set before his students the goal of genuine philosophy, the attainment of the good life. Only those who aim at living an upright life, he taught, can live worthy of reasonable creatures and seek to know first themselves and then what is good and what man ought to strive for, what is evil, and what man ought to flee. Ignorance, he said, is a great barrier to godliness. There can be no genuine piety toward God in the man who despises the gift of philosophy. But true philosophy, said Origen, always focuses on the Word, "who attracts all irresistibly to himself by his unutterable beauty."

Origen's philosophy, then, was more than a matter of ideas; it was a way of forming character. Here his example proved to be his most powerful lesson. He stimulated us, says Gregory, "by the acts he performed more than by the theories he taught." He urged his students to examine the springs of their conduct, to note the impulses that led them out of confusion into moral order, and to resist the seeds of evil and cultivate the growth of goodness, which was what Origen meant by reason. Thus he instilled in his students a love for virtue, and they came to see that their teacher was himself a model of a truly wise man.

Thanks to the generosity of a wealthy friend, Origen gained the services of seven shorthand writers, to work in relays. Books began to pour from his literary workshop. His fame soared to extraordinary heights. Jerome later asked, "Who could ever read all that Origen wrote?"

The great Alexandrian addressed a wide range of subjects for Christians and against pagans, but he always considered the exposition of Scripture his primary task. He is practically the only Greek-speaking Christian to study the Old Testament in its original Hebrew language. He produced a book entitled *Hexapla*, which displayed six versions of the Old Testament in six parallel columns. He added to this scores of commentaries and hundreds of sermons on particular books. The Scriptures, he believed, are the treasury of divine revelation. Students, therefore, must see them as a whole. Any occasion where the apparent sense of a passage contradicted the morality or nature of God was a God-given sign that there must be some deeper lesson underneath the surface of the passage.

This conviction led Origen into what we usually call the "allegorical interpretation" of Scripture. He held that there are three levels of meaning in the Bible: the literal sense; the moral application to the soul; and the allegorical or spiritual sense, which refers to the mysteries of the Christian faith. These senses corresponded to common notions that people were composed of a mind, soul, and a body. In practice, Origen typically appealed to the literal and spiritual senses. Origen believed that interpreting the Bible was a great intellectual endeavor, but the ability to see the spiritual sense was given to him by the Holy Spirit as a gift.

Origen's overriding concern was to allow the whole Bible to speak for itself, whatever a single text may seem to say, for when the Bible speaks it speaks for God who inspired it.

Here Origen scored a telling point against the heretics. The persistent tendency of heresy, whether ancient or contemporary, is to lay hold upon a few impressive texts and to wrench some rigid and erroneous interpretation from these. This Origen would not allow. He wanted the whole Bible to speak, because he knew that what the Bible taught in its entirety is the central Christian truths of catholic Christianity.

Origen's enormous work in the Scriptures was immensely important. It enabled intelligent Christians to believe the Bible and so to remain Christians. What would have happened to Christianity without a rationally interpreted Bible to feed the mind and control the development of Christian thought? Origen saved the Scriptures for the church and thus protected the historical foundation of the Christian faith.

A THEOLOGY FOR THINKERS

The great scholar's achievements in Bible study were matched by his pioneering work in systematic theology. Most earlier Christian theology aimed at the refutation of heresy. Origen was the first theologian to set forth his whole intellectual framework of the Christian faith. He produced his work on *First Principles* early in his ministry, but he never found the need to modify it to any degree. It was addressed to educated readers and dealt with ideas they would recognize. Origen felt no contempt for the simple faith of peasants, but he realized that if Christianity were to succeed in shaping civilization, it must justify itself to the intellect as well as to the heart of mankind.

The rule of faith was an unofficial restatement of the Christian teaching or story found in several early Christian teachers. Origen was grateful to proclaim that he had never abandoned the rule of faith. He, however, also felt free to offer "speculative" teaching when the rule was silent on a particular matter.

Origen's vision, it seems, knew no limits. It extended so far as to teach that all creatures, including the devil himself, would one day be restored to communion with God. Hell would be emptied. That doctrine, above all others, caused him no end of trouble. Many humane souls in the history of the church have dreamed that God's love would someday triumph over all sinful rebellion. Origen's error lay in turning a dream into a doctrine. Orthodox Christians felt that they could not turn the dream into a doctrine because such an idea almost always tends to deny man's free will and its eternal consequences.

If God has character, as Charles Williams argued in *Descent of the Dove*, and if man has choice, an everlasting rejection of God by man must be admitted as a possibility; that is, hell must remain. Origen simply went too far. He proposed as a doctrine what can only remain as a desire.

The end of all desires for Origen came in 254. In the persecution instigated by Emperor Decius, Origen was singled out for special attack. He was flung into prison, chained, and tortured. The authorities made him as miserable as possible while preserving his life in constant torment. Decius's reign of terror for the church ended in 251 and Origen was released. The torture, however, had taken its toll on the white-haired professor. He died three years later, at the age of sixty-nine, at Tyre.

Origen's expansive mind and Clement's generous spirit have always made orthodox Christians uncomfortable. Did they go too far in their accommodation to the Hellenistic environment? Did the language and concepts of Greek philosophy invade Christian ranks and lead the original gospel into captivity? Sincere Christians raise these questions because they know that love of the world can compromise the revealed articles of faith.

It is clear, however, that Clement and Origen were true to the faith as it was understood. Even though they entered seriously into the spiritual world of their listeners, they were aware of the meaning of salvation. Just as Christ in his incarnation adopted human existence, so his people in the course of history adopt the humanity of all peoples and civilizations. Like Paul, who was "all things to all men" (1 Cor. 9:22), Clement repeatedly declared, "For the Hellenes one must become a Hellene in order to win them all. One must offer to those who demand it the kind of wisdom with which they are familiar so that as easily as possible they can make their way through their own world of ideas to the belief in the truth."

On the positive side, what Clement and Origen did was preserve humanism for Christianity. They made possible the careers of other great Christian leaders—Athanasius and Gregory of Nyssa and John Chrysostom—who followed them. And they demonstrated that the best of classical culture could find a home and a future within the church.

Suggestions for Further Reading

Davidson, Ivor J. *The Birth of the Church: From Jesus to Constantine, AD 30–312. Baker History of the Church.* Vol. 1. Grand Rapids: Baker, 2004.

Danielou, J. *Origen. Translated by W. Mitchell.* New York: Sheed and Ward, 1955.

Franzen, August. *A History of the Church: Revised and Edited by John P. Dolan.* New York: Herder and Herder, 1969.

Oulton, J. E. L., and Henry Chadwick, eds. *Alexandrian Christianity.* Philadelphia: Westminster, 1954.

Patzia, A. C. *The Emergence of the Church.* Downers Grove, IL: InterVarsity Press, 2001.

Prestige, G. L. *Fathers and Heretics.* London: S.P.C.K., 1963.

*Trigg, Joseph Wilson. *Origen: The Bible and Philosophy in the Third Century Church.* Atlanta: John Knox, 1983

THE AGE OF THE CHRISTIAN ROMAN EMPIRE

312–590

The Emperor Constantine is one of the major figures of Christian history. After his conversion Christianity moved swiftly from the seclusion of the catacombs to the prestige of palaces. The movement started the fourth century as a persecuted minority; it ended the century as the established religion of the empire. Thus the Christian church was joined to the power of the state and assumed a moral responsibility for the whole society. Initially under the instruction of Constantine, the church refined its doctrine and developed its structure. Some, such as the historian Eusebius, saw Constantine's embrace of Christianity as its victory over the empire. Others, such as the monks, believed the culture was capturing Christianity. The story that follows is the "Christianizing" of the great Hellenistic mindset and world. When the empire gave way to barbarian invaders (known as Europeans today), the monks ironically won over the conquerors; the monks displayed the dignity of a well-ordered life in community with deep roots in the Christian faith.

The Age of the Christian Roman Empire

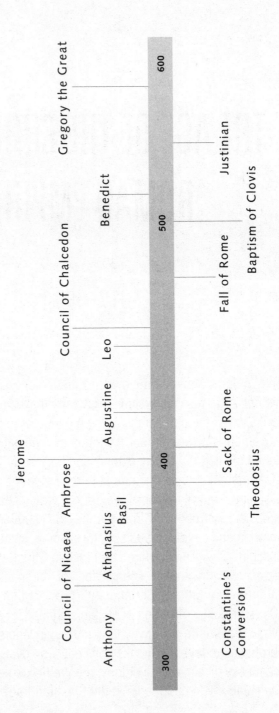

CHAPTER 9

LAYING HER
SCEPTRE DOWN

The Conversion of the Empire

U NLESS HE HAS SOME special interest in history or in sculpture, today's tourist in Rome will marvel at the size of the Triumphal Arch of Constantine. But if he stops to read his guidebook carefully he will recognize the Latin at the top of the arch is praising "The Emperor Caesar Flavius Constantine the Great" for some impressive victory over "the enemy and his whole troop."

A frieze on the town side of the arch shows the enemy, a rival Caesar named Maxentius, and his troops falling from the Milvian Bridge into the Tiber River. They are the battered and bleeding victims of the victorious Constantine.

Eusebius of Caesarea, the Christian historian and biographer of Constantine, compared Maxentius's destruction in the Tiber to the Pharaoh's in the Red Sea. Many contemporaries recognized that Constantine's conversion to Christianity and his victory over his enemies was "inspired by the Godhead" and marked a turning point in history.

Constantine represents the passing of the Age of Catholic Christianity and the beginning of the Age of the Christian Empire (312–590). Courageous martyrs were a thing of the past. The Christianization of the empire and the imperial interference in the affairs of the church begins. We can detect the fallout of these two developments to this day.

How could such a turn of events even come about? Why did the despised and persecuted "superstition" called Christianity rather suddenly arise from the shadows of Roman society and assume, almost overnight, the spiritual leadership of the vast and powerful empire?

TURNING AROUND AN EMPIRE

To catch the significance of this shift in Christianity's fortunes we need to go back to Constantine's predecessor in the imperial palace, a general named Diocletian.

All the signs of a crumbling empire were there in 284, when Diocletian first donned the purple. Thirty emperors had claimed the throne in the third century, and many others tried. The Roman Senate scarcely pretended any longer to go through the motions of electing the Caesars. Kinship to a reigning emperor counted for nothing in determining the succession. On the contrary, the sons or near relatives of one Caesar usually found themselves in danger of a speedy execution when the next emperor assumed the crown.

As Hutchinson and Garrison describe the crisis,

Chaos and anarchy spread throughout the empire. The slaying of one Caesar was a signal to Roman troops somewhere to acclaim a new ruler. Sometimes the Praetorian Guards stationed in Rome itself made the choice; sometimes it came from the armies on the frontiers. As the third century drew toward its close, most thoughtful Romans were in despair. They saw the empire on a swift slide into ruin and the once proud civilization about to plunge into a barbarian sea.

That of course was what eventually happened. But the collapse did not come in AD 300. In the west it was delayed for another 175 years. And in the east an empire that claimed to be Roman continued almost until the day Columbus hauled up anchor to sail to the discovery of the New World. "This sudden about-face in Rome's history, from chaos and encroaching disintegration to a new surge of vigor and stability, was largely the product of one reign, that of Diocletian," who occupied the throne for 20 years (284–305), just before Constantine.

Diocletian has not enjoyed what is called a "good press" in Christian circles because he was the most savage of the persecutors of the church. Given the anarchy he inherited and the revived empire he passed on to his successors, "Diocletian deserves to be ranked among the truly great emperors."

The son of slaves in Dalmatia (today's Balkan area), Diocletian embarked on a military career and became commander of the army before he was forty. Raised to the purple "by the election of generals and officers," he settled any possible competition for the imperial power by leaping on his nearest rival as he stood before the tribunal of the Senate and running him through. "From that moment on, this rough-handed soldier proceeded to take the disintegrating empire as it were by the scruff of its neck and shake it into new life." He not only turned back the retreat in Germany and along the Danube; he even reconquered most of distant Britain and Persia.

Diocletian, however, was more than a victorious general. In the long run, his skill as a statesman proved more significant. He was convinced that the empire was unmanageable. The constant frontier attacks called for reorganization. So, he divided the imperial power with three others and established four imperial courts, none of them in Rome. His own court he placed in Nicomedia, in the northwest corner of Asia Minor. From there he could keep a close watch on the ever-threatening invaders along the eastern borders.

Diocletian's plan aimed to protect the empire from the anarchy created by the constant assassination of emperors. The shrewd old emperor believed that the division of the imperial rule among four men—two "Augusti," each with his slightly subordinate "Caesar"—would control the ambitions of his most likely rivals. Since each had hopes of becoming emperor he would no longer be tempted to promote his fortunes by killing the older rulers.

CHRISTIANS TO THE FLAMES

No one seems to know exactly why, but Diocletian, two years before the end of his highly effective reign, suddenly ordered the most vicious of all persecutions of the Christians. For eighteen years Diocletian, although himself a convinced and practicing pagan, paid no attention to the growing Christian power. His court was full of Christian officials, and his wife Prisca and his daughter Valeria were considered Christians. Impressive church buildings appeared in the principal cities of the empire, the largest in his capital of Nicomedia.

Then, suddenly, the old emperor ordered his army purged of Christians. Imperial edicts followed, commanding officials to destroy church buildings, prohibit Christian worship, and burn the Scriptures. Bishops were rounded up wholesale, imprisoned, tortured, and many put to death, while the power of the imperial throne was turned loose to wipe out the rest of the Christian community in blood.

In 305 Diocletian, following a long-established plan, abdicated and forced his fellow Augustus, Maximian, to do likewise. What history recalls as "the Diocletian persecution" was still raging. In fact, the new Augustus in the east, Galerius, was more intent than ever on pushing ahead to the complete extermination of Christianity. Christians said he was the original instigator of the purge.

The pagans themselves, however, were sickened by so much bloodshed. The other new Augustus, Constantius Chlorus, in far-off Britain, who had never pushed the persecution very hard in his district of Gaul, suspended all measures against the Christians and began to show them signs of favor.

In 311, on his deathbed, Galerius realized that his attempt to do away with the upstart religion had failed. "Thousands upon thousands of terrified Christians had, to be sure, recanted, but other thousands had stood fast, sealing their faith with their blood." So eager, in fact, did many Christians prove to suffer for their faith the bishop of Carthage demanded that those who needlessly rushed into martyrdom should not be revered as martyrs.

The effect on public opinion throughout the empire was tremendous. "Even the throne could no longer take the risk of continuing the torturing, maiming, and killing. So, in his last official act, Galerius, reluctantly, grudgingly, issued an edict of toleration," and for all practical purposes, the last and worst persecution of Christians by Rome came to an end.

Upon the death of Galerius, a struggle for imperial power broke loose. In the spring of 312, Constantine, the son of Constantius Chlorus, advanced across the Alps to dislodge his rival Maxentius from Italy and to capture Rome. It was a daring gamble; and when he came upon his militarily superior enemy at the Milvian Bridge, just outside the walls of Rome, he found help in the God of the Christians. In a dream he saw a cross in the sky and the words, "In this sign conquer." This convinced him to advance. When on October 28, 312, he achieved his brilliant victory over the troops of Maxentius, Constantine looked upon his success as proof of the power of Christ and the superiority of the Christian religion.

Some historians have considered Constantine's "conversion" a purely political maneuver. Plenty of paganism remained. He conspired; he murdered; he even retained his title *Pontifex Maximus* as head of the state religious cult. But a purely political conversion is hard to maintain in the light of his public and private actions. From the year 312, he favored Christianity openly. He allowed Christian ministers to enjoy the same exemption from taxes as the pagan priests; he abolished executions by crucifixion; he called a halt to the battles of gladiators as a punishment for crimes; and in 321 he made Sunday a public holiday. Thanks to his generosity, magnificent church buildings arose as evidence of his support of Christianity.

Care for the Dying

Unbelieving Romans, like many ancients, would abandon unwanted children to die. Girls, who were less economically desirable, were especially likely victims. Christians holding each person's worth as one created in the image of God would rescue these abandoned children. Romans objected to Christians engaging in this practice, and eventually laws were crafted to penalize believers who rescued the children. Constantine ruled that the abandoned children belonged to the finder. This ruling, like many others, favored Christians.

This public Christianity was matched by changes in Constantine's private life. Making no secret of his Christian convictions, he had his sons and daughters brought up as Christians and led a Christian family life. Bishop Eusebius of Nicomedia baptized him shortly before he died in 337. After his baptism, Constantine refused to wear again the imperial purple and thus left this life dressed in his white baptismal robes.

The emperor's conversion inspired Matthew Arnold, the nineteenth-century poet, to write:

> She heard it, the victorious West,
>   In crown and sword array'd!
> She felt the void which mined her breast,
>   She shiver'd and obey'd.
>
> She veil'd her eagles, snapp'd her sword,
>   And laid her sceptre down;
> Her stately purple she abhorr'd
>   And her imperial crown.

A NEW CAPITAL FOR CHRISTIANITY

Along with his new religion, Constantine provided the Roman world with a new capital city. The empire's enemies tended to gather in the east and now the official religion was eastern. A move to the east was natural. The site Constantine chose could hardly have been more perfect for a city that would grow rich through trade. The narrow neck of the Bosporus, the waterway between the Black Sea and the Mediterranean, is a natural crossroads between Asia and Europe, either by land or by water. Neatly placed to one side of the straits is an ideal natural harbor, narrow enough for a chain to be stretched across it in the old days to keep out intruders. For centuries a town had been there. Byzantium it had been called, until the day in 330 when Constantine was ready to inaugurate his new city. Exactly 1,600 years later, in 1930, the

Turks changed its name to Istanbul. But for the greater part of its long history the place has been known as Constantine's city, Constantinople, the capital of the Byzantine (or eastern Roman) Empire.

Today, after all the intervening years, we find it almost impossible to grasp what this change in imperial leadership meant for the church. Prior to 312, Christianity had been outlawed and persecuted. Suddenly it was favored and pampered. Constantine thrust it into public life. As a result, the church re-envisioned its image and mission.

The church historian Eusebius probably spoke for the majority of Christians when he represented the emperor as the ideal Christian ruler and envisioned the beginning of a new age of salvation. The new opportunity to preach publicly and to develop unmolested surely meant that God had a new and greater mission for the church. The divinely ordained moment had arrived for the infusion of public life with the spirit of Christianity.

Some Christians found special meaning in the fact that Jesus and his message appeared at the very hour when the Roman Empire provided the world with political, economic, and cultural unity. The empire seemed to carry the providential task of preparing the way for Christianity to fulfill its mission to all men. Now, with Constantine, the conversion of the world seemed near.

The advantages for the church were real enough, but there was a price to pay. Constantine ruled Christian bishops as he did his civil servants and demanded unconditional obedience to official pronouncements, even when they interfered with purely church matters. There were also the masses who now streamed into the officially favored church. Prior to Constantine's conversion, the church consisted of convinced believers who were willing to bear the risk of being identified as Christians. Now many came who were politically ambitious, religiously disinterested, and still half-rooted in paganism. This threatened to produce not only shallowness and permeation by pagan superstitions but also the secularization and misuse of religion for political purposes.

THE CHURCH COMES TO POWER

By 380, rewards for Christians had given way to penalties for non-Christians. In that year the emperor Theodosius made belief in Christianity a matter of imperial command:

> It is Our Will that all the peoples we rule shall practice that religion which the divine Peter the Apostle transmitted to the Romans. We shall believe in the single Deity of the Father, the Son, and the Holy Spirit, under the concept of equal majesty and of the Holy Trinity.

We command that those persons who follow this rule shall embrace the name of Catholic Christians. The rest, however, whom We adjudge demented and insane, shall sustain the infamy of heretical dogmas, their meeting places shall not receive the name of churches, and they shall be smitten first by divine vengeance and secondly by the retribution of Our own initiative, which We shall assume in accordance with divine judgment.

Theodosius takes for granted the close link between his own will and God's. It was a connection implicit in the Christian empire.

Church buildings in the Christian empire were carefully designed to emphasize the new hierarchy of Christ and emperor. The style was borrowed from the East. A Greek traveler visited Persia in the second century and described a palace in which there was "a hall covered with a dome; the inside was adorned with sapphires sparkling with a celestial blue brilliance, and standing out against the blue background of the stones were golden images of the gods, glittering like stars in the firmament." This became the pattern for the mosaic-encrusted interiors of Byzantine churches, displaying, if not "golden images of the gods," at least God and the "demigod" emperor who represented him on earth.

In the west, farther from the imperial courts, some churchmen dared to challenge the demigod. Ambrose, Bishop of Milan, was one. The incident that led to the clash was, on the surface, hardly a matter for imperial concern. In the year 390 a charioteer in a Greek city was accused of homosexual practices. The governor of the area threw him into prison but did not count on the reaction of the people. With the chariot races about to begin, the people asked for the charioteer's freedom. The governor refused. So the people rose in arms, murdered the governor, and freed their hero.

Theodosius, then in Milan, was incensed. He ordered that the people be punished, so at another chariot race in the circus at Thessalonica the gates were closed and the soldiers of Theodosius were stationed at the entrances. At a signal they fell upon the people. In three hours seven thousand Thessalonians fell by the sword.

A cry of horror rose through the empire. Ambrose, who regarded himself as the imperial conscience, felt utterly ashamed. In the name of common humanity and the church, he had to speak out. Theodosius would have to admit he had committed a crime and repent. Ambrose decided to write Theodosius.

"I cannot deny that you have a zeal for the faith," he wrote,

and that you fear God, but you have a naturally passionate spirit which becomes un-governable when you are excited. I call on you to repent.

You can only atone for your sin by tears, by penitence, by humbling your soul before God. You are a man, and as you have sinned as a man so you must repent. No angel, no archangel can forgive you. God alone can forgive you, and He forgives only those who repent.

Ambrose refused the emperor Communion until he had confessed his sin. For a while Theodosius stayed away from church, but in the end he accepted Ambrose's terms. In front of a crowded congregation he took off his splendid imperial robes and asked pardon for his sins. He had to do so on several occasions until at last, on Christmas Day, Ambrose gave him the sacrament.

It required unusual courage to humiliate a Byzantine emperor. Ambrose had hit upon the weapon—the threat of excommunication— that the Western church would soon use again and again to humble princes. But at the center of the Christian empire, in Constantinople, no bishop ever stepped so far out of line.

Today, as Bamber Gascoigne points out,

In the Milan church named after St. Ambrose, the services are Roman Catholic—recognizably different from the form of worship associated with the Byzantine emperors, which we now know as Greek Orthodox. But orthodox merely means correct; catholic is a word for universal. We might equally well refer to them as Greek Catholic and Roman Orthodox.

It was just a case of each side, East and West, claiming to have the right form of Christianity. In their contrasting attitudes toward the Christian emperors, however, we have a symbol of their diverging destinies.

Suggestions for Further Reading

Baynes, Norman H. *Constantine the Great and the Christian Church.* 2nd ed. London: Oxford University Press, 1972.

Cochrane, Charles Norris. *Christianity and Classical Culture.* New York: Oxford, 1957.

Coleman, Christopher Bush. *Constantine the Great and Christianity.* New York: AMS Press, 1968.

Davidson, Ivor. *A Public Faith: From Constantine to the Medieval World, AD 312– 600, Baker History of the Church.* Vol. 2. Grand Rapids: Baker, 2005.

Kee, Allistair. *Constantine Versus Christ: The Triumph of Ideology.* London: SCM Press, 1982.

*Leithart, Peter. *Defending Constantine: The Twilight of an Empire and the Dawn of Christendom.* Downers Grove, IL: InterVarsity Press, 2010.

*Yoder, John Howard. *Christian Attitudes to War, Peace, and Revolution.* Ed. By Theodore Koontz and Andy Alexis-Baker. Grand Rapids: Brazos, 2009.

CHAPTER 10

SPLITTING
IMPORTANT HAIRS

The Doctrine of the Trinity

Of all the things that Christians say about God, the most distinctive is that God is three persons. Worshipers stand and sing:

> Holy, holy, holy! Lord God Almighty!
> All Thy works shall praise Thy name
> in earth and sky and sea;
> Holy, holy, holy! merciful and mighty!
> God in three persons, blessed Trinity.

No other major religion confesses or worships a three-in-one deity. Muslims and Jews find the doctrine offensive; Unitarians and Jehovah's Witnesses find it deplorable.

Most Christians themselves acknowledge the doctrine is a mystery. When believers tried to identify God or address God in worship, they inevitably spoke of Father, Son, and Spirit. When asked whom they encountered in the Christian story, they answered in liturgy and preaching, "Father, Son, and Spirit." Thinking more abstractly about what God's nature is like, they answered that God was one—a unity. Fourth-century Christians felt a nagging restlessness about the doctrine, like scholars who have a piece of unfinished research. Three in One and One in Three, each identical and yet different?

One bishop described Constantinople as seething with discussion:

If in this city you ask anyone for change, he will discuss with you whether God the Son is begotten or unbegotten. If you ask about the quality of

105

bread, you will receive the answer that "God the Father is greater, God the Son is less." If you suggest that a bath is desirable, you will be told that "there was nothing before God the Son was created."

This is the age that formulated the doctrine. But what did they mean by Trinity? What is the orthodox Christian understanding of the triune God?

MAKING SENSE OF MYSTERY

The belief assumed major importance after Constantine's conversion. When the emperor turned to the Christian faith he hoped the church would bring new life into the weary empire. But, to do that, the church itself had to be united. A quarreling, divided Christianity could not bind the crumbling empire together.

That is why Constantine was troubled by reports from all quarters of the bitterness Christians were displaying over theological issues. The same believers who had been the victims of terrible persecution under Diocletian and Galerius were now demanding that their fellow Christians be suppressed or banished from their churches by the power of the state over disagreements concerning points of doctrine. Constantine had no choice but to intervene to stop this constant bickering (or worse) and to make his Christian subjects agree on what their own beliefs were.

Rejected Trinitarian Schemes

Progress toward appreciating the doctrine of the Trinity can be made by understanding what it is not. The early church typically believed the Trinity to be a mystery that is honored or respected, and not a simple riddle to be solved or explained by some logical exercise.

Two approaches sought to protect the idea of one great ruling (monarch) God, but rejected the importance of the Father, Son, and Spirit necessary to tell the Christian story. These theorists are called *Monarchians*. One monarchial approach is called *modalism*. This version of modalism saw Father, Son, and Spirit as modes or roles that God assumes in consecutive periods, like an actor playing different characters in successive acts of a drama. Important theologians of the second century led the attack against modalism. The theory did not successfully account for the interaction of Father, Son, and Spirit pictured in the New Testament (consider Jesus' baptism). Also, the genuine God behind the masks of Father, Son, and Spirit is left unrevealed. The church soundly rejected modalism.

A second monarchial approach, *subordinationism,* proved much more difficult to assess. This approach pictured a genuine and powerful ruling God assisted by lesser gods of inferior potency and rank. The Father was fully God and the Son and Spirit were lesser deities. The famous council of Nicaea in 325 rejected the subordinationist theology of Arius. The dispute continued for another half century until Nicaea's verdict became the consensus of the church. Both modalism and subordinationism are rejected in the Christian affirmation of the Trinity.

The most troublesome dispute in the East centered in Alexandria, where Arius, pastor of the influential Baucalis Church, came into conflict with his bishop, Alexander. Sometime around 318 Arius openly challenged teachers in Alexandria by asserting that the Word (Logos) who assumed flesh in Jesus Christ (John 1:14) was a lesser god that had a different nature than God the Father. The Son is neither eternal nor omnipotent. To Arius, when Christians called Christ God, they did not mean that he was deity except in a sort of approximate sense. He was a lesser being, not the eternal and changeless Creator. He was a created Being—the first created Being and the greatest, but nevertheless himself created. In explaining his position to Eusebius, the bishop at the empire's capital of Nicomedia, Arius wrote, "The Son has a beginning, but . . . God is without beginning."

Such teaching appealed to many of the former pagans; it was so much like the religion of their youth. Gnosticism, for example, as we have seen, taught that there is one supreme God who dwells alone and then a number of lesser beings who do God's work and pass back and forth between heaven and earth. Converts from paganism found it hard to grasp the Christian belief that the Word existed from all eternity, and that he is equal with the Father. Arius made Christianity easier to understand. It seemed more reasonable to think of Christ as a kind of divine hero: greater than an ordinary human being, but of a lower rank than the eternal God. At issue were the Son's exact status as a divine being and the unity of the idea of God; if the Son was of a different nature than the Father, then there are at least two Gods. Arius affirmed the Father as the genuine, great God, and the Son as a lesser god.

Arius's views were all the more popular because he combined an eloquent preaching style with a flair for public relations. In the opening stages of the conflict, he put ideas into jingles, which set to simple tunes like a radio commercial, were soon being sung by the dockworkers, the street hawkers, and the schoolchildren of the city.

Bishop Alexander, however, would have none of it. He called a synod at Alexandria about 320, and the assembled churchmen condemned Arius's teaching and excommunicated the former pastor. Arius turned to his friend, Eusebius, Bishop of Nicomedia, and won his backing. Thus the theological quarrel became a test of strength between the two most important churches in the East: Nicomedia, the political capital, and Alexandria, the intellectual capital. With the backing of his friends, Arius returned to Alexandria, and riots erupted in the streets.

Constantine recognized that the explosive issue had to be defused. So, in 325, he called for a council to meet at Nicaea not far from Nicomedia in Asia Minor. What a vivid picture that first imperial synod made! Most of the 300 or so bishops had fresh memories of the days of persecution. Some bore the crippling disfigurement of suffering and prison. One had lost an eye during the persecution. Another had lost the use of his hands under torture. But the days of suffering seemed over now. The bishops did not set out for Nicaea secretly, as they used to do, fearing arrest. They did not painfully walk the long miles as once they did. They rode in comfort to the council, all their expenses paid, the guests of the emperor.

In the center of the conference hall at Nicaea sat Constantine, who had at first thought that the whole issue was a mere difference in terms. Presiding over the early sessions, he appeared as a glittering figure in his imperial robes, which were no longer the austere purple garment worn by the emperors in Rome but were the jewel-encrusted, multicolored brocades thought proper to an Eastern monarch.

He spoke briefly to the churchmen, reminding them that they must come to some agreement on the questions that divided them. Division in the church, he said, was worse than war. Having made his point, he stepped aside, committing the resolution of the conflict into the hands of the church leaders.

TRUE GOD OF TRUE GOD

According to one report from the council, some bishops who supported Arius went for a complete victory by stating the case for Arius in a bold and confident manner. The council at large was so upset that they loudly interrupted the presentation. On the face of it, all these bishops came from churches where Jesus was worshipped. To emphasize Jesus as a different type of being may have seemed irreverent.

In one sense, the council was already over; Arius's teaching had lost this round. Next came the hard work of crafting a statement that the council would embrace but that would also exclude the teachings of Arius.

In the course of the debate that followed, the most learned bishop present, the church historian Eusebius of Caesarea, a personal friend and admirer of the emperor and a somewhat halfhearted supporter of Arius, put forward his own creed, perhaps as evidence of his own questioned orthodoxy.

Most of the pastors, however, recognized that something more specific was needed to exclude the possibility of Arian heresy. For this purpose they produced another creed, probably from Palestine. Into it they inserted an extremely important series of phrases: "True God of true God, begotten not made, of one substance with the Father."

The expression *homo ousion*, "one substance," was probably introduced by Bishop Hosius of Cordova (in today's Spain). Since he had great influence with Constantine, the imperial weight was thrown to that side of the scales. Thus there emerged that Nicene Creed, which to this day is the standard of orthodoxy in the Roman, Eastern, and Anglican churches, as well as some others:

> I believe in one God the Father Almighty; Maker of heaven and earth, and of all things visible and invisible.
>
> And in one Lord Jesus Christ, the only-begotten Son of God, begotten of the Father before all worlds. God of God, Light of Light, very God of very God, begotten, not made, being of one substance with the Father; by whom all things were made; who, for us men and for our salvation, came down from heaven, and was incarnate by the Holy Ghost of the Virgin Mary, and was made man; and was crucified also for us under Pontius Pilate; he suffered and was buried; and the third day he rose again, according to the Scriptures; and ascended into heaven, and sitteth on the right hand of the Father; and he shall come again, with glory, to judge both the quick and the dead; whose kingdom shall have no end.
>
> And I believe in the Holy Ghost, the Lord and Giver of Life; who proceedeth from the Father and the Son; who with the Father and the Son together is worshiped and glorified; who spake by the Prophets. And I believe in one Holy Catholic and Apostolic Church. I acknowledge one Baptism for the remission of sins; and I look for the resurrection of the dead, and the life of the world to come. Amen.

All but two bishops present signed the Creed, and these two, along with Arius himself, were soon afterward sent into exile. Meanwhile, Constantine was joyful, thinking the issue settled. He held a great banquet. Such an event defied the Christian imagination. The head of the empire and the bishops of the church sitting together, celebrating the coming happy days of the church of Christ?

"No bishop was absent from the table of the emperor," Eusebius of Caesarea wrote enthusiastically.

Bodyguards and soldiers stood guard, with sharp swords drawn, around the outer court of the palace, but among them the men of God could walk fearlessly and enter the deepest parts of the palace. At dinner some of them lay on the same couch as the emperor, while others rested on cushions on both sides of him. Easily one could imagine this to be the kingdom of Christ or regard it as a dream rather than reality.

Bishop Paphnutius from Egypt, who had lost one eye under the Emperor Diocletian, was singled out for special honor by the new emperor. As a sign of friendship between the empire and the church, Constantine kissed the bishop's eyeless cheek.

After Nicaea, however, first Constantine and then his successors stepped in again and again to banish this churchman or exile that one. Church teaching too often depended on control of the emperor's favor. The court was overrun by spokesmen for some Christian party. As a result, the imperial power was forever ordering bishops into banishment and almost as often bringing them back again when some new group of ecclesiastical advisers got the upper hand in the palace.

No career better illustrates the way in which imperial power took over actual control of the church than that of Athanasius. He may well have attended the council as secretary to Alexander, bishop of Alexandria. If so he could claim to be a contributor to Nicene faith as well as its champion defender. Soon after that, at the age of thirty-three, he succeeded Alexander upon his death. For the next fifty years, however, no one could predict who would win in the struggle with Arianism. During these decades, Athanasius was banished no fewer than five times, each banishment and return to Alexandria representing either a change in emperors or a shift in the makeup of the palace ecclesiastical clique that had the emperor's ear. At times Athanasius was so completely out of imperial favor that he felt deserted by all his supporters. During one such hour he uttered his famous defiance, *Athanasius Against the World.* He would stand alone, if need be, against the whole empire.

These fifty years continued the heated debate over the Arian question. Not long after the Council of Nicaea a moderate group, sometimes called the Semi-Arians, broke away from the strict Arians and attempted to give a new interpretation to the *one substance* statement. They defended the use of *homoios*, meaning "similar," to describe the Word's relation to the Father. Thus two parties arose. The one led by Athanasius insisted upon using *homoousios* because they believed that the Word (Christ) was of the "same" nature as the Father. If Christ had not been fully God, they said, he could not have fully saved us. The other party, the Semi-Arians, argued for *homoiousios* because they held that the Word was a being "like" God the Father. Edward Gibbon, in his memorable history of the fall of the Roman Empire, passed on a sneer that, in this struggle, Christians fought each other over a diphthong. Well, so it was—a diphthong. But that diphthong carried an immense meaning.

In one of his books, William Hordern tells a story about a woman touring in Europe, who cabled her husband: "Have found wonderful bracelet. Price seventy-five thousand dollars. May I buy it?" The husband promptly cabled back, "No, price too high." The cable operator, in transmitting the message, missed the signal for the comma. The woman received a message that read, "No price too high." She bought the bracelet; the husband sued the company and won.

The anecdote reminds us that the importance of a message cannot be weighed by the size of the punctuation or the number of letters used. Although only an iota (in English the letter *i*) divided the parties after Nicaea, the issues involved represented two sharply different interpretations of the Christian faith. At stake were the full deity of Jesus Christ and the essence of the doctrine of the Trinity.

If the Semi-Arians had succeeded in getting their iota into the Creed, their point of view would have become orthodox Christianity. It would have meant that Christianity had degenerated to a form of paganism. The Christian faith would have had two gods and a Jesus who was neither God nor man. It would have meant that God himself was unapproachable and totally removed from man. The result would have been a Christianity like a host of pagan religions. In the Arian struggle accuracy was everything. But how does one speak of three in one without spouting nonsense?

THE MYSTERY OF THE TRINITY

In attempting to explain the doctrine of the Trinity, Christians today occasionally appeal to patterns of threeness in the world: the yolk, white, and shell of an egg; the root, tree, and fruit of a plant; or water in its three forms of ice, liquid, and vapor. These are all fascinating ideas, and under certain circumstances might be useful as illustrations of the Trinity. But they miss completely the personal element in the Christian doctrine of the Trinity.

Why Is the Trinity Important?

The New Testament documents and earliest teachers recognized that Father, Son, and Spirit were not just three among the many terms used to describe God. Father, Son, and Spirit were necessary to tell the basic Christian story. God had exercised oversight or managed the course of history to bring about our salvation.

Trinity and Salvation: Salvation for the early church was about more than going to heaven; it was about being united in communion with God. Father, Son, and Spirit had to be divine to include us and make us ready to share in the already existing divine fellowship. We would not be made into God or equal to God, but we must be transformed to belong to the rich, eternal communion that awaits Christians.

A simple story about a grandson who spends time at his grandparents' farm may illustrate. To the young boy, his grandparents are bigger than life. They work the farm, enjoy his stories, and allow him to share in their everyday adventures. After evening meal and long conversation, the couple sit on a front porch swing and grow silent. They seem to take joy in this satisfying silence and communion. The boy can sense the bond, love, and union between them. He longs to become part of this great love and life that the old couple share together. Finally, the boy wedges himself between the couple and they make room for him. He sits with them in silence, soaking up the love and fellowship drawn from life lived together. Early Christians saw their destiny as being included into fellowship of the triune God.

Trinity and Worship: Father, Son, and Spirit are ingrained into the essential Christian story and worship. Almost all Christians are baptized into the name (singular) of the Father, Son, and Spirit. The Trinity is present in the earliest Christian voices; even the apostle Paul gives a Trinitarian blessing in 2 Corinthians 13:14.

Trinity and Human Dignity: Subordinationists imagined that if Jesus served the Father he was beneath the Father. In most ancient cultures, a person's rank was determined by family status and achievement. In this mindset, great people were distinguished from lesser persons who would inevitably serve the greater people. The radical Christian notion of God honors the dignity of the Son serving the Father out of love, not because of inferiority. Christians, following Jesus, see service as the evidence of Christlikeness, not of weakness or inadequacy.

The true foundation upon which the doctrine rests is God himself. It is God as he acted in history, revealing himself to Israel. It is God as he acted in history, entering our world as a Jewish carpenter named Jesus, dying and rising again to save. It is God as he acted in history at Pentecost, descending as the Spirit to share life with the Christian church.

But if God is eternally one and God is eternally three persons, how are we to understand this? Since God is personal, any example we use to think or speak of God ought to be personal.

When we search for personal analogies, we find that there are only two options. We may think of God as three persons or we may think of God as one person.

If we think of God as three persons, then God's threeness is clear, and we have to account for God's unity. Theologians usually point out that three persons can become so close they may be said to share a common life. They may be bound together so closely that it is actually a distortion to speak of them separately. Because this analogy rests on a society of three persons, theologians call it the social analogy. Its strength lies in its clarity regarding the threeness of God. Its problem is to account clearly for God's unity.

If we think of God as one person, we have to try to account for his threeness. One way of doing this is to say that a person may have several distinct functions such as mind, emotions, and will.

Because this analogy draws on psychological functions, theologians call it the psychological analogy. Its strength is its clarity about God's unity: He is one person. Its problem is its vagueness about God's threeness.

Both of these analogies were used in the early church, just as modern theologians like Leonard Hodgson and Karl Barth use them.

As the decades passed between 325 and 381, when the second general council of the church met, leaders in the Arian debate slowly clarified their use of *person*. Three so-called Cappadocian Fathers—Gregory of Nazianzus, Gregory of Nyssa, and Basil the Great—led in this achievement. The Cappadocians used the social analogy, but they saw that the distinctions between the three divine persons were solely in their inner divine relations. There are not three gods. God is one divine Being in three "persons."

The word *person*, however, did not mean to the early Christians what it means today. To us, a person means someone like Tom, Dick, or Harry. But the Latin word *persona* originally meant a mask worn by an actor on the stage. Despite the possible misunderstandings suggested by the term, Christians used this term to describe the dynamic inner, communal life of Father, Son, and Spirit.

A bit later Augustine, Bishop of Hippo near Carthage, used the psychological analogy. He believed that if man is created in the image of God, he is created in the image of the Trinity. His analogy for the Trinity, then, was from the human mind. God, said Augustine, is like the memory, intelligence, and will in the mind of a man. In short, we do not have to think of three persons when we think of God; we may think of one person. Of course, Augustine made it clear that this was only an analogy; he was far too profound a thinker to suppose that God was a glorified man sitting in heaven. We are finite human beings seeking to speak faithfully about the mystery that is God.

The World in Which the Early Church Developed Its Doctrine

As it turned out, then, Athanasius was not all alone against the world. He lived to see the triumph of the cause he championed. When he died at the age of seventy-five, his death was peaceful. He had been at last secure in his office as bishop of Alexandria in the closing years, and, what mattered more to him, he could rest assured that the creed he had fought for at Nicaea and ever afterward was the creed of the church. "God in three persons, blessed Trinity."

Suggestions for Further Reading

*Anatolios, Khaled. *Athanasius: The Coherence of His Thought*. London: Routledge, 1998.

*———. *Athanasius. The Early Church Father Series*. New York: Routledge, 2004.

Cranfield, C. E. B. *The Apostles' Creed: A Faith to Live By*. Grand Rapids: Eerdmans, 1993.

Kelly, J. N. D. *Early Christian Creeds*, 3rd ed. New York: D. McKay, 1972.

———. *Early Christian Doctrine*, 5th ed. New York: Harper, 1978; London: Continuum, 2000.

———. *Early Christian Doctrine*. New York: Harper, 1978.

*Leithart, Peter. *Athanasius*. Grand Rapids: Baker, 2011.

McGrath, Alister E. *"I Believe": Exploring the Apostles' Creed*. Downers Grove, IL: InterVarsity, 1998.

Van Harn, Roger E., ed. *Exploring and Proclaiming the Apostles' Creed*. Grand Rapids: Eerdmans, 2004.

Young, Frances M. *The Making of the Creeds*. London: SCM Press, 1991.

CHAPTER 11

EMMANUEL!

Christ in the Creeds

I N THE FOOTHILL REGION of Mount Hermon, Jesus once asked his disciples, "Who do men say that I am?" They told him that most people associated him with the prophets of Israel. When he pressed them further, "And how about you? Who do you say I am?" Peter responded, "You are the Messiah, the Son of the living God."

Men have given a thousand answers to Jesus' question. Some have said, "He is an unusual Jewish rabbi preaching a kingdom of love." Others answer, "No, he is a social revolutionary whose primary purpose is the overthrow of Rome's tyrannical rule." Still others claim, "He is a misguided dreamer who looked for God to step into history and establish justice on the earth."

Whatever the views of men, the church through the centuries has confessed with Peter, Jesus Christ is the Messiah, the Son of the living God. He is more than a subject for Christian study: he is the object of Christian devotion. Theologians call this mystery the *incarnation*, the *enfleshment* of God. Hymn writers extol the merits of "Emmanuel," meaning "God with us."

During the Imperial Age of the church, when emperors pressed the pastors for creedal statements accurately expressing the Christian faith, the church came to speak of the God-man. In 451 a general council at Chalcedon, not far from Constantinople, affirmed that Jesus Christ was "complete in Godhead and complete in manhood, truly God and truly man . . . in two natures, without confusion, without change, without division or without separation . . . coming together to form one person."

Most Roman Catholic, Eastern Orthodox, and Protestant Christians to this day consider that statement orthodox Christian belief. Sadly,

116

some Christians in Egypt and Syria and India do not. The reasons for their disagreement lie in the fifth-century attempts to speak clearly about the Event. How did the classic doctrine of the incarnation come to be formulated? What does it mean?

THE WORD BECAME FLESH

We call this area of theology Christology because it raises the question, "Who was Jesus Christ?" What was the relation of the divine life and the human life in this unique person, the Christian Savior?

The very existence of this question in the life of the church is profoundly significant. So far as I know, Islam has no Mohammedology and Buddhism has no Buddhology. The debate in the history of Christianity is a monument to the uniqueness of the One Christians call the Son of God.

The Imperial Age did not create the question of the incarnation; it simply debated it. The mystery of the God-man was central to Christian worship long before it became central to Christian thinking. "A deep instinct," J. S. Whale once told the undergraduates at Cambridge University, "has always told the Church that our safest eloquence concerning the mystery of Christ is in our praise. A living Church is a worshiping, singing Church; not a school of people holding all the correct doctrines."

Whale meant that the most treasured hymns of the church have always treated Christ as an object of worship. We find the beating heart of Christian experience not in the church's creed but in its music.

A major task remains for devout scholarship, however, because God in flesh is more than Christian sentiment; he is Christian reality. The apostles spoke of "the Image of the Invisible God," "the Word made flesh," and "the Lamb slain from the foundation of the world." Second- and third-century believers rejected Ebionism and Gnosticism because they were so clearly distortions of this truth.

The fourth- and fifth-century debates about the meaning of the incarnation were not aimed at an explanation of Christ. These Christians knew that Jesus Christ defies explanation because he fits no class. He is unique. The great merit of the creeds is that they left the mystery intact.

It is no surprise, however, that the human mind revolts against these creeds from Nicaea and Chalcedon. Any professor who has tried to trace the Christological debates for first-year seminarians has seen the reaction. But as Charles Williams once pointed out, it is a revolt of "immature sensibility." It is natural.

The church councils appear beyond feeling. As a result we have the immature and romantic devotions to "the simple Jesus, the spiritual genius, the broad-minded international Jewish workingman, the falling-sparrow and grass-of-the-field Jesus." But, said Williams, these will not serve the faith because the Christian idea from the beginning believed that in Jesus Christ earth and heaven meet, both man and God.

Christians of an earlier day felt this reality deeply. They also knew that the obligation to be intelligent is a moral obligation, so they searched for some statement that would correlate the human life and the divine life in Jesus Christ.

In the early church two famous schools of theology offered contrasting emphases on the Word becoming flesh (John 1:14). One of these was at Alexandria; the other was at Antioch. The Alexandrians emphasized how the divine Word assumed human flesh (humanity in general). The Antiochians emphasized how the divine Word was joined to the man named Jesus. The inherent danger or risk for the Alexandrians was to so emphasize the union of the divine and human that the humanity was overshadowed by the divinity of Jesus. The inherent danger for the Antiochians was to underemphasize the union of the divine and human in Jesus to the point that his divinity was overshadowed by his humanity.

The early, leading voice at Alexandria was Origen, who, in speaking of Jesus Christ, coined the term *God-man*. Drawing upon ideas from the famous Greek philosopher Plato, Origen developed a deep, fervent mysticism centering in the divine Word (Logos). His ideas focused on the thought that in Christ the encounter between God and mankind had taken place perfectly and that Christians must strive to imitate it.

Later Christians developed this mystical idea. One of the Cappadocian fathers, Gregory of Nyssa, taught that in Christ, the Logos—the *one* divine person—had united in himself the divine and human natures. Both natures existed by themselves and distinct from one another, yet they were not separated but arranged in such a way that their attributes were mutually exchangeable.

The Antioch school of theologians normally interpreted the Scriptures in a more straightforward historical manner. Major teachers of this position tended to stress the human figure of the Gospels. They found saving virtue in Jesus' example and achievement. In Christ the human will, which in other men turns freely to sin, proved obedient and victorious.

Antiochene theologians consequently stressed the concrete manhood of Christ. As David F. Wright explains it, the union of body and soul did not in any way affect the completeness and normality of the human nature. After the Word became flesh, the two natures remained distinct. In Antiochene teaching they could easily seem like two beings, God and man, Son of God and son of Mary, joined or associated rather than personally united. As a vessel indwelt by the Word, Jesus was not unlike prophets and apostles, except that he enjoyed perfect fullness of grace and power. According to one theologian the Word lodged in the man Jesus as in a temple.

The debate over the meaning of the Event raged for generations in part because political influence was at stake. After Christianity emerged as the official religion of the empire under Theodosius, the structure of the church centered upon a few powerful figures. The bishops in the chief towns of the imperial provinces came to be called *archbishops*. The term for the official center of a bishop's jurisdiction and authority is *see*. Those bishops in the premier cities of the empire—Rome, Constantinople, Alexandria, and Antioch—were considered highest of all and were called *patriarchs*. Throughout the fourth and fifth centuries these four powerful patriarchs were attempting to extend the prestige and power of their spiritual offices.

Generally speaking, Alexandria and Rome tended to support each other, and Antioch to go along with Constantinople. On Alexandria's part this reflected the jealousy that proud and ancient city felt at the rise of the upstart capital in the east, Constantinople. Rome, too, while for the time content to extend its influence over the imperial dominions in the west, was not happy with the growing arrogance of the "new Rome" in the east. On the other hand, Antioch and Alexandria had long been at loggerheads as rivals in the east. If Antioch could not gain preeminence, it preferred to see it go to the church in the new capital rather than to its old rival on the Nile.

MAJOR HERESIES ABOUT CHRIST

In this climate the Christological debate stretched over a century and was the primary passion in the churches of the East. Between 350 and 450 heresies arose, each of them forcing the churches to greater clarity in their answer to the question, "Who is Jesus Christ?"

The first position advanced and rejected was associated with a pastor of Laodicea named Apollinaris, a younger friend of Athanasius. Reacting to the teaching from Antioch, Apollinaris struck upon the idea of approaching the question from the view of what we would call psychology. He felt that human nature embraced the body and the soul. At the incarnation, however, the divine Word (Logos), according to Apollinaris, displaced the animating and rational soul in a human body, creating a "unity of nature" between the Word and his body. Humanity, he felt, was the sphere, not the instrument of salvation, so he could speak of "one enfleshed nature of the divine Word." Here was the Alexandrian stress on the deity of Christ, but only a body represented Christ's human nature.

Objections to Apollinaris's position quickly arose. Does not the gospel picture Jesus as a complete and genuine human? And if the Word displaced the rational soul of human nature, with its powers of choice and sin, how can man be fully redeemed? Without complete solidarity with humanity, how could the Word secure the salvation of mankind? As Gregory of Nazianzus put it, "What has not been assumed cannot be restored."

In this atmosphere of criticism, the second general council of the church, meeting at Constantinople in 381, effectively silenced the Apollinarian teaching. It simply was not an adequate description of the incarnation.

The second heresy was associated with the name Nestorius, a famous preacher at Antioch before the emperor, in 428, made him bishop of Constantinople. The imperial capital gave Nestorius a platform. From it he tried to defend the position of his teacher in the faith, Theodore, bishop of Mopsuestia, near Antioch. Like his instructor, Nestorius rejected a popular designation of Mary as the "God-bearer, Mother of God."

In rejecting the phrase, Nestorius made it appear that he held that Christ joined two persons. He did not deny the deity of Christ; but in emphasizing the reality and integrity of the Savior's humanity, Nestorius pictured the relation between the two natures in terms of a moral conjunction or a merging of wills rather than that of an essential union. Although he never divided Christ into two sons, Son of God and son of Mary, he refused to attribute to the divine nature the human acts and sufferings of the man Jesus. Once he said, "I hold the natures apart, but unite the worship." He insisted that calling Mary "Mother of God" was tantamount to declaring that the divine nature could be born of a woman, or that God could be three days old.

As it turned out, Nestorius was condemned more for political than for doctrinal reasons. In the hot seat of Constantinople, he was soon widely hated for his assaults on Jews and heretics. He speedily incurred the hostility of Cyril, the patriarch of Alexandria (412–44). Cyril was a distinguished preacher and theologian, but ruthless in debates. He was especially alarmed by Nestorius's teaching and outraged when Nestorius listened to the complaints of some Alexandrian clergy Cyril had disciplined.

Thus, late in 428, Cyril opened his attack on Nestorius. He stirred up charges against him and slandered him in Rome where Patriarch (Pope) Celestine was upset about Nestorius's welcome of certain exiles from Rome.

At the General Council of Ephesus (431), called by Emperor Theodosius II, who had until then supported Nestorius, Cyril got Nestorius deposed before the late arrival of his Syrian supporters. When the Syrians arrived, under the leadership of John, Patriarch of Antioch, they proceeded to condemn Cyril and his followers. Finally, the Roman legates arrived and approved Cyril's action. The whole affair was disgustingly riddled with power politics. American church historian Williston Walker called it "one of the most repulsive contests in church history."

Eventually Theodosius II surrendered to pressure and expelled Nestorius from the capital. He died around 450, an exile in Egypt. Most of his supporters, however, refused to accept his excommunication. To this day it remains unclear to what extent Nestorius's teachings were actually heretical and to what extent he suffered as a victim of misunderstanding and misrepresentation.

Nestorius's followers fled to Persia and founded there the Nestorian Church, which soon enjoyed an active life. A vital monasticism, an eminent theology, and an imposing missionary activity testify to its strength. Its missionaries penetrated to Malabar, India, and Turkestan. Between 780 and 823 Nestorian believers even made their way to Tibet and central China. At the beginning of the fourteenth century the Nestorian Church in central Asia could count ten major churches and numerous native clergymen. Unfortunately, during the bloody persecution of the Muslim conqueror Tamerlane (1380), this mission was destroyed.

Today the Nestorian Church in the Near East and India still counts about eighty thousand members, and in America twenty-five thousand.

In his autobiography Nestorius insisted that he did not oppose the use of God-bearer because he denied the Godhead of Christ but to emphasize that Jesus was born as a genuine human being with body and soul. His concerns were not unfounded. Nevertheless, even if unfairly, the church has attributed the name Nestorius to the failure to view the divine and human natures as truly united.

Some recent liberal understandings of Christ are labeled as Nestorian. They reason, if Nestorius believed that only the will power of the human man Jesus held him in a moral and volitional union with divine

Word, then the difference between Christians and Christ himself is one of degree. Jesus was more attentive and submissive to God than we are. Jesus was not divine but only a loftier picture of how close a person can be to God; Jesus is a human model but not a divine savior.

Sadly, some evangelical believers fall sway to the same failure in doctrine; they seek Jesus as a role model for self-help and ignore the life-giving transformation offered by Emmanuel: God with us.

ESTABLISHING THE BOUNDARIES OF TRUTH

Soon after the Council at Ephesus (431), the third heresy arose. Eutyches, the spiritual leader of a monastery near Constantinople, defended the one nature in Christ (monophysitism). He combined the two natures so intimately that the human nature appeared completely absorbed by the divine one. Just "as a drop of honey, which falls into the sea, dissolves in it," so the human nature in Christ is lost in the divine. Thus Eutyches denied the central prerequisite for the mystery of Christ and his mission as Savior and Redeemer. The whole Christian doctrine of redemption was in danger.

Patriarch Flavian of Constantinople called Eutyches before a synod and when he refused to recant, Flavian condemned him as a heretic. Eutyches, however, found support in Dioscorus, Patriarch of Alexandria, who followed Cyril's ideas. At Dioscorus's request, Emperor Theodosius II once again summoned an imperial council. It assembled under Dioscorus's leadership in Ephesus (449) and rehabilitated Eutyches, even though it was not recognized by the rest of the church. Pope Leo I (440–461) called it the "Robber Council." He supported the patriarch of Constantinople and asked the emperor for a new council. The successor of Theodosius, Emperor Marcian (450–457), granted the request and in 451 called the fourth General Council of Chalcedon.

At this town not far from Constantinople, nearly four hundred bishops gathered and quickly indicted Dioscorus for his actions at the robber council. Then the assembled fathers, despite some reluctance to supplement Nicaea, set forth a new definition:

> We all with one voice confess our Lord Jesus Christ one and the same Son, at once complete in Godhead and complete in manhood, truly God and truly man, . . . acknowledged in two natures, without confusion, without change, without division, or without separation; the distinction of natures being in no way abolished because of the union, but rather the characteristic property of each nature being preserved, and coming together to form one person.

Christology of the Early Councils

"In Jesus Christ, true deity [against Arius] and full humanity [against Apollinaris] are indivisibly united in one person [against Nestorius] without being confused [against Eutyches]."

Council	Year	Accused Heretic	Accused Heretic Failed to Affirm . . .	Accused Heretic . . .
Nicaea	325	Arius	Full deity of the Son	• Taught that Son is begotten/created/a created being. • Son is not eternal or coeternal; "there was a time when he was not." • Son does not share in the Father's essence or nature. • Son is a lesser god.
Constantinople	381	Apollinaris	Full humanity of the Son	Taught that Jesus had a human body and a lower soul; his human higher soul—his rationality or mind—had been replaced by the divine word or logos; this logos was steady and immutable.
Ephesus	431	Nestorius	The union of the divine and human natures	Held only a moral or volitional union between divine and human; danger inherent in typically Antiochian conjunctive Christologies (illustration: man and woman choosing to be married).
Chalcedon	451	Eutyches	The distinctiveness and coexistence of the divine and human natures	Held to a mingling of both into one; danger inherent in typically Alexandrian unitive Christologies (illustration: drop of honey added to the ocean).

So against Arius the church affirmed that Jesus was truly God, and against Apollinaris that he was truly man. Against Eutyches it confessed that Jesus' deity and humanity were not changed into something else, and against Nestorius that Jesus was not divided but was one person.

From that date forward most Christians in Catholicism, Protestantism, and Orthodoxy looked to Chalcedon for the foundation of the doctrine of salvation, a unique God-man, Jesus Christ.

Numbers of Christians in the Near East, however, rejected the work of Chalcedon. They held that instead of the divine and human natures joining to form one person in Jesus, he possessed but one nature in which divine life and human were indistinguishable. This monophysite (one nature) teaching was an important factor contributing to the breaking away of the Monophysite Churches from the rest of Eastern Orthodoxy. Coupled with the decline of the Byzantine power in the outlying areas of the Eastern Empire, monophysite doctrine led to the Coptic Church, the largest Christian body in Egypt today, with a related church in Ethiopia, and the so-called Jacobite Church of Syria, which has most of its adherents in South India.

Obviously Chalcedon did not solve the problem of how deity can unite with humanity in a single person. At the human level the problem resists explanation. The Bible regards the Event as absolutely unique. The merit of the Chalcedonian statement lies in the boundaries it established. In effect, it erected a fence and said, "Within this lies the mystery of the God-man." Fifteen hundred years after the event we may wish for more understandable terms, but we dare not say less than the church said then.

Suggestions for Further Reading

Bevan, Edwyn. *Christianity.* New York: Henry Holt & Co., 1932.
*Ferguson, Everett. *Church History, Volume 1: From Christ to the Pre-Reformation.* Grand Rapids: Zondervan, 2005.
Hardy, Edward R., ed. *Christology of the Later Fathers.* Philadelphia: The Westminster Press, 1954.
Kelly, J. N. D. *Early Christian Doctrines,* 5th ed. New York: Harper, 1978. Continuum, 2000.
Prestige, G. L. *Fathers and Heretics.* London: S.P.C.K., 1963.
Wand, J. W. C. *Four Great Heresies.* London: A. R. Mowbray, 1955.

CHAPTER 12

EXILES FROM LIFE

The Beginnings of Monasticism

O NE NIGHT, EARLY IN the fourth century, Anthony, the revered Egyptian monk, was standing in the desert engaged in earnest prayer. Satan seized the opportunity to rally the wild beasts of the area and to send them against Anthony. As they surrounded him on every side,

> and with threatening looks were ready to leap upon him, he looked at them boldly and said unto them, "If ye have received power over me from the Lord, draw nigh, and delay not, for I am ready for you; but if ye have made ready and come at the command of Satan, get ye back to your places and tarry not, for I am a servant of Jesus the Conqueror." And when the blessed man had spoken these words, Satan was straightway driven away by the mention of the Name of Christ like a sparrow before a hawk.

That is the stuff ideals are made of. The words are from Athanasius's *Life of Saint Anthony*, but the vision of greatness could be from a thousand fourth-century preachers of righteousness.

The model Christian was no longer the courageous bishop dragged before wild beasts in a Roman arena. He was now a lonely hermit in the forsaken Egyptian desert defying the devil. The moral of the scene was as clear as a Hollywood western shoot-out in Dodge City. There was Satan and there was Christ, struggling for a man's soul.

Modern men are not sure what to make of the monks. Most feel about like Edward Gibbon who scoffed "at the unhappy exiles from social life, impelled by the dark and implacable genius of superstition." Why would anyone want to renounce sex? And if there is any axiom of modern times it is this: the good life is found in a spacious home, well stocked with all the latest labor-saving conveniences.

Even Christians—Catholic and Protestant—disagree over the pros and cons of monasticism. Roman Catholics are inclined to argue that the church is big enough for both ascetics, who strive for spiritual perfection, and weak and sinful members, who show few signs of grace. The church, they say, must be for all, regardless of moral attainments or spiritual failures.

Protestants have felt differently. The Reformation of the sixteenth century struck a heavy blow against monasticism. Martin Luther, who had himself been a monk, declared war on the cloister. Monasticism, said Luther and the other Reformers, encourages the idea of two roads to God, a higher and a lower. But the gospel knows only one way to salvation. It is by faith alone in the Lord Jesus Christ. This faith is no dead faith, however; it is active in love for God and one's neighbor.

Naturally, these conflicting views of the place of monasticism in the church have led to conflicting interpretations of the history of the movement. Everyone agrees that the monks were ascetics. They renounced the comforts of society and sought the spiritual rewards of self-discipline. Their theory held that renunciation of the body frees the soul to commune with God. The key question is how does renunciation relate to the gospel? Is it a form of self-salvation? Is it a works righteousness, an atonement for sin based upon denial of the self? Or is it a legitimate form of repentance, an essential preparation for joy in the good news of God's salvation?

THE MONASTIC IDEAL

Certainly ascetic notes resound from the preachers of the apostolic age. John the Baptist, roaming the Judean desert with crude garb and shouts of repentance, was an ascetic figure. Jesus himself urged at least one young man to get rid of his possessions if he wanted to find eternal life. And the apostle Paul argued that "the flesh lusteth against the Spirit, and the Spirit against the flesh: and these are contrary the one to the other" (Gal. 5:17 KJV).

Shortly after the days of the apostles the idea of a lower and a higher morality appeared. We find it in a document, written about 140, called *The Shepherd of Hermas*. The New Testament, *The Shepherd* says, teaches precepts of faith, hope, and love binding upon all. But it also offers advice for those who aspire to do more than what is required of the ordinary Christian.

Soon other Christians sang the praises of self-denial, especially of celibacy, the renunciation of marriage. Once it was introduced, the practice of penance encouraged acts of exceptional virtue as a means of removing sin. Thus Tertullian, Origen, Cyprian, and other leaders threw their support behind the idea of a higher level of sanctity. Long before Constantine's conversion many believers took vows of abstinence, though at first without withdrawing from the ordinary life of the cities.

The first form of monasticism was the lonely hermit. The word *hermit* comes from the Greek word for desert and is a reminder that the monastic flight from the world began in Egypt, where a short journey either east or west from the narrow ribbon of Nile fertility would put the monk in a rigorous desert.

Anthony, whom many regard as the first monk, was born about 250 in the village of Koma. Under the impulse of Christ's words to the rich young ruler—"go, sell your possessions and give to the poor, and you will have treasure in heaven. Then come, follow me"—Anthony, when twenty years of age, gave away his wealth and soon took up the life of solitude in a tomb. Later legends recount his battles with temptations assailing him in visible forms: devils, beasts, and women. In spite of such stress he apparently lived a full life of 105 years.

Anthony's example proved contagious; he had hundreds of imitators. His friend, Athanasius, wrote, "The sign of solitary ascetics rules from one end of the earth to the other." This sudden surge of self-denial coincides, roughly, with the equally sudden popularity of Christianity.

Whatever Constantine's motives for adopting the Christian faith, the result was a decline in Christian commitment. The stalwart believers whom Diocletian killed were replaced by a mixed multitude of half-converted pagans. Once Christians had laid down their lives for the truth; now they slaughtered each other to secure the prizes of the church. Gregory of Nazianzus complained, "The chief seat is gained by evil doing, not by virtue; and the sees belong, not to the more worthy, but to the more powerful."

The hermit often fled, then, not so much from the world as from the world in the church. His protest of a corrupt institution led him into the dangers of a pronounced individualism. Against the great imperial institution, the channel of divine grace, the early monks set the life of the soul, face to face with God.

Temptations of the outer world were replaced by temptations of the inner world: pride, rivalry, and eccentricity. Many of the monks in Egypt and in Syria went to extremes in enduring hardships. Some ate nothing but grass, while others lived in trees. Still others refused to wash.

The reputations of some hermits attracted vast crowds of people from the cities. One, Simeon Stylites, was so troubled by crowds around the mouth of the cave where he lived, that he put up a pillar and made his home on the top of it for over thirty years. Disciples sent up food to him in a basket, and from time to time, so we are told, he preached to the multitudes below, converting thousands to Christianity.

THE MOVE TO COMMUNITY LIFE

While the hermit's popularity continued in Egypt, the monastic movement took a significant step forward when, around the year 320, a former soldier named Pachomius instituted the first Christian monastery. Instead of permitting the monks to live singly or in groups of hermits, each a law to himself, Pachomius established a regulated common life, in which the monks ate, labored, and worshiped. His plan called for fixed hours, manual work, dress in uniform garb, and strict discipline. It is called coenobitic monasticism, from the Greek terms for common life—*koinos bios.*

The reform was an immense improvement over the hermit's life with its dangers of idleness and eccentricity. It made the monastic life easy for women, for whom the isolated life of a hermit was all but impossible. And it brought monasticism into some system of restraint. Pachomius saw clearly "to save souls you must bring them together."

From these beginnings in Egypt, the ascetic movement spread to Syria, to Asia Minor, and eventually throughout Western Europe. Asia Minor was won to the monastic ideal especially through the influence of Basil, Gregory of Nazianzus, and Gregory of Nyssa, the champions of the Nicene faith in the generation that succeeded Athanasius. Basil, who died in 379, was especially important as the designer of the Rule of Discipline under which the monasticism of Greek Orthodoxy is organized to this day.

The monastic ideal struck imperial Christianity with unprecedented power, and during the fourth and fifth centuries it swelled into a movement affecting all levels of the Christian population. Many found the ascetic way an acceptable substitute for the spiritual heroism required during the days of persecution. The monks revived the Christian enthusiasm and the end-time piety of an earlier, more demanding age. They transformed the spirit of martyrdom into the final full commitment to God and the ascetic imitation of Christ.

The aim of the imitation of Christ was to exist only for God and to live from the strength of his grace alone. To reach this goal and not be hindered on their way, the monks assumed a threefold vow: poverty, chastity, and obedience. Thus the true spiritual warriors tried to divest themselves of their possessions, their marital happiness, and their freedom to choose. Today we call these "basic rights." The monk considered them the roots of ego and obstructions to communion with God.

Once the early extravagances had subsided and monks began to live under stable and livable rules, the monastery began to assume tasks of enormous benefit to the church and to the world. In the fifth and sixth centuries, practically every leader in the church was either a monk himself or was closely linked to monasticism. The monastic cell became a study and the monks became scholars.

As Roland Bainton says,

> The pioneer in monastic scholarship was Jerome (340–420), who began his career as a hermit in the Syrian Desert but found that he could exorcise his sexual temptations only by occupying his mind with a tough intellectual discipline. He took up the study of Hebrew and found it so effective that he could even venture to return to the world. At Rome, he became a teacher to Bishop Damasus and to a circle of high-born ladies."

They studied the problems of biblical interpretation. In time, however, hostility toward the monks in Christian Rome, which Jerome thought still resembled Babylon, led him to withdraw to a monastery at Bethlehem, where his linguistic skills were put to use in translating the Old and the New Testament from the original tongues into literary Latin. The result was the so-called Vulgate, the authorized version of the Bible in Roman Catholicism until recent years.

The first to introduce monasticism to the West was Athanasius. In 335, when he was banished to Trier (in modern Germany), he was accompanied by two monks. The circulation of his *Life of Saint Anthony* also spread the idea in the West. Bishop Ambrose of Milan and Augustine in North Africa were eager supporters of monasticism. Augustine wrote the first western monastic rule for his community of clerics at Tagaste and at Hippo. A bit later, in 415, the monk John Cassian, who had visited Egypt, founded the monastery of St. Victor near Marseille and wrote two valuable books of meditation, which could be regarded as Rules. Above all, however, Benedict of Nursia provided the constitution for Western monasticism.

THE GENIUS OF THE WEST

Benedict was born in Nursia, about eighty-five miles northeast of Rome, late in the fifth century. His education in Rome was still in its early stages when he adopted the most extreme form of asceticism and lived as a hermit high in a lonely cave in wild country south of Rome. He spent three years there in the study of the Scriptures and in severe self-denial, until "the monks of a neighboring monastery chose him for their abbot," the fatherly spiritual leader of a monastic group. Benedict's strict discipline proved irksome to them, however, and he narrowly escaped death when the monks tried to poison him. For a time he found solitude in a cave, but jealous opposition drove him from the region, a wiser man.

In 529, on the heights of Monte Cassino, eighty-five miles southeast of Rome, he laid the foundations of what became the most famous monastery in Europe, the motherhouse of the Benedictine order. For this monastery he wrote his famous Rule. Here he taught, preached, and lived a pattern of monastic piety until his death in 542.

"Benedict was no scholar," says Williston Walker, "but he had the Roman genius for administration, an earnest belief in monasticism as the ideal Christian life, and a profound knowledge of people." In drawing up his set of regulations—the Rule—he built on the work of earlier leaders of monasticism, but he revealed a sense of moderation and good judgment that came from keen observation of human nature. Monasticism, he recognized, had its perils. Many monks lived unworthy of their profession. "Some were no better than vagabonds." These evils, he said, were due to lack of discipline. So Benedict made discipline a fundamental; yet he saw that it must not be too heavy a yoke for ordinary men. It was this remarkable "combination of restraint with some degree of freedom" that distinguished Benedict's Rule.

The saint apparently thought of the monastic life as a kind of spiritual garrison for Christ in a hostile world. As such, its discipline was a necessary part of its life. None should enter its service until he had tried the life fully for at least a year. During this time the novitiate was free to leave. After this time of testing, the would-be monk took the threefold vows that forever cut him off from the world and bound him to permanent life in the monastery: poverty, chastity, and obedience to the Rule and the monastery's leaders.

The government of the monastery was vested in an abbot, and nowhere does Benedict's wisdom more vividly appear than in his provision for the exercise of authority. While each monk vowed absolute obedience to the abbot's commands, even if they seemed to him impossible to fulfill, the abbot was chosen by the monks themselves, and he could decide major matters only after calling for the judgment of the whole body. "Benedict was wise enough to know that a sensible man, even if given absolute authority in theory," should not refuse the advice of others in matters of great importance.

As Walker explains, to maintain this spiritual fortress apart from the world, "Benedict prescribed that each monastery, wherever feasible, should be equipped to furnish all the necessities of life." Monks wove their own cloth, made their own wine, and were their own carpenters and masons. Benedict considered wandering outside the walls a great spiritual danger for a monk.

Since worship was a large part of monastic life, the Rule made special plans for its observance. On the supposed authority of Scripture, Benedict required not only seven services in the twenty-four hours, but made a special obligation for two o'clock in the morning, the "vigil." In contrast to the requirements of some other Rules, however, the Benedictine services, except the vigil, were exceptionally brief. They took about twenty minutes each and consisted primarily of reciting Psalms.

Benedict's most fruitful requirements, says Walker, were regarding labor. "Idleness," he said in the Rule, "is hostile to the soul, and therefore the brethren should be occupied at fixed times in manual labor, and at definite hours in religious reading." He saw clearly the moral value of work; and he was broad-minded enough in his conception of labor to include work of the mind as well as work of the hands. The proportion naturally varied with the seasons. In the harvest time of summer the manual labor of the fields came first, but in the comparative rest of winter, especially in Lent, opportunities for reading increased.

A Benedictine monastery that was true to the purposes of the founder was, therefore, "a little world in itself, in which the monks lived a strenuous but not overburdened life, involving worship, vigorous labor in the shop and fields, and serious reading." Every Benedictine monastery, therefore, included a library, and, though Benedict himself says nothing about classical learning, Benedictine monks soon copied and read the great literary works of Latin antiquity. We are indebted to them for preserving the writings of the Latin church fathers and the masterpieces of Roman literature.

SOME PROS AND CONS

From Italy the Benedictine Rule spread rapidly over Western Europe. It is almost impossible to exaggerate the service these monks rendered in the period after the ruin of the old Roman civilization and the growth in its place of the new nations of German conquerors. The Middle Ages preserved so much of the best in Christianity and the ancient world because Benedictine monasteries filled the European countryside. They gave the only opportunity the Middle Ages had for study, for protection amid constant warfare, and for rest. They were a great missionary force and a constant reminder to a rude population that man does not live by bread alone.

As Williston Walker says, it is easy to see monasticism's faults. While the individual monk took the vow of poverty, the monasteries often grew immensely rich through gifts, especially land. Their discipline frequently became lax. Their original rigor often declined. The history of the Middle Ages shows constant efforts toward their reform and the foundation of new houses designed to eliminate the corruption of the older ones.

Above all, the Benedictine conception of the Christian life was essentially unnatural. "To enter a monastery was to separate from the world, to abandon the ordinary relationships of social life," to shun marriage and all that the Christian home signifies. And supporting the whole endeavor was an erroneous view of man. The soul, said the monk, is chained to the flesh as a prisoner to a corpse. That is not the biblical view of human life, and it created a fundamental flaw in monasticism.

To recognize these errors today, however, is not to say that the faults were apparent to the men of the declining Roman Empire or the Middle Ages. For them, generally, the monastic calling seemed the truest form of the Christian life. Nor should we, in noting the evils of monasticism, underrate in the least the immense service the monks rendered in the spread and development of Christianity and of civilization in a trying period of European history.

Suggestions for Further Reading

*Burton-Christian, Douglas. *The Word in the Desert—Scripture and the Quest of Holiness in Early Christian Monasticism*. New York: Oxford University Press, 1993.

Chittister, Joan. *The Rule of Benedict: Insights for the Ages*. New York: Crossroads, 1992.

Deferrari, Roy J., ed. *Early Christian Biographies*. Washington, DC: Catholic University Press, 1952.

Dowley, Tim, ed. *Eerdmans' Handbook to the History of Christianity*. Grand Rapids: Eerdmans, 1977.

Noll, Mark A. *Turning Points: Decisive Moments in the History of Christianity*. Grand Rapids, Baker Books, 2000.

Waddell, Helen. *The Desert Fathers*. London: Constable, 1936.

Workman, Herbert B. *The Evolution of the Monastic Ideal*. Boston: Beacon Press, 1962.

CHAPTER 13

THE SAGE
OF THE AGES

Augustine

T HEY CALLED ROME THE Eternal City. For 620 years, since the days
of Hannibal, Rome had seen no foreign invader outside its walls.
Then suddenly in 410 Alaric, the Visigoth leader, with his Arian hordes
was besieging the city. The storm would soon break. Everyone knew
that, but when?

The first peace party ventured beyond the wall to bargain with
Alaric. They begged for mercy. They asked for terms. All your gold, all
your silver, came the reply. Above all, your German slaves! The Romans
continued to plead as the misery within the walls mounted.

Finally, the Visigoths charged through the gates and plundered the
city, temple by temple, palace by palace. Devastation and ruin were
everywhere—except in the churches. When Alaric, proclaiming himself a Christian, inspected the booty, he separated the church treasures
from the rest and had his soldiers carry the sacred vessels through the
streets to the churches dedicated to Peter and to Paul and leave them
there.

A short time later the Visigoth and his troops withdrew from Rome,
but the world would never be the same. The glory of "the queen of
cities" was gone. Eternal Rome was not eternal. "My voice sticks in my
throat," said Jerome. "The City that took the whole world captive is
itself taken." He uttered the sentiments of all, Christians and heathen.

Shocked Romans pointed to the spots where statues of the ancient
gods had stood. They had made Rome great. Perhaps they would have

saved the city. Were they angry because the emperors had so recently turned to the Christian God?

Refugees from Rome fled in all directions. In the little North African seaport of Hippo, a slim and beardless figure, with a shaven head and sharp features, watched the arrival of the troubled refugees. He heard their probing questions, their expressions of doubt. Someone should offer an explanation for the ravaging of Rome. Then and there Aurelius Augustinus, the Bishop of Hippo, decided to pursue the questions: Why had Rome fallen? Would the ruin of the Eternal City mean the collapse of Christianity? Was the end of the world at hand?

Augustine's answer to these questions not only provided light for the dark days just ahead, but a philosophy for the foundations of Christendom. To this day Christians feel the impact of his mind and soul. Roman Catholicism draws upon Augustine's doctrine of the church and Protestants upon his views of sin and grace.

PREPARATION FOR GREATNESS

The great North African was born on November 13, 354, in Tagaste, a little town in the hill country of Numidia, a region we know as Algeria. His father, Patricius, was an easygoing heathen; his mother, Monica, an eager Christian. In spite of their limited resources, the couple was determined to give Augustine the best education available. Thus he went to school, first near home and then in the North African capital, Carthage. In the capital he found sexual temptations irresistible. He fell in love with a girl who gave him a son, Adeodatus. They lived together for thirteen years, but Augustine always felt that sex was his defiling passion. It colored his conceptions of sin, and it marked the depravity from which he later felt himself rescued by God's grace.

His higher nature, however, constantly asserted itself. A treatise by Cicero, the Latin author, fell into his hands in his nineteenth year and convinced him intellectually that he should make truth his life's search. The old temptations, however, still assailed him, and like Paul, he felt that two warriors, a higher and a lower, were struggling in him for mastery. In his conflicts he turned to the Bible, but it had no appeal to him. Its style seemed crude and barbarous to him.

For a time Augustine tried Manicheanism, a persecuted faith in the Roman Empire, but one peculiarly appealing to a man of passion who felt two tendencies at war within him. Mani, its founder, had taught in Persia and had met there a martyr's death by crucifixion in 276 or 277. The fundamental belief of the religion pictured the universe as the scene of an eternal conflict of two powers, the one good and the other evil. Man, as we know him, is a mixed product: the spiritual part of his nature consists of the good element, the physical of the evil. His task, therefore, is to free the good in him from the evil, and this can be accomplished by prayer, but especially by abstinence from all the enjoyments of evil: riches, lust, wine, meats, luxurious houses, and the like.

Manichaeism, like Gnosticism, taught that the true spiritual Jesus had no material body and did not actually die. His purpose was to teach men the way out of the kingdom of darkness into the kingdom of light. Like the Gnostics, the Manicheans held that much of the New Testament is true, but they rejected everything in it that seemed to suggest Christ's real sufferings, and they discarded the Old Testament altogether.

Augustine remained an eager Manichean for nine years, from 374 to 383, before dissatisfaction with its teachings arose in his mind. During these years he taught grammar in his native Tagaste, and rhetoric in Carthage, and though inwardly doubting the truth of the Manichean philosophy, it was at the suggestion of Manichean friends in 383 that he moved to Rome.

Shortly after his arrival in the capital he secured a professorship in the State University in Milan (384) and moved to the northern city. His widowed mother and some of his African friends soon joined him. He was now thirty years old, at the summit of a career, with dazzling prospects of success before him. More than ever, however, he was deeply dissatisfied with his life. He callously separated from his mistress, Adeodatus's mother, to become engaged to a young woman of wealth and position; but he could not master his passions. He found himself in "a whirl of vicious love-making." "There's nothing so powerful," he later observed, "in drawing the spirit of a man downward as the caresses of a woman." His inner conflicts became almost unbearable.

While living in Milan, however, Augustine came under the powerful preaching of Bishop Ambrose. He went to church first to study Ambrose's preaching style, but before long the message reached his soul. In Ambrose he discovered that Christianity could be both eloquent and intelligent, and that the troublesome stories in the Old Testament could be interpreted as allegories.

The final stimulus to Augustine's conversion seems to have been the personal example of the monks. When a friend told him the story of Anthony and the Egyptian hermits—how they withstood the temptations of the world—Augustine felt a burning sense of shame. How could these unlearned men win such spiritual victories when he, with all his education, knew only defeat? His sense of sin and his powerlessness were profoundly stirred.

Matters came to a head as he walked through his garden in agony. He heard the singsong voice of a child saying, "Take it and read it." He picked up a New Testament. His eyes fell on the words perfectly suited to his mood: "not in rioting and drunkenness, not in chambering and wantonness, not in strife and envying. But put ye on the Lord Jesus Christ, and make not provision for the flesh, to fulfil the lusts thereof" (Rom. 13:13–14, KJV). "Instantly," said Augustine, "as I reached the end of this sentence, it was as if the light of peace was poured into my heart, and all the shades of doubt faded away."

On the eve of the following Easter, 387, Augustine, with his son, Adeodatus, and his friend, Alypius, was baptized by Ambrose in Milan. "The unrest of our past life," he said, "receded from us." A few months later, accompanied by his mother, he set out for North Africa a different man. On the journey, however, near Rome, his mother died. And during the autumn of 388, once again settled in Tagaste, he lost his son, adding to the grief he already felt from the death of his mother. Augustine was now as eager to leave the world as he had once been to plunge into it. It was not to be. His gifts were too well-known and the need for leadership in the church was too great for him to be left in peace.

Three years later at Hippo, by popular demand but against his will, Augustine was ordained a priest. Soon, at the request of Bishop Valerius, he was chosen assistant bishop of the church, and a year later, upon the death of Valerius, Augustine succeeded to the leadership of the church in Hippo. He was forty-three years old and for the next thirty-three years, until his death in 430, he stood in the center of the storms of his time.

THE DONATIST CONTROVERSY

North African Christianity was still torn by a passionate conflict between Catholics and a movement called Donatism. The controversy was long-standing and deep-seated. A bishop of Hippo could scarcely avoid speaking to the issue.

When Augustine stepped into church leadership, Donatism was almost a hundred years old. The movement stood for a holy church, for church discipline, and for the unflinching resistance of unworthy bishops. The Catholics, said the Donatists, had surrendered all of these by ordaining immoral priests and bishops.

The *Donatist* name arose from Donatus, an early bishop of Carthage (313–355) who led the protest against Catholic practices. Donatist charges centered on the fact that certain Catholic bishops had handed over the Scriptures to be burned during the persecution under Diocletian. Such an act, the Donatists insisted, was a serious sin of apostasy. Since the Catholic pastors were ordained by bishops who had sinned so grievously, the Donatists believed they, rather than the Catholics, constituted the true church of Christ. During Augustine's time the Donatists were still widespread in North Africa, and in some areas they constituted a majority.

Augustine rejected the Donatist's view of a pure church. Until the day of judgment, he said, the church must be a mixed multitude. Both good and bad people are in it. To support this idea he appealed to Jesus' parable of the wheat and tares (Matt. 13:24–30), overlooking the fact that Jesus was not speaking of the church but of the whole world.

Augustine also set forth a different understanding of the sacraments. The Donatists argued that the validity of the sacrament depends upon the moral standing of the minister. Augustine said no. The sacrament does not belong to the minister but to Christ. The priest's acts are really God's because he has placed the sacraments in the hands of the properly ordained minister. All that is required of the priest is his awareness that he administers God's grace for the whole church.

Such a view makes the priest the channel for grace to the members of the church. Thus Augustine added his considerable influence to his priestly (sacerdotal) view of the church that reached such unfortunate extremes in medieval Catholicism.

His defense of the Catholic Church in the Donatist controversy also led Augustine to support the use of force in the suppression of the rivals. Initially he was strongly opposed to coercion. But step by step he came to another view. In the face of Donatist resistance to the government's mounting pressure, he came to accept the use of force in a religious issue. What looks like harsh action, he said, may bring the offender to recognize its justice. Had not the Lord himself in the parable said, "Compel people to come in" (Luke 14:23)? Thus Augustine's prestige was made available for those in later ages who justified the ruthless acts of the Inquisition against Christian dissenters.

OF SIN AND GRACE

If the Donatist controversy called forth the churchman in Augustine, the Pelagian debate evoked his emphases on salvation by grace.

Pelagius was a British monk who came to North Africa from Rome. A disciple who accompanied him, Coelestius, had hopes of securing ordination as a priest in Carthage, but he found little support in lands dominated by Augustine. As soon as Coelestius's views appeared in Carthage, they were repudiated.

As a result Coelestius headed for the East where Pelagius had gone. Churches there were more receptive to Pelagius's teaching. But Augustine launched a strenuous literary attack on Pelagianism. By 419 the

Pelagians were banished by the Emperor Honorius, and in 431 they were condemned by the General Council of the Church meeting at Ephesus.

Why? What did Pelagius teach to arouse Augustine's vigorous opposition? The monk denied that human sin is inherited from Adam. Man, he said, is free to act righteously or sinfully. Moreover, death is not a consequence of Adam's disobedience. Adam, indeed, introduced sin into the world, but only by his corrupting example. There is no direct connection between his sin and the moral condition of mankind. Almost all the human race has sinned; but it is possible not to sin, and some people have in fact lived without sin. God predestinates no one, except in the sense that he foresees who will believe and who will reject his gracious influences. His forgiveness comes to all who exercise "faith alone"; but, once forgiven, man has power of himself to live pleasing to God. Thus Pelagius found no real need for the special enabling power of the Holy Spirit. His idea of the Christian life was practically the Stoic conception of ascetic self-control.

All this was in sharp contrast to Augustine's own experience. He sensed profoundly the depth of his sin and hence the greatness of God's salvation. He felt that nothing less than irresistible divine power (grace) could have saved him from his sin and only constantly inflowing divine grace could keep him in the Christian life. His Christian ideal was no Stoic self-control but love for righteousness infused by the Spirit of God.

In Augustine's view, Adam's sin had enormous consequences. His power to do right was gone. In a word, he died—spiritually, and soon physically. But he was not alone in his ruin. Augustine taught that the whole human race was "in Adam" and shared his fall. Mankind became a "mass of corruption," incapable of any good (saving) act. Every individual, from earliest infancy to old age, deserves nothing but damnation.

Since man of himself can do nothing good, all power to do good must be the free gift of God, that is, grace. Out of the mass of the fallen race, God chooses some to receive this grace, which comes to them from the work of Christ, and ordinarily through the church and especially through its sacraments. All who receive baptism receive regenerating grace, which gives man back his freedom to serve God, though that service is imperfect even at best, and is maintained only by the constant gift of more grace.

As Williston Walker explains, "Those to whom God does not send his grace are lost. Nor can any man be sure, even if he now enjoys God's grace, that he will be saved. Only those to whom God gives the added grace of perseverance, that is, who have divine aid to the end of life, will be redeemed." Man, therefore, has no power or worthiness of himself; his salvation is fully from God.

Augustine, like Paul, had been "apprehended" by the grace of God. He entered the Christian faith by what seemed to him catastrophes. The great original catastrophe was his condition at birth, sinful alienation from God. And the only freedom from that catastrophe was a new birth.

The Protestant Reformers would depend greatly upon Augustine's view that mankind is incapacitated by sin's grip and the notion that only God's grace could rehabilitate man. These teachings fit well with Augustine's teaching of predestination, which the Reformers expanded. They disregarded how Augustine tied salvation and grace to the sacraments of the church.

Pelagius's teaching was condemned by the great council of Ephesus in 431. He had failed to grasp sin's great distorting effect and how turning toward God without his grace was impossible. Yet over the next century the church expressed independence from Augustine's ideas of irresistible grace and predestination. Some critics argued that Augustine had broken the longstanding practice of embracing human freedom. Vincent of Lerins complained of this innovation when he wrote that a Christian should believe what has been believed "always, everywhere, and by all."

THE CITY OF GOD ON THE RUINS OF ROME

Augustine was fifty-six years old when he was told that Rome had been sacked. It must have been a dramatic moment in his life. He welcomed the first refugees from Rome and set to work finding quarters for them and encouraging his enlarged flock. In a sermon delivered at the time, he compared the capture of Rome with the judgment of Sodom. There had been a great deal of destruction, but cities, he said, consist of men, not walls. Unlike Sodom, Rome had been chastised but not destroyed.

Soon, he turned to the deeper questions of the relations between earthly cities like Rome, which have their day, rising and falling like everything in time, and the Heavenly City or City of God, which is everlasting. This question occupied him for sixteen years, almost to the end of his life, and resulted in his great work, *The City of God*, which directly or indirectly influenced the thought of Christians on what they owed to God and what to Caesar through the succeeding fifteen centuries.

From Adam to the end of time, Augustine wrote, humanity falls into two cities: the mass of the godless, who live the life of earthly men; and the company of spiritual men, born of grace and called to the City of God for all eternity. The Worldly City, said Augustine, is united by the common love for temporal things. The City of God is bound together by the love of God.

What drove the Romans to their great achievements except the praise of men?

> What else was there for them to love save glory? For, through glory, they desired to have a kind of life after death on the lips of those who praised them . . . . The Heavenly City outshines Rome, beyond comparison. There, instead of victory, is truth; instead of high rank, holiness; instead of peace, felicity; instead of life, eternity . . . .

And what about the church and state? Augustine considered the church the only human community that worked for the building of the City of God. The state had its place in suppressing crime and preserving peace, but since the state was based on the power of sin, it must submit to the laws of the Christian church.

The grandeur of this spiritual vision made *The City of God* the most beloved of Augustine's works throughout the early Middle Ages. It gave a spiritual interpretation to the woes the world was suffering. The present might be bad, but better things are to come. The golden age—the kingdom of God—is in the future, not in the fading splendors of a worldly kingdom that could only crumble and fall.

The older Augustine became, the more difficult his life became. In his seventy-sixth year the barbarian Vandals had crossed the Straits of Gibraltar and were sweeping east toward Hippo. In his closing days he had the penitential psalms copied on parchment and fixed to the wall of his room so he could read them in bed. The dying man believed the end of the world to be at hand. On August 28, 430, Augustine found peace at last in Christ.

The Vandal siege of Hippo lasted fourteen months. When they finally breached the walls in August 431, they found most of the people dying or dead from hunger.

Suggestions for Further Reading

*Bonner, Gerald. *St. Augustine of Hippo: Life and Controversies*. London: SMC, 1963.

Brown, Peter. *Augustine of Hippo: A Biography*. Berkeley: University of California Press, 2000.

Hansel, Robert R. *The Life of Saint Augustine*. New York: Franklin Watts, 1969.

Knowles, Andrew and Pachomius Penkett. *Augustine and His World*. Downers Grove, IL: InterVarsity Press, 2004.

Martin, Thomas F. *Our Restless Heart: The Augustinian Tradition*. Maryknoll, NY: Orbis, 2003.

O'Meara, John J. *The Young Augustine*. Staten Island: Alba House, 1965.

CHAPTER 14

PETER AS "PONTIFEX MAXIMUS"

The Beginnings of the Papacy

"**Y**OU ARE THE SCOURGE of God," cried a hermit as Attila the Hun led his cavalry and well-armed foot soldiers out of the endless pastures of central Asia to invade the western half of the Roman Empire. The Hun's march up the Danube in the fifth century forced inhabitants on both sides of the valley to flee, until he confronted Roman legions and their Gothic allies in central Europe. "Yes, you are the scourge of God," the hermit had prophesied, "but God will break the tool of his revenge. Know that you will suffer defeat!"

In June 452 the Scourge of God advanced on Rome. A sudden raid over the Alps brought him into northern Italy, where he met with resistance at only a few places. The weakened Roman army kept out of range and the population fled. In spite of pestilence and mutiny, Attila drove his horses and men on.

At a fordable spot on the Po River, Attila met an embassy from Rome, the usual peace delegation. He was about to send them away when he heard that Bishop Leo was there as emissary for the Roman emperor.

Leo was commissioned to negotiate with one of the mighty men of the panic-stricken world in the hope of avoiding chaos. He must save what there was to save. The Roman emperor was doing nothing to preserve the ancient capital of the empire and its surrounding territories from devastation. So Peter's deputy, now acting in the name of the emperor, sat facing Attila alone.

Man to man, the contest seemed unequal. On the one side, the law of conquest; on the other, the law of faith. On the one side, triumph

141

over the wounded, the ravaged, the dying; on the other, submission to the divine mysteries of the church. A foreign king and a ruling pope.

Long before the arrival of the embassy from Rome, Attila had probably made up his mind about further military thrusts. Epidemics in his army added to widespread famine were forcing him to break off the advance. But nobody knew it. So he willingly granted an interview to the imperial envoy, and in the course of it he granted the pope's plea that the capital should be spared. He even promised to withdraw from Italy, and he kept his word. The bishop of Rome had assumed a new role and staked a fresh claim on the future.

The papacy is a highly controversial subject. No other institution has been so loved and so hated. Some Christians have revered the pope as the "Vicar of Christ"; others have denounced him as the "Anti-Christ."

All sides agree, however, that Leo represents an important stage in the history of this unique institution. He demonstrates the papacy's capacity to adapt to different environments in its long history: the Roman Empire, the Germanic kingdoms of the Middle Ages, the national states of modern times, and today the developing worlds of Asia and Africa. What is the foundation of the papal office, and when was it laid?

THE ROMAN CATHOLIC CLAIM

According to the official teaching of the Roman Catholic Church, defined at the First Vatican Council (1870), Jesus Christ established the papacy with the apostle Peter, and the bishop of Rome as Peter's successor bears the supreme authority (primacy) over the whole church. Both Eastern Orthodox churches and Protestant denominations deny both of these claims. For this reason any study of the history of the papacy creates controversy, comparable to sticking your hand into a hornet's nest.

Our primary concern, however, is neither the vindication nor the refutation of the Roman Catholic claims. It is a survey of Christian history. Whatever the absolute claims of church authorities, history indicates that the concept of papal rule of the whole church was established by slow and painful stages. Leo is a major figure in that process because he provides for the first time the biblical and theological bases of the papal claim. That is why it is misleading to speak of the papacy before his time.

The term *pope* itself is not crucial in the emergence of the doctrine of papal primacy. The title *papa* originally expressed the fatherly care of any and every bishop of his flock. It only began to be reserved for the bishop of Rome in the sixth century, long after the claim of primacy.

We must also separate the honor of the church of Rome from the authority of its head. The early centuries of Christian history offer abundant evidence of Rome's prominence among the churches of the western regions of the empire. Honor surrounded her name for several reasons. First, Rome was the imperial capital, the Eternal City, and the church of Rome was the largest and wealthiest church, with a reputation for orthodoxy and charity. It stood without a rival in the West.

Second, despite persecutions of all kinds, the Roman congregation quickly grew in numbers and significance. By the middle of the third century its membership probably approached 30,000; it counted 150 clerics and 1,500 widows and poor people. Then, just as today, size meant influence.

Third, several early Christian writers, beginning with Irenaeus in the second century, referred to Peter and Paul as founders of the church in Rome and to subsequent bishops as successors of the apostles. These roots in the apostolic age were important in a day when gnostic teachers appealed to a secret tradition arising from Christ. Many catholic Christians felt that a list of bishops traced back to Peter and Paul was a sure means of safeguarding the apostolic message.

This respect for Rome's traditions, however, did not prohibit able men like Irenaeus and Cyprian from disagreeing with Rome when they felt the church or her bishop was in error. Up to the time of Constantine, history offers no conclusive evidence that the bishop of Rome exercised jurisdiction outside of Rome. Honor, yes; jurisdiction, no.

Rome's growing influence was a part of the increasingly complex church structure emerging in the third and fourth centuries. Church organization developed in two important ways: the authority of church councils and the authority of certain bishops over other bishops.

Councils arose when churches in various areas began sending their pastors (or bishops) to meetings to discuss common problems. These were at first irregular, but during the third century these provincial councils began to meet annually. In theory, the bishops from the churches were all equal, but in practice this was seldom the case. The pastors of the churches established by the apostles possessed an informal spiritual prestige, and the bishops from the larger cities exercised authority in certain matters over the pastors from smaller towns.

As the church grew it adopted, quite naturally, the structure of the empire. This meant that the provincial town of the empire became the episcopal town of the church. Above the provinces in the empire was the metropolis, so bishops in these larger cities soon supervised the bishops in the provinces of that area. Finally, the empire was divided into several major regions, so within the church people came to think of the church at Rome exercising authority in Italy, Carthage in North Africa, Alexandria in Egypt, Antioch in Syria, and so on.

As the churches within the province thrust out into the countryside, usually through a preaching tour of the bishop, other churches were established to meet the needs of the converts. At first these churches were cared for by clergy sent out from the city. Ministers who served them, however, were not bishops. They were called priests from *presbyter*, the Greek word for elder. These priests in the country parishes were consecrated and controlled by the city bishop, but they could administer the sacraments.

Thus, as the fourth century began, the catholic churches were establishing general policies by regular regional councils of bishops and handling day-to-day affairs under the oversight of bishops in each area.

General councils of the church arose only after Constantine's conversion. To settle major issues troubling the churches, the emperor convened synods of bishops from a wide area. Arles, in 314, was a general council of the churches in the West, and Nicaea, in 325, the first general council of the whole church. The decrees of these and later councils became the law of the church.

The bishop of Rome soared to major importance on the wings of these developments. The Council of Nicaea recognized the bishops of Alexandria, Antioch, and Rome as preeminent in their own areas. Jerusalem was granted an honorary primacy. Thus by 325 the policy of patriarchates, that is, the administration of church affairs by bishops from three or four major cities, was confirmed by conciliar action.

THE IMPERIAL MOVE EAST

In 330 an important new factor appeared. Constantine moved his imperial residence to the New Rome, to the ancient city Byzantium on the Bosporus. The City of Constantine (Constantinople) shifted the political center of gravity to the East, and as Constantinople's power increased, the political importance of Old Rome declined. Soon the churches looked to the bishop of Constantinople for spiritual and doctrinal leadership equal to that of the other major cities.

Shortly after the Emperor Theodosius entered Constantinople he published legislation making Christianity the state church. Pagan sacrifices were forbidden; the temples were closed, some of them destroyed by Christian fanatics.

In May 381 the new emperor called a general council at Constantinople. As Constantine had done sixty years earlier, Theodosius made a personal appearance at the opening. He wanted to bring order into his

Christian church. He invited, however, only bishops from the eastern part of the empire. The Italians were absent, notably Damasus, Bishop of Rome, who did not even send a representative.

What did the emperor want? The confirmation and renewal of the Nicene Creed. That was the basic action of the council, but it also asserted, "The bishop of Constantinople shall take precedence immediately after the bishop of Rome, because his city (Constantinople) is the New Rome."

In the West they realized at once the significance of the confrontation of Old Rome and New Rome and of the bishop of Constantinople's promotion. It was obviously a political move to buttress the episcopal power in the East. Was Rome to be left alone to go its own way?

Damasus, the bishop of Rome, objected to the Council's action. Does the position of the church and its bishops depend upon the status of some city in the empire? Rome's preeminence, he insisted, does not rest upon any such historical accident, or on the decrees of a council.

At a synod in Rome the next year, bishops from the West argued, "The Holy Roman Church takes precedence over the other churches, not on the ground of any synodal decisions, but because it was given the primacy by the words of our Lord and Redeemer in the gospel, when he said, 'Thou art Peter, and upon this rock I will build my church.' " Thus we have the first mention of the "primacy of the Roman Church."

The church at Constantinople and the church at Rome were headed in different directions. That was clear by the end of the fourth century. Strains that would eventuate in a complete break between the Christianity of the East and the West were already apparent.

Constantinople relied more and more on its political position and was drawn into the orbit of eastern imperial politics. The more religion and politics became intertwined in the East, the less independent became the patriarch of the capital.

In Rome, the conditions were markedly different. The weakness of the Roman Empire in the West led to a growing independence of the bishop of Rome, the patriarch of the West. The pope had no strong rival. Deprived of the old argument of primacy based on Rome the imperial city, the bishops of Old Rome relied more heavily upon an argument from Scripture and tradition, the primacy of Peter.

Bishop Damasus (366–384) marked the transition to the new day for Old Rome. He was able to fuse the old Roman civic and imperial pride with Christianity. He could point to the noble basilicas dedicated to Peter and Paul. Built by Constantine, the churches rested on the shrines thought to mark the graves of the two saints. "Although the East sent the apostles," said Damasus, "yet because of the merit of their martyrdom, Rome has acquired a superior right to claim them as citizens." Such was the prelude to Leo.

LEO'S CASE FOR PRIMACY

Before his election to the papal office, Leo, a nobleman from a region north of Rome, had been sent by the emperor to Gaul to arbitrate a dispute. When the bishop of Rome died the Roman clergy sent a delegate to inform Leo that the choice of a new bishop had fallen to him.

In the sermon Leo preached on the day of his entrance into office he extolled the "glory of the blessed Apostle Peter . . . in whose chair his power lives on and his authority shines forth." The city that had once enjoyed the favor as capital of the empire, the scene of the martyrdom of Peter and Paul, was now granted a powerful new leader. Leo made his entrance into world history as the Supreme Head of all Christendom. Appealing to the threefold gospel testimony (Matt. 16:13–19; Luke 22:31, 32; and John 21:15–17) the new pope laid the theoretical foundation for papal primacy: Christ promised to build his church on Peter, the rock for all ages, and the bishops of Rome are his successors in that authority.

This was a complete reversal of the policy of Constantine, who used Christianity as a tool. He had put political and religious pressure on the bishops at the Council of Nicaea to preserve the unity of the church, which he considered the cement of the empire. A century later Leo raised the status of the bishop's office in Rome once and for all. He carried the papacy as far theoretically as it could go. The dynasty of Peter, Prince of the Church, was established, solemnly, decisively.

Leo's use of the gospel texts to support Peter's primacy flew in the face of several difficulties, however: first, the Gospels make clear that preeminence among the followers of Christ was not to be according to the pattern of the princes of the world who exercise lordship and authority. Christ's disciples must lead by humble service. Second, Peter continued to be notoriously unstable. Even in the Matthew 16:23 passage Jesus rebuked him and called him "Satan" for not understanding "the things that be of God." Later he denied his Lord in the moment of crisis, and Paul criticized him as an unreliable disciple. Third, the theory assumes that the grant of authority was not to Peter personally but to his office as bishop of Rome, but this identification of authority with a particular office is nowhere evident in the text.

Leo's argument, however, seemed to be sent from God to an uncertain hour in the Church of Rome. The barbarian attacks in Italy made the imperial court at Ravenna desperate for the support of any authority that might help to hold the empire in the West together. Thus in 445 the Emperor Valentinian III issued a decree instructing Aetius, the Roman commander in Gaul, to compel the attendance at the papal court of any bishop who refused to come voluntarily. The emperor's edict turned Leo's claim into law.

The imperial document ran,

> As the primacy of the Apostolic See is based on the title of the blessed Peter, prince of the episcopal dignity, on the dignity of the city of Rome, and on the decision of the Holy Synod, no illicit steps may be taken against this See to usurp its authority. For the only way to safeguard peace among the churches everywhere is to acknowledge its leadership universally.

Peter's title was clear; the dignity of the city was history. But just which "Holy Synod" the emperor had in mind is not at all clear.

Leo's vision of the papacy seemed to have the support not only of the emperor but of the sacred fathers meeting at Chalcedon. A year before the encounter with Attila, in October 451, the suburb of Constantinople on the Asiatic shore of the Bosporus drew 350 bishops to defend the true faith against false interpretations of the life of Jesus Christ.

Even though the emperor had called the council to Chalcedon and visited it personally, the spirit of Pope Leo was dominant. His letters, decisions, and actions were quoted so frequently that sometimes a mere reference to him sufficed for the majority of the bishops to shout jubilantly, "That was the faith of the Fathers, that was the faith of the Apostles . . . . Peter has spoken through Leo."

In the historic session on October 30, 451, however, the same council gave the bishop of Constantinople, as bishop of New Rome, authority equal to Leo's. Constantinople became for the East what Rome was for the West. The sole and independent leadership of the Eastern Church by the patriarch of Constantinople was confirmed.

Leo's representative to the council immediately protested, but the council fathers would not alter their decision. It was an obvious reversal for Leo. Christianity acquired not one but two heads: the Roman Church of the Western Empire and the Greek Church of the Eastern Empire.

STANDING AMIDST THE RUINS

The Western Empire was a shadow of its former self. Three years after Leo's successful negotiations with Attila, he faced another test of his diplomacy. A fresh enemy threatened Rome.

This time it was the Vandals, a migrating tribe from Scandinavia, driven southwestward by the Goths advancing from Hungary through Gaul and Spain. The Vandals, expelled for a time from Europe, settled down in the weakest corner of the Roman Empire, in North Africa, and for years they waited for the right moment to strike at Rome.

At the end of March 455, Gaiseric, King of the Vandals, set sail with a hundred ships manned by Carthaginian sailors. His army landed north of the Tiber, creating panic in Rome. Rumors swirled about that Gaiseric intended to burn the city. Many tried to flee. The imperial troops mutinied. While attempting to escape, the Emperor Maximus was slain by one of his own bodyguards. His body was dragged through the streets, torn to pieces, and thrown in the river. No general took over the defense; the troops were disorganized. On June 2, 455, the Vandals entered Rome, meeting no resistance.

At the city gate, Leo met Gaiseric. He was leading not soldiers but priests. The Vandal king was about sixty-five years of age; Leo about the same. An illegitimate offspring of an old Germanic family and a nobleman's son from Tuscany, Gaiseric had been lamed by a fall from his horse, but his reputation as master of the western Mediterranean preceded him.

When they faced each other, Leo begged for mercy. He urged the king to restrain his troops; he implored him not to burn the city. He offered money. Gaiseric nodded silently. Then, spurring his horse away, he called out to the pope, "Fourteen days' looting!"

The Vandals plundered the city systematically, palace by palace. Insignia, gold and silver plate, anything belonging to the emperor was fair game. Temple after temple was sacked. The gilded roof of the Capitol was carried off and the sacred vessels from the Temple of Solomon, brought from Jerusalem. Equestrian figures, marble and bronze columns, images of the gods: everything was loaded on the Vandals' ships.

The Vandals took human booty too: first, political prisoners, like the empress and her daughters, then senators and members of the Roman aristocracy to be held for ransom. For fourteen days the Vandals occupied the city. Then the ships were loaded and the expeditionary force withdrew to Carthage.

After the Vandals were gone, the Romans held a solemn service of thanksgiving. Rome had not been burned down, massacre had been avoided, and only a few Christian churches had been plundered.

All the Romans knew what their bishop had done for them, but only a few of the faithful were present for the service. They were still terrified by the memory of the foreign soldiers and the constant looting. Not a single house had been spared. Would Rome ever recover from such a catastrophe?

Leo reminded his audience of the "days of our chastisement and liberation." He longed for his voice to carry through the walls of the church, out into the streets, into the hearts of those who should have been present.

> One is ashamed to say this, and yet one dares not be silent. You value the devils higher than the Apostles. Who has restored security to the city? Who has liberated it, preserved it from massacre? Turn to the Lord, acknowledge the miracles he has manifestly wrought on our behalf, and ascribe our liberation not, as the godless do, to the influence of the stars but to the ineffable mercy of the Almighty, who has softened the rage of the barbarians.

Though he had saved Rome for a second time, Leo made no reference to himself. It wasn't really necessary. He had assumed the old heathen title, *Pontifex Maximus*, the high priest of religion throughout the empire, and everyone understood. Leo, not the emperor, had shouldered responsibility for the Eternal City. Peter had come to power.

Suggestions for Further Reading

Barraclough, Geoffrey. *The Medieval Papacy*. New York: Harcourt, Brace & World, 1968.

Hollis, Christopher, ed. *The Papacy*. New York: Macmillan, 1964.

Jalland, T. G. *The Church and the Papacy*. London: S.P.C.K., 1944.

Kidd, B. J. *The Roman Primacy to AD 461*. London: S.P.C.K., 1936.

Ullmann, Walter. *A Short History of the Papacy in the Middle Ages*. London: Methuen, 1972.

CHAPTER 15

SOMEWHERE BETWEEN HEAVEN AND EARTH

Eastern Orthodoxy

ONE SUMMER AFTERNOON IN the year 1054, as a service was about to begin in the spacious Church of Holy Wisdom at Constantinople, Cardinal Humbert and two other representatives (legates) of Pope Leo IX entered the building and made their way up to the sanctuary. They had not come to pray. They placed a Bull (an official papal document) of Excommunication upon the altar and marched out once more. As he passed through the western door, the cardinal shook the dust from his feet with the words, "Let God look and judge." A deacon ran after him in great distress and begged him to take back the Bull. Humbert refused, and it was dropped in the street.

For centuries Christians have considered this incident the beginning of the great division between Eastern Orthodoxy and Western Catholicism. Its counterpart in the sixteenth century was Martin Luther's tacking the 95 Theses on the church door in Wittenberg, Germany, precipitating the schism between Protestantism and Roman Catholicism. This confrontation in Constantinople came only after a long and complicated process.

Of the three major divisions in Christianity today—Roman Catholicism, Eastern Orthodoxy, and Protestantism—the least known in the West is Eastern Orthodoxy. Most Christians in Europe and North America, if they think of Orthodox Christians at all, think of Orthodoxy as a kind of Roman Catholicism without the pope.

Such an uninformed response is understandable. Christians in the West, both Protestant and Catholic, generally start by asking the same questions: How is a person saved? What is the church? Where does religious authority lie? Protestant and Catholic simply disagree about the answers. In Orthodoxy, however, it is not merely the answers that are different. The questions themselves are not the same. Orthodoxy reflects a distinctive history and a unique culture.

Important Events in Early Orthodoxy

1. This confession of the church honors the Greek traditions of the early church. Orthodox believers remind us that the New Testament, the Old Testament commonly used by the ancient church (the Septuagint is a translation of Hebrew Scriptures into Greek), and the church's early statements of faith are all in Greek. By contrast, the Western church is influenced greatly by the Latin language and influences.
2. The Orthodox Church was instrumental in the conversion of the Slavic people. Prince Vladimir was baptized in 988 and earnestly promoted the church. For the next one thousand years, Orthodoxy shaped the mindset of this great people.
3. In 1054, the leaders of Catholic and Orthodox confessions officially broke communion.
4. The Orthodox brothers more directly faced the militaristic expansion of the Muslims. The West took advantage of their Orthodox brothers in their time of need; the crusades injured the Eastern believers instead of helping them. In 1453, Constantinople fell to the Turks. Orthodoxy was somewhat tolerated by Muslim rulers, though Orthodox believers were recognized as inferior subjects to the rule of the Turks.

THE CLUE TO ORTHODOXY

What is Eastern Orthodoxy? Today it is about fifteen distinct churches, mostly in Eastern Europe, bound together by a common faith and a common history. The best starting point for understanding Orthodoxy, however, is probably not its basic doctrines but its holy images called icons. Most westerners can recall those characteristic pictures of the saints with the golden nimbuses encircling their heads. These are basic to understanding Orthodoxy. The Orthodox believer who enters his church to attend services, for example, goes first to the iconostasis, the wall of paintings that separates the sanctuary from the nave. There he kisses the icons before taking his place in the congregation. Or a guest who enters an Orthodox home finds an icon hanging in the eastern corner of the living room and bedroom. If he is himself an

Orthodox believer he will, upon entering a room, greet the icons first by crossing himself and bowing. Only then will he greet his host.

An Orthodox believer does not consider these images of Jesus and the saints the works of men but as manifestations of the heavenly ideal. They are a kind of window between the earthly and the celestial worlds. Through the icons the heavenly beings manifest themselves to the worshiping congregation and unite with it. Thus it is impossible to understand Orthodox worship apart from the icons.

In Orthodoxy the idea of image is the key to understanding the ways of God with man. Man is created "in the image of God"; he carries the icon of God within himself.

Thus a rather sharp difference between Eastern Christianity (Orthodoxy) and Western Christianity (Roman Catholicism and Protestantism) appears. Western Christians are inclined to understand the fundamental relationship between God and man in legal terms. Salvation addresses how a person may acquire the righteousness or justice of God. A later division over this issue will furnish an important theological dispute between Catholics and Protestants.

The same Roman sense of legal order is reflected in Roman Catholicism's view of the papacy. According to Rome, Jesus Christ established on Peter a jurisdictional supremacy for the whole church. At its heights, as we shall see, the theory made the pope the supreme ruler of the world!

Orthodoxy represents an interesting contrast to Roman Catholicism. The great theme of Orthodox theology is the incarnation of God and the re-creation of man. According to Orthodoxy when man sins he does not violate the divinely established legal relationship between God and man (a dominant image in Catholicism and Protestant teaching); he reduces the divine likeness; he inflicts a wound in the original image of God.

Salvation, therefore, consists of the perfection or completion of the full image. Christ, the incarnate God, came to earth to restore the icon of God in man. The major themes of Orthodoxy, then, are rebirth, re-creation, and the transfiguration of man. The church is not a formalized institution, it is the mystical body of Christ constantly renewed by the life of the Holy Spirit flowing through it. And it is within this community of love that man is made ready to join the preexisting fellowship among Father, Son, and Spirit. Orthodox believers call the process *Theosis* or deification. The language of "becoming gods" troubles Western believers. But Orthodox teachers do not claim that believers become Father, Son, or Spirit, but use the language to picture the transformation of believers to become fit companions for an eternal communion with and in the triune God. A champion Greek theologian, Athanasius, pictured Jesus fully sharing in the corrupted world of humans so that we could fully share in the incorruptible fellowship of God; he becomes man so that men can become gods. Western theologians also taught other concepts that would picture an unavoidable and necessary transformation prior to our sharing eternity with God; recent Protestant voices have compared *theosis* to the union that Christ establishes with believers.

These fundamental differences were present in the church as soon as the gospel reached Rome and Corinth. But the distinctively Eastern Christian faith appeared first under Constantine.

Constantine's conversion was vital for the development of Orthodoxy because he created, for the first time, an alliance between state and church, and he made purity of Christian doctrine a central concern of the empire. Few events have introduced greater change in the church.

Some independent-minded Christians regard these changes as the beginning of an enslavement of the church by the state, or even the *fall* of the church from the heights of primitive Christian freedom. For Eastern Christians, however, Constantine remains the holy initiator of the Christian world, the hero of that victory of light over darkness that crowned the courageous struggle of the martyrs.

Orthodoxy tends to view Constantine's reign as the climax of the evolution of the Roman Empire. Rome had gradually become a religious monarchy. The emperor served as the connecting link between God and the world, while the state was the earthly reflection of divine law. The cult of the Invincible Sun, which Emperor Aurelian had made the imperial religion in the middle of the third century, was by Constantine's day closely connected with the new religious view of monarchy. The emperor in the world was the same as the sun in heaven; he was a participant in its glory and its representative on earth. Then came Constantine's victory over his rivals—after he turned for help to the Christian God. God himself placed the emperor under the protection of the cross and in direct dependence upon Christ.

GOD'S WILL IN HUMAN SOCIETY

This meant, however, that Constantine was converted, not as a man, but as an emperor. Christ himself had sanctioned his power and made him the divine representative, and through Constantine's person the God of heaven bound the empire to himself by special ties. That, at any rate, is how Eastern Christians saw it.

The Christian mind was fascinated by the conversion of Constantine. Not only did this mood prevent the church from modifying the absolutism of the empire in terms of the gospel, but on the contrary, that absolutism itself became an inseparable part of the Christian view of the world. Constantine believed in the state as the *bearer* of religion because it directly reflected and expressed the divine will for the world in human society. Long after Constantine, that conviction remained a hallmark of Eastern Christianity. This view of the world is very different and distant from the modern emphasis upon the individual, and a nation-state whose power is limited by the individual's inviolable rights.

The symbol of the new era for the church in society was Constantinople, the new capital of the empire, New Rome. During its long and illustrious history as the center of a thriving civilization and the seat of economic and political power, Constantinople was the home of the Eastern Christian tradition and the hub of the new Byzantine civilization. It left a thousand-year mark on the pages of history.

Through the centuries this mystical vision of Constantinople as a holy city broadened and deepened, but it undoubtedly originated with its first emperor. From the first it was to be the Christian center of the empire. In the Church of the Twelve Apostles, which he had built, Constantine prepared in the midst of the twelve symbolic tombs of the apostles a thirteenth, for himself. Did not the conversion of the empire fulfill the prophecy of the apostles? This thirteenth tomb gave rise to the emperor's title as "equal to the apostles."

Fifty years after the founding of the city the religious significance of New Rome was clear to all. The fathers of the second general council proclaimed that the bishop of Constantinople held primacy of honor after the bishop of Rome, because Constantinople was the "New Rome, the city of the Emperor and the Senate."

Constantine discovered, however, that Christianity itself was divided and torn over differences in traditions of doctrine and practice. He was superstitiously anxious that God would hold him personally responsible for these divisions and quarrels among the Christians. If Christianity lacked cohesion and unity, how could it be a proper religion for the empire? Thus Constantine and the emperors who followed him made every effort to secure agreement about the Christian faith.

Constantine adopted a procedure already developed by the Christians to settle differences of opinion at a local or regional level. He called the leaders of the entire church to assemble in his presence to agree upon and define the correct tradition. This procedure itself became a part of the Eastern Christian tradition. From the first General (or Ecumenical) Council at Nicaea (325) to the seventh, also held at Nicaea in 787, it was the emperor who called the council and presided over it, either personally or by deputy. Eastern Christians today place great emphasis on these seven general councils. They sometimes refer to themselves as "The Church of the Seven Councils."

The history of the councils, ranging over five centuries, gave us the elevating writings of the Fathers and the creeds of the ecumenical assemblies. But this struggle to attain the truth also heightened the role of state power. It ceased to be a purely church matter; it acquired a new, political dimension. Thus Eastern Orthodox Christianity came to a painful fruition through these controversial centuries.

The symbol that East and West were headed in two diverging directions came in 395 when Emperor Theodosius the Great, on his deathbed, divided the empire between his two sons. Honorious received the West and Arcadius the East. Theoretically the empire continued to be one state with two emperors, but in practice, from that point on, the Eastern and Western roads inevitably diverged.

JUSTINIAN AND THE REMOVAL OF BOUNDARIES

Clear evidence of the Byzantine character of Eastern Christianity appeared under a second powerful emperor, Justinian, who ascended the royal throne in 527. Under Justinian (527–565) the unique Byzantine blend of Roman law, Christian faith, and Greek (Hellenistic) philosophy—with a pinch of the Orient—came to tasteful excellence. In Byzantine art, greatly encouraged by Justinian, Christianity expressed its distinctively Eastern style. The familiar, physical world of human experience was subordinated to the supernal, transcendent world. And no work made heaven more real than the church building in the heart of the empire.

When Justinian rebuilt Constantine's Church of Holy Wisdom, *Hagia Sophia*, and consecrated it in 538, he exclaimed that he had outdone Solomon. The dome, said contemporaries, hung as it were by a golden chain from heaven, a link in the hierarchy rising from the finite to the infinite and descending from the Creator to the creature. It appeared unfathomable as the sky. The mosaics under it shone with dazzling brilliance. In them, Constantine and Justinian were portrayed, the one offering to the Mother of God a model of Constantinople, the new Rome, and the other a model of the Church of Holy Wisdom.

The link with Constantine was apropos, for Justinian brought the plans of Constantine to their logical conclusion, and in turn defined the future course of Eastern Orthodoxy.

Justinian never distinguished Roman state tradition from Christianity. He considered himself to be completely a Roman emperor and just as fully a Christian emperor. Here lay the source of his whole theory, the unity of the empire and the Christian religion. He defined the mission of the pious emperor as "the maintenance of the Christian faith in its purity and the protection of the Holy Catholic and Apostolic Church from any disturbance."

Justinian always felt himself to be the servant of God and the executor of his will, and the empire to be the instrument of God's plan in the world. The empire had placed itself irrevocably under the symbol of the cross, so its purpose was to guard and spread Christianity among men. The changes from the early days of the faith were remarkable.

The early church considered itself a body, a living organism, a new people, completely incompatible with any other people or any natural community. Theoretically all men in the empire were called and could become members of this body, but even then the world would not become the church, because in the family of God and through it men commune with another world, another life, one to come in glory only after the end of this age.

In official Byzantine doctrine, however, the state was compared to a body not in this early Christian sense, nor because all subjects of the empire had become genuine church members. The figure of the imperial body arose from pagan thinking. The state itself was conceived as a community established by God, and it embraced the whole life of man. The visible representative of God within it, who performed his will and dispensed his blessings, was the emperor. Thus the old boundaries of the church were gradually effaced; the Christian community increasingly coalesced with Byzantine society as a whole.

In Justinian's theory the church almost dissolves in Christian society. Certainly any awareness that the church is radically alien to the world and the empire disappears once and for all from state thinking.

The fragile balance of these major elements in Eastern Christianity was easily upset. The power of the Christian emperor, the state concern over purity of doctrine, and popular belief in icons as windows into the unseen world—all tumbled in violent disarray during the famous (or infamous) iconoclastic controversy.

THE CONFLICT OVER ICONS

On the surface this conflict, which raged for over a century, was a disagreement over the use of icons. But at a deeper level it was a disagreement over which things were sufficiently sacred or holy to deserve worship. Some said the Christian clergy are set apart by ordination; hence, they are holy. Church buildings are set apart by dedication; thus they are holy. The martyrs and heroes of the faith are set apart by their deeds, and they are normally called *saints*. Do they not deserve the same reverence as the clergy?

From the sixth century, the church and the imperial government as well encouraged the development of both Christian icon making and the honoring of monastic holy men. They did not realize that the uncontrolled multiplying of icons and holy men would make people confine their Christian devotion to local shrines and figures. Ordinary Christians may fail to distinguish between the holy object or holy person and the spiritual reality it stood for and fall into idolatry.

This kind of idolatry had its precedents. In ancient Rome the icon of the emperor was revered as if the emperor himself were present. Even after the emperors became Christian, the imperial icon continued to appear in army camps, courthouses, and prominent places in the major cities. Coins also displayed the emperor's image as a mark of authenticity.

During Justinian's reign the emperor erected a huge statue of Christ over the main gate, "the Bronze Gate" of the imperial palace in Constantinople. By the end of the sixth century, icons of Christ or Mary replaced the imperial icon in many situations. Eventually, the icon of Christ appeared on the reverse side of coins.

Early in the eighth century, however, Emperor Leo III (717–41) launched an attack on the use of icons. Perhaps he was motivated by a sense of the empire's wrongdoing. Christianity taught that God punished the children of Israel because of their idolatry. Perhaps the humiliating defeats and losses of the previous century, as well as the calamitous earthquake early in Leo's reign, were intended to bring "God's new chosen people" to their senses. In any case, before the end of the seventh century, feeling against the icons developed and spread.

After successfully repulsing the Muslim armies in their second major attack on Constantinople (717–18), Leo openly declared his opposition to icons for the first time. An angry mob murdered the official who was sent to replace the icon of Christ with a cross over the Bronze Gate. Whole sections of the empire rebelled vigorously. Mosaics were gouged from the walls; icons were daubed with whitewash. Leo secured the retirement of the patriarch of Constantinople and the consecration of a new one who favored his own views.

The iconoclasts (or image breakers) wanted to replace the religious icons with the traditional Christian symbols of the cross, the Book (Bible), and the elements of the Lord's Supper. These objects alone, they insisted, should be considered holy. Beyond this, only ordained clergy and dedicated buildings possessed a kind of holiness.

As Harlie Kay Gallatin explains the crisis, the monks and ascetics, along with an uneducated public, supported the icons; even the monks were not all supportive, though some monasteries made and sold icons. A thoughtful defense of their position came from a distant source:

> John Mansour (about 730–60), in a monastery far away in Arab-controlled Palestine, formulated the ideas that were eventually used to justify religious icons. Mansour, better known as John of Damascus (his birthplace), was the greatest theologian of the eighth century. He is recognized today by the Orthodox churches as the last of the great teachers of the early church, the so-called Fathers.
>
> John explained that an image was never of the same substance as its original, but merely imitated it. An icon's only significance is as a copy and reminder of the original. His argument is based on Plato's notion that everything we sense in this world is really an imitation of the eternal, original "form," which can be known only by the soul in the nonmaterial world.
>
> To deny, as the iconoclasts did, that any true icon could depict Christ, was, in effect, to deny the possibility of the Incarnation. Although it was wrong to worship an icon, the presence of an icon of Christ could instruct and assist the believer in the worship of the true Christ. Icons should be honored and venerated in much the same way as the Bible, or the symbol of the Cross.

Thus John cleared the ground for the acceptance of the icons of Mary, the apostles, the saints, and even the angels. But the pictures themselves were only reminders to help the faithful give proper respect and reverence.

The later course of the iconoclastic controversy is long and complicated. With the assistance of Patriarch Tarasius (784–806), the seventh general council of 350 bishops finally assembled at Nicaea in 787. The Council condemned the whole iconoclastic movement and backed the position presented by John of Damascus.

Iconoclasm, however, was not so easily eliminated. Strong iconoclastic tendencies remained in Asia Minor and among the professional military class. But as the ninth century wore on, the heat of controversy subsided. A synod called early in 843 deposed John Grammaticus, elected Methodius as patriarch, condemned all the iconoclasts, and confirmed the rulings of the seventh council. Orthodox churches today still celebrate the first Sunday in Lent each year as the Feast of Orthodoxy, to commemorate the triumph of icons.

EAST AGAINST WEST

Through these years of Justinian's greatness and the iconoclastic conflict, differences between the Orthodox Church in the East and the Catholic Church in the West widened. The doctrines and practices of the two halves of the Christian church drifted slowly apart. They protested insertions in the Creed; they insisted on different practices for Lent; they disagreed over the type of bread to use in celebrating the Eucharist. Given their different cultures and histories, it only took two ambitious leaders to drive a permanent wedge between the churches.

In 1054 Pope Leo IX sent the firebrand Cardinal Humbert to Constantinople with terms that were doomed to fail and insult. The emperor had interest in cooperation with the West, but the patriarch of Constantinople, Michael Cerularius, returned Humbert's intolerance and humiliated the papal party. Humbert delivered the Pope's Bull of Excommunication to the altar of the Church of Holy Wisdom during worship!

In time military losses, as well as heresies, whittled away the great empire of Constantine and Justinian. Hordes of barbarians were followed by the spread of Islam. In the late Middle Ages the original territories of Greek Orthodoxy were reduced to western Turkey, the Balkans, and Cyprus. In 1453 even Constantine's city itself fell to the Islamic Turks. After eleven centuries the original Christian empire was at an end, and the Christians became a minority in a community run by Muslims. Without an emperor as their head, they looked to the patriarch for political guidance. Muslims tended to follow the Christian lead and consider him the spokesman for the Christian community.

Today, out of the vast empire that was diverted into Christian paths by Constantine, only Greece and half of Cyprus are still Greek Orthodox. But Orthodox Christianity had found one new area for expansion. In spite of pressures from Roman Catholic Europe in the west and from Islam in the east, a narrow corridor remained open to the north. Boris, king of the Bulgarians, was converted in the ninth century, and Vladimir, grand prince of Kiev and of all Russia, in the tenth.

The breathtaking magnificence of Constantinople and the awe inspiring liturgy captured the loyalties of the envoys Vladimir had sent to investigate the Christian faith in New Rome.

After they had attended services in the great Church of Holy Wisdom, the envoys told their master, "We know not whether we were in Heaven or on earth, for surely there is no such splendor or beauty anywhere upon earth. We cannot describe it to you; only we know that God dwells there among men, and that their service surpasses the worship of all other places. For we cannot forget that beauty."

THE GREEK
EASTERN CHURCH

THE LATIN
WESTERN CHURCH

ISLAM

THE GREEK
EASTERN
CHURCH

ISLAMIC TERRITORY

ISLAMIC TERRITORY

The Church Is Divided   1054

Over the years Russia made the aesthetic glories of Orthodox Christianity her own. Gradually Moscow came to see herself as the leader of the Orthodox world. A theory developed that there had been one Rome, in Italy, that had fallen to the barbarians and to the Roman Catholic heresy. There had been a second Rome: Constantinople. And when that fell to the Turks, there was a third Rome: Moscow. The emperor took his title from the first Rome—Tzar is the same word as Caesar—just as he had taken his religion from the second.

Even in recent decades the Kremlin has stood as a reminder of the rich and inspiring past. The onion domes of Orthodoxy's former glory remain and point toward heaven.

Suggestions for Further Reading

Benz, Ernst. *The Eastern Orthodox Church: Its Thought and Life.* Garden City, NY: Doubleday, 1957.

Clendenin, Daniel B. *Eastern Orthodox Christianity: A Western Perspective.* 2nd ed. Grand Rapids: Baker, 2003.

Fairbairn, Donald, *Eastern Orthodoxy through Western Eyes.* Louisville: Westminster John Knox Press, 2002.

Pelikan, Jaroslav. *The Spirit of Eastern Christendom (600–1700).* Chicago: University of Chicago Press, 1974.

Ware, Timothy. *The Orthodox Church.* Baltimore: Penguin, 1963.

CHAPTER 16

BENDING THE NECKS
OF VICTORS

Mission to the Barbarians

THE BRISTLING FORESTS OF northern Europe were inhabited by bar-barian tribes who sacrificed animals and worshiped nature spirits among the trees and beside the streams. Any missionary who ventured among them, with any hope of conversions, had to demonstrate the superior power of the Christian spirits.

The most famous incident tells of one eighth-century missionary named Boniface who marched into a shrine in Germany, the sacred forest of Thor, the god of thunder. The cult object was a massive oak. Boniface, so the story goes, took an axe to it. Just as he leveled the first stroke, a mighty breath of wind from God toppled the tree. The pagans marveled and were converted. Boniface used the wood to build a cha-pel to St. Peter.

That is the stuff that made Europe Christian. The missionary monks overthrew barbarian magic by calling down superior powers. God blew, and the tree fell. A miracle here and a victorious battle there; and the Germans were ready for baptism.

The point is, Christianity faced a new and enormous challenge when the German tribes swept across the Rhine and Danube frontier and left the once mighty empire of the Romans in shambles. The civiliza-tion that arose on those ruins was Christian in character because the invaders surrendered, not their arms, but their gods.

How did the barbarians come to accept the chapel dedicated to St. Peter where the sacred oak of Thor once stood? Why did the Ger-mans come to worship the God of their defeated foes?

THE COMING OF THE BARBARIANS

The year 476 usually marks the end of the Christian Roman Empire in the West. That is the year the long line of emperors inaugurated by Augustus (27 BC–AD 14) ended, and the undisguised rule by German leaders began.

The event was about as unspectacular as events can be. The mercenary soldiers wielding the real power in the name of the emperor were mainly German. Germans were killing Germans.

In 475 Orestes, the barbarian commander of the imperial troops, forced the Senate to elect his young son Romulus Augustulus (Little Augustus) as emperor in the West. In the following year, however, another Germanic commander, Odovacar, slew Orestes and, seeing no reason for continuing the sham of an imperial line, he deposed Romulus Augustulus and proclaimed himself head of the government. That was it. No one was particularly shocked. That had all come a generation earlier with Alaric and Gaiseric and Attila.

Who were these new masters of Europe? The Romans had called them "barbarians" because during early contact with the Romans they spoke no Greek and no Latin. But for the most part they were tribes from the north, originally in or near Scandinavia: Vandals, Franks, Angles, Saxons, Goths, Lombards, Burgundians, and others.

When they started to give the Romans problems in the third century they were at a cultural stage midway between a pastoral and an agricultural economy. They engaged in so little commerce that cattle, rather than money, marked the man of wealth and power among them.

According to the Roman historian Tacitus, the Germans were notoriously heavy drinkers and gamblers. On the other hand, Tacitus praised their courage, respect for women, and freedom from many Roman vices. A favorite amusement was listening to the tribal bards recite ancient tales of heroes and gods. Today the tales are long lost, but we retain Thor's day in our *Thursday* and another god's name, Wodin, in our *Wednesday*.

The Germans lived to fight. Every warlord had a retinue of warriors linked to their leader by a personal oath of loyalty. According to Tacitus, any warrior leaving a battle alive after his chief had fallen was consigned to lifelong infamy. "The chiefs fight for victory, the companions for their chief."

During the centuries that the Romans and Germans faced each other across the Rhine-Danube frontier, they had countless contacts with each other, peaceful as well as hostile. Roman trade reached into Germany, and Germans entered the empire as slaves. During the troubled third century, many barbarians were invited to settle on vacated lands within the empire or to serve in the Roman legions. By the end of the fourth century the Roman army and its generals in the West had become almost completely German.

The crisis of mass invasions came with the sudden appearance of a new uncontrollable force: the Huns. Late in the fourth century, this wave of Asiatic people crossed the Volga and soon subjugated the easternmost Germanic tribe, the Ostragoths. Terrified at the prospect of conquest by the advancing Huns, the Visigoths (or West Goths) petitioned the Romans to allow them to settle as allies inside the empire. Rome granted the request, and in 376 the entire tribe crossed the Danube into Roman territory. Shortly, however, corrupt Roman officials mistreated the Visigoths, and the proud barbarians went on a rampage. The inept Eastern emperor Valens tried to quell them, but in 378 he lost both his army and his life in the battle of Adrianople (in today's Turkey).

Some historians regard Adrianople as one of history's decisive battles: it destroyed the legend of the invincibility of the Roman legions and ushered in a century and a half of chaos. For a few years the able emperor Theodosius I held back the Visigoths, but after his death in 395 they began to migrate and pillage under their leader, Alaric. He invaded Italy, and in 410 his followers sacked Rome.

To counter Alaric's threat to Italy, the Romans had withdrawn most of their troops from the Rhine frontier in 406 and from Britain the following year. The momentous consequence of this action was a flood of Germanic tribes across the defenseless frontiers. The Vandals pushed their way through Gaul to Spain and, after pressure from the Visigoths, moved on to Africa. In 455 a Vandal raiding force sailed over from Africa, and Rome was sacked a second time.

Meanwhile the Burgundians settled in the Rhone valley, the Franks gradually spread across northern Gaul, and the Angles, Saxons, and Jutes invaded Britain. Although each of these several tribes set up a German-ruled kingdom within the confines of the empire, only the Franks in Gaul and the Angles and Saxons in Britain managed to perpetuate their kingdoms longer than a few centuries.

Today we can see that the Germanic invasions were not as cataclysmic as men once thought. The invaders seized a great deal of land, but most of this was either vacant or belonged to the emperors; few private landowners were displaced. In most areas the Germans still represented a minority of the population, and a gradual blending and fusing of the cultures and the blood of the two peoples began. Thus the barbarians in time lost their Germanic customs, religion, and speech. That is why hardly a trace of the Germanic languages remains in Italy, France, and Spain.

MISSIONS TO THE NORTH

The task of converting these northern peoples was enormous. To bring them to a nominal adherence to Christianity was not so difficult, because they wanted to enter into the grandeur that was Rome. Christianity was, in their eyes, the Roman religion. But to tame, refine, and educate these peoples; to transmit to them the best of the culture of antiquity; to teach them the Christian creed; and, above all, to instill in them even a modicum of Christian behavior—all that was another matter.

The barbarians were brought to orthodox Christianity in two ways: directly from paganism and indirectly through Arianism, a heresy that denied the eternality of Jesus Christ as the Son of God. Arius's doctrine spread among them from the time in the fourth century when Arianism was strong in the empire. This Arianism, however, was more ecclesiastical than theological, because the Germans were not interested in the niceties of abstract theology. Their Christ was the firstborn creature. They tended to think of him as a glorified warlord. But the main difference between the Arians and the orthodox in the West lay in the structure of the church. The Arians had no ecclesiastical center. They did not recognize orthodox Rome, and they had no counterpart of their own. Their churches belonged to the clan. Even after the conversion of these Arian Germans to orthodoxy, they were still loath to accept centralization through Rome.

The Arian influence apparently began with missionary work among the Visigoths. A half century after the Council of Nicaea (325), a missionary named Ulfilas (or Wulfila) crossed the Danube to work among them for forty years. Aided by other unknown missionaries, Ulfilas led them to faith in Christ as Arius had preached him. This conversion of the Goths must have been something more than surrender to social pressures. We know that Ulfilas translated the Bible into the Gothic language, with the exception of the books of Kings, which he thought too bellicose to be edifying for a people already extremely fierce and warlike. From the Goths, then, Arian Christianity spread to other German tribes.

Some of the earliest northern peoples to come to Christ were beyond the borders of the empire and were not themselves German. The Irish were Celtic people, and their conversion is traced to Patrick early in the fifth century. From his brief autobiography we learn that when the Roman legions were withdrawn for the defense of the Continent, the

Irish, then called Scots, began swooping down on the English coast, sailing up the rivers, raiding the settlements, and carrying off plunder and slaves. Among the captives was Patrick. So Ireland's patron saint was not Irish! He had been reared a Christian. His father was a deacon, but Patrick's religion sat lightly until, as a swineherd, he prayed ardently for his freedom. His conversion dates from this captivity. "The Lord opened to me the sense of my unbelief," he says, then. After six years he managed to escape and found his way to the coast where a ship carrying a cargo of hounds was about to sail to France or Scotland. We don't know which. Stories about his trips to France may be sheer fancy, but we do know that he was eager to see his family, and after many hardships reached home once again.

He would have gladly remained in England had he not had a dream one night in which the babies of Ireland pleaded with him to come back to their country and tell them about Christ. Patrick decided to return, but first he had to learn more about Christianity. At length he was sent out, some say with the approval of the pope, to be a missionary to the people among whom he had once been a slave.

At this point his account ends, and from then on we have only legends. We know, however, that a century later the structure of the church in Ireland was predominantly monastic. Presumably the monastic community, maintaining itself on the land, fitted the agricultural communities of the Celts better than the parish-church system so common in the Roman Empire.

We also know that Ireland became the base for the evangelization of Britain. The Irish have a habit of leaving Ireland. And the missionary monks were no exception. As we have seen, there were Christian churches in Britain before Patrick's day, but a century after Patrick's time, an Irish monk named Columba led in the founding of a monastery on Iona, an island off the coast of Scotland. Iona, in turn, gave a new and vital impulse to the preaching of Christ in Britain.

Surprisingly, Celtic monks from Ireland and Britain also became missionaries to the Continent. Their itching feet carried them farther and farther from home. They established monasteries in Germany and Switzerland and even in northern Italy. These became centers of evangelization and devout learning. Columbanus is the great name in this mission, though he was only one among many; and St. Gall and Bobbio were two of the most famous Celtic monasteries. These were the days before the bishops of Rome gained general recognition as popes, so this Celtic influence on the Continent and the independent spirit of the Irish and British monks became in time a disturbing factor to Roman Christianity.

THE GOSPEL AMONG THE FRANKS

Roman Catholic influence began in the northern half of Gaul, among the Franks, the one tribe destined to greatness in the shaping of Christian Europe. The founder of the nation was Clovis (481–511), who was the first barbarian chief of any importance to convert to orthodox Christianity. It happened that he was married to a Burgundian princess who was a Christian. Clothilda often spoke to Clovis about the one God who created heaven and earth out of nothing and had fashioned man. Clovis replied, "Nonsense!" But when their first son was born, he allowed the child to be baptized. The babe died in his baptismal robes. Clovis blamed the baptism, but Clothilda rejoiced that God had taken a soul directly to heaven to eternal bliss.

Another son was born, baptized, and fell sick. Clovis claimed that baptism would kill him, too, but the mother prayed and he recovered. Then, in a battle with the Alamanni tribe, Clovis was facing a terrible defeat. He cried, "Jesus Christ, Clothilda says thou art the Son of the living God, and thou canst give victory to those who hope in thee. Give me victory and I will be baptized. I have tried my gods and they have deserted me. I call on thee. Only save me." The king of the Alamanni fell, and his army fled. Clovis returned and told Clothilda.

She summoned the bishop of Rheims, who exhorted the king to renounce his gods. "Yes, holy father," said Clovis, "but my people will not consent. However, I will speak to them." He did, and with one accord they renounced their German gods. The baptistry was hung with tapestries, fragrant candles flared, the aroma of incense filled the shrine with fragrance so that many thought they were amid the odors of paradise. Clovis advanced like another Constantine to the baptismal font and the bishop said, "Bend your neck. Worship what you burned and burn what you worshiped." Thus the king was baptized in the name of the Father and of the Son and of the Holy Spirit. Three thousand of his army followed him in baptism.

This first of many mass conversions during the Middle Ages raises important questions about the paganizing of Christianity. Missions can proceed in two ways. One is the way of *individual conversion* with a period of instruction prior to baptism. In general this is the method used by Protestant missions under the evangelical movements of the nineteenth century, with their emphasis upon individual change of heart. The disadvantage of this method is that the Christian converts in a pagan culture become, by reason of their change in faith, uprooted from their own culture and compelled to move into an alien enclave.

The other method is *mass conversion*, and it was this method that converted Europe. Kings like Clovis embraced the faith, and their people followed them into the spiritual City as into the earthly. This meant that individuals were not uprooted from their culture, but it also meant that the converts brought with them into the church their superstitions and behavior.

This is evident in many instances, starting with Clovis himself. Jesus was for him a tribal war-god. The Franks especially admired St. Peter, whose noblest exploit in their eyes was his eagerness to wield his sword to protect the Lord Jesus and to slice off the ear of the high priest's servant. This admiration for militant religion is also reflected in St. George, a military saint who became the patron of England, and St. James, the patron saint of Christian Spain in the struggle against Islam.

The saints, with their particular assignments, may well have meant more to the people than Christ himself. St. Anthony took care of pigs, St. Gaul looked after hens, St. Apollonia, whose jaw had been broken in the persecution, cured the toothache, St. Genevieve cured fever, and St. Blaise was responsible for sore throats. For almost every human need these tenuously converted Germans could find a saint.

Many tales circulated about the miraculous powers of the saints. The story was told of two beggars, one lame, the other blind. They happened to be caught in a procession carrying the relics of St. Martin and were fearful lest they be cured and so deprived of their alms. The one who could see but not walk mounted the shoulders of the one who could walk but not see, and they hurried to get beyond the range of the saint's miraculous powers, but, poor fellows, they failed to make it.

PASSAGE TO ENGLAND

In spite of the shallow impact of the gospel among the Franks, their conversion did provide a passage through Gaul to Great Britain. The invasion of Britain by the Anglo-Saxons (or English) made hostilities so great that any idea of the Britons evangelizing the Germans was unthinkable. The initiative for the conversion of the English came from Rome. In 596 Pope Gregory the Great (596–604) sent a party of Benedictine monks to distant and barbaric England under the leadership of Augustine—another St. Augustine, who would become known as St. Augustine of Canterbury.

Augustine and his monks began their ministry in Kent, one of the twelve areas controlled by the Anglo-Saxon invaders of England. Under the favor of Queen Bertha, another of those Christian queens eager to convert a pagan husband, Augustine secured a hearing from King Ethelbert, but only out of doors where Augustine would be less able to exercise his magical powers. Rumor had it that he was able to make tails grow on the backs of those who displeased him. The king was so persuaded by Augustine that he granted land for the foundation of a monastery at Canterbury, ever after to be the seat of the English religious leader. Gregory appointed Augustine the first archbishop of Canterbury.

The missionaries who followed Augustine worked farther north. By the time of King Oswy in the late seventh century, the two missionary thrusts converged, Celtic followers of Columba working toward the south and those of Augustine toward the north. Oswy's queen was from the south and followed the Roman practices, but Oswy had received his Christian beliefs from the north and observed the Celtic way. Among the points of dispute was the date for Easter. When the King had ended Lent and was keeping Easter, the Queen and her household were still fasting: enough to ruin any family's Easter!

At the Synod of Whitby in 664, Oswy brought the matter to a decision. The Celtic advocate appealed to the authority of Columba, the Romans to that of Peter, to whom Christ gave the keys. "Is that really so? Does Peter guard the gates to heaven?" Oswy asked the Celtic defender. He, of course, agreed. Oswy promptly resolved to take no chances of alienating the doorkeeper of heaven! He agreed to follow Roman practices. After Whitby the British Isles moved relentlessly into the orbit of Rome.

Once securely rooted in Anglo-Saxon England, Christianity returned in fresh vigor to the Continent. The most famous British missionary of the Middle Ages was Winfrid, better known as Boniface. Born in Devonshire, Boniface was commissioned by Pope Gregory II in 729 to evangelize Germany. His primary task was to convert the pagan population, and in this he had great success. Besides that, however, he brought the British and Irish missionary monks and their converts into closer relations with the bishop of Rome.

Boniface was deeply devoted to the cause. He could not only chop down a sacred tree while the shuddering multitude watched to see him struck dead by fire from heaven; he could also win the masses to the faith and organize the districts in which he exercised his powers so as to leave behind him a church structure bound firmly to the central authority at Rome.

Boniface became archbishop of Mainz and would have ended his splendid career there in peace if final qualms about the failure of his early efforts in Frisia (the Netherlands) had not drawn him back to that still pagan field. There he sealed his faith with martyrdom. If that was in the year 754, as is generally supposed, the young Frankish prince Charles, who was destined to become the Emperor Charlemagne and architect of a new—Christian—Europe, was twelve years old at the time.

Suggestions for Further Reading

Davis, R. H. C. *A History of Medieval Europe.* London: Longmans, 1957.

Deanesley, Margaret. *A History of the Medieval Church 590–1500.* London: Methuen, 1969.

Neill, Stephen. *A History of Christian Missions.* Middlesex: Penguin, 1964.

Pirenne, Henri. *A History of Europe from the Invasions to the XVI Century.* New York: Murray Printing Company, 1938.

*Southern, R. W. *Church and Society in the Middle Ages.* New Haven, CT: Yale University Press, 1992.

THE CHRISTIAN MIDDLE AGES

590–1517

Europe owes more to the Christian faith than most people
realize. When the barbarians destroyed the Roman Empire in the
West, it was the Christian church that put together a new order
called Europe. The church took the lead in rule by law, the
pursuit of knowledge, and the expressions of culture. The
underlying concept was Christendom, which united empire and
church. It began under Charlemagne in the eighth century, but
the popes slowly assumed more and more power until Innocent
III (1198–1216) taught Europe to think of the popes as world
rulers. Later centuries, however, saw the popes corrupted by
power, and increasingly militant reformers cry out for change.

Early Middle Ages

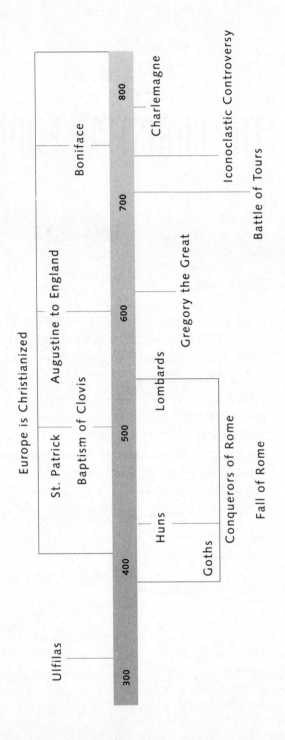

CHAPTER 17

GOD'S CONSUL

Gregory the Great

E ARLY IN AD 590 Rome was in agony. The city suffered through the tragedies of floods and the atrocities of war only to be smitten by the relentless spread of the plague. Men felt hardly more than a little soreness of the throat; afterward came the black eruptions and a swift death. The carts were piled high with corpses. People went insane. Rome became a desert, and the pope himself, Pelagius II, died, screaming in agony.

For six months no pope ruled in St. Peter's Basilica. When church leaders decided to elect a monk named Gregory, he refused the office and even fled from the city, hiding in the forest, until he was found and dragged back to Rome. After notifying Constantinople, officials consecrated him St. Peter's successor on September 3, 590.

Gregory was a most unlikely candidate for greatness. Fifty, balding, and frail, he had no craving for the papal office. He complained that he was "so stricken with sorrow that he could scarcely speak." Yet he began his administration with a public act of humiliation because the plague had taken the life of his predecessor. Seven processions filed through the streets for three days. Prayers were said; hymns were sung. But to no immediate avail. The plague continued to ravage the city. Then, mercifully, it seemed to subside.

A later legend traced the staying of the calamity to Gregory's action and told of the appearance of the archangel Michael, who put back his drawn sword into its sheath over the mausoleum of the emperor Hadrian. Since that time Romans have called it the Castle of St. Angelo. They adorned it with the statue of an angel. Tourists can still find it on the banks of the Tiber.

173

Rome was a symbol of the continent. What we now call Europe arose like a phoenix from the blazing ruins of a devastated empire. And more than any other force, it was Christianity that brought life and order out of the chaos.

How? What did Christianity bring to the devastation to erect a new order called Christian Europe?

GREGORY'S PLACE IN HISTORY

The church enlisted the Celtic and Benedictine monks to serve as a spiritual militia for winning the barbarians to the Christian faith. It turned to the papal office to provide some stable structure for a new way of life. And it read and recounted the ideals of Augustine's theology to maintain a framework of spiritual meaning. No man mastered these instruments of the future better than Gregory.

In his book *Pastoral Care*, Gregory stressed that the spiritual leader should never be so absorbed in external cares as to forget the inner life of the soul, nor neglect external things in the care for his inner life. "Our Lord continued in prayer on the mountain," Gregory wrote, "but wrought miracles in the cities; showing to pastors that while aspiring to the highest, they should mingle in sympathy with the necessities of the infirm. The more kindly charity descends to the lowest, the more vigorously it recurs to the highest." The words were autobiographical.

When Gregory died in 604, worn out after thirty years of prayers on the mountains and miracles in the cities, his epitaph proclaimed him "God's Consul." It was a singularly appropriate description of the man who had exerted himself to the utmost to be solely God's while ruling church and world like a Roman statesman, the last of his line.

Not long after his death the churches came to speak of him as "Gregory the Great." And in time the Catholic Church added his name to those of Augustine, Ambrose, and Jerome to speak of the "Latin Fathers of the Church." In terms of intellectual powers alone, Gregory probably doesn't belong in such company. But he combined great executive ability with warm sympathy for human need. And if goodness is the highest kind of greatness, then the church moved rightly in according him the title "Great." Certainly no other man or woman better represents the early Middle Ages. Gregory was born about AD 540 from an old and wealthy senatorial family of Rome and was educated for government service. He could hardly have stepped on the pages of history at a more angry time. In his childhood Rome changed hands over and over again. He was fourteen in the year 554 when Narses became viceroy of Italy under the Emperor Justinian in Constantinople. Then at last, with the Visigoth rule over Italy destroyed, a few brief years of peace followed before the savage Lombards began their campaign of burning churches, slaying bishops, robbing monasteries, and reducing cultivated fields to a wilderness. Rome was clearly no longer the metropolis Ambrose and Augustine had known. The city of the caesars was fast becoming the city of the popes; and it was Gregory's fate to appear at the hour of transition.

Suddenly, at the age of 33, Gregory found that the Emperor Justin had appointed him prefect (or mayor) of Rome, the highest civil position in the city and its surrounding territory. The whole economy of Rome—the grain supplies, the welfare program for the poor, the construction of buildings, baths, sewers, and riverbanks—rested on Gregory's shoulders. To make the burden even heavier, his appointment in 573 came just as both the pope and Narses died.

Gregory was never comfortable with worldly power, however. He preferred the solitude of a monastic cell. Within a few years he stepped down from public office and broke with the world. Upon the death of his father, he spent the greater part of his personal fortune in founding seven monasteries. He distributed the rest in alms for the poor, then laid aside all vestiges of rank and transformed his father's palace into a monastery dedicated to St. Andrew. He exchanged the purple toga for the coarse robe of a monk and began to live with extraordinary asceticism, eating only raw fruit and vegetables, praying most of the night, wearing a hair shirt, throwing himself into the many duties of a Benedictine. He had never been strong, and now unceasing fasting ruined his digestion and played havoc with his heart. Yet Gregory looked upon these years as the happiest of his life.

Gregory's gifts, however, could not remain hidden. In 579 Pope Pelagius II made him one of the seven deacons of the Roman church and sent him as ambassador to the imperial court in Constantinople. His political training and executive ability fitted him eminently for this post. He returned in 585 and was appointed abbot of his convent, St. Andrew, but remained available for important public business.

Gregory was perfectly content to be an abbot, and he would probably have continued stretching for the other world if the terrible plague had not swept through the city and snuffed out the life of Pope Pelagius II (579–590).

PICKING UP THE PIECES OF A SHATTERED WORLD

Soon after Gregory's election the Lombards laid siege to Rome, and the new pope was forced to cut short his preaching on Ezekiel: "I am constrained to cease from my exposition, for I am weary of life. Who can expect me now to devote myself to sacred eloquence, now that my harp is turning to mourning, and my speech to the voice of them that weep?"

All of Western Europe was in chaos. Serious men, and Gregory was among them, thought that the end of the world was at hand. "What is it," he asks in one of his sermons, "that can at this time delight us in this world? Everywhere we see tribulation, everywhere we hear lamentation. The cities are destroyed, the castles torn down, the fields laid waste, the land made desolate. Villages are empty, few inhabitants remain in the cities, and even these poor remnants of humanity are daily cut down. The scourge of celestial justice does not cease, because no repentance takes place under the scourge. We see how some are carried into captivity, others mutilated, others slain. What is it, brethren, that can make us contented with this life? If we love such a world, we love not our joys, but our wounds."

The church of Rome survived these attacks, almost the only vestige of organized civilization in the West that did so. While Gregory regarded his elevation to the papacy as a punishment, he immediately threw himself into the struggle for order in the midst of chaos.

He wrote urgent letters to the managers of his estates in Sicily: "You sent me a sorry nag and five good asses: the nag is too wretched to ride, and I simply can't ride the asses because they are asses."

He began a vast correspondence with his bishops: "You evidently paid no attention to my last letter."

And he set forth the principles for Christian ministry in his *Pastoral Rule:* "He who, by the necessity of his position, is required to speak the highest things, is compelled by the same necessity to exemplify the highest."

The prestige of the papacy in the Middle Ages rests in large part on the practical government maintained by Gregory through these troubled times. He was incessantly busy. Nothing seemed too great, nothing too little for his personal care. His labors are all the more astonishing when we consider that he was in poor health and often confined to bed. "For a long time," he wrote to a friend in 601, "I have been unable to rise from my bed. I am tormented by the pains of gout; a kind of fire seems to pervade my whole body: to live is pain; and I look forward to death as the only remedy." In another letter he says: "I am daily dying, but never die."

During Gregory's time the Church of Rome controlled extensive lands around Rome, in the toe and heel of Italy and on Sicily. These were called "the patrimony of St. Peter." Taken together these estates—something like 1,800 square miles—made the Church the richest landowner in Italy. Quite naturally, then, when the Lombards invaded central Italy, destroying the imperial administration in the process, officials of the patrimony stepped in to feed the population and to collect the land taxes, just as imperial officers had once done. The head of this tax and welfare system was Gregory.

Moreover, when Lombard attacks moved closer and closer to Rome, Gregory undertook the defense of central Italy. He appointed a military governor and arranged peace with two Lombard leaders. As a result, after 595, the pope was more important in Lombard politics than any imperial representative.

This participation in the political fortunes of Italy became a significant element for the papal office in the centuries that followed. After Gregory, the pope was no longer only a Christian leader; he was also an important political figure in European politics: God's Consul.

Gregory's vigorous leadership magnified the authority of the papal chair. One significant clash with the patriarch of Constantinople reveals his view of the office. In his letters, John IV, the patriarch, repeatedly used the title *universal bishop*. It was an honorary title, given to patriarchs by the emperors Leo and Justinian and confirmed to John and his successors by a Constantinopolitan synod in 588.

Gregory, however, was provoked and irritated by the assumption of his Eastern rival. He strained every nerve to get the title revoked. He characterized it as a foolish, proud, profane, wicked, pestiferous, blasphemous, and diabolical usurpation, and compared anyone who used it to Lucifer. He threatened to break off communion with the patriarch. He called upon the emperor to punish such presumption.

In opposition to these high-sounding titles, Gregory called himself simply, "the servant of the servants of God." This became one of the standing titles of the popes, although it sounds like irony when linked with later astounding claims. When a churchman addressed Gregory himself as universal pope, he strongly repudiated the title, saying, "I have said that neither to me nor to any one else ought you to write anything of the kind. Away with words which inflate pride and wound charity!"

On the other hand, while Gregory protested high-sounding titles, he claimed and exercised, as far as he had the opportunity and power, the oversight over the whole church of Christ.

No wonder, therefore, that the successors of Gregory had no scruple in using even more arrogant titles than the one against which he so solemnly protested with the warning "God resisteth the proud, but giveth grace to the humble."

To Gregory pride was a vicious hound that dogged him relentlessly. He speaks of it so often that he was clearly obsessed with it. He sees pride in all its moods. In his commentary on Job called *Moralia* he examines it from every angle: "Pride, which we have called the root of vices, far from being satisfied with the extinction of one virtue, raises itself up against all the members of the soul, and as a universal and deadly disease corrupts the whole body."

It is clear that Gregory himself suffered from the disease. All his frenzy, the continual urgent letters sent all over Christendom, the determination never to rest for a moment—all these seem to spring from his knowledge of his own pride, from his desperate desire to face the evil and vanquish it. Such a lifelong struggle was in perfect harmony with his dedication to monasticism.

MISSIONARY STATESMAN

With Gregory, monasticism for the first time ascended the papal throne. He continued the austere simplicity of monastic life, surrounded himself with monks, made them bishops and legates, confirmed the rule of St. Benedict at a council of Rome, guaranteed the liberty and property of convents, and by his example and influence rendered the highest service to the monastic life.

A story circulated, probably part fact and part fiction, that Gregory, before he assumed the papal office, happened upon three young English boys for sale on the Roman marketplace. Gregory was immediately attracted to them.

"Alas! alas!" he exclaimed, "that such bright faces should be the slaves of an inward darkness. So beautiful they are and yet their minds are sick and without God's grace." He asked the slave owner what nation they came from.

"They are Angles," answered the man.

"Yes, indeed," Gregory went on, "they have the appearance of angels and they should be co-heirs of the angels in Heaven. What province do they come from?"

"From Deira," said the slave owner, mentioning the ancient name for what is now Northumberland.

"From Deira? Then indeed they should be saved from God's anger (*dei ira*) and called to the mercy of Christ. Who is their King?"

"Aella."

"Then," said Gregory, "must Alleluia be sung in Aella's land."

Gregory attempted to go to England himself as a missionary monk but was hindered by God and the pope. But once on the papal throne himself, he sent the Benedictine Augustine and forty monks to replant the gospel on English soil. The success of that mission in Kent, as we have seen, provides a direct link for all Anglo-American Christianity with the early church.

DEFENDER OF ORTHODOXY

Gregory not only yearned to advance the faith in distant places, but he took seriously his calling as defender of orthodoxy. His teachers in the faith were Ambrose, Augustine, and Jerome, but he lacked their intellectual abilities. He contributed no new ideas and created no epoch in theology. But he formulated the common faith of his day and handed it on to the Catholic Church of the Middle Ages. This faith embraced not merely the official pronouncements of the councils and the teachings of the Fathers, but also the notions of the illiterate populace, often crude and superstitious, at times even pagan. To this mass of material he lent the weight of his authority, and as a consequence it became an integral part of the faith of the Western church, of theologians and bishops as well as of monks and laymen. It is impossible to follow the thinking of the Middle Ages without the guidance of Gregory.

In his doctrine of man, Gregory stressed that Adam's fall affected all his descendants, weakening but not destroying their freedom of will. Thus once man has been moved by grace, he may cooperate with it and win merit for himself by his good works, which are the joint product of divine grace and human will.

In baptism, God grants forgiving grace freely without any merit on man's part, but for sins committed after baptism man must make atonement by penance, which is simply a form of punishment inflicted by the man himself instead of by God: "For either man himself by penance punishes sin in himself, or God taking vengeance on him smites it." Penance involves repentance, which must be sincere and of the heart, and also confession and meritorious works.

The meritorious works, without which penance is not complete, are deeds involving sacrifice or suffering, such as almsgiving, ascetic practices, and prayers at all hours of the day. The greater our sins the more we must do to make up for them, and the more careful we must be to avoid them in the future. Whether we have done enough to atone for them we cannot know until after death.

Fortunately, sinners have the help of the saints. The belief in the intercession of the saints and the custom of appealing to them to use their influence with Christ did not originate with Gregory; both the belief and the custom were much older than he. But he emphasized them and made them central for Christian piety. "Behold," he wrote, "the severe judge Jesus is about to come; the terror of that mighty council of angels and archangels is at hand. In that assembly our case will be tried and yet we are not seeking patrons who will then come to our defense. Our holy martyrs are ready to be your advocates; they desire to be asked, indeed if I may say so, they entreat that they may be entreated. Seek them as helpers of your prayer; turn to them that they may protect you in your guilt."

Another aid to devotion was the holy relics. Gregory encouraged the collection and veneration of holy remains of the saints and martyrs: locks of hair, fingernails, toes, pieces of clothing. Gregory taught—and most of his contemporaries believed—that these items possessed great powers, including that of self-defense.

And if the saints and relics were not sufficient for righteousness in this life, sins could still be atoned in purgatory. This is a place of purification and suffering, not for those who die with serious offenses still charged against them, but for those who are not as yet altogether righteous. At death the perfectly holy go at once to heaven and the wicked to hell, while those of an intermediate character, who still have minor sins for which penance must be done, spend a season in purgatory.

Surely, however, the supreme miracle, the key to all the other expressions of divine power, was the Holy Eucharist. According to Gregory, the Eucharist is a communion with Christ whose body and blood are really present in the bread and wine. Feeding upon them we nourish and strengthen our spiritual life.

The marvelous power of the Eucharist, however, lies in its sacrificial character. It is offered by the priest for the sins of men—not like Christ's death upon the cross, for the sins of all men, but only for the sins of the participants, or of those for whose benefit it may be specifically offered. For all such it has the same effect as penance, taking the place of a certain amount of suffering that they would otherwise have to undergo because of their sins. It may benefit the dead as well as the living, the dead, that is, in purgatory not in hell. If offered for anyone in purgatory, it will hasten the time of his release.

One of the better examples of Gregory's belief in the power of the sacred mass is found in his *Dialogues*. While the incident is a bit long, it serves as a revealing picture of medieval piety. After telling of the death of one of his monks who had been found guilty of hoarding money and had been severely punished, Gregory writes,

> Thirty days later, I began to feel strong compassion for the deceased Justus. As I considered with deep anguish the penalty he was enduring,

I thought of a way to relieve him of his suffering. With this in mind, I called Pretiosus, the prior, and said to him sadly, "Justus has now been suffering the torments of fire for a long time and we must show him our charity by helping as much as we can to gain his release. Beginning today, offer the holy Sacrifice for his soul for thirty consecutive days. Not one of these days is to pass without a Mass being celebrated for his release." The prior obediently accepted the instructions and left.

Days passed, and being busy with other affairs, I lost count of them. Then, one night, Justus appeared to his brother Copiosus, who asked him at once why he came and how he was. "Up to this moment I was in misery," he said, "but now I am well, because this morning I was admitted to communion."

Copiosus hurried to tell the monks the good news. Taking exact count of the days, they discovered that this was the thirtieth consecutive day on which mass had been offered for him. Previous to this Copiosus did not know that the brethren were offering masses for Justus, nor did the brethren know that Copiosus had seen him in a vision. At the very moment, therefore, when they became mutually aware of what had taken place, they realized that the vision and the completion of the thirty masses occurred at one and the same time. They were now convinced that the brother who had died was freed from punishment through the Sacrifice of the Mass.

The doctrine was widely accepted in the Western church from Gregory's time on and helped to give its peculiar tone to the Christianity of the Middle Ages.

Suggestions for Further Reading

Deanesly, Margaret. *A History of the Medieval Church 590–1500*. London: Methuen, 1969.

Duckett, Eleanor Shipley. *The Gateway to the Middle Ages: Monasticism*. Ann Arbor: University of Michigan Press, 1961.

Gontard, Friedrich. *The Chair of Peter*. New York: Holt, Rinehart, and Winston, 1964.

*Kardong, Terrence G. *Together Unto Life Everlasting: An Introduction to the Rule of Benedict*. Richardton, ND: Assumption Abbey, 1984.

*Markus, Robert A. *Gregory the Great and His World*. Cambridge: Cambridge University Press, 1997.

Zimmerman, Odo John, trans. *Saint Gregory the Great: Dialogues*. New York: Fathers of the Church, 1959.

CHAPTER 18

THE SEARCH
FOR UNITY

Charlemagne and Christendom

THE DATE WAS APRIL 25, 799, St. Mark's Day, a customary day of repentance and prayer. This year, however, the faithful had been plagued by accidents and severe crop damage. So Pope Leo III (795–816) was leading a procession through Rome for God's blessing upon the fields and their harvest.

The procession led from the Church of the Lateran through the middle of the city to St. Peter's. As it turned the corner by the monastery of Saints Stephen and Silvester, armed men rushed at the pope. They drove off his attendants and pulled Leo off his horse and whisked him away to a Greek monastery.

It was mutiny led by ranking officials and dignitaries loyal to the previous pope, Adrian I. Perjury and adultery were among the charges leveled at Leo. Using the cover of darkness, the pope's supporters were able to rescue him and to bring him back to St. Peter's. But continued fighting in the streets convinced Leo that he needed outside help. His appeal went to the traditional protector of the papacy, the king of the Franks, Charles the Great.

The next year Charles crossed the Alps with an army, prepared to settle the pope's problem once and for all. In December the king presided over a large assembly of bishops, nobles, diplomats, members of the royal household, and rebels. On December 23 the pope, holding the gospel in his ringed hand, took an oath purging himself of the accusations against him. With that the mutiny waned, but the stage was set for a more important development.

182

On Christmas Day, Charles came to St. Peter's with a large retinue for the Christmas worship. Leo sang the mass and Charles prayed on his knees in front of the crypt of the apostle. Charles saw the pope approach. In his hands was a golden crown. Leo placed it on Charles's head as the congregation cried, "To Charles, the most pious, crowned Augustus by God, to the great peace-making Emperor, long life and victory!" The pope prostrated himself. Charles the Great, King of the Franks, had restored the Christian Roman Empire.

Modern times are marked by the idea of autonomous, sovereign states without religious affiliation and by the concept of the church as a voluntary association apart from the rest of organized society. But neither of these ideas existed in the Middle Ages.

Drawing upon Augustine's vision of the "City of God," Charles the Great engrafted the Christian concept of a universal Catholic Church on the stock of the traditional Roman view of empire and gave to the medieval world Christendom, a unified society mingling religious (or eternal) concerns with earthly (or temporal) affairs.

How did it happen? How could the kingdom that Jesus said was "not of the world" become so much a part of worldly power?

The answer lies in the persistence of an idea and the rise of a powerful kingdom.

IDEAS DIE SLOWLY

Centuries after its fall to barbarism, the Roman Empire in the West continued its sway over the imaginations of men. The barbarians had many kingdoms and were often at war with one another. But men still longed for the unity that had once marked the empire, and they looked for the day when a new Roman Empire would appear. As the Greeks believed that Rome had passed over to Constantinople, so the Roman people and their German neighbors thought that the empire would live again among them.

In the blending of Roman and Germanic peoples and cultures, the Franks ascended above the others and seemed destined to restore the imperial authority. Clovis, with the active support of the Catholic Church, had made the kingdom of the Franks a dominant power among the German tribes.

After the death of Clovis, however, his dynasty began to decay from inner weakness. The Germanic practice of treating the kingdom as personal property and dividing it among the king's sons resulted in constant and bitter civil war. So the royal heirs plotted murders and became adept at intrigue and treachery.

At the same time a new center of power arose from the landed aristo-crats. More and more authority shifted into their hands. Among these powerful landowners, one emerged as the most influential figure in the kingdom. He was called "mayor of the palace."

A new day dawned for the kingdom of the Franks in 714, when Charles Martel, Charlemagne's grandfather, became mayor of the pal-ace. Martel allowed the Merovingian kings to retain their claim to the throne. But they were mere figureheads; the real power rested with the mayor of the palace.

Many students remember Charles for his victory over the Muslim invaders of Europe. This triumph earned him the surname Martel, "The Hammer." In 711 a Muslim army from North Africa had invaded Spain, and by 718 the weak kingdom of the Visigoths had collapsed. With most of the peninsula under their control, the Muslims began making raids across the Pyrenees Mountains. In 732 Charles Martel met them near Tours, deep within the Frankish kingdom. He inflicted heavy losses upon them, so during the night they retreated toward Spain and were never again a major threat to central Europe.

Charles Martel's son, Pepin the Short (741–768), was a worthy suc-cessor to his father. He thought the time had come, however, to legalize the regal power exercised by the mayors of the palace. He turned to the pope for a ruling stipulating that whoever had the actual power should be the legal ruler. He got what he wanted. With the papal blessing, Boniface, the great English missionary among the Germans, in 751 crowned Pepin king of the Franks. The last Merovingian was quietly shelved in a secluded monastery. Three years later the pope blessed this *coup d'etat* by crossing the Alps and personally anointing Pepin, in the Old Testament manner, as the Chosen of the Lord.

As one historian explains it, behind the pope's action lay his need for a powerful protector. In 751 the Lombards had conquered the imperial territory at Ravenna, the seat of Byzantine government in Italy, and were demanding tribute from the pope and threatening to take Rome. Following Pepin's coronation, the pope secured his prom-ise of armed intervention in Italy and his pledge to give the papacy the territory of Ravenna once it was conquered. In 756 a Frankish army forced the Lombard king to surrender his conquests, and Pepin offi-cially conferred the Ravenna territory upon the pope. Known as the "Donation of Pepin," the gift made the pope a temporal ruler over the Papal States, a strip of territory that extended diagonally across Italy from coast to coast. Peter recovered his sword.

This alliance between the Franks and the papacy affected the course of European politics and Christianity for centuries. It accelerated the separation of the Latin from the Greek Church by providing the papacy with a dependable western ally in place of the Byzantines, hitherto its only protector against the Lombards; it created the Papal States, which played a major role in Italian politics until the late nineteenth century; and, by the ritual anointing, it provided western kingship with a religious sanction that would in time contribute to the rivalry between pope and emperor.

Only one significant step remained to restore the Christian Empire to the West. That came with the rise to power of Pepin's illustrious son, Charles. Today, we know him as Charlemagne, Charles the Great.

When Charles succeeded his father in 768 his mind was set on three goals: military power to crush his enemies, religious power to direct his people's souls, and intellectual power to instruct both souls and minds. Charlemagne's success in these areas made Europe—the new political order—nominally Christian, for better or for worse, for a thousand years.

ARCHITECT OF AN EMPIRE

Einhard, in his famous biography of Charlemagne, pictured his king as a natural leader of men—tall, physically strong, and a great horseman who was always in the van of the hunt. Although he was preeminently a successful warrior-king, leading his armies on yearly campaigns, Charlemagne also sought to provide an effective administration for his realm.

Four areas were successfully annexed to his kingdom by military might. First was his southern border. Taking advantage of feuds among the Muslims in Spain, Charlemagne sought to extend Christendom into that land. In 778 he crossed the Pyrenees with only minor success. On later expeditions, however, he drove the Muslims back to the Ebro River and established a frontier area known as the Spanish Mark (or March) centered around Barcelona.

Second, Charlemagne conquered the Bavarians and the Saxons, the last of the independent Germanic tribes.

It took thirty-two campaigns to subdue the staunchly pagan Saxons, who lived between the Rhine and Elbe rivers. Charlemagne divided Saxony into bishoprics, built monasteries, and proclaimed harsh laws against paganism. Eating meat during Lent, cremating the dead (an old pagan practice), and pretending to be baptized were offenses punishable by death.

His brutality in conquering and converting the Saxons was extreme by any measure.

A third trouble spot was the kingdom's eastern frontier, which was continually threatened by the Slavs and the Avars, Asiatic nomads related to the Huns. "In six campaigns Charlemagne decimated the Avars and then set up his own military province in the valley of the Danube to guard against any possible future plundering by eastern nomads. Called the East Mark, this territory later became Austria."

Finally, like his father before him, Charlemagne intervened in Italian politics. Expansionist ambition drove the Lombard king to invade again the papal territories. At the behest of the pope, Charlemagne defeated the Lombards in 774 and proclaimed himself their king. While in Italy, he cemented his father's alliance with the Church of Rome by confirming the Donation of Pepin.

That first incursion into Italy proved to be the prelude to the one in 800 that resulted in his coronation as emperor. The pope needed protection. Charlemagne needed divine sanction.

After his Christmas coronation Charlemagne said that he did not know it had been planned. But he lived up to it. He wrote in his dispatches, "Charles, by the will of God, Roman Emperor, Augustus . . . in the year of our consulship I." He had an oath taken to him as Caesar by all officers, lay or ecclesiastical. He sent ambassadors to soothe the anger of the emperor in Constantinople and in 812 the Eastern court acknowledged him.

The ceremony in St. Peter's demonstrated that the memory of the Roman Empire survived as a vital tradition in Europe and that there was a strong desire to reestablish political unity. The coronation also inaugurated, however, a long-standing struggle between the revived empire and the papacy.

In medieval theory church and state were but two aspects of Christendom: the one representing Christian society organized to secure spiritual blessings, the other the same society united to safeguard justice and human welfare. Theoretically church and state were in harmonious interplay, each aiming to secure the good of mankind.

In fact, however, the pope and emperor were contestants. The ever-present question was, should the church rule the state or the state control the church? This contest was illustrated on countless fields, large and small, throughout the Middle Ages. Since time depended upon eternity, the papal party held that the emperor depended on the pope. But since Constantine and Charlemagne revealed that God also ordained the Christian state, the imperial party argued that the emperor was independent of the pope; and if the Holy Father neglected his eternal office in time, the emperor might even correct or control the pope.

In his lifetime Charlemagne left no doubts about sovereignty in his empire. He gave Europe a dominating father figure. Everyone within the realm was answerable to him. To solve the problem of supervising local officials, a concern that plagued all German rulers, Charlemagne issued an ordinance creating the *missi dominici*, the king's envoys. Pairs of these itinerant officials, usually a bishop and a lay noble, traveled throughout the realm to check on the local administration. Even the pope could not hide from Charles's watchful eyes.

Charlemagne also fostered a revival of learning and the arts. His efforts have prompted historians to speak of this period as a "cultural rebirth." In 789 Charlemagne decreed that every monastery must have a school for the education of boys in "singing, arithmetic, and grammar." At Aix-la-Chapelle, his capital, the emperor sponsored a palace school for the education of the royal household and the stimulation of learning throughout the realm. His importation of scholars from Italy and Ireland promoted studies in Greek and Latin. Alcuin, an Anglo-Saxon scholar in charge of the school, began the arduous task of reviving learning by undertaking the first step of writing textbooks on grammar, spelling, rhetoric, and logic. Alcuin exhorted his students, "Ye lads whose age is fitted for reading, learn! The years go by like running water. Waste not the teachable days in idleness!"

Few historians challenge Charlemagne's claim to greatness as a major constructive figure of world history. From the new center in the north, rather than on the Mediterranean, he extended Christian civilization in Europe. After three centuries of disorder, he restored a measure of law and order. His patronage of learning left a cultural heritage that later generations could build upon. And the imperial ideal that he revived persisted as a political force in Europe until 1806, when the Holy Roman Empire was terminated by another self-styled emperor, Napoleon Bonaparte.

THE DECLINE INTO FEUDALISM

Unfortunately, Charlemagne's empire afforded no more than a breathing space. Its territories were too vast and its nobility too powerful to be held together under existing conditions after the dominating personality of its creator had passed from the scene. Under his weak successors the empire disintegrated amid the confusion of civil wars and devastating new invasions. When Vikings began sweeping out of the Northland, people increasingly surrendered both their lands and their persons to the many counts, dukes, and other local lords in return for protection. These disintegrating conditions presented a new challenge to the church and to the unity of Europe. We call it feudalism.

Feudalism was a type of government in which political power was exercised locally by private individuals rather than by the agents of a centralized state. One popular text explains it this way: "Fully developed feudalism was a fusion of three basic elements: (1) the personal element, called lordship or vassalage, by which one nobleman, the vassal, became the loyal follower of a stronger nobleman, the lord (or suzerain); (2) the property element, called the fief (usually land), which the vassal received from his lord to enable him to fulfill the obligations of vassalage; and (3) the governmental element, meaning the private exercise of governmental functions over vassals and fiefs. The roots of these three elements ran back to late Roman and early Germanic times."

Central to feudalism was the personal bond between lord and vassal. In the ceremony known as the act of *homage*, the vassal knelt before his lord and promised to be his "man." In the oath of fealty that followed, the vassal swore on the Bible, or some other sacred object, that he would remain true to his lord. Next, in the ritual of *investiture*, a lance, a glove, or even a bit of straw was handed the vassal to signify his jurisdiction (not ownership) over the fief.

Praying Hands

By the end of the eleventh century, the ceremony included the vassal kneeling before the feudal lord. The vassal would join his hands and extend them. The feudal lord would clasp his hands around the vassal's hands, pull him up, and kiss him. The vassal's hands joined and extended have become the symbol and posture of prayer today.

The feudal contract thus entered into by lord and vassal was considered sacred and binding upon both parties. Breaking this tie of mutual obligations was considered a felony, because it was the fundamental bond of early medieval society. The lord, for his part, was obliged to give his vassal protection and justice. The vassal's primary duty was military service. He was expected to devote forty days' service each year to the lord without pay.

Since the church was so much a part of medieval life, it could not escape inclusion in the feudal system. The unsettled conditions caused by new invaders (Vikings from the north and Magyars from Asia) forced church officials to enter into close relations with the only power able to offer them protection: the feudal barons in France and the kings in Germany. Bishops and abbots thus became vassals, receiving fiefs for which they were obligated to provide the usual feudal services. This loyalty to higher lords created unusual conflicts for those bishops who looked to the pope as God's appointed shepherd of the church. In the tenth and early eleventh centuries the pope was in no position to challenge anyone. The office fell into decay after becoming a prize sought by local Roman nobles.

On the positive side, however, the church in time sought to influence for the better the behavior of the feudal barons. In addition to attempting to add Christian virtues to the code of knightly conduct called chivalry, the church tried to impose limitations on feudal warfare. In the eleventh century bishops inaugurated the Peace of God and Truce of God movements. The Peace of God banned from the sacraments all persons who pillaged sacred places or refused to spare noncombatants. The Truce of God established "closed seasons" on fighting: from sunset on Wednesday to sunrise on Monday and certain longer periods, such as Lent. Unfortunately, both movements were generally ineffective.

Only after the German king Otto the Great revived the Roman Empire in the West in 962 was some sense of unity restored. With the renewal of the empire, however, came the old rivalry between church and state.

Otto claimed to be the successor of Augustus, Constantine, and Charlemagne, although his actual power was confined to Germany and Italy. At first the papacy looked to the German king for protection against the unruly Italian nobles who for a century had been making a prize of the papacy. From the church's viewpoint, however, this arrangement had its drawbacks, for the German kings continued to interfere in ecclesiastical affairs—even in the election of popes.

During the eleventh century the controversy between church and state centered on the problem of lay investiture. Theoretically, on assuming office a bishop or abbot was subject to two investitures: his spiritual authority was bestowed by a church official and his feudal or civil authority by the king or a noble. In actual fact, however, feudal lords and kings came to control both the appointment and the installation of churchmen. This practice was most pronounced in Germany, where control of the church was the foundation of the king's power. The German church was in essence a state church.

SETTING IN ORDER THE HOUSE OF GOD

The church was ill prepared to challenge kings and emperors; it needed to set its own house in spiritual order. This began with a far-reaching revival within the reformed Benedictine order of Cluny, founded in 910. From the original monastery in Burgundy, a powerful impulse radiated for the reform of the feudalized church. The Cluniac program began as a movement for monastic reform, but in time it called for the enforcement of clerical celibacy and the abolition of simony, the purchase or sale of a church office. (The term *simony* comes from Simon the magician, who tried to buy the gift of the Holy Spirit from the apostles, Acts 8:9–25.) The ultimate goal of the Cluniac reformers was to free the entire church from secular control and subject it to papal authority. Some three hundred Cluniac houses were freed from lay control, and in 1059 the papacy itself was removed from secular interference by the creation of the College of Cardinals, which henceforth elected the popes.

The man behind the reform of the papacy was an arch-deacon named Hildebrand. In 1073 he was elected pope, and as Gregory VII (1073–1085) he claimed unprecedented power for the papacy. Gregory held as his ideal the creation of a Christian commonwealth under papal control. Instead of conceding equality between the church and the state, he insisted that the spiritual power was supreme over the temporal. In 1075 he formally prohibited lay investiture and threatened to excommunicate any layman who performed it and any churchman who submitted to it. This drastic act virtually declared war against Europe's rulers, since most of them practiced lay investiture. The climax to the struggle occurred in Gregory's clash with the emperor Henry IV.

The pope accused Henry of simony and lay investiture in appointing his own choice to be the archbishop of Milan. Gregory summoned Henry to Rome to explain his conduct. Henry's answer was to convene in 1076 a synod of German bishops that declared Gregory a usurper and unfit to occupy the Roman See: "Wherefore henceforth we renounce, now and for the future, all obedience unto thee." In retaliation Gregory excommunicated Henry and deposed him, absolving his subjects from their oaths of allegiance.

At last, driven to make peace with the Holy Father by a revolt among the German nobles, Henry appeared before Gregory in January 1077 at Canossa, a castle in the mountains of Italy. Dressed as a penitent, the emperor stood barefoot in the snow for three days and begged forgiveness until, in Gregory's words "We loosed the chain of the anathema and at length received him . . . into the lap of the Holy Mother Church."

"This dramatic humiliation of the emperor," says one historian,

> did not resolve the quarrel, nor do contemporary accounts attach much significance to the incident—public penance was not uncommon in those days even for kings. Yet the pope had made progress toward

freeing the church from interference by laymen and toward increasing the power and prestige of the papacy. The problem of lay investiture was settled in 1122 by the compromise known as the Concordat of Worms. The church maintained the right to elect the holder of an ecclesiastical office, but only in the presence of the emperor or his representative.

Later popes added little to Gregory's theories of the office. They, like Gregory, insisted that Christian society was organized under the pope, its visible head, and he was guarded against all possibility of error by the presence of Peter perpetually present in his successors, the bishops of Rome.

Many of Gregory's claims now appear intolerable. Yet we must agree that Gregory and his powerful successors stood for two principles that to the Christian are incontestable: (1) In the loyalties of men, the spiritual has the primacy over the secular; and (2) the families of men can find true unity only in Christ and in obedience to the law of God. Medieval society was far from perfect. But during the Middle Ages, Europe became conscious of itself as a unity, far beyond the uncertain limits of the Holy Roman Empire; and the church attained a level of power and influence over the lives of men, for the most part used helpfully, such as it has never known since that time.

Suggestions for Further Reading

Baldwin, Marshall W. *The Mediaeval Church*. Ithaca, NY: Cornell University Press, 1953.

Barraclough, Geoffrey. *The Crucible of Europe*. Berkeley: University of California Press, 1976.

Barraclough, Geoffrey. *The Medieval Papacy*. New York: Harcourt, Brace & World, 1968.

Fremantle, Anne. *Age of Faith*. New York: Time-Life Books, 1968.

*Logan, Donald. *History of the Church in the Middle Ages*. New York: Routledge, 2003.

Noll, Mark A. *Turning Points: Decisive Moments in the History of Christianity*. Grand Rapids: Baker Books, 2000.

Russell, Jeffrey Burton. *A History of Medieval Christianity: Prophecy and Order*. Arlington Heights, IL: AHM Publishing Corporation, 1968.

*Southern, R. W. *Western Society and the Church in the Middle Ages: The Penguin History of the Church*, Vol. 2. New York: Penguin, 1990.

CHAPTER 19

LIFTED IN A MYSTIC MANNER

The Papacy and the Crusader

Iɴ Pᴀʀɪs, ᴏɴ ᴀ small island in the Seine, stands an edifice of weather-beaten stone, the Gothic Cathedral of Notre Dame. Dedicated to the glory of God and the veneration of "Our Lady," this well-known sanctuary reflects a fascinating image of the life and spirit of the Christian Middle Ages.

Notre Dame was erected between 1163 and 1235 during some of the most epoch-making years of Western Christianity. While workmen were constructing a flying buttress or carefully fitting a beautiful window in place, students reclined on the Petit Pont, a bridge that led to the Left Bank, and exchanged reports of crusader victories in the Holy Land or wrangled over one of the theological virtues. Some of these students would shortly wear the colors of the Episcopal office, and one of them would carry the papal office to the zenith of worldly power as Pope Innocent III.

Notre Dame was only one symptom of a veritable fever of church building then infecting Europe. Between 1170 and 1270 more than five hundred great churches were built in Gothic style in France alone. Gothic first appeared in the restoration of the abbey church of St. Denis near Paris. The abbot of St. Denis, Suger, conceived the project and guided the work of rebuilding between 1137 and 1144. He described his reaction to the restoration in terms seldom surpassed in praise of the Gothic: "I seem to find myself, as it were, in some strange part of the universe which was neither wholly of the baseness of the earth nor wholly of the serenity of heaven, but by the grace of God I seemed lifted in a mystic manner from this lower towards the upper sphere."

Lift. Reach. Aspiration. These are the terms for the age. The Middle Ages were not all dark, as the hundreds of Gothic cathedrals so readily testify.

What can Christians hope for in human society? If God's will were done on earth as it is in heaven, what would earth look like? Believers in every age have asked that question, but no age has reached for the stars quite like the so-called High Middle Ages.

THY KINGDOM COME

During the twelfth and thirteenth centuries, the papacy led an admirable attempt to constitute a perfect society on earth. The church achieved an incomparable power and majesty. Like the Gothic cathedral the medieval church shot upward into the heavens, calling all below it to the glory of God. But like the cathedrals, the papacy reached for the impossible and first cracked, then, in time, crumbled to earth.

It happened often with the churches. Early Gothic builders tried to attain the utmost height possible with the materials at hand. The Cathedral of Chartres, for example, equals the elevation of a skyscraper of thirty stories. The Strasbourg Cathedral rises forty stories. Many such efforts resulted in repeated failures in church construction. One historian of cathedrals has remarked that the question to put to a tourist guide is, "When did the tower fall down?"

By reaching the greatest height possible, the architect tried to create the illusion of soaring. The use of flying buttresses eliminated the massive walls of earlier churches and made possible slender pillars that, in turn, were carved in the form of a cluster of still more slender shafts reaching up, up into infinity. Even the sculptured forms of saints or angels standing in the niches were elongated: the neck, the arms, the legs seemed to be soaring heavenward.

That is probably the best way to understand Western Christianity in the twelfth and thirteenth centuries. The papacy ascended high above European society, mounting upon the fading glory of the empire. The emergence of unified national states reduced the empire to a shadow of its former universal power. Emperors continued to call themselves "ever-august Roman Emperors" and continued to go to Rome for their coronations, but they were actually merely the sovereigns of the cluster of kingdoms and municipal republics that constituted the Germany of the late Middle Ages.

The papacy, by contrast, built upon the reforms of Pope Gregory VII and emerged as the most powerful office in Europe. The pope's government was a truly universal monarchy, steadily becoming completely centralized. All the bishops swore fealty to the pope, no religious order could be founded without his authorization, the papal court in Rome heard appeals from all over Christendom, and in every country legates from Rome watched over the execution of papal orders.

In the hands of a strong leader, the papacy could overshadow all secular monarchs. Such a leader was Pope Innocent III (1198–1216), a new type of administrator-pope. Unlike Gregory VII and other earlier reform popes who were monks, Innocent and other great popes of the later twelfth and thirteenth centuries were trained as canon lawyers, experts in church government. Innocent was like Gregory VII, however, in holding an exalted view of his office. "The successor of Peter," he announced, "is the Vicar of Christ: he has been established as a mediator between God and man, below God but beyond man; less than God but more than man; who shall judge all and be judged by no one."

Innocent III told the princes of Europe that the papacy was like the sun, while kings were like the moon. As the moon received its light from the sun, so kings derived their powers from the pope. The papacy's chief weapons in support of this authority were spiritual penalties. Almost everyone believed in heaven and hell and in the pope's management of the grace to get to one and avoid the other.

Thus the pope's first weapon in bringing peasants and princes to their knees was the threat of excommunication. He could pronounce their anathema and they would be "set apart" from the church, deprived of the grace essential for salvation. After some bishop read the solemn sentence of excommunication, a bell rang as for a funeral, a book was closed, and a candle was extinguished, all to symbolize the cutting off of the guilty man. If he entered a church during mass he was expelled or the mass was halted.

While under excommunication, persons could not act as judge, juror, witness, or attorney. They could not be guardians, executors, or parties to contract. After death they received no Christian burial, and if, by chance, they were buried in consecrated ground, the church had their bodies disinterred and destroyed.

The second weapon in the papal arsenal was the interdict. While excommunication was aimed at individuals, the interdict fell upon whole nations. It suspended all public worship and, with the exception of baptism and extreme unction, it withdrew the sacraments from the lands of disobedient rulers. Pope Innocent III successfully applied or threatened the interdict eighty-five times against uncooperative princes.

So successful was the pontiff in asserting his temporal as well as spiritual supremacy that many states, both large and small, formally acknowledged the pope as their feudal lord. In England, King John differed with Innocent over the election of the archbishop of Canterbury, and Innocent placed England under interdict and excommunicated John. Under attack from his barons, John capitulated to Innocent by becoming his vassal, receiving England back as a fief, and paying him a sizable annual tribute.

In France, Innocent forced King Philip Augustus to comply with the church's moral code by taking back as his queen the woman he had divorced with the consent of the French bishops.

And within the Holy Roman Empire (Germany), Innocent intervened in a civil war between rival candidates for the throne, supporting first one, then the other. In the end Innocent secured the election of his ward, the young Hohenstaufen heir Frederick II, who promised to respect papal rights and to go on a crusade.

Wielding these spiritual weapons, Innocent and his successors in the papal office during the thirteenth century led Christianity to its peak of political and cultural influence. We simply cannot understand the pope's place in our own times without some understanding of these years.

The soaring dreams—and delusions—of the papacy in this period appear preeminently in the crusades and in Scholasticism. In one the pope claimed power over the holy cause in history; in the other he maintained authority over the souls of men even in eternity. We will look at the crusades in this chapter and examine Scholasticism in the next.

TAKING UP THE CROSS FOR CHRIST

The crusades reflected the new dynamism in Christianity. Islam had come to birth through the visions and revelations claimed by its prophet, Muhammad, who was born in AD 570. At the age of twenty-five he suddenly moved from being a keeper of camels to overseeing the business affairs of a wealthy widow. She was impressed by his character, and though fifteen years his senior, soon proposed married to him. Although after she died he took numerous wives, while she was alive she remained his only wife.

At the age of forty Muhammad began to retire into a cave for extensive periods of contemplation and meditation. After one of these occasions he told his wife that he had been visited by an angel who ordered him "to recite," and from that command came the Koran, which literally means *to recite.*

At first he was perplexed by it all, but his wife told him this could well be the call of God upon him. She became his first follower, and then a handful of family members followed suit. Many resisted his claim to be God's spokesman, and it was only after various battles, arguments, and wars that Muhammad was able to gain a vast following in Arabia.

In the first one hundred years of this Arabic movement, numerous capitals, such as Jerusalem, Damascus, and Cairo, fell to Islam. But the succession to Muhammad after his unexpected death in AD 632 became a serious, divisive issue. He had not named a successor, and an immediate struggle for the leadership of the movement ensued. One group, the *Sunnis*, insisted that the first caliph should be elected. *Shiahs* or *Shiites* argued that the successor must come from Muhammad's own bloodline, which would have been Ali, his cousin and son-in-law.

Now, in the age of the grand cathedral, crusaders from Western Europe attempted to expel the Muslims from the Holy Land. Historians have attributed numerous motives to the crusaders beyond their religious fervor. Did they seek adventure in these strange foreign lands? Would they find personal gain or spiritual advantage? While few contemporary Christians would defend the idea of the crusades or its most gross offenses, we must not overlook a simple reality. The Christians sought to counter Islam's remarkable military conquest and preserve their geographic strongholds from being overrun. By the eighth century, one half of all Christians lived under Islamic rule. All the great and colorful figures of this era were caught up in this consuming cause, from Peter the Hermit, who enflamed the First Crusade, to the saintly Louis IX, King of France, who inspired the Sixth and Seventh.

For centuries peaceful pilgrims had been traveling from Europe to worship at the birthplace of Christ. The rise and spread of Islam in the Near East during the seventh century did not interrupt this traffic. By the tenth century bishops were organizing mass pilgrimages to the Holy Land; the largest, which set out from Germany in 1065, included about seven thousand pilgrims.

During the eleventh century, however, Christian pilgrims began to encounter persecution, and when the Seljuk Turks, new and fanatical converts to Islam, came sweeping and plundering into the Near East, the situation became especially tense. The Seljuks seized Jerusalem from their fellow Muslims and then swept north into Asia Minor.

Forces of the Eastern Empire desperately tried to bar the invader, but at the battle of Manzikert (1071) the Turks captured the eastern emperor and scattered his army. Within a few years Asia Minor, the chief source of Byzantine revenue and troops, was lost, and the emperor was writing to western princes and to the pope seeking mercenaries to aid in the rescue of lost territories. In addition, tales of alleged Turkish mistreatment of Christian pilgrims circulated throughout Europe, and though there is evidence that these stories were propaganda, rumors themselves were sufficient to inflame men's minds.

In 1095, after the Eastern Emperor Alexius I sent out an urgent appeal for help, Pope Urban II proclaimed the First Crusade to regain the Holy Land. Preaching at the Council of Clermont in southeastern France, the pope urged Christians to take up the cross and strive for a cause that promised not merely spiritual rewards but material gain as well:

> For this land which you inhabit . . . is too narrow for your large population; nor does it abound in wealth; and it furnishes scarcely food enough for its cultivators. Hence it is that you murder and devour one another . . . enter upon the road to the Holy Sepulchre; wrest that land from the wicked race, and subject it to yourselves.

As Urban ended his impassioned appeal a roar rose from the multitude: "Deus Vult!" "God wills it!" So there on the spot Urban declared that *Deus Vult!* would be the crusader battle cry against the Muslim enemy.

For seven centuries Christians have tried to forget the crusades, but neither Jew nor Muslim will allow them to do so. In our liberated generation it is easy to dismiss the whole bloody affair as insane religious bigotry, forgetting the context in which it occurred.

But the crusaders were human beings, so their motives, like our own, were mixed and often in conflict. The word *crusade* itself comes from "taking the cross," after the example of Christ. Thus on the way to the Holy Land the crusader wore the cross on his breast. On his journey home, he wore it on his back.

The crusaders were fully aware of the spiritual rewards Urban promised them, including full forgiveness of their past sins. And most of them shared a profound personal reverence for the soil that Christ had trod.

The intensity of this emotion was later caught by Shakespeare in words of that pugnacious English monarch Henry IV:

> We are impressed and engag'd to fight . . .
> To chase those pagans in those holy fields,
> Over whose acres walked those blessed feet,
> Which fourteen hundred years ago were nail'd,
> For our advantage on the bitter cross.

For Urban and the popes who followed him, the crusades were a new type of war, a Holy War. Augustine had laid down the principles of a "just war": It was conducted by the state; its purpose was the vindication of justice, meaning the defense of life and property; and its code called for respect for noncombatants, hostages, and prisoners. All these evaporated in the heat of the holy cause. Urban appealed for crusaders in the name of the church; the purpose of liberating fellow Christians morphed into the conquest of the infidels in the Holy Land; and this high calling excused somehow the total disregard for noncombatants and prisoners.

The inception of the crusades ignited horrible attacks against the Jews, and even fellow Christians were not exempt from rape and plunder. Incredible atrocities befell the Muslim foes. Crusaders sawed open dead bodies in search of gold, sometimes cooking and eating the flesh—a delicacy they found "better than spiced peacock," as one chronicler chose to describe it.

EVENTS OF THE CRUSADES

From the end of the eleventh century to the end of the thirteenth, Christian Europe, led by the popes, launched seven major crusades, as well as various small expeditions.

The First Crusade was composed of feudal nobles from France, parts of Germany, and southern Italy, where the Norman (or Viking) invaders had settled. The armies proceeded overland to Constantinople. Having expected the help of European mercenaries against the Seljuks, the emperor Alexius Comnenus was taken aback when confronted by an unruly horde of what Pope Urban himself had called "aforetime robbers." The emperor hastily directed the crusaders out of Constantinople to fight the Turks.

The First Crusade was the most successful of the seven; with not more than five thousand knights and infantry, it overcame the resistance of the Turks, who were no longer united. Above all, it captured the Holy City, Jerusalem. A contemporary account of the Christian entrance into Jerusalem reads,

> Some of our men . . . cut off the heads of their enemies; others shot them with arrows, so that they fell from the towers; others tortured them longer by casting them into the flames. . . . It was necessary to pick one's way over the bodies of men and horses. But these were small matters compared to what happened at the Temple of Solomon [where] . . . men rode in blood up to their knees and bridle reins. Indeed it was a just and splendid judgment of God that this place should be filled with the blood of the unbelievers, since it had suffered so long from their blasphemies.

At nightfall the crusaders' hands were still bloody when they folded them in prayer and knelt at the Church of the Holy Sepulchre, "sobbing for excess of joy."

The First Crusade captured a long strip of territory along the eastern coast of the Mediterranean and created the feudal Latin kingdom of Jerusalem. It survived until 1291 when its last remnant fell to the Muslims.

When the kingdom of Jerusalem faced its first crisis, tottering on the brink of destruction in 1147, Bernard, the powerful mystic of Clairvaux, called for the Second Crusade. Despite Bernard's rhetoric and the presence of royalty, the crusade achieved nothing. After two years it simply melted away.

The original frenzy had clearly cooled, and the signs of corruption of the holy cause were apparent. The popes needed money to meet such obligations as providing legates for the new Christian lands in the East. So they turned spiritual benefits into moneymaking advantage.

In the Middle Ages sins to be forgiven had to be confessed. Upon hearing a confession the priest not only pronounced the penitent's guilt for sin forgiven (thanks to the merit of Christ) but also required a penalty or *satisfaction*—some "act of penance"—as a mark of the penitent's sincerity. If the penitent died before performing this penance, purgatory afforded him an opportunity in the life after death. Such penance, whether in this life or in purgatory, was called "temporal" punishment.

For years the church had claimed the power to remit part of this temporal punishment, but no complete remission had been granted until Urban II at Clermont offered total remission or "indulgence" for crusaders who headed for Jerusalem "out of pure devotion."

It was only a slight step farther to confer like benefits upon those who were unable to go on a crusade but who contributed to the cause. A man could virtually buy a substitute. Thus the possibilities for fund-raising opened in all directions, including construction of a hospital here or a cathedral there.

In 1187 Saladin, the Sultan of Egypt and Syria, brought fresh and vigorous leadership to the Muslims. When Jerusalem fell to the infidels, Christians with some reluctance responded to the cry for the Third Crusade (1189). Its leaders were three of the most famous medieval kings: Frederick Barbarossa of Germany, Richard the Lion-Hearted of England, and Philip Augustus of France. Frederick was drowned in Asia Minor; and, after many quarrels with Richard, Philip returned home. Saladin and Richard remained the chief protagonists.

To keep the Muslims united, Saladin proclaimed a *jihad*, or holy war, against the Christians, but he remained a patient statesman and chivalrous warrior. "Abstain from the shedding of blood," he once said, "for blood that is spilt never slumbers." His commonsense approach to a settlement was evident when he proposed that Richard should marry his sister and be given Palestine as a wedding present, a proposal that shocked the Europeans.

Richard and Saladin finally agreed to a three-year truce and free access to Jerusalem for Christian pilgrims. Since Saladin would have granted this concession at any time, the truce scarcely compensated for the cost of such an expensive crusade.

The Fourth Crusade revealed the harsh realities of papal aspirations in the East and the degradation of the crusading zeal. Upon ascending the papal throne in 1198, Innocent III threw himself into the effort of reviving the crusading spirit, but the few knights who answered his call were unable to meet the outrageous shipping charges demanded by the Venetians. To secure the costs of shipping, the Venetians persuaded the crusaders to capture the Christian town of Zara on the Adriatic coast.

The town had been a nuisance to Venetian vessels for years. So in 1202 the crusaders sacked Zara. Innocent complained that Satan was behind the whole rapacious affair and proceeded to excommunicate all who participated.

The Venetians, however, followed their advantage by pressuring the crusaders to attack Constantinople itself. Torn by warring parties within, Constantinople fell to the crusaders and, after ravaging the city, the crusaders set up the Latin Empire of Constantinople in 1204 and promptly forgot about "the deliverance of the Holy Land."

Upon hearing of the conquest Innocent wrote in rage, "You have spared nothing that is sacred, neither age nor sex. You have given yourselves up to prostitution, to adultery and to debauchery in the face of all the world." Never one to pass a political advantage, however, Innocent appointed an archbishop of Constantinople to serve Roman interests.

The Latin Empire in Constantinople lasted until 1261, but the ancient city never fully recovered. The conquest widened the schism between the Greek and the Latin churches and hastened the fall of the city in 1453 to the Turks.

Other crusaders marched and meandered east during these years but none of the holy efforts postponed the predictable, the return of the Holy Land to Muslim control. The era of crusades ended in 1291 when Acre, the last stronghold of the Christians in the land where Jesus walked, fell to those who denied his deity.

RESULTS OF THE HOLY CAUSE

The long-range results of two centuries of crusading zeal are not impressive. If the primary purposes of the crusades were to win the Holy Land, to check the advance of Islam, and to heal the schism between the Eastern and Western churches, then the crusades failed miserably.

The crusades created three semimonastic military orders: the Templars (or Knights of the Temple) whose first headquarters were on the

The Age of Crusades

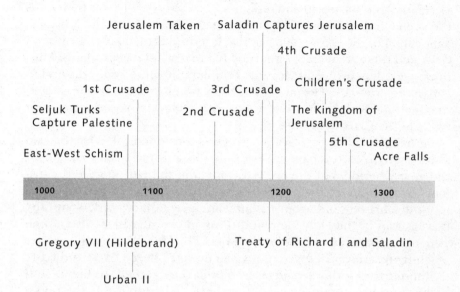

The High Middle Ages

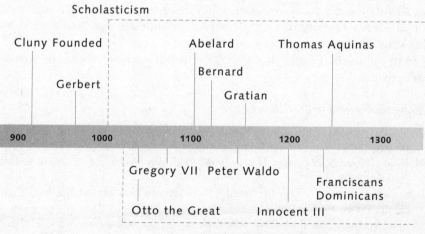

site of the old Temple of Jerusalem; the Hospitalers (or Knights of St. John of Jerusalem) who were founded originally to care for the sick and wounded; and the Teutonic Knights, exclusively a German order. Combining monasticism and militarism, these orders had as their aims the protection of all pilgrims and perpetual war against the Muslims. These men of the cross could put five hundred armed knights into the field, and their great castles guarded the roads and passes against Muslim attack. For two centuries the Templars in white robes decorated with a red cross, the Hospitalers in black robes with a white cross, and the Teutonic Knights in white robes with a black cross were common sights in the Crusader States.

Perhaps the most significant result was the added splendor the crusades brought to the papacy. Not only did a pope, Urban II, launch the First Crusade, but the popes throughout the period were the primary inspiration for fresh expeditions. They, not the emperors, strove to unite Christendom against Islam. The new military orders and the new bishops in the Holy Land and those in Constantinople for a time were under papal protection and service. The Holy War was the papacy reaching for universal sovereignty, one united Church, West and East.

But like the Gothic architects who built their cathedrals higher and higher until the towers cracked and then crashed to earth, the popes tried the impossible. Christian Europe had no need for Syria or Jerusalem. She took them in a fit of enthusiasm and had no power to retain them. When trade and towns turned rulers and people to new interests at home, the popes remained faithful to the old ideal, Christian control of the Holy Land. It was their constant preoccupation.

Unfortunately the popes never held two basic truths that we must never forget: Christianity's highest satisfactions are not guaranteed by possession of special places, and the sword is never God's way to extend Christ's church. This fault assured the religious collapse of the whole structure.

Suggestions for Further Reading

Barraclough, Geoffrey. *The Medieval Papacy*. New York: Harcourt, Brace & World, 1968.

Madden, Thomas. *A Concise History of the Crusades*. New York: Rowman & Littlefield, 1999.

Riley-Smith, Jonathan. *The Crusades: A Short History*. New Haven, CT: Yale University Press, 1987.

*Stark, Rodney. *The Battalions: The Case for the Crusades*. New York: Harper One, 2012.

CHAPTER 20

THE NECTAR
OF LEARNING

Scholasticism

FOR EIGHT CENTURIES GOTHIC cathedrals throughout Europe have inspired worshipers, and awed tourists. The medieval masters of Gothic style tried to portray in stone and glass man's central religious quest. They wanted to depict a tension: on the one hand was man aspiring to reach the heights of heaven; on the other hand was God condescending to address the least of men.

The movement of the Gothic, therefore, is two-way. The pillars, arches, and steeples, aligned like rows of rockets ready to ascend to heaven, point skyward. But through colorful windows of leaded glass the light of God descends to meet the lowly. It is an architect's version of human reason and divine revelation.

Windows in the Gothic structure could be plentiful and large because the outside pillars and buttresses eliminated the need for thick walls. Between the shafts of slender stone, architects could set windows of colored glass. Artists used brilliant colors—crimson, blue, purple, ruby—to tell the story of redemption from creation to the Last Judgment. Worshipers, then, could ponder the sacrifice of Isaac, the crossing of the Red Sea, the birth of Jesus, or Saint Anthony's struggle with devils.

The total effect was breathtaking. As the evening sun cast its warm enchanting rays upon the cold gray stone, even the cobbler from his pew could sense his kinship with Moses, Isaiah, Jesus, Paul, Augustine, and Benedict.

Light, which played upon the multicolored windows, had been a constant symbol of God and his ways with men. "God is light," wrote the apostle. "In him is no darkness at all" (1 John 1:5). And Jesus himself used this image of his own incarnation when he announced, "I am the light of the world."

The Gothic cathedral, therefore, displayed the spiritual tension of the Christian drama: the highest aspirations of man and the descending light of God. Man, in effect, ascends while God descends. Such language is, of course, figurative. God is no more above than below in any spatial sense. But man has always described his need in terms of reach, and God's truth in terms of descent.

THE RISE OF UNIVERSITIES

Appropriately, therefore, schools in these cathedrals gave birth to medieval universities, for the supreme task of the university was to understand and explain the light of God's revealed truth. Just as the crusades reflected a widespread passion to extend the authority of God in Muslim lands, so the universities reveal an intense hunger to understand the truth of God received from any land.

But just how did the world of ideas bow to the rule of God? How was reason made the servant of faith? We call this period in the history of Christian thought "Scholasticism" because a distinctive method of scholarship arose and because a unique theology of the Middle Ages emerged. The aim of the Schoolmen, as these teachers are sometimes called, was twofold: to reconcile Christian doctrine and human reason, and to arrange the teachings of the church in an orderly system.

A free search for the truth was never in view since the chief doctrines of the Christian faith were regarded as fixed. The purpose of discussion was to show the reasonableness of the doctrines and to explain their implications.

The whole endeavor surged forward on the winds of intellectual curiosity. One eleventh-century scholar from Liege represents hosts of others:

> Olbert was not able to satiate his thirst for study. When he would hear of someone distinguished in the arts he flew there at once, and the more he thirsted the more he absorbed something delightful from each master . . . . Afterwards just like the bees among flowers, gorged with the nectar of learning, he returned to the hive and lived there studiously in a religious way, and religiously in a studious manner.

Living "religiously in a studious manner" was the hallmark of medieval education. Its central aim was eternal salvation. Originally, however, learning had been limited primarily to the clergy. Benedict of Nursia had insisted that his monks read and study for their own spiritual development. As a result, Benedictine abbeys created a kind of rudimentary schooling in Latin.

Later, in the eighth century, Charlemagne, dreaming of a Christian empire, had widened the opportunities for study through a decree that every monastery have a school to teach all those "who with God's help are able to learn." The emperor himself set an example with a palace school for his own children and those of his courtiers.

The best chance for learning among laymen came from cathedral schools. Since cathedrals, churches of the bishops, were located in towns, their schools to train parish priests were in time opened to all.

The curriculum of the cathedral school was limited to grammar, rhetoric, logic, arithmetic, geometry, music, and astronomy—the seven liberal arts, so called because in ancient Rome their study had been reserved for *liberi, freemen.* The few texts available were writings of a handful of scholars of the early Middle Ages. One was Cassiodorus, a sixth-century Roman whose *Handbook of Sacred and Secular Learning* defined the liberal arts and interpreted the Bible. Another was Boethius, a contemporary of Cassiodorus, whose *Consolation of Philosophy,* written while he was in prison for an alleged plot against the barbarian King Theodoric, attempted to reconcile the misfortunes of man with the concept of a benevolent, omnipotent God. These men, along with Augustine, Pope Gregory the Great, and a few other church fathers, were known as *auctores, authorities,* whose words the medieval student would not lightly presume to contradict.

THE MAGNETISM OF AN ABLE TEACHER

A new day dawned, however, with the coming of the great schoolmasters. We can trace the birth of universities to the magnetism of popular teachers whose skill and enthusiasm for learning attracted students wherever they happened to be.

As Anne Fremantle describes them, the first of this new breed was Gerbert, master of the cathedral school at Rheims in the latter half of the tenth century. The son of a serf, Gerbert was destined to end his days as Pope Sylvester II (999–1003). But he left a deeper mark upon history through his scholarship. "As a young monk, Gerbert had been so brilliant a student that his abbot had taken the unusual step of sending him to Spain to study mathematics. Although Gerbert's mentor there was a Christian bishop, he was also exposed to the broad and tolerant culture of the ruling Muslims." This was the first of a number of significant contributions Muslims made to the Christian intellectual awakening.

Gerbert returned to Rheims deeply impressed by the inquisitive, questing spirit of Muslim scholarship. When he began to teach at Rheims, he announced that quotations of traditional church authorities no longer sufficed; his pupils were henceforth to study Roman classics in the original. "To this end Gerbert collected manuscripts wherever he could and built a sizable library—no mean feat at a time when a manuscript sometimes took a year to copy, and cost at least the equivalent of a churchman's yearly income."

The liveliest figure in this early stage of intellectual revolution was Peter Abelard (1079–1142). The eldest son of a minor noble of Brittany (northwestern France), "Abelard for love of learning had given up his inheritance rights to younger brothers, and roamed France to sit at the feet of the great masters, now listening, now openly challenging them in class." In time he established himself as a lecturer in Paris, where he attracted a host of students. He also began to write.

In a treatise entitled *Sic et Non* (*Yes and No*), he posed 158 questions from Christian teaching and answered them with conflicting quotations from the Scriptures, the church fathers, and pagan classics. "The first key to wisdom," Abelard asserted, "is assiduous and frequent questioning . . . . For by doubting we come to inquiry, and by inquiry we arrive at the truth." This idea, commonplace to the Greeks, was hardly so to medieval Europeans. Abelard's zest for doubt won the applause of some, but alarmed as many others. Another of his books, on the nature of the Trinity, invoked condemnation by a church council at Soissons in 1121, and the brilliant scholar found himself behind the walls of a monastery.

Resourceful as usual, Abelard secured the monastery's permission to leave a year later to live in the wilderness southeast of Paris. "Students flocked to his side. They built him a shelter, tilled his land, and begged him to teach once more. Resuming his pursuit of reason, Abelard again and again fell afoul of conservatives in the church, this time including Abbot Bernard of Clairvaux, the most influential churchman in Christendom." Bernard pursued Abelard as devoutly as he preached the Second Crusade. "The faith of the righteous believes," he declared, "it does not dispute." At Bernard's instigation, a church council at Sens in 1140 condemned Abelard for heresy. Abelard retired to the abbey of Cluny, where he stayed in seclusion for the remaining two years of his life.

No one, however, could stifle the growth of the seeds he had scattered. Schools sprouted all around the Continent. Fewer than one hundred years after his death, universities flourished at Paris, Orleans, and Montpellier in France; across the English Channel at Oxford and Cambridge; at Bologna and Padua in Italy.

The event that marked the flowering of the universities was the grouping of students and masters into guilds. "As craftsmen had done before them," explains Fremantle, scholars banded together for mutual interest and protection, and called themselves a *universitas*, the medieval name for any corporate group.

In Italy, where the majority of students were mature men pursuing advanced study in law and medicine, their guilds came to exercise great power. Students hired and paid teachers, determined the courses to be given, and fined any lecturer who skipped a chapter in expounding his subject.

At French and English universities, where students were younger, masters' guilds had the upper hand. They forbade students to swear or gamble, fined them for breaking curfews, and prescribed table manners. "Cleanse not the teeth," one rule went, "with the steel that is sharpened for those that eat with thee."

Upon hearing "university" we tend to envision ivied halls and grassy quadrangles. Medieval universities, however, had not even the semblance of permanent quarters. At first lectures were given in wayside sheds at Oxford and Cambridge, in the cathedral cloisters in Paris, and in the squares in Italy. In time teachers rented rooms. Students sat on the floor, which was usually covered with straw to protect against the dampness. Unencumbered with athletic stadiums, libraries, or other equipment, universities could pick up and move elsewhere at any time if they found themselves at odds with local citizens.

In addition to lectures, the method of teaching was the *disputation*. Two or more masters, and occasionally the students, debated text readings, employing Abelard's question-and-answer approach. *Scholasticism* developed in this context and came to stand for painstaking arrival at logical conclusions through questioning, examining, and arranging details into a system of logic. The Scholastic disputation stirred heated clashes and bitter feelings. Wars of logic ran for years between master and master, with adherents of each cheering their hero on with tumultuous stomping and whistling. Something important was happening in this raucous atmosphere. Students were learning to think. Unquestioning acceptance of traditional authorities was no longer assured; even the conclusions of Christian doctrine were being investigated.

SUPPORT FOR THE PAPAL MONARCHY

All of this feverish activity proceeded, however, under the watchful eye of the papacy. Some debates continued for generations, but the popes worked to make sure that the net result was a new philosophical framework that supported the papal monarchy. On the one hand was a new formulation of canon law, and on the other hand a systematic statement of Christian theology.

The University of Bologna in Italy emerged in the later years of the twelfth century as the center of the study of Roman civil law and church or, as it is called, *canon law.*

Canon law served the church just as civil law supported a secular government. It defined the rights, duties, and powers of all people and priests within the church. It was the law administered in all ecclesiastical courts, from those of the bishop up to that of the pope.

Sometime around 1140 Gratian, a monk of the monastery of St. Felix at Bologna, published a *Harmony of Discordant Canons*, which tried to coordinate all previous collections of church law. Since he arranged his quotations of authorities subject by subject, his *Harmony* soon emerged as the sole manual for teachers and for judges in the church.

It served as the base for later additions to the *Body of Canon Law.* Thus by the fourteenth century the Roman Church had at its disposal—until 1918, when it was revised—an authoritative body of laws to control and direct the lives of men.

Canon law interfered in wars and recognized the care of widows. It decreed fasting and feasting. It ordained confession and communion at least once a year. It specified which actions excommunicated a Christian from the church.

But it also directed man's most intimate relationships. By virtue of its concern with baptism it established standards for all births—and all that led to births. The first inviting smile between man and woman brought the couple under its watchful shadow. It directed penance for fornication and adultery; it laid down the conditions in which a marriage could exist.

Canon law, in short, reached not only to every priest, but to every layman, plowman, or prince. And it professed to declare not only the necessary path to salvation but the very nature of the most intimate organs of men and women.

This craving to control, the zeal to reach every aspect of life, may reflect a Christian legalism. It tried to reduce human freedom to a miserable minimum and forgot that God designed freedom as the forerunner for the coming of true faith.

Canon law, however, gave to the papacy a rational legal basis, something the medieval state did not yet possess. As a result the papacy rose to preeminent power in the public life of Europe and achieved an international prestige that far outweighed that of any feudal kingdom.

On the day of Innocent III's consecration to the papal office, he took as the text of his sermon God's words in Jeremiah 1:10: "I have this day set thee over the nations and over the kingdoms, to root out, and to pull down, to destroy and to throw down, to build, and to plant." For three decades that is what he did. He was the "Vicar of Christ" on earth, thanks in large part to the universal authority conveyed in canon law.

The second way the universities served the universal papacy was to provide an unshakable, rational theological construction of Christian society. By the thirteenth century, the universities faced a controversial issue. Several writings of Aristotle had been re-introduced to the West in the new universities, lost works that had survived the decline of Rome among the eastern Christians, and especially among the Muslims. The prospect of employing Aristotelian philosophy, however, raised challenges. For example, the new Aristotelian approach called for a new matrix or framework, a revised worldview, whereas most theologians had previously assumed a Platonic frame of reference.

A basic dualism followed: theologians distinguished between the basic material stuff of the world we live in and the mental or intellectual realm (Plato's world of Forms). The conceptual realm held basic ideas, everything from the idea of a circle (circularity) to the idea of justice in and of itself. The ideas are perfect, non-material, and eternal. Our concrete world is composed of imperfect, material, and corruptible (not eternal) copies of these perfect ideas. This world contains many circles, but every physical, tangible circle is imperfect (out of round) and temporal (subject to time and its effects; not eternal).

Theologians such as Origen and Augustine had told the Christian story with this philosophical backdrop in place. One might picture God and his ideas in an eternal realm and the corrupt and compromised physical world below. While Aristotle did not overturn everything about Platonism, he thought that the ideas or forms were present in the concrete physical realities. Discovering the forms then called for one to investigate the concrete world or tangible creation. The overall thrust for Aristotle was not to separate two unfitting dimensions (the conceptual and material), but was to discover and admire how the best thinking integrated or fit with the material world by God's special design. This shift in viewing the world and reason was challenging in its scale, its novelty, and its uncertain future.

Many scholars only knew Aristotle as he was presented by a famous Muslim interpreter named Averroes. He stressed philosophy or reason's independence from revelation or faith. His work left the impression that one might follow reason to one conclusion, while revelation might point the learner in a completely different direction. At times, Averroes would follow Aristotle and reason to conclusions contradicting Christian truth, such as matter being eternal (not created). Things changed with the arrival of Thomas Aquinas. His life work was to insist that good thinking never leads the learner away from God's truth. The truth that God reveals surpasses the truth we can achieve by reasoning, but they never contradict. As the popular saying goes, "All truth is God's truth."

THE PEAK OF RATIONAL REACH

To address controversies concerning doctrine, Thomas Aquinas (1224–1274) was dispatched to Paris from Italy. Thomas Aquinas (for his father's home, Aquino) was a Dominican monk of noble birth, brilliant mind, tireless industry, and gentle disposition: he, too, had turned to Aristotle but he had distinguished himself for his fidelity to the church. Unlike Averroes, Thomas taught that reason fit with revelation. The result was his *Summa Theologica* (a summation of theological knowledge).

The *Summa* has in view the whole universe. Thomas says at the beginning, "In sacred doctrine (theology) all things are treated from the standpoint of God, and the content of theology is in part God Himself and in part other beings in as far as they are ordained unto God."

Aquinas made a clear distinction between philosophy and theology, reason and revelation, but there is no contradiction between the two. Both are fountains of knowledge; both come from the same God.

St. Thomas Aquinas by Piero della Francesca, Poldi-Pezzoli Museum, Milan.

Thomas Aquinas (1224–1274) formulated Christian doctrine using the rational method. His masterpiece, Summa Theologica, *is still widely read by theologians and philosophers.*

The two differ in their methods of searching after truth. Reason is based upon the visible creation and can reach ideas that deal with "the vestibule of faith." Revelation looks to God as he is in himself and so is superior to reason both in its certainty and in its subject matter.

Reason, for example, can prove God's existence. Accepting Aristotle's principle (every effect has a cause, every cause a prior cause, and so on back to the First Cause) Thomas declared that creation traces back to a divine First Cause, the Creator.

However, the full knowledge of God—the Trinity, for example—comes only through revelation. From this knowledge we discover man's origin and destiny.

Man is a sinner and in need of special grace from God. Jesus Christ, by his sacrifice, has secured the reconciliation of man and God. All who receive the benefits of Christ's work are justified, but the key, as in traditional Catholic teaching, lies in the way the benefits of Christ's work are applied. Christ won grace; the church imparts it. Aquinas taught that Christians need the constant infusion of "cooperating grace," whereby the Christian virtues—above all, love—are stimulated in the soul. Assisted by this cooperating grace, a Christian can do works that please God and gain special merit in God's sight.

This saving grace, said Aquinas, comes to men exclusively through the channel of divinely appointed sacraments placed in the keeping of the church, the visible, organized Roman body, led by the pope. So convinced was Aquinas of the divine sanction of the papacy that he insisted that submission to the pope was necessary for salvation.

Aquinas followed Peter Lombard who had written the standard textbook for theology, in holding to seven sacraments: baptism, confirmation, the Lord's Supper, penance, extreme unction, marriage, and ordination.

The sacrament of all sacraments, however, is the Lord's Supper, which is more than the communion of the early church. As the Roman Church had for centuries, Aquinas held that it is a true sacrifice, continuing that of Christ on the cross, and predisposing God to be gracious to those for whom it was offered. In the Supper the essence or genuine being of the bread and wine are changed miraculously into the actual body and blood of Christ while the exterior remains unchanged. Thomas gives the classic presentation of this doctrine known as *transubstantiation*. Since sin remains a problem for the baptized Christian, God provided penance, the sacrament of spiritual healing. According to Thomas it consists of three elements: contrition or sorrow for the sin; confession to the priest as the spiritual physician who can apply the appropriate remedy and pronounce absolution; and satisfaction,

Magdeburg
Cologne Efurt
Rheims Worms BOHEMIA
Paris Spires
FRANCE Constance
Lyon
Cluny Milan Venice
Bologna
Albi Avignon Canossa
Florence
ARAGON Pisa Assisi
Rome

Significant Cities
of the Medieval Church

by which the Christian makes good the evil effects of the sin, usually called an "act of penance."

With some cautions Thomas also accepted the practice of indulgences that had gained prominence during the crusades. Aquinas taught that thanks to the work of Christ and the meritorious deeds of the saints, the church has access to a "treasury of merit," a great spiritual reservoir. Priests may draw from this to aid Christians who have insufficient merit of their own.

Death is the great divide. The wicked, said Thomas, pass into hell. The faithful who have wisely used the means of grace pass immediately to heaven. But the mass of mankind, who while Christian in desire and participants in the sacraments, have followed Christ inadequately, must suffer further purification in purgatory before attaining the joys of heaven. Thankfully these souls are not beyond the help of the church on earth. Prayers to the saints in heaven can prevail to relieve the pains of souls in purgatory.

Thus we come to the peak of ecclesiastical aspiration—and arrogance. Earth alone is not enough! The pope and his priests not only mediate the grace of God to sinners on earth by the miracle of the Blessed Sacrifice and by their prayers for the dead; they reach beyond the grave to minister to suffering souls.

There is nothing new in this. It had been said many times before. But Thomas set the traditional teachings of the church in a grand, almost cosmic, framework. Like the Gothic cathedral, his system aimed at a perfect harmony between the aspirations of man and the light of God's truth. It provided the papal monarchy an impressive supernatural view of this world and the next.

But like the crusades, Scholastic theology may have reached too far, claimed too much for itself and the church. A clue to the heights of arrogance lies in Innocent III's claim that the pope is the judge of the world, "set in the midst between God and man, below God and above man." The boast did not go unchallenged. A growing host of unlettered laymen remembered the apostolic testimony, "There is one God and one Mediator."

Suggestions for Further Reading

*Barron, Robert. *Thomas Aquinas: Spiritual Master.* 2nd ed. New York: Crossroad, 2008.

*Bauerschmidt, Frederick. *Holy Teaching: Introducing the Summa Theologiae of St. Thomas.* Grand Rapids: Brazos, 2005.

Daniel-Rops, H. *Cathedral and Crusade.* London: J. M. Dent, 1957.

Dauphinais, Michael, and Matthew Levering. *Knowing the Love of Christ: An Introduction to the Theology of St. Thomas Aquinas.* Notre Dame: University of Notre Dame Press, 2002.

Fremantle, Anne. *Age of Faith.* New York: Time-Life Books, 1968.

Haskins, Charles Homer. *The Rise of the Universities.* Ithaca, NY: Cornell University Press, 1957.

*Healy, Nicholas. *Thomas Aquinas: Theologian of the Christian Life.* Burlington, VT: Ashgate, 2003.

McGiffert, Arthur C. *A History of Christian Thought: From Tertullian to Erasmus.* New York: Scribner's, 1954.

Nichols, Aidan. *Discovering Aquinas: An Introduction to His Life, Work, and Influence.* Grand Rapids: Eerdmans, 2003.

CHAPTER 21

A SONG
TO LADY POVERTY

The Apostolic Lifestyle

E VERYONE, WE KNOW, LOVES a lover. Songs of endless devotion are not
new. The ballads of the troubadours filled the twelfth century.
They were all about courtly love: gallant knights, sinister magicians,
enchanted castles, talking animals, and, always, beautiful damsels.

Perhaps that is why so many felt drawn to St. Francis of Assisi. His
song was of Lady Poverty, his ideal for true Christianity and personal
holiness. Early in his preaching career, "Christ's very courageous
knight," as his first biographer called him, gave himself devotedly,
ardently to Poverty.

According to one of many stories told about him, Francis, with some
companions, went out in search of Poverty. Two old men told Francis
that she lived high in the mountains. Scaling the peaks, Francis found
her there "on the throne of her neediness." She welcomed the travel-
ers and Francis immediately praised her as "the queen of the virtues."
She replied that she had indeed been with Adam in Paradise, but after
he sinned she had become a homeless wanderer. Then Jesus came. He
made her his elect one, and through her believers multiplied. Monks
especially joined her until her enemy Avarice made them rich and
worldly. Then she no longer had a choice; she withdrew from monasticism. Upon hearing Poverty's story, Francis vowed to be faithful to her.
He took her as his bride, and she descended the mountain with him.

Francis was not the only spiritual knight devoted to Lady Poverty.
In the twelfth and thirteenth centuries she had a host of admirers.

Itinerant preaching and voluntary poverty appealed to the imaginations and consciences of many Christians. Growing numbers of laymen, instead of relying on the prayers of monks and bishops, read the
Bible in the vernacular and vowed to follow the gospel mandate: "Sell
what you have, give it to the poor, and come follow me." Some of these
believers chose orthodoxy, others opted for heresy, and at times only a
knife edge seemed to separate the two.

One thing was clear: Innocent III's vision of the ascended Christ who
ruled, through his Vicar, all nations, all learning, and all grace in this
life and the next, faced a formidable rival in the ancient image of the
Savior who said, "Foxes have holes and birds of the air have nests but
the Son of man has no place to lay his head." Where, after all, is true
Christianity? In a sacramental institution or in a self-denying lifestyle?

POVERTY, HERESY, AND VIOLENCE

The medieval poverty movement is a timeless reminder that political
Christianity is only partial Christianity. The Christian faith is more
than papal policy—much more. What shall it profit the church, as well
as men, to gain the world and lose her soul? What advantage are canon
laws, holy crusades, episcopal appointments, and scholastic disputa-
tions if common people receive a stone when asking for bread?

The gospel of voluntary poverty drew its strength from a deep and
widespread resentment of a corrupt and neglectful priesthood. The
back-to-the-apostles movement was often allied with political and economic restlessness in a rapidly changing and expanding society. But at
its heart was the spiritual hunger of people.

At a time when it was desperately needed, pastoral care was a lost art.
Robert Grosseteste, the able bishop of Lincoln, England (1235–1253),
decried the covetousness, greed, and immorality of the clergy: "As the
life of pastors is the book of the laity, it is manifest that such as these
are the preachers of all errors and wickedness." And the foundation of
all of this, said Grosseteste, is the Roman Court. It appoints not pastors
but destroyers of men.

Grosseteste's complaint had a familiar ring to it. As early as the tenth
century, monastic reformers had called for a return to the poverty of
the early church. Every zealous preacher knew if apostolic poverty
is the Christian ideal then bishops in their embellished palaces and
monks in their wealthy cloisters were not living the Christian life.

In earlier centuries, however, all such appeals to sacrifice were conveniently channeled into some new monastic reform. Within the church
itself, it was business as usual. The twelfth and thirteenth centuries

proved to be different. Not all preachers of apostolic poverty were willing to remain within the acceptable boundaries of the church. When they turned against the church they entered the ranks of heretics.

Modern Christians find it all but impossible to understand the medieval attitude toward heresy. We believe deeply that religious faith is a matter of personal choice but we seldom think of religious beliefs as life-and-death matters. Why should anyone either die for his own faith or kill another for his?

Medieval Christians, however, never considered faith strictly private. Christian beliefs were the cement of society; denying a doctrine was tantamount to treason. Christendom was, to shift the image, a sociopolitical body, and the Christian faith was its life-giving soul. So heresy in Christendom was no more acceptable than cancer in the flesh.

But what is heresy? In the twelfth century, it was the denial by a baptized person of any revealed truth of the Christian faith. Among these truths were the unity of the church and the divine appointment of the pope as head of the Christian body. Therefore, disobedience to established authority was itself heresy.

In dealing with heretics, then, the church had two primary objectives: the conversion of the heretic and the protection of Christian society. But how far can the church go to protect society? Is it right to take a life in order to protect other lives?

Heresy drove the Catholic Church to her most serious internal conflict: how can the church employ violence to safeguard a peaceful society? The church deliberately accepted a line of action all but impossible to reconcile with the eternal kingdom toward which she aspired. She created the Inquisition, not only to execute heretics but to subject them to deliberate and prolonged torture. In driving out one devil the church opened the door for seven others.

The contradiction was not widely apparent at the time. The same church that sent crusading armies against the infidels could command the burning of heretics. Almost everyone agreed that a pure church was the will of God.

THE POOR IN THE KINGDOM

But where is the one pure church? Is it in the papal palace in Rome? Is it in the blood of crusading armies or in the sale of indulgences to the poor? What if the one pure church is in none of these, but is in fact in the hungry who find bread, the naked who are clothed, and the stranger who finds rest? What if the kingdom of heaven does belong to the poor in spirit? That was the question Lady Poverty raised.

One of the earliest voices against the worldliness of the Catholic Church was Arnold, an abbot at Brescia, a town in northern Italy. In a series of sermons at Brescia, Arnold insisted that clerical vice was a result of the church's attempt to control the world. He urged the church to surrender its property and secular dominion to the state and return to the poverty and simplicity of the early church. The true church and its ministers, he said, should shun wealth, for wealth and power nullify salvation.

By 1139 Arnold succeeded in turning the people against their bishop. For this, the pope, Innocent II, banished Arnold from Italy. He apparently fled to Paris where he studied under Abelard and aroused the wrath of Bernard of Clairvaux, just as his teacher had succeeded in doing. Another "ravening wolf in sheep's clothing" Bernard called him.

After five years in exile Arnold showed up in Rome and immediately joined a movement to overthrow papal dominion. The Romans, filled with dreams of the ancient Roman republic, seized power during the pope's preaching tour for the Second Crusade and Arnold stepped into leadership of the new purely secular government. He preached that clergy should live in apostolic poverty, and he denounced the College of Cardinals as a den of thieves.

The experiment lasted about ten years before Pope Hadrian IV placed Rome under an interdict and secured the help of Emperor Frederick Barbarossa in capturing Arnold. In 1155 he was executed by burning and his ashes were thrown into the Tiber River.

People had scarcely forgotten Arnold when another voice for poverty arose in eastern France: Peter Waldo (c. 1140–1218), a rich merchant of Lyons.

One day Waldo heard a wandering troubadour singing the virtues of the monastic life. The ballad was about young Alexis whose patrician Roman parents pressed him into marriage. The reluctant groom, however, was dedicated to the ideal of chastity, so on his wedding night he made a pact of virgin purity with his bride and immediately left for the Holy Land.

Alexis' parents searched for him in vain. Years later he returned home a beggar, so emaciated from his life of self-denial that no one recognized him. He existed in the courtyard on scraps from the family table.

Only as he lay dying did he reveal his true identity, too late for the grieving family to claim him. The moral was pointed: a true Christian must be willing to sacrifice everything in this life for the sake of the next.

Struck to the heart by the story, Waldo sought a priest to find out how to live like Christ. The priest turned him to the answer Jesus gave to the rich young ruler: "If you would be perfect, go, sell what you possess and give to the poor, and you will have treasure in heaven; and come, follow me" (Matt. 19:21). The same text nine centuries before had launched the monastic movement with Anthony in Egypt.

Waldo decided to follow the counsel. He provided an adequate income for his wife, placed his two daughters in a cloister, and gave the rest of his estate to the poor.

To launch his mission to the poor, Waldo enlisted two priests to translate portions of the Bible into French. After memorizing long passages, Waldo began to teach common folk to imitate Christ by practicing voluntary poverty. Thus his innovations lay in applying the life of poverty, discipleship, and preaching to all true Christians, not just monks.

As he gained a few followers, Waldo sent them out two by two, after the apostolic pattern, into villages and marketplaces, to teach and explain the Scriptures. They called themselves the "Poor in Spirit." We know them as Waldenses.

Waldo's unauthorized preaching soon met the stiff opposition of the Archbishop of Lyon, who ordered him to stop. Waldo refused, quoting St. Peter: "We must obey God rather than men" (Acts 5:29). The Archbishop proceeded to excommunicate him.

Waldo and his followers decided to appeal to the pope. They arrived in Rome and found it crowded with churchmen attending the Third Lateran Council (1179). They were able to gain a hearing before the Council but had the misfortune to be ridiculed by a smooth, fast-talking Englishman named Walter Map.

Pope Alexander III found no evidence of heresy among them and was impressed by their poverty. They were mere laymen, however, so he ruled that they could preach only by the invitation of bishops, a very unlikely prospect.

Waldo was convinced that the Scriptures commanded him to preach to the poor with or without bishops' approval. Along with a growing number of followers, he continued to preach and practice apostolic poverty. The movement spread into southern France and across the Alps into Italy. By 1184 their disobedience compelled Pope Lucius III to excommunicate them from the holy Catholic Church.

The conflict is understandable. The Waldenses wanted to purify the church by a return to the simple life of the apostles. This meant the surrender of worldly power. Their aim, like that of the Roman church, was salvation. But their means were radically different. The papacy could not renounce its sacraments or its priesthood, nor admit that faith in God might be something other than the mandates of Rome. From their side, the Waldenses came to feel more and more that no teaching except Christ's was binding. The Scriptures must rule. But how could they find support for their cause if everyone lived in apostolic poverty? Slowly they came to accept, just as early monastic houses had, two levels of Christian commitment. The "Poor in Spirit," the society proper, was bound by special vows and worshiped together in simple services. Another circle of "friends" remained in the Catholic Church but supplied recruits and support for the movement.

The Waldenses were so clearly a back-to-the-Bible movement that over the years many evangelical Christians have tried to present them as "reformers before the Reformation." Compared to the Roman church's doctrine of papal authority, the Waldensian call to return to the Bible does indeed sound like Luther or Calvin. But their view of salvation, a life of penance and poverty, lacks the clear note of God's grace that sounded so powerfully in the Reformation.

THE PERIL OF NEW HERESIES

A third dissenting movement, and by far the most troublesome for the Catholic Church, was the group commonly called *Cathari*, which means *pure ones*. Since they were especially influential in and about the town of Albi in southern France, some people called them Albigenses.

Most of what we know about the Albigenses comes through their enemies and, as Charles Williams once observed, not one mind in a thousand can be trusted to state accurately what one's opponent says, much less what he thinks.

Very likely, however, the Cathari infiltrated Europe from Bulgaria, where one of their chief branches bore the name Bogomiles. Like the Gnostics in the early church, the Cathari held that the universe is the scene of an eternal conflict between two powers, the one good, the other evil. Matter, including the human body, is the work of this evil power, the god of the Old Testament. He had, they claimed, imprisoned the human soul in its earthly body.

To escape from the power of the flesh, the true Cathar was supposed to avoid marriage, sexual intercourse, eating of meat, and material possessions. Here was a radical poverty, but not one based on the example of Jesus so much or the nature of the universe. A cosmic civil war raged between matter and spirit, and the Cathari joined the ranks of spirit.

The good God, they taught, sent Christ to reveal the way of salvation to man; Christ, to a Cathar, was not a human being but a life-giving spirit. A human Christ was an impossibility, and salvation by death on the cross was unthinkable. Christ taught the way, like a Buddha rather than the God-man of Christian creeds.

Obviously the Cathari were heretical in a way Arnold of Brescia and Peter Waldo were not. Arnold and Waldo refused to submit to church authorities, but the Cathari rejected not only popes and bishops but basic Christianity. They tried to escape from evil, not by repentance and faith but by discovering and liberating the pure self.

The Cathari were an immense peril to the Roman church. Not only had they revived the ancient dualist heresy; by 1200 they had gained the protection of the princes of Toulouse, a cultural area in southern France, and were spreading at an alarming rate. Three weapons were at the Catholic Church's disposal: preaching to return them to the truth, a crusade to crush all hardened resistance, and the Inquisition to uproot heresy completely.

RISE OF THE DOMINICANS

The popes tried sending preachers among the Cathari, but they were notoriously ineffective, at least until a Spaniard named Dominic Guzman (1170–1221) struck upon the reason. In 1206 Dominic was helping in efforts to convert the Albigenses when he realized that the papally assigned preachers were depending upon their ecclesiastical pomp and dignity. The Albigenses considered such show a sure sign of false religion. Dominic believed that the heretics would listen if the preachers themselves were committed to poverty. To win the heretics, Dominic went forth among them as a poor man, barefoot and begging.

Dominic's peaceful mission lasted only two years in southern France before it was forced aside by Innocent III's get tough policy. However, the zealous Spaniard was convinced that poverty and preaching belonged together. He gathered a group of like-minded men and continued his work among the heretics in other places. In 1220 the Dominican mission and lifestyle gained official approval. The new preaching order that we know as Dominicans was called *mendicant*, meaning begging, and the term *friar* (or brother) distinguished them from monks because, unlike monks, they went forth to live among people to preach and teach. Just as monastic houses had once arisen to minister in the countryside, so the mendicant friars now emerged to meet the spiritual needs of townspeople.

Meanwhile, Innocent III was determined to crush the Albigensian heresy. The northern French were itching for a chance to gobble up southern France, which was then a separate country. When Innocent called for a crusade—not against the Muslim Turks but against Christian heretics—the northern French came pillaging and murdering. It isn't often that good Christian men can save their souls and at the same time enlarge their kingdoms by butchering unbelievers. Even Innocent was shocked by the brutality. But the crusade was eminently successful. By 1215 the Albigenses were uprooted in Toulouse and the northern French had claimed the ravaged territories of the south.

ENTER THE INQUISITOR

The scattered heretics had to be hounded out of hiding. That was the purpose of the Inquisition. The infamy of this institution has left its mark on the memories and vocabularies of men everywhere. We equate it with the ruthless miscarriage of justice.

The early form of the Inquisition appeared in 1184 when Pope Lucius III required bishops to "inquire" into the beliefs of their subjects. In short, they held an inquiry or inquest. Heresy or harboring a heretic brought immediate excommunication.

The spread of the Albigenses and their own violence toward loyal Catholics called for stricter measures. In 1215 the Fourth Lateran Council, under Innocent III's leadership, provided for the state's punishment of heretics, the confiscation of their property, excommunication for those unwilling to move against the heretic, and complete forgiveness of sins for those cooperating.

In 1220 the pope took the Inquisition from the hands of the bishops and turned it over to the newly-formed Dominicans, and nine years later the Synod of Toulouse systematized inquisitorial policies, leaving the alleged heretic with virtually no rights. The inquisitor was subject to no law, only to the pope. He was prosecutor and judge. The "trial" was secret, and the accused had to prove his innocence, as in all courts following Roman law, without the benefit of counsel or knowledge of his accusers.

The final significant step came in 1252. Pope Innocent IV authorized torture as a means of getting information and confessions from accused heretics. Popes, saints, and theologians had in the past rejected with horror the very thought. But no such reserve remained after Innocent III had ascended the papal throne and the Catholic Church had achieved its majestic and powerful unity.

Canon Law, it is true, forbade a cleric from shedding blood. He who served the altars of the One Sacrifice must not sacrifice men. He could only hound and interrogate and torture the prisoner. If he found the unfortunate person guilty of heresy, he turned him over to civil authorities, usually for burning at the stake.

It was an ugly business, but almost everyone, after Augustine, agreed that saving the body by amputating a rotten limb was the path of wisdom. Clearly the Church of Rome was the body and the heretic the rotten limb.

The combination of the crusade against heresy in Toulouse and the Inquisition brought an end to Catharism before the thirteenth century closed. The doctrine that matter was incapable of salvation was, until the coming of Mary Baker Eddy, a thing of the past. The Waldenses, who were often targets of the same Inquisition, survived in the mountains of Italy and welcomed the Reformation when it broke over Europe in the sixteenth century.

The Inquisition also survived, even with its serious weakness. It could amputate, but it could not heal. The ministry of healing arose in a village surrounded by vineyards eighty-five miles north of Rome. Assisi was the hometown of Giovanni Bernardone; we know him as St. Francis of Assisi. Francis (1182–1226) was the son of a wealthy Italian cloth merchant. Francis' father had dreams of knighthood for his son. Francis pursued the glory of military service, but his capture, illness, and a series of visions led him to turn his back on his father's dreams. The re-orientation was dramatic. Before his turning he benefited from wealth, sought honor, and was repulsed by illness like leprosy. With Christ as his model, he abandoned the security of wealth, lived a humble life dedicated to benefiting others, and embraced lepers. Leaving home in a ragged cloak and a rope-belt taken from a scarecrow, he wandered the countryside with a few followers, begging from the rich, giving to the poor, and preaching the joys of apostolic poverty.

FOUNDING THE FRANCISCANS

In 1209 Francis prepared a simple Rule for his little brotherhood. It consisted chiefly of Christ's appeal to take up the cross, his advice to the rich young ruler, and his directions on sending out the apostles. With this Rule, Francis and his companions went to Pope Innocent III for approval. The scene was almost a reproduction of Waldo before Alexander III in 1179, but times had changed. Innocent saw the mistake others had made, so he approved the little preaching band. Francis called his group the Friars Minor (Lesser Brothers). We call them the Franciscans.

Almost from the start Francis' vision was for the world. He tried to go to Syria and to Morocco but was thwarted by misfortune. Then in

1219 a crusading expedition to Egypt gave him his opportunity. With eleven companions he accompanied the army to the Middle East where he tried unsuccessfully to convert the Sultan of Egypt. From Egypt he visited the holy places in Palestine, and it was more than a year before he again saw Italy.

During his absence differences arose among the brothers. Some felt that their rapid growth demanded more organization, more rules, more supervision. Others tried to cling to the original principles of Christ-like poverty.

Upon Francis' return to Italy, he saw that the problems were more than he could handle. He was a model, not a manager. So he appealed to the pope to appoint Cardinal Ugolino as his adviser and soon he surrendered the administration of the brotherhood to his associate Peter de Cataneo. "Lord Jesus," he prayed, "I give Thee back this family which Thou didst entrust to me. Thou knowest that I have no longer the strength or the ability to take care of it." It is a familiar scene in Christian organizations. One man establishes; another man administers.

Ugolino, who later became Pope Gregory IX, admired Francis greatly, but he was above all a prince of the church. He saw the possibilities of the movement as an agent for the advancement of the Roman church, especially where its authority had been undermined by Arnold, Waldo, and the Cathari. He would reform the church by giving the Franciscans authority; Francis wanted to reform the world by preaching Christ-like humility.

In 1223 Pope Honorius III confirmed a new Rule for the order, which allowed for an elaborate organization and made begging a fundamental trait of the order. Thus Franciscans joined Dominicans in a great mendicant counteroffensive in preaching, doctrine, and dedication. As his end drew near, he was carried back to Assisi and died there on October 3, 1226, in full humility and song.

Francis was a product of his age, a lover of Lady Poverty, but he belongs to all the Christian centuries. "For a few years," wrote Herbert Workman, "the Sermon on the Mount became a realized fact. But the dream passed" from all but a few.

For another century the Franciscans were divided between the Conventuals, who allowed the church to hold property for Franciscan use, and the Spirituals, who argued that complete poverty was an indispensable note of the true church.

Thus Lady Poverty remained a challenge to the church of wealth and power, but like Innocent III's vision of universal dominion, it proved an impossibility for the whole church for all times.

Suggestions for Further Reading

Baldwin, Marshall W. *The Mediaeval Church*. Ithaca, NY: Cornell University Press, 1953.

Gobry, Ivan. *St. Francis Assisi*. San Francisco: Ignatius, 2006.

Lambert, Malcolm. *Medieval Heresy*. New York: Holmes & Meier, 1976.

Runciman, Steven. *The Medieval Manichee*. London: Cambridge University Press, 1955.

Thompson, Augustine. *Francis of Assisi: A New Biography*. New York: Cornell University Press, 2012.

Turberville, A. S. *Medieval Heresy and the Inquisition*. London: Archon, 1964.

Westin, Gunnar. *The Free Church through the Ages*. Nashville: Broadman, 1958.

Workman, Herbert B. *The Evolution of the Monastic Ideal*. Boston: Beacon Press, 1962.

CHAPTER 22

SLEEPING MEN AND THE LAW OF NECESSITY

The Decline of the Papacy

THE FOURTEENTH CENTURY APPEARED to break upon Europe on a triumphant note. On February 22, 1300, Pope Boniface VIII proclaimed a Jubilee—a Holy Year—to celebrate the new centenary of Christ's birth. It was the first of its kind. The official decree announced "a full and copious pardon of all their sins" for all who reverently visited the churches of St. Peter and St. Paul during the Holy Year. Joyous throngs poured into the Eternal City.

Six and three-quarter centuries later, Pope Paul VI echoed Boniface's words in announcing that 1975 would be another Holy Year. The "gift of the Plenary Indulgence" were Paul's words. And as in the first Holy Year Rome threw open her arms to the throngs who came.

Boniface VIII (1294–1303), the founder of the Holy Years, had a flair for pomp and circumstance. Several times he appeared before the pilgrims in imperial robes crying "I am Caesar. I am emperor." According to reports his papal crown contained forty-eight rubies, seventy-two sapphires, forty-five emeralds, and sixty-six large pearls. He could afford to be generous with pardons for spiritual pilgrims. At the Church of St. Paul, according to one chronicler, generous celebrants kept two priests busy night and day "raking together infinite money."

The decades ahead looked bright to Boniface because for two centuries the papacy had held an unrivaled peak of power, religious and political. The pope had before him the sparkling example of Innocent III, a pope highly skilled at imposing his will upon emperors and kings. Boniface naturally assumed that he could continue the same practice.

Within three years of the Jubilee, however, Boniface was to die of the shock of the greatest personal insult ever inflicted upon a pope. Even as Jubilee celebrants rejoiced, forces were at work that marked the beginning of the end of medieval papal sovereignty.

How could such a thing happen? Why did men and nations come to challenge the worldly power of the popes?

SLEEP AND CHANGE IN THE KINGDOM

Jesus once told a parable about a man who scattered seed on the ground (Mark 4:26–29). Night and day, whether the man was asleep or awake, the seed sprouted and grew. At times the man had no idea how the grain grew. The soil simply produced the stalk then the head and finally the full kernel in the head all by itself. This is what Jesus said the kingdom of God was like.

Significant changes often take place in the church and in the world, and men are totally unaware of what is happening. The fourteenth century was such a time. The papacy in particular continued its business-as-usual attitude while important ideas and social forces changed the face of Christianity. We call the period between 1300 and 1500 the age of "the decline of the Middle Ages" because the idea of Christendom, which unified the millennium between the fourth and fourteenth centuries, was under vigorous attack.

Christendom was made possible by the harmony of two ideas, the Christian empire and the Catholic Church. The image of a Christian empire, so useful in creating a unified Europe in the seventh and eighth centuries, slowly faded in importance in the twelfth and thirteenth centuries as the papal influence spread. Innocent III demonstrated that papal sovereignty was far more effective in rallying princes for a crusade or defending the faith against heretics.

The significance of the fourteenth and fifteenth centuries lies not only in the further decline of the empire, but in the dramatic loss of papal prestige.

The fourteenth century is too early to speak of *nations* in the modern sense of the term, but more and more people were getting used to the idea that they were English or French whenever their thoughts reached beyond their own town or religion. And perhaps more importantly they found it possible to think of their "state" functioning without direct papal guidance. In modern terms, they began to think of secular and sacred affairs, a realm for the state as well as a realm for the church. This new way of looking at the world appears most vividly in the events swirling about the popes.

Europe was slowly moving away from its feudal past. Land was less important; hard cash was the new thing. Increasingly, men at the top of the medieval power structure realized that they had to command ever-larger sources of revenue. This, in turn, required a broader authority to tax. The struggle between the church and the brash national monarchies of England and France touched off the turmoil of the fourteenth century.

Edward I ruled in England; Philip the Fair in France. Both were strong and self-assured and at odds with each other over lands in France still under English control. To finance their costly campaigns, Edward and Philip hit upon the same solution: tax the clergy within their realms. But, in the pope's view, church revenues were exempt from compulsory assessments and taxable only by the church.

In 1296 Boniface VIII had issued *Clericis laicos*, a document threatening excommunication for any lay ruler who taxed the clergy and any churchman who paid those taxes without papal consent. But Edward and Philip were a new breed of secular monarch, unimpressed by threats from Rome. Edward's retort was to decree that if the clergy did not pay, they would be stripped of all legal protection and their extensive properties would be seized by the king's sheriffs. Phillip's answer was to place a complete embargo on the export of all gold, silver, and jewels from his domains, thus depriving the papal treasury of a major source of revenue from church collections in France.

Faced with such stiff opposition, Boniface had backed down, explaining that he had not meant to cut off clerical contributions for defense in times of dire need. Since the kings could decide what constituted "defense" and "dire need," the victory for Edward and Philip was clear.

A NEW VOICE IN CHRISTENDOM

The royal victory, however, was far from complete. Buoyed by the smashing success of the Jubilee year, Boniface concluded that the spiritual reverence manifested for him in every corner of Christendom extended to the civil sphere as well. He had a second circlet added to his crown as a symbol of his temporal sovereignty. Concentrating his fire upon Philip, the pope determined to teach the French monarch a lesson. Philip, however, represented a strident new voice in Christendom. Jesus Christ, he held, gave the church no temporal authority.

In 1301 the king imprisoned a French bishop on charges of treason. Boniface ordered the official's release and rescinded his earlier concession on taxation of church lands. The next year Philip responded by summoning representatives of the French nobility, clergy, and bourgeoisie (the debut of his national assembly, the Estates-General) and mustering their unanimous support in his quarrel with the pope. One of Philip's ministers put the choice baldly: "My master's sword is made of steel; the pope's is made of words."

Several months later Boniface issued *Unam sanctam*, the most extreme assertion of papal power in all church history. This time Boniface made his meaning unmistakable. "It is altogether necessary," he declared, "for every human being to be subject to the Roman pontiff." The king's countermove was no less drastic. He prepared to have Boniface deposed on the ground that his election had been illegal. To execute this plan he chose William of Nogaret, a shrewd lawyer who was helping Philip build the foundations of his nation.

Nogaret was also a master of the trumped-up charge. He had been known to approve the use of "voluntary" testimony obtained by such a device as stripping a witness, smearing him with honey, and hanging him over a beehive. His case against Boniface included not only the illegitimacy of his election, but heresy, simony, and immorality. Armed with authority from an assembly of French churchmen and nobles, he rushed to Italy determined to bring the pope to France for trial before a special church council.

Boniface, now eighty-six, had left the heat of Rome to summer in the foothills of the Apennine Mountains at his birthplace, Anagni. Nogaret and some troops he had marshaled broke in on the aged Boniface in his bedroom. Whether they actually manhandled him is in dispute. But certainly they heaped abuse upon him. They kept him prisoner for several days. When the plain people of Anagni realized what was happening, they rose up and rescued Boniface. Numbed and humiliated, the aged pope died within weeks. Contemporaries said, "He crept in like a fox, reigned like a lion, and died like a dog."

What is the significance of the Anagni episode? It reveals that European Christians no longer accepted papal interference in what they regarded as purely political matters. No one could say with certainty what a purely political matter was, but a king's power within his own country was a generally accepted fact. At the same time an outrage against a pope, even an unpopular one, was widely resented. Boniface was not a beloved pope; he was a target of widespread criticism. Dante, the Italian genius who wrote *The Divine Comedy*, reserved a place in hell for him! Yet he was the Vicar of Christ. Not many men at that time could conceive of Christianity without the Holy Father.

Thus, even when they had no political terms for it, men in the early fourteenth century were beginning to distinguish secular and religious authority and to recognize the rights of each in its own place. And that was new.

Anagni came to symbolize the descent of papal power, even as Canossa, some two centuries before, had symbolized its ascent. When Boniface's successor in Rome died after a brief, ineffectual reign, Philip's daring coup bore its fruit. In 1305 the College of Cardinals elected a Frenchman, the Archbishop of Bordeaux, as Pope Clement V. Clement never set foot in Rome, preferring to stay closer to home, where he was always accessible to royal bidding.

THE CAPTIVITY OF THE HOLY FATHER

Clement's election marked the start of the seventy-two-year period in church history called, after the long exile of the ancient Jews in Babylon, the Babylonian Captivity of the papacy. Following Clement, six successive popes, all of French origin, chose to reside in a little town called Avignon rather than in Rome. Avignon was located on the Rhone River just across from the borders of Philip's domain. Under the popes the town grew to a busy city of eighty thousand with its immense clerical bureaucracy and the sumptuous papal palace.

This removal of the papacy to Avignon was more than a matter of geography. In the thinking of European people, Rome, the Eternal City, stood not only for the idea of the apostolic succession of the church founded upon St. Peter, but also the concept of western universality, Roman *imperium*. Avignon, on the other hand, was surrounded on all sides by the French kingdom and was a mere tool in the hands of one nation, the power-hungry French.

The Avignon papacy was bitterly resented in Germany. In 1324 the emperor Louis the Bavarian (1314–1347) moved against Pope John XXII by appealing to a general council. Among the scholars supporting such a move was Marsilius of Padua who had fled from the University of Paris. In 1326 Marsilius and his colleague John of Jandun presented Louis with a work titled *Defender of the Peace*, which questioned the whole papal structure of the church and called for a democratic government. *Defender of the Peace* asserted that the church was the community of all believers and that the priesthood was not superior to the laity. Neither popes nor bishops nor priests had received any special function from

Christ; they served only as agents of the community of believers, which was represented by the general council.

This radical and revolutionary view of the church transformed the papacy into the executive office of the council and subordinated the pope to the authority of the council. The theory, called conciliarism, would soon find a place not only in theory but in fact.

Most of the hostility aimed at the Avignon papacy complained of the use and abuse of money. The decline in revenues from the Papal States in Italy had brought the papal court to bankruptcy. To replace these funds and raise new ones the Avignon popes resorted to a host of moneymaking schemes, some old, some new. There were fees for this privilege and taxes for that. For example, the popes introduced the rule that whenever a bishop was appointed, the first year's income, called an *annat*, should go to the pope. To fill a vacancy popes often transferred a bishop from another city and thus created more *annates*. Or perhaps the pope delayed the appointment and received all the income in the interim. This was called a *reservation*.

The most lucrative practice, however, was the granting of indulgences. These were dispensed for the most minor reasons, from building bridges to waging war, and extravagant claims of their spiritual benefits mounted with each generation. Bitter feelings against the papacy increased, especially when the Holy Father demanded this tax or that revenue under threats of excommunication.

By 1360 turmoil in Italy over the Papal States plus the outcries against the French domination of the papacy made it clear that the Avignon papacy could not continue indefinitely. No one could foresee, however, the outrageous events the return to Rome would bring.

In 1377 the aged Pope Gregory XI reentered Rome. The joy over the reestablishment of the papacy in the Eternal City was short-lived. Gregory's death within a year required a new papal election. The College of Cardinals, still heavily weighted with Frenchmen, yielded to the clamor of a Roman mob and chose an Italian. On April 18, Easter Sunday, the new pope, Urban VI, was crowned. All the cardinals were present. The summer months, however, along with Urban's dictatorial ways, brought second thoughts about his selection. In August the cardinals suddenly informed all Europe that the people of Rome had forced the election of an apostate to the chair of Peter and the proceedings were invalid.

A month later the "apostate" responded by creating practically a new College of Cardinals. For their part the French cardinals chose from their own number another pope, Clement VII, and announced this fact to the various civil and church authorities. Clement VII moved about Italy and eventually sailed for France and Avignon.

THE GREAT PAPAL SCHISM

Thus, with Urban ruling from Rome and Clement from Avignon, the murky chapter in papal history called the Great Schism of the papacy begins. It lasted for thirty-nine years. Each pope had his own College of Cardinals, thereby insuring the papal succession of its own choice. Each pope claimed to be the true Vicar of Christ, with the power to excommunicate those who did not acknowledge him.

Such breaches had occurred before. Both before and after this schism there were pious souls who rejected the claims of the Roman church. But now no one was rejecting any such claims—no one except the Church of Rome itself. It was engaged both in promoting and rejecting its own pontiff.

The proper identity of the true pope was a matter of considerable importance to Christendom. Unfortunately, the only witnesses to the problem, the cardinals, contradicted themselves flatly. If what they said in April was true, then what they said in September was not true. If what they said in September was accurate, then what they said in April was not. It was left to universities, kings, bishops, dukes, and just about everyone else to decide who was the true Vicar of Christ.

France went with Clement; Italy with Urban. The empire went with Urban; so did England. Scotland went with Clement. But within each country minorities existed. Tumults and riots broke out. Property was burned and crusades were preached. A house divided against itself could not stand.

In 1395 leading professors at the University of Paris proposed that a general council, representing the Universal Church, should meet to heal the schism. But difficulties immediately arose. Canon Law said that only the pope could call a general council; and only the pope could ratify any decision of a general council. Which pope had those rights? In effect Canon Law prohibited the reunion of Christendom! Was necessity a higher law?

A NEW POPE ELECTED

By 1409 a majority of the cardinals from both camps agreed that it was. They met for a general council at Pisa, on the west coast of Italy. They deposed both claimants to the papal chair, and elected a third man, Alexander V. Neither of the two deposed popes, however, would accept the action of the council. So the church now had not two, but three claimants to the chair of Peter.

Three popes at a time are too many by almost anyone's standards, especially so when one of the popes preaches a crusade against another and starts selling indulgences to pay for it. This bizarre spectacle stirred Europe sufficiently to goad its leaders into firm action. In 1414 the Holy Roman Emperor assembled at the German city of Constance, the most impressive church gathering of this era. Even the Greek Ortho- dox Church sent representatives.

The Decline of the Middle Ages

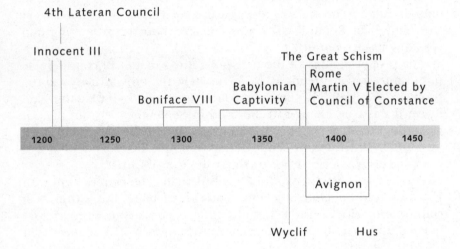

For the first time voting took place on a purely national basis. Instead of the traditional assembly of bishops, the council included lay representatives and was organized as a convention of "nations" (Ger- man, Italian, French, and English, the Spanish entering later). Each nation had one vote. The national structure of the council was highly significant. It shows that the church was reluctantly coming to realize the new national alignment of power.

At length, in 1417, the council got one papal incumbent to step aside, deposed the other two and chose a new Vicar of Christ, Martin V. One of the deposed popes, Benedict XIII of Avignon, clung to his claim, but for all practical purposes, the council in Constance ended the Great Schism.

Necessity had triumphed; yet it was promptly denied. Martin reigned precisely because of the council's action. Yet as soon as he was pope, he repudiated all acts of the council, except the one by which he ruled. The legal mind of the Roman church had never encountered so great a contradiction, not of theory, but of practice.

Martin had good reason to deny the work of the council for it raised a very important question: who is greater, a general council that creates the pope, or the pope who claims supremacy over councils?

The conciliar movement aimed at transforming the papacy into something like a limited monarchy. Constance solemnly decreed that general councils were superior to popes and that they should meet at regular intervals in the future. The pope called this heretical. His return to power plus the inability of later councils to introduce much-needed reforms enabled the popes, by 1450, to discredit the conciliar movement. They busied themselves not with religious reforms but with Italian politics and patronage of the arts. The pope often could not make up his mind whether he was the successor of Peter or of Caesar. Political corruption and immorality in the Vatican reached unbelievable heights under Roderigo Borgia, who ruled as Alexander VI (1492–1503). He was grossly immoral and obsessed with his passion to provide wealth and power for his children.

Thus, Constance could be denied, but it could not be forgotten. Estrangement from the pope was growing. Men began to think in terms of "national churches," and the church governed by representative bodies. The challenge of the Protestant Reformation was already prepared.

Suggestions for Further Reading

Baldwin, Marshall W. *The Mediaeval Church*. Ithaca, NY: Cornell University Press, 1953.

Deanesly, Margaret. *A History of the Medieval Church 590–1500*. London: Methuen, 1969.

Heinze, Rudolph W. *Reform and Conflict: From the Medieval World to the Wars of Religion, AD 1350–1648, Baker History of the Church*. Vol. 4. Grand Rapids: Baker, 2004

Hollis, Christopher, ed., *The Papacy*. New York: Macmillan, 1964.

*Logan, F. Donald. *A History of the Church in the Middle Ages*. New York: Routledge, 2013.

Schaff, Philip. *History of the Christian Church, Volume V, The Middle Ages (Part I), AD 1049–1294*. Grand Rapids: Eerdmans, 1957.

*Southern, R. W. *Western Society and the Church in the Middle Ages. The Penguin History of the Church*. Vol. 2. New York: Penguin, 1990.

CHAPTER 23

JUDGMENT IN THE PROCESS OF TIME

Wyclif and Hus

IN HIS INSIGHTFUL LITTLE volume *Christianity and History*, Herbert But-terfield observes that human systems rise and thrive and then fall because the processes of time have their own built-in "judgment." Institutions, which at first glance seem to be quite worthy, eventually crumble to ruins because the centuries themselves bring out the flaws.

The Babylonian Captivity at Avignon and the Great Schism of the papacy that followed revealed fundamental flaws. Basic reforms were in order, but after the failure of the conciliar movement no significant reforms came from within the Church of Rome. The idea that the papal office was the channel of God's will died slowly. Men believed that the papacy was essential not only for the religious life of men but as a means of sanctioning political rule. He was the center of the Christian society on earth.

Two brave souls—John Wyclif, an Englishman, and John Hus, a Czech—dared to toy with the idea that the Christian church was something other than a visible organization on earth headed by the pope. They paid dearly for even raising the possibility, but they saw clearly that the hour had come for judgment to fall upon the house of God. Who were they? And how did they point the way to the future?

THE ENGLISH ZEALOT, WYCLIF

John Wyclif was a zealot. Like most zealots, he despised neutrality, and he got as much as he gave. Since his day, men have either praised him to high heaven or consigned him to outer darkness.

Confusion about the real Wyclif is understandable. We really know little about the man. He had an exasperating habit of burying his character beneath pages of scholarly discourse, and while historians can follow his arguments well enough, few claim they understand *him*.

Wyclif's early life is as obscure as his personality. We are not even sure of his date of birth. He was reared in northern England but only emerged from the medieval mists as a student at Oxford. He secured his doctoral degree in 1372 and rose immediately to prominence as the leading professor at the university.

The hottest issue at that hour was *dominion* or *lordship* over men. All thinkers agreed that lordship arose from God. But how was this right to rule transmitted from God to earthly rulers? One widely held view argued that lordship was only just when it derived from the Roman church. God had entrusted the pope with universal dominion over all temporal things and persons. Any authority exercised by sinful rulers was unlawful.

Other teachers insisted that lordship depended less on the mediation of the church than on the fact that its possessor was in a state of grace, that is, he had committed no grievous sin. One of Wyclif's professors, Richard FitzRalph, had argued, "Why should the state of grace be required only of temporal rulers? Do churchmen have the right to rule when they live in mortal sin?" If grace is essential in a lay ruler, said FitzRalph, it is no less necessary in a churchman.

Undoubtedly influenced by his professor, Wyclif plunged into this debate and added an important idea. He argued that the English government had the divinely assigned responsibility to correct the abuses of the church within its realm and to relieve of office those churchmen who persisted in their sin. The state could even seize the property of corrupt church officials.

Not surprisingly, the pope in 1377 condemned the Oxford Reformer's teaching. The church might have moved against Wyclif at that moment, but influential friends in England saw to it that the condemnation never went beyond threats.

The long-range significance of Wyclif's teaching on dominion lies in its link with the Reformation. It was the English Reformer's way of emphasizing the spiritual freedom of the righteous man. He is a possessor of "a dominion founded on grace": "God gives no lordship to

His servants without first giving Himself to them." Every man, therefore, priest or layman, holds an equal place in the eyes of God. This personal relation between a man and God is everything; character is the one basis of office. The mediating priesthood and the sacrificial masses of the medieval church are no longer essential. Thus Wyclif anticipates Luther's doctrine of justification by faith alone. Both men destroy the medieval barriers between God and his people.

This doctrine of "dominion founded in grace" proved to be only the first of Wyclif's thunderbolts. The decisive year of his reforming career was 1378, the date of the Great Schism in the papacy. Faced with the comic-tragedy of one pope in Rome excommunicating another pope in Avignon, Wyclif became more radical in his assessment of the church and its need for reform.

Wyclif's early views of the papacy were shaped by his emphasis on apostolic poverty. He insisted that those who sat in St. Peter's chair should be, like the apostle, without silver or gold. According to Wyclif the "Bible papacy" consisted in a poor and humble life, spent in the service of the church, setting before God's people an example of Christian goodness. The pope should be the shepherd of the flock and the preacher who brings men to Christ.

Such a view leaves no room for the temporal power of the pope. The conception of the papacy as a political force was anathema to Wyclif. He detested the trappings of power; he denounced the worldliness and luxury of the popes.

In one sense Wyclif welcomed the Great Schism. The spectacle of two rival popes excommunicating each other seemed to him to be a confirmation for all to see of the spiritual bankruptcy of the office and the need to put something else in its place. As the schism continued, however, Wyclif's view hardened. He came to believe that the pope was Antichrist. If there were two of them railing at each other, they simply shared the unholy title.

In a steady stream of charges Wyclif showed how far the papacy had departed from the simple faith and practice of Christ and his disciples. "Christ is truth," he wrote, "the pope is the principle of falsehood. Christ lived in poverty, the pope labors for worldly magnificence. Christ refused temporal dominion, the pope seeks it."

The Oxford Reformer poured scorn on the idea that because Peter died in Rome therefore every bishop of Rome is to be set above all of Christendom. By the same reasoning the Muslim might conclude that his "prelate of Jerusalem," where Christ died, is greater than the pope. Christ alone, said Wyclif, is the head of the church. The papal institution is "full of poison." It is Antichrist itself, the man of sin who exalts himself above God. Let judgment fall!

FROM REFORMER TO PROTESTANT

Thus the Reformer took the great step of his life. He passed from an orthodox preacher eager for the reform of the existing international Roman church, into a Protestant, to use a later term.

The Oxford scholar's break with the papacy was part of a new idea that he had formed of the church. He accepts the ancient division of the church into three parts: "one triumphant in heaven," "one militant here on earth," and the third "asleep in purgatory." But the church on earth he defines as the whole number of the elect, containing "only men that shall be saved." So absolute is his predestinarianism that he adds that no man, not even a pope, knows whether he is of the church, or whether he is "a limb of the fiend." Wyclif guards his doctrine from some of its dangers by adding that "as each man shall hope that he shall be safe in bliss, so he should suppose that he be a limb of holy church," and even maintains that "each man that shall be damned shall be damned by his own guilt, and each man that is saved shall be saved by his own merit."

From this doctrine of an invisible church of the elect, Wyclif drew some practical conclusions. The church is a unity that knows nothing of papal primacies and hierarchies, and of the "sects" of monks, friars, and priests; nor can the salvation of the elect be conditioned by masses, indulgences, penance, or other devices of priestcraft.

In time Wyclif challenged the whole range of medieval beliefs and practices: pardons, indulgences, absolutions, pilgrimages, the worship of images, the adoration of the saints, the treasury of their merits laid up at the reserve of the pope, and the distinction between venial and mortal sins. He retained belief in purgatory and extreme unction, though he admitted that he looked in vain in the Bible for the institution of extreme unction. Images, he said, if they increased devotion, need not be removed; and prayers to saints were not necessarily wrong. Confession he held to be useful, provided it was voluntary and made to a suitable person, best of all if it were made in public. Compulsory confession he considered "the bondage of Antichrist." We can catch the spirit of his revolt in his declaration that preaching "is of more value than the administration of any sacrament."

The standard Wyclif used to judge the Roman Church was the teachings of Scripture. "Neither the testimony of Augustine nor Jerome," he said, "nor any other saint should be accepted except in so far as it was based upon Scripture." "Christ's law," he held, "is best and enough, and other laws men should not take, but as branches of God's law."

John Wyclif (1300–1384), the English reformer, denounced the worldliness of the popes and emphasized the spiritual freedom of the righteous man.

John Hus (1369–1415), the Czech reformer, viewed Christ, not the pope, as the head of the church.

The Oxford Reformer went even further in his assertion of the right of every man to examine the Bible for himself: "The New Testament is of full authority, and open to the understanding of simple men, as to the points that be most needful to salvation . . . . He that keepeth meekness and charity hath the true understanding and perfection of all Holy Writ," for "Christ did not write his laws on tables, or on skins of animals, but in the hearts of men."

In all of his puritan outcry, Wyclif aroused no hostility like that sparked by his attack upon the traditional doctrine of transubstantiation. In the summer of 1380 he published twelve arguments against the idea that the bread and wine of Holy Communion were transformed into the physical body and blood of Christ. He asserts that the early church held that the consecrated elements of bread and wine were efficacious symbols of Christ's body and blood. Hence, Christ is present in the elements sacramentally, not materially. The end of the sacrament is the presence of Christ in the soul.

Wyclif's denial of transubstantiation gave his enemies their opportunity. His support dwindled to a small minority at Oxford. First the chancellor and a small council condemned his doctrines and forbade him to lecture. Then the Archbishop of Canterbury, William Courtenay, followed with another council that condemned ten of Wyclif's doctrines as heretical. By 1382 the Reformer was effectively silenced at Oxford.

Before his defeat at the university, however, Wyclif had turned for support to the people in cottages and towns. His mission called for the Bible in the language of craftsmen and peasants, so he led a handful of scholars at Oxford in the translation of the Latin Bible into the English language and copied the methods of St. Francis and the friars.

From Oxford, as from Assisi two centuries before, Wyclif sent out "poor priests" into the byways and village greens, sometimes even to churches, to win the souls of the neglected. Clad in russet robes of undressed wool, without sandals, purse, or scrip, a long staff in their hand, dependent for food and shelter on the good will of their neighbors, Wyclif's poor priests soon became a power in the land. Their enemies dubbed them *Lollards*, meaning *mumblers*. They carried a few pages of the Reformer's Bible and his tracts and sermons as they went throughout the countryside preaching the Word of God. One panic-stricken observer claimed that "every second man" he met was a Lollard. Despite Wyclif's academic environment, his legacy was carried on largely by lay-proclaimers who sought to model and proclaim a simple dependence upon the Bible. Its influence is an example of the recurring empowerment of the Scriptures when read in the language of the people.

Wyclif gained enough support that church authorities had the good sense not to move against him. His followers were hunted down, were expelled from Oxford, or forced to renounce their views, but Wyclif, though driven from the university, was left to close his days in peace at his parish at Lutterworth. He died there in 1384.

THE PASSAGE TO BOHEMIA

The movement Wyclif launched continued in England under restrictions but found an even greater opportunity for expansion in Bohemia. The two nations were linked in 1383 by the marriage of Anne of Bohemia and King Richard II of England, so students of both countries went back and forth between Oxford and Prague.

The Wyclif revolt met greater success in Bohemia because it was joined to a strong national party led by John Hus. The Czech Reformer came from peasant parents in southern Bohemia, a small town called Husinetz. He studied theology at the University of Prague, earning both a bachelor of arts (1394) and the master of arts (1396) before beginning his teaching in the faculty of arts and plunging into the reform cause.

His student days introduced Hus to the philosophical writings of Wyclif, but only after his ordination and appointment as rector and preacher at Bethlehem Chapel did he come upon Wyclif's religious writings. He adopted at once the English Reformer's view of the church as an elect company, with Christ, not the pope, its true head.

Bethlehem Chapel near the university gave Hus an unrivaled opportunity to circulate Wyclif's teachings, including his criticisms of the abuses of power in the papacy. On the walls were paintings contrasting the behavior of the popes and Christ. The pope rode a horse; Christ walked barefoot. Jesus washed the disciples' feet; the pope preferred to have his kissed. The Chapel had been founded in 1391 for the express purpose of encouraging the national faith in Bohemia, so Hus's fiery sermons in the Bohemian language fanned widespread popular support. Soon there were student riots for and against Wyclif, much as today they might be for or against some revolutionary figure.

The Archbishop of Prague grew restless and complained to the pope about the spread of Wyclif's doctrines. Root out the heresy, replied the pope. So Archbishop Zbynek excommunicated Hus. As a result a great popular tumult erupted. Hus made matters worse when he openly attacked the pope's sale of indulgences for support of his war against Naples. This move cost Hus the support of his king Wenceslas, and when Prague fell under a papal interdict because of Hus, the Reformer left for exile in southern Bohemia. During this period of retirement, Hus, drawing heavily upon Wyclif, wrote his major work, *On the Church.*

The Council of Constance was now fast approaching, and Hus yielded to the urging of the emperor Sigismund and agreed to appear at the council. He had hopes of presenting his views to the assembled authorities, but upon his arrival he found himself instead a victim of the Inquisition.

> ## Inquisition
>
> Inquisition is a strategy from ancient Roman law; it is a trial before a panel of judges. While one judge may present the evidence, all the judges interrogate witnesses, decreasing the prospect that the court might receive false testimony. Romans required confession or two eyewitnesses as evidence in capital cases. Without witnesses or a confession the accused was sometimes tortured to secure a confession when circumstances seemed to suggest guilt. This ancient arrangement was adopted by the church.

The rule of the Inquisition was simple: if sufficient witnesses testified to the guilt of the accused, then he had to confess and renounce the errors or be burned. The reward for confession was life imprisonment instead of the stake. In accordance with this rule, the panel of judges appointed by the council believed the witnesses against Hus and condemned him for heresies he had never taught.

AWAY WITH HERETICS

Hus was willing to yield himself to the teaching of the church, when instructed by Scripture in what way his teaching was wrong. But he could not agree to recant heresies that he had always stoutly disclaimed. For Hus truth was supreme: "I have said that I would not, for a chapel full of gold, recede from the truth." "I know," he wrote in 1412, "that the truth stands and is mighty for ever, and abides eternally, with whom there is no respect of persons." Throughout his letters from Constance, his chief anxiety is "lest liars should say that I have slipped back from the truth I preached." Few scenes in church history are more touching than Hus's fidelity and refusal to swerve from absolute truth, even to save his life.

For eight months he lay in prison in Constance. His letters during his last month rank among the greatest in Christian literature. If the Reformer had added nothing to our intellectual heritage, he would still have enriched our moral outlook.

"O most holy Christ," he prayed,

draw me, weak as I am, after Thyself, for if Thou dost not draw us we cannot follow Thee. Strengthen my spirit, that it may be willing. If the flesh is weak, let Thy grace precede us; come between and follow, for without Thee we cannot go for Thy sake to cruel death. Give me a fearless heart, a right faith, a firm hope, a perfect love, that for Thy sake I may lay down my life with patience and joy. Amen.

Finally, July 6, 1415, the day for his burning came. On the way to the place of execution he passed through a churchyard and saw a bonfire of his books. He laughed and told the bystanders not to believe the lies circulated about him. On arriving at the execution ground, familiarly known as the Devil's Place, Hus knelt and prayed. For the last time the marshal of the empire asked him if he would recant and save his life. Said Hus, "God is my witness that the evidence against me is false. I have never thought nor preached except with the one intention of winning men, if possible, from their sins. In the truth of the gospel I have written, taught, and preached; today I will gladly die."

The Bohemian rebellion refused to die with Hus. It developed a moderate and a militant wing. The moderates were called *Utraquists*, a term from Latin for "both" since their primary protest called for freedom to receive Communion in *both* the bread and the cup.

The militants were called Taborites after the city in Bohemia that served as their chief stronghold. These followers of Hus struggled against the Roman Church and the German Empire until several wars reduced their number and influence. Despite the best efforts of the papacy to bring an end to the Bohemian heresy, however, an independent church survived known as the *Unitas Fratrum* or Unity of the Brotherhood. Until the coming of Luther, it remained a root in dry ground.

If the Church of Rome was to be reformed from within, it had ample opportunities in the fourteenth and fifteenth centuries. But by the end of the fifteenth century, the dreams of Marsilius of Padua had vanished, the leaders of reform by church councils were frustrated and repudiated, and the revolts of Wyclif and Hus were crushed. The value of the period lies in the demonstration it gives that reform of the papal church from within was impossible. The time of judgment had come. The Unity of the Brotherhood was witness to that fact, and a promise of things to come.

Suggestions for Further Reading

*Evans, G.R. *John Wyclif: Myth and Reality.* Downers Grove, IL: IVP, 2006.

*Fudge, Thomas A. *The Magnificent Ride: The First Reformation in Hussite Bohemia*, St. Andrews Studies in Reformation History. Aldershot, Vermont: Ashgate, 2008.

Heinze, Rudolph W. *Reform and Conflict: From the Medieval World to the Wars of Religion, AD 1350–1648, Baker History of the Church.* Vol. 4. Grand Rapids: Baker, 2004

McFarlane, John. *Wycliffe and the Beginnings of English Nonconformity.* London: English University Press, 1952.

Spinka, Matthew, ed. *Advocates of Reform.* Philadelphia: Westminster, 1953.

———. *John Hus: A Biography.* Princeton, NJ: Princeton University Press, 1968.

Workman, Herbert B. *The Dawn of the Reformation: The Age of Hus.* London: Epworth, 1933.

———. *The Dawn of the Reformation: The Age of Wyclif.* London: Epworth, 1933.

THE AGE OF THE REFORMATION

1517–1648

The spirit of reform broke out with surprising intensity in the sixteenth century, giving birth to Protestantism and shattering the papal leadership of western Christendom. Four major traditions marked early Protestantism: Lutheran, Reformed, Anabaptist, and Anglican. After a generation, the Church of Rome itself, led by the Jesuits, recovered its moral fervor. Bloody struggles between Catholics and Protestants followed, and Europe was ravaged by war before it became obvious that western Christendom was permanently divided and a few pioneers pointed toward a new way: the denominational concept of the church.

The Age of the Reformation

Luther's Theses	Diet of Augsburg	Peace of Augsburg	Edict of Nantes
	Calvin's *Institutes*	Presbyterianism in Scotland	
1500	1550	1600	1650
Cortés Takes Mexico	Society of Jesus	Ricci in Peking	30 Years' War
Pizarro Takes Peru	Council of Trent		Peace of Westphalia

CHAPTER 24

A WILD BOAR
IN THE VINEYARD

Martin Luther and Protestantism

IN THE SUMMER OF 1520 a document bearing an impressive seal circulated throughout Germany in search of a remote figure. "Arise, O Lord," the writing began, "and judge Thy cause. A wild boar has invaded Thy vineyard."

The document, a papal bull—named after the seal, or bulla—took three months to reach Martin Luther, the wild boar. Long before it arrived in Wittenberg where Luther was teaching, he knew its contents. Forty-one of his beliefs were condemned as "heretical, or scandalous, or false, or offensive to pious ears, or seductive of simple minds, or repugnant to Catholic truth." The bull called on Luther to repent and repudiate his errors or face the dreadful consequences.

Luther received his copy on the tenth of October. At the end of his sixty-day period of grace, he led a throng of eager students outside Wittenberg and burned copies of the Canon Law and the works of some medieval theologians. Perhaps as an afterthought Luther added a copy of the bull condemning him. That was his answer. "They have burned my books," he said; "I burn theirs." Those flames in early December 1520 were a fit symbol of the defiance of the pope raging throughout Germany.

The Church of the popes no longer hurls anathemas at Protestants, and Lutherans no longer burn Catholic books, but the divisions of Christians in Western Christianity remain. Behind today's differences between Catholics and Protestants lie the events of the age of Luther, a period of church history we call the Reformation (1517–1648).

THE MEANING OF PROTESTANTISM

What is Protestantism? The description from Ernst Troeltsch has served as a standard. In the early twentieth century he called Protestantism a "modification of Catholicism" in which Catholic problems remain but different solutions are given. The four questions that Protestantism answered in a new way are, (1) How is a person saved? (2) Where does religious authority lie? (3) What is the church? and (4) what is the essence of Christian living?

Protestant reformers throughout sixteenth-century Europe came to hold similar convictions about these questions, but fresh answers emerged first in Martin Luther's personal conflict with Rome. Other men and women felt deeply the need for reform, but none matched the bold struggle of soul within the burly German.

Born in 1483, the son of a Saxon miner, Luther had every intention of becoming a lawyer until one day in 1505 he was caught in a thunderstorm while walking toward the village of Stotternheim. A bolt of lightning knocked him to the ground, and Luther, terrified, called out to Catholicism's patroness of miners, "St. Anne, save me! And I'll become a monk."

Much to his parents' dismay, Luther kept the vow. Two weeks later, obsessed with guilt, he entered the Augustinian monastery at Erfurt and proved to be a dedicated monk. "I kept the rule so strictly," he recalled years later, "that I may say that if ever a monk got to heaven by his sheer monkery, it was I. If I had kept on any longer, I should have killed myself with vigils, prayers, reading, and other work."

Luther pushed his body to health-cracking rigors of austerity. He sometimes fasted for three days and slept without a blanket in freezing winter. He was driven by a profound sense of his own sinfulness and of God's unutterable majesty. In the midst of saying his first mass, said Luther, "I was utterly stupefied and terror-stricken. I thought to myself, 'Who am I that I should lift up mine eyes or raise my hands to the divine majesty? For I am dust and ashes and full of sin, and I am speaking to the living, eternal and true God.'" No amount of penance, no soothing advice from his superiors could still Luther's conviction that he was a miserable, doomed sinner. Although his confessor counseled him to love God, Luther one day burst out, "I do not love God! I hate him!"

The troubled monk found the love he sought through the study of Scripture. Assigned to the chair of biblical studies at the recently established Wittenberg University, he became fascinated with the words of Christ from the cross, "My God, my God, why hast Thou forsaken me?" Christ forsaken! How could our Lord be forsaken? Luther felt forsaken, but he was a sinner. Christ was not. The answer had to lie in Christ's identity with sinful humanity. Did he share mankind's estrangement from God in order to assume the punishment required of sin?

A new and revolutionary picture of God began to develop in Luther's restless soul. Finally in 1515 while pondering St. Paul's Epistle to the Romans, Luther came upon the words, "For therein is the righteousness of God revealed from faith to faith: as it is written, The just shall live by faith" (1:17, KJV). Here was his key to spiritual certainty.

Night and day I pondered," Luther later recalled, "until I saw the connection between the justice of God and the statement that 'the just shall live by his faith.' Then I grasped that the justice of God is that righteousness by which through grace and sheer mercy God justifies us through faith. Thereupon I felt myself to be reborn and to have gone through open doors into paradise.

Luther saw it clearly now. Man is saved only by his faith in the merit of Christ's sacrifice. The cross alone can remove man's sin and save him from the grasp of the devil. Luther had come to his famous doctrine of justification by faith alone. He saw how sharply it clashed with the Roman church's doctrine of justification by faith and good works: the demonstration of faith through virtuous acts, acceptance of church dogma, and participation in church ritual. Later, in a hymn that reflects his vigorous style, Luther described his spiritual journey from anxiety to conviction:

> In devil's dungeon chained I lay
>   The pangs of death swept o'er me.
> My sin devoured me night and day
>   In which my mother bore me.
> My anguish ever grew more rife,
>   I took no pleasure in my life
> And sin had made me crazy.
>
> Thus spoke the Son, "Hold thou to me,
>   From now on thou wilt make it.
> I gave my very life for thee
>   And for thee I will stake it.
> For I am thine and thou art mine,
>   And where I am our lives entwine.
> The Old Fiend cannot shake it."

The implications of Luther's discovery were enormous. If salvation comes through faith in Christ alone, the intercession of priests is superfluous. Faith formed and nurtured by the Word of God, written and preached, requires no monks, no masses, and no prayers to the saints. The mediation of the Church of Rome crumbles into insignificance.

LUTHER'S ATTACK ON PAPAL AUTHORITY

Luther had no idea where his spiritual discovery was leading him. It took a flagrant abuse of church finances to propel him into the center of religious rebellion in Germany, and into another revolutionary position regarding papal authority.

The sale of indulgences, introduced during the crusades, remained a favored source of papal income. In exchange for a meritorious work—frequently, a contribution to a worthy cause or a pilgrimage to a shrine—the church offered the sinner exemption from his acts of penance by drawing upon its "treasury of merits." This consisted of the grace accumulated by Christ's sacrifice on the cross and the meritorious deeds of the saints.

All too often zealous preachers of indulgences made them appear to be a sort of magic, as though a good deed, especially a contribution, automatically got its reward, regardless of the condition of the doer's soul. Sorrow for sin was completely and conveniently overlooked. That troubled Luther deeply.

Armed with his newfound understanding of faith, Luther began to criticize the theology of indulgences in his sermons. His displeasure increased noticeably during 1517, when the Dominican John Tetzel was preaching throughout much of Germany on behalf of a papal fundraising campaign to complete the construction of St. Peter's basilica in Rome. In exchange for a contribution, Tetzel boasted, he would provide donors with an indulgence that would even apply beyond the grave and free souls from purgatory. "As soon as the coin in the coffer rings," went his jingle, "the soul from purgatory springs."

To Luther, Tetzel's preaching was bad theology if not worse. He promptly drew up ninety-five propositions (or theses) for theological debate and on October 31, 1517, following university custom, he posted them on the Castle Church door at Wittenberg. Among other things, they argued that indulgences cannot remove guilt, do not apply to purgatory, and are harmful because they induce a false sense of security in the donor. That was the spark that ignited the Reformation.

Within a short time the German Dominicans denounced Luther to Rome as a man guilty of preaching "dangerous doctrines." A Vatican theologian issued a series of counter-theses, arguing that anyone who criticized indulgences was guilty of heresy. Initially willing to accept a final verdict from Rome, Luther began to insist on scriptural proof that he was wrong—and even questioned papal authority over purgatory. During an eighteen-day debate in 1519 with theologian John Eck at Leipzig, Luther blurted out, "A council may sometimes err. Neither the church nor the pope can establish articles of faith. These must come from Scripture."

Thus Luther had moved from his first conviction—that salvation was by faith in Christ alone—to a second: that the Scriptures, not popes or councils, are the standard for Christian faith and behavior.

John Eck did not miss Luther's likeness to John Hus. After the Leipzig debate he moved to have Rome declare Luther a heretic. Luther in turn decided to put his case before the German people by publishing a series of pamphlets. In his *Address to the Nobility of the German Nation*, the Reformer called on the princes to correct abuses within the church, to strip bishops and abbots of their wealth and worldly power, and to create, in effect, a national German Church.

In his *The Babylonian Captivity of the Church* Luther made clear how justification by faith reshaped his doctrine of the church. He argued that Rome's sacramental system held Christians captive. He attacked the papacy for depriving the individual Christian of his freedom to approach God directly by faith, without the mediation of priests, and he set forth his own views of the sacraments. To be valid, he said, a sacrament had to be instituted by Christ and be exclusively Christian. By these tests Luther could find no justification for five of the Roman Catholic sacraments. He retained only Baptism and the Lord's Supper, and he placed even these within a community of believing Christians, rather than in the hands of an exclusive priesthood.

Important Theological Themes for Luther

Justification by Faith

Catholics typically followed Augustine who taught that righteousness was imparted. This righteousness is an internal possession of the believer acquired during his or her life. By contrast, Luther taught that one comes to be right in the eyes of God by *imputation*. Imputation is a bookkeeping term. It pictures God adding the righteousness that belongs to Jesus to a believer's personal account. This "God-declared" righteousness is external to the believer, who continues experientially to be a sinner. One can only come to be righteous by God crediting his or her account. Only then can a declared saint start to become righteous experientially. Protestants call the event of being declared righteous *justification*; they call the subsequent process of growing to be more holy *sanctification*. Luther condemned efforts to grow in holiness apart from being declared righteous.

Summary of Righteousness	
Augustine's view of righteousness (Catholic model)	Luther's view of righteousness (Protestant model)
Faithful followers are made righteous in the spiritual pilgrimage	Believers are declared righteous and only then can progress to become more holy experientially
Righteousness is acquired in a process	Righteousness is received in an event
Righteousness is imparted	Righteousness is imputed
Righteousness is an inner state, infused or implanted	Righteousness is external to the believer
Justification and Sanctification are a seamless unity	Justification and Sanctification are vigorously distinguished[1]

Law and Gospel

Luther distinguished two different working systems or orientations scattered throughout the Bible: Law and Gospel. Law and Gospel both hold the promise of blessings. For Luther, the Law's promises are conditioned upon keeping the covenant stipulations. You could enjoy covenant fellowship with God if you could keep the covenant rules. The Law's promise becomes almost torturous if you cannot keep the stipulations. Yet the Law does serve a vital role in revealing one's spiritual bankruptcy and need for gospel grace. By contrast, the gospel makes an even greater promise of fellowship with God; it is greater still because God in his mercy meets every condition: an unconditional promise. Luther experienced the life-giving joy of the gospel; he went from a tortured man who could not keep the rules to a recipient of an unconditional promise. Gospel-proclaiming passages were found in both the Old Testament (concentrations in Isaiah, for example) and the New Testament (concentrations in John and Paul, but no gospel in James).

Theology of the Cross

The cross reveals a mystery at the heart of Christianity. An eyewitness of the crucifixion would naturally conclude that this event was the lowest point in history. This great injustice (the crucifixion of an innocent man) appears as the defeat of God's purpose: utter darkness. Only later does one learn that in witnessing the cross one witnessed God defeating evil and wrongdoing. With a cross as a new paradigm or lens for seeing the world, one's sense of values, justice, and hope is transformed. The reversal in our assessment of the cross (from the triumph of evil to the triumph over evil) leads to a reassessment of the world. For example, it was not the disciplined and decent who had progressed to be closer to God. The cross reveals false pride and shows that it was the humble who know their spiritual and moral incapacity. The humble sinners were ready for God's grace. We see the world differently when looking through the lens of the cross: God makes sinners saints, and the dead come to life.

Luther criticized Catholic theology as being confident in mankind's capacity to progress (or ascend) toward God. He called this a theology of glory, and said that our theology must be rooted in the reorienting cross.

Thus Luther brushed aside the traditional view of the church as a sacred hierarchy headed by the pope and returned to the early Christian view of a community of Christian believers in which all believers are priests called to offer spiritual sacrifices to God.

In his third pamphlet published in 1520, *The Freedom of a Christian Man*, Luther set forth in conciliatory but firm tones his views on Christian behavior and salvation. This is probably the best introduction available to his central ideas. He did not discourage good works but argued that the inner spiritual freedom that comes from the certainty found in faith leads to the performance of good works by all true Christians. "Good works do not make a man good," he said, "but a good man does good works."

Thus, on the threshold of his excommunication from the Roman Church, Luther removed the necessity of monasticism by stressing that the essence of Christian living lies in serving God in one's calling, whether secular or ecclesiastical. All useful callings, he said, are equally sacred in God's eyes.

HERETIC, OUTLAW, AND HERO

In June 1520 Pope Leo X issued his bull condemning Luther and giving him sixty days to turn from his heretical course. The bonfire at Wittenberg made clear Luther's intent, so his excommunication followed. In January 1521 the pope declared him a heretic and expelled him from the "one holy, catholic and apostolic Church."

The German problem now fell into the hands of the young emperor, Charles V, who was under oath to defend the church and remove heresy from the empire. He summoned Luther to the imperial Diet (or assembly) meeting at Worms to give an account of his writings. Before the assembly Luther once again insisted that only biblical authority would sway him. "My conscience is captive to the Word of God," he told the court. "I will not recant anything, for to go against conscience is neither honest nor safe. Here I stand, I cannot do otherwise. God help me. Amen."

Charles V was not impressed. He declared Luther an outlaw. "This devil in the habit of a monk," his pronouncement said, "has brought together ancient errors into one stinking puddle, and has invented new ones." Luther had twenty-one days for safe passage to Saxony before the sentence fell. It never came. Luther was saved from arrest and death by the prince of Saxony, Duke Frederick the Wise, whose domains included Wittenberg. The Duke gave Luther sanctuary at his lonely Wartburg Castle. Disguised as a minor nobleman, Junker George, the Reformer stayed for nearly a year; during the time, he translated the New Testament into German, an important first step toward reshaping public and private worship in Germany.

Meanwhile the revolt against Rome spread; in town after town, priests and town councils removed statues from the churches and abandoned the mass. New reformers, many of them far more radical than Luther, appeared on the scene. Most important, princes, dukes, and electors defied the condemnation of Luther by giving support to the new movement.

In 1522 Luther returned to Wittenberg to put into effect a spiritual reform that became the model for much of Germany. He abolished the office of bishop since he found no warrant for it in Scripture. The churches needed pastors, not dignitaries. Most of the ministers in Saxony and surrounding territories abandoned celibacy. Monks and nuns also married. After exhorting others to marry, Luther himself finally agreed to take a former nun, Katherine Von Bora, as his wife. A new image of the ministry appeared in Western Christianity: the married pastor living like any other man with his own family. "There is a lot to get used to in the first year of marriage," Luther said later. "One wakes up in the morning and finds a pair of pigtails on the pillow which were not there before."

Luther also revised the Latin liturgy and translated it into German. He abandoned the Catholic practice of only partaking of the bread at the supper. The laity received the Communion in bread *and* wine, as the Hussites had demanded a century earlier. And the whole emphasis in worship changed from the celebration of the sacrificial mass to the preaching and teaching of God's Word.

All, however, was not well in Germany. During 1524 Luther revealed how much he had surrendered in gaining the support of the German princes. Encouraged by the Reformer's concept of the freedom of a

Christian man, which they applied to economic and social spheres, the German peasants revolted against their lords. Long ground down by the nobles, the peasants included in their twelve demands abolition of serfdom—unless it could be justified from the gospel—and relief from the excessive services demanded of them.

At first Luther recognized the justice of the peasants' complaints, but when they turned to violence against established authority, he lashed out against them. In a virulent pamphlet, *Against the Thievish and Murderous Hordes of Peasants*, Luther called on the princes to "knock down, strangle, and stab . . . and think nothing so venomous, pernicious, or Satanic as an insurgent."

In 1525 the princes and nobles crushed the revolt at a cost of an estimated one hundred thousand peasant lives. The surviving peasants considered Luther a false prophet. Many of them returned to Catholicism or turned to more radical forms of the Reformation.

Martin Luther (1483–1546), was the father of the Reformation, which transformed not only Christianity but all of Western civilization.

Major Traditions of the Reformation

Roman Catholicism

Medieval Christianity   { Lutheran
                                     Reformed
                                     Roman Catholic
                                     Anglican
Eastern Orthodoxy   Anabaptist

Luther's conservative political and economic views arose from his belief that the equality of all men before God applied to spiritual not secular matters. While alienating the peasants, such views were a boon to alliances with the princes, many of whom became Lutheran in part because Luther's views allowed them to control the church in their territories, thereby strengthening their power and wealth.

LUTHER'S LASTING INFLUENCE

By 1530, when a summit conference of Reformation leaders convened in Augsburg to draw up a common statement of faith, leadership of the movement had begun to pass out of Luther's hands. The Reformer was still an outlaw and unable to attend. The task of presenting Lutheranism fell to a young professor of Greek at Wittenberg, Philip Melanchthon. The young scholar drafted the Augsburg Confession signed by Lutheran princes and theologians, but the emperor was no more inclined to conciliation than he had been at Worms.

After Augsburg Luther continued to preach and teach the Bible in Wittenberg, but even sympathetic biographers have found it hard to justify some of the actions of his declining years. As *Time* once put it, "He endorsed the bigamous marriage of his supporter, Prince Philip of Hesse. He denounced reformers who disagreed with him in terms that he had once reserved for the papacy. His statements about the Jews would sound excessive on the tongue of a Hitler." By the time of his death in 1546, says biographer Roland Bainton, Luther was "an irascible old man, petulant, peevish, unrestrained, and at times positively coarse."

Fortunately, the personal defects of an aging rebel do not in any way detract from the grandeur of his achievement, which ultimately transformed not only Christianity but all of Western civilization.

After 1530 the emperor, Charles V, made clear his intention to crush the growing heresy. In defense, the Lutheran princes banded together in 1531 in the Schmalkald League, and between 1546 and 1555 a sporadic civil war raged. The combatants reached a compromise in the Peace of Augsburg (1555), which allowed each prince to decide the religion of his subjects, forbade all sects of Protestantism other than Lutheranism, and ordered all Catholic bishops to give up their property if they turned Lutheran.

The effects of these provisions on Germany were profound. Lutheranism became a state religion in large portions of the empire. From Germany it spread to Scandinavia. Religious opinions became the private property of the princes, and the individual had to believe what his prince wanted him to believe, be it Lutheran or Catholic.

Luther's greatest contribution to history, however, was not political. It was religious. He took four basic Catholic concerns and offered invigorating new answers. To the question, how is a person saved? Luther replied, "not by works but by faith alone." To the question, where does religious authority lie? he answered, "not in the visible institution called the Roman church but in the Word of God found in the Bible." To the question, what is the church? he responded, "the whole community of Christian believers, since all are priests before God." And to the question, what is the essence of Christian living? he replied, "serving God in any useful calling, whether ordained or lay." To this day any classical description of Protestantism must echo those central truths.

Suggestions for Further Reading

Bainton, Roland. *Here I Stand: A Life of Martin Luther.* Nashville: Abingdon Press, 1950.

Chadwick, Owen. *The Reformation.* Middlesex: Penguin Books, 1964.

Dillenberger, John. *Martin Luther: Selections from His writings.* Garden City, NY: Doubleday & Company, Inc., 1961

Heinze, Rudolph W. *Reform and Conflict: From the Medieval World to the Wars of Religion, AD 1350–1648. Baker History of the Church.* Vol. 4. Grand Rapids: Baker, 2004

Marty, Martin. *Martin Luther.* New York: Penguin, 2004

*McGrath. *Theology of the Cross: Martin Luther's Theological Breakthrough.* 2nd ed. Malden, MA: Wiley-Blackwell, 2011.

CHAPTER 25

RADICAL DISCIPLESHIP

The Anabaptists

U NDER THE COVER OF darkness, a dozen or so men trudged slowly
through the snow falling in Zurich on January 21, 1525. Quietly
but resolutely they made their way through the narrow streets. The
wintry chill blowing off the lake seemed to match their mood as they
approached the Manz house near the Great Minster, the largest church
in town.

The City Council of Zurich had that day ordered their leaders Conrad Grebel and Felix Manz to stop holding Bible classes. Opposition
was mounting! Only four days before, the council had warned all parents to have their babies baptized within eight days of birth or face
banishment from the territory. What were the brethren going to do?
They agreed to meet at the Manz house to decide.

Once inside they shared their rumors and reports, and then they
called upon God to enable them to do his will. They arose from prayer
to take one of the most decisive actions in Christian history.

George Blaurock, a former priest, stepped over to Conrad Grebel
and asked him for baptism in the apostolic fashion: upon confession
of personal faith in Jesus Christ. Grebel baptized him on the spot and
Blaurock proceeded to baptize the others. Thus Anabaptism, another
important expression of the Protestant Reformation, was born.

Today the direct descendants of the Anabaptists are the Mennonites and the Hutterites. Americans probably think of them as bearded
farmers and their bonnet-covered wives driving their horses and bug-
gies across some Pennsylvania or Iowa countryside. No automobiles; no
buttons; no zippers.

In fact only one section of the Mennonites, the Old Order Amish, holds tenaciously to the old ways. The majority of Mennonites looks like any other Americans and consume their share of energy like the rest of us.

What unites the various types of Mennonites is not a style of dress or a mode of transportation but a shared set of beliefs and values. Many of these beliefs are now accepted by other Christians. So the distant relatives of the Anabaptists today include the Baptists, the Quakers and, in one sense, the Congregationalists. In fact, in their belief in the separation of church and state the Anabaptists proved to be forerunners of practically all modern Protestants.

Why is that? How could a people so intent upon restoring New Testament Christianity come to be so far ahead of their time? Like the Benedictine monks of an earlier day, the Anabaptists demonstrate that those who live most devoutly for the world to come are often in the best position to change the present.

BASIC BELIEFS OF ANABAPTISTS

In a sense the rise of Anabaptism was no surprise. Most revolutionary movements produce a wing of radicals who feel called of God to reform the reformation. And that is what Anabaptism was, a voice calling the moderate reformers to strike even more deeply at the foundations of the old order.

Like most counterculture movements, the Anabaptists lacked cohesiveness. No single body of doctrine and no unifying organization prevailed among them. Even the name *Anabaptist* was pinned on them by their enemies. It meant *rebaptizer* and was intended to associate the radicals with heretics in the early church and subject them to severe persecution. The move succeeded famously.

Actually, the Anabaptists rejected all thoughts of rebaptism because they never considered the ceremonial sprinkling they received in infancy as valid baptism. They much preferred *Baptists* as a designation. To most of them, however, the fundamental issue was not baptism. It was the nature of the church and its relation to civil governments.

They had come to their convictions like most other Protestants: through Scripture. Luther had taught that common people have a right to search the Bible for themselves. It had been his guide to salvation; why not theirs?

As a result, little groups of Anabaptist believers gathered about their Bibles. They discovered a different world in the pages of the New Testament. They found no state-church alliance, no Christendom. Instead they discovered that the apostolic churches were companies of committed believers, communities of men and women who had freely and personally chosen to follow Jesus. And for the sixteenth century, that was a revolutionary idea.

In spite of Luther's stress on personal religion, Lutheran churches were established churches. They retained an ordained clergy who considered the whole population of a given territory members of their church. The churches looked to the state for salary and support. Official Protestantism seemed to differ little from official Catholicism.

Anabaptists wanted to change all that. Their goal was the "restitution" of apostolic Christianity, a return to churches of true believers. In the early church, they said, men and women who had experienced personal spiritual regeneration were the only fit subjects for baptism. The apostolic churches knew nothing of the practice of baptizing infants. That tradition was simply a convenient device for perpetuating Christendom: nominal but spiritually impotent Christian society.

The true church, the radicals insisted, is always a community of saints, dedicated disciples in a wicked world. Like the missionary monks of the Middle Ages, the Anabaptists wanted to shape society by their example of radical discipleship—if necessary, even by death. They steadfastly refused to be a part of worldly power including bearing arms, holding political office, and taking oaths. In the sixteenth century this independence from social and civic society was seen as inflammatory, revolutionary, or even treasonous.

The radicals found their best opportunities to preach in Switzerland, the Rhineland, and Holland. By mid-century three groups appeared in German-speaking Europe: (1) the Swiss Brethren, led by Conrad Grebel and Felix Manz at Zurich; (2) the Hutterite brethren in Moravia; and (3) the Mennonites in the Netherlands and North Germany.

RADICALS IN THE SWISS ALPS

Conrad Grebel and Felix Manz were at first supporters of the fledgling reformation in Zurich led by Ulrich Zwingli (1484–1531). In 1519, the year Luther debated John Eck at Leipzig, Zwingli became the people's priest at the Great Minster Church in Zurich. He launched the reformation not by posting theses on the church door but by preaching biblical sermons from the pulpit. Under the influence of the famous scholar Erasmus, Zwingli had come to revere the language and message of the New Testament. So his messages created quite a stir in Zurich. One of his listeners, a young man named Thomas Platter, said when he heard the long-neglected Bible explained, he felt as if Zwingli were lifting him by the hair of his head.

In one important respect Zwingli followed the Bible even more stringently than did Luther. The Wittenberger would allow whatever the Bible did not prohibit; Zwingli rejected whatever the Bible did not prescribe. For this reason the reformation in Zurich tended to strip away more traditional symbols of the Roman church: candles, statues, music, and pictures. Later, in England, men called this spirit Puritanism.

Grebel and Manz, both well-educated men of standing in Zurich, supported Zwingli's initial reforms. But following the Reformer's lead—the study of the Bible—they came to see the obvious differences in the apostolic churches and those of their own day.

In Zurich's city-state, as in the rest of the Christian world, every newborn child was baptized and considered a member of the church. As a result, church and society were identical or interchangeable. The church was simply everybody's church. In the New Testament, however, the church was a fellowship of the few, a company of true believers committed to live and die for their Lord.

That is the kind of church Grebel and Manz wanted in Zurich: a church free from the state, composed of true disciples. The baptism of believers was merely the most striking feature of this new kind of church. Zwingli, however, would have no part of this revolution. He needed the support of the city fathers.

In the fall of 1524, when Grebel's wife gave birth to a son, all the theories faced the test of action. Would the baby be baptized? The Grebels refused, and other parents followed their example.

To deal with the crisis, the City Council of Zurich arranged a public debate on the question for January 17, 1525. After hearing arguments on both sides of the issue, representatives of the people declared Zwingli and his disciples the winners. As a result the council warned all parents who had neglected to have their children baptized to do so within a week or face banishment from Zurich.

That was the background for the historic baptism at the Manz house on January 21. It was clearly an act of defiance. But it was much more. Grebel, Manz, and their followers had counted the cost. That is why shortly after the baptism the little company withdrew from Zurich to the nearby village of Zollikon. Here, late in January, the first Anabaptist congregation, the first free church (free of state ties) in modern times, was born.

The authorities in Zurich would not overlook the rebellion. They sent police to Zollikon and arrested the newly-baptized men and imprisoned them for a time. But as soon as they were released the Anabaptists went to neighboring towns in search of converts.

Finally, the Zurich council lost all patience. On March 7, 1526, it decided that anyone found re-baptizing would be put to death by drowning. Apparently their thought was, "If the heretics want water, let them have it." Within a year, on January 5, 1527, Felix Manz became the first Anabaptist martyr. The Zurich authorities drowned him in the Limmat, which flows through the city. Within four years the radical movement in and around Zurich was practically eradicated.

Many of the persecuted fled to Germany and Austria, but their prospects were no brighter there. In 1529 the imperial Diet of Speyer proclaimed Anabaptism a heresy, and every court in Christendom was obliged to condemn the heretics to death. During the Reformation years, between four and five thousand Anabaptists were executed by fire, water, and sword.

To us the Anabaptists seem to have made a simple demand: a person's right to his own beliefs. But in the sixteenth century the heretics seemed to be destroying the very fabric of society. That is why the voice of conscience was so often silenced by martyrdom.

We hear that voice in a moving letter written by a young mother in 1573, to her daughter only a few days old. The father had already been executed as an Anabaptist. The mother, in an Antwerp jail, had been reprieved only long enough to give birth to her child. She writes to urge her daughter not to grow up ashamed of her parents:

> My dearest child, the true love of God strengthen you in virtue, you who are yet so young, and whom I must leave in this wicked, evil, perverse world.
>
> Oh, that it had pleased the Lord that I might have brought you up, but it seems that it is not the Lord's will . . . . Be not ashamed of us; it is the way which the prophets and the apostles went. Your dear father demonstrated with his blood that it is the genuine faith, and I also hope to attest the same with my blood, though flesh and blood must remain on the posts and on the stake, well knowing that we shall meet hereafter.

Among the early Anabaptist missionaries who carried their message east along the Alps to the region called Tyrol was George Blaurock. Catholic authorities there persecuted the Anabaptists intensely. On September 6, 1529, Blaurock himself was burned at the stake.

The persecution forced the Anabaptists north. Many of them found refuge on the lands of some exceptionally tolerant princes in Moravia. There they founded a long-lasting form of economic community called the *Bruderhof*, a Christian commune. In part they aimed to follow the pattern of the early apostolic community. But they sought community for practical reasons too, as a means of group survival under persecution. Their communities attempted to show that in the kingdom of God brotherhood comes before self. Consolidated under the leadership of Jakob Hutter, who died in 1536, these groups came to be known as Hutterites.

KINGDOM BUILDING GONE MAD

Catholic and Lutheran fears of the Anabaptist radicals deepened suddenly in the mid-1530s with the bizarre Munster rebellion. Munster was an episcopal city in Westphalia near the Netherlands. In 1532 the Reformation spread rapidly throughout the city. A conservative Lutheran group was at first strong there. But then new immigrants, who were apostles of a strange figure called Jan Matthijs, led to fanaticism among those in power. Many looked for the creation of the Lord's earthly kingdom in Munster. Church historians call such views *chiliasm*, meaning belief in a thousand-year earthly kingdom of Christ.

When the bishop of the region massed his troops to besiege the city, these Anabaptists uncharacteristically defended themselves by arms. As the siege progressed, the more extreme leaders gained control of the city. In the summer of 1534 a former innkeeper, Jan of Leiden, seized the powers of government and ruled as an absolute despot. Claiming new revelations from God, Jan introduced the Old Testament practice of polygamy and by September took the title "King David."

With his harem "King David" lived in splendor, yet by a strange cunning he maintained morale in the city in spite of widespread hunger. He was able to keep the bishop's army at bay until June 24, 1535. The fall of the city brought an end to David's reign. But for centuries thereafter Europeans, upon hearing "Anabaptist," thought of the Munster rebellion. It stood for wild-eyed religious fanaticism.

In the aftermath of the suppression of Munster, the dispirited Anabaptists of the lower-Rhine area gained new heart through the ministry of Menno Simons (about 1496–1561). Although always in great personal danger, Menno, a former priest, traveled widely to visit the scattered Anabaptist groups of northern Europe and inspire them with his nighttime preaching. Menno was unswerving in commanding pacifism. As a result, his name in time came to stand for the movement's repudiation of violence. Although Menno was not the founder of the movement, most of the descendants of the Anabaptists are to this day called Mennonite.

Surviving only as bands of outlaws in Switzerland, Moravia, and the Netherlands, these Anabaptist groups had little opportunity to coordinate their evangelistic efforts or to give united expression to their beliefs. On one important occasion, however, they did attempt to agree upon a common basis of fellowship.

PIONEERS OF MODERN CHRISTIANITY

John H. Yoder and Alan Kreider look to this early conference for a summary of Anabaptist beliefs. In 1527 at Schleitheim (on today's Swiss-German border, near Schaffhausen) the Anabaptists met in the first synod of the Protestant Reformation. The leading figure at this meeting was the former Benedictine monk Michael Sattler who, four months later, was burned at the stake in nearby Rottenburg-am-Neckar. The "Brotherly Union" adopted at Schleitheim proved to be a highly significant document. We call it the Schleitheim Confession. During the next decade most Anabaptists in all parts of Europe came to agree with the beliefs it laid down.

First among these convictions was what the Anabaptists called *discipleship*. The Christian's relationship with Jesus Christ must go beyond inner experience and acceptance of doctrines. It must involve a daily walk with God, in which Christ's teaching and example shape a transformed style of life. As one Anabaptist put it, "No one can truly know Christ except he follow him in life." This meant resolutely obeying the "bright and clear words of the Son of God, whose word is truth and whose commandment is eternal life." Usually, Christians think one must understand (interpret) then obey; Anabaptist instinct is the opposite: only obedience yields understanding.

The consequences of being a disciple, as the Anabaptists realized, were wide-ranging. To choose only one, the Anabaptists rejected the swearing of oaths, because of Jesus' clear commandment in the Sermon on the Mount: "Do not swear at all, either by heaven . . . or by the earth . . . or by Jerusalem" (Matt. 5:34, 35). For the Anabaptist there could be no gradation or levels of truth-telling.

A second Anabaptist principle, the principle of love, grew logically out of the first. In their dealings with non-Anabaptists, they acted as pacifists. They would not go to war, defend themselves against their persecutors, or take part in coercion by the state.

The love ethic, however, was also expressed within the Anabaptist communities, in mutual aid and the redistribution of wealth. Among Moravian Anabaptists, as we have seen, it even led to Christian communal living.

The third Anabaptist principle is what we have come to call the *congregational* view of church authority, toward which Luther and Zwingli inclined in their earliest reforming years. In the Anabaptist assemblies all members were to be believers baptized voluntarily upon confession of personal faith in Christ. Each believer, then, was both a priest to his fellow believers and a missionary to unbelievers.

Decision making rested with the entire membership. In deciding matters of doctrine, the authority of Scripture was interpreted, not by a dogmatic tradition or by an ecclesiastical leader, but by the consensus of the local gathering in which all could speak and listen critically. In matters of church discipline, the believers also acted corporately. They were expected to assist each other in living out faithfully the meaning of their baptismal commitments.

A fourth major Anabaptist conviction was the insistence upon the separation of church and state. Christians, they claimed, were a "free, unforced, uncompelled people." Faith is a free gift of God, and civil authorities exceed their competence when they "champion the Word of God with a fist." The church, said the Anabaptist, is distinct from society, even if society claims to be Christian. Christ's true followers are a pilgrim people; and his church is a marching demonstration of perpetual aliens.

By separating church and state the Anabaptists became the first Christians in modern times to preach a thoroughgoing religious liberty: the right to join in worship with others of like faith without state support and without state persecution.

Over the centuries the descendants of Anabaptism lost many of the characteristics of their founders. In their search for a pure church, they often became legalistic. In the interests of sheer survival, they lost their evangelistic zeal and became known simply as excellent farmers, good people, and the "Quiet in the Land." Not until the late nineteenth century did they experience revival and fresh growth. By the late twentieth century their worldwide membership had reached over a half million. Far beyond the boundaries of the Mennonite and Hutterite communities, however, Christians have embraced one or more of those principles for which the first generation of radicals were willing to die.

Suggestions for Further Reading

Clasen, Claus-Peter. *Anabaptism: A Social History, 1525–1618.* Ithaca, NY: Cornell University Press, 1972.

Estep, William R. *The Anabaptist Story.* Grand Rapids: Eerdmans, 1975.

Hershberger, Guy F. *The Recovery of the Anabaptist Vision.* Scottdale, PA: Herald Press, 1957.

Littell, Franklin H. *The Origins of Sectarian Protestantism*. New York: Macmillan, 1964.

Wenger, John Christian. *Even unto Death*. Richmond: John Knox Press, 1946.

*Weaver, Denny. *Becoming Anabaptist: The Origin and significance of Sixteenth Century Anabaptism*. 2nd ed. Scottsdale, PA: Herald Press, 2005.

Williams, George H. and Angel M. Mergal. *Spiritual and Anabaptist Writers*. Philadelphia: The Westminster Press, 1957.

*Van Braght, Thieleman J. *Martyrs Mirror: The Story of Seventeen Centuries of Christian Martyrdom from the Time of Christ to AD. 1660*. Trans. Joseph F. Sohm. Scottsdale, PA: Herald Press, 1950.

CHAPTER 26

THRUST INTO THE GAME

John Calvin

THE WAR RAGING BETWEEN Spain and France had closed the road to Strasbourg. So the young scholar from France, hoping to continue his studies, was forced to go through Geneva. He planned to stay only one night. He knew that the town wasn't the best place for solitude.

Geneva was in disarray. It was notoriously pleasure-loving, but its recent rejection of the Duke of Savoy and the pope in Rome had left public affairs in shambles, torn by dangerous factions.

An inflammatory Reformer named William Farel had been preaching in Geneva for four years, and Catholic masses had ceased. But Geneva's Protestantism rested chiefly on political hostility to the bishop, not doctrinal convictions. No one had stepped forward to shape the city's religious institutions along biblical lines.

Farel knew the city needed a manager. So during the "chance" visit of the young Frenchman John Calvin, Farel made a point to call upon the visitor. He found in Calvin the answer to Geneva's need, and he urged the young scholar to go no farther but to stay in the city and help establish the work there.

Calvin protested that he had some special studies he wanted to pursue. But Farel responded, "You are only following your own wishes! If you do not help us in this work of the Lord, the Lord will punish you for seeking your own interest rather than His."

Calvin was terror-stricken. The last thing he wanted was to offend Almighty God! So he consented to stay and immediately took up the reforming cause in Geneva.

267

Years later, looking back over his career, Calvin observed, "Being by nature a bit antisocial and shy, I always loved retirement and peace . . . . But God has so whirled me around by various events that He has never let me rest anywhere, but in spite of my natural inclination, has thrust me into the limelight and made me 'get into the game,' as they say."

Calvin's leadership in "the game" shaped a third reformation tradition. Today we call it Reformed or Calvinistic Christianity. It includes all Presbyterians, Dutch and German Reformed Churches, and many Baptists and Congregationalists.

THE MEANING OF REFORMED CHRISTIANITY

What are the unique features of Reformed Christianity? We can trace the dominant characteristics to the life and teachings of that young scholar who heard the call of God in William Farel's warning.

God had a game. Calvin was convinced of it. He called it God's sovereign will. Just as Luther's central doctrine was justification by faith, so Calvin's was the sovereignty of God. Both Reformers had an overwhelming sense of the majesty of God, but Luther's served to point up the miracle of forgiveness, while Calvin's gave the assurance of the impregnability of God's purpose.

Calvin (1509–1564) shared with Luther the four central Protestant beliefs, but he was born a generation after Luther in a different land and was a far different sort of person.

Luther was a peasant, a monk, and a university professor; Calvin, a scholar and lawyer called to a turbulent public ministry in a flourishing business community. Naturally they were impressed by different needs and emphasized different Christian solutions. Their foundations were the same, but the structures of doctrine and practice they erected at Wittenberg and Geneva were different in many important respects.

Calvin's organizing and executive abilities enabled him to build on the work of Zwingli. The reform movement started at Zurich spread rapidly in German-speaking Switzerland. Bern and its surrounding territories (the canton) joined the Protestant ranks in 1528. Basel followed in 1529. Soon Appenzell, St. Gall, and Schaflhausen joined the movement.

The Zwinglian type of reformation found support also outside of Switzerland in the important German city of Strasbourg. There Martin Bucer (1491–1551), surpassed in influence throughout Germany only by Luther and his associate Melanchthon, was inclined to sympathize with Zwingli rather than with Luther.

Controversy between the Protestant and Catholic cantons in Switzerland led, however, on October 11, 1531, to a battle at Kappel between

Zurich and its Catholic neighbors. In the course of the battle Zwingli lost his life. Thus the leadership of the reformation in Zurich fell to Heinrich Bullinger. By the 1540s, however, Geneva, in French-speaking Switzerland, had emerged as the international center of Reformed Christianity under Calvin's disciplined hand.

John Calvin came from a small town sixty miles northeast of Paris. His father was anxious for his son to have the advantages of a good education. Calvin entered the University of Paris at fourteen and mastered not only a brilliant writing style but a skill in logical argument. In later years men might not like what Calvin said, but they could not misunderstand what he meant. He left the university in 1528 with his Master of Arts degree.

After Paris, at his father's insistence, John turned to the study of law in the universities of Orleans and Bourges, but his father's death in 1531 left Calvin free to pursue his own interests. Thus he returned to Paris as a student of the classics, intent upon a scholar's career.

His studies brought Calvin into touch with reforming ideas circulating in Paris, and shortly thereafter an event in Calvin's life turned him in a new direction. He called it an "unexpected conversion." We can't be certain about the date, but it was clearly more than a kind of spiritual enlightenment or the recognition of the supreme authority of the Scriptures. Calvin surrendered his will to God. He gave up his career as a classical scholar and identified with the Protestant cause in France.

In the autumn of 1533 Calvin was so closely linked with his friend Nicholas Cop that when Cop gave a strongly Protestant address as rector of the university, some suspected Calvin wrote the speech. The vigorous address threw the institution into an uproar, and Calvin was forced to flee from Paris. The young Reformer found refuge in Basel where in March 1536 he published the first edition of his highly influential *Institutes of the Christian Religion*.

The work was the clearest, most logical, and most readable exposition of Protestant doctrine that the Reformation age produced, and it gave its youthful author European fame overnight. Calvin labored on its elaboration nearly all his active life. Twenty years later it was a much larger work but its interpretation of Christian truth remained essentially the same.

As a preface to the *Institutes*, Calvin addressed a remarkable letter to Francis I, King of France, defending the Protestants in that land from the criticisms of their enemies and vindicating their rights to a respectful hearing. No one had spoken so effectively in their behalf, and with this letter Calvin assumed a position of leadership in the Protestant cause.

GENEVA: HOME OF CALVINISM

He could no longer remain in France. This is why after some months of travel he was headed for Strasbourg that fateful night in July 1536 when William Farel enlisted him for the work of God in Geneva.

The city councils offered Calvin a position, Professor of Sacred Scriptures, and he began his work with vigor. He prepared a confession of faith to be accepted by everyone who wished to be a citizen, he planned an educational program for all, and he insisted on excommunication, particularly expulsion from the Lord's Supper, for those whose lives did not conform to spiritual standards.

It was the most strenuous program of moral discipline within Protestantism, a bit more than the city fathers had bargained for. Opposition arose, especially over who had the power to excommunicate, the church or the magistrates. After a year of struggle Calvin and Farel were defeated on the issue, and in April 1538 the city councils ordered the two Reformers to leave Geneva. Calvin appeared to be a failure.

The next three years spent in Strasbourg were probably the happiest in Calvin's life. As pastor of the church of French refugees, he was free to carry out his disciplinary measures; he was a successful teacher of theology; he was honored by the city and was made its representative to important religious conferences in Germany. He married a widow with two children during these years and she remained his helpful companion until her death in March 1549.

Meanwhile Calvin's friends in Geneva regained power in the city government and urged him to return and resume his reform efforts. In September 1541, with great reluctance, he once again took up the Geneva burden, practically on his own terms. The church constitution accepted by the city put into practice Calvin's leading ideas.

Four offices governed the church: pastors, teachers, elders, and deacons. The twelve elders, together with the ministers, formed the Consistory, which was responsible for the moral supervision of the city. Offenses ranged from absences from public worship to drinking, adultery, gambling, and dancing.

Naturally, opposition continued. Many times Calvin was on the brink of banishment. But he fought his way through courageously, and the influx of exiles for their faith, chiefly from France, whom Calvin attracted to Geneva constantly increased his following.

During one low point in Calvin's influence, in 1553, the brilliant but erratic Spanish physician Michael Servetus sought refuge in Geneva. Servetus was fleeing Catholic persecution for his heresy of denying the doctrine of the Trinity. He arrived in Geneva just as Calvin's enemies were challenging his authority. While Calvin wanted a more merciful death than burning for the heretic, he did support the silencing of the ill-balanced thinker. Servetus was burned at the stake, and many in later generations remembered Calvin primarily as "the man who burned Servetus."

Two years later Calvin's position in Geneva was secure, and until his death he enjoyed significant influence over religious and moral issues in the city. For Calvin, however, Geneva was never an end in itself. He considered the city a refuge for persecuted Protestants, an example of a disciplined Christian community, and a center for ministerial training. Enthusiastic students from all over Europe came to Geneva to see what John Knox called "the most perfect school of Christ that ever was on earth since the days of the Apostles." They received Calvin's theology firsthand and obediently lived the city's rigorous lifestyle.

THE SOVEREIGNTY OF GOD

The Calvinism the students imbibed flowed from Calvin's central belief in the absolute sovereignty of God. "God asserts his possession of omnipotence," he wrote, "and claims our acknowledgement of this attribute." God is the "Governor of all things." In his own wisdom, from the remotest eternity, he decreed what he would do, and by his own power he executes what he has decreed.

This is more than a general guidance. The Bible teaches God's particular direction in individual lives. We read that not a sparrow falls to the ground unknown to the Father. We read, too, that he has given babies to some mothers and withheld them from others. Such events represent no relentless fatalism in nature, but the personal decrees of Almighty God, who moves men to walk in his ways.

If Luther's ultimate text was "the just shall live by faith," Calvin's was, "Thy will be done, on earth as it is in heaven." Calvin saw the old doctrine of predestination taught by Paul, Augustine, and Luther as a source of religious devotion. More than a problem of the mind, Calvin considered divine election to eternal life the deepest source of confidence, humility, and moral power.

While Calvin did not profess to know absolutely who were God's chosen (the elect) he believed that three tests constituted a good yardstick by which to judge who might be saved: participation in the two sacraments Baptism and the Lord's Supper, an upright moral life, and a public profession of the faith. These were adequate for a disciplined church on earth.

The consequence of faith to Calvin, far more than to Luther, is strenuous effort to introduce the kingdom of God on earth. Though no longer judged by the law of God, the true Christian finds in the law the divine pattern for moral character. Man is not justified by works, yet no justified man is without works. No one can be a true Christian without aspiring to holiness in his life. This rigorous pursuit of moral righteousness was one of the primary features of Calvinism. It made character a fundamental test of genuine religious life and explains Calvinism's dynamic social activism. God calls the elect for his purpose!

Calvinism's emphasis upon the sovereignty of God led in turn to a special view of the state. Luther tended to consider the state supreme. The German princes often determined where and how the gospel would be preached. But Calvin taught that no man, whether pope or king, has any claim to absolute power. Calvin never preached the "right of revolution," but he did encourage the growth of representative assemblies and stressed their right to resist the tyranny of monarchs. Calvinist resistance to the exercise of arbitrary power by monarchs was a key factor in the development of modern constitutional governments.

The church, said Calvin, is not subject to secular government except in obviously secular matters. On the other hand, the church has the obligation under the sovereign God, to guide the secular authorities in spiritual matters. Such a vision sent Calvin's followers throughout Europe as a spiritual conspiracy seeking the overthrow of false religion and restrictive governments.

Many zealous disciples considered Geneva a beachhead established by God. It was a promise that the kingdom would someday be organized. When they left Geneva they returned to their own countries to establish Calvinist principles there. As a result, Calvinism rapidly assumed international dimensions.

In France Calvinism remained a minority, but, thanks to influential converts among the nobility, the movement gained an importance out of all proportion to its numbers. Known as Huguenots, French Calvinists were threatening to seize leadership of the country when thousands of them were ruthlessly massacred on St. Bartholomew's Day in 1572. They remained a significant minority but never again a serious challenge to the Catholic throne.

In the Netherlands Calvinism offered a rallying point for opposition to the oppressive rule of Catholic Spain. Calvinist ministers were among the earliest leaders of resistance groups. Today we would call them freedom fighters or perhaps guerrillas. The liberation leader of the national party in the northern province of the Netherlands was

William the Silent. He joined the reformed church in 1573 and during the next decade helped to fashion a Dutch republic. Today's national anthem of the Netherlands, "The Song of the Prince," was written for William's followers.

In Scotland the Calvinists created something unique in sixteenth-century Europe: a land of one religion ruled by a monarch of another.

The monarch was Mary Queen of Scots, an eighteen-year-old girl living abroad. She married into the French royal family, and the Scots as well as many Englishmen feared that she might deliver Scotland to the French. One man, however, preached everywhere the notion that the people of Scotland could challenge the rule of their queen. That man was John Knox.

JOHN KNOX'S SCOTLAND

Knox was a restless activist who had tried earlier to point England in the direction of Calvinism. Like many others, however, he was forced to flee England overnight when, in 1553, the country returned to the Catholic faith under Henry VIII's daughter, Mary I. The queen's persecution of Protestant leaders earned her the title Bloody Mary.

Knox escaped to the Continent, where he developed the theory that Protestants had the right to resist, by force if necessary, any Roman Catholic ruler who tried to prevent their worship and mission. That was farther than Calvin himself was willing to go, but many of the nobles in Scotland found the idea attractive.

When civil war broke out in Scotland in 1559, Knox rushed home. By the summer of 1560 the Calvinists were in control of Edinburgh. Knox drafted the articles of religion that parliament accepted for the country, thereby abolishing Roman Catholicism.

Next year when Mary Queen of Scots, now a nineteen-year-old widow, decided to return to her kingdom, she found it in the lap of Protestant "heresy." Over the next few years Knox, the passionate preacher of Calvinism, and Mary, the young queen of Scotland, came to symbolize the Reformation conflict: Protestant against Catholic, but also the democratic claims of Calvinism against the monarchy's power to appoint bishops. Events in Scotland moved in Knox's direction. Even though Mary's descendants tried to turn back the clock, Scotland remained the most devoutly Calvinist country in the world.

Thus, when Calvin died in 1564, he left far more than a reformed Geneva. All over Europe, and soon in distant America, he had followers who were eager to continue the game he had entered that fateful night in Farel's rowdy and restless Geneva.

Suggestions for Further Reading

*Cottret, Bernard. *Calvin: A Biography.* Eerdmans, Grand Rapids, 2000.

Ferm, Vergilius. *Classics of Protestantism.* New York: Philosophical Library, 1959.

Harbison, E. Harris. *The Christian Scholar in the Age of the Reformation.* New York: Charles Scribner's Sons, 1956.

McGrath, Alister. *A Life of John Calvin: A Study in the Shaping of Western Culture.* Oxford: Basil Blackwell, 1990.

McNeill, John T. *The History and Character of Calvinism.* New York: Oxford University Press, 1967.

Parker, T. H. L. *Portrait of Calvin.* Philadelphia: Westminster, John Knox Press, 2007.

Walker, Williston. *John Calvin, the Organizer of Reformed Protestantism.* New York: Schocken, 1969.

CHAPTER 27

THE CURSE
UPON THE CROWN

The Church of England

O N A SATURDAY AFTERNOON in June 1533, a dark-eyed English lady, surrounded by the nation's nobility, rode through London's crowded streets and triumphal arches. Anne Boleyn, mounted on a chair draped in silver and gold, was on her way to Westminster Abbey where, next morning, she would be solemnly anointed and crowned Queen of England.

Behind that entourage was a series of fast-paced events that carried England into the reformation of Christianity in its own distinctive way and created the historic background for a host of Anglo-American denominations including Episcopalians, Congregationalists, and Baptists.

If the Lutheran reformation began in a monastic cell, the Anabaptist reformation in a prayer meeting, and the Calvinistic reformation at a scholar's desk, then the English reformation began in the affairs of state, specifically with the problem of succession to the royal throne.

In a sense England had two reformations: a constitutional one under King Henry VIII (1509–1547) and a theological one under the Puritans almost a century later. Under Henry nothing changed doctrinally. England simply rejected the authority of Rome. In this move, however, England forecast the future of Christianity in modern nations. She made Christian beliefs almost altogether a private affair and considered the practice of religion an instrument of the state. Later generations called it *civil religion*.

275

How could such a thing happen? Why did England, even without any great theological issue, overthrow the longstanding authority of the Church of Rome?

ENGLAND'S BREAK WITH ROME

The idea arose out of the marital problems of King Henry, whom Charles Dickens once described as "a most intolerable ruffian and a blot of blood and grease on the history of England." Other influences, to be sure, contributed to the break with Rome, but succession to the throne was the primary constitutional factor in the transformation of the Church *in* England into the Church *of* England.

For centuries the Church in England had been moving toward independence from Rome. By Luther's time, most patriotic Englishmen had a sense of the distinctive character of the faith in their fatherland.

Cardinal Thomas Wolsey (1474–1530) is probably the best symbol of the independence England had achieved even prior to Henry's break with Rome. Wolsey was the Archbishop of York, a Cardinal in the Church of Rome, and the chancellor of the English realm. So in his own person, he combined the Church in England, the Church of Rome, and the Kingdom of England. Yet in all of these offices he was the king's henchman, subject to honor or disgrace at the royal whim.

Understandably, the schism in the church came over a royal problem, not over theological conflicts. Putting it simply, Henry VIII, King of England, revolted against the pope because he passionately desired the dark-eyed Anne Boleyn, a lady-in-waiting of the court.

But that is only the headline. The important facts surround the royal succession to the English throne, not the personal lust of the king. Henry knew how to satisfy his lusts. He shared the customary royal pastime with mistresses and had at least one illegitimate son. His problem was he had no son born of his queen, Catherine of Aragon.

Catherine, daughter of Ferdinand and Isabella of Spain, had delivered five children, but the only survivor beyond infancy was the princess Mary. Unfortunately, England was in no mood to accept a girl as heir to the throne because the nation's only previous queen had occasioned bloody wars of succession.

Thus, as Catherine grew older Henry grew more troubled. In 1525 the queen was forty and Henry pondered more and more the ways of the Almighty: "Am I under some curse of God?"

The question arose because prior to their marriage Catherine had been Henry's deceased brother Arthur's wife, at least for several months, and Henry believed that the curse of God fell on any marriage to a brother's wife. According to the book of Leviticus: "If a man shall take his brother's wife, it is an unclean thing . . . they shall be childless" (Lev. 20:21, KJV).

Naturally, the Church of Rome had also recognized the curse, and at the time of Henry's wedding Pope Julius II had found grounds for granting special permission for the wedding. But with the passing of the barren years, Henry wondered if Julius had not overstepped his sacred rights. Was Catherine's inability to bear a son evidence of God's curse upon the union? If so, why couldn't the pope divide asunder what he had joined?

In 1527 Henry asked the Holy Father, Clement VII, to revoke the special dispensation and declare the marriage of eighteen years invalid from the outset. The pope might have been open to the idea had not Catherine been the aunt of Charles V, Holy Roman Emperor and King of Spain. At that moment the pope could ill afford to offend the emperor, so he stalled. Henry's personal reasons for desiring the annulment were matched by the pope's political reasons for refusing the request.

Henry decided to take matters into his own hands. He eagerly adopted the suggestion of one of his advisers, Thomas Cranmer, that he present his case to the European universities for their scholarly opinion. The response, as one might expect, was mixed, but Henry had his cover for imposing his will upon the nation.

In January 1533 the king secretly married Anne. In May an English church court declared Henry's marriage to Catherine null and void. And in September the new queen gave birth to a child. Contrary to the forecasts of astrologers, it was a girl, Elizabeth.

When the pope countered Henry's move by excommunicating him, Henry realized that papal authority in England had to be overthrown. The king knew the antipapal sympathies in England were running high. At Cambridge, for example, certain instructors were so taken with Luther that the favorite gathering place, the Inn of the White Horse, was called "Little Germany." So the king calculated that he would face little popular opposition so long as he renounced papal authority in England and avoided troublesome doctrinal questions.

Henry moved briskly on a series of fronts. He discovered an old fourteenth-century law prohibiting dealings with foreign powers and used it to insist that the English clergy stop their dealings with the pope. The clergy offered surprisingly little resistance.

A year later, 1534, the Act of Supremacy declared, "The king's majesty justly and rightly is and ought to be and shall be reputed the only supreme head in earth of the Church of England called *Anglicana Ecclesia.*"

It was done. The break with Rome was complete. England now had a national church with the king as its head. The head, however, was not a priest. He could appoint, but he could not consecrate bishops. He could defend, but he could not formulate the faith. The king looked to the archbishop of Canterbury, the highest office in the Church of England, to serve the purposes of the priesthood and secured the services of Thomas Cranmer in that post.

HENRY'S DUAL POLICY

The sole religious issue, then, in England's initial reformation was papal supremacy. Henry intended no break with the old faith. He considered himself, in fact, a guardian of Catholic dogma. In 1521, in answer to Luther's attack upon the seven sacraments, the king had written a *Defense of the Seven Sacraments.* In it he had castigated Luther as a "poisonous serpent" and a "wolf of hell." In gratitude, the pope had bestowed on Henry the title "Defender of the Faith"—a title still carried by English monarchs.

After the break with Rome, England's orthodoxy remained intact. Henry continued to insist upon Catholic doctrine within the realm. Apparently his goal was an English Catholic Church instead of a Roman Catholic one. The Statute of Six Articles in 1539 upheld such Catholic articles as clerical celibacy, the private mass, and confessions to a priest.

Only two serious changes marked the new way within the Church of England. The first was the suppression of the monasteries; the second was the publication of the English Bible for use in the churches.

Monks in England were neither popular nor devout. One author called them "foul, unhappy lepers who . . . despoiled poor wives of the tenth egg." Their lack of dedication to their calling was evident in 1536 when Henry suppressed the smaller monasteries. The king gave the monks the opportunity either of transferring to other houses or of entering secular life; fully one-half chose society over another cloister.

Henry used the monastic properties—almost one-tenth of the national wealth—to replenish the royal coffers and to gain support from favored barons and gentry who were given or purchased the property. Monks received a reasonable pension, but Henry succeeded by this one stroke in reducing the opposition to his policy and gaining new friends.

The second change in the Church of England occurred when Henry ordered that an English Bible be installed in all the churches. In principle, the Church of Rome did not object to versions in the native tongue provided they were orthodox and authorized. Translations from the Hebrew and Greek, however, were bound to offend Rome because she had for centuries based crucial doctrines on questionable translations found in the Latin version. The most noteworthy example is the Latin rendering "do penance" where the Greek means simply "repent." Rome, therefore, could hardly welcome news of another English Bible, especially in the wake of Wyclif's heresy.

Nevertheless, shortly after the publication of Erasmus's Greek New Testament in 1516, with its preface urging the translation of Scripture into the common tongues of Europe, new versions appeared in German, French, and English. These fed the rising national sentiments and Protestant convictions.

WILLIAM TYNDALE'S BIBLE

The pioneer in the translation of the English Bible was William Tyndale. A zeal to place the English Scripture into the hands of the common man burned in Tyndale's soul. After receiving his ordination, he once expressed his frank amazement at the ignorance of the clergy. When a fellow priest resented this observation, Tyndale hotly replied, "If God spares my life, before many years pass I will make it possible for a boy behind the plow to know more Scripture than you do."

Tyndale soon learned, however, that such an undertaking was not welcome in England. After study at Oxford and Cambridge he was forced to flee to the Continent to live, labor, and print the New Testament. Early in 1526 he began smuggling the first copies of his work into his homeland.

In the following years Tyndale translated portions of the Old Testament and brought out an improved edition of the New. Church officials continued to hound him, however, and in 1536 he fell into their hands. After seventeen months in prison Tyndale went to his death at the stake. His dying prayer was, "Lord, open the king of England's eyes."

Events in England were already moving swiftly toward an answer to Tyndale's prayer. During his months of imprisonment, another Cambridge graduate and Reformer, Miles Coverdale, had published the first edition of his complete translation of the Bible. The edition was basically Tyndale's work, supplemented by Latin and German versions.

Then, a year after Tyndale's death, the Matthew Bible appeared. It was the work of another English reformer named John Rogers, who thought it wise to send forth his translation without his name attached. The Matthew Bible was virtually a well-edited compilation of Tyndale and Coverdale's work. At Thomas Cranmer's request, however, Henry VIII authorized that this Bible, revised by Coverdale and called the "Great Bible," be bought and read throughout the realm. Tyndale's dying prayer was answered, at least in part. The sudden access to the Scriptures created widespread excitement, so much so that Henry issued new regulations limiting the reading of the Bible to wealthy merchants and aristocrats. Greater freedom, however, was just a matter of time.

THE SWING TO PROTESTANTISM

After the king's death in 1547, his only son, frail ten-year-old Edward VI, followed his father to the throne. Edward's mother was Jane Seymour, whom Henry had married after he had executed Anne Boleyn on charges of adultery. The power of government under young Edward rested with a group of royal advisers who were in sympathy with the Protestant Reformation, so official English policy shifted abruptly in a Protestant direction.

During Edward's brief years England saw the Six Articles repealed, priests allowed to marry, and the old Latin service of worship replaced by Cranmer's Book of Common Prayer in English. In 1553 Cranmer also produced the Forty-Two Articles, which defined the faith of the Church of England along Protestant lines.

This swing in a Protestant direction came to a sudden halt when Edward died in 1553 and Mary, the daughter of Catherine, ascended the throne. Devoutly Catholic, Mary tried to lead England back to the ways of Rome. In four short years she outdid her father in intolerance. She sent nearly three hundred Protestants, including Archbishop Cranmer, to the burning stake.

Later John Foxe collected the vivid reports of these martyrdoms in his *Book of Martyrs* (1571) and incited the English people to a longstanding horror of Catholicism. He succeeded in giving Mary the name by which history still remembers her, Bloody Mary.

Though Mary was probably the only really pious English monarch of the sixteenth century, she committed an unforgivable blunder in making martyrs. By the 1550s England had enjoyed almost a generation without interference from Rome, so the country interpreted her devotion and her marriage to Philip of Spain as a betrayal of her people. She died a broken and disappointed queen.

With the accession to the throne of Anne Boleyn's redheaded and fiery-tempered daughter, Elizabeth I (1558–1603), the Anglican Church assumed its distinctive character, neither Roman nor

Reformed. Realizing the political necessity for religious peace, Elizabeth worked hard to achieve a compromise settlement. Although the Church of England remained a state church under the control of the monarch, Elizabeth astutely changed her title from Supreme Head to the more modest Supreme Governor.

In accepting the Bible as the final authority, and in recognizing only Baptism and the Holy Eucharist as Christ-instituted sacraments, Elizabeth's Thirty-Nine Articles (1563) were essentially Protestant, but many articles were worded in a way that would satisfy both Catholics and Protestants. The liturgy of the Church retained many Catholic elements and bishops in apostolic succession governed the Church. Elizabeth, like the monarchs after her, received and believed advice that a bishop-led church would be easier to control. In time English churchmen spoke of this compromise as the best of both worlds, the *Via Media*, the Middle Way between Protestantism and Catholicism.

Some of the exiles who were forced out of England during Mary's reign were not so sure. When they returned from the Continent to Elizabeth's establishment, they began to cry out against "the ease in Zion." They had read their Bibles and had developed their own ideas about a true reformation in England. We know these Reformers as Puritans, preachers of personal and national righteousness. The future was dawning.

Suggestions for Further Reading

*McCulloch, Diarmaid. *Thomas Cranmer: A Life*. New Haven, CT: Yale, 1996.

Mozley, J. F. *William Tyndale*. New York: The Macmillan Company, 1937.

Parker, T. M. *The English Reformation to 1558*. London: Oxford University Press, 1960.

Rupp, E. G. *The English Protestant Tradition*. Cambridge: Cambridge University Press, 1966.

Rupp, Gordon. *Six Makers of English Religion: 1500–1700*. New York: Harper & Brothers Publishers, 1957.

Woodbridge, U. K. *Thomas Cranmer: Churchman and Scholar*. Rochester: Boydell Press, 1993.

CHAPTER 28

"ANOTHER MAN" AT MANRESA

The Catholic Reformation

IN 1521, THE YEAR that Martin Luther stood before the Emperor Charles V at the Diet of Worms, a young Spanish nobleman was fighting on the emperor's borderlands against the invading French at Pamplona. A cannonball shattered one of his legs. During a long, painful convalescence he turned, out of boredom, to two popular inspirational works, one on the lives of the saints and the other a life of Christ. With these his long process of conversion began.

Months later, at the Benedictine abbey of Montserrat, he exchanged his gentleman's clothes for a rough pilgrim's garb and dedicated his sword and dagger to the shrine's Black Virgin. For nearly a year, in a little town called Manresa, thirty miles north of Barcelona, he gave himself to an orgy of austerity: begging door to door, wearing a barbed girdle, fasting for days on end. For months he endured the terrible depressions of the mystic's dark night of the soul, even contemplating suicide at one point. But what followed was the mystic's singular reward, an immense breakthrough to spiritual enlightenment. In a wave of ecstatic illumination one day at the River Cardoner, the wounded nobleman, Ignatius Loyola, became, in his own words, "another man."

Loyola (1491–1556) transformed his rebirth at Manresa to a plan for spiritual discipline, a military manual for storm troopers at the service of the pope. The result was the Jesuits, the Society of Jesus, the greatest single force in Catholicism's campaign to recapture the spiritual domains seized by Protestantism.

How did the Church of Rome respond to the Protestant challenge? It didn't, not immediately. But when it finally realized the seriousness of the revolt, it called upon its spiritual warriors, it convened a new militant council, and it reformed the machinery of the papal office. Faced by the rebellion of almost half of Europe, Catholicism rolled back the tide of Protestantism until by the end of the sixteenth century Protestantism was limited roughly to the northern third of Europe, as it is today.

Some historians have interpreted the Catholic Reformation as a counterattack against Protestantism; others have described it as a genuine revival of Catholic piety with few thoughts of Protestantism. The truth is the movement was both a Counter Reformation, as Protestants insist, and a Catholic Reformation, as Catholics argue. Its roots run back to forces before Luther's time, but the form it took was largely determined by the Protestant attack.

Facets of the Counter Reformation

1. Ignatius became an important voice for Catholic spirituality, as well as organizing the influential Jesuit order.
2. The Counter Reformation also contributed to the emergence of other important voices in spirituality, including St. Teresa of Avila.
3. Catholics answered the academic and scholarly work of the Protestants with work in language (especially in Spain) and training for priests.
4. The council of Trent offered an articulation of doctrines in reaction to the Protestant teaching.
5. The Catholic Church initiated a global missionary expansion.
6. The Inquisition, an adaptation of an ancient Roman legal format, proved an effective yet brutal strategy to discover and stop heresy.

RETURN TO THE SPIRITUAL

Strange as it may seem the mystical experience was a large part of Catholicism's recovery. The sixteenth century produced a remarkable variety of Catholic saints: the English lawyer and statesman, Thomas More; the cheerful and imaginative missionary to the Calvinists, Francis of Sales; the somber reforming archbishop of Milan, Charles Borromeo; the rapturous Spanish mystic, Teresa of Avila; and, most influential of all, the Spanish soldier of Christ, Ignatius Loyola.

Even before Luther posted his theses on the church door, a distinguished and aristocratic group at Rome had formed a pious brotherhood called the Oratory of Divine Love. Their guiding belief was that the reformation of the church and society begins within the individual soul.

The Oratory was never large in number, perhaps fifty, yet it had enormous influence. It stimulated reform in the older monastic orders and contributed leaders to the Church of Rome as it laid plans for a general council to deal with internal reform and the Protestant heresy. Among the members of the Oratory who later emerged as significant figures were Jacopo Sadoleto, who debated with Calvin; Reginald Pole, who tried under Bloody Mary to turn England back to Rome; and Gian Pietro Caraffa, who became Pope Paul IV.

Throughout the 1520s and 1530s, however, the Church of Rome took no significant steps toward reform. The question is why. Why was she so slow to respond to the Protestant challenge?

One simple answer is politics. The Emperor Charles V and the popes fought a running battle over the calling of a general council that stretched over two decades. Luther had called for a council of the church as early as 1518. The idea gained the support of the German princes and the emperor, but the popes had fears of such an assembly. They remembered too well the councils at Constance and Basel. They also knew that many in Germany had in mind a council without the pope.

Equally important, the popes in the 1520s and 1530s were preoccupied with secular and political affairs. Clement VII (1523–1534) is a prominent example. He regarded concern for the Papal States in Italy as a supreme law, and his passion for papal political fortunes drew him into an alliance with France against Charles V, leader of the Hapsburg interests in Italy. The pope's treachery and disloyalty enraged Charles, and he threatened Clement with a trial before a general council unless he broke his alliance with Francis I, King of France.

To show the pope he meant business Charles ordered his troops to march on Rome. As it turned out he got more than he had planned. The commanders of his troops were killed. As a result, the rough and undisciplined Spanish and German mercenaries were leaderless when they stormed Rome on May 6, 1527. Their pillaging, plundering, and murdering in the Eternal City lasted for weeks. The pope took refuge in the Castle of St. Angelo, but finally had to surrender and endure half a year of harsh imprisonment. Many considered this sack of Rome a terrible visitation by God, a clear call to repentance and change in the worldly papacy.

No serious reform came until Pope Paul III (1534–1549) ascended the papal throne. Paul appeared to be a most unlikely candidate for spiritual leadership. He had three illegitimate sons and a daughter, four striking reminders of his pursuit of pleasure. The sack of Rome, however, seems to have sobered him. He realized that the time had come for reform to begin in the House of God. He started where he felt a change of heart was most urgently needed, in the College of Cardinals. He appointed to the college a number of champions of reform. Among them were leaders in the Oratory of Divine Love: Sadoleto, Pole, and Caraffa.

Paul then appointed nine of the new cardinals to a reform commission. The head of the commission was another former member of the Oratory, Gasparo Contarini. A peacemaker by temperament, Contarini stood for reconciliation with the Protestants and advocated a return to the faith of the apostles.

After a wide-ranging study of conditions in the Church of Rome, the commission issued in 1537 a formal report, *Advice . . . Concerning the Reform of the Church.* Disorder in the Church, the report said, could be traced directly to the need for reform. The papal office was too secular. Both popes and cardinals needed to give more attention to spiritual matters and stop flirting with the world. Bribery in high places, abuses of indulgences, evasions of church law, prostitution in Rome: these and other offenses must cease.

CALL FOR A GENERAL COUNCIL

Pope Paul took action on a few of these items, but his most significant response was a call for a general council of the Church. After intense negotiations he agreed with the emperor on a location for the assembly, a town in northern Italy under imperial control called Trent.

Even then, however, no council assembled for years because Francis I did everything in his power to prevent such a gathering. In his passion for leadership of Europe, he feared a council would only strengthen Charles's hand. Francis even stooped to incite the Turks against the emperor. Two wars between Francis and Charles delayed the opening of a council until 1545, almost three decades after Luther's theses appeared.

By 1545 Rome was under the spell of a new austerity. Reform was on the rise. The immoralities of Paul's younger days were no longer acceptable behavior. The pope's new rigor was apparent in the institution of the Roman Inquisition and in the Index of prohibited books: works that any Catholic risked damnation by reading. All the books of the Reformers were listed, as well as Protestant Bibles. For a long time merely to possess one of these banned books in Spain was punishable by death. The Index was kept up to date until 1959 and was finally abolished by Pope Paul VI.

IGNATIUS LOYOLA

It was this city, a new militant Rome, and this pope, Paul III, who approved Ignatius Loyola's new Society of Jesus. These daring soldiers of Christ promised the pope that they would go wherever he might send them "whether to the Turks or to the New World or to the Lutherans or to others, be they infidel or faithful." They said it and they meant it, for the Jesuits were a fitting likeness of their founding general.

As a boy Ignatius had left the gloomy castle of Loyola near the Pyrenees to enter the court of his father's noble friend. He had grown into little more than an engaging playboy, spending his days in military games or reading popular chivalrous romances, his nights pursuing less noble adventures with local girls.

But all that was before Ignatius met God at Manresa. Martin Luther emerged from his spiritual struggle convinced that the human will is enslaved, that man cannot save himself. God, and God alone, must deliver him. Loyola came out of his struggle believing that both God and Satan are external to man, and man has the power to choose between them. By the disciplined use of his imagination man can strengthen his will so as to choose God and his ways.

One of Loyola's spiritual exercises, for example, aimed to make the horrors of hell real:

> Hear in imagination the shrieks and groans and blasphemous shouts against Christ our Lord and all the saints. Smell in imagination the fumes of sulphur and the stench of filth and corruption. Taste in imagination all the bitterness of tears and melancholy and growing conscience. Feel in imagination the heat of the flames that play on and burn the souls.

The same technique, of course, could be used to represent the beauties of the Nativity or the glories of heaven. By proper discipline the imagination could strengthen the will and teach it to cooperate with God's grace.

For Ignatius personally surrender to the will of God meant more education. He entered a school in Barcelona to sit with boys less than half his age to study Latin, then threw himself into a dizzying year of courses at the University of Alcala. Out of it came his conviction that learning must be organized to be useful. The idea eventually grew into the Jesuits' famed plan of studies, which measured out heavy but manageable doses of classics, humanities, and sciences.

Ignatius became such a fervent evangelist that the Inquisition imprisoned and examined him more than once about his life, teaching, and theology. Perturbed, he left for Paris where he spent seven years at the university, became "Master Ignatius," and gathered around him the first of his permanent companions: Peter Faber, Diego Laynez, Alfonso Salmeron, Simon Rodriguez, Nicholas Bobadilla, and, above all, the young Spanish nobleman, Francis Xavier.

Ignatius shared with them his remarkable program for sainthood, his *Spiritual Exercises*. A distillation of his own religious experiences during and following his conversion, the *Exercises* prescribe four "weeks" of meditations, beginning with sin, death, judgment, and hell, and then moving on to Christ's life, death, and resurrection.

Ignatius intended a path to spiritual perfection: rigorous examination of conscience, penance, and a resolute amnesia about guilt once the spiritual pilgrim confronted God's forgiveness. The *Exercises* became the basis of every Jesuit's spirituality. Later popes also prescribed them for candidates for ordination, and Catholic retreats applied them to lay groups.

In his *Portrait of the Artist as a Young Man*, James Joyce describes his young hero, Stephen Dedalus, reduced to horror by a sermon on hell: "A wave of fire swept through his body . . . flames burst forth from his skull." After he had gone to confession, however, "the past was past." That is just the way Ignatius planned it. "Send no one away dejected," Loyola wrote. "God asks nothing impossible." Thus his followers became the great apostles of the possible.

THE SOCIETY OF JESUS

In 1540 Pope Paul III approved the little Society of Jesus as a new religious order. In Ignatius's metaphor, they were to be chivalrous soldiers of Jesus, mobile, versatile, ready to go anywhere and perform any task the pope assigned. As a recognized order, they added to their earlier vows of poverty and chastity the traditional vow of obedience to their superiors and a fourth vow expressing their special loyalty to the pope. They gave command to a superior general elected for life. Their choice for the first general was Ignatius.

The aim of the order was simple: to restore the Roman Catholic Church to the position of spiritual power and worldly influence it had held three centuries before under Innocent III. Everything was subordinated to the Church of Rome because Ignatius believed firmly that the living Christ resided in the institutional church exclusively.

Perhaps the most fascinating feature of the Jesuits was their perilous attempt to live energetically *in* the world without being *of* it. Loyola wanted them to be all things to all men, and they nearly succeeded.

Their efforts have rallied defenders who assign them the highest posts in heaven and critics who consign them to the lower regions of hell. Writing to Thomas Jefferson in 1816, John Adams said, "If ever any congregation of men could merit eternal perdition on earth and in hell, it is the company of Loyola." Whatever their destination, the Jesuits were from their beginning unique.

That first generation under Loyola's zealous leadership rode full gallop into their new assignments: convert the heathen, reconvert Protestant Europe. Francis Xavier leaped from India to Southeast Asia to Japan, a country that had never before heard the Christian message. More than any others, the Society of Jesus stemmed, and sometimes reversed, the tide of Protestantism in France, the Low Countries, and Central Europe. When Ignatius died in 1556, his order was nearly one thousand strong and had dispatched its apostles to four continents.

No mission in that first generation proved more decisive than the band of Jesuits assigned to the Council of Trent. Only thirty-one council fathers led by three papal legates were present for the opening ceremonies of the council. None of them could have guessed that their modest beginning would lead to the most important council between Nicaea (325) and Vatican II (1962–1965). Under the influence of the Jesuits, Trent developed into a powerful weapon of the Counter Reformation. Two suave, intelligent, and highly influential members of the society, Diego Laynez and Alfonso Salmeron, guided the agenda more and more toward "the correct churchly attitude" of the followers of Loyola.

The council fathers met in three main sessions: 1545–1547, 1551–1552, and 1562–1563. Throughout the sessions the Italians were strongly represented. Other areas, notably France, were significantly underrepresented. Compared to other councils, Trent was never well attended. During the second series of sessions a number of Protestants were present, but nothing came of it. From start to finish the council reflected the new militant stance of Rome.

THE SHAPE OF MODERN CATHOLICISM

Everything the Protestant Reformation stood for was vigorously—one could almost say violently—rejected at Trent. The Protestant Reformers emphasized justification by *faith alone*. The council rejected a potential compromise holding that justification is the result of two causes: 1) a righteousness that is external to the disciple but added to our account in the eyes of God, and 2) a righteousness that is internal, infused into the disciple. The Protestant's external righteousness was an event whereby God counted the person right in his eyes. For Catholics internal righteousness was the process whereby God imparted righteousness within the disciple during the course of their life. Trent emphatically linked justification to the process of becoming righteous, leaving the notion of being declared righteous to the Protestant proclaimers.

Luther, Calvin, and Grebel stressed salvation by *grace alone*; the council emphasized grace and human cooperation with God to avoid, in Loyola's terms, "the poison that destroys freedom." "Pray as though everything depended on God alone;" Ignatius advised, "but act as though it depended on you alone whether you will be saved."

The Protestants taught the religious authority of *Scripture alone*. The council insisted on the supreme teaching office of the Roman Church, popes and bishops, as the essential interpreters of the Bible.

ANGLICAN

CATHOLIC

CALVINIST

LUTHERAN

Religious Divisions at the End of the 16th Century

Thus the Council of Trent guaranteed that modern Roman Catholicism would be governed by the collaboration between God and man. The pope remained, the seven sacraments remained, the sacrifice of the mass remained. Saints, confessions, indulgences remained. The council's work essentially narrowed the range of options previously available to medieval Catholics; the anti-Protestant reactionary tone was unmistakable. After four centuries, we can look back to the Reformation age and see that the religious unity of western Christendom was permanently shattered. Men and women in Loyola's lifetime did not see that truth. The fact dawned upon Europe slowly.

At first Luther's followers thought him so obviously right that the Catholic Church would inevitably adopt his ideas. Others thought him so obviously wrong that sooner or later he would be burned as a heretic and his movement wither away. After all, the past was strewn with the corpses of heretical bodies. The point is both parties, Catholic and Protestant, thought that they represented the true, catholic church of Christ and their enemies a false version of it. That was the spirit of Trent as well.

As time went on, however, the thinking of ordinary men reached, almost imperceptibly, a second stage. The uneasy, half-conscious conviction grew that the conflict had reached a stalemate. Catholicism could not crush the new heresy, and Protestantism could not overthrow Rome. In this second stage men had no real emotional or intellectual acceptance of a stalemate, only a bitter admission of the fact.

The vast majority of people were still convinced that religious truth was identifiable. Truth stood on one side, error on the other. Error meant not only individual damnation, but infection of others and destruction of society. Resistance of these dreadful evils took the form of inquisitions, civil wars, and persecutions.

In this ideological warfare, Calvinists and Jesuits led the charge. Each embodied a militant organization calling for loyalty above and beyond national and political ties. At this stage almost no one could imagine that truth could lie on both sides of the battlefield or that both parties could peacefully coexist in the same state or even on the same continent.

The third stage of religious toleration, based upon the full acceptance of religious diversity within a nation, appeared before 1600 only in hints in the attitudes of mystics, Christian humanists like Erasmus, radical Protestants like the Anabaptists, and practical politicians like Queen Elizabeth of England.

Perhaps more powerful still were the political and economic forces committed to the emergence of the nation-state. Europe now had small political areas (the size of large counties or small states in the U.S.) under the umbrella of an emperor and the Catholic Church. These smaller realms under lords were merging into what we recognize today as nations, such as Germany. A state with geographic boundaries and more people would require both Protestant and Catholic citizens to coexist and cooperate.

Some voices, anticipating later Enlightenment thinking, called for a generic concept of God shared by virtually all believers in the West to become a new public standard: God is eternal, one, etc. Distinctive beliefs and social practices would be tolerated if they could be transformed to become a matter of private devotion. Feeble as it was, this whisper was the voice of the future. No company of Christians resisted it more doggedly than the Jesuits.

Suggestions for Further Reading

*Bireley, Robert. *The Refashioning of Catholicism, 1450–1700.* Washington, D.C.: Catholic University of America Press, 1999.

Brodrick, James. *The Origin of the Jesuits.* London: Longmans, Green and Co., 1949.

Daniel-Rops, Henry. *The Catholic Reformation.* New York: E. P. Dutton, 1962.

Franzen, August. *A History of the Church: Revised and Edited by John P. Dolan,* New York: Herder and Herder, 1969.

Noll, Mark A. *Turning Points: Decisive Moments in the History of Christianity.* Grand Rapids: Baker Books, 2000.

*O'Malley, John W. *The First Jesuits.* Cambridge, MA: Harvard University Press, 1993.

Thompson, Francis. *Saint Ignatius Loyola.* Westminster, MD: Newman Press, 1950.

Wakefield, James L. *Sacred Listening: Discovering the Spiritual Exercises of Ignatius Loyola.* Grand Rapids: Baker Books, 2006.

CHAPTER 29

OPENING THE ROCK

America and Asia

O N THURSDAY OCTOBER 11, 1492, a new world opened for the Christian faith. On that day Christopher Columbus, "Admiral of the Ocean Sea, Viceroy and Governor of whatever territory he might discover," sighted sandpipers, green reeds, and finally land in what we call the West Indies.

Next morning Columbus stepped on the island's shore, named it San Salvador (Holy Savior), and took possession of it in the name of King Ferdinand and Queen Isabella of Spain. He offered to the curious natives "red caps and glass beads to put round their necks." This gave them such obvious pleasure that Columbus surmised that they could easily be "converted to our holy faith by love" rather than by force.

Historians speak of the next 150 years as the age of discovery because during these decades Europeans planted colonies in the Americas and found new trade routes to the riches of the Far East. In the history of Christianity we might call these years "the age of global expansion" since between 1500 and 1650 Roman Catholic monks and friars carried the gospel to Spanish colonies throughout Latin America and Portuguese ports along the coasts of Africa and Asia.

Through all these exhilarating years Columbus's original alternative troubled Christian missionaries. Should the natives be won to the holy faith by love or by force? At times it was some courageous and selfless Franciscan or Jesuit winning by persevering love. At others, it was some troop of ruthless Christian conquerors forcing baptism upon natives at the point of the sword.

The problem arose because missionaries must always decide what heathenism is. Is it mankind stumbling in uncertain quest of the true God? Or is it humanity organized in hardened resistance to the gospel? Should the Christian ambassador seek the good in heathen religions and use this as a foundation for building a Christian community? Or should he suppress, destroy if necessary, all forms of heathen religion in order to plant the true faith? We can call one approach the policy of adaptation and the other the policy of conquest.

THE GOSPEL AND CULTURE

Adaptation or conquest rests in turn upon a broader question: how does the gospel relate to culture? The church is often in danger of identifying the gospel with some cultural form in which the faith has found a home. And thus missionaries failed to adapt to the ways of another people. They felt constrained to insist upon the expression of the faith in familiar ways.

In the age of the apostles, Jewish Christians initially believed devoutly that the faith was identical with Hebrew rites and covenants and sabbaths. Only when the good news broke free from its Jewish forms was it able to take root in the Greco-Roman world. The same was true when the invading Germanic tribes destroyed many of the institutions of Roman life. The Christian faith had to find new ways to speak effectively to medieval people. The early and high Middle Ages were times of dedicated missionary efforts.

During the Middle Ages, however, an important attitude developed among European Christians. The rise of Islam in the seventh century drove a wedge between Christians in Europe and their fellow believers in Asia and Africa. Only a few outposts of Christianity survived in the Islamic countries of North Africa and the Near East. Christianity was confined almost exclusively to Europe.

The crusades were the convulsive attempt of Christian Europe to batter down the barriers of Islam by military force. The long struggle in Spain and Portugal to drive out the Moors, as the Muslims were called there, created an especially militant attitude toward the unbelieving outsider. Conquest and evangelization slowly intertwined; few minds recognized a difference.

The new age of worldwide missions opened with the era of great discoveries. The Portuguese and Spaniards first turned their ships south about the middle of the fifteenth century. The French, Dutch, and English soon joined the colonizing venture. Following the west coast of Africa, the Portuguese reached the southern tip of the continent in

1486 and named it the Cape of Good Hope. In 1495 Vasco da Gama continued around Africa in the direction of Asia and first sighted land on the western or Malabar Coast of India. It was a spot ideally suited to serve as a base of operations for Portuguese expansion in the Far East. For centuries in Malabar ports Arab merchants had picked up spices, gems, ivory, Indian cottons, and Chinese silks and had shipped them through the Red Sea or the Persian Gulf, then overland to the Mediterranean world. The Portuguese realized that these ports were centers of exchange between the East and the West, the heart of the Eastern trade.

In short order the Portuguese drove the flimsy Arab vessels from the Indian Ocean. They made Goa on the Malabar Coast the center of their eastern commercial empire and moved on eastward to plant strategic bases in the Malay Archipelago and the Molucca Islands. By 1516 they had reached China and by 1543 Japan.

The Portuguese, unlike the Spanish, made no attempt to conquer or colonize on a large scale. They had no interest in land, no visions of gold. They wanted a trade monopoly. That meant control of the seas.

So Portuguese ports sprang up along the coasts of West Africa, the Congo and Angola; in India and Ceylon; in Brazil, Mozambique, and Malaya. In every trading settlement little Catholic churches appeared.

SPANIARDS IN THE NEW WORLD

Meanwhile the Spaniards were following up the discoveries of Columbus. The redheaded Genoese made three more trips to the New World in a vain attempt to find an opening to the Asian mainland. On the second of these trips, he sailed with seventeen ships bearing 1500 men. And on Haiti, he found gold—lots of it.

After tracing the coast of Cuba, which he thought was southern China, Columbus set sail for Spain. In spite of an oath of secrecy, the magic word *gold* leaked out in the homeland and the most violent gold rush in history was underway.

Within fifty years of the first sighting of San Salvador, the Spaniards had plundered and conquered the New World from California to the tip of South America. The work of these courageous and brutal conquerors planted the word *conquistadores* in our vocabularies. By 1521 Hernando Cortes, equipped with horses, armor, and gunpowder, had destroyed the great Aztec empire in Mexico, and by 1533 Francisco Pizarro had treacherously murdered Atahualpa, the monarch of the Incas, and brought the once mighty empire to its knees.

All this, it is worth noting, happened in Martin Luther's lifetime. Charles V, who succeeded Ferdinand and Isabella and fell heir to the enormous wealth of the New World, was the same prince before whom Luther stood at the Diet of Worms. So while Charles struggled to keep Germany from slipping from his imperial grasp into Protestant hands, he found comfort in the laden Spanish ships arriving from the West Indies and Mexico.

This great global venture, however, was far from a breathless race for spices and gold. Deep within the hearts of the Portuguese merchants and the Spanish *conquistadores* was the zeal to extend the holy faith, the Roman Catholic faith of their fathers. Thus Dominicans, Franciscans, Augustinians, or Jesuits sailed on nearly every ship, as eager to convert the heathen as any captain to find a new port for trade.

The sacrifices that many of these monks and friars made were extraordinary. The voyages at sea were risky, and there were no furloughs. Out of 376 Jesuits who sailed for China between 1581 and 1712, 127 died en route.

Thanks to such men, the sixteenth century, which saw Europe divided between Catholic and Protestant, also saw Christianity become catholic in a new way. Just when it was painfully apparent that *catholic* no longer meant *united*, the Christian faith appeared catholic in its mission to distant peoples. To avoid rivalry between Portugal and Spain, the pope drew a line on the map from the North Pole to the South, just west of the Azores. All to the west of the line, he said, belonged to Spain; all to the east belonged to Portugal. That boundary explains why Brazil is a Portuguese-speaking country today and the rest of Latin America is Spanish.

By papal commission the kings of Portugal and Spain were responsible to evangelize the lands conquered by their soldiers. The Catholic Church expected these princes to send out missionaries and maintain them in India or Peru. The monarchs had exclusive control over the missionaries and could name bishops to lead their newly baptized subjects.

Thus the underlying idea of this new missionary era was the extension of the concept of the Christian prince, the divinely appointed spiritual guide of his people, who was expected to remove all signs of idolatry from his lands and bring his subjects to the rule of Christ through the holy Catholic Church.

The violent nature of Spanish expeditions may be rooted in Spain's devotion to the mother church and to Islam's military encroachment into Spain. Sadly the expeditions assumed the violent fanaticism of a crusade. Cortes, the ruthless and skillful conqueror of Mexico, for example, was devoted to the Virgin Mary and always kept a statuette of her upon his person. He said his prayers and attended mass daily. Upon one flag he carried a cross and upon the other, a picture of the Virgin.

Spain's first policy toward the Indians, called *encomienda*, granted the Spanish colonists a number of Indians who were supposed to toil in the mines and on the plantations of their captors. For their trouble the Indians received protection and instruction in the holy faith. Since the Indians were guilty of gross crimes such as human sacrifice and idolatry, the Spanish felt duty-bound to stop these barbarities. Wars against the Indians, then, in their minds, were righteous wars like Israel's against the godless Canaanites. In 1531 Bishop Zumarraga wrote from Mexico that they had destroyed more than five hundred temples and twenty thousand idols.

CHAMPION OF THE OPPRESSED

One champion of the oppressed Indians was Bartholomew de Las Casas, whose father had accompanied Columbus on that second voyage to the West Indies. At first Bartholomew was as much a part of Christian imperialism as the next Spaniard in the West Indies or Mexico. In his middle thirties, however, he had a spiritual conversion and was ordained to the priesthood, the first such ordination in the New World. He began to feel pangs of conscience. In a sermon before the governor and leading settlers he denounced the cruelties he saw about him. How could the Christian's God ordain brutality as an instrument of Christian conversion?

Las Casas met widespread resistance; many considered him a visionary and a menace to New Spain. Some missionaries argued that wild and barbarous peoples could not come to the faith without the force necessary to show them the error of their ways. Some colonists insisted that Las Casas' opposition to *encomienda* could bring the colonies to economic ruin.

Las Casas, however, persisted in his views. He made fourteen trips across the Atlantic to urge Spanish leaders to consider another way to win the Indians to the faith. Thanks in part to his appeals, Charles V in 1542 issued a series of new laws, *The Laws of the Indies*, which softened the severity of the *encomienda* system and established the principle that Indians had human rights too.

Laws in Spain, however, were one thing; practice in Mexico was another. In a famous debate held at Valladolid on the Yucatan Peninsula in 1550, Las Casas argued for the equality and freedom of the

Indians. The only way to convert them, he said, is by peaceful preaching of the Word and by example of holy living. His opponent was a theologian, Juan Gines de Sepulveda, who used Aristotle's argument that certain peoples are by nature born to slavery. "The Spanish," he said, "are as much above the Indians as man is above the ape." So in spite of Las Casas' best effort, Christian imperialism continued in the New World and hampered the spread of the gospel among the Indians.

The Indians were eager enough to accept the Christian faith; but they were just as ready to abandon it. Between 1524 and 1531 the Franciscans baptized more than a million Mexicans. The practice of mass baptisms reminds the reader of the mass conversions in Europe during the early Middle Ages. Such practices seem perfunctory or even superstitious to modern believers who emphasize an individual's standing before God.

One well-known story has it that Cortes left the strictest instructions in one town that the citizens were to worship the Christian God and to care for one of his horses, which was lame. The Indians faithfully obeyed. They fed the horse on fruit and flowers until it died; they supposed that the horse and the Christian God were the same. Later, two Franciscans discovered that the Indians had made an image of the horse and were worshiping it as the god of thunder and lightning.

In the East the Portuguese, like the Spanish, took the view that a Christian king was responsible to God for the spiritual welfare of his subjects. As a result, Goa, the center of the Portuguese commercial empire in the Orient, became a city of great baroque churches. It had an archbishop who served as the representative of the authority of the Catholic Church throughout East Asia, and Portuguese authorities saw that no idolatry defiled the territory of their Christian king.

The Portuguese faced a problem, however, that the Spanish never encountered in the Americas. They met highly developed civilizations and ancient religions far stronger than those of the Incas and Aztecs. These had a significant impact on the way many Christian missionaries approached Asian peoples. In India, Japan, and China the policy of conversions by conquest was modified, and in some cases abandoned, in favor of the policy of adaptation. Jesuits in particular asked which Japanese, Chinese, or Indian customs were merely social or civil and which were incompatible with Christian baptism.

FRANCIS XAVIER

The great pioneer of Christian missions in the Far East landed in Goa in 1542. Francis Xavier (1506–1552), the associate of Ignatius Loyola, was commissioned as a papal legate in the service of the king of Portugal. Officials everywhere were obligated to assist him in his preaching mission. He found Goa, like most seaports, filled with riffraff from a thousand shores, catering to lustful appetites. Xavier stayed in Goa only a few months, but in that short time he sparked something of a moral revolution in the port. Then, eager to break new ground, he turned his eyes to a more demanding field of labor, this time on the southern tip of India.

In 1534 some fisherfolk, living on the southeast coast, had sought the protection of the king of Portugal. Robbers on land and sea had been making their lives miserable. The Portuguese agreed to protect them providing they would accept Christian baptism. They did, but for the first eight years of their Christian profession they had no one to explain to them the mysteries of their new faith. Xavier, "the little dark man," stepped into that need. He went everywhere over the burning sand hills where the fisher villages were scattered. He would ring a handbell to call the villagers together and recite the Creed, the Lord's Prayer, the Ten Commandments, and the Rosary. When the fisherfolk had learned the words and professed their belief in the Creed, Xavier would baptize them by the hundreds until his hands dropped from exhaustion. After three years he had an organized church to pass on to his successors.

The Paravars, as these fisherfolk were called, numbered perhaps thirty thousand. Since Christianity among them was restricted to one caste, they had little contact with their neighbors outside of trade. The church survived, therefore, only as an island surrounded by the sea of Hinduism.

The Jesuits who followed Xavier, supported by the Portuguese authorities, gathered the Paravars into villages and slowly fashioned their lives according to Christian standards. No boat set out to fish on Sunday; a part of each Friday's catch went to the church. Gradually all memory of a time when the Paravars were not Christian died away. The center of their life was the church, the one stone building around which their huts of palm leaf and thatch were clustered.

Roman Catholics and Protestants unite in praising Francis Xavier's missionary zeal and personal charm. He was a man of his time, however. His years in India show that he at first shared the religious intolerance of his age. In a letter written on May 16, 1546, he told the king of Portugal that to have good Christians in India the king should establish the Inquisition to suppress Muslims. The king granted his request and the Inquisition continued in Goa until early in the nineteenth century.

Xavier, however, had no intention of remaining in Goa or its region. His commission from pope and king extended to the whole of the Far East, so in 1546 he moved on from India to Malaya. After nearly two years of ministry there he was ready to find new worlds to conquer. He returned to Goa and in 1549, with letters from the authorities, he sailed for Japan, the isle of Marco Polo's dreams.

With two companions Xavier landed on Japan on August 15. It proved to be an opportune time. Governed only by feudal barons and eager for trade with the outside world, Japan welcomed the strangers. Buddhism was out of favor and no national religion presented stiff opposition to the gospel.

The years in Japan changed Xavier's view of Christian missions. During his earlier days in India he had held the imperialist position. Heathenism had nothing in common with the true faith. Everything had to be leveled to the ground before anything Christian could be erected: the view of most missionaries in Latin America.

In Japan, however, Xavier confronted a people with so many marks of nobility, he shifted his ground. He saw that while the gospel must transform and refine the Japanese, it need not discard as worthless everything in Japanese life and culture. Surrounded by the impressive ancient religions of the East, many Jesuits who followed Xavier developed a quality totally uncharacteristic of the Counter Reformation: compromise in religious matters.

The Society of Jesus dominated the Christian mission in Japan until the end of the sixteenth century. Their work met with remarkable success. In 1577 one Jesuit wrote optimistically, "In ten years all Japan will be Christian if we have enough missionaries." Two years later the Jesuits did establish a new town as a home for Christian converts. They called it Nagasaki. Before the end of the century missionaries could count three hundred thousand converts, hundreds of churches, and two Christian colleges.

Through the years the Jesuits followed Xavier's lead and looked for ways to express the Christian faith in the culture of their hosts. They adapted to local customs and values in every way they could. And they moved as rapidly as possible to train Japanese leaders for the churches.

Unfortunately, early in the seventeenth century new rulers, fearful that foreign missionaries meant foreign invaders, launched a policy of persecution of Christians. Between 1614 and 1642, no fewer than 4,045 martyrs made the ultimate witness for Christ, some by sword, some by the stake, some by the boiling cauldron. The once thriving Christian work in Japan disintegrated. Only a remnant survived in the hills near Nagasaki.

THE DOOR TO CHINA

In China the story of Christian missions during this era parallels the saga in Japan. Once again the visionary was Francis Xavier. After two years preaching in the streets of Japan, the intrepid Xavier decided it was time to enter China. He returned to Goa to secure the necessary authority, but on the passage east he found it difficult to get beyond Singapore. Hoping to smuggle himself into Canton, he took a ship as far as an island off the coast of south China. There he fell ill and died, bringing to an end one of the most imaginative careers in missionary annals. The year was 1552.

The doorway to China that Xavier failed to find opened to his spiritual successor, Matthew Ricci (1552–1610). In 1567 a small island off the coast of China, Macao, became a Portuguese colony. For years, however, entrance to China seemed impossible. The ruling Ming dynasty had no interest in contacts with the outside world. They considered the Chinese as the givers of culture, not the receivers. Confucianism was dominant in the empire and the state; the family and ethics were governed by its ideals and teachings. .

According to one story Allessandro Valignani, a leader of the Jesuits in the Orient, looking out his window at Macao in 1579 cried out toward the Chinese coast, "Oh, Rock, Rock, when will you open?"

Valignani recalled a thirty-year-old Italian Jesuit teaching at the time in a seminary in Goa. Matthew Ricci had studied mathematics, astronomy, and cosmology in Rome before heading for India. He seemed unusually prepared for work among the Chinese, so Valignani called Ricci to Macao and placed the burden of China upon his shoulders.

Ricci's first task was to settle in Macao to learn the Chinese language and customs—and to wait for the Rock to crack. In 1583 he secured permission to settle in Chaoch'ing, the provincial capital. With their traditional respect for the scholar, the Chinese responded to a man who dressed in the garb of a Mandarin, spoke their language, and was able to open to them new fields of learning. Ricci made a map of the world for them and introduced them to the new science of the calendar.

Such contacts proved useful for gaining toleration from the Chinese, but Ricci was convinced that China could never be won to the Christian faith from an outlying province. Step by step he moved toward the capital of the empire. In 1600 he gained permission to enter Peking itself.

Ricci used two clocks to gain imperial favor. He brought the clocks with him as gifts to the emperor. They pleased the monarch very much, but when they ran down, the Chinese experts had no idea how to restart them. Ricci's skill in keeping them in working order gained the emperor's warm approval and allowed Ricci to remain in the capital for ten years as an astronomer and mathematician.

Under Ricci's wise guidance the Jesuit mission in Peking took root and flourished. A number of notable families and scholars were baptized. At the time of Ricci's death in 1610, the church numbered two thousand.

Ricci's successor, Adam Schall, carried the scholarly work to an even higher level. He won the admiration of the Chinese scholar class by accurately predicting the time of an eclipse of the moon and became the Director of the Imperial Astronomical Service. In 1650 Schall built a public church in Peking and gained religious freedom for Christianity in the whole of the empire (1657). At Schall's death there were almost 270,000 Christians in China. The imperial edict of toleration in 1692 rewarded the service of the Jesuits on behalf of China and the imperial house, and thus an independent Chinese church approached reality.

The Chinese mission, however, also met with misfortune, this time not from external pressures but from Dominican and Franciscan missionaries who argued that adaptation to Chinese ways had gone too far.

Ricci had tried to avoid presenting Christianity to the Chinese as something new. He refused to consider these advanced and religious people as atheists, so he taught that traditional Chinese devotion reached perfection in the Christian faith. The "Lord of Heaven," whom the Chinese had so long revered, was God. Ricci contended that the reverence for ancestors, so common in China, was not a religious act but a social one, and therefore acceptable to Christians.

Had adaptation gone too far? In 1631 a Franciscan and a Dominican arrived in Peking and were shocked at what they found. The word used to translate the Christian *mass* in the Jesuit catechism was the Chinese character for the ceremony of ancestor worship! One night the friars went in disguise to such a ceremony; they watched as Chinese Christians participated and were scandalized at what they saw. They reported their experience to Rome and the quarrel over "the rites" began. One pope approved, another disapproved, until after a century the whole mission in China fell into a serious decline.

The conflict between the policy of adaptation and the policy of conquest did not end with the seventeenth century. It is raging today, only conquest is usually in terms of economic control rather than political. But the age of global expansion was special in one sense: in opening up huge areas of the earth's surface to the Christian message it displayed some of the most innovative and creative missionary leaders found in any age.

Suggestions for Further Reading

Gascoigne, Bamber. *The Christians*. New York: William Morrow & Co., Inc., 1977.

Latourette, Kenneth Scott. *A History of the Expansion of Christianity*. Vol. 3. New York: Harper, 1939.

Neill, Stephen. *A History of Christian Missions*. Edited by Owen Chadwick. Middlesex: Penguin Books, 1986.

———. *The Christian Society*. New York: Harper & Brothers, 1952.

CHAPTER 30

THE RULE
OF THE SAINTS

Puritanism

I N 1630 MORE THAN four hundred immigrants gathered at Southampton, England, preparing to sail to the New World. John Cotton, a distinguished minister who would later join them on the other side of the sea, preached a farewell sermon. His text for the occasion summed up the spirit of the great adventure. He took it from 2 Samuel 7:10:

> Moreover I will appoint a place for my people Israel, and will plant them, that they may dwell in a place of their own, and move no more; neither shall the children of wickedness afflict them any more, as beforetime (KJV).

Cotton declared that like the ancient Israelites these immigrants were God's chosen people, headed for the land he had promised and prepared. In this new land they would be able to labor undisturbed for the glory of God.

There you have a snapshot of Puritanism: the Bible is the guidebook providing concrete instruction for the believer's conversion and the construction of a society designed to reinforce a biblical view of the state; the church, often pictured analogously to ancient Israel, is also rightly pictured in the Scriptures and should function as the agent for individual and societal reform; the society and nation should also be ordered to bolster the purpose of God being played out in history. While it endured as a distinct historic movement between 1560 and

1660, Puritanism provided for Christians of every generation a model of the Christian faith as a decisive commitment to Jesus Christ and how that life of the soul expresses itself in the public arena in a nation governed by the truths of the Bible.

PURITANISM: NEW LIFE AND NEW WORLD

In more recent centuries Christians have renewed from time to time the Puritan experience of the soul, a type of piety arising from the purely gracious work of God in the heart of the believer. But no later Christian movement has had the vision or the opportunity to apply the law of God to the life of a nation.

In modern times, marked by zeal for individual rights and sexual freedom, *puritan* has come to refer to a person who is self-righteous, hyper-religious, or sexually repressed: one who does his best to keep people from having fun. This view of the puritan as a moss-backed moralist captured popular thinking in the backlash of Victorian stuffiness. Early in the twentieth century American journalist H. L. Mencken summed up the popular image in his quip that Puritanism was "the haunting fear that someone, somewhere may be happy."

But is that fair? What was Puritanism originally? Whatever it was, it was not straitlaced. It stood for change and a new day in England. The first Puritans had little confidence in traditional religion. Their plans for a new England arose from a deep conviction that spiritual conversion was crucial to Christianity. This rebirth separated the Puritan from the mass of mankind and endowed him with the privileges and the duties of the elect of God. The church may prepare a man for this experience, and, after it, the church may guide him, but the heart of the experience, the reception of the grace of God, is beyond the church's control.

In its quest to reshape England, the Puritan movement passed through three rather clearly marked periods: First, under Queen Elizabeth (1558–1603) it tried to purify the Church of England along the lines of Calvin's Geneva. Second, under James I and Charles I (1603–1642) it resisted the claims of the monarchy and suffered under royal pressures designed to force conformity to a high-church style Christianity. Third, during England's Civil War and Oliver Cromwell's rule (1642–1660), Puritans had a chance to shape the national church in England but failed because of their own internal dissensions.

Such an outline suggests, as it should, that Puritanism had a public side as well as a personal side. It began with an individual's experience of the redeeming grace of God but moved on to stress the elect's mission in the world, the shaping of society according to biblical principles.

In its emphasis upon the interior life of the saint, Puritanism was a taproot of later evangelical Christianity with its born-again message. In its stress upon a disciplined "nation under God" and his laws, it contributed significantly to the national character of the American people.

Puritanism, England's second reformation, first appeared during the reign of Elizabeth. It had a new style of preaching: a message aimed not at the head but at the heart. This "spiritual brotherhood," as William Haller the Puritan authority once called it, included names like Greenham, Rogers, Chaderton, and Dod. Many of these first Puritans had been Protestant exiles of the reign of Bloody Mary (1553–1557). Hounded out of their homeland by their Catholic queen, these Protestant sympathizers had gone to Geneva and mobilized as a vanguard for a fresh Calvinist assault on England.

The military image is appropriate, for in the late 1550s Geneva had become a center for international subversion—a Protestant Moscow, if you please—sending out cadres of students enflamed with a passion to overthrow Catholicism in their homelands. In 1560 John Knox was successful in Scotland, and the English Reformers hoped for as much in their own country.

Queen Mary's death and the crowning of Elizabeth appeared to be an invitation to the exiles to return to England. They took up their work, still convinced that the Bible gave specific guidance for the ordering of personal life, the structuring of the church, and the regulation of society. They discovered that the most explosive political issue was the authority to choose ministers for the churches. The Puritans wanted the selection of their ministers to rest with the people; the queen insisted that the appointment of bishops was a responsibility of rulers.

As long as Elizabeth lived she allowed these Puritan dogs to bark so long as they did not bite. The queen's tolerant policy permitted them to complain about prayers from a book and special clothing for ministers and the sign of the cross during baptisms—just about any practice that looked like Roman Catholicism—but she would not hear of their control of the Church. She allowed them to lecture for hours on the importance of preaching and the biblical office of elder, but she made sure the Church of England remained firmly in the hands of bishops, and therefore in the control of the crown.

A PEOPLE OF THE BOOK

The Puritan's zeal to purify the Church of England was fired by eager reading of popular versions of the Bible. Chief among these was the Geneva Bible. The name came from the fact that it was the work of several of those English exiles in Geneva during the reign of the Catholic Mary. Miles Coverdale, who had translated the first complete Bible into English in 1535, was in this group. Once printed during the early years of Elizabeth's reign, the Geneva Bible's numbered verses, lucid prose, improved scholarship, extensive prologues, and marginal notes gave it wide popularity. Until its eventual replacement by the King James Version (1611) it was the most widely distributed Bible in English and was the one the Puritans carried to America.

The Puritans, however, had more than their Geneva Bibles. They had a sense of destiny, a vision of God's purpose among men and nations. The idea that the Almighty moves in the affairs of men is traceable, to be sure, to the Bible. But the concept that the pilgrimage of God's people spanned the centuries and led at last to England was from another book. John Foxe, in his highly popular *Book of Martyrs*, planted this idea in the minds of Englishmen.

Like the Geneva Bible, *The Book of Martyrs* was a product of the English exile during the reign of Bloody Mary. Foxe marshaled account after account of the suffering of faithful Protestants who dared to die, if need be, for the triumph of God's kingdom. According to Foxe, this trail of martyrs led to the shores of England and to the reign of Mary. The conclusion seemed clear: God had a special place for the English people in his worldwide plan of redemption.

The influence of *The Book of Martyrs* proved enormous. Generation after generation of Englishmen saw history, and read their Bibles, through Foxe's eyes. Aside from the Bible, his book probably did more to shape the mind of Englishmen than any other single volume. Less than half a century after Foxe's death, Puritans carried his work and his philosophy of history, along with their English Bibles, across the Atlantic into the American wilderness.

Thanks to their study of the Bible and their reading of *The Book of Martyrs,* Puritans came to think of themselves as God's new Israel. Most Christians in the seventeenth century believed that the Bible was God's inspired Word and revealed will. The key to the Puritan view of the Bible and of themselves lies in their understanding of that fundamental biblical concept called *covenant.*

The Puritans, like the ancient Hebrews, believed that *spiritual contracts* exist between God and men. The most fundamental was the covenant of grace. This was the spiritual contract by which true Christians were bound to God. While they believed that God sovereignly elected men to salvation, they also held that anyone by personal faith in Jesus Christ could be added to the covenanted company. By grace believers became God's people and he their God.

This "near bond" obligated the saint to walk in all of God's ways made known in his Word. On the other hand, it opened the Scriptures as a deeply felt source of spiritual and emotional strength, a fountain of that rugged determination for which the Puritan became famous. To live within the covenant of grace was to live within the light of the Word and according to the plan of Almighty God.

CONFLICTS WITH THE KING

In 1603 the long reign of Queen Elizabeth came to a close when she died without an heir. James VI of Scotland, the son of Mary Queen of Scots, became James I of England, uniting for the first time the two kingdoms. Any Puritan hopes for James bringing Presbyterianism from Scotland to England were dashed early. He welcomed a chance to deal with bishops. Rule in Scotland had been a constant struggle with Presbyterian ministers. A Scottish presbytery, he said, "agrees with monarchy as well as God and the devil."

At the Hampton Court Conference in 1604 some leading Puritans had a chance to present to the king their ideas for change in the Church of England. But James, who had an inflated view of his own intelligence, dismissed most of their opinions rather rudely. On only one point did he consent to the demands of the Puritans. He was willing to have a new translation of the Scriptures made. From this decision came what we call the King James Version of the Bible.

On nothing else of significance would the king yield to the Puritans. The ceremonies, the Prayer Book, and the bishops of the Church of England were going to stay. And if the Puritans did not like it, they would still submit or, said the king, "I will drive them out of this land—or else worse." With that threat the conference broke up.

James's initial contact with Parliament was equally tactless. In his first address to the body he defended the divine right of kings. "The state of monarchy," he said, "is the supremest thing upon earth, for kings are not only God's lieutenants upon earth and set upon God's throne, but even by God himself they are called gods."

Sweeping aside English institutions and ignoring the mood of the English people, James made it plain that he meant to be an absolute monarch. In 1611 he dissolved Parliament and for the next ten years he ruled England without it. Thus the leaders of the Puritans and the advocates of parliamentary authority in England tended to merge in their resistance to royal power.

Some in the Puritan movement, however, grew impatient for change in the Church. Shortly after the Hampton Court Conference little groups of believers began to meet for worship as they felt the Bible taught them, not according to bishops and prayer books. They were determined to obey God even if their nation's leaders were not. We call this movement Separatism because the groups were intent upon leaving (to build a separate church) the Church of England.

One of these groups was in the village of Scrooby in northern England. Another was not far away at Gainsborough. By 1608 both congregations had moved to Holland for safety and freedom of worship. The Scrooby group settled at Leyden; the Gainsborough group found a home in Amsterdam.

After ten years in Holland the Scrooby congregation, led by Pastor John Robinson, realized that their children were growing up out of touch with their homeland, forgetting even their native tongue. But to return to England meant a return to the evil ways of English society. They had heard of the English colony in Virginia planted in 1607. Perhaps the new continent of America was their answer. It was a daring thought, full of unknown terrors, but a small number was willing to try. These returned to England, where they were joined by another group of like-minded pilgrims. In September 1620 a company of about a hundred souls set sail from Plymouth in a ship called the *Mayflower*. In November the crew sighted the rocky shore of New England. The Pilgrim Fathers stepped ashore at what we call Plymouth, Massachusetts.

Meanwhile, the second group sought safety from persecution in Holland. These separatists had been given aid by local Mennonites. We know little about their association, but we know they exchanged confessions to compare doctrines. The pastor of the flock, a Cambridge graduate, John Smyth, studied his Greek New Testament and discovered that the practice of baptizing babies never appeared in its pages. If babies were not included in the covenant of grace, only mature believers in Jesus Christ, then shouldn't churches be constituted by confession of faith rather than ties of covenants? Upon their profession of faith they constituted the first Baptist church. Smyth baptized himself and then the other forty members of his congregation by pouring. The year was 1609. The question of Baptist origins and identity are closely tied. Are Baptists to be understood as English Separatists or English Separatists who mingled with Anabaptists?

ATTACK UPON THE LORD'S ANOINTED

Separation from the Church of England, however, was far too drastic for the vast majority of Puritans. They remained hopeful for some alternative to schism. All grounds for hope in earthly rulers appeared to vanish in 1625, however, when Charles I followed his father James to the English throne. James had his theories about the divine right of kings; Charles was determined to put them into practice. No law and no parliament would restrain him. To make matters worse in the eyes of the Puritans, his wife, Henrietta Maria, was a French Roman Catholic princess.

To enforce his will upon the Puritans, Charles found a ready servant in Archbishop William Laud, who believed that God had ordained bishops to govern his church. Led by the archbishop, an episcopal party arose to resist the Puritans. With the king's support they reintroduced stained glass windows, crosses—even crucifixes. They elevated the Communion table and called it an altar and they insisted that worship be conducted according to the Prayer Book and no other.

Laud's high-minded and high-handed policy drove some Puritans toward Separatism and others across the Atlantic to America. Within ten years after Laud became archbishop, twenty towns and churches had sprung up in Massachusetts Bay: in all sixteen thousand people including the four hundred who heard John Cotton's farewell at Southampton.

The straw that broke the back of restraint within the two kingdoms came when Charles tried to force his high church brand of Anglican religion upon the Presbyterian Scots. He insisted that they conduct their worship services from the Book of Common Prayer. John Milton called it "the skeleton of a Mass-book." That is the way the Scots took it. They rose in opposition to the move and joined in a "National League of Covenant." To defend their Church, they dared to take up arms against their king.

To put an army in the field Charles was forced to convene Parliament, which he, like his father, had tried to ignore for over a decade. Once Parliament assembled, conflicting loyalties led to a Royalist Party and a Parliamentary Party. The Parliamentarians, clearly a majority, were agreed on the broad Puritan principles but were divided over the form of the church. On the one hand were Presbyterians; on the other were Independents (or Congregationalists). United in their hatred of Archbishop Laud, the Parliamentarians succeeded in bringing him to trial and seeing him beheaded.

When Charles tried to punish the leaders of this opposition, civil war erupted. The Royalist members of Parliament left London to join the forces defending the king. So Parliament was free at last to institute the reform of the Church the Puritans had always wanted. It called to

Westminster scores of Puritan theologians and assigned to them the creation of a new form of worship and a new form of church government for the Church of England.

The Westminster Assembly, meeting from 1643 to 1649, produced the Westminster Confession of Faith to replace the Thirty-nine Articles, as well as a Larger and Shorter Catechism for use in the churches. These writings alone made the assembly one of the most significant gatherings of Christian history. Many orthodox Presbyterians and Congregationalists use these documents to this day.

In 1645 Parliament ordered the creation of presbyteries throughout the land and the election of elders for the churches. The system, however, was never fully in force because Parliament never ruled the entire country, and even when the king was defeated, the Army, not Parliament, wielded the power.

THE RULE OF THE SAINTS

The war itself brought forward one of the towering figures of Christian history, a country gentleman named Oliver Cromwell (1599–1658). As a colonel in the Parliamentary forces he proved to be a military genius. His regiment, known as Ironsides, was never defeated, in part because Cromwell instilled in his men a sense of discipline and Christian mission.

The rise of Cromwell's star brought him in time to the leadership of the New Model Army, a force of twenty-one thousand men, who considered their role in English history a call from God. In their eyes, the war was a Puritan crusade against the enemies of righteousness. The just end sanctified force as a means. That is why the Army prayed before battles and plunged into conflict singing Christian hymns.

By the end of 1646 Cromwell's Army had forced Charles to surrender. For the next two years the king tried to play off his enemies against each other: the Scots, the Presbyterians (who controlled Parliament), and the Independents (who dominated the Army). He succeeded in splitting Parliament and making a secret alliance with the Scots. But fierce resentment against Charles broke out in the Army, and in 1648 war erupted anew.

This time the Army defeated the allies of the king, and the Presbyterians were purged from the House of Commons. This so-called Rump Parliament, a tool of the Army, created a high court of justice to try the king. In January 1649 Charles was led to the scaffold in front of the royal palace of Whitehall in London, and, before an assembled throng, he was executed.

It was a brash move, a sure sign of Puritanism's ultimate fall from power, for it gave the royalists their own martyr. Centuries of English royal tradition could not be erased, even by the saints of God.

The Reformation in England

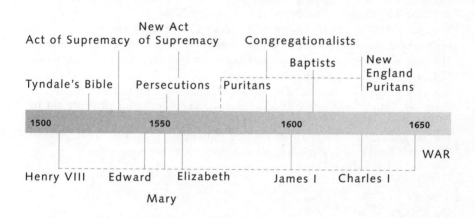

Shortly after the king's execution a portrait appeared, allegedly depicting his last hours. He was kneeling at a table; on it rested the Bible. The royal crown lay on the floor. In the king's right hand was a crown of thorns. His eyes were lifted to a crown of glory above.

The widely distributed picture and its attendant sentiment unmasked Puritanism as no battlefield could. It changed Charles from a king executed by rebels into the martyr persecuted by fanatics. That is how many Englishmen chose to remember the Puritans.

For the moment, however, the Army of saints had their say. After abolishing the House of Lords, the House of Commons proclaimed England a republic: the Commonwealth. But in 1653 the Army, still distrusting Parliament, overthrew the Commonwealth and set up a form of government called the Protectorate. Cromwell held the Office of Lord Protector, virtually a military dictator of England.

The Lord Protector tried to achieve a religious settlement for the nation by granting liberty to a wide variety of Christian groups now growing on the religious landscape: Presbyterians, Independents, Baptists, Quakers, Levellers, and others. Unfortunately he found the task impossible, and the last three years of his life were filled with disappointment and trouble. When he died in 1658 the rule of the saints in old England died with him. Within two years the country welcomed the return of the monarchy, and with the king the office of bishop. Far across the Atlantic, however, tens of thousands of saints were happily settled in New England where they were devoutly erecting the kingdom of God in the American wilderness.

Suggestions for Further Reading

*Bebbington, David. *Baptists through the Centuries: A History of a Global People.* Waco, TX: Baylor Press, 2010.

*Brackney, William H. *The Baptists.* Westport, CT: Praeger, 1995.

Haller, William. *The Rise of Puritanism.* New York: Harper & Brothers, 1938.

Morgan, Edmund S. *Visible Saints: The History of a Puritan Idea.* Ithaca, NY: Cornell University Press, 1963.

Rutman, Darrett B. *American Puritanism.* Philadelphia: Lippincott, 1970.

Simpson, Alan. *Puritanism in Old and New England.* Chicago: University of Chicago Press, 1955.

Torbet, Robert G. *A History of the Baptists.* Philadelphia: Judson Press, 1963.

Watkins. Owen C. *The Puritan Experience.* New York: Schocken, 1972.

CHAPTER 31

UNWILLING TO DIE
FOR AN OLD IDEA

Denominations

FOR DECADES CRITICS HAVE called them "a scandal," "a blight," "faction-alism," and "a caste system," but denominations remain the institutional hallmark of modern Christianity.

Criticism is understandable. Any Christian reading his New Testament senses the difference between the faith of the apostles and the Christianity of our day. The apostle Paul, for example, speaks of the church as the temple of God, unified in devotion to the Lord Jesus Christ, but we find in our time only a menagerie of cults, sects, denominations, and isms. We sense deeply that this divided state of Christianity *ought* not be, but it is.

Why? How did denominations come to be the primary expression of Christianity in modern times?

The simple fact is Christians are divided today, in part at least, because they have the freedom to differ. In earlier centuries they did not. We may curse denominations or try to ignore them, but they are not going to disappear soon because the cost of their removal is greater than most of us want to pay. We are shocked by this fruit of modern Christianity, but few of us want to lay the ax at its root.

The Age of the Reformation (1517–1648) did not suddenly end and the Age of Reason and Revivals (1648–1789) appear overnight as historians' dates might suggest, but times do change, and one marked difference between the sixteenth century and the seventeenth was the acceptance of religious differences.

313

We often hear, "I disapprove of what you say, but I will defend to the death your right to say it." And most Christians today, even if they cannot identify its source, accept the sentiment of that oft-quoted manifesto. They accept it not because it is Christian but because it is modern.

SUPPRESSION OF THE NONCONFORMIST

The statement probably belongs to Voltaire (1694–1778), the proud, self-sufficient humanist of the Age of Reason. It is the kind of thing Martin Luther or Ignatius Loyola would never say, because neither believed it. In the light of the Reformation, dissent was neither a Christian virtue nor a human right. The Reformers were as eager as Catholics to suppress nonconformity.

That was because both camps believed that Christian truth held societies together. It was an instrument of power. And only one side in a religious conflict had the truth. The idea that God's Word could be found on both sides of a battle line was a revolutionary concept that only gained a hearing after both sides fell from exhaustion.

In the 1540s and 1550s, when both Protestants and Catholics still believed in a united Christendom, Lutheran princes fought Catholic Imperial forces to a stalemate in Germany. In the Peace of Augsburg (1555) both sides agreed to stop fighting only after adopting the territorial principle: the ruler in each region could decide the faith of his subjects, Lutheran or Catholic.

The compromise was a spin-off of the idea of the Christian prince. It was a guarantee to a number of people the right to worship according to their consciences, but it also recognized the right of the prince to persecute those who didn't happen to agree with him. It led to suffering and hardship for many innocent people whose only offense was religious dissent.

The principle of territorialism was the herald of the approaching death of Christendom. If one Christian prince of a small territory can lay down the law of one religion for his subjects and another ruler a dozen miles away can lay down another law for another religion, then the norm of Christian truth is shattered and Christian society crumbles to pieces.

Of course, events were running ahead of new ideas, so other wars were fought all over Europe and new territories were fashioned according to the old concept that only one religion could exist in one region.

From 1562 to 1598 France suffered a series of civil wars between Roman Catholics and French Calvinists (or Huguenots). When both parties reached the point of utter fatigue they agreed to a territorial compromise in the royal Edict of Nantes (1598). The Huguenots gained religious freedom and political control of certain parts of the country while Roman Catholicism remained the official religion of the realm and in the greater portion of the nation.

In a similar way between 1560 and 1618 in the Netherlands, the strongly Calvinistic Dutch fought a war of independence from Catholic Spain and won. In the southern territories, however, the area we call Belgium, the people remained Catholic and did not gain their independence from Spain until much later.

THE THIRTY YEARS' WAR

All of these conflicts were a bloody prelude to the last and most devastating of the so-called wars of religion: the Thirty Years' War (1618–1648). This conflict began primarily as a religious struggle with political overtones and ended as a barbarous political power struggle with religious overtones. That shift in dominant motives makes the Thirty Years' War a fitting symbol of the transition from the Age of Reformation to the Age of Reason and Revivals.

The war was as complex as it was long. This is no place for military or political details. We are interested in the change in ideals, and we can find this in the simplest highlights.

One of the glaring weaknesses of the Peace of Augsburg (1555) was that it completely ignored the Calvinists. Given their sense of holy mission, it was merely a matter of time before hostilities erupted anew. Preparations for war were laid early in the seventeenth century when Protestants formed a league of German princes and the Catholics created a similar Catholic League. Fighting broke out in 1618.

A zealous supporter of the Counter Reformation, the Jesuit-educated Ferdinand II, was named the king of Bohemia only shortly before he was also elected Holy Roman Emperor. Moving under the concept of one religion for one realm, Ferdinand attempted to uproot Protestantism from Bohemia and impose Catholicism upon his subjects.

The Bohemian nobles, mostly Protestants, rose in revolt and offered their crown to Frederick V, the ardent Calvinist ruler of the Palatinate, one of the major German territories. Frederick's acceptance touched off the fighting between Catholics and Calvinists.

In 1620 near Prague the Catholic Imperial forces, surging forward to the cry, "For the Virgin Mary," crushed the Bohemians and confiscated most of the estates of the insurgents. The victors added salt to the wounds by awarding the Jesuits control of the University of Prague, the old haunt of John Hus.

Appalled by this Catholic victory and eager to annex German territory, King Christian IV of Lutheran Denmark entered the war against Ferdinand and the Catholic forces. Without adequate support, however, his venture was doomed from the start. In 1626 the Danes were completely routed in the Harz Mountains and forced to withdraw to Denmark like a pack of whipped pups.

Imperial control of the southern shores of the Baltic and deep religious convictions compelled the able Lutheran warrior, King Gustavus Adolphus of Sweden, to enter Germany as the new leader of the Protestant cause. A series of smashing victories carried him south as far as Munich. "The Lion of the North" Protestants called him, but even regal courage meets its end. At the Battle of Lutzen (1632), southwest of Leipzig, the Swedish army was again victorious, but Adolphus was cut down in combat.

Without Adolphus the war wore on, but the outcome was already clear. The Catholic forces could not subdue the Protestants in northern Germany and the Protestants could not control the Catholics in the south.

In the final years of the conflict, religion faded to insignificance. For the most part France and Spain, both nominally Catholic, struggled for political advantages in the Rhineland.

When the swords fell silent, Germany lay ravaged. Ferdinand's dream of a revival of imperial authority there was gone, and in its place were 300 independent states. Out of sheer futility the religious zeal of Catholics and Calvinists cooled, and men began to question the territorial idea. Denominationalism was an alternative.

The terms of peace, called the Peace of Westphalia (1648), reflect the passing of an age. Calvinism joined Lutheranism and Catholicism as a recognized expression of the Christian faith. Princes, if they chose, could, for the first time, allow Protestants and Catholics to exist within their territories. And the pope was excluded from any interference in the religious affairs of Germany. Naturally Pope Innocent X condemned the treaty, but both Catholics and Protestants ignored his protests. After more than a thousand years the state was free to transact its business as though the pope did not exist.

Christianity's alliance with civil power was changing. Christians in the West would now live in nation-states, the real victor in the Thirty Years' War. The emerging nation-states would require Christians to live under a government whose citizens belonged to a variety denominations and faiths. In time, some of these nation-states required citizens to affirm a generic version of God in order to hold office or attend college; but distinctive beliefs and practices, such as being Catholic or Presbyterian, were strictly a private, individual matter.

THE NEW WAY IN AMERICA

By 1648, far across the Atlantic in the English colonies of North America, men were seeking to build distinctly religious societies. At first, they came to fashion places of devout Christian character and witness. Eventually the goal of building a holy city that nurtures holy men was amended to building a city where people could be holy. Waves of newcomers, the indifference of the second generation, and the wide open frontier all weighed against a religious uniformity.

During the sixteenth century both England and France had sent courageous explorers to North America searching in vain for the Northwest Passage to China. But not until the London Company landed its first colonists at Jamestown, Virginia, in 1607 did permanent settlements begin drawing Englishmen to the New World. The Pilgrims landed in 1620, and ten years later the Massachusetts Bay Company began attracting thousands of frustrated Puritans to Boston and its surrounding towns. Between 1629 and 1642 some twenty-five thousand Puritans migrated to New England. Other than in Virginia, the English authorities made no attempt to impose a pattern of religious uniformity in the New World.

The colonies were commercial ventures designed to contribute to the prosperity of a developing English empire. To be profitable the colonies needed settlers to clear the forests and till the fields. So the promise of religious toleration provided a powerful incentive to accept the hazards of life in the American colonies. Quakers came to Pennsylvania, Catholics to Maryland, and Dutch Reformed to New York. Later came Swedish Lutherans and French Huguenots, English Baptists and Scottish Presbyterians.

The prominent exception to this general policy of religious toleration were the Congregational Puritans of Massachusetts Bay, who were determined to establish a new Zion in the American wilderness: a "due form of government both civil and ecclesiastical" is the way Governor John Winthrop put it.

The opportunity to create the rule of the Puritan saints in New England arose from the curious omission from the charter of the customary clause requiring the headquarters of the company to be in England and thus subject to the authority of the king. As a consequence of the omission, the Massachusetts Bay Company, controlled by the saints, was in effect an independent republic, for all the members of the company migrated to New England and took the charter with them.

Thus for two generations the saints in New England ruled by a policy of religious conformity even as the same policy proved futile in old England. Individuals could face severe punishment on numerous

grounds: for failing to attend church services, for denying Christ's resurrection, or for showing irreverence for the Bible.

Yet even here, within the heart of New England Puritanism, were
impulses for religious toleration. One of them was in the Puritans'
devotion to Scripture.

Pastor John Robinson told the Pilgrim Fathers, "the Lord hath more
truth yet to break forth out of his Holy Word." The Puritan was ever
ready "to receive whatever truth shall be made known . . . from the written word of God." Not surprisingly then, New England Puritans were
always spawning their own dissenters, men and women who appealed
to the truth that had been made known to them from "the written word
of God." Roger Williams was one of these; Anne Hutchinson another.

A second check on Puritan intolerance was hidden in the wilderness. Dissenters in New England did not need to go underground; they
could just move on—across the river, through the woods, or over the
mountain. Sanctuary was always possible in open space.

Thus Puritan devotion to the Bible, the presence of the wilderness,
and the English policy of toleration combined to undercut the intolerance of the New England Puritans.

The end of their attempt to enforce conformity in New England was
foreshadowed by the loss of their charter in 1684. The colony's return
to royal control was dramatically signaled in 1687 when the governor
seized the Old South meeting house for Anglican worship. Thereafter
New Englanders had to conform to English policy.

THE IDEA OF DENOMINATIONS

The religious diversity of the American colonies, though largely within
the Puritan tradition, called for a new understanding of the church. We
may call it the *denominational theory* of the church. The use of the word
denomination to describe a religious group came into vogue about 1740
during the early years of the Evangelical Revival led by John Wesley and
George Whitefield. But the theory itself was hammered out a century
before by a group of radical Puritan leaders in England and America.

Denominationalism, as originally designed, is the opposite of sectar-
ianism. A sect claims the authority of Christ for itself alone. It believes
that it is the true body of Christ; all truth belongs to it and to no other
religion. So by definition a sect is exclusive.

The word *denomination* by contrast was an inclusive term. It implied
that the Christian group called or *denominated* by a particular name
was but one member of a larger group, the church, to which all denominations belong.

The denominational theory of the church, then, insists that the true church cannot be identified with any single ecclesiastical structure. No denomination claims to represent the whole church of Christ. Each simply constitutes a different form, in worship and organization, of the larger life of the church.

The Reformers had planted the seeds of the denominational theory of the church when they insisted that the true church can never be identified in any exclusive sense with a particular institution. The true succession is not of bishops but of believers. Luther insisted that some institutional expression "in a place and in the things and activities of the world" was inevitable; but "in this life the church is not properly understood in terms of all this." The outward forms of the church, said Luther, ought to give the Word of God free course in the world, not block its power to save.

In a similar way Calvin, in the preface to his *Institutes*, indicated that it is impossible to draw precise boundaries to the church of Christ. No one can determine with precision who is numbered among the elect of God.

The Reformers, however, never followed this lead. When religious dissent arose within a particular area, they tried to suppress it. They were still convinced that only one religion could exist in one region.

The real architects of the denominational theory of the church were the seventeenth-century Independents (Congregationalists) who represented the minority voice at the Westminster Assembly (1642–1649). The majority at the Assembly held to Presbyterian principles and expressed these convictions classically in the Westminster Confession of Faith and in the Westminster Larger and Shorter Catechisms.

The Independents, however, who held to congregational principles, were keenly aware of the dangers of "dividing the godly Protestant party" in England, so they looked for some way to express Christian unity even when Christians did not agree.

These Dissenting Brethren of Westminster articulated the denominational theory of the church in several fundamental truths:

First, considering man's inability to always see the truth clearly, differences of opinion about the outward form of the church are inevitable. Second, even though these differences do not involve fundamentals of the faith, they are not matters of indifference. Every Christian is obligated to practice what he believes the Bible teaches. Third, since no church has a final and full grasp of divine truth, the true church of Christ can never be fully represented by any single ecclesiastical structure.

Finally, the mere fact of separation does not of itself constitute schism. It is possible to be divided at many points and still be united in Christ.

Thus the denominational theory of the church looked for Christian unity in some inward religious experience and allowed diversity in the outward expressions of that personal faith.

This tolerant attitude was not born of doctrinal indifference. The Independent had no intention of extending Christian unity to all religious professions. The identity of the "one true church" was restricted to those who shared a common understanding of the core of the Christian faith.

This denominational view of the church found only limited acceptance in England where the Church of England retained a favored position, even after the Act of Toleration in 1689 recognized the rights of Presbyterians, Congregationalists, Baptists, and Quakers to worship freely. In the English colonies of America, however, the denominational theory gained increasing acceptance. It seemed to be God's answer for the multiplying faiths in the New World.

Few advocates of the denominational view of the church in the seventeenth century envisioned the hundreds of Christian groups included under the umbrella today. They had no intention of reducing the basic beliefs of Christianity to a general feeling of religious sincerity. But they could not control the future. They simply knew that the traditional bigotry and bloodshed in the name of Christ was not the way forward.

In the end, then, the denominational form of the church has marked the recent centuries of Christian history, not because it is ideal, but because it is better than any alternative the years have offered.

Suggestions for Further Reading

Ahlstrom, Sydney E. *A Religious History of the American People*. New Haven, CT: Yale University Press, 1972.

Buschart, W. David. *Exploring Protestant Traditions*. Downers Grove, IL: IVP Academic, 2006.

*Gaustad, Edwin S. and Leigh E. Schmidt. *The Religious History of the America: Revised Edition*. San Francisco: Harper Collins, 2004.

Hudson, Winthrop S. *American Protestantism*. Chicago: University of Chicago Press, 1961.

Littell, Franklin H. *From State Church to Pluralism*. Garden City, NY: Doubleday, 1962.

Mead, Sidney E. *The Lively Experiment: The Shaping of Christianity in America*. New York: Harper & Row, 1963.

THE AGE OF REASON AND REVIVAL

1648–1789

The Age of Reformation was marked by debate among Christians about the way of salvation. The Age of Reason was highlighted by the denial of any supernatural religion. Respect for science and human reason replaced the Christian faith as the cornerstone of Western culture. Many Protestants met this crisis of faith not by arguments, but by the experience of supernatural conversion. Faith was less dogma and more experience. This evangelical Christianity spread rapidly by the power of preaching alone. And many Christians came to see that state support was no longer essential for Christianity's survival. Modern Christians could accept religious freedom.

The Age of Reason and Revival

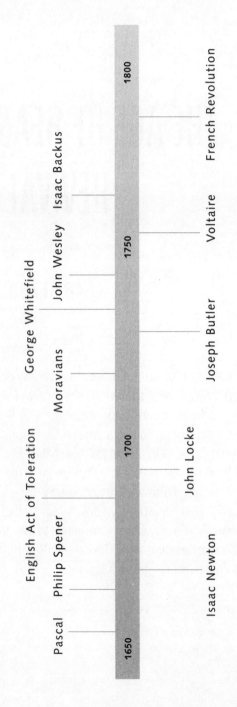

Pascal

Philip Spener

English Act of Toleration

Moravians

George Whitefield

John Wesley

Isaac Backus

Isaac Newton

John Locke

Joseph Butler

Voltaire

French Revolution

1650

1700

1750

1800

CHAPTER 32

AIMING AT THE FOUNDATIONS

The Cult of Reason

IF AMERICANS BELIEVED IN saints, Benjamin Franklin would be among them. He exemplified so many virtues Americans have come to admire. People found him practical, earthy, affable, witty and, above all, tolerant.

A few weeks before he died, Ben responded to an inquiry by President Ezra Stiles of Yale concerning his religious faith. Said Franklin,

> As to Jesus of Nazareth . . . I have . . . some doubts as to his Divinity, tho' it is a question I do not dogmatize upon, having never studied it, and think it needless to busy myself with it now, when I expect soon an opportunity of knowing the truth with less trouble. I see no harm, however, in its being believed, if that belief has the good consequence . . . of making his doctrines more respected and better observed.

Something of the American spirit is there. It is the spirit of Franklin's time, the Age of Reason (1648–1789). Questions of dogma seemed unimportant, hardly worth fretting about. What was immensely more important was behavior. Do our beliefs make us more tolerant, more respectful of those who differ with us, more responsive to the true spirit of Jesus?

If that hatred of religious bigotry, coupled with a devotion to tolerance of all religious opinions, has a familiar ring, it is because the

323

attitudes of the Age of Reason are not a thing of the past. They live on today in the values of the Western world.

The Age of the Reformation proved again that faith and power are a potent brew. As long as Christians had access to power, they used it to compel conformity to the truth: Catholic, Lutheran, or Reformed. So men died for their faith, tens of thousands of them, until something general but very deep in man awoke to revolt.

THE SPIRIT OF THE AGE OF REASON

We call that revolt the Age of Reason—or as some prefer, the Enlightenment—when, as Charles Williams put it, "national interests and mental relaxations combined to exclude metaphysics from culture."

The spirit of the Age of Reason was nothing less than an intellectual revolution, a whole new way of looking at God, the world, and oneself. It was the birth of secularism.

The Middle Ages and the Reformation were centuries of faith in the sense that reason served faith, the mind obeyed authority. To a Catholic it was church authority, to a Protestant biblical authority, but in either case God's Word came first, not man's thoughts. Man's basic concern in this life was his preparation for the next.

The Age of Reason rejected that. In place of faith it set reason. Man's primary concern was not the next life, but happiness and fulfillment in this world; and the mind of man, rather than faith, was the best guide to happiness, not emotions, or myths, or superstitions.

The spirit and purpose of the Enlightenment were eloquently expressed by one of its spokesmen, Baron von Holbach, who wrote,

> Let us endeavor to disperse those clouds of ignorance, those mists of darkness, which impede Man on his journey, . . . which prevent his marching through life with a firm and steady step. Let us try to inspire him . . . with respect for his own reason—with an inextinguishable love of truth . . . so that he may learn to know himself . . . and no longer be duped by an imagination that has been led astray by authority . . . so that he may learn to base his morals on his own nature, on his own wants, on the real advantage of society . . . so that he may learn to pursue his true happiness, by promoting that of others . . . in short, so that he may become a virtuous and rational being, who cannot fail to become happy.

THE RENAISSANCE

How did this new spirit take root and grow? Its seeds probably lie in the Reformation era itself, in a movement historians call the Renaissance.

The word means *rebirth* and refers to the recovery of the values of classical Greek and Roman civilization expressed in literature, politics, and the arts. In one sense, the Reformation is not possible without the influence of Renaissance humanism, which seeks human flourishing, a well-rounded person who possesses a full complement of virtues and abilities. Reading classic texts from the ancient Greek and Roman glory days was thought to be a crucial step towards living well. To read was to engage a famous author in a conversation, an experiential encounter with both author and culture. Reading a text in its original language was the gold standard in this soul-building venture. Each of the major Reformers embraced this Renaissance humanist approach to texts. Each came to believe that they must encounter the Bible in its original languages.

Perhaps the best example of the rebirth of the classical spirit was Erasmus of Rotterdam (1467–1536). In a series of best-selling satires highlighted by *Praise of Folly*, Erasmus ridiculed monasticism and Scholasticism by the use of irony, wit, and enlightened common sense.

Erasmus's followers thought they heard a true reformer in him. He laid the egg, they said, that Luther hatched. But in 1524 a significant conflict between Luther and Erasmus erupted. In that year Erasmus's *Diatribe on Free Will* appeared. It made clear the cardinal differences between the two men. Luther believed that the human will was enslaved, totally unable, apart from an enabling grace, to love or serve God. But Erasmus considered this a dangerous doctrine since it threatened to relieve man of his moral responsibility.

The differences in the Reformation and the Renaissance lie right there, in the view of man. The Reformers preached the original sin of man and looked upon the world as fallen from God's intended place. The Renaissance had a positive estimate of human nature and the universe itself. This confidence in man and his powers flowered and filled the air with fragrance during the Enlightenment.

Another root of the Enlightenment runs through the century (1550–1650) of appalling religious conflicts: the English Civil War, the persecution of the French Huguenots, and the Thirty Years' War in Germany. Common decency cried out against the power of fanatical clerics. More and more people felt only disgust at the burning or drowning of an elderly woman accused of witchcraft or heresy. Religious prejudice seemed like a far greater danger than atheism. So a thirst for tolerance and truths common to all men spread.

Enlightenment

The Enlightenment was actually a series of enlightenments. It influenced England, France, and elsewhere before finally beginning in Germany. Its basic insight was captured in the first French Enlightenment thinkers. They made several observations from their experiences in England, which fascinated them. They saw greater prosperity and greater liberty. In England, the institutions of government and church did less to restrict individual citizens who were free to reason for themselves to a greater degree. These several elements were finally gathered into a central conviction: if individuals were not constrained and restricted by the burden of cultural traditions and were allowed to freely reason for themselves, they would enjoy prosperity. Freedom to think for oneself, independent from tradition, yields truth and prosperity. This insight is expanded and extended in endless varieties.

Finally, the Age of Reason sprang from the soil of a new faith in law and order. Modern science arose in the sixteenth and seventeenth centuries and filled men with visions of a new day of peace and harmony. These pioneers of modern science forced men to think in a new way about the universe: Copernicus (1473–1543), who insisted that the sun, not the earth, was the center of our universe; Johann Kepler (1571–1630), who concluded that the sun emitted a magnetic force that moved the planets in their courses; and Galileo Galilei (1564–1642), who made a telescope to examine the planets and proved that the acceleration of falling bodies is constant.

All these discoveries, however, had to be united in one all-embracing principle that would explain the motion of bodies in the heavens and present the universe as one great machine operating according to unalterable laws. This was the feat of the most illustrious scientist of the Age of Reason, Isaac Newton (1642–1727).

In 1687 Newton published his momentous work, *Mathematical Principles of Natural Philosophy*, in which all laws of motion, in the heavens and on the earth, were harmonized in a master principle for the universe, the law of gravitation.

THE WONDER OF THE WORLD-MACHINE

The reading public of Europe was captivated by the wonder of Newton's world-machine. The medieval world of unseen spirits—angels and demons—seemed less plausible or even superstitious. In its place was a sun-centered universe that operated by physical laws explained and justified by mathematics.

In the new model, the sun displaced the earth as the center. Some believed that mankind had been displaced as the crowning apex of creation in the center of God's world. Some felt that God had been displaced as well. God seemed less necessary to sustain the world when one observed that the world operated by discernible laws. Readers today should be reminded that the rise of modern science is absolutely dependent upon Christian convictions and is carried on by minds trained in Christian environments and institutions. Also worth noting is the re-envisioning of God. In these discussions, God is often pictured as one more actor on the stage and not the majestic Lord overseeing the entire project.

This vast unfolding universe filled some men with dismay. Blaise Pascal (1623–1662), the French physicist, recoiled before "the terrifying expanses which engulf us as a fleeting atom." But others accepted it as an invitation to discover the secrets of cosmic existence. Alexander Pope wrote:

> Nature and Nature's laws lay hid in night;
> God said, "Let Newton be!" and all was light.

This sudden access to the mysteries of the universe seemed to magnify the role of human reason. If the universe is a smooth-running machine with all its parts coordinated by one grand design, then man only has to think clearly to find life's meaning and true happiness. This fundamental idea, that man has the ability to find the truth by the use of his senses and reason, gave rise to the label Age of Reason.

The term should not suggest that every blacksmith and village priest suddenly assumed the airs of an intellectual. Many Christians lived and died in the faith of their fathers, totally unconscious that a new age had dawned. But the outlook and direction of Europe had changed.

Christianity could scarcely escape the fallout from this intellectual revolution. For 1,200 years Augustine's ideas had ruled Christendom. Man was an enslaved sinner who needed, above all else, the supernatural grace of God. To insure the availability of this grace through the Christian church, God had ordained the powers of the state to protect truth and punish error.

But now intellectuals were arguing something else: Man is no sinner. He is a reasonable creature. Now he seemed to need common sense more than God's grace.

Christians found themselves in two contrasting climates. At first, during the closing years of the seventeenth century, some believers, especially in England, tried to harmonize reason and faith. They argued that Christianity is totally reasonable but some truths come by reason and some by revelation. Some things, like the existence of God, come by observing the heavens; while other things, like the resurrection of Christ, come by the witness of Scripture.

In time, however, after the beginning of the eighteenth century, the climate changed. In France confidence in reason soared and Christians found that many intellectuals dismissed all appeals to revealed Scripture as superstitious nonsense. The climate was obviously more hostile.

The best representative of the first generation is John Locke (1632–1704). The highly influential philosopher never minimized the importance of belief. In his *Essay Concerning Human Understanding*, he not only shows how reason functions; he indicates that the existence of God is "the most obvious truth that reason discovers." Closer examination, however, shows that the God Locke had in mind has little in common with the God of the Exodus or of Jesus' resurrection. Attempts to rationally justify Christianity sadly often led to a revising of Christianity to what seems rational at the time. A profound ancient Christian wisdom is forgotten. Christians do not arrive at Christian conviction as the conclusion of a long argument; they believe because they received witness from the first eye witnesses. This witness was powerfully vindicated by the ongoing power of God. The New Testament is a book of powerfully vindicated testimony of God's action, not a book of deductive logic. Reason may serve revelation, but it can never replace revelation.

To Locke's credit, he endorses revelation and never doubts its importance. Fulfilled prophecies and the miracles of Jesus are proof of Jesus' authority. But what Scripture actually shows is that few dogmas are necessary. And these are simple and intelligible to ordinary men. Christianity, in fact, has only one essential doctrine: Jesus is the Messiah. Most of traditional theology Locke casually dismisses as irrelevant.

Locke also spoke for his generation in his emphasis upon moral conduct. Christianity, he says, adds to its belief in Jesus as Messiah the imperative of a good life. Jesus often spoke of rewards and punishments for Christian behavior. And that, too, is entirely reasonable because reason shows that moral standards must be reinforced by strong incentives.

Thus, according to Locke, revelation shows Christianity's reasonable character. Belief in Jesus as Messiah and man's ethical behavior are all Jesus and the apostles required for righteousness. Both of these are basically rational.

THE RISE OF THE RADICALS

"The fathers have eaten sour grapes, and the children's teeth are set on edge" (Ezek. 18:2). Many in the next generation, the first of the eighteenth century, felt fewer obligations to the Christian past, so instead of trying to harmonize nature and Scripture, they simply set aside revelation. Many intellectuals claimed that the parts of the Bible that agree with reason are clearly unnecessary. The parts that contradict reason—the myths, miracles, and priestly mumbo jumbo—are simply untrue. This more militant attitude toward the faith was especially evident in France.

In the eighteenth century Paris arose as the capital of a new cosmopolitan culture. Ideas circulated freely throughout Europe and the American colonies. To a degree unmatched before or since, the social and intellectual leaders of Europe were united in a community of thought and interests.

In Paris a group of thinkers and writers known as the *philosophes* brought the Age of Reason to its climax. The *philosophes* were not philosophers devoted to an academic discipline. They were men of letters, students of society who analyzed its evils and advocated reforms. They aimed to spread knowledge and emancipate the human spirit.

Curiously enough, atheism was not at all fashionable in this "polite society." Most of the prominent "infidels" who ridiculed Christianity during the eighteenth century believed in a supreme being but regarded it superstitious to hold that he interfered with the world-machine. This belief comes to be called *deism*, a movement especially popular among English speakers. Deism served as a halfway house on the road to atheism. One could keep the idea of God and dismiss the concept that God would engage or interfere with the world.

The God of the deists has sometimes been called the watchmaker God. God created the world as a watchmaker makes a watch, and then wound it up and let it run. Since God was a perfect watchmaker, there was no need of his interfering with the world later. Hence the deists rejected anything that seemed to be an interference of God with the world, such as miracles or special revelations recorded in the Bible.

The deists believed that their religion was the original religion of man. From it had come, by distortion, all other religions. These distortions were the work of priests who concocted the theologies, myths, and doctrines of the various religions to enhance their own power.

The most influential propagandist for deism was Voltaire (1694–1778), who personified the skepticism of the French Enlightenment. Above all others, Voltaire popularized Newton's science, fought for

personal liberty and freedom of the press, and spread the cult of reason. He turned out a prodigious number of works: histories, plays,
pamphlets, essays, and novels. In his correspondence, estimated at ten
thousand letters, he wittily spread the virtues of Enlightenment and
scathingly attacked the abuses of his day.

Voltaire achieved his greatest fame as the most relentless critic of the
established churches, Protestant and Catholic alike. He was sickened
by the intolerance of organized Christianity and disgusted by the petty
squabbles that seemed to monopolize the time of many priests and
clergymen. Yet, in spite of his biting criticism of Christianity, his aim
was not religion's destruction. He once said that if a God did not exist,
it would be necessary to invent one.

Voltaire had many disciples, but his only serious rival in spreading
the gospel of deism was a set of books: the famous French *Encyclopedia*
edited by Denis Diderot (1713–1784). The seventeen volumes of the
Encyclopedia constituted the chief monument of the *philosophes*. They
heralded the supremacy of the new science, championed tolerance,
denounced superstition, and expounded the merits of deism. Diderot's
article on Christianity professed high regard for the religion of Jesus,
but its effect was to stir the reader to a profound contempt for Christianity's social failures.

Unlike most previous critics of the church, the *philosophes* were not
heretics or dissenters who attacked the church in the name of Christ.
These men launched their attack from outside the church. And they
aimed their missiles not at a single point of dogma but at the foundation of all Christian truth. Their well-publicized purpose was to demol-
ish the citadel.

CHRISTIANITY ON TRIAL

Christianity, they insisted, was a pernicious plot designed to turn the
earth over to the oppressive powers of a priestly caste. Revealed religion was nothing less than a scheme to exploit the ignorant. Voltaire
liked to refer to Christianity as the "infamous thing." His most ruthless charge against the faith pictured the thousands upon thousands
of victims of Christianity's intolerance. Ironically, Christianity's critics
measured Christian behavior by standards they called human. These
critics ignored the fact that these human standards were actually the
legacy of Christian teaching.

These intellectuals judged Christianity by the simple human standards of good and evil. If the church, in the name of purity of doctrine,
sanctioned the bloody carnage of fellow Christians, as it had in the
wars of religion, then Christianity, far from being sacred and holy, was

a wicked institution. It had prevented peace, harmony, and progress among the peoples of the earth.

The primary weapon aimed at the church was truth. "We think that the greatest service to be done to men," said Diderot, "is to teach them to use their reason, only to hold for truth what they have verified and proved."

But the standards of truth ruled out Christian doctrine from the start. When the orthodox tried to reason from their basic premises, the infidels only scoffed because they refused to allow arguments drawn from authority or tradition embodied in the Bible or the church. These simply were not "reasonable."

Appeals to miracles met with similar disdain. The proof of a position was found in reason or human experiences, and since miracles failed this test they were dismissed as medieval nonsense.

"You see," Diderot argued,

once one sets foot in this realm of the supernatural, there are no bounds, one doesn't know where one is going nor what one may meet. Someone affirms that five thousand persons have been fed with five small loaves; this is fine! But tomorrow another will assure you that he fed five thousand people with one small loaf, and the following day a third will have fed five thousand with the wind.

The critics were thoroughly aware that they were fomenting a revolution in the fundamental beliefs of Europeans. Voltaire reported on each new triumph of reason over the church with the exultation of a commander winning battles.

THE FUTILITY OF EMPTY CONFIDENCE

These attacks upon Christian convictions demanded a vigorous and well-reasoned response from orthodox Christians. Unfortunately in Catholic countries, like France, the reaction was woefully inadequate. Church leaders were not indifferent to the rising tide of infidelity, but they tried to check it by traditional means. They appealed to secular authorities to censor the "dangerous" books, but they were usually unfamiliar with the primary issues the scoffers raised.

In England it was different. Several men wrote effectively against deism, none more so than Bishop Joseph Butler (1692–1752). His monumental work, *The Analogy of Religion*, virtually ended the debate for thinking people. Skirmishes continued for years, but after Butler it was clear the fundamental issues had been settled.

The deists, with their confident optimism, assumed that they knew all about God's wisdom and purpose. They read it all in the pattern of nature. Butler, however, saw with disarming clarity that life is filled with perplexities and enigmas.

He did not try to prove the existence of God. Deists never denied this premise. Nor did he reject reason; he accepted it as man's natural light. But he did challenge reason's sovereignty. Reason, said Butler, provides no complete system of knowledge, and in ordinary life it can offer us only probabilities.

Thus Butler undermined deism's fortress, its confidence in reason. Nature, he said, is not a realm in which reason is supreme. It is filled with obscurities and unexplained mysteries. We meet perplexity at every turn. And if we meet problems in nature, should we be surprised if we encounter difficulties in religion?

But take one further step. We know the ordinary course of nature because it is disclosed to us by experience, including our problems and perplexities. If religious truths encounter similar difficulties, isn't it reasonable to assume that one kind of knowledge is as dependable as the other? We normally act on the basis of probability. Why not in religion?

In the end, however, deism collapsed from its own weaknesses. It was based on a false optimism. It had no explanation for the evils and disasters of life. Because the laws of nature were clear and unalterable, deists assumed that man's moral choices drawn from nature were also simple and unchanging. If asked, "Why don't men always see clearly the religious truths in nature?" the deist could only respond with, "the lies of priestcraft." But that was too simple to be true, and few were convinced.

The eventual rejection of deism, however, did not restore Christianity to a central place in Western culture. The negative work of the Age of Reason endured. Modern culture—its art, its education, its politics—was freed from formal Christian influence. Men made a deliberate attempt to organize a religiously neutral civilization. This meant that faith was to function in the private realms confined to church, home, and heart. That is what we find today in modern secular societies.

This leaves Christians with a basic problem in the modern era: How far can believers go in trying, as citizens, to get the state to enforce Christian standards of conduct? Or if Christians give up the idea of enforcing Christian behavior, then what norm of conduct should they, as citizens, try to make an obligation for everyone?

Suggestions for Further Reading

Brinton, Crane. *The Shaping of the Modern Mind*. New York: The New American Library, 1953.

Cragg, Gerald R. *The Church and the Age of Reason: 1648–1789.* Middlesex: Penguin Books, 1960.

Gay, Peter. *Age of Enlightenment.* New York: Time-Life Books, 1966.

———. *The Enlightenment: An Interpretation: The Rise of Modern Paganism.* New York: Alfred A. Knopf, 1966.

McGrath, Alister. *Science and Religion: A New Introduction*, 2nd edition. Malden MA: Blackwell, 2010.

Pearse, Meic. *The Age of Reason: From the Wars of Religion to the French Revolution, AD 1570–1789, Baker History of the Church.* Vol. 5. Grand Rapids: Baker, 2006.

CHAPTER 33

THE HEART AND ITS REASONS

Pascal and the Pietists

WHAT DOES ONE DO with the personal belongings of a deceased loved one? It is an all but universal problem.

A few days after Blaise Pascal's death, a servant of the house noticed by chance a curious bulge in the great scientist's jacket. Opening the lining, he withdrew a folded parchment written in Pascal's hand. Within the parchment was a scribbled sheet of paper, a faithful copy of the words of the parchment:

> The year of grace 1654.
> Monday, November 23rd., . . . from about half past ten in
>   the evening until about half past twelve
> God of Abraham, God of Isaac, God of Jacob,
>   not of the philosophers and scholars.
> Certainty, certainty, feeling, joy, peace.
>   God of Jesus Christ . . .
> I have separated myself from Him, I have fled from Him,
>   renounced Him, crucified Him.
> May I never be separated from Him . . .
> Renunciation, total and sweet.

The words were the record of Pascal's mystical illumination, two hours in the presence of God! For eight years he had hidden them in his coat, sewing and unsewing them as he had need. It was his personal secret, his memorial of the coming of grace to his soul.

Even in the Age of Reason the thirst of the soul could not be ignored. An important new movement called Pietism arose as a reminder of that fact.

The Roman Catholic Blaise Pascal and the early Pietists, mostly professing Lutherans, would not seem to belong in the same stream of Christian history. With the hostility of faith prevalent in the seventeenth and eighteenth centuries, traditional religious labels meant less and less. Pascal's powerful critiques of the Enlightenment showed that Enlightenment thinkers could not consistently defend their narrow technical understanding of reason without major assumptions or leaps of faith. Pascal's important witness did not rest in some pretentious, omniscient, self-sufficient version of human reason, but in a deeper wisdom of reason's link to the heart. Pascal and the Pietists held to the heart's essential role in knowing God. How, then, in the Age of Reason did they sustain the life of the soul?

APPEALS TO "CHEAP GRACE"

The Catholic Church of the seventeenth century did not lack spiritual heroes in Europe or in the new worlds of Asia, Africa, and America. In France, however, she jealously guarded her traditional powerful alliances. The higher clergy of the church knew their importance in the political order. They shared with nobles and kings the revenues of the nation and the splendors of the court.

Frequently the teachers of the wealthy and the confessors of the powerful, the Jesuits, were trained to function in the urbane world of royalty. Their role as spiritual guides of nobles and kings made the followers of Loyola experts in psychology. They learned to deaden the thunder of Sinai and to heal the neuroses of remorse by developing the skills of casuistry, the science of right and wrong for the Christian conscience.

As confessors Catholic priests were expected to know just what was mortal sin or a venial sin or no sin at all. They had to apply this knowledge and the proper penance to the special experience of each penitent. In what cases might the letter of the law be set aside for its spirit? When might a Christian lie or steal or kill for a higher purpose?

Some experts in this science of casuistry were strict interpreters of the moral law; others were lenient. The Jesuits were lenient—very lenient. They argued that it might be possible to withhold the truth by "mental reservation" or even tell a lie if some high purpose called for it. They made so many allowances for sinful human nature that many earnest people protested what seemed to them "cheap grace," forgiveness without contrition.

Mental Reservation and Probabilism

Wide mental reservation allows the speaker's ambiguity to deceive the listeners. With Roman soldiers pursuing Athanasius, his friend told the soldiers that Athanasius was "not far away" when the bishop was actually hidden in his boat. The soldiers hurried ahead, thinking that they might still overtake Athanasius' boat. *Strict* mental reservation allows the speaker to mislead the listener in light of a significant qualification that he held in mind. The speaker might reason, "I must not admit that I told a lie because I had a very noble reason for telling it." Jesuits reasoned an answer under such circumstances may not be counted as a lie or a sin.

Jesuits also proposed the theory of probabilism. This theory justified behavior on the grounds that such behavior had even a remote probability of being morally acceptable.

The most aggressive opposition to the Jesuits came from a movement called Jansenism. Cornelius Jansen (1585–1638) was a Dutchman who had adopted St. Augustine's views of sin and grace at the University of Louvain. He came to believe that the best way to defend Catholicism against the Calvinist challenge was to return to the doctrines of the great North African and establish a rigorous moral code for the Catholic clergy to combat the easygoing ethics of the Jesuits.

Jansen carried on his campaign against the Jesuits as professor of Scripture at Louvain and later as Bishop of Ypres. At his death in 1638 he left, not quite finished, a major treatise, *Augustinus*, which soon after its publication in 1640 became the platform for Jansenism in France.

To correct the errors of Catholicism in his own day, Jansen went back to Augustine and argued that God, before the foundation of the world, had chosen those men and women who should be saved. The good works of men could never earn salvation without the help of divine grace because man's will is not free and his nature is corrupt beyond self-salvation. Only God's grace, available through Christ's death, can save him.

The Catholic Church had never explicitly repudiated these doctrines of Augustine, but she had let them slip into the background of her teaching. After the Council of Trent the Jesuit defense of free will magnified man's good works to the point of cheapening the redeeming work of Christ—at least so it seemed to Jansen. The Jesuits, he said, made far too much of human reason and woefully little of a trustful, unquestioning faith in God.

JANSENISM AT PORT-ROYAL

Jansen's close friend, Jean DuVergier, abbot of Saint-Cyran, carried the Jansenist message to France in 1633 when he was appointed confessor of a Cistercian convent called Port-Royal, sixteen miles from Paris. The youthful abbess of the nunnery, Jacqueline Arnauld, had led her flock in the ways of Christ totally, yet humbly. The reputation of the convent's devotion attracted not only other women but a group of devout laymen called Solitaries who pursued personal holiness in the low marshy valley surrounding Port-Royal.

Among the notable friends of the convent was Jacqueline's brother, Antoine Arnauld II, a member of the Sorbonne, the theological faculty of the University of Paris. After Jansen's death in 1638, Arnauld assumed leadership of the Jansenist cause. In 1643 he leveled his theological guns at the Jesuits. Without naming them he blasted the idea that frequent confession could compensate for frequent sinning.

The Jesuits could scarcely sidestep the charge. They turned to the pope and impressed upon him the dangers of Jansenism. Calvinism, they called it, in Catholic garb. In 1653 the pope condemned five propositions allegedly taken from *Augustinus*.

Arnauld, however, continued his attack on the Jesuits. He published two *Letters to a Duke and Peer* attacking what he claimed were Jesuit methods in the confessional. The Sorbonne now considered a move to expel him from the faculty.

Arnauld needed a defender, so he turned to a new friend of Port-Royal, a young scientist and master of French prose, Blaise Pascal (1623–1662). He could not have made a better choice. From childhood Pascal had known few things other than problems.

The boy's mother died when he was only three. His father, Stephen Pascal, undertook the education of the three children, Gilberte, Blaise, and Jacqueline. Occasionally Stephen took his son with him to the meetings of the Academy of Science and soon the youth's scientific curiosity was aroused.

Before he reached the age of twenty-seven Pascal had gained the admiration of mathematicians in Paris, had invented the calculating machine for his father who was a burdened tax collector at the time, and had discovered the basic principles of atmospheric and hydraulic pressures. He belonged to the age of scientific greats.

Blaise's initial contact with the Jansenists came as the result of an accident to his father. One icy day in January 1646, Stephen hurried out on foot to prevent a duel about to take place. He fell on the hard frozen ground and dislocated a hip. The two physicians who treated him were devoted Jansenists. They succeeded not only in curing their patient but also in winning his son to their doctrines.

They taught the Pascals that physical sufferings were but illustrations of a basic religious truth: man of himself is a helpless and miserable creature. Blaise had seldom enjoyed a day without pain. He knew how helpless physicians could be, so the argument struck him with unusual force. It deepened his sense of the tragic mystery of life.

Blaise also learned from these Jansenist physicians how profoundly the Bible speaks to the human condition. He became an avid student of Scripture, pondering its pages as he had atmospheric pressures. The Bible, he felt, was the way to a transformed heart.

In 1651, however, Pascal's personal tragedy deepened with the death of his father. The loss brought Blaise to a crisis in his life. His sister, Jacqueline, renounced the world by entering the Port-Royal convent, and Blaise was left alone in Paris.

He now gave himself to worldly interests. He took a sumptuously furnished home, staffed it with servants, and drove about town in a coach drawn by four horses. He pursued the ways of "proper society" as he had once studied geometry. But after a year of pleasure he found only a "great disgust with the world," and he plunged into a day-to-day "quiet desperation." He felt abandoned by God.

CERTAINTY, JOY, PEACE

Alone in the darkness of his soul, Blaise turned again to the Bible, to the seventeenth chapter of the gospel of John where Jesus prepares for his sacrifice on the cross. All of a sudden the Fire appeared, as he described in his scribbled memorial: "Certainty, certainty, feeling, joy, peace."

Pascal's new faith drew him magnetically into the orbit of Port-Royal. Late in 1654 he joined his sister, Jacqueline, as a member of the community. That is where Arnauld found him when he needed an advocate in his case against the Jesuits.

Pascal responded brilliantly. He penned eighteen *Provincial Letters* exposing the Jesuit theology and practices by flashes of eloquence and sarcastic wit. As each letter appeared, the public snatched them up. They were instant best sellers. Port-Royal was no longer an obscure monastery; it was the center of public interest. The pope condemned the letters, predictably, but all educated France read them, as succeeding generations did for two centuries.

After writing the last of the letters in March 1657, Pascal looked forward to a projected book on the evidences for Christianity. He was never able to complete the manuscript. In June 1662 he was seized with a violent illness, and after lingering two months he died on August 19 at the age of thirty-nine.

Friends found portions of his writing on faith and reason, and eight years after his death they published these notes under the title *Thoughts* (*Pensées*). In these Pascal is the religious genius who cuts across doctrine and pierces to the heart of man's moral problem. He appeals to the intellect by his passion for truth and arouses the emotions by his merciless descriptions of the plight of man without God.

In the Age of Reason Pascal insisted that nature is no sure clue to God. "I look on all sides," says Pascal,

> and everywhere I see nothing but obscurity . . . . If I saw no signs of a divinity, I would fix myself in denial. If I saw everywhere the marks of a Creator, I would repose peacefully in faith. *But seeing too much to deny (Him), and too little to assure me, I am in a pitiful state, and I would wish a hundred times that if a God sustains nature it would reveal Him without ambiguity.*

Man, caught in this ambiguous universe, is himself the greatest mystery. He is part angel and part beast. He reminds Pascal of the Chimera, which, in Greek mythology, was a she-goat with a lion's head and a serpent's tail: "What a Chimera is man! What a novelty, a monster, a chaos, a contradiction, a prodigy! The glory and refuse of the universe. Who shall unravel this confusion?"

Even reason is no sure guide. If we trust reason alone, we will doubt everything except pain and death. But our hearts tell us this cannot be true. That would be the greatest of all blasphemies to think that life and the universe have no meaning. God and the meaning of life must be felt by the heart rather than by reason: "The heart has its reasons which reason does not know."

Pascal saw the human condition so deeply yet so clearly that men and women in our own time, after three centuries, still gain perspective from him for their own mysterious pilgrimage.

After Pascal's death, the combined opposition of the Catholic Church and King Louis XIV succeeded in forcing Jansenism out of France. Port-Royal was destroyed and the movement forced to take refuge in Holland.

In the seventeenth century, however, Roman Catholic France was not the only area in need of heart. Any religion that becomes the religion of the majority and slowly turns into a social habit tends to grow humdrum and flat, regardless of its original glow of enthusiasm. So it proved in many areas of Lutheran Germany.

Protestant Scholasticism

During the one hundred years after Luther and Calvin taught, a substantial change came over the Protestant movement. The dynamic character of early Protestant calls for believers to entrust themselves to God's transforming mercy was eclipsed by doctrinal discussions that seemed abstract and lifeless. Luther had read the Bible to discern its life-giving witness to Jesus. The Protestant Scholastics fashioned involved, tedious arguments that depended upon Aristotle's logic (which Luther had condemned) and not upon Scripture. When later Protestants did appeal to the Bible, they often abstracted statements as if they were atomic, logical bits of data and not part of the great historical flow of God's story. Scripture seemed to be viewed as a self-sufficient body of material and not the book that came alive by the witness of God's Spirit. With God seen in less personal terms, Scripture seemed different: a source, but not a life-changing witness. Also, theology was shaped by the schools and less by the church. In time, even sermons seemed like lectures or theoretical ponderings. What Luther and Calvin said mattered less than what they would have said if they had addressed the speculative topics of Protestant Scholastics. Sadly, this theological undertaking did not distinguish them from unbelievers or even Catholics, but from one another. Confessions and creeds divided the church more and more.

On the heels of the vigorous, creative movement called the Reformation came a cautious period called Protestant Scholasticism or confessionalism. Out of the depths of his own experience, Luther had proclaimed a robust doctrine of justifying faith. In the seventeenth century, however, his dedicated followers, under the spell of the intellect, turned faith into a mental exercise. No longer an act of surrender to the mercy of God revealed in Christ, faith was now a formal assent to doctrinal truths set forth by scholars.

The Christian life was less a personal relation to Christ and more a matter of membership in the state church. Faithful attendance at public worship and reception of the sacraments offered by orthodox ministers were the essential marks of a good Christian.

Pietism arose as a reaction to this ossification of the Reformation. Just as Jansenism opposed the cheap grace of the French Jesuits, so the Pietists challenged the nominal faith of German Lutheranism.

The aims of the Pietists were twofold. First, they stressed the importance of personal faith. They left behind all dreams of Catholic

Christendom and Puritan commonwealths. They believed that Christianity started with the individual. So, for the first time in Christian history, the idea of conversions of baptized Christians (as well as pagans) came to prominence. The essence of faith, said the Pietist, is a personal experience of God's grace in the believer's heart.

Second, the Pietists wanted to shift the center of the Christian life from the state churches, in which a person was born and brought up, to intimate fellowships of those who had a living faith in God. Revitalized laymen from these centers were expected to spread the Word of God through all classes of men.

Three men—Philip Jacob Spener, August Hermann Francke, and Count Nikolaus von Zinzendorf—highlight the history of Pietism.

THE SOUL'S RETURN TO LIFE

Philip Spener (1635–1705) grew up under strong religious influences, including the writings of the German mystic Johann Arndt and the English Puritans. Later, at the University of Strasbourg, he met professors who introduced him to Luther and understood justification by faith not simply as a doctrine but as a spiritual rebirth.

After three years in a pastorate at Strasbourg, Spener accepted a call to the important Lutheran city of Frankfort. He was shocked by conditions in the town. He abandoned the prescribed texts and began to preach from the whole Bible. He called for repentance and discipleship. For several years nothing earth-shaking happened. Then in 1669 he preached from the Sermon on the Mount and response was sudden and surprising. People were converted and family life changed.

Spener gathered a little company of dedicated believers in his house twice weekly for reading of Scripture and religious conversation. These meetings were soon called, in scorn, "gatherings of the pious," and Pietism was born.

As interest in devotional literature grew, Johann Arndt's sermons were published and Spener wrote an introduction to them. He called it *Pious Desires*. In it he recommended the establishment of Bible study groups for spiritual development; a strenuous, rather ascetic, Christian life; greater care for the Christian character of theological students; and simpler and more spiritual preaching. Spener's thought was that a cell of experiential Christians should be gathered in each congregation to cultivate a stricter and warmer Christian life. He hoped that this leaven would permeate the whole church. He felt that only those who had been born again by a conscious Christian experience, conversion, were fitted for this work or should have a place in the ministry.

In 1686 Spener accepted a call to become court preacher at Dresden. But because of his uncompromising preaching he was often in trouble with the authorities, and in 1692 he welcomed an invitation from the elector of Brandenburg to move on to Berlin. That same year he persuaded Frederick, the future king of Prussia, to invite August Hermann Francke (1663–1727) to become a professor at the new University of Halle. In this Spener showed great wisdom and humility. Francke soon rose to leadership of the Pietist movement, though Spener continued writing and preaching until his death in February 1705.

Francke's arrival in Halle followed several years at the University of Leipzig, where his spiritual emphasis had created tensions with his faculty colleagues.

He traced his zeal to a life changing conversion that had come after two years of inner struggle and doubt. While writing a sermon on John 20:31, Francke had dropped to his knees in great fear. "I implored," he said, "the God, whom I did not yet know and whom I did not believe, that, if there really is a God, he should save me from this wretched condition." God heard him! Sadness left his heart and he was "suddenly overwhelmed by a flood of joy." When he arose, he knew he was saved and from that time on, it was "easy to live righteously and joyfully in this world."

At Halle, Francke pioneered an array of spiritual and social ministries. The university became the hub of a host of Pietist ministries. Francke's compassion for the neglected led him to begin a school for the poor. He also established an orphanage and bought a tavern and adjunct land to build a hospital. His ongoing work included a Latin school for talented boys, a house for widows, a house for unmarried women, a medical dispensary, a book depot, a printing establishment, and a Bible house. When King Frederick IV of Denmark wished to establish one of the earliest of Protestant missions in India in 1705, it was among Francke's disciples in Halle that he found his first missionaries.

THE CARPENTER AND THE COUNT

The later phase of Pietism is dominated by Count von Zinzendorf (1700–1760), an ardent and emotional man who believed that the mark of true Christianity is a simple, childlike faith in the blood of Jesus. In vivid, almost erotic images he sang of the soul's relation to Christ.

Zinzendorf was the grandson of a nobleman who had left Austria for his religious convictions. When young Nikolaus's father died and his mother remarried, his training fell into the hands of his devout grandmother who was an admirer of the Halle Pietists. Nikolaus studied law for three years at the University of Wittenberg, but the ministry remained his soul's concern.

An opportunity for service came in an unexpected way with the remains of the old Hussite movement, the Bohemian Brethren (*Unitas Fratrum*). The brethren flourished in Bohemia and Moravia at the time of the Reformation but had been nearly crushed during the Thirty Years' War, and were subject to severe persecution. Under a Moravian carpenter, Christian David, the Brethren had experienced the stirring of revival and were casting about for some place of refuge in Protestant lands. They found it on Zinzendorf's estates, and in 1722 David established a community called *Herrnhut*, "The Lord's Watch." Zinzendorf entered into the community and soon devout people of various backgrounds were flocking to Herrnhut. The Moravians had in mind a town inhabited only by Christians, separate from the World, a real "communion of saints." It was a free and social monasticism, without celibacy. But like monasticism, they sought to live the Christian life under peculiarly favorable conditions and apart from grosser temptations.

From 1727 Zinzendorf was the guiding spirit of Herrnhut, and ten years later he received formal ordination in the reorganized Moravian Church, or United Brethren as the believers preferred to call it. Zinzendorf's impulses were always strongly missionary. As a result the Moravians became the first large-scale Protestant missionary force in history.

On a visit to the Danish capital, Copenhagen, for the coronation of King Christian VI in 1731, Zinzendorf met a black man from the Danish West India Islands and was impressed with the needs of the enslaved people. As a result, in 1732 the first of an army of Moravian missionaries, Leonhard Dober and David Nitschmann, set forth from Herrnhut on their way to St. Thomas. The establishment of other missions speedily followed: Greenland, Lapland, the American Indians in Georgia, the African Guinea Coast, the Hottentots of South Africa, South American Guiana, Ceylon, and Algeria.

Zinzendorf's character, like most, had its light and its shadow. He was inclined to a sentimental type of religion. Yet some of his emotional hymns, such as "Jesus still lead on, till our rest be won," have found a place in the worship of many churches. Few men have shown such personal devotion to Christ, and he gave the true cornerstone of his character in his declaration to his Herrnhut congregation: "I have only one passion. It is He, none but He."

VIEW FROM A REARVIEW MIRROR

Pietism made an enormous contribution not only to the German people but to Christianity worldwide. It shifted emphasis in eighteenth-century churches from avid controversy to the care of souls. It made preaching and pastoral visitation central concerns of the Protestant ministry. It enriched Christian music enormously. And it underscored the importance of a spiritual laity for a revived church. Perhaps its greatest legacy was its emphasis on small groups and the devotional reading of Scripture. Church meetings did not offer enough systematic exposure to Scripture, while small groups focused attention on supplementing and encouraging personal Scripture reading and corporate worship. Personal copies of Scripture were more accessible to believers than ever before in history. Personal engagement with the Bible became a focal point of discipleship. Groups would highlight a word or thought from Scripture. A well-chosen hymn would reinforce the daily meditation from Scripture.

Supporting all these emphases was the Pietist's dominant theme: regeneration. And they meant by this not a theological doctrine but the indispensable experience of the Christian. They believed this spiritual rebirth was the true fulfillment of the Protestant Reformation. In the heart Christian doctrine became Christian reality.

The intensely personal way the Pietist described regeneration often made Christianity a drama of the human soul. The heart of man was the scene of a desperate struggle between the powers of good and evil.

In this sense Pietism was the fountain of all modern revivals. It set the experience of new life in Christ at the center of the Christian message and the Christian ministry. For this reason it is impossible to think of evangelical Christianity today without the imprint of Pietism.

Evangelicals inherited two important traits from Pietism. First, emotion played so large a part in the Pietist's religious life that reason was endangered. Since the mind of man could not fathom the mysteries of human destiny, feelings were left to carry the meaning of faith. Consequently Pietism had little to say about God's place in nature or human history. And it presented few challenges to the spread of secularism. Evangelicals often surrendered to the same weakness.

Second, Pietism assumed the existence of the institutional church. It made no frontal attacks upon it. But it shifted what was essential to Christianity—the new birth and the spiritual life—from the traditional state churches to intimate fellowship groups or voluntary associations of believers. In the United States, where no state church ever prevailed, Evangelicals made an alliance with the denominational concept of the church and simply multiplied religious movements stressing evangelism or some aspect of the Christian life.

Clearly, then, Pietism lives on, not only in the Moravian denomination, but also in evangelical Christianity at large, the spiritual descendants of John Wesley and George Whitefield.

Suggestions for Further Reading

Brown, Dale. *Understanding Pietism.* Revised Edition. Nappanee, IN: Evangel Publishing House, 1996.

Cailliet, Emile. *Pascal: The Emergence of Genius.* New York: Harper & Brothers, 1961.

Groothuis, Douglas. *On Pascal.* Melbourne: Thomson/Wadsworth, 2003.

*Hammond, James. *The Cambridge Companion to Pascal.* Cambridge: New York, 2003.

McGiffert, A. C. *Protestant Thought Before Kant.* New York: Harper & Brothers, 1961.

McNeill, John T. *Modern Christian Movements.* New York: Harper & Row, 1954.

*O'Connell, Marvin. *Blaise Pascal: Reasons of the Heart.* Grand Rapids: Eerdmans, 1997.

*Shantz, Douglas H. *An Introduction to German Pietism: Protestant Renewal at the Dawn of Modern Europe.* Baltimore, MD: Johns Hopkins, 2013.

Stoeffler, F. Ernest. *The Rise of Evangelical Pietism.* Leiden: E. J. Brill, 1965.

CHAPTER 34

A BRAND FROM
THE BURNING

Wesley and Methodism

Toward the end of January 1736, the good ship *Simmonds*, bound for Savannah, Georgia, sailed into a series of violent Atlantic storms. The wind roared; the ship cracked and quivered; the waves lashed the deck.

A young, slightly built Anglican minister on board was frozen in fear. John Wesley had preached the gospel of eternal salvation to others, but he was afraid to die. He was deeply awed, however, by a company of Moravian Brethren from Herrnhut. As the sea broke over the deck of the vessel, splitting the mainsail in pieces, the Moravians calmly sang their psalms to God.

Afterward, Wesley asked one of the Germans if he was frightened.

"No," he replied. "Weren't your women and children afraid?" Wesley asked.

"No," said the Moravian, "our women and children are not afraid to die."

"This," Wesley wrote in his *Journal*, "was the most glorious day I have ever seen."

At that glorious moment Wesley was a most unlikely candidate for leadership in a spiritual awakening soon to shake England to its moorings. He had a form of godliness, but he had yet to find its power.

THE EVANGELICAL AWAKENING

The Age of Reason saw a dramatic spiritual renewal in Western Christianity called the Evangelical Awakening. The movement was interlaced

346

by personal ties of the leaders, but three regions were significantly changed: Germany by the rise of Pietism, the British Isles by the preaching of the Methodists, and the American colonies by the impact of the Great Awakening.

The Methodist revival in England not only explains the origin of the Methodist denomination (numbering over twenty million in the world today), it also throws light on the movement we call evangelical Christianity. Who were these Evangelicals, and how did they gain major significance in Christian history?

Those singing Moravians who sailed to Georgia with Wesley represent one important wing of evangelicalism. They were, we know, Pietists. The main body of Evangelicals, however, came from Great Britain and her colonies.

The 1730s in America, Scotland, Wales, and England saw a sudden explosion of apostolic concern to preach the gospel to the unconverted. Jonathan Edwards in Northampton, Massachusetts; Ebenezer and Ralph Erskine in Scotland; Howel Harris in Wales; and George Whitefield in England all preceded John Wesley in the evangelical awakening.

Most of the basic beliefs of the Evangelicals could be found in Puritanism: the sinfulness of man, the atoning death of Christ, the unmerited grace of God, the salvation of the true believer. But Puritanism was more concerned with politics. It tried to create the holy commonwealth, the true Bible society, in England and America.

The Evangelicals were not detached from politics as the Pietists were, but their controlling passion was the conversion of the lost. They were less concerned about the reform of churches and more intent upon the preaching of the gospel to all: nominal Christians, scoffers, and heathen. John Wesley lacked that passion in Georgia, but when he found it, all England knew it.

In the early decades of the eighteenth century, England was a most unlikely place for a nationwide revival of vital faith. Among the rich and well educated the Enlightenment had shoved religion from the center of life to its periphery.

In the established Church, the Anglican Church, and in the Nonconformist denominations such as the Baptists and Congregationalists, the zeal of the Puritans seemed to be a thing of the past. England had known her fill of holy causes. The order of the day was moderation in all things.

An English sermon, said Voltaire, was a "solid but, sometimes dry dissertation that a man reads to the people without gesture and without particular exaltation of the voice." Ministers blandly ignored the traditional Christian doctrine of man's sinfulness. Instead, men approached God with gentle awe and cheerfulness. Joseph Addison's famous hymn published in his periodical, *The Spectator*, is typical of this new attitude:

> The Spacious Firmament on high
> With all the blue Etherial Sky,
> And spangled Heav'ns, a Shining Frame,
> Their great Original proclaim:
> Th' unwearied Sun, from Day to Day
> Does his Creator's Power display,
> And publishes to every Land
> The Work of an Almighty Hand.

Signs of reason's deadening influence upon the churches appeared in a large group within the Church of England called the Latitudinarians. The eloquent John Tillotson, the Archbishop of Canterbury (1691–1694), was among them. He vigorously denounced what he called religious "enthusiasm." This included any emotional expression encouraged by fervent preachers. He and his fellow Latitudinarians stressed instead proper behavior. Men should reform their conduct; they should be generous, humane and tolerant, and avoid bigotry and fanaticism.

THE LITTLE GIANT

John Wesley (1703–1791) came from a home steeped in decency and order. It combined strains of Anglican and Nonconformist piety. His father, the Reverend Samuel Wesley, was a learned and devout high-churchman ministering at Epworth in Lincolnshire. John's mother, Susanna, was the daughter of a Nonconformist minister in London. She was a remarkable woman who bore nineteen children. John was the fifteenth. She taught them "to fear the rod and cry softly." Every week she made time for religious instruction for each child separately. To do so, she had to be methodical! John looked to her for guidance to the day of her death.

When John was six the rectory at Epworth burned down; he was left alone amid the flames, but he appeared at a second-story window and was rescued by a neighbor standing on the shoulders of another. Thereafter John called himself "a brand plucked from the burning." He never doubted God's providential hand upon his life.

At seventeen he was off to Oxford University where he studied first at Christ Church and later at Lincoln College. He found little at Oxford to stimulate his mind or his soul, but he read widely and was especially impressed by the early church fathers and the great devotional classics. The early Greek fathers taught him that the goal of the Christian life was perfection, a process of disciplined love rather than a religious state.

From Jeremy Taylor's *Holy Living*, Thomas à Kempis's *Imitation of Christ*, and William Law's *Serious Call to a Holy Life*, Wesley learned that the Christian life is the consecration of the whole man in love to God and neighbor. These men, he said, "convinced me of the absolute impossibility of being *half a Christian*. I determined, through His grace, to be all devoted to God." So he catalogued his weaknesses and established his rules to overcome them.

In 1726 Wesley was elected a fellow of Lincoln College. This gave him not only academic standing at the University but assured him of a steady income. Two years later he was ordained to the Anglican ministry and returned to Epworth for a time to serve as his father's assistant.

When he resumed his duties at Oxford, he found that his brother, Charles, alarmed at the spread of deism at the University, had assembled a little band of students determined to take their religion seriously. John proved to be just the leader they needed. Under his direction they drew up a plan of study and rule of life that stressed prayer, Bible reading, and frequent attendance at Holy Communion.

The little group soon attracted attention and some derision from the lax undergraduates. "Enthusiasm" at Oxford? Holy Club, they called them—and Bible moths, Methodists, and Reforming Club. The Methodist label is the one that stuck.

The members of the little society were ardent but restless souls. They found fresh enthusiasm when a townsman or new student joined them, such as the bright and brash undergraduate from Pembroke College, George Whitefield. But they were constantly in search of ways to make their lives conform to the practice of early Christians. They gave to the poor and they visited the imprisoned. But John was quick to confess that he lacked the inward peace of a true Christian. God must have something more in mind.

Then came the invitation to Georgia. A friend, Dr. John Burton, suggested that both John and Charles could serve God in the new colony led by General James Oglethorpe. Charles could be the General's secretary and John a chaplain to the colony. John welcomed a chance to preach to the American Indians so the brothers boarded the *Simmonds* in October with youthful idealism and missionary zeal, totally unaware of the storms on sea and soul just ahead.

The whole Georgia episode proved to be a fiasco. John discovered that the noble American savages were "gluttons, thieves, liars and murderers." And his white colonists deeply resented his rigid high church ways, his refusal to conduct the funeral of a Nonconformist, and his prohibition of the ladies' fancy dresses and gold jewelry in church.

John's frustrations were compounded by his pitiful love affair with Sophy Hopkey, the eighteen-year-old niece of Savannah's chief magistrate. Wesley was so mixed up emotionally and spiritually that he didn't know his own mind. Sophy finally resolved the affair by eloping with John's rival. The jilted lover then barred her from Holy Communion, and her incensed husband sued John for defaming Sophy's character. The trial dragged out, and after six months of harassment, Wesley fled the colony in disgust.

On his way home he had a chance to ponder the whole experience. "I went to America," he wrote, "to convert the Indians, but, oh, who shall convert me?"

THE HOLY HEART WARMING

He landed back in England on February 1, 1738, sadly discredited and painfully uncertain of his faith and his future. For a dozen years he had been toiling up the path to perfection, striving by the best models he knew to attain true blessedness. And the Georgia mission only revealed his spiritual bankruptcy.

He found one positive experience in the Georgia episode, his contact with the Moravians. He was determined to learn their secret of spiritual power. In London he met Peter Bohler, a young Moravian preacher who impressed upon Wesley his need of a new birth, a strong personal faith in Christ that would enable him to overcome sin and attain true holiness. Justification by faith, said Bohler, is not merely a doctrine. It is a personal experience of God's forgiveness. But how, asked Wesley, can faith be given in a moment of time?

He discovered the answer for himself on May 24, 1738. "In the evening," he wrote,

> I went very unwillingly to a society in Aldersgate Street, where one was reading Luther's preface to the *Epistle to the Romans*. About a quarter to nine, while he was describing the change which God works in the heart through faith in Christ, I felt my heart strangely warmed. I felt that I did trust in Christ, Christ alone, for salvation; and an assurance was given me that he had taken away *my* sins, even *mine*, and saved me from the law of sin and death.

Wesley's journal entries after Aldersgate reflect an ongoing lack of security that gave way when God used his own evangelistic preaching to great effect.

Thus Wesley found the assurance that he had lacked, a sense of purpose that would sustain him for half a century of unparalleled energy. He had discovered his life's message. He needed now to find his method.

Later that summer Wesley visited the Moravians in their Saxon homeland. He wanted to see firsthand the power of the piety he had witnessed aboard ship and in Georgia. His impressions of Herrnhut were mixed. On the one hand, he met many remarkable people who exemplified "the full assurance of Christian faith." On the other hand, he was quick to spot the signs of self-righteousness among them. He was especially repelled by the cult of personality that had grown up around their leader, Count von Zinzendorf. "Isn't the Count all in all?" Wesley asked.

Thus Wesley and the Moravians soon parted ways. He owed much to them, especially their message of justification by faith and their system of small groups for spiritual growth. But Wesley could not see himself as a Moravian.

Wesley returned to London and resumed his preaching in the churches. His zeal was undiminished, but his results were no more satisfying than before. An inner sense of reality and outward impact were still missing. Then, almost by chance, while walking from London to Oxford he began to read Jonathan Edwards's account of the recent conversions in Northampton, Massachusetts. It struck Wesley with terrific force. In this instance, the Great Awakening in New England had a direct influence upon the Wesleyan revival in the mother country. In a matter of weeks Wesley was caught up in a similar movement of the Spirit. It started when he received a surprising invitation from a member of the Holy Club.

George Whitefield, nine years younger than John Wesley, had followed him to Georgia in 1738 but returned in the fall of that year to be ordained. Not satisfied with the opportunities given him in pulpits and eager to reach the masses of people, he began in February 1739 to preach in the open fields near Bristol to coal miners who seldom dared or cared to enter a church. His voice was clear and strong, and his fervent oratory so moved these hardened and weary men that he could see "the white gutters made by their tears" falling down their black cheeks as they emerged from the coal pits.

Whitefield's preaching was unforgettable. Using startling images he could make his listeners feel the pain of sin and the terror of hell. Then with tears in his voice he could describe the love of Christ until his audience cried with him for forgiveness. "I would give a hundred guineas," said the actor David Garrick, "if I could only say Oh! like Mr. Whitefield."

When the hardened miners of Bristol pled for God's mercy in such great numbers Whitefield urged Wesley to follow his lead into the open fields. John knew he was no match for Whitefield's oratory. He spoke as an Oxford scholar and a gentleman. But he hesitated chiefly because he had never dreamed of preaching under the sky. "Having been all my life so tenacious of every point relating to decency and order," he wrote, "I should have thought the saving of souls almost a sin if it had not been done in a church."

TO THE FIELDS, TO THE WORLD

In spite of his brother Charles's opposition, John reluctantly decided to go to Bristol, more like a martyr than a joyous messenger. As it turned out, "the brand from the burning" was carried across the threshold of his true mission in life. He preached to over three thousand in the open air, and the reaction of these common folk was amazing. Conversions, as real as those in New England, took place on every hand. The Methodist revival had begun.

The effects on Wesley were equally remarkable. Up to this point he was filled with anxiety, insecurity, and futility. After Bristol he was a firebrand for God.

Peter Bohler had exhorted him to "preach faith till you have it and then because you have it, you will preach faith." At Aldersgate he had passed from virtual to real faith, from hoping to having. Edwards and Whitefield had shown him that the Word rightly preached bears visible fruit. And now, before his eyes, was a harvest of such fruit. He had preached faith until others had it, and now his own was confirmed by theirs!

After that spring of 1739 in Bristol, Wesley set out to carry the gospel to the poor wherever they were willing to listen. In June he wrote, "I look upon all the world as my parish; I judge it my bounden duty, to declare unto all that are willing to hear, the glad tidings of salvation."

He preached in jails to prisoners, in inns to wayfarers, on vessels crossing to Ireland. At a natural amphitheater in Cornwall he preached to 30,000 at once, and when he was refused admission to the Epworth Church he preached to hundreds in the churchyard while standing on his father's tombstone. In his diary for June 28, 1774, Wesley claims that his minimum mileage per year was 4,500. That means he must have traveled in his lifetime 250,000 miles, ten times around the world! He traveled mostly on horseback, and he soon learned to give the horse plenty of rein so that he could read a book or prepare a sermon on his way to the next town.

In Wesley's early years of itinerating, the crowds were not always friendly. Rocks and stones or other missiles would come flying at the preacher. Sometimes he was mobbed and beaten by gangs incited by a hostile squire or parson. But Wesley feared no man. By a strange personal magnetism he often awed turbulent crowds, and in time the violence subsided. Before his death, statuettes in China and mementoes of his likeness were produced in large numbers to satisfy public demand.

In 1751 Wesley married Molly Vazeille, the widow of a London merchant, who nursed him back to health after a fall on the ice. He was not an easy man to live with. For two years she tried to travel with him on his hectic rounds, but her health and nerves broke and she left him. As late as 1777 Wesley was considering the possibilities of a reconciliation, but when Molly died in 1781 he was unaware of her death and did not attend the funeral. She had simply married a man who was wed to his mission.

In his tireless preaching Wesley stressed what we now call *Arminian* beliefs; he was the only prominent leader of the Awakening who did. The name came from Jacob Arminius (1560–1609), a Dutch professor who tried to modify the Calvinism of his time. Wesley felt no special debt to Arminius, but he did staunchly oppose Calvin's doctrine of predestination. He thought the belief made God appear arbitrary. He insisted that God willed the salvation of *all* men and that men could receive or refuse divine grace.

This conviction brought his friendship with Whitefield to the breaking point. Whitefield defended the doctrine of predestination because it underscored God's sovereign authority. He felt Wesley's "Arminianism" dulled the all-important sense of sin and compromised the vital concept of an almighty God.

Both men sought to advance the work of the awakening, so they agreed to differ in mutual respect. In Wesley's sermon at Whitefield's funeral in 1770, he spoke of the evangelist's "most generous and tender friendship." But the controversy did lead to two camps among the Methodists: Arminian societies following Wesley and Calvinist societies following Whitefield.

THE METHODIST STRUCTURE

Whitefield had no real taste for organization, but Wesley was an administrative genius. Following his trail Methodist societies appeared all over England, Ireland, and Wales. These were not yet congregations in our sense of the term. Most of the believers were members of the Anglican Church, and Wesley urged them to attend their parish churches for worship and Holy Communion. He was still the devout churchman from Epworth rectory. But his converts found the center of their Christian experience in the Methodist societies where they confessed their sins to one another, submitted to the discipline of their leader, and joined in prayer and song.

Charles Wesley, who had experienced God's forgiving grace three days before John, wrote over seven thousand hymns and gospel songs for these Methodist meetings. Perhaps his best loved was "Jesus Lover of my Soul." It was sung in societies all over Britain and America. Some historians believe Charles's hymns are the revival's greatest legacy.

Following the Moravian example John divided his societies into smaller groups of twelve or so members called *classes*. The term was from the Latin *classis* meaning division and had no overtones of schools. Wesley originally used them to encourage financial support, a penny a week for the work. But he soon realized that the collector might also serve as the spiritual guide of the sheep and that members of the classes could encourage one another in their Christian experience. The result was the "class meeting" for testimonies, prayer, and spiritual encouragement, a highly successful feature of the Methodist awakening.

As the work grew Wesley decided to employ laymen from the societies and classes as preachers and personal assistants. He carefully avoided calling them ministers and he refused them any authority to administer the sacraments. They were, he said, his personal helpers directly responsible to him in their work, as he was responsible to the Anglican Church.

By 1744 he found it impossible to maintain personal contact with all these preachers. With a few ordained colleagues and still fewer lay preachers, he created the Annual Conference. This gathering helped to shape the policy and doctrine of the movement; however, always as Wesley decided.

He deployed his assistants as a sort of militia, moving them frequently from one assignment to another but insisting on their common task: evangelism and Christian nurture: "We look upon ourselves, not as the authors or ringleaders of a particular sect or party—it is the farthest thing from our thoughts—but as messengers of God, to those who are Christians in name but heathens in heart and life, to call them back to that from which they are fallen, to real, genuine Christianity."

Thus by 1748 "the people called Methodists," like the Pietists in Germany, were a church within the church. For the next forty years Wesley resisted all pressures from his own followers and all charges from Anglican bishops that suggested separation from the Church of England. "I live and die," he said, "a member of the Church of England."

Toward the end of his days, however, the needs of the Methodists in America led him to significant steps toward separation. Long before the American cries of "liberty" Wesley had sent Francis Asbury to the colonies, and the work had grown. In 1773 the first American Methodist conference was held in Philadelphia, but the societies needed ordained leaders. Wesley's appeals to the Bishop of London proved fruitless, so he took matters into his own hands.

Wesley decided to appoint two of his lay preachers, Richard Whatcost and Thomas Vasey, for the American ministry and to commission Dr. Thomas Coke as superintendent of the American Methodists. This was an important breach in Anglican policy. The Methodist Church in America became a new, distinct denomination when the Christmas Conference meeting at Baltimore in 1784 selected Coke and Francis Asbury as superintendents.

Wesley continued preaching almost to the end of his days. He died in London, March 2, 1791, approaching eighty-eight years of age. When the burning brand finally went out, he left behind seventy-nine thousand followers in England and forty thousand in North America. If we judge greatness by influence, he was among the greats of his times.

After his death the English Methodists followed their American brethren into separation from the Anglican Church. But Wesley's impact and the revival he represents carried far beyond the Methodist Church. It renewed the religious life of England and her colonies. It elevated the life of the poor. It stimulated missions overseas and the social concerns of Evangelicals in the nineteenth and twentieth centuries.

Suggestions for Further Reading

*Collins, Kenneth J. *The Theology of John Wesley: Holy Love and the Shape of Grace.* Nashville, TN: Abingdon, 2007.

Edwards, Maldwyn. *John Wesley and the Eighteenth Century.* London: Epworth, 1955.

Green, V. H. H. *John Wesley*. London: Nelson, 1964.

Outler, Albert C., ed. *John Wesley*. New York: Oxford, 1964.

Pudney, John. *John Wesley and His World*. New York: Scribner, 1978.

*Rack, Henry D. *Reasonable Enthusiast: John Wesley and the Rise of Methodism*. 3rd ed. London: Epworth Press, 2002.

Tomkins, Stephen. *John Wesley: A Biography*. Grand Rapids: Eerdmans, 2003.

Wood, A. Skevington. *The Inextinguishable Blaze*. Grand Rapids: Eerdmans, 1960.

CHAPTER 35

A NEW ORDER
OF THE AGES

The Great Awakening

O N JULY 4, 1776, Benjamin Franklin, John Adams, and Thomas Jefferson were appointed as a committee to prepare a Seal of the United States of America.

Various suggestions were offered. Franklin wanted a design featuring Moses. In the background, the troops of Pharaoh would be seen drowning in the Red Sea and the message would read, "Rebellion to tyrants is obedience to God." Jefferson suggested that the Seal show that the children of Israel in the wilderness were "led by a cloud by day and a pillar of fire by night."

By the time of final adoption the biblical content nearly evaporated, but it is significant that these American patriots, themselves distant to their Jewish-Christian heritage, found in the Bible those symbols that would unite and interpret their people's experience. The Latin on the Seal, found today on United States currency, reads,

E PLURIBUS UNUM—ANNUIT COEPTIS—MDCCLXXVI—
NOVUS ORDO SECLORUM

A rough translation would be:

one out of many—(God) has smiled on our undertakings—
1776—a new order of (or for) the ages.

357

No one knows all that these patriots meant by "a new order of the ages." It is the rhetoric of a revolution. But certainly the Christian churches faced a new and strikingly different mission in the emerging American nation. No event marked the new order for Christianity more clearly than the religious explosion we call the Great Awakening, the first in the long history of American revivals. What was the Great Awakening and why was it crucial to the development of Christianity in America?

NEW ORDER FOR THE CHURCHES

For thirty generations Christian people had found a meaningful place under God's heaven by holding the idea of Christendom. No one seriously challenged it. Generation after generation were born and baptized in Christian society where church and state found a working harmony for the good of all. Through her teaching and sacraments the church dispensed saving grace to prepare men for the life to come. The state maintained Christian laws and political order for the earthly welfare of her citizens.

The Reformation unintentionally shattered traditional Christendom. It prayed and preached and fought for the true faith until no single church remained, only what we now call denominations. But in the place of Christendom strong national princes arose to perpetuate the alliance of church and state in their realms for the supposed good of their subjects. These churches, established and supported by law, tended to swing between the extremes of repression and relaxation.

The "new order" for Christianity in the American colonies threw the churches into another arena. After the first generation of settlers a wide variety of national and religious strains made an established church implausible in all but a few colonies. By 1646, for example, eighteen languages echoed from the banks of the Hudson River alone. Probably all the Christian groups were unanimous on one thing: each wanted the liberty to proclaim its own view. In time it became obvious, however, that the only way each group could attain religious liberty for themselves was to grant it to all the others. They had come to America to build a government that would produce holy people; eventually, they would need to cooperate with many different kinds of people to achieve a revised dream. They settled to live in a society where people could still practice holiness.

Thus the churches were forced to shoulder the burden alone for evangelizing the unconverted and nurturing the believers: no state support, no state protection. Christianity was on its own.

We call this condition *voluntaryism* because the churches, deprived of state support, were compelled to maintain their mission of preaching and teaching on a voluntary basis. Men could accept or reject the gospel as they pleased. The state had nothing to do with it. The denominations had to win converts and raise funds without state aid.

The Great Awakening proved crucial in this new order. It convinced hosts of Christians that voluntaryism could work. After the first ecstatic waves of the Spirit, many believers considered revivals God's gift for the creation of a Christian America. Jonathan Edwards even preached that America would be the scene of the coming millennium!

It did not come easily. The revival met resistance, especially in Puritan New England. The reasons are no great mystery. Puritanism established by law represented the old order: Christianity allied with the state. Yet even in Puritanism seeds for revival were liberally scattered.

The Puritan view of the church rested upon their understanding of the covenant of grace. Early New Englanders realized that the visible church could never be an exact copy of the truly elect, but God willed the church so far as possible to be a church of visible saints. That is why the first generation insisted that conversion precede church membership, a practice reaffirmed in 1648 with the adoption of the Cambridge Platform.

"The doors of the churches of Christ upon earth," they said, "do not by God's appointment stand so wide open, that all sorts of people good or bad, may freely enter therein at their pleasure." Those seeking admission, they declared, must be "examined and tried first" to see that they possess, above all else, "repentance from sin and faith in Jesus Christ." This usually meant that potential members made "a personal and public confession," detailing "God's manner of working upon the soul."

GOD'S WILL IN SOCIETY

The colony in Massachusetts, however, was more than a string of Christian congregations around Boston harbor. Like the Pilgrims in their Mayflower Compact, the Puritans aimed to knit the whole community together according to God's design. That was the purpose of the civil covenant. A Christian people, if they are to enjoy the corporate blessings that God alone can give, must walk in his ways and fulfill his commands, even in their civil government.

God's will was embodied in "wholesome laws." Puritans held that law without a moral base is no law at all. Since the "sins of men are like raging sea(s), which would overwhelm all if they have not banks," the Puritan knew that laws were necessary to curb the lusts of men and to restrain outward expressions of human depravity. Such laws are drawn from Scripture or from nature and right reason. The test of any law, however, was whether or not it advanced "the public good," which was another way of saying, "fulfilling God's will in society."

Puritans were in a position to say which laws were for the public good because they had secured the charter granting them the right to settle in New England. Thus in their colony in Massachusetts they had the authority to permit only freemen to vote for the governor and magistrates and to insist that all freemen be church members. So the vote and public morality were controlled by the churches.

This attempt to legislate morality is one reason later Americans came to hate the Puritans. Most twentieth-century Americans prized their personal freedoms above the character of the society in which they lived. The Puritan "holy experiment," blending belief in a church of the truly converted with the idea of a Christian state, seemed destined to fail almost from the start. There are problems in operating any church on earth when only God knows who the real members are. Not everyone in Massachusetts or Connecticut could boldly testify of experienced grace. As the zeal of the New England founders cooled, fewer men and women could bear public witness to grace in their souls. To keep membership from shrinking drastically, many churches in 1662 had to settle for the Half-Way Covenant. Under this policy the "unawakened" could enjoy a kind of partial membership, baptizing their children and joining in congregational activities, but not taking full Communion. This was enough church affiliation for most political and social purposes, so that gradually the "saints" sank to a tiny minority. When a new charter in 1691 based the right to vote on property rather than on church membership, New England had reached a spiritual crossroads.

Shortly after the dawn of the eighteenth century, two types of Puritan heirs were visible. The spiritual heritage fell to the children of the Great Awakening. The call for personal conversion as the basis of church membership soon echoed throughout the Connecticut River valley through the preaching of Jonathan Edwards.

The "worldly puritans" continued the Puritan sense of civic responsibility and concern for lawful government. Even when they could no longer feel the dread of living before an awesome Lord of history, these colonialists still held that empires rose or fell depending on whether men obeyed or disobeyed the designs of Divine Providence. They believed, for example, that God smiled upon the quest of liberty.

The Great Awakening knew both the frown and the smile of God. It restored both the tears of repentance to colonial Christianity and the joy of salvation.

For twenty years (1720–1740) the awakening appeared as a series of regional breezes. According to George Whitefield, "the beginner of the great work" was Theodore J. Frelinghuysen, a minister of the Dutch Reformed Church in New Jersey. Shortly after arriving in the colonies he stirred the feelings of his solid Raritan valley farmer parishioners with his impassioned appeals and enjoyed a great "ingathering of new members."

The winds moved on to the Scotch-Irish Presbyterians in the area. In a little school, dubbed a "Log College" by more bookish clergymen, a Pennsylvania preacher named William Tennent started turning out a number of ministers with evangelical zeal. His alumni soon had the winds of revival whipping through a number of churches, particularly in New Jersey. In a short time a controversy arose over the question of "educated" versus "converted" ministers, and the whole Presbyterian Church divided into "New Side" men favoring the revival and "Old Side" men opposing it.

Undaunted by opposition, the New Side forces sent missionaries into the Southland. Under the leadership of the Reverend Samuel Davies, revivalistic Presbyterian congregations took root in Virginia. And not to be outdone, Baptists began multiplying in Virginia and the Carolinas under uneducated but zealous preachers led by Shubael Stearns.

In New England the breezes came from the west, from a little Massachusetts town called Northampton where Jonathan Edwards had spiritual charge of two hundred families, suffering an "extraordinary dulness in religion." Edwards complained of "licentiousness . . . night walking, and frequenting the tavern, and lewd practices." In December 1734, however, "the Spirit of God began extraordinarily to set in." A "great and earnest concern about the great things of . . . the eternal world" swept the town. "There was scarcely a single person in the town, old or young," Edwards wrote, "left unconcerned about the great things of the eternal world . . . . The work of conversion was carried on in a most astonishing manner; souls did, as it were, come by flocks to Jesus Christ."

THE GREAT REVIVALIST

New Jersey. Virginia. Massachusetts. The winds remained vigorous but regional until the Atlantic currents carried to America the father of modern mass evangelism, George Whitefield. In 1739 the Wesleys' friend brought his powerful voice and magnetic style to the colonies and preached his way through Georgia, the Carolinas, Virginia, Maryland, Pennsylvania, and New York.

In Philadelphia he spoke out of doors. Even the worldly wise Benjamin Franklin was impressed, especially when the audience "admir'd and respected him, not withstanding his . . . assuring them they were naturally *half beasts and half devils*." It was a surprise to the deistic Franklin to walk through the streets of his city and hear psalms ringing out from house after house.

Whitefield moved on north and in 1740 he united the New England revival with that of the Middle Colonies and the South. A number of Boston ministers invited him to their town and unknowingly set a precedent. In later years every outstandingly successful revivalist would find his way to the largest cities. Whitefield spoke in Boston itself and at Harvard and finally went to Northampton to deliver four talks to Edwards's congregation. Then he journeyed on through the towns of Connecticut where the crowds came in from the surrounding farms so thickly that it was "like a steady stream of horses and their riders."

Whitefield left New England after a month, but the regional awakenings were no longer refreshing breezes. They had churned up a spiritual hurricane called the Great Awakening.

Edwards and other ministers began to visit neighboring towns to deliver revival sermons. When Edwards spoke at Enfield, Connecticut, about "Sinners in the Hands of an Angry God," he was merciless. He described God holding men over the flames in the way that one held a loathsome spider over a candle. He speculated on how it would feel to have the searing agony of a burn drawn out through eternity. He told listeners that the ground beneath their feet was a rotten flooring over a blazing pit, ready to give way in seconds.

This was powerful preaching for men and women to whom those flames were unmistakably real. Sobs and gasps rose to such a climax that Edwards sometimes had to pause in his delivery, his voice drowned out. The sermon was almost his undoing. Later generations of Americans almost forgot that he was a keen psychologist, a brilliant theologian, and the third president of Princeton. They remembered him, inaccurately, only as one more dramatic preacher of hellfire and brimstone.

By 1741 all the elements of the revival were in play: the visitors in the pulpits, the threats of perdition, the traveling spellbinders, the prayer meetings, and the rush of members—and also the controversies and church splits.

The dramatic changes the Great Awakening brought to Puritan New England are evident in the life of a Connecticut farm boy. In a one-room schoolhouse young Isaac Backus learned that the good order of Connecticut society was safeguarded by the religious training of the churches and the laws of the colony.

The Great Awakening, however, rolled through peaceful Norwich in 1741 and seventeen-year-old Isaac's mother was converted. Soon he realized "the appointed time" for him to repent had come. He was "born again" without the usual emotion and ecstasy as he was mowing alone in the field. "I was enabled by divine light," he said, "to see the perfect righteousness of Christ and the freeness and riches of his grace, with such clearness, that my soul was drawn forth to trust him for salvation."

This "new light" or "inward witness" was the key to the revival in New England. The revivalists pointed out that their fathers had left the Church of England to come to America precisely because they believed it was contrary to the Word of God to permit the unconverted to enter the church. The Awakening, they felt, was a call from God to begin a "new reformation" in New England.

Thus New Lights began separating from parish churches and organizing their own congregations using the methods of the founding fathers of New England. They heard testimonies of conversion experiences and then signed a covenant agreeing to walk together in the ways of the Lord as a church of visible saints.

Not long after his conversion Isaac Backus felt called of God to join the ranks of the revivalists. He plunged into the work of itinerant evangelism in the towns of southeastern New England. Additional light brought him to Baptist convictions. So with a handful of others he formed the First Baptist Church of Middleborough, Massachusetts.

ADVOCATE OF RELIGIOUS FREEDOM

Thus the stage was set for Backus's significant role in American history as advocate for religious freedom. More than any other man he formulated and publicized the evangelical position of church and state that was ultimately to prevail throughout America.

In 1769 Baptists in New England formed the Warren Association to advance their cause. Two years later the association created a grievance committee and charged it with the task of advocating religious freedom throughout New England. Backus became the key member of this committee.

He wrote tracts, drew up dozens of petitions, obtained factual evidence of persecution, appeared in court as a witness, worked on committees to formulate policies, and carried on a constant warfare of words in newspapers, public disputes, and private letters. The imprisonment of his mother, brother, and uncle in Connecticut, and his own deep pietistic convictions produced in him a passionate opposition to the established system.

Basic to the Baptist position was the belief that all direct connections between the state and institutionalized religion must be broken in order that America might become a truly Christian country. Backus, like Jefferson and Madison, believed that "Truth is great and will prevail." But unlike his "enlightened colleagues," by *truth* he meant the revealed doctrines of Scripture. His fundamental assumption was that "God has appointed two different kinds of government in the world which are different in their nature and ought never to be confounded"; one is civil, the other ecclesiastical.

"Our civil legislature," said Backus, does not function as "our representatives in religious affairs." They were elected as representatives for civil or secular affairs, and when they act in ecclesiastical affairs, they meddle in matters upon which their constituents did not empower them to legislate. Furthermore, legislative power is inappropriate for faith. "Religion is a voluntary obedience unto God which force cannot promote."

By resisting established churches the revivalists never intended to surrender their dream for a Christian America. They had found in the Great Awakening the answer to their needs. The kingdom of God would come to America if a majority of the citizens could be persuaded to submit voluntarily to the laws of God. Revivals were God's means to that end.

In 1760 that was more than an empty dream. From 1740 to 1742 the Awakening had swept 25,000 to 50,000 members into the New England churches alone. Between 1750 and 1760, 150 new Congregational bodies were formed, to say nothing of the steadily proliferating Baptists.

A clue to the depth of the Awakening's break with the past, however, lies in the revivalists' message. By concentrating on the individual's need for salvation, the Awakeners tended to neglect the Puritan concern for the political and social implications of the gospel. With the "covenant of grace" limited to individuals, twice-born men and women, the "covenant people" idea shifted easily from the church to the American people in general. As a result the mission of the "elect people" shifted subtly from a Puritan "holy commonwealth" to the American people's struggle for "liberty."

The revivalists, of course, were not the only colonists in favor of voluntaryism. Other lines of thinking of the eighteenth century reinforced the idea of free, uncoerced, individual consent as the only proper basis for man's civil and ecclesiastical organizations.

Many of the Sons of Liberty were infected with the spirit of the Enlightenment. Like their French and English tutors, these patriots—Jefferson, Franklin, Madison—assumed that man could use his reason and by it he could arrive at a reasonable or "natural" understanding of himself and his world.

These enlightened patriots held that the individual could be moved and guided only by the weight of the evidence in his own mind. Coercion of opinion by the state in the interest of uniformity, Jefferson thought, had served only "to make one half the world fools, and the other half hypocrites."

This is where the "reasonable men" of the Enlightenment and the "revival men" of the Great Awakening found common ground. The revival also developed the idea of freedom, only this liberty of the individual was under a special ministry of the Spirit checked, of course, by the objective revelation of Scripture. The convert's personal experience of grace brought him spiritual freedom—not from reason, however, but "in Christ."

Thus, as Sidney Mead once said, the revivalist "did not have the heart" and "the rationalist did not have the head" to justify any longer the coerced uniformity under an established religion. That is why during the eighteenth century rationalists and revivalists could combine forces on the practical and legal issue of religious freedom against the defenders of religious establishments.

Their temporary alliance was successful. The birth of the United States of America brought the adoption of the First Amendment of the Constitution, "Congress shall make no law respecting an establishment of religion, or prohibiting the free exercise thereof . . . ."

A century after the American Revolution, a discriminating observer of the American people, Lord James Bryce, wrote his penetrating *The American Commonwealth*. He succeeded in highlighting the assumptions Americans take for granted. The American view of church and state, said Bryce, is rooted in "the conception of the church as a spiritual body existing for spiritual purposes, and moving along spiritual paths," and consequently it never occurred to "the average American that there is any reason why state churches should exist . . . . Compulsion of any kind is contrary to the nature of such a body . . . . It desires no state help . . . . It does not seek for exclusive privileges."

Nothing in the new order of the ages was newer than that!

Suggestions for Further Reading

*Kidd, Thomas S. *The Great Awakening: A Brief History with Documents.* New York: St. Martins, 2007.

————. *The Great Awakening: The Roots of Evangelical Christianity in Colonial America.* New Haven, CT: Yale, 2007.

Marsden, George. *Jonathan Edwards: A Life.* New Haven, CT: Yale University Press, 2003.

Marty, Martin E. *Religion, Awakening and Revolution.* Wilmington: McGrath 1977.

McLoughlin, William G. *Isaac Backus and the American Pietistic Tradition.* Boston: Little, Brown and Co., 1967.

Parrish, Archie. *The Spirit of Revival: Discovering the Wisdom of Jonathan Edwards.* Wheaton, IL: Crossway, 2000.

Stearns, Monroe. *The Great Awakening 1720–1760.* New York: Franklin Watts, 1970.

Stott, Harry S. *The Divine Dramatist: George Whitefield and the Rise of Modern Evangelicalism.* Grand Rapids: Eerdmans, 1991.

THE AGE OF PROGRESS

1789–1914

Christians saw new social unrest added to the intellectual challenges stemming from the rise of modern science. The French Revolution unleashed new hopes and expectations for the common man. Power now seemed in reach for the masses. How are Christians supposed to meet the needs of the urban masses? Was man simply a product of evolutionary forces? Christians were seriously divided over ways to face these problems. Without the traditional support of the state many Protestants turned to voluntary societies to minister to the poor and the oppressed as well as to carry the gospel to foreign lands.

The Age of Progress

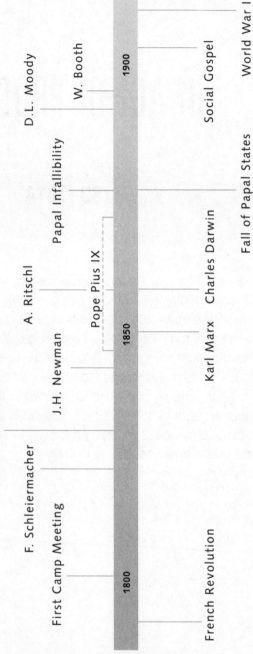

French Revolution

First Camp Meeting

F. Schleiermacher

William Wilberforce

J.H. Newman

A. Ritschl

Pope Pius IX

Papal Infallibility

Karl Marx

Charles Darwin

D.L. Moody

W. Booth

Fall of Papal States

Social Gospel

World War I

1800

1850

1900

Chapter 36

THE RESTORATION
OF FORTRESSES

Catholicism in the Age of Progress

O N THE EASTERN EDGE of Paris stood an old feudal fortress, long used as a prison. Popular propaganda had made it a symbol of royal tyranny. Languishing in its dungeons were supposed to be virtuous defenders of oppressed people. Governor de Launay held the Bastille with a garrison of 110 soldiers.

Early in the morning, July 14, 1789, a crowd began gathering in a small square before the prison's outer gate. It grew in numbers and in excitement. People started pushing toward the great gate. Some adventurous patriots climbed up and cut the chains to the drawbridge, giving the attackers access to the outer court.

Sensing the vicious mood of the mob, de Launay agreed to surrender the fortress on terms of a safe withdrawal for himself and his men. But as soon as the gates of the inner court were opened the attackers swept in, seized de Launay, and murdered him.

The dungeons yielded seven victims of tyranny: five ordinary criminals and two madmen. No learned patriots among them! The sordid facts of July 14, 1789, were speedily transformed into heroic deeds of the French Revolution.

BIRTH OF A NEW AGE

Historians look to that fateful event as the birth of a new age: the Age of Progress (1789–1914). The Bastille was a symbol of the Old Regime:

the absolute rule of monarchs and the traditional feudal society consisting of the Catholic Church, wealthy aristocrats, and powerless commoners. The tumultuous crowd was a token of the new age, the nineteenth century, and its rights of the common man.

The firm ground of popular belief in the new era was the doctrine of human progress. If the riot and the bloodshed that followed the fall of the Bastille raised questions about the conditions on the road to progress, few doubted that history moved relentlessly upward. The human race was getting better and growing happier. That, at any rate, was the new creed.

Christianity made its way through this tumultuous period but under adverse conditions. The nineteenth century was swept by currents and cross currents, and Christians found it hard at times to find the right way. Protestants felt the impact, but the Roman Catholic Church, due to its long association with the old order, found that many of its treasures from the past were swept violently away by the winds of modern times.

The democratic gospel of the French Revolution rested upon the glorification of man rather than God. The Church of Rome recognized this and struck back at the heresy as she had always done. She saw more clearly than did most Protestant churches that the devil, when it is to his advantage, is democratic.

Ten thousand people telling a lie do not turn the lie into truth. That is an important lesson from the Age of Progress for Christians of every generation. The freedom to vote and a chance to learn do not guarantee the arrival of utopia. The Christian faith has always insisted that the flaw in human nature is more basic than any fault in man's political or social institutions.

Alexis de Tocqueville, a visitor in the United States during the nineteenth century, issued a warning in his classic study, *Democracy in America*. In the United States, he said, neither aristocracy nor princely tyranny exist. Yet, asked de Tocqueville, does not this unprecedented "equality of conditions" itself pose a fateful threat: the "tyranny of the majority"? In the processes of government, de Tocqueville warned, rule of the majority can mean oppression of the minority, control by erratic public moods rather than reasoned leadership.

Unfortunately, in resisting the gospel of the common man, the Church of Rome tried to turn back the clock. She tried to erect a medieval fortress on the road to progress, and masses of secular men and women simply passed by on the other side. The question is why. Why did Catholicism look with such fear upon the popular movements of the time?

The winds of the new age were forecast in the clarion call of the French Revolution: "Liberty, Equality and Fraternity."

Liberty stood for individual freedoms in the political and economic arenas. The terms *liberty* and *liberalism* are used with a confusing variety. Liberty in a social sense might include Ronald Reagan and Ted Kennedy, because both men sought (and their respective parties still seek) to maximize and extend personal liberty; they differ on what liberty looks like and how to achieve it. Yet we still speak of liberty as the goal. Theologically and politically, the terms also demand careful attention.

Liberals in early nineteenth-century politics were voices for the middle class. They wanted the right to vote and the control of representative governments. In matters of money, they wanted freedom to build factories and amass wealth without the interference of governments (*laissez faire*).

Equality, the second term, stood for the rights of men, irrespective of their family background or financial standing. During the nineteenth century peasants and urban workers attempted to gain political equality with the middle class, so they supported social philosophies that advanced their rights. But whereas the middle class, property owners, and business barons championed the doctrine of *laissez faire*, the working class demanded equality by a rival philosophy called *socialism*. Advantages for the workers could come either by evolution within a democratic framework or by revolution in a Marxist pattern.

Fraternity, the third idea, represented a powerful sense of brotherhood unleashed in the nineteenth century. The rebels who stormed the Bastille were united by an ambition to be masters of their own territory and national destiny. In short, they were driven by *nationalism*, which not only swept across nineteenth-century Europe, but in the twentieth century went on to engulf Asia and Africa.

All these currents and more swirled about the churches in the Age of Progress, but no one predicted the devastation they would bring to the tradition-bound Church of Rome.

On the eve of the French Revolution the Roman Catholic Church basked in the glory of the old order. For a thousand years she had sanctified the structures of feudal Europe. She gave divine blessing to the rule of kings and the marriages of nobles. Like these monarchs and aristocrats, the Church gave little thought to the powerlessness of the peasants and the growing middle class. In eighteenth-century European society, noble birth and holy calling were of greater consequence than intelligence, achievement, or the accumulation of wealth. In France's total population of twenty-five million, only two hundred thousand belonged to the privileged classes, the nobility and clergy. These two groups controlled nearly half of the nation's land and held the best positions in the government. The peasants, 80 percent of the population, staggered under intolerable burdens including heavy taxes to church and state. The middle class had wealth without responsibility, intelligence without authority, and ability without recognition. Drastic change was simply a matter of time—less time than anyone dreamed.

THE REVOLUTIONARY FEVER

The Age of Enlightenment created the ferment for change, but most of that ferment was expressed in words rather than action. Beginning in the 1760s, country after country felt the fever of political unrest. In little states like Geneva and large states like England, radical politicians challenged the established order. Everywhere their basic demands were the same: the right to participate in politics, the right to vote, the right to greater freedom of expression.

The American Revolution in the 1770s inspired these radicals in Europe. It offered a great lesson to ponder and perhaps to imitate. To European observers, the American settlers were true men of the Enlightenment: rational yet passionately concerned about equality, peaceful yet ready to go to war for their freedom. By wresting independence from a formidable imperial power, the colonists had proved that the Enlightenment ideas worked. They had been tested in the hardest laboratory of all, the laboratory to which the Enlightenment liked to submit all its ideas: experience.

In France, the most populous country in Europe, evidence of political and economic bankruptcy mounted. The government was borrowing huge sums from European bankers and falsifying records to hide the true state of its finances. In addition, high living among church officials and a series of bad harvests in the strategic French wine industry contributed to an atmosphere of restlessness.

King Louis XVI tried to make repairs. In 1789 he convened the Estates-General, a national assembly representing the three traditional divisions, or Estates, in French society: the clergy, the nobility, and the common people.

Controversy sprang up immediately over how the assembly should conduct its business. It had not met for 175 years, and its powers had never been clearly defined. As Peter Gay describes it,

> The aristocracy and the clergy, seeking to preserve their traditional privileges, wanted each Estate to vote as a unit. This would have left

control of the assembly with the upper classes. The common people, comprising the Third Estate, wanted each man to vote as an individual. Since their representation in the assembly had recently been enlarged to 50 percent of the total membership, and they figured on the support of liberals in the other two Estates, this would have given them numerical control.

Popular agitation over this issue grew intense, and revolutionary sentiments spread. When the king would not honor the Third Estate's demands, the commoners broke away from the Estates-General to form their own National Assembly.

On July 14, 1789, the enraged Parisian mob stormed the Bastille: the Crown could no longer keep order; from then on, the French populace had to be counted as a political force. By the end of August of the same year most of the French aristocracy's traditional feudal privileges had been wiped out and a bold "Declaration of the Rights of Man and of the Citizen" had passed into law.

The Declaration codified most of the demands of the Enlightenment: it declared that the natural rights of man, "liberty, property, security, and resistance to oppression," were sacred and inalienable; it established men's right to express their opinions freely; it prohibited arbitrary arrest and protected the rights of the accused. It also declared that France was not the private property of its monarchs, but a sovereign nation owned by its people!

In the brief ten years before the century ended, France formed a republic, executed a king, established an effective if faction-ridden revolutionary regime, and passed from that through a period of confusion that ended with a *coup d'etat* and General Napoleon Bonaparte's accession to power. Through it all, the French nation continually fought the rest of Europe.

The Church of Rome was so much a part of the old order that the revolutionaries made it a special object of their rage. In the early 1790s the revolutionary National Assembly attempted to reform the Church along the lines of Enlightenment ideals. It provided a decent income for pastors and reshaped the diocesan boundaries, all for the good. But when the Assembly eliminated all control by the pope in the French Church and imposed a loyalty oath on Church officeholders, it split the Church down the middle. Two Catholic camps faced each other in almost every town and village of France: the constitutional clergy who took the oath and the non-constitutional who refused.

The leaders of the revolution soon drove thirty to forty thousand priests out of their native towns into exile or hiding. And that proved to be only a prelude. The revolution began to take on a religious character all its own. A new calendar removed all traces of Christianity and elevated the cult of Reason. Soon parish churches were converted to Temples of Reason, and in the cathedral of Notre Dame revolutionaries enthroned an actress on the high altar as the Goddess of Reason. This set the pattern for the provinces. Young girls decked out as Reason or Liberty or Nature led processions through towns to altars erected to the new religion of the revolution.

By 1794 this parody of Christianity had spent its force and a decree early the following year guaranteed the free exercise of any religion in France. All over the country Catholics returned to the altar. The Church of Rome, however, never forgot: Liberty meant the worship of the goddess of Reason!

When Napoleon seized the reins of power he had the good sense to work out an agreement with the pope, the Concordat of 1801, that restored the Church of Rome to a special place in France. It was called "the religion of the great majority of Frenchmen," but the Church had lost forever its position of power. France and the rest of Europe could never return to a society held together by an alliance of throne and altar. And the Church of Rome never developed a taste for liberalism. The reasons are not hard to find.

CATHOLICISM VERSUS LIBERALISM

The Lord and his apostles had spent little time talking about freedom and personal independence and a man's right to his own opinions. And through the Middle Ages and the Reformation, Augustine's axiom that liberty comes by grace and not grace by liberty had been at the bottom of the organization and imposition of Christian belief. To be properly free man must be in a state of salvation, so throughout these centuries Christians had little enthusiasm for the idea of man's improper freedom—free in a political sense.

During the nineteenth century, however, the idea that everyone ought to be as free as possible was in the air. But how far is possible?

Liberty in an Ancient Sense

Liberty in numerous ancient settings meant more than the mere notion that an individual may choose a course of action. Liberty was typically tied to nature. Mankind possessed a nature or essence. Consequently, in keeping with the nature of humans, people could, for example, think and reason with great potential.

Liberty was linked to a person being able to live up to and according to their nature. A man crawling on hands and knees in slop would not be praiseworthy on the grounds that some human had decided to act like a pig. Freedom was noble and important because a person could pursue the goal of living up to their nature or potential. Social barriers restricting a person's progress should be removed when possible. People today often understand liberty apart from nature. They do not wish to be free so they can become a good version of what they are (by nature); they think freedom is being able to choose what they want to be. On a similar note ancient understandings of human flourishing or happiness were tied to being or becoming good, not just to feeling good. Aristotle, for example, would think it odd that our contemporary culture might take satisfaction in someone feeling good while not being good. Again living in sync with one's nature was foundational for liberty and happiness. Our founding fathers assumed this ancient notion of nature when speaking of life, liberty, and happiness. Contemporary notions of liberty are often impoverished by comparison.

"The liberty of each," wrote John Stuart Mill, "limited by the like liberty of all." That defined the possible. Liberty meant to have a right to have your own opinions, to propagate your own opinions, and to behave according to your own opinions, subject to a similar freedom for each member of the community. In practice this meant a constitutional government that guaranteed civil liberties to all, including the freedom to worship according to personal choice. The popes despised the thought.

When Napoleon's empire collapsed in 1815 and he was banished to a bleak island in the Atlantic, absolutist kings tried to regain their lost ground. But the return to monarchies met stiff resistance from liberals all over Europe.

The first liberal uprisings in Spain and Italy were easily suppressed. But the liberal success in overturning the restored kings of France (1830) gave the promise of change. The important year was 1848, when liberal revolution temporarily triumphed in almost every capital in Europe.

Through all those years the popes—Leo XII, Pius VIII, and Gregory XVI—were not bad men. They simply refused to join the nineteenth century. They continued to defend the past and lost touch with the movements of their own time. None of them really understood the new world introduced by the French Revolution. They never figured out how to fight it or how to convert it.

Liberalism proposed to overthrow the evils that afflict mankind, and in this battle it not only refused the assistance of the Roman Catholic Church, it insisted that the church had no right to express its views on the morality of public life. Politics is independent of Christian ethics. Roman Catholics are private citizens with all the rights of private citizens, but nothing more.

The most obvious symbol of the papal ties to the past was the Papal States in Italy, for in these the pope was not only a spiritual leader but an earthly sovereign. For centuries and centuries Italy had been nothing more than a geographical expression. It embraced seven Italian states in addition to the papal territories running northeast from Rome across the peninsula.

In the middle of the nineteenth century, however, a movement for Italian unity arose in Sardinia. It was called *risorgimento*: rebirth. It aimed at the overthrow of all alien powers in Italy and the unity of the whole peninsula in a modern Italian nation. This revolutionary spirit could not tolerate the continuation of the Papal States, a medieval state in the heart of Italy governed by strict absolutist principles. After 1849 the Papal States were so hated they could be defended only by French bayonets.

Liberals initially welcomed Pope Pius IX (1846–1878). He was a warm, kindly, well-meaning man, and the liberals took him for a true reformer when, on March 14, 1848, he gave the Papal States a constitution that permitted the people a moderate degree of participation in their government. Some dreamed of an Italian federation under the pope. But Pius suddenly changed his mind about the Papal States when revolutionaries assassinated the first papal prime minister, Count Pellegrino Rossi. Revolution broke out in Rome, and Pius was forced to flee. With French military help he regained Rome and the Papal States, but this time Pius insisted on a return to the old absolutist rule.

The irritation of his opponents mounted, and the national unity movement, headed by King Victor Emmanuel II of Sardinia (1849–1878), grew into an avalanche that could not be diverted. In 1859–1860 large portions of the Papal States fell to the nationalists. In Florence in March 1861 Victor Emmanuel was proclaimed King of Italy.

Rome itself was still protected by a French garrison, but when the Franco-Prussian War forced the withdrawal of the French troops to their homeland, Italian nationalists immediately invaded Rome. After a short bombardment on September 20, 1870, the city surrendered. After more than one thousand years, the Papal States came to an end.

Pius IX withdrew into the Vatican. In June 1871 Victor Emmanuel transferred his residence to Rome, ignoring all protests and excommunications of the pope. The new government offered the pope an annual subsidy together with the free and unhindered exercise of all his spiritual functions. But Pius angrily rejected the offer and continued his protests as the "prisoner of the Vatican." He forbade Italy's Catholics to participate in political elections. But this only left a free field to the radicals. The result was an increasingly anticlerical course in the Italian government. This unpleasant condition, the "Roman Question," reached no solution until Benito Mussolini concluded the Lateran Treaty in February 1929. In the treaty, the pope renounced all claims to the former Papal States and received full sovereignty in the small Vatican State.

THE INFALLIBILITY OF THE POPE

The year 1870, however, marks not only the end of the earthly rule of the pope; it also signifies the declaration of the supreme authority of the Bishop of Rome and the doctrine of papal infallibility. That is more than symbolic. The First Vatican Council represented the culmination of a movement called *ultramontanism*. It means "across the mountains" (the Alps) and stands for devotion to Rome.

After the French Revolution a peculiar loyalty to the papacy had developed in that troubled country. After the turmoil of the revolutionary and Napoleonic years, some Catholics extolled the papacy as the only source of civil order and public morality. They claimed that only the popes were capable of restoring the disordered human society and only a clergy independent from the state and firmly led by an infallible pope, the un-contested master of the Church, had the required prestige and strength to protect spiritual freedom from the tyranny of political power.

Infallibility, therefore, had appeared as the unavoidable, necessary, and obvious prerequisite of an effective papacy. The Church must be a monarchy according to the will of God. What sovereignty was to secular kings, infallibility was to the popes; infallibility was nothing more than sovereignty in the realm of the spirit and the Church. In this way convinced monarchists could transfer their concepts of political authority to the Church and the papacy.

By mid-century this line of thinking attracted a sizable Catholic following. The pope encouraged it in every way possible. A Jesuit publication explained that when the pope meditated, God was thinking in him. Hymns appeared addressed, not to God, but to Pius IX; and some dared to speak of the Holy Father as "the vice-God of humanity."

On December 8, 1854, Pius IX declared as dogma the traditional belief that Mary had been conceived without original sin: "It is a divinely revealed truth of faith that Mary in the first moment of her conception was freed by special grace from the stain of original sin in view of the merits of Christ." The subject of the decision was not new. It was the way it was proclaimed. This was not a decision by a council, but an *ex cathedra* definition by the pope. The expression means "from the chair," the official teaching role within the Church.

Questions arose from all sides. Can the pope alone, without council, decide and proclaim dogma? The one great topic of the First Vatican Council was before the Church. The solemn proclamation of Mary's immaculate conception was attended by 54 cardinals and 140 bishops, but the decision was made by the pope alone.

Ten years later, December 1864, as the Italian nationalists tightened their noose around the neck of the Papal States, Pope Pius IX sent an *encyclical*, or papal letter, to all bishops of the Church.

In it he enclosed a *Syllabus of Errors*, a compilation of eighty evils in modern society. In no uncertain terms, he declared war on socialism, rationalism, freedom of the press, freedom of religion, public schools, Bible societies, separation of church and state, and a host of other demons in the Age of Progress. He concluded by denying that "the Roman pontiff can and ought to reconcile himself and reach agreement with progress, liberalism, and modern civilization."

Pius IX wanted no peace talks with the modern world. The Church had to close its ranks around its infallible leader and brace itself for a long struggle.

To strengthen the hands of the Vicar of Christ, Pius laid plans for a general council of the Church. He appointed a preparatory congregation of cardinals (March 9, 1865), took additional bishops into his confidence, and, on the occasion of the eighteen hundredth anniversary of the martyrdom of Peter and Paul (1867), announced to more than five hundred bishops his plan to convoke a council. The council opened in Rome on December 8, 1869.

The question of the definition of papal infallibility was in the air. The concept as such posed no great difficulties; Catholics had little doubt that the pope as successor of Peter possessed special teaching authority. The only question was how far this authority extended, whether it could be exercised independently from councils and the college of bishops, and what special preconditions would have to be met.

In the council Bishop Hefele of Rottenburg, the learned author of the famous *History of the Councils,* and Bishop Strossmayer of Djakovar in Bosnia led the opposition against a definition; they were supported also by numerous other cardinals and bishops, among them the majority of the Germans.

At the first balloting on July 13, 1870, 451 council fathers voted in favor of the definition of infallibility, 88 opposed it, and 62 accepted it with reservations. Many who opposed simply thought that the time was not right.

After further discussion a number were still uncertain, but rather than create a scandal, 55 bishops, with the consent of the pope, left Rome before the final vote. The vote for the record, on July 18, was 533 for the doctrine of infallibility. Only two against.

Thus the Council asserted two fundamental truths: the primacy of the pope and the infallibility of the pope.

First, as the successor of Peter, Vicar of Christ, and supreme head of the Church, the pope exercises full and direct authority over the whole Church and over the individual bishops. This authority extends to matters of faith and morals as well as to discipline and church administration. Therefore, the individual bishop owes the pope obedience, "not only in matters concerning faith and morals, but also in those of habits and administration of the church."

Second, when the pope in his official capacity (*ex cathedra*) makes a final decision concerning the entire Church in a matter of faith and morals, this decision in itself is infallible and immutable and does not require the prior consent of the Church.

Immediately after the vote on infallibility, the Council had to discontinue its work. The outbreak of the Franco-Prussian War (July 19, 1870) forced many council fathers to return home. And later, the occupation of Rome by the Italian nationalists on December 20, 1870, destroyed any hopes of continuing. No matter: the really vital work had been done. The Council succeeded in restoring, so to speak, the Bastille.

The whole strategy of the ultramontanists, led by Pius IX, shaped the lives of Roman Catholics for generations to come. Surrounded by the hostile forces of liberalism, socialism, and nationalism, Rome chose to withdraw for safety behind the walls of an exalted and infallible papacy.

Unfortunately, fortresses have a decided disadvantage. They grow stuffy. They allow no enlargement of thinking, and after a time you begin to imagine that the only world of any importance lies within the walls.

Suggestions for Further Reading

Bokenkotter, Thomas. *A Concise History of the Catholic Church*. New York: Doubleday, 1977.

Hughes, Philip. *A Popular History of the Catholic Church*. New York: MacMillan, 1957.

*Jadock, Darrell. *Catholicism Contending with Modernity*. Cambridge: Cambridge University Press, 2000.

Johnson, Paul. *A History of Christianity*. New York: Atheneum, 1983.

Vidler, Alec R. *The Church in an Age of Revolution: 1789 to the Present Day*. New York: Penguin Books Inc., 1961.

CHAPTER 37

A NEW SOCIAL FRONTIER

Nineteenth-Century England

> Lead, kindly Light, amid th' encircling gloom,
> Lead Thou me on!
> The night is dark, and I am far from home!
> Lead Thou me on!

THESE LINES, TODAY SUNG by millions, were written in 1833 by John Henry Newman while traveling home to England from Sicily. The somber mood reminds us of the many troubled souls in nineteenth-century England. A decade later Newman fled to the Church of Rome for safety, but the same sense of impending gloom appears in the Evangelical Henry Francis Lyte's popular hymn "Abide with Me":

> Swift to its close ebbs out life's little day;
>   Earth's joys grow dim, its glories pass away;
> Change and decay in all around I see:
>   O Thou who changest not, abide with me!

No one in nineteenth-century England could ignore the pace of change. But two outstanding Christian movements helped literally millions of their fellow believers adjust to "life's little day" and in the process won for themselves a respected place in Christian memory.

I speak of the Clapham Sect of Evangelicals and the Oxford movement of Anglican high-churchmen. Neither was, at first, numerically large. They remind us of Professor Gilbert Murray's observation that "the uplifting of man has been the work of a chosen few." Yet to this day evangelical Christians regard the Clapham Sect as a model of Christian social concern, and "High Church" Anglicans look back to the Oxford movement as a wellspring of devout churchmanship.

A comparison of the two movements creates some interesting insights into the continuing questions about Christianity's place in society. How, after all, are Christians to view the world?

EVANGELICALS IN THE WORLD

We know that the church is under a twofold commission: God has sent his people *into* the world to proclaim salvation and to serve the needy. But he has also called his own *from* the world to worship and learn of him. Mission without worship can produce empty service, just as worship without mission can lead to careless religion. Thus the church's life in the world involves a constant conversation: a yes here and a no there. Protestants in nineteenth-century England found society changing so rapidly that they were not always sure whether they were talking to friends or to enemies.

Evangelicals

Contemporary descriptions often depend upon the four characteristics offered by David Bebbington. These include conversionism, activism, Biblicism (confidence in the Bible as a source for devotion, guidance, and theology), and crucicentrism (emphasis upon the sacrificial nature of the cross). Thomas Kidd adds an emphasis upon the Holy Spirit as manifested in revivals, Spirit outpourings, and transforming encounters with God's love.

In many ways the nineteenth century belonged to Britain. England was the cradle of the Industrial Revolution. London became the largest city and the financial center of the world. British commerce circled the globe; the British navy dominated the seas. By 1914 Britannia ruled the largest empire in extent and in population ever fashioned by man.

This rapid industrial and commercial growth, however, left many Britons breathless. Every hallowed institution seemed to be cracking at the foundation. Some men, remembering the terrifying days of the

French Revolution, feared the future. Other men sang the praises of change and called it progress. To them England was the vanguard of a new day of prosperity and liberty for all. Thus fear and hope were curiously mingled.

The dawning of the Age of Progress found English Protestants either in the established Church, Anglicanism, or in the nonconforming denominations: Methodist, Baptists, Congregationalists, and a few smaller bodies. The striking movements of the nineteenth century, however, did not surge along traditional denominational lines. The increasing liberties of the age allowed Christians to form a host of religious societies to minister to English life in some vital way or to spread the gospel overseas. These societies were not churches in the traditional sense of sacraments, creeds, and ordained ministers. They were groups of individual Christians working for some specific objective: the distribution of Bibles, for example, or the relief of the poor.

At the opening of the Age of Progress, the greatest power in English religious life was the evangelical movement, sparked and spread by John Wesley and George Whitefield. The chief marks of the movement were its intense personal piety, usually springing from a conversion experience, and its aggressive concern for Christian service in the world. Both of these were nourished by devotion to the Bible, and both were directed by the central themes of the eighteenth-century revival: God's love revealed in Christ, the necessity of salvation through faith, and the new birth experience wrought by the Holy Spirit. This evangelical message echoed from a significant minority of pulpits in the Church of England and from a majority in the nonconforming denominations.

The Evangelicals of the Church of England were thoroughly loyal to their church and approved of its episcopal government. But they were willing to work with Nonconformist ministers and churches because their chief interest was not the church and its rites. They considered the preaching of the gospel more important than the performance of sacraments or the styles of ritual. Such a position was called "Low Church."

Impelled by the enthusiasm of the Methodist revival, the Evangelicals viewed the social ills of British society as a call to dedicated service. They threw themselves into reform causes for the neglected and the oppressed.

THE CLAPHAM COMMUNITY

The general headquarters for Evangelical crusades was a hamlet then three miles from London called Clapham. The village was the country residence of a group of wealthy and ardent Evangelicals who knew what it was to practice "saintliness in daily life" and to live with eternity in view. A number of them owned their own magnificent houses in the village, while others in the group visited Clapham often and lived with their co-laborers. Historians have come to speak of them as the "Clapham Sect," but they were no sect; they were more like a closely knit family.

The group found a spiritual guide in the minister of the parish church, John Venn, a man of culture and sanctified good sense. They often met for Bible study, conversation, and prayer in the oval library of a wealthy banker, Henry Thornton.

The unquestioned leader of the Sect was William Wilberforce (1759–1833), the parliamentary statesman. But Wilberforce found a galaxy of talent for Evangelical causes in his circle of friends: John Shore (Lord Teignmouth), the Governor General of India; Charles Grant, Chairman of the East India Company; James Stephens Sr., Undersecretary for the Colonies; Zachary Macauley, editor of the *Christian Observer;* Thomas Clarkson, an abolitionist leader; and others.

At twenty-five Wilberforce had experienced a striking conversion after reading Philip Doddridge's *Rise and Progress of Religion in the Soul;* but he also possessed all the natural qualities for outstanding leadership: ample wealth, a liberal education, and unusual talents. Prime Minister William Pitt once said he had the greatest natural eloquence he had ever known. Some called him "the nightingale of the House of Commons." Many testified to his overflowing capacity for friendship and his high moral principles. For many reasons Wilberforce seemed providentially prepared for the task and the time.

"My walk," he once said, "is a public one: my business is in the world, and I must mix in the assemblies of men or quit the part which Providence seems to have assigned me."

Under Wilberforce's leadership the Clapham friends were gradually knit together in intimacy and solidarity. At the Clapham mansions they held what they chose to call their "Cabinet Councils." They discussed the wrongs and injustices of their country and the battles they would need to fight to establish righteousness. And thereafter, in Parliament and out, they moved as one body, delegating to each man the work he could do best to accomplish their common purposes.

"It was a remarkable fraternity," says Reginald Coupland, the biographer of Wilberforce. "There has never been anything like it since in British public life."

EVANGELICALS AND SOCIAL ISSUES

A host of evangelical causes sallied forth from quiet little Clapham: The Church Missionary Society (1799), the British and Foreign Bible

Society (1804), The Society for Bettering the Condition of the Poor (1796), The Society for the Reformation of Prison Discipline, and many more.

The greatest labor of all, however, centered on the campaign against slavery. The first battle was for the abolition of the slave trade, that is, the capturing of Negroes in Africa and shipping them for sale to the West Indies.

The English had entered this trade in 1562 when Sir John Hawkins took a cargo of slaves from Sierra Leone and sold them in St. Domingo. Then, after the monarchy was restored in 1660, King Charles II gave a charter to a company that took three thousand slaves a year to the West Indies. From that time the trade grew to enormous proportions. In 1770, out of a total of one hundred thousand slaves a year from West Africa, British ships transported more than half. Many Englishmen considered the slave trade inseparably linked with the commerce and national security of Great Britain.

In 1789 Wilberforce made his first speech in the House of Commons on the traffic in slaves. He recognized immediately that eloquence alone would never overthrow the commercial interests in the sale of human beings. He needed reliable information, so he called upon his Clapham colleagues for assistance.

Two years later, after exhaustive preparation, Wilberforce delivered another speech to Commons seeking to introduce a bill to prevent further importing of slaves into the West Indies. "Never, never," he said, "will we desist till we have wiped away this scandal from the Christian name, released ourselves from the load of guilt, and extinguished every trace of this bloody traffic."

Once again oratory was inadequate, but support was growing. The workers for abolition came to see that hopes of success lay in appealing not only to Parliament but to the English people. "It is on the feeling of the nation we must rely," said Wilberforce. "So let the flame be fanned."

Stage by stage the Clapham Sect learned two basics of politics in a democracy: how to create public opinion and how to bring the pressure of that opinion on the government.

The Evangelicals secured petitions; they published quality abolitionist literature; they lectured on public platforms; they campaigned on billboards. They used all the modern means of publicity. Nonconformists rallied in support, and for the first time in history women participated in a political contest. The Evangelicals fanned the flame, then they carried the fire to Parliament where Wilberforce and four colleagues from Clapham—the "Saints" in Commons—tried to arouse complacent leaders to put a stop to the inhumane slave trade.

THE END OF SLAVE TRADE

Finally, victory crowned their labors. On February 23, 1807, the back of the opposition was broken. Enthusiasm in the House mounted with the impassioned speeches of supporters of abolition. When one member reached a brilliant contrast of Wilberforce and Napoleon, the staid old House cast off its traditional conventions, rose to its feet, burst into cheers, and made the roof echo to an ovation seldom heard in Parliament. Wilberforce, overcome with emotion, sat bent in his chair, his head in his hands, and the tears streaming down his face.

That halted the legal traffic in human lives, but the slaves were still in chains. Wilberforce continued the battle for complete emancipation until age and poor health forced him from Parliament. He enlisted the skills, however, of a young Evangelical, Thomas Fowell Buxton, to assume leadership of the "holy enterprise." Buxton was a wise choice. The certainty of the passage of the Emancipation Act, freeing the slaves in the sprawling British Empire, came on July 25, 1833, four days before Wilberforce died.

The significance of this action before the European colonial powers partitioned Africa is enormous. No one has described the impact better than Professor G. M. Trevelyan in his *British History in the Nineteenth Century*:

> On the last night of slavery, the negroes in our West Indian islands went up on the hill-tops to watch the sun rise, bringing them freedom as its first rays struck the waters. But far away in the forests of Central Africa, in the heart of darkness yet unexplored, none understood or regarded the day. Yet it was the dark continent which was most deeply affected of all. Before its exploitation by Europe had well begun, the most powerful of the nations that were to control its destiny had decided that slavery should not be the relation of the black man to the white.

For this reason above all others, the Clapham Sect remains the shining example of how a society, perhaps the world itself, can be influenced by a few men of ability and devotion.

THE OXFORD MOVEMENT

Another Christian movement, the Oxford movement, represents a contrasting response to the social crisis of nineteenth-century England. Like its predecessor, the Evangelical movement, it was more a movement of the heart than of the head. But unlike the Clapham group, the Oxford men were deeply troubled by the direction of English society.

They saw the reforms of the government as attacks upon the sanctity of the Church of England, and they determined to resist the intrusions of the world.

"We live in a novel era," John Henry Newman wrote to his mother in March 1829. "Men have hitherto depended on others, and especially on the clergy, for religious truth; now each man attempts to judge for himself . . . . The talent of the day is against the Church."

For generations the strength of the Church of England had rested with landed aristocrats who were strong in Parliament. The Industrial Revolution created rapidly growing industrial towns, such as Manchester and Birmingham, but these had no representatives in Parliament. The cry for reform mounted.

The Reform Act of 1832 shifted the balance of power from the landed gentry to the middle class and signified a new sensitivity to democratic forces. This action meant that many of the new members of Parliament, though not members of the Church of England, wielded significant power over the Church. Some devout churchmen recoiled in horror. Dare profane politicians lay hands on the holy things of God?

One group of gifted and deeply religious men at Oxford University raised a cry against the thought. John Keble, Fellow of Oriel College, preached in the University Pulpit, July 14, 1833, a sermon titled "National Apostasy." A nation stands convicted of the denial of God's sovereignty, he said, when it shows disrespect for the successors of the apostles, the bishops of the Church, and appeals only to reasons based on popularity or expediency.

Keble found a staunch supporter in John Henry Newman (1801–1890), vicar of the University Church and a commanding figure in the academic community. Before long an older man joined them, Edward Pusey, professor of Hebrew. By their preaching and writing, these three influential men turned their protest into a movement.

The Oxford men felt that the Church of England needed to affirm that its authority did not rest on authority from the state. It came from God. Bishops of the Church were not empowered by social position but by an apostolic commission. Even if the Church were completely separated from the state, the Church of England could still claim the allegiance of Englishmen because it rested on divine authority.

To spread their views the Oxford men launched, in 1833, a series of "Tracts for the Times," a move that gave rise to the label "Tractarians." In these writings the Oxford leaders published their convictions on a single article of the Creed: belief in "one, holy, Catholic and apostolic Church." They emphasized the apostolic succession of bishops through history and the Church's God-given authority to teach the truth and rule men's lives. They magnified the place of the sacraments, ascribing to them an actual saving power. As an ideal for the Church of England, they held up the church of the first five Christian centuries. Then, they said, the Christian church was undivided and truly catholic.

While some of these historical ideas were fanciful, the Tractarians believed them enthusiastically. They called themselves Catholics, on the ground that they were in agreement with this early catholic Christianity, and they shunned the name Protestant because it referred to a division in the church.

Public worship was vital to the Oxford men. They believed strongly in the religious value of symbolic actions in worship such as turning toward the altar, bending the knee, and elevating the cross. The worship of God, they said, demands the total response of man, so ritual should appeal to the senses: rich clerical garments, incense on the altar, music by trained voices. In short, Tractarian Christianity was a zealous version of High Church Christianity.

Step by step the Oxford men moved toward the Church of Rome. Then came the thunderclap. In 1841 John Henry Newman wrote Tract 90 and asserted that the Thirty-Nine Articles of the Church of England were not necessarily Protestant. They could be interpreted in the spirit of the Catholic Church. Did Newman really believe that a person could be a Roman Catholic and remain in the Church of England?

A storm of protest fell upon the Oxford movement. The Bishop of Oxford forbade Newman to publish other tracts. Newman concluded that the only way to be truly Catholic was to enter the Roman Catholic Church. He converted to Rome in 1845, and during the next six years hundreds of Anglican clergymen followed him. In time Newman became rector of the new Catholic University in Dublin, and in 1877 he was made a cardinal in the Church of Rome.

The great majority of the Tractarians, however, stayed in the Church of England and saw an increasing number of clergymen adopt their High Church views. Religion for many focused on ritual, priests, and sacraments. The concern for beauty brought improvements in architecture, music, and art in the churches. Gradually the names "Oxford movement" and "Tractarian" gave way to "Anglo-Catholic," which meant Anglicans who valued their unity with the catholic tradition in Eastern Orthodoxy and Roman Catholicism but who refused to accept the supremacy of patriarch or pope.

The Evangelical and Anglo-Catholic views of Christianity's role in society are alive, though not always well, in our time. Few generations can claim a Wilberforce or a Newman. Their convictions survive, however, because they are so basic to Christianity in any age: mission and worship. Early Christians believed that, amid his encircling gloom, the Lord Jesus himself prayed for his disciples: "Father, . . . My prayer is not that you take them out of the world but that you protect them from the evil one. They are not of the world, even as I am not of it. Sanctify them by the truth; your word is truth. As you sent me into the world, I have sent them into the world" (John 17:11–18, NIV).

Suggestions for Further Reading

Church, R. W. *The Oxford Movement*. Chicago: University of Chicago Press, 1970.

Coupland, Reginald. *Wilberforce: A Narrative*. Oxford: Clarendon Press, 1923.

Howse, Ernest Marshall. *Saints in Politics*. London: George Allen, 1960.

Johnson, Paul. *A History of Christianity*. New York: Atheneum, 1983.

Ollard, S. L. *A Short History of the Oxford Movement*. London: Faith Press, 1963.

Symondson, Anthony, ed. *The Victorian Crisis of Faith*. London: S.P.C.K., 1970.

*Tomkins, Stephen. *William Wilberforce: A Biography*. Grand Rapids: Eerdmans, 2007.

CHAPTER 38

TO EARTH'S
REMOTEST PEOPLE

Protestant Missions

In an English village, late in the eighteenth century, stood a humble workshop. Over its door a sign announced, "Secondhand shoes bought and sold." Inside, the shoemaker, William Carey, repaired a neighbor's boot or, when time allowed, continued his study of Latin and Greek. Over the workbench was a crude map of the world. On it Carey had penned bits of information from the voyages of Captain James Cook or some other world traveler. A friend, Thomas Scott, called the workshop "Carey's College."

Carey's workbench and map are fit symbols of the awakening interest in distant peoples during the Age of Progress and in the means of getting the gospel to them. At the beginning of the nineteenth century, Protestant Christianity scarcely existed outside Europe and America. Asia was almost untouched by the gospel, except for small traces in India and in the East Indies where the Dutch had taken over from the Portuguese. Africa was the "dark continent" except for the ancient Copts in Egypt and Ethiopia. After eighteen centuries Christianity was far from being a world religion.

It is a different story today. The front page of almost any metropolitan newspaper carries news, daily, of events vitally linked with Christianity somewhere on the earth.

The great era of Christian expansion was the nineteenth century. "Never had any other set of ideas, religious or secular, been propagated over so wide an area by so many professional agents maintained by the unconstrained donations of so many millions of individuals." That is the informed judgment of Kenneth Scott Latourette, the foremost historian of Christianity's expansion. For sheer magnitude the Christian mission in the nineteenth century is without parallel in human history.

How do we explain this sudden explosion of Protestant energy aimed at winning the world for Christ?

THE PIONEER IN MODERN MISSIONS

During the first century of Protestant history, the Roman Catholic countries, Spain and Portugal, dominated the commercial and imperial expansion of European peoples. The great missionary names were Xavier, Las Casas, and Ricci. Only after the English defeat of the Spanish Armada (1588) and the emergence of the British and Dutch as colonial powers do new continents and peoples open to Protestant missionaries.

The first Protestants to attempt to reach distant peoples with the gospel were the Pietists. Moravian concern, however, was focused on individuals in some European colony perishing without the knowledge of Christ. The Christian groups created by Pietists were tiny islands in the surrounding sea of "heathenism."

William Carey introduced Christians to missions on a grander scale. He thought in terms of the evangelization of whole countries and of what happens when whole populations become Christian. He held that the foreign missionary can never make more than a small contribution to the accomplishment of the work that has to be done, and that therefore the development of the local ministry is the first and greatest of all missionary considerations. Above all, he saw that Christianity must be firmly rooted in the culture and traditions of the land in which it is planted. For all these reasons and more Carey gained the title "Father of Modern Missions."

The English cobbler was a most unlikely candidate for greatness. He was married to a poor, uneducated girl, and what Carey earned as a shoemaker was often too little to provide enough to eat. Yet the greatness of the man was within, not in his circumstances. He had a ravenous hunger for knowledge and would go without food to buy a book. Columbus and Captain James Cook were his great heroes.

In 1779, through a fellow shoemaker, he was converted to faith in Christ, and in 1783 he was baptized as a believer. After gaining some preaching experience he became pastor of the Moulton Baptist Chapel, supporting his family by teaching and shoemaking.

In Baptist circles he met fellow pastor Andrew Fuller. Fuller, a strong Calvinist, broke with some of his fellow Calvinists who pictured vigorous evangelism and appeals to conversion as inconsistent with God's election of certain individuals to salvation. Fuller held to both his belief in a Calvinist version of election and the mandate to follow Jesus and the apostles in the practice of evangelism.

"We have sunk into such a compromising way of dealing with the unconverted," Fuller complained, "as to have well nigh lost the spirit of the primitive preachers, and hence it is that sinners of every description can sit so quietly as they do, year after year, in our places of worship."

From Fuller's teaching Carey drew the inescapable inference that if it is the duty of all men to repent and believe the gospel, as Fuller argued, it is also the duty of those entrusted with the gospel to carry it to the whole world.

In 1792 Carey published *An Enquiry into the Obligation of Christians to Use Means for the Conversion of the Heathen*. It created an epoch. In it Carey took up the five objections that people raised against missions to heathen lands: their distance, their barbarism, the danger that would be incurred, the difficulties of support, and the unintelligible languages. One by one he answered these. The same obstacles had not prevented the merchants from going to distant shores. "It only requires," he wrote, "that we should have as much love to the souls of our fellow-creatures, and fellow sinners, as they have for the profits arising from a few otter skins, and all these difficulties could be easily surmounted." He ended his appeal with practical proposals for the preaching of the gospel throughout the world.

By encouraging each other Carey and Fuller succeeded in breaking free from the restrictive theology of their time. They went back to the New Testament, especially to Jesus' injunction to preach the gospel to all the world and to the apostle Paul's declaration of God's intention: "that at the name of Jesus every knee should bow, in heaven and on earth and under the earth, and every tongue confess that Jesus Christ is Lord, to the glory of God the Father" (Phil. 2: 10, 11). Such texts were read with a sense of immediacy, as if Jesus were speaking to them and not merely the disciples long ago.

As a result, in October 1792 Carey, Fuller, and eleven Baptist colleagues formed the Baptist Missionary Society, and within a year Carey and his family were on their way to India. His wife Dorothy had planned to stay behind, but she reversed her decision and accepted a final appeal to join her husband. Almost immediately, she regretted her decision. Eventually she lived out her life in her room in bitterness and perhaps insanity.

The British East India Company, which had been the virtual ruler of India since 1763, was exercising its full power at that time. It was not enthusiastic about missions. Its interest was in profits. Most of its representatives, living free and easy lives and enjoying to the full their sense of racial superiority, considered "the sending out of missionaries into our Eastern possessions to be the maddest, most extravagant, most costly, most indefensible project which has ever been suggested by a moonstruck fanatic. Such a scheme is pernicious, imprudent, useless, harmful, dangerous, profitless, fantastic."

The Company refused Carey permission to live in Calcutta, so he settled instead in Serampore, under the Danish flag. He secured employment as foreman of an indigo factory in Bengal. Since the position demanded only three months of the year, he found plenty of time for intensive study of the oriental languages. In 1799 two fellow Baptists, Joshua Marshman and William Ward, joined Carey at Serampore. For the next quarter-century the three men worked together to organize a growing network of mission stations in and beyond Bengal.

Carey and his companions plunged courageously into all the intricacies of Hindu thought. They did not regard these studies as in any way a distraction from their missionary work. On the contrary, they regarded a full understanding of Hindu thought as an essential part of their equipment, not only because the preacher of the gospel cannot be clearly understood if he speaks merely out of the self-confidence of his own knowledge, but also because they understood that it is not only the souls and bodies of men that need to be redeemed; the thought-world of a non-Christian nation is also one of those realms that are to be taken captive and brought into subjection to Christ. By 1824 Carey had supervised six complete and twenty-four partial translations of the Bible, as well as publishing several grammars, dictionaries, and translations of Eastern books.

THE CONTAGION OF MISSIONARY SERVICE

The example of the Serampore trio proved contagious. The beginning of the nineteenth century found a new and pervasive determination in Protestantism to carry the gospel to all men. The earlier prevailing attitude of the major churches had considered missions an unnecessary and hopeless undertaking. Now voices were raised on all sides proclaiming the duty of all Christians to share in the conversion of the peoples of the whole world. The gospel was not the private possession of European peoples.

The list of missionary pioneers would run into the hundreds: Henry Martyn in India, Robert Morrison in China, John Williams in the South Seas, Adoniram Judson in Burma, Alexander Duff in India, Allen Gardiner on Tierra del Fuego, Robert MoVat in South Africa, and many more. Scores of other missionaries and their wives are long forgotten because they died in a matter of months in some malaria-infested tropical climate or at the hands of some savage tribe.

In large part this new passion to preach the gospel to the heathen sprang from those portions of Protestantism deeply influenced by the eighteenth-century evangelical revivals in England and America. For the first three decades of the new missionary era the endeavor was almost exclusively evangelical.

This is hardly surprising. The evangelical awakenings revolution-ized preaching and its objectives. Traditional churchmen usually limited the minister's task to nurturing the seed of faith planted at baptism in virtually all members of the parish. Such men could not imag-ine preaching the gospel in a tribal society. At the same time those Christians who held a rigid doctrine of predestination never seemed to concern themselves with the elect in India or China. Evangelicals, however, like Carey, saw preaching as calling sinners to God through faith in Christ. They felt a personal responsibility to do this and saw no difference in principle between "baptized heathen" in Britain and non-Christian peoples overseas.

Only in the 1820s and 1830s did interest in overseas missions become a general feature of British church life. This was due in part to the suc-cess of Evangelicals in influencing English and Scottish society. Many of their values were adopted outside their circle. In particular the idea of Britain as a Christian nation, with Christian responsibilities over-seas, took root.

The vision of this missionary task is expressed in thousands of ser-mons and hundreds of hymns of that time. Reginald Heber, who gave his life for India serving as Bishop of Calcutta, provides an example in his widely sung "From Greenland's Icy Mountain":

> Can we, whose souls are lighted
>   With wisdom from on high;
> Can we to men benighted
>   The lamp of life deny?
> Salvation, O salvation!
>   The joyful sound proclaim,
> Till earth's remotest nation
>   Has learnt Messiah's Name.

Two emphases led to this new Protestant world vision. One, as Carey and Fuller illustrate, was evangelical. The Bible teaches that men are lost without faith in Christ, and the Lord commands believers in every age to make salvation known in all the world.

The other was prophetic. Many Christians in the nineteenth century followed Jonathan Edwards in the belief that the knowledge of the Lord would fill the earth as the waters cover the sea, and this spread of the gospel was preparation for the coming reign of Christ upon the earth. This belief in a future reign of Christ was called *millennialism*.

The Protestant mission to all the world was no empty dream. The dedication of the missionary movement blended with the optimism of the Age of Progress to make the achievement of the goal seem quite possible. Thus the Student Volunteer Movement for Foreign Missions took as its watchword, "the evangelization of the world in this generation."

The vision was constantly renewed by some fresh account from Africa or the South Pacific. None of these proved more inspiring than the reports of the spiritual darkness of Africa or the horrors of the Arab slave trade sent home by David Livingstone (1813–1873).

The great explorer of the dark continent came from a hardy clan of Scotsmen. When he was nineteen, he determined to devote his life to the "alleviation of human misery." He studied as a doctor to prepare himself for the work of a missionary, and, attracted by the fame of Robert MoVat in South Africa, he went to Africa to help in the work.

LIVINGSTONE IN AFRICA

Arriving in 1841, Livingstone served for ten years in the ordinary routine of missionary work. But he was not a man to stay long in any one place. The mind and impulse of the explorer were in him, and he was always drawn on, in his own words, by "the smoke of a thousand villages" that had never seen a missionary.

The first great journey that made him famous led him through the jungles to the west coast in Angola, and then, because he would not desert the African carriers who had accompanied him, right across the continent to Quilimane on the east coast. On this journey he showed all the qualities of a great explorer. His manner with the Africans was so patient that he never had to use violence. And his scientific and geographical observations were minutely accurate. This one trip opened the heart of Africa to the modern age.

But Livingstone was at all times more than a traveler. His cause was the gospel. His journal abounds in passages of almost mystical devotion. Shortly before setting out on his great journey he wrote, "I place no value on anything I have or may possess, except in relation to the kingdom of Christ."

What moved him more than anything else was what he called "this open sore of the world," the devastating slave trade of central Africa. Speaking to the students at Cambridge in 1857 he said, "I go back to Africa to try to make an open path for commerce and Christianity: do your best to carry out the work which I have begun, I leave it to you."

Commerce and Christianity? Was Livingstone simply a forerunner of those colonialist exploiters who made life in so many parts of Africa a nightmare? No, far from it. Livingstone realized that the slave trade could not continue apart from the African's own participation in it. When slave raiding was the way to wealth, the temptation was always present to engage in those raids on weaker neighboring tribes that made life perilous for the defenseless. Only if the Africans could be persuaded to engage in legitimate commerce, exchanging the products of their own fields and forests for those desirable things the white man could supply, would the evil and destructive commerce be brought to an end. That, at any rate, was Livingstone's conviction, a central part of his dream for Africa.

How was this missionary vision turned to action? What were the channels for this burst of spiritual energy? The traditional denominations used one of three forms of church government: episcopal, presbyterian, or congregational. The supporters of each claimed to be following the Bible, and all the main arguments on each side were well-known. Men had suffered, some even shed blood, for each form of government.

But as the conviction of the responsibility to spread the gospel world-wide began to dawn on British and American Christians it became clear that none of the traditional forms of church government would enable the church to embark on a world mission. Supporters of global evangelism were driven to find another form of cooperation: the voluntary society.

CREATION OF THE VOLUNTARY SOCIETY

Again, Carey proved the pioneer. When he wrote his *Enquiry* he asked, what would a trading company do? From this he proposed the formation of a company of serious-minded Christians, laymen and ministers. The group should have a committee to collect and sift information and to find funds and suitable missionaries to send to foreign lands.

The voluntary society, of which the missionary society was one early form, transformed nineteenth-century Christianity. It was invented to meet a need rather than for theological reasons, but in effect it undermined the established forms of church government. It made possible interdenominational action. Anglican, Baptist, Congregationalist, and Methodist could work together for defined purposes without raising troublesome questions of church structure. It also altered the power base in the church by encouraging lay leadership. Ordinary Christian men, and later women, came to hold key positions in the important societies, something thought impossible elsewhere in the church.

These features appeared early in the history of missionary societies. The London Missionary Society adopted in 1795 its "fundamental principle that our design is not to send Presbyterianism, Independency, Episcopacy or any other form of church government . . . but the glorious gospel of the blessed God to the heathen." One of the founders called for "the funeral of bigotry."

Thanks to the creation of the societies, the missionary enthusiast who collected a penny a week from members of his local missionary society auxiliary and distributed the missionary magazine participated fully in the work of missions. Through the labors of such people, candidates for service often came forward. The American missionary, Rufus Anderson, wrote in 1834, "It was not until the present century that the evangelical churches of Christendom were ever really organized with a view to the conversion of the world." They became organized by means of the voluntary society.

In the United States the first foreign missionary society was the American Board of Commissioners for Foreign Missions (1810). It was formed on the initiative of a group of students at the newly created Congregational Andover Theological Seminary. The leader of the group was Samuel J. Mills, who while at Williams College had instigated the formation of a small society in which each member pledged to devote his life to missionary service. At Andover, the society included the later famous missionary to Burma, Adoniram Judson. Students, then, as so many times in later years, laid the foundation for a missionary advance, this one for the youthful American nation.

In a few years Baptists, Presbyterians, and other major denominations followed the Congregationalists in creating missionary agencies. The conversion of the heathen became one of the major concerns of local congregations in every city and town in the country, stimulated by the continuous activity of local societies and women's organizations, "children's days for foreign missions," occasional visits from missionaries on furlough, periodical campaigns for offerings, and, more recently, the inclusion of support of foreign missions as a large item in regular church budgets.

By the end of the nineteenth century, almost every Christian body, from the Orthodox Church of Russia to the Salvation Army, and almost every country, from the Lutheran Church of Finland and the Waldensian Church of Italy to the newest denomination in the United States, had its share in the missionary enterprise overseas.

Many times these early missionaries were unaware of the conflicts that the gospel produced in other cultures. To most of them, Christianity in its Western form was Christianity. Therefore to make an Indian or a Malaysian a Christian was in great measure to turn him into a Dutchman or a Portuguese.

It is easy today to condemn this attitude. Yet every Christian society, and every individual Christian, combines with the faith much that is cultural tradition. The problem has pursued all missionary work from the beginning. Nevertheless, the consequences of such an alien presentation can be disastrous to the progress of the gospel. If Christianity appears in Western habits that other people find shocking, such as eating of meat or a greater familiarity between the sexes than is permitted in most Eastern societies, then the faith is condemned before it is even examined.

On the other hand there is a distinctiveness of the Christian community that arises from the distinctiveness of the gospel itself. The gospel is a revolutionary power and any attempt to disguise this fact is likely to change the Christian faith into something else.

THE MARKS OF MODERN CHRISTIANITY

In spite of all barriers, however, the Protestant missionary movement continued to expand. In the process it highlighted several characteristics of modern Christianity:

First, the worldwide expansion usually came by voluntaryism not by compulsion. Since the time of Constantine the propagation of the faith had had the active support of rulers in Christian countries and often resulted in mass conversions. Protestant missionaries in the nineteenth century, however, went, with few exceptions, without state support or state control. They advanced only by the power of persuasion. Thus Christians found a way to engage in missions while upholding religious freedom.

Second, this missionary movement tapped the wealth and talents of rank and file Protestants. Unlike earlier missionary expansion led by monks and bishops, the new societies were organized on the widest base possible. So the primary task of the churches, preaching the gospel, fell upon the people of the churches.

Third, a wide variety of humanitarian ministries accompanied the widespread preaching of the gospel. Mission agencies established schools, hospitals, and centers for training nurses and doctors. They reduced many languages and dialects to writing and translated not only the Bible but other Western writings into these languages. And they introduced public health measures and better agricultural techniques. In some cases these activities were closely related to the goal of conversion, but many sprang simply out of the recognition of social and physical needs that no Christian could in good conscience ignore.

In many respects, then, the missionary movement restored the gospel to its central place in Christianity. And in this important sense the movement recovered an element in the concept of the holy catholic church that the splintering of the Reformation had obscured. A catholicity or universality that inspired Carey's workshop map reached out to embrace new peoples in many new lands.

Suggestions for Further Reading

Drewery, Mary. *William Carey: Shoemaker and Missionary.* London: Hodder and Stoughton, 1978.

George, Timothy. *Faithful Witness: The Life and Mission of William Carey.* Birmingham, AL: New Hope, 1991.

Gascoigne, Bamber. *The Christians.* New York: William Morrow, 1977.

Huxley, Elspeth. *Livingstone and His African Journeys.* New York: Saturday Review Press, 1974.

Neill, Stephen. *A History of Christian Missions.* Edited by Owen Chadwick. Middlesex: Penguin Books, 1986.

Northcott, Cecil. *David Livingstone: His Triumph, Decline and Fall.* Philadelphia: Westminster, 1973.

CHAPTER 39

THE DESTINY
OF A NATION

A Christian America

" SHALL THE EARTH BE made to bring forth in a day? Or shall a nation be born at once?" Isaiah's question seemed unusually appropriate for the youthful American nation. In 1835 Lyman Beecher, the well-known Presbyterian and Congregational minister in New England, preached a sermon from the text, Isaiah 66:8, and he called it *A Plea for the West.*

Beecher believed firmly that a vast new empire was opening in the American wilderness. Nothing less than a whole culture was at stake. Christians should seize the opportunity, he said, and shape the "religious and political destiny of the nation."

And how did he propose to do that? He called for the preaching of the gospel, the distribution of Bibles, the planting of churches, the establishing of schools, and the reform of American morals. Puritan that he was, Beecher knew that a free society needed just laws, and in a democracy just laws required popular support informed by Christianity.

Beecher spoke for a host of evangelical Christians: Baptists, Methodists, Congregationalists, Presbyterians, and Episcopalians. In fact, his views were so widely shared that historians speak of this era as the age of the "righteous empire." The vision for a Christian America is a dominant theme in nineteenth-century American Protestantism. We can trace its rise, its major crisis, and the elements of its decline. Without some knowledge of this century, today's Christians find it almost

400

impossible to understand the social forces and religious figures of their own times.

THE CHALLENGE OF THE AMERICAN WEST

The evangelical campaign to shape the destiny of the young American nation was not new. Like Innocent III's vision of medieval Europe and Calvin's design for a Christian Geneva, the evangelical dream for America was an expression of Christian concern for society. The American West provided evangelical Christianity with its greatest opportunity ever to press the claims of the gospel upon a whole nation.

If this vision has faded in our time—and it has—the basic impulse remains, for it is part of the Lord's purpose for his people: "Ye are the light of the world . . . ye are the salt of the earth." How can Christians not be concerned for the world around them?

The great fact of the nineteenth-century world in America was the West, the ever moving frontier. Early visitors beyond the Allegheny Mountains sang the praises of the region. In 1751 Christopher Gist described it as "watered with a great number of little streams and rivulets, and full of beautiful natural meadows, covered with wild rye, blue grass, and clover."

After the Revolutionary War so many Americans poured into the territory that the whole continent seemed to tilt toward the Pacific. Between 1792 and 1821, nine new states were added to the original thirteen. By mid-century half of the American people were west of the Appalachians.

It was a violent shift. Between the rough tasks of expelling the Native American Indians and subduing the wilderness, the frontiersman gained a reputation for wild and lawless living. His barbarian manner never failed to shock the occasional European who ventured beyond the mountains.

One English visitor found that the

> backwoodsmen . . . fight for the most trifling provocations. Their hands, teeth, knees, head and feet are their weapons, not only boxing with their fists, . . . but also tearing, kicking, scratching, biting, gouging each others' eyes out by a dexterous use of a thumb and finger, and doing their utmost to kill each other . . . .

At the birth of the United States of America, the denominations seemed ill prepared to face the opportunities of the West. Christian influence was at an all-time low. Only 5 or 10 percent of the American people were church members. In time, however, the crude, turbulent, and godless society of the West was tamed and, more than any other single force, it was evangelical Christianity that did it.

As Evangelicals faced the challenge of winning a nation to Christian obedience, two instruments were available to them: the voluntary society and the revival.

The Bill of Rights, with its provision of religious liberty for all, had in effect sanctioned the denominational concept of the church and had ruled out any direct influence of the churches upon the government. The denominations were free, therefore, to define their own faith and practices. But what about Christian responsibility for public life and morals? That is where the voluntary society came in.

William Carey and other English Evangelicals had designed the voluntary society to carry the gospel to India and to fight the slave trade in the West Indies. American Evangelicals seized the idea for their own purposes. It seemed to be the perfect instrument for the free society in America to exert influence upon public opinion, to provide support for far-reaching missionary and educational activities, and to spread reform ideals in the youthful nation. The voluntary societies allowed Christians from the various denominations to unite in some matter of common concern: temperance, for example, or the observance of the Sabbath.

Thus early in the nineteenth century a host of societies appeared seeking to shape some aspect of American life: the American Bible Society, the American Colonization Society, the American Sunday School Union, the American Education Society, and hosts of others. "One thing is becoming daily more evident," Beecher observed in 1830 "that the grand influence" of the church and the triumphs of the last forty years are the result of the "voluntary association of Christians."

The second instrument evangelicals used to subdue the wilderness was the revival. Beecher argued that the churches could look to revivals "for their members and pastors, and for that power upon public opinion which gives energy to law, and voluntary support to religious institutions."

In 1790 Evangelicals faced a dual evangelistic challenge: to regain the East and to win the West. In the East, especially in a number of colleges, fresh enthusiasm for the life of the Spirit was apparent before 1800. This revival came to be known as the Second Great Awakening. It provided the next generation with skilled and dedicated leaders for the western crusade.

The great western frontier revival took place in newly settled regions between the Alleghenies and the Mississippi and centered in Kentucky and Tennessee. This awakening took on the characteristics of the inhabitants. It was rugged, wild, and boisterous.

Timothy Flint, who knew the region well, left us a portrait of the western preacher:

> Travelling from month to month through dark forests . . . the men naturally acquire a pensive and romantic turn of thought and expression . . . . Hence the preaching is of a highly popular cast and its first aim is to excite the feelings . . . . The country opens a boundless theatre for strong, earnest and unlettered eloquence; and the preacher seldom has extensive influence, or usefulness who does not possess some touch of this power.

In a largely illiterate population this frontier preacher, whether white or black, became the primary channel for the spread of Christianity. One of the most pungent of these roughhewn western revivalists was a tall, angular Presbyterian with keen black eyes and a "bold and uncompromising manner": the Reverend James McGready.

THE INFLAMMABLE JAMES MCGREADY

McGready came from Scotch-Irish stock in Pennsylvania, but he hurled his first thunderbolts in North Carolina. Stressing the wrath of the Lord against stiff-necked sinners, McGready ignited a revival that drove scores of penitents to conversion.

He found, however, that frontier congregations did not always wilt under torrid preaching. When McGready abruptly moved to Kentucky in 1798, a tale circulated that the suggestion he move west had come from an anonymous letter written in blood!

In Kentucky the inflammatory McGready preached to three small congregations at Red River, Gasper River, and Muddy River. All three were in Logan County, in the southwestern corner of the state. That area was described by one frontier parson as a "Rogues' Harbor," abounding in horse thieves, desperados, and murderers. Surprisingly, lawless backwoodsmen there responded enthusiastically to McGready's pictures of heaven and hell.

He would describe heaven so vividly that his calloused congregation would almost see its glories and long to be there. Then he would paint hell and its horrors so effectively that sinners would tremble and quake, imagining a lake of fire and brimstone yawning to overwhelm them, and the wrath of God thrusting them down into the abyss.

In July 1800, McGready had his Pentecost—and changed the course of American history. After an initial revival at Red River, he decided to send out advance notice of the next sacramental service at the Gasper River church. When the word spread through the settlements, scores of pioneers headed in wagons, in the saddle, and on moccasined feet, for Gasper River, ready for the Spirit to work. They came from as far away as one hundred miles. Scores of families came to Gasper River with tents and vittles—cold pork, slabs of corn bread, and roasted birds—ready to stay a while to see, hear, and feel the hand of God.

We now look back to Gasper River as the first "camp meeting," that is, the first religious service of several days' length held outdoors for people who had traveled a distance to attend. They camped on the spot, thus the name.

McGready was a pacesetter. For almost two centuries the revival preacher and the camp meeting have endured in America. Time, however, had its way and the intensity of the preaching cooled. It was inevitable. Man does not live by fire alone. Under the leadership of men like Charles Finney, D. L. Moody, and Billy Graham, the camp meeting moved indoors and continued its winning ways in rural chapels and urban auditoriums.

Not everyone, of course, favored revivals. Many Lutherans and Presbyterians felt that they slighted sound doctrine. Roman Catholics and Episcopalians considered them emotional eruptions, not true worship.

Such criticisms, however, were largely ignored as enthusiastic revivalists and increasing numbers of missionaries moved west, preaching the gospel, planting churches, and founding colleges. By the 1830s Alexis de Tocqueville, a keen observer from abroad, discovered that "there is no country in the world in which the Christian religion retains a greater influence over the souls of men." Many others agreed.

A deadly cancer, however, spread through the tissues of "Christian America." How could a democracy infused with Christian principles continue to sanction the enslavement of millions of human beings?

The American practice of slavery had begun on August 20, 1619, when twenty Negro slaves were unloaded from a Dutch frigate at Jamestown, Virginia. By 1830 their number had increased to about two million. As a nation spread west, the institution became the issue. Every time a new state came into the Union, every time settlers moved out to fresh land, the white-hot issue of slavery burned the national conscience more deeply. Should the new territory be slave or free? Was slavery to be extended indefinitely? In the passion to preserve both liberty and union, if one must choose, which must come first?

The dimensions of this struggle were so basic to human existence, so religious in character, that all sides turned to the Scriptures to interpret their experiences.

CHRISTIANITY AMONG THE SLAVES

The slave turned to the Bible for meaning to fill his emptiness. He turned mostly out of necessity because his white master had stripped him of all else, including his African gods.

The uprooting of Negroes and their transportation to an alien land had a shattering effect upon their lives. In destroying their African culture and in breaking up their social organization, slavery deprived them of their sense of place in the world.

Some slaves committed suicide during the "middle passage," the crossing of the Atlantic. Others tried to escape from bondage in their new environment. The vast majority of them, however, submitted to their fate and, in their confusion and bewilderment, sought a meaning for their existence in the white man's world.

Christianity gave the slave a new center for his new life in a new land. At first some owners strongly opposed teaching the Scriptures to the Negro. They feared that the slave might find in the Bible ideas of human equality that could incite him to rebellion. Opposition declined, however, as masters became convinced that the New Testament itself offered arguments in support of slavery. Some masters, in fact, were persuaded that the best slaves—that is, those willing to accept the control of their white masters—were those who knew the Bible best.

From the Bible, then, slaves learned about the white man's God and his ways with men. Since all other forms of organized social life were forbidden among the slaves, the Negro preacher arose as the important figure in the "invisible institution," the slave church. Reflecting the revival spirit of the frontier, the Negro preacher was "called" to his office, nearly always through some experience that indicated God had chosen him as a spiritual leader. Such dramatic callings gave the black pastor unprecedented influence. In time he learned to dramatize biblical stories for blacks and to interpret many characters and events in terms of the slave's experiences.

As Dean Willard Sperry once explained, chief among these events was the Exodus, and first among the biblical characters was Jesus. The Egyptian bondage of God's people, the deliverance from Egypt, the passage of the Red Sea, the destruction of Pharaoh's host in that Sea, the wanderings in the desert, and the final crossing of Jordan into the Land of Promise: these were the parables of life that furnished the constant themes for slave sermons and spirituals. In the days of bondage there seemed little hope of deliverance here on earth, so emancipation came to be linked with death, when Jesus would strike the shackles from the slave and release him into another and happier world.

Looking back on it, it is difficult to see how any Christian could ever have defended slavery. Most didn't try until the 1830s. We sometimes forget that during the first three decades of the nineteenth century the antislavery movement was stronger in the South than in the North. For a combination of reasons, however, the antislavery movement faded and a Southern defense of the institution arose. Some of the arguments for slavery were drawn from the Bible, thanks to Southern churchmen.

At the root of the Southern defense of slavery was the fact that the Bible by precept and example supported the right to hold slaves. Richard Furman, South Carolina's leading Baptist, argued that the Israelites in the Old Testament were directed to purchase their bondmen and once purchased they were to be "bondmen for ever" (Lev. 25:46, KJV). Similarly in the New Testament, Furman reasoned, the inspired apostles never demand the emancipation of slaves. Masters are only required "to give them the things that are just and equal, forbearing threatening . . . ."

The associations of evangelical religion and race came to be a distinctive feature of the southern way of life during the years of the Cotton Kingdom. The South became increasingly isolated, not only from the North but from much of the rest of the Western world where strong judgments against slavery were often expressed. This isolation led to defensiveness. The region seemed obsessed with the institution. Harriet Martineau, a visitor from abroad in the 1830s, observed, "A magic ring seems drawn around those who live amidst slavery; and it gives a circular character to all they think and do upon the subject. There are but few who think within it who distinctly see anything beyond it." One thing Southerners saw beyond their "magic ring" were threats and attacks.

A primary fountain of the evangelical sentiment against slavery in the North can be traced to the revival preaching of Charles G. Finney. Through the broad impact of Finney strong antislavery feelings built up in the Midwest, especially around Oberlin College where Finney served as president. At the forefront of this crusade was one of Finney's disciples, Theodore Weld. His powerful writings, *The Bible against Slavery* (1837) and *Slavery as It Is*, served as a catalyst for abolitionism.

Lyman Beecher's daughter Harriet was especially impressed with *Slavery as It Is*. According to Weld's wife, Angelina Grimke Weld, "Harriet Beecher Stowe lived with *Slavery as It Is* day and night till its facts crystallized into *Uncle Tom's Cabin*." In her famous anti-slavery book Harriet Beecher Stowe appeals, "Christians! Every time that you pray that the kingdom of Christ may come, can you forget that prophecy associates, in dread fellowship, the day of vengeance with the year of His redeemed?" She was referring to the violent overthrow of evil, Babylon, predicted in the last book of the Bible. According to the widely held millennialist interpretation of Revelation, the death throes of Babylon, which began with the Protestant Reformation, would be marked by the "convulsion" of nations.

Thus the American nation, destined to play a key role in the divine plan, must be purged of its guilt as it rushes toward the climax of human history. Slavery is not a sin of the South alone. The guilt is national; the purgation must be national. In *Uncle Tom's Cabin*, then, Mrs. Stowe was striking at the national conscience in the hope that a cleansing of the nation's soul would avert a divine scourging of the body politic.

All sides in the struggle, then, used the same set of symbols. There was one Bible, one heaven, one hell, one Jesus Christ, one path of salvation. Yet the symbols were employed for opposite causes. How could God be the God of the South against the North and of the North against the South? How could He have sponsored slavery, as Southerners said, and opposed slavery, as Northerners contended?

No one was more aware of these questions than the man who bore the burden of reconciliation, President Abraham Lincoln. Although shaped by evangelical culture, Lincoln never joined a church and found himself at home with no particular creed. His language and thought, however, were formed by the Bible, and from it he learned that no one could interpret precisely what the will of God was for the nation.

Lyman Beecher (1775–1863), a Puritan, held firmly to a vision for a Christian America.

"In great contests," he once said, "each party claims to act in accordance with the will of God. Both may be, and one must be wrong." Another time, in his second Inaugural Address, he observed, "Both [Union and Confederacy] read the same Bible, and pray to the same God; and each invokes his aid against the other . . . . The prayers of both could not be answered . . . . The Almighty has his own purposes." Lincoln knew that men should try to do God's will as well as they could determine what it was for them, but the Almighty has his purposes that go beyond the plans of men.

So it proved. The war was fought; blood was shed; the nation endured. The vision for a Christian America also survived, but like the nation itself it was greatly weakened. Black churches arose in large numbers, the primary institutional expression of freedom, and the constant reminder of the blind spot in the vision for a Christian America.

CULTURAL SHOCKS FOR EVANGELICAL AMERICA

The streets of Atlanta were scarcely cleared before a series of cultural shocks raised widespread questions about the truth or relevance of traditional evangelical beliefs.

The first shock came from Charles Darwin's pen. In 1859 he published *The Origin of Species*, perhaps the most important book of the century. Darwin's evolutionary theory presented a major challenge to Evangelicals. The book argued that evolution took place by a mechanism called natural selection. Various species seek to survive. The stronger ones that can adapt to their environment endure; species that are weaker and prove unable to adapt die off. Many believers anticipated where this idea would lead. Would such a theory eventually leave room for a creating or sustaining God? How was the biblical story of creation to be understood?

The second shock to the traditional faith came from the increasing industrialization of American society and the rush to the cities. Small towns became big cities overnight. People came not only from America's hinterland but from Germany, Norway, Italy, and other European countries. Most of the new immigrants brought religious opinions alien to the traditional way Protestant Americans had viewed their country and their Bibles.

The third and most direct assault on confidence in the Scriptures came in the form of higher criticism of the Bible. As more and more seminary and college professors took advanced degrees in the leading European universities, critical views became increasingly dominant in American higher education and eventually in many major denominations. Imagine the jolt to the churches when it was suggested that Moses did not author the first five books of the Bible and that Jesus himself was a somewhat deluded visionary and not the Son of God in the flesh.

Taken together these shocks were part of the general shift in Western culture from Christian to secular forms of thought and behavior. And Christians disagreed about what actions they should take to meet the new challenges.

Among traditionally evangelical denominations, two rather distinct parties developed. One party chose to embrace the changes as blessings sent from God; another chose to resist the changes as threats to the biblical message.

The major urban revivalist during the generation following the Civil War was Dwight L. Moody. Moody and scores of lesser known preachers felt that their primary task was the winning of souls to Christ and preparation of saved men and women for Christ's second coming.

Clearly, however, Beecher's dream of a Christian America was fast fading. Millennialist hopes dissolved in the hatred of the war between the states, the trauma of strikes and financial panics in the 1870s and 1880s, and the formation of an urban world with its rejection of Christian values. In increasing numbers Evangelicals, especially in the urban North, turned to speculation about the future and to the cultivation of the inner life.

The decisive character of the half century between the Civil War and World War I is evident in two statements, one at the beginning of this period and the other at the end.

In an 1873 address to the Evangelical Alliance, the Reverend Theodore Woolsey, retired President of Yale, asked, "In what sense can this country be called a *Christian* country? In this sense certainly," he answered, "that the vast majority of the people believe in Christ and the gospel, that Christian influences are universal, that our civilization and intellectual culture are built on that foundation . . . ."

Fifty years later in 1924, H. L. Mencken, the widely read critic of American ways, remarked that "Christendom may be defined briefly as that part of the world in which, if any man stands up in public and solemnly swears that he is a Christian, all his auditors will laugh."

Beecher would never have believed it.

Suggestions for Further Reading

Frazier, E. Franklin. *The Negro Church in America*. New York: Schocken, Books, 1963.

George, Timothy, ed. *Mr Moody and the Evangelical Tradition*. New York: T & T Clark International, 2004.

Handy, Robert T. *A Christian America*. New York: Oxford University Press, 1971.

Marty, Martin E. *Righteous Empire: The Protestant Experience in America*. New York: Dial Press, 1970.

McLoughlin, William O. *The American Evangelicals: 1800–1900*. New York: Harper & Row Publishers, 1968.

Noll, Mark A. *A History of Christianity in the United States and Canada*. Grand Rapids: Eerdmans, 1992.

CHAPTER 40

A BRIDGE
FOR INTELLIGENT
MODERNS

Protestant Liberalism

O N HIS EIGHTY-FIFTH BIRTHDAY in 1920, Lyman Abbott, who had been one of America's most influential ministers in the 1890s, looked back three-quarters of a century to his staunch Puritan upbringing. He recalled his youthful view of God as "a kind of awful and omnipresent police justice" and his own self-image as "a scared culprit who knows he is liable to punishment but does not clearly know why."

Long before 1920, however, along with many other Americans and Europeans, Abbott had ceased to think of God as an "omnipresent policeman" and man as a "scared culprit." The Western world had undergone too many changes and adopted too many new ideas in the last quarter of the nineteenth century.

Abbott was typical of a large number of American ministers whose background included a pious Protestant home but who had studied in Germany or in an American seminary where continental scholarship was treasured and who had adopted "liberal" religious convictions.

The events of the twentieth century have been unkind to the liberal creed, but every major Protestant denomination continues to reflect the impact of liberal theology. It is hard to argue with Professor Sydney E. Ahlstrom's judgment when he says the liberals "precipitated the most fundamental controversy to wrack the churches since the age of the Reformation." The reason lies in their ambitious objective. They tried to lead the Protestant churches into the new world of modern science, modern philosophy, and modern history. In his autobiography *The Living of These Days*, Harry Emerson Fosdick, minister at the influential Riverside Church in New York City, put it well when he said the central aim of liberal theology was to make it possible for a man "to be both an intelligent modern and a serious Christian."

THE AIMS OF PROTESTANT LIBERALISM

Protestant liberalism, then, engaged a problem as old as Christianity itself: how do Christians make their faith meaningful in a new world of thought without distorting or destroying the gospel? The apostle Paul tried and succeeded. The early Gnostics tried and failed. The jury is still out on liberalism, but Christian public opinion tilts heavily in the direction of failure. No one expressed the irony of liberalism better than H. Richard Niebuhr when he said in liberalism "a God without wrath brought men without sin into a kingdom without judgment through the ministrations of a Christ without a Cross."

Beyond its rather clear goal, definitions of religious liberalism are as varied as those of political liberalism. Many deny that Protestant liberalism is a theology. They prefer an *outlook* or an *approach* or a *spirit*. Thus Henry Sloane Coffin at New York's Union Seminary once said liberalism is that spirit that reveres truth supremely and therefore craves freedom to discuss, to publish, and to pursue what it believes to be true.

Theological Liberalism

Theological Liberalism promotes a progressive ethical vision derived from the Christian message, while denying Christianity's traditional understanding of doctrine.

Liberalism's perfect exemplar is Adolf von Harnack (1851–1930). He made pioneering contributions to New Testament studies, theology, ethics, and historical theology (a field he revolutionized). He argued that Jesus had been misunderstood and misrepresented in most Christian sources, including the Gospels. Jesus had been a simple Hebrew prophet calling people to moral awakening. The message of the genuine Jesus could be recovered, however, once the corrupt layers of tradition had been removed, extracting husk from the kernel of enduring value.

According to Harnack, Jesus taught that the kingdom of God was not a coming supernatural cataclysm but an ethical kingdom. He taught about the fatherhood of God and the brotherhood of mankind; each and every soul was of infinite value. Jesus also called his followers to a higher righteousness (beyond that of the Pharisees) that was rooted in God's command to love.

No doubt this is the outlook of liberals, but is that all? Doesn't this spirit lead to identifiable convictions? I think so. And that spirit and those convictions together constitute Protestant liberalism.

It might be helpful to think of liberal theology as a suspension bridge. The footing of one tower is planted upon modern thought and the foundation of the other rests upon Christian experience. Unfortunately, the ground around both towers is shifting soil, and those who take the bridge disagree over which is the safer side. That is why Professor Kenneth Cauthen finds two fundamental types of liberalism. He calls them "evangelical liberalism" and "modernistic liberalism."

Cauthen suggests that the evangelical liberals were "serious Christians," to borrow Fosdick's terms, who were searching for a theology that could serve "intelligent moderns." Evangelical liberals, then, took greater confidence in the tower resting on Christian experience.

On the other side of the bridge were modernistic liberals who were intelligent moderns hoping to be considered serious Christians in some sense. They found greater support in the tower resting on modern thought.

Perhaps the best way to explore theological liberalism, then, is to take a close look at *modern thought* and then at *Christian experience.*

Liberals believed that Christian theology had to come to terms with modern science if it ever hoped to claim and hold the allegiance of intelligent men of the day. They refused, therefore, to accept religious beliefs on authority alone. They insisted that faith had to pass the tests of reason and experience. Man's mind, they believed, was capable of thinking God's thoughts after him, and the best clues to the nature of God were human intuition and reason.

The Christian, they said, should keep his mind open to truth from any source. New facts may well change traditional beliefs that rest on no more than custom and time, but unexamined faith is not worth having.

By surrendering so completely to the modern mind liberals accepted the assumption that the universe was one grand, harmonious machine, or perhaps an extremely complex growing organism. Whatever the image, a watch or a plant, the point is unity, harmony, coherence.

The biblical account of creation, however, recognizes certain important orders in the universe: inanimate matter, plants, animals, man, and God. That didn't bother liberal theology. It pressed on for unity or continuity. It reduced distinctions between revelation and natural religion, between Christianity and other religions, between saved and lost, between Christ and other men, between man and God.

Two technical theological terms are crucial here: *immanence* and *transcendence.* Immanence carries the idea of God's presence in the world and working through nature. An extreme version of immanence is found in pantheism, which claims that God and the world are identical. Transcendence implies the reality of God apart from the world. An extreme version of transcendence is found among the deists, for whom God is as separate from the world as a watchmaker from his watch.

Liberals felt that the old orthodox Christian idea of a God somewhere beyond the universe was unacceptable to modern men. Some liberals criticized seeing God as a distant and remote being, though this view may have more to do with deism than genuine Christian theology. Opposed to a remote understanding of God, they linked the divine with mankind's conscious being. The life coursing through nature and man they called God.

This immanent view of God seemed to fit the results of scientific studies. Instead of suddenly breaking through the clouds to create the world, God, they said, had been working for ages through natural law, slowly building the universe as we find it today. Most liberals agreed with the poet who said, "Some call it evolution, and others call it God."

Evolution was the theory that held that all complex living things have developed from simple forms through the operation of natural selection. Thus no species is fixed and changeless. In 1785 James Hutton had attributed the earth's development to natural rather than supernatural causes. Confirmation of the view came in Sir Charles Lyell's epoch-making *Principles of Geology* (1830). Lyell showed that the earth's surface had been formed by natural causes operating over a vast period of time. Such a conception of geologic time was essential for any theory of evolution based on changes in species over many thousands of generations.

ENTER CHARLES DARWIN

The scientist whose name became synonymous with evolution was Charles Darwin (1809–1882). After studying medicine and preparing at Cambridge University for the ministry, Darwin became a naturalist. From 1831 to 1836 he studied the specimens he had collected while on a surveying expedition with the ship *Beagle* along the coast of South America.

In 1859 Darwin's views appeared in his *Origin of Species*. He contended "that species have been modified during a long course of descent . . . chiefly through the normal selection of numerous successive, slight, favourable variations." *The Origin of Species*, the most important book of the century, revolutionized the concepts about the origin and evolution of life on planet earth. Darwin followed his first bombshell by a second. In 1871 his *Descent of Man* applied the natural selection to human beings and reached the controversial conclusion that man's ancestors were probably monkey-like animals.

Such conclusions threw many religious people on the defensive. Some vigorously rejected the new scientific views. If man is not specially created by God and fallen from God's favor, where is the need for Christ's salvation? Others attempted to reconcile their religious beliefs with evolution. As time went on liberals came to believe that the evolutionary theory supplemented rather than contradicted the basics of Christianity. They considered growth and development as God's way of revealing himself to man. In 1892 Lyman Abbott, then minister at the Plymouth Church in Brooklyn, New York, wrote *The Evolution of Christianity* and attempted to show that "in the spiritual, as in the physical, God is the secret and source of light." He spoke of the evolution of the Bible, of the church, and even of the soul.

As serious as the challenge of science was to orthodox Christianity, it was clearly secondary to the new views of history. Science could only question God's rule in the physical world, but historical criticism advanced directly to the domain of the Christian faith, to the revelation of God in the Bible.

The term for the application of the principles of history to the Bible is *biblical criticism*. The term *criticism* may be somewhat misleading. It is true that many critical scholars reach conclusions that challenge the Bible's veracity and value as a witness to God's purpose. But the term actually identifies a strategy for knowing and learning. A scholar is critical if he or she subjects the material to an inspection of careful (critical) scrutiny. For example, a modern or critical scholar may inspect the New Testament materials to see if there actually is historical evidence to support the church's teaching that the Son was God or if this doctrine rests upon tradition. Although less believable in our day, this movement assumed that it was immune from corrupting traditions itself.

Biblical criticism came to be expressed in two forms, what is sometimes called *lower* and *higher* criticism. Lower criticism tried to reconstruct the precise wording of the originals (presently lost) from an inspection of the many surviving ancient manuscripts. This scholarly pursuit may alarm conservative Christians initially; but conservatives have contributed significantly to this endeavor. After all, they have a great interest in the discernment and discovery of the exact wording of the originals.

Higher criticism, however, proved another matter. The higher critic is not primarily interested in the original wording of the text;

he is interested in the meaning of the text. The higher critic wants to inspect the text historically to see if the event which it reports really happened. To achieve this, he studies the background, authorship, and setting of the text. The higher critic believes that we can only understand the Bible if we see it against its background. The methods of higher criticism were not new, but they had been limited to writings other than Scripture. In the nineteenth century the method was applied to the Bible as if the Bible were any other ancient book whose credentials had to pass the standards of historical methods. In actual practice the critics did not apply critical methodology as they would to any other book. Many held assumptions that God could not act in history in miraculous or routine ways. Others assumed the Bible story and teaching to be untrue unless it could be shown true by an independent source beyond the Bible. This did result in conclusions that shook orthodoxy.

Several critical conclusions troubled believers. Critics believed that the books of Moses were actually the product of a centuries-long composition that included four great literary traditions being combined throughout Israel's history. Some critics speculated that some prophecies seemed true because they were actually written after the events occurred. Others challenged the accuracy of the Gospels, especially John. One of the central concerns of higher criticism was the search for the "historical Jesus." The critics assumed that Jesus, as he lived in history, was different from the Jesus whom we find portrayed in the Gospels. They assumed that the early church and the gospel writers had added many things to the biblical account so that the problem was to sift the authentic sayings and doings of Jesus from the later additions.

The work of Strauss (1809–1874) rejected the previous approaches. He held that it was no longer possible to embrace a straightforward supernaturalist approach or the face-saving approach of rationalism. The rationalists held that readers could discover rational explanations for Jesus' miracles that the gospel writers misunderstood; for example, Jesus was walking on a jetty and not on the water. Also unsatisfactory was the notion that the gospel writers were intentionally fraudulent in creating Jesus' story. Strauss argued that the gospel's representation of Jesus reflects a mythological perspective of the ancients.

Myths were the vehicles that ancient people employed to grasp great people and events; the awareness of the myth-shaped understanding of the world gave the modern reader the necessary insight to appropriately assess the important ideas carried in the ancient myth stories.

THE IMPACT OF BIBLICAL CRITICISM

As important, however, than any of the particular conclusions of biblical critics was the fact that criticism threw into question the general trustworthiness of the Bible. Liberals welcomed higher criticism because they recognized a radically different view of the Bible was necessary for intelligent moderns. They felt free from the need to apologize for the whole Bible as the infallible Word of God. They no longer had to defend a God who ordered the Israelites to kill their enemies to the last woman and child or who sent bears to maul children who poked fun at a prophet.

The studies of the higher critics, said the liberals, make it clear that God has revealed himself through an evolutionary process. It began with primitive, bloodthirsty ideas and showed how the Jews slowly came to grasp the idea of a righteous God who can be served only by one who does justly, loves mercy, and walks humbly with his God. This evolutionary revelation of God finds its fulfillment in Jesus, where God is portrayed as the loving Father of all men.

When liberals could no longer rest in the traditional doctrines of orthodoxy, which they felt science and history had destroyed, they found their needed assurance in the other pillar of their bridge: Christian experience.

In the early nineteenth century an artistic and intellectual movement arose called Romanticism. While it is popularly understood as a protest against the overly rationalistic mindset of the Enlightenment, Romanticism discerned a dynamic energy and force surging within nature. This strong vitality was not exactly irrational but rather beyond reason. Romantic paintings often represent this vital force as a great storm that is at once dangerous and fascinating to the onlooker. People could discern this and be swept up into its creative and mental powers. Encountering and engaging this vitality came to be of first importance. It was engaged by an intuitive awareness or sense and not as a logical deduction. Why trouble about formal and external creeds when so intimate and so undeniable a certainty ruled every soul? As Tennyson wrote:

Speak to Him, thou, for He hears, and Spirit can meet—
 Closer is He than breathing, and nearer than hands and feet.

When he was asked to interpret the American situation before the International Congregational Council in London in 1891, Dr. Lewis F. Stearns of Bangor Seminary in Maine said,

We are coming to understand that it is the recognition of the invincible reality of spiritual Christianity which is going to give our theology its great power in the future . . . . Criticism may assail the historical facts of revelation: rationalism may urge objections to its doctrines; but the surf on our coast of Maine might as easily overthrow the granite cliffs against which it breaks as criticism and rationalism disturb the Christian realities which stand firm in the experience of the individual believer and the church.

INFLUENTIAL SPOKESMEN FOR LIBERALISM

The two most influential spokesmen for Christian experience were Friedrich Schleiermacher (1768–1834) and Albrecht Ritschl (1822–1889). Both were German theologians. Schleiermacher taught at the newly founded University of Berlin and Ritschl at Bonn and Gottingen.

According to Professor William Hordern, Schleiermacher attempted to rehabilitate religion among intellectuals, insisting that the great debates over proofs of God and the abstract doctrinal descriptions of faith were, at best, a secondary expression of religion. At the heart of religion was an awareness of our absolute dependence and vulnerability before the grandeur of God. He appealed to sophisticated intellectuals that they were right to reject the abstract versions of Christianity seen in Protestant Scholasticism. In fact, their romantic sensibilities were inherently religious, and Christianity, rightly understood, accounts for this experience better than any other religion. After Schleiermacher, the idea became commonplace that religions are differing expressions of the same inner religious experience shared by all people. The uniqueness of Christ, says Schleiermacher, is not in some doctrine about Jesus or in some miraculous origin such as the Virgin Birth: "The real miracle is Jesus himself. In Jesus we find a man who had the sense of God-consciousness to a supreme degree." Where we all have flashes of God, he had complete knowledge. Where we give fitful obedience, he gave complete obedience. "As the Godfilled man," Jesus was "our great pioneer" in the realm of the spirit and morality.

Since Jesus has the full and complete knowledge of God, he is able to communicate the consciousness of God to others. Through Jesus we can come into a vital and living relationship with God. The church is the living witness to the fact that down through the centuries men have come to a vital God consciousness through their contact with the life of Jesus. This leads to a true reunion with our fellow men in brotherly living.

Schleiermacher was "the father of modern theology" primarily because he shifted the basis of the Christian faith from the Bible to "religious experience." Albrecht Ritschl, the most influential theologian in the late nineteenth century and the principal teacher of American liberals, focused religious experience upon the historical Jesus.

To Ritschl religion had to be practical. It must begin with the question, What must I do to be saved? But if that question means, How can I go to heaven when I die? then it is a theoretical question. To be saved means to live a new life, to be saved from sin, selfishness, fear, and guilt.

According to Hordern, "To be practical, Christianity must be built upon fact, so Ritschl welcomed the search for the historical Jesus. The great Christian fact is the impact that Jesus has made upon the church through the centuries." Nature cannot introduce us to God because it speaks ambiguously about God. "We find God instead in history, where movements arise dedicated to the values that make life meaningful. The task of theology is to turn men again to Jesus and remind them anew of what it means to follow him."

For Ritschl religion rests upon the values of men, not upon the truth of science. Science tells us the facts, things as they are; but religion weighs the facts and counts some more valuable than others. "The great fact about man is that, although he is a product of nature and evolution, he has a sense of values." We can explain this only if we recognize that the universe creates not only atoms and molecules but also values. "God is the necessary postulate to explain this sense of worth in man."

Many Christians in the late nineteenth century, says Hordern, found Ritschl's approach helpful. It appeared to free the Christian faith from the destructive impact of history and science. It allowed biblical criticism to take the way of science: to decide the facts about authorship, date, and meaning of the biblical books. But it also recognized that religion is much more than facts. Science cannot rule on values, the stuff of religion.

If biblical criticism denies Jesus' miracles, his Virgin Birth, his pre-existence, this does not make Jesus less valuable to us. Belief in the divinity of Jesus does not rest in any of these; it rests solely on the fact that he is the source of a value-creating movement; he has led men to find the God of values. That is, Jesus' life was the embodiment of such high ethical ideals and attainment that we are inspired to live as he did. Jesus is divine in the sense that he can do for us what God does; he makes us conscious of the highest in life. From Jesus' influence, then, comes the church, a value-creating community: the spearhead for building a society inspired by love, the kingdom of God upon earth.

The impact of liberalism was not limited to any single denomination or country. It challenged traditional orthodox bodies all over Europe and North America. We may take the Congregationalists in the United States as an example of many other Christian groups.

AN EXAMPLE OF LIBERAL CHANGE

Liberal theology appeared among New England churches under the title New Theology. The leading advocates of the New Theology emerged from within traditional New England Calvinism. Theodore Thornton Munger was minister of the United Church (Congregational) in New Haven, Connecticut. Newman Smyth, his colleague in New Haven, served the Center Church (Congregational) for twenty-five years. George Angier Gordon was minister of historic Old South Church in Boston. Washington Gladden early served in New England but found his greatest success at the First Congregational Church in Columbus, Ohio. George Harris was Abbott Professor of Theology at Andover Theological Seminary and, supported by his colleagues, was spokesman for the New Theology through *The Andover Review*. Finally, there was the great popularizer of the movement, Lyman Abbott. "Probably no man," said F. H. Foster, "ever wielded in America so powerful an influence in the direction of a liberal theology."

Scores of men clustered around these early leaders—Henry Ward Beecher, Egbert Smyth, William Jewett Tucker, Lewis French Stearns, William Newton Clarke, and others—but the character of the movement remained basically the same. It was a protest in the interests of modern thought against the "old theology" of evangelical Puritanism, usually called *New England Theology*.

In 1881 Edwards Amasa Park, perhaps the last outstanding spokesman for New England Theology, resigned from the influential Abbot Professorship of Theology at Andover. Two years later Harris succeeded him. We may consider that event the watershed of the old and the new.

Prior to 1880 most New England ministers held to the sovereignty of God; to the innate depravity of mankind (which they traced to the sin of the first man); to the atonement of Jesus Christ, the ground of man's forgiveness of sin; to the Holy Spirit as essential to conversion; and to the eternal separation of the saved and lost in heaven or hell.

After 1880 every one of these beliefs came under heated fire from the liberals. The most celebrated controversy erupted at Andover Seminary. The seminary had been established by New England Congregationalists in 1808 to counter the Unitarian tendencies of Harvard. Attempting to preserve Andover's orthodoxy, the founders required faculty subscription to a creed summarizing their inherited Calvinism. By 1880, however, faculty members, under the influence of liberalism, found this requirement impossible and said so. The spark that lit the flames of controversy was a series of articles in the *Andover Review*. Egbert C. Smyth, William Jewett Tucker, and George Harris of the faculty argued that heathen who die without any knowledge of the gospel will have an opportunity in the future life either to accept or to reject the gospel before facing final judgment. Step by step in the debate that followed faculty members moved toward the public defense of liberal theology.

The Board of Visitors, one of the ruling bodies of the seminary, finally brought charges against Smyth for his departure from the Creed: a kind of test case. After years of moves and counter-moves, the Supreme Court of Massachusetts in 1892 voided the action of the Board of Visitors in dismissing Smyth. By that time almost every American denomination had on its hands its own celebrated case of heresy.

Suggestions for Further Reading

Ahlstrom, Sydney E. *A Religious History of the American People*. New Haven, CT: Yale University Press, 1972.

Cauthen, Kenneth. *The Impact of American Religious Liberalism*. New York: Harper & Row, 1962.

Dorrien, Gary J. *The Making of American Liberal Theology, 1900–1950*. Louisville, KY: Westminster John Knox Press, 2003.

Hordern, William E. *A Layman's Guide to Protestant Theology*. New York: MacMillan, 1968.

Shriver, George H. *American Religious Heretics*. Nashville: Abingdon Press, 1966.

CHAPTER 41

NOTHING TO LOSE
BUT CHAINS

The Social Crisis

IN HIS NOVEL *HARD Times* Charles Dickens described a typical English factory town in the early nineteenth century:

> It was a town of red brick, or of brick that would have been red if the smoke and ashes had allowed it; but as matters stood it was a town of unnatural red and black, like the painted face of a savage. It was a town of machinery and tall chimneys, out of which interminable serpents of smoke trailed themselves forever and ever, and never got uncoiled. It had . . . a river that ran purple with ill-smelling dye, and vast piles of buildings full of windows where there was a rattling and a trembling all day long . . . .

The scene is a snapshot of the industrial revolution, a term historians use for the rapid changes in European and American societies in the nineteenth century. They call it industrial because most of the changes can be traced to new methods of manufacturing. Factories meant cities, cities meant people, and people meant problems—lots of them.

The sudden growth of cities and the multiplication of machines presented Christianity with a new and complex challenge, a kind of book-end to match the conflict with modern thought. How did Christians respond to this social crisis?

Many critics insist, to this day, that Christianity has not confronted the crisis. It has only fled from it. In our times large territories once

422

shaped by Christian values are now controlled by a Marxist government. And even in the so-called Christian West, few people see any connection between their religion and their employment. What fellowship hath light with darkness, or the union hall with the church sanctuary?

THE NEW WORLD OF FACTORIES

The industrial city is a riddle for many believers. They do not understand its workings; they fear its sins and crimes. Throughout its history, however, Christianity has been both a conservative and a radical force. And it proved so in the industrial crisis.

France had a political revolution, Germany an intellectual revolution, but England gave birth to the industrial revolution. As the leading commercial and financial power, England had the markets and the money for industrial production. Late in the eighteenth century industry after industry had some breakthrough to greater productivity, but none was more important than the harnessing of steam. James Watt (1736–1819), the Scottish genius at the University of Glasgow, found a way to control the supply of steam and drive a piston back and forth in a closed cylinder. Soon steam engines were employed in manufacturing textiles and later in driving locomotives and ships.

For the first time a manufacturer had a source of power that did not depend upon the climate or the seasons for driving windmills or waterwheels. The factory became the symbol of the new industrial order. Here the power and the machinery made productivity possible. So people to run the machines were forced to leave their cottages, looms, and fields to join the work force in some factory.

Life was suddenly changed. Gone, for many, was rural or small-town life where the pace of work was determined by night and day, sowing and harvest. In its place people found the precision and the regimen of the factory world. God's sun was hid behind the smoke and in its place was the factory whistle: symbol of man's time, not God's.

The Industrial Revolution greatly increased the wealth of mankind, but it brought a host of evils for the workers massed together in the ever expanding factories of European and American cities. The early factories were without the most elementary sanitary and safety facilities. Horrible cases of mangling were common, and under English common law any accident a worker might suffer was considered a result of his own negligence. The employer could not be held responsible. There was no system of workmen's compensation or health insurance. An injured worker was likely to be thrown out in the street destitute and his job given to one of the thousands who had flocked to the new cities in search of employment.

Women and children worked alongside of men. Poverty often forced women to toil until a day or two before delivery of their children and then to report back to work shortly after the baby was born. Many mills employed youngsters only four or five years of age. And the work days were twelve to fifteen hours of hard labor for minimum wages.

The workers and their families lived in a single room in a dirty tenement and were fortunate if they didn't have to share it with other families. The squalid streets around them were littered with garbage. Without adequate sewers, they reeked with the smell of excrement.

The old class conflict between the aristocrats and the middle class that had raged in Western Europe during the early years of the nineteenth century had ended in the triumph of the bourgeoisie. With their victory had come an economic philosophy called *laissez faire*. The theory held that the social ills of industrialism defied correction. Every individual should be left alone to pursue his own interests: then everything was supposed to work out for the happiness of the greatest number.

The textbook of this school of thought, Adam Smith's *Wealth of Nations*, argued that society benefited most from competition. The more efficient individuals gained the greater rewards. Although governments were responsible for the protection of life and property, the hands of government should be kept out of business. The best interests of society are served by the free operation of the laws of supply and demand.

The urban working force, however, had no access to the benefits of this competition. They were without property and, therefore, without the vote to change conditions. Their struggle in the nineteenth century was for access to the ballot, or other means of power.

The early attack upon the capitalist's laissez faire philosophy came from a new concept called *socialism*. At this early stage the term did not stand for a militant workers' movement. It was mostly a theory that condemned the concentration of wealth and called for public or worker ownership of business. Above all the socialist insisted that harmony and cooperation, not ruthless competition, should control economic affairs.

These early socialists were utopians because their theories of model communities were based upon the naïve notion that men naturally loved one another and that they could live happily together. It was capitalist competition, they said, that set man against man.

Thus the many problems of industrial society tended to concentrate on one question: property. Is there in man a natural and inalienable right to own things? The church had always said there was. It seemed to be embodied in the tenth commandment: "Thou shalt not covet thy neighbor's house . . . nor his ox . . . nor anything that is thy neighbor's." Those who had rejected the principle had been treated as heretics.

But never before the nineteenth century had there been so much property to be owned or so few allowed to own it. Millions instead of thousands were dispossessed, and wholly dispossessed. The Roman people had of old been appeased with bread and circuses. But in this later age both had vanished. The poor were allowed neither corn nor carnival. Hunger preoccupied the lowest classes, and insecurity crept more and more among the middle classes.

The churches were not in a strong position to speak to the crisis. The trend in modern times to separate the church and the state had left the churches without a political platform. The Constitution of the United States forbade the federal government to make any church the religion of the land. The English reforms of the 1830s stripped the Church of England of many traditional privileges. And in countries where Roman Catholics were numerous, especially France and Italy, anticlerical feelings limited Church authorities. In short, the churches had been excluded from the arena where crucial decisions were made.

Men inside and outside the churches came to think of Christianity in narrower and narrower terms. Almost everything not obviously "spiritual" was left free from criticism. Thus a growing body of industrial workers regarded the churches and the Christian message as largely irrelevant or powerless to speak to the difficulties they suffered in the age of the machine.

MARX, PROPHET OF THE NEW AGE

The age, however, was not without voices. Almost unnoticed, in 1848, a prophet named Karl Marx arose preaching a new form of socialism. Marx criticized Christianity, claiming it was untrue to its own vision: it had taken the side of the wealthy oppressors. Like religion generally, Christianity was a tool in the hands of the rich to oppress the poor. Christian preaching exhorted the poor to suffer injustice in the here and now, promising a reward in heaven. Christianity also misguided people by lofty and distracting conversation about noble ideas; Marx argued instead that the current circumstances were the result of the conflict between the social classes. He taught that the time had come for the poor to rise up to engage in history-changing violence.

Born in the Rhineland, at Trier, of German-Jewish parents who had been converted to Christianity, Marx (1818–1883) obtained his doctoral degree after studying the ideas of philosopher Georg Hegel.

Failing to find a career in university teaching, he was forced to make a precarious living as a journalist. He went to Paris, where he became interested in socialistic ideas and, while there, he began his lifelong friendship with Friedrich Engels (1820–1895), the son of a wealthy German factory owner. In 1845 French authorities expelled Marx and with Engels he went to live in Brussels.

In January 1848 Marx and Engels published the famous *Communist Manifesto*. This stirring document contained practically all the elements of what they came to call "scientific" socialism. It opened with an ominous declaration: "A spectre is haunting Europe—the spectre of Communism." The *Manifesto* called for an implacable struggle against the bourgeoisie. It proclaimed the inevitable revolution and the triumph of the masses and closed with a stern warning:

The Communists disdain to conceal their views and aims. They openly declare that all their ends can be attained only by the forcible overthrow of all existing social conditions. Let the ruling classes tremble at a Communistic revolution. The proletarians have nothing to lose but their chains. They have a world to win. Working men of all countries, unite!

After a short time in Germany, Marx spent the rest of his life in London, most of it on the edge of survival. Supported largely by contributions from friends, especially Engels, Marx almost daily made his way to the British Museum where he collected material for his various books, especially *Das Kapital* (*Capital*).

Whatever one may think of Marxist socialism, no one can doubt that *Das Kapital* (1867–1894) constitutes one of the most influential books of modern times. For a season in the twentieth century nearly half of the world was organized under governments rooted in Marxism.

As in the slavery controversy, Christian movements fell on all sides of the social crisis. Many church members were capitalists. They owned factories and had several influential positions in society. Many were eager to defend the *laissez faire* philosophy.

After the middle of the nineteenth century, however, an increasing number of Christians, Catholic and Protestant, worked zealously for improved conditions for laborers. Four lines of action were open to them: (1) they could challenge the *laissez faire* philosophy in the name of Christian principles; (2) they could establish Christian institutions to relieve the suffering of the poor and powerless; (3) they could support the formation of labor unions; and (4) they could appeal to the state for legislation aimed at the improvement of working conditions.

In Roman Catholic circles, as early as 1848, a German bishop, Wilhelm Ketteler (1811–1877), addressed the problem of the factory worker in sermons and books. He sketched out a Catholic solution that pointed out the dangers in both the unlimited competition of capitalism and the exaggerated state control of the socialists. He defended the right of state intervention against the capitalists and the right of private property against the totalitarian tendencies of the socialists. Above all, he insisted on the right of workers to form their own associations, and he called for a whole series of reforms, including profit sharing, reasonable working hours, sufficient rest days, factory inspection, and the regulation of female and child labor.

In England the workers found a friend among Roman Catholics in Henry Edward Cardinal Manning (d. 1892), a convert from evangelical Anglicanism. As early as December 1872, Manning appeared at a meeting held to promote the cause of farm workers. It was a courageous act since it was the first time in England that a Roman Catholic prelate had so openly taken the side of labor. He followed this up with a letter to Prime Minister Gladstone urging two things: the passage of laws prohibiting the labor of children under a certain age, and the regulation of housing.

In 1874 Manning delivered a lecture, "The Rights and Dignity of Labour," in which he forcefully defended the right of the worker to organize, called for laws to regulate the hours of work, and made a plea for people to look into the horrible abuses associated with child labor.

In the United States, a Roman Catholic layman, Terence Powderly, was the leader of the first really effective labor union, The Knights of Labor. The union was open to Americans of all beliefs, but it had a large Catholic membership from its earliest days.

In the nineteenth century, however, officials of the Roman Church, including the pope, feared labor unions. They remembered too well the conflicts with Italian Masons and the political forces to unite Italy. The Knights of Labor were in danger of papal condemnation and probably only avoided it when the Archbishop of Baltimore, who later became Cardinal Gibbons, came to their defense.

Not until 1891 did the pope speak to the social crisis. The aging Leo XIII (1878–1903) outlined what has become the basic Catholic position on the relationship between capital and labor. The encyclical *Rerum Novarum*, after calling attention to the evil conditions resulting from the industrial revolution, rejects socialism and takes a strong stand for the Christian family as the most essential unit of society.

Leo stresses, however, the capitalist's obligation to deal justly with workers. He defends the rights of Catholic workers to organize and to bargain with owners, as well as their right to a living wage and reasonable leisure. Thus monopoly capitalism and industrial slavery came under papal criticism as well as what he called socialism.

LABORING MEN IN ENGLAND

In largely Protestant England support for the laboring man came primarily from the Nonconforming denominations. Until the middle of the nineteenth century labor unions were illegal, but the labor movement found strong support among Nonconformists, especially the Primitive Methodists. Many of the leaders of the labor movement had their apprenticeship as Methodist lay preachers. They simply carried into the workingmen's associations the zeal, the organizing skills, and the preaching experience found in the Methodist chapels.

Nonconformists were also leaders in the temperance crusade and in the founding of orphanages. George Müller of the Plymouth Brethren; Charles Haddon Spurgeon, the leading Baptist preacher in London; and T. B. Stephenson, a Methodist, were all instrumental in creating Christian orphanages.

ONWARD, CHRISTIAN SOLDIERS!

The most outstanding example of ministry to the dispossessed was the work of a pietistic Evangelical, William Booth (1829–1912). He started his ministry with the Methodist New Connection but soon withdrew to work with London's poor. His street preaching in London's East End in 1864 met with phenomenal success. Within eleven years he had thirty-two stations promoting evangelism and social service among London's destitute. His workers, organized like a military unit, were soon called the Salvation Army. Evangelist Booth became General Booth.

By 1888 the General had established 1,000 British corps and had dispatched patrols to many other nations. His book *In Darkest England and the Way Out* appeared in 1890, graphically comparing the social darkness in England to Africa's darkness pictured by David Livingstone. In London, in one year, he reported 2,157 people had been found dead, 2,297 had committed suicide, 30,000 were living in prostitution, 160,000 had been convicted of drunkenness, and more than 900,000 were classed as paupers. Booth went on to describe the Army's enormous rescue efforts. The whole picture was one of dire need.

The Church of England was so wed to the past that it had great difficulty adjusting to the social crisis. New parishes in the mushrooming industrial towns required an act of Parliament. This was time-consuming and costly. As a result the new urban masses usually grew up beyond the care of the Church of England.

One movement in the Anglican Church proved to be a striking exception: the Christian Socialist group. F. D. Maurice (1805–1872), a theologian; Charles Kingsley (1819–1875), a novelist; and John Malcolm Ludlow (1821–1911), a lawyer, were churchmen who felt that the gospel had something to say to the working people of England.

During its brief period of activity, 1848 to 1854, the Christian Socialist movement attacked the whole *laissez faire* outlook. "Competition," Maurice wrote to Kingsley, "is put forth as the law of the universe. That is a lie. The time is come for us to declare that it is a lie, by word and deed."

The true law of the universe, he claimed, is that man is made to live in community. Men realize their true nature when they cooperate with one another as children of God and brothers in Christ.

The leaders of Christian Socialism adopted the socialism label to be provocative. It means no more, they said, than the science of making men partners. They considered it a development of Christianity and believed that the Christian faith stood for a society that would enable men to work with one another instead of against one another.

The practical results of the Christian Socialist movement were limited. Their cooperative workshops were poorly organized and unduly optimistic about the role of laborers. Their greatest contribution was probably in the ideas that carried across the Atlantic to the United States.

In general, workers in nineteenth-century England slowly gained both political power and better working conditions. Step by step, act by act, England whittled away at the old *laissez faire* doctrine and improved life for her working citizens: no children under ten could work, women and children were limited to a ten-hour day, safety inspections were introduced in factories, and many others. England had provided many benefits for laboring people before many in the United States recognized a social crisis existed.

SOCIAL GOSPEL IN AMERICA

The major movement for social justice in the United States was called the Social Gospel, a movement among liberal Protestant pastors and theological professors. They formed no outstanding organization but chose to work through established denominations and political agencies.

The crux of the Social Gospel was the belief that God's saving work included corporate structures as well as personal lives. If it is true that social good and evil are collective in nature, not simply the total of good and evil individuals, then Christians are obliged to work for the reconstruction of the social order. It is part of their religious responsibility.

The prophets of the Social Gospel drew upon a range of sources. Revivalism itself, which under Dwight L. Moody became heavily individualistic, had originally had a vision for a moral and Christian America. Before the Civil War, revivals and reforms went hand in hand. Charles Finney, for example, encouraged his converts to move from the personal regeneration experience to the social mission of the antislavery crusade.

Social Gospel leaders also read, however, the works of the European Christian Socialists: J. F. D. Maurice, Charles Kingsley, and others.

Finally, there was the New Theology. The "progressive orthodoxy" of Andover Seminary and the pulpits of New England provided a general pattern of beliefs for the early preachers of the Social gospel.

The father of the movement was Washington Gladden (1836–1918), who published the first of his many books on the Social gospel in 1876. A transplanted New Englander, he spent his most influential years at the First Congregational Church of Columbus, Ohio. In the Ohio capital he encountered the labor struggle firsthand.

In his congregation were both employers and employees, so during times of industrial strife Gladden witnessed with alarm "the widening of the breach between these classes." In a number of evening addresses he focused on the labor problem and expressed his conviction that the teachings of Jesus contained the principles for the right ordering of society.

We catch something of the Reformer's spirit in his widely sung hymn:

> O Master, let me walk with Thee
> In lonely paths of service free;
> Tell me Thy secret; help me bear
> The strain of toil, the fret of care.

Gladden was no socialist. He held to private property and private enterprise. Yet he believed many industries could be run cooperatively and that railroads, mines, and public service industries of the cities should be operated by the government.

In terms of lasting influence, the outstanding prophet of the Social Gospel was Walter Rauschenbusch (1861–1918). As a young German Baptist pastor in a tenement section of New York City called Hell's Kitchen, he struggled with the Christian response to urban problems. The books that made him nationally prominent came during his years as professor of church history at Rochester Theological Seminary. His three major works were *Christianity and the Social Crisis* (1907), *Christianizing the Social Order* (1912), and *A Theology for the Social Gospel* (1917).

Avoiding the comforting doctrine of human progress, Rauschenbusch anchored his appeal to social responsibility in the concept of the kingdom of God.

> The social gospel," he wrote, "is the old message of salvation, but enlarged and intensified. The individualistic gospel has taught us to see the sinfulness of every human heart and has inspired us with faith in the willingness and power of God to save every soul that comes to him. But it has not given us an adequate understanding of the sinfulness of the social order and its share in the sins of all individuals within it . . . . The social gospel seeks to bring men under repentance for their collective sins and to create a more sensitive and more modern conscience.

The prime example of sin in society, according to the preachers of the Social Gospel, was the capitalist system. Man's salvation, they said, was impossible as long as that system remained unchanged. Social Gospelers differed among themselves over how much change was necessary for the regeneration of the American system, but they agreed the kingdom of God could not come without it.

How far did the Social Gospel penetrate the denominations? Many theological seminaries reshaped their curricula to address social concerns. The primary sign of change, however, came in 1908 with the formation of the Federal Council of Churches. Almost the first act of the Council was the adoption of a "Social Creed of the Churches." It called for many benefits later American workers considered basics: occupational safety, old age security, minimum wage, and the rights of arbitration.

Throughout its history the church had tried to improve man's life on earth even as it prepared him for the world to come. It was always possible to concentrate on the next life so much that Christians appeared insensitive to the pain of the present. Certainly, the Social Crisis of the last century made that obvious.

The various Christian movements for social concerns faced the danger of reducing the gospel to social activism. They left us all an important reminder, however, that Christians cannot show their concern for people's eternal destiny unless they also demonstrate their concern for people's earthly needs.

Suggestions for Further Reading

Carter, Paul A. *The Decline and Revival of the Social Gospel.* Hamden, CT: Archon Books, 1971.

Dayton, Donald W. *Discovering an Evangelical Heritage.* New York: Harper & Row, 1976.

George, Timothy, ed. *Pilgrims on the Sawdust Trail: Evangelical Ecumenism and the Quest for Christian Identity.* Grand Rapids: Baker, 2004.

Handy, Robert, ed. *The Social Gospel in America 1870–1920.* New York: Oxford University Press, 1966.

*Rauschenbusch, Walter. *Christianity and the Social Crisis in the 21st Century: The Classic that Woke up the Church.* With essays edited by Paul Raushenbush. New York: Harper Collins, 2007.

White, Ronald C., Jr. and C. Howard Hopkins. *The Social Gospel.* Philadelphia: Temple University Press, 1976.

THE AGE OF IDEOLOGIES

1914–1989

The twentieth century brought the colossal struggles of political and military giants: Communism, Nazism, and Americanism. A new paganism appeared in appeals to the laws of economics, the passions of race, and the inviolable rights of individuals. Christians were forced to suffer, to think, and to unite in new ways. Protestants reached out to each other in the movements of unity. Roman Catholics struggled to update their Church. The fall of the Berlin Wall signals a decline in the power of ideologies. And the "new" Christianity in the Third World and beyond emerges and expands at an incalculable rate. This new Christianity eclipses inflamed Muslim voices in which it discerns both danger and call to mission.

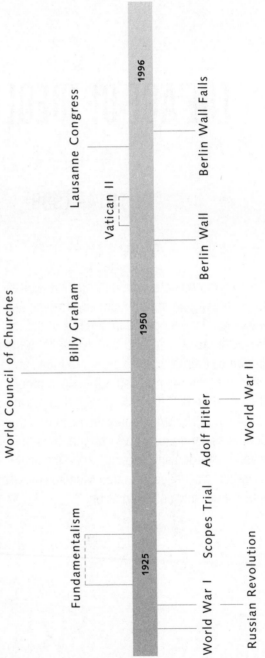

The Age of Ideologies

Fundamentalism

World Council of Churches

Billy Graham

Lausanne Congress

Vatican II

1925

1950

1996

World War I

Scopes Trial

Adolf Hitler

Berlin Wall

Berlin Wall Falls

Russian Revolution

World War II

CHAPTER 42

GRAFFITI ON A WALL OF SHAME

Twentieth-Century Ideologies

DURING THE SUMMER OF 1961 East German police, instigated by Soviet Premier Nikita Khrushchev, tried to turn back the surge of East Germans fleeing to West Berlin. When tighter travel restrictions failed, the police erected twenty-six miles of barbed wire and concrete running like an ugly scar across the face of the city. Furious Berliners labeled it *Schandmaurer,* a wall of shame. What a symbol of the twentieth-century world!

On the east side of the Berlin Wall stood the somber buildings of the Communist world with its gospel of an earthly utopia in some future classless society. On the west side were the shops and movies of the "free West" with its endless search for wealth and happiness now. Alongside the wall lay unmarked bunkers, the silent memorials to Adolf Hitler's once invincible Third Reich.

How has Christianity, with its message of peace and freedom, endured through these years of international hostilities? Like other gospels it has had to fight for space on the bloodstained walls of human conflicts. A backward glance over the last two generations reveals the Christian message scribbled across the decades like so much graffiti, surrounded by other messages equally arresting and perhaps more demanding: Nazism, Marxism, Capitalism.

435

POST-CHRISTIAN GODS FOR THE MASSES

Arnold Toynbee, the eminent historian, once suggested that the twentieth century marked the displacement of the great world religions by three post-Christian ideologies: nationalism, communism, and individualism. These ideologies assume the character of a religion. Each makes ultimate demands: patriotism, class struggle, or secular humanism. Each has its sacred symbols and ceremonies, inspired writings, dogmas, saints, and charismatic leaders.

Toynbee's theory, however, is only partly right. People in the West seem to rightly understand the twentieth century in terms of this secularizing process; the emerging ideologies of nationalism, communism, and individualism largely displaced or tamed the great religions, making them appear marginally important. Many predicted that this process would continue. Reason and science would explain more and more about the world and its people. As people became more educated, they would not need religion, at least not in the same way. Voices of secularization forecasted that fewer people would believe in God, and the God they believed in would be less of a God. Although many Westerners continue to embrace the secularization model, the theory is ridiculously inaccurate when the entire world is considered. The world is more religious than ever, even hyper-religious. Believers in the West may still believe that Christianity is in retreat and be unaware of its unparalleled expansions. Before the century was finished, theorists reversed much of Toynbee's theory; we will understand the future better by paying attention to religious and cultural issues rather than to the political and economic ones.

Nevertheless, numerous totalitarian governments emerged. They were often led by a dictator or small ruling elite in control of an armed force. By the use of sophisticated psychological methods the rulers are able to direct the minds and the emotions of the people against the enemies of the regime. Propaganda and control of the media, along with the regulation of the economy, are aimed at producing a new type of people utterly lacking any hunger for personal freedoms. That is the totalitarian way.

Roots of these twentieth-century ideologies and their totalitarian regimes run back into the blood-drenched soil of World War I. The new religion of early twentieth-century Europe was nationalism. Pan-Germanism and Pan-Slavism brought the great powers of Europe into conflict in the Balkans. Growing militarism, economic imperialism, and power politics created a tinderbox for war. The spark to ignite it came on June 28, 1914, when a young student inspired by Serbian nationalism assassinated the Crown Prince of Austria-Hungary. By August, Germany and Austria (the Central Powers) were arrayed against France, Russia, and Britain (the Allies). Before the war was over twenty-seven nations were caught up in the conflict, ranging from Tokyo to Ottawa.

For the first time the world knew "total war." Soldiers and airmen died as men had always died. But civilians now surrendered civil liberties and sacrificed personal possessions for the war effort. On both sides of the battle lines people believed they were engaged in a righteous crusade. When the United States entered hostilities on April 6, 1917, President Woodrow Wilson, son of a Presbyterian minister, said it was a war "to make the world safe for democracy."

While the Americans mobilized manpower and material, the Russian war effort collapsed. In a revolution in November 1917, the Bolsheviks—the militant, self-appointed vanguard of a new socialist society—wrested power from the Tzar, and early in 1918 the revolutionaries made peace with Germany.

The landing of one million American doughboys in Europe enabled the Allies to bring Germany to the armistice table and eventually to the Paris Peace Conference. But the terms of peace wrung from the Germans proved to be a curious blend of naïve idealism and eager revenge.

Woodrow Wilson secured the creation of a League of Nations only to see the American people refuse to support it. The other Allies were more intent upon extracting a confession of guilt from Germany and crippling the country for years to come. They succeeded on both scores, but the Germans never forgot. Nazism came about as a result of this vindictiveness.

THE RISE OF NAZISM

The Nazis taught the world the meaning of totalitarianism. They were a right wing version of dictatorial rule. We call this *fascism*. Such governments counter personal frustration and alienation, as well as social and economic tensions, by stressing class unity and reaffirming traditional values. Fascist movements glorify the nation, defining it in terms of its mission or racial uniqueness or the state itself. Fascist rulers permit private property and capitalist enterprise, but they tightly control them.

After World War I right wing governments sprang up all over Europe, but the greatest was German National Socialism, better known as Nazism. The Protestant churches in the lands of Luther lost millions of people to this new political religion. Many were compromised or co-opted; others abandoned traditional Christianity.

Most of the Protestant clergy in postwar Germany were monarchists. They had no sympathy for socialism or for democracy. But many people did. The industrial workers came to hate a socially and politically reactionary church. At the same time the German cultured class were ripe for Nazism because they had turned to a romantic view of Germany's past. It was a heroic view, aristocratic and often pantheistic.

The leader of the Nazi movement was Austrian-born Adolf Hitler who was named chancellor of the German Republic on January 30, 1933. Two years later he gained complete control of the government.

The Nazis believed in the absolute unity of the German people under the leader (*der Führer*) and the expression of this leadership principle in all structures of the nation. By integrating all social, economic, and political instruments of the country, they intended to create an ideal super-community.

Nazis abandoned some goals of Enlightenment thinkers, such as individual freedom and tolerance. They employed the general Enlightenment methodology to critique the traditions of the Bible by the exercise of reason. A newly invented version of Christianity followed in which The "Nazi Jesus" had nothing but contempt for the Jews and their corrupted testament. Nazi theologians believed that Christians missed the point of Jesus' teaching, and mistakenly pictured him within a Jewish framework. Typical for Enlightenment thinkers, they only pretended to critique tradition; in practice, they rejected the tradition of Jesus and the Jewish people and turned to embrace yet another tradition. They magnified, instead, a primitive, idealized past portrayed in Wagnerian operas and ancient Germanic sagas where the complexities of modern life had no place. The concern with race was central to Nazi ideology. They preached that Germans possessed unique qualities arising from their homeland. "Soil" and "blood" set the Germans apart from all other people, so the Nazis considered foreign ideas and persons as corrupting, especially Jewish people and ideas.

Nazi theoreticians developed a barbaric doctrine of anti-Semitism. To regain the lost innocence of the past, they argued, Germany had to purge the present of its impurities. The Jews served as scapegoats. They were the source of all modern evils, the "culture-destroying race" that gave the world both capitalism and Marxism. Hitler declared that even the Christian faith was a Jewish plot: "The heaviest blow that ever struck humanity was the coming of Christianity. Bolshevism is Christianity's illegitimate child. Both are inventions of the Jew." The eradication of the Jewish race was the act of social purification necessary to restore Germany to her uncorrupt past.

The Nazis first deprived German Jews of their rights as citizens and pressured them to emigrate. When armies of the Third Reich overran eastern Europe, which had a much larger Jewish population, anti-Semitism mounted in violence. Nazi death squads liquidated thousands of Jews on the spot. The infamous concentration camps, originally created to break the spirits of Nazism's opponents, had even more ominous overtones for the Jews.

In 1940 the Nazis designed a new type of camp for their "final solution," the extermination of the entire Jewish population of Europe. The largest was Auschwitz in Poland. They rounded up men, women, and children and transported them to these "death factories" where in cold-blooded fashion they starved, shot, gassed, or performed medical experiments on the Jews. Reasonable estimates put the number of Jewish deaths in the Holocaust at six million.

CHRISTIANS UNDER HITLER

The dedicated Christian's place in the Nazi world was no more secure than that of the Jew. Born and reared a Catholic, Hitler completely abandoned whatever Christian principles he ever held for his new faith in Germany's regeneration through National Socialism.

During his rise to power Hitler courted Christian support by emphasizing national pride and pretending to favor the churches' role in the state. Like millions of other Germans, churchmen had shared the shock of the nation's defeat in World War I. They, too, dreamed of Germany's new birth.

Catholics, who had been strong in the German republic during the 1920s, endorsed the new Nazi government and supported the agreement (*concordat*) the *Führer* signed with the pope in 1933 guaranteeing the freedom to practice the Catholic religion.

The *concordat* was an important milestone for Hitler. It greatly increased his prestige, and it successfully excluded Catholics from German politics. Hitler, however, had no intention of keeping his part of the bargain.

At the same time a movement called the German Christians arose among Protestants aimed at closer ties with the Nazis. The German Christians wanted to unite the twenty-eight regional Protestant bodies under a single bishop. They elected to this post Ludwig Müller, a fervent Nazi. They also introduced the *Führer* principle into the church government and adopted the "Aryan paragraph," which called for the dismissal of all people of Jewish origin from church positions. In 1933 the German Christians claimed three thousand out of a total of seventeen thousand Protestant pastors.

To counter the German Christian movement, a group of ministers, led by Martin Niemöller, formed the Pastor's Emergency League and set up an alternative church government known as the Confessing Church. The movement at its height was probably about the same size as the German Christian group. In between the two parties were the timid majority of Protestant ministers who eventually obeyed Hitler's commands without open protest.

In May 1934 the Confessing Church spelled out its theological convictions in the *Barmen Declaration*. Largely written by Karl Barth, the *Declaration* called the German churches back to the central truths of Christianity and rejected the totalitarian claims of the state. The statement called the church to depend on revelation, especially as revealed in Jesus. It ruled against natural theology. The natural theologian might use some phenomena of nature to prove that God exists or to observe some good quality in nature (such as creativity) and to conclude that God must be its source. Barth rejected natural theology completely. He saw it as inevitably declining into idolatry, describing God in our own terms. Liberalism employed a similar strategy of seeing God through human lenses. Liberals embraced only the biblical teaching that fit with their sophisticated understanding of God. They abandoned unseemly descriptions of God found in Scripture and tradition and embraced a vision of God that met their own standards. The outcome was the same as with the Nazi theology: unchecked idolatry. God not only likes us, he is like us. It takes little imagination to understand the Nazi policy of genocide as a demonic form of idolatry. Tragically, Nazi believers saw their crime as divinely sanctioned cleansing. Aberrant theology has consequences.

The Confessing Church planned no campaign of resistance to Nazism. It was mainly directed against the heretical distortions of the German Christians, and in fact the leaders repeatedly affirmed their loyalty to the state and congratulated Hitler on his political moves. Because Lutherans traditionally supported the ruling power, the Confessing Church decided not to set itself up as a rival church but simply as a body to defend the orthodox Christian faith against innovations.

Harassed by the Gestapo and repudiated by most Protestant leaders, the Confessing Church led a perilous existence. In 1935 no fewer than seven hundred Confessional Church pastors were arrested. The movement's presence was an embarrassment to the Nazis, and its witness to Christ's Lordship over the world implicitly challenged Hitler's totalitarianism.

When it was obvious that Hitler's friend Ludwig Müller had failed to unite the Protestant churches, the *Führer* turned more and more to his anti-Christian Nazis who claimed that Nazism itself represented the true fulfillment of Christianity. In 1935 the Nazis created their own Ministry of Church Affairs under a Nazi lawyer, Hanns Kerrl. When Kerrl met resistance from churchmen he declared, "National Socialism is the doing of God's will. God's will reveals itself in German blood. True Christianity is represented by the party."

Hitler's intentions were now clear to all. Catholic churchmen expressed alarm over the spread of "new heathenism" and increasing restrictions on their work; finally they turned to the Vatican for help.

On May 14, 1937, with the assistance of Eugenio Cardinal Pacelli, the papal secretary of state who was soon to be Pope Pius XII, Pius XI drafted the encyclical *Mit brennender Sorge* (With deep anxiety). It was the first major church document to criticize Nazism. Smuggled into Germany, it was read on Palm Sunday from every Catholic pulpit before a single copy had fallen into Nazi hands. As Richard Pierard explains, the encyclical protested the oppression of the church and called upon Catholics to resist the idolatrous cult of race and state, to stand against the perversion of Christian doctrines and morality, and to maintain their loyalty to Christ, his church, and Rome. Hitler reacted furiously at first, but then decided to avoid a break with Rome by treating the encyclical with complete silence. Knowing that he had the support of the German Catholic lay people, Hitler simply stepped up the pressure on the churches to eliminate the possibility of organized resistance.

THE RUSSIAN REVOLUTION

Meanwhile, through the same troubled twenties and thirties, the Russian Bolsheviks (or Communists) created another totalitarian system, a left wing regime. The Communist system had many of the same traits as Hitler's Germany: dictatorial leadership, a single centralized party, ruthless terror, propaganda, censorship, a controlled economy, and hostility to all organized religion.

The difference was that Communist ideology emphasized the working class, revolution as a means of social change, and the utopian ideal of a classless society. From 1917 to 1924 the mastermind of the Russian Revolution was Vladimir Ilich Ulyanov (1870–1924). We know him as Lenin, an exiled socialist leader who returned from Switzerland in 1917 to take charge of events in his homeland.

Lenin believed in violence as the chief weapon of Marxism. He took nothing for granted. To destroy capitalism he created a highly disciplined Communist party, first to overthrow all traditional institutions and then to control the machinery of the new government. Party and state became one.

When Lenin died in 1924, a bitter struggle for Soviet leadership raged between Leon Trotsky and the ambitious Joseph Stalin. By 1927 Stalin was the unrivaled dictator. He was determined to transform the Soviet Union, as it was then called, into an industrial nation so it could compete with the capitalist countries.

Stalin proved, if anything, even more ruthless than Hitler. He used secret police terror and labor camps to suppress even the slightest dissent and to eliminate all potential rivals.

The Communist Revolution confronted Christianity with an enormous challenge because it was a worldview clearly based on atheism. The Marxist-Leninist theory claimed that religion is false consciousness, an illusory reflection of the world resulting from class divisions. When society is restored to a "normal" state in communism, religion will die a natural death. That is the theory. And yet Communists actively struggle against religion. The party regards itself as the embodiment of the ideals of Marxism and cannot allow any part of society to operate outside its control. Institutional religion is a reactionary social force that only impedes progress toward the classless society, and it must be smashed.

For centuries before the Revolution, the Russian Orthodox Church had been the state church. The Tzar was, in theory, the head of the church. But when the Bolsheviks took over, they confiscated church lands, cancelled state subsidies for the church, decreed civil marriage, and prohibited religious education for the young. How could a church survive when it could not teach its own children in a society filled with atheistic indoctrination?

The Orthodox Church replied to these decrees with defiance. Newly elected Patriarch Tikhon, in his first pastoral letter, declared war on the state. Riots in almost every city followed. In the unorganized violence of the first six years of the Revolution twenty-eight bishops and over one thousand priests were killed.

In 1929 the state's Law on Religious Associations placed strict limits on the activities of churches, effectively denying them any influence on Russian society. More years of intense persecution followed. Thousands of clergymen were imprisoned or liquidated during the collectivization of agriculture and Stalin's purges.

The new Soviet constitution of 1936 restored voting rights to the clergy, but the "servants of religion" continued to be second-class citizens, members of a profession that "exploited the backwardness and ignorance of the toilers." They were constantly harassed by the secret police as "clerico-fascists."

By 1939 the atheistic propaganda, the rigid anti-religion laws, and the Stalinist terror brought the Russian Orthodox Church to the brink of disintegration. The Lutherans were almost wiped out, and Baptists and Evangelical Christian denominations were ravaged.

In the West, however, revulsion against the Soviet regime grew with the reports of persecution. The Roman Catholic Church expressed its alarm. In March 1937 Pius XI issued the encyclical *Divine Redemptoris* condemning the "errors of communism." He criticized the spread of communism, expressed sympathy for the Russian people, and offered the doctrines of the Catholic Church as the alternative to communism. To counter the then-current "popular front" policy of Stalin, the pope declared that "communism is intrinsically wrong and no one who would save Christian civilization may collaborate with it in any undertaking whatsoever." Coming only four days after his encyclical criticizing Nazi Germany, this placed the Vatican firmly on the side of persecuted believers in the totalitarian countries.

THE IMPACT OF WORLD WAR II

World War II broke out in 1939 when German forces invaded Poland. Hitler had made common cause with Mussolini's fascist regime in Italy and a militaristic clique ruling in Japan. All three nations were enflamed by ideas of expansion. Hitler also signed a nonaggression pact with Stalin just before his troops marched into Poland, but within two years he had turned on his former ally. Communist Russia was forced into alliance with France, Great Britain, and the United States to check the expansion of Japan in the Orient and the Nazis in Europe and North Africa.

Just as in World War I, Christians on both sides of the conflict participated in the war effort, but this time with less crusading zeal. German believers were in a special dilemma. German church officials remained conciliatory toward the Nazi state but failed to relieve the suffering of Christians in Germany. Hitler's closest advisers, Bormann, Himmler, and Heydrich, systematically worked toward the "final settlement" of the church question. The churches were to be subordinated to the new order, the clergy stripped of all privileges, and Christianity left to suffer what Hitler called "a natural death."

In the occupied areas of eastern Europe, priests and pastors, along with devout laymen, were treated as common criminals. Thousands were executed or sent to concentration camps. Only the demands of the war and need for popular support prevented the Nazis from eradicating religion in Germany itself.

The German churches' resistance to Hitler was amazingly meager. They were exclusively concerned with individualistic personal faith, traditional submission to the state, and a conservative outlook that rejected all left wing proposals for social and political reform and enabled them to accept the Nazis' claim to be the only alternative to Communism.

The situation in wartime Soviet Russia was a striking contrast. Stalin realized the value of the churches' contribution to public morale in the war and how they could help integrate the territories acquired during the war and promote later Soviet foreign policy.

Stalin allowed the churches to set up their organizations again, collect funds, and give some private religious instruction to children. In 1945 the Orthodox Church and other religious groups regained status as a legal corporation and with it the right to possess property and produce liturgical objects. While still closely supervised, the Orthodox Church enjoyed the most favorable position since the Revolution.

In 1943 the government created The Council for Affairs of the Russian Orthodox Church and a year later established a similar council for other religious groups. These maintained relations between the government and the churches, drafted regulations on religion, and ensured that the laws were enforced.

Overall, however, World War II had a devastating impact on Christianity, both physically and morally. Thousands of churches were destroyed, clergymen killed, and faithful believers persecuted or uprooted from their homes. The level of violence escalated with the use of armored vehicles, incendiary bombing, guided missiles, and the atomic bomb. Millions lost their lives. A popular assessment in American universities pictured the Russian regime as corrupt but morally equivalent to the United States; Russia was a flawed example of Socialism and the United States was an imperfect version of Capitalism. Such a theory seems implausible, given the brutality that extended beyond the church; Communist deaths are still being calculated, but surpass the Nazi death toll (six million) by a factor of ten or more.

This carnage led many to question whether a just war could any longer be possible. They suggested that Christian endorsement of war only led to its intensification. Although some Christians were involved in attempts to bring nations and churches together, such as the United Nations (1945) and the World Council of Churches (1948), continued national passions frustrated their work.

After the atomic bomb drove Japan to the peace table and Communist and allied forces toppled the Third Reich, the victors entered what came to be called the "Cold War."

As leader of the Western democracies, the United States took the initiative through the containment policy to counter Soviet expansion. America was prepared to resist Communism almost everywhere, even if this meant military intervention, but eventually the development of the H-bomb and long-range ballistic missiles made armed conflict between the superpowers costly beyond calculation.

Professor Richard Pierard sums up the conditions this way:

> Although the Cold War started as a rivalry between the great powers it rapidly took on an ideological dimension. Both sides in the polarized world received support from their Christian populations. In a messianic manner, the Soviets preached the doctrines of Communism and the necessity of freeing peoples oppressed by "imperialists."
>
> The Russian Orthodox leaders meanwhile sought to bring churches in other countries under their jurisdiction. Orthodox representatives traveling abroad invariably proclaimed the Moscow 'line' on world issues and praised conditions in the Soviet Union. They were especially active in the Soviet-sponsored peace campaigns. With the emphasis on "peaceful coexistence" following Stalin's death in 1953, the Orthodox Church participated in ecumenical affairs, and finally joined the World Council of Churches in 1961.
>
> The West reacted with the counter-ideology of Anticommunism. The basic assumption was that there was a universal communist conspiracy centered in Moscow, which master-minded all revolutionary unrest in the world. Anticommunism was, particularly, an American response to the East-West stalemate after World War II. An anxious frustration resulted from America's inability to spread the virtues of liberal democracy to all nations.

Thus the wall remained.

Suggestions for Further Reading

Detzler, Wayne A. *The Changing Church in Europe.* Grand Rapids: Zondervan, 1979.

Dowley, Tim. ed. *Eerdmans' Handbook to the History of Christianity*. Grand Rapids: Eerdmans, 1977.

Franzen, August. *A History of the Church: Revised and Edited by John P. Dolan*. New York: Herder and Herder, 1969.

Hardon, John A. *Christianity in the Twentieth Century*. Garden City, NY: Doubleday & Company, Inc., 1971.

Johnson, Paul. *A History of Christianity*. New York: Atheneum, 1983.

CHAPTER 43

ROOTLESS IMMIGRANTS IN A SICK SOCIETY

American Evangelicals

URING THE 1976 PRESIDENTIAL campaign in the United States, Jimmy
Carter's evangelical faith arose as one of the major issues. Aware
that the Watergate scandal had toppled the Nixon administration a
short time before, many Americans felt that morality in government
was of supreme importance. Others, however, warned that religion
could divide the nation and had no place in an American political
campaign.

Historian Arthur M. Schlesinger Jr., once an advisor to Presidents
John Kennedy and Lyndon Johnson, said bluntly, "I don't think
Carter should have brought in his intimacy with God, Jesus and so
forth . . . . If he feels that, bully for him, but it's totally irrelevant to
the campaign!"

In terms of a checklist for public service, Schlesinger was undoubtedly right. The American Constitution prohibits religious tests for public office. But serious-minded Christians found it impossible to look at
government or any other social institution (the family, the courts, the
schools) through totally secular eyes.

That was the Evangelical's dilemma in the Age of Ideologies. They
offered millions of people a consoling personal faith in the face of

447

apocalyptic fears, but could they also lead America in another great awakening of social ideals?

RETURN OF THE OLD-TIME RELIGION

In the 1970s, Jimmy Carter, the former Georgia governor, was a symbol of a revitalized evangelical Christianity in the United States. The old-time religion was showing remarkable signs of new life.

Many Americans found this surprising. They had been brought up to think that revivalism was the province of faith healers, holy rollers, and counterfeit preachers: a thing of high emotions, bad taste, and simplemindedness. Yet in the 1970s prominent figures by the scores—in politics, sports, and entertainment—spoke freely about their faith in Christ.

Religion that was supposedly confined to the Bible Belt suddenly appeared all over the country. America, it seemed, had discovered born-again Christianity. After a generation of steady growth, Evangelicals numbered forty-five million in the United States and had changed the face of American Protestantism.

The so-called mainline—or to use Martin Marty's term, *public*—Protestants belonged to the major denominations in the National Council of Churches: Episcopalians, Methodists, Presbyterians, American Baptists, United Church of Christ. But in most of the denominations Evangelicals formed a conservative minority, so that about one-third of the thirty-six million Protestants in the National Council were evangelical. When these were added to about thirty-three million Evangelicals outside the Council, the so-called Private Protestants constituted a major religious body, close in number to the forty-six million Roman Catholics.

Of course, Evangelicals represented no single approach to America's problems. The movement included a number of distinct subgroups. Among them were the fundamentalists, the militant right wing churchmen who opposed all accommodation to contemporary culture, and the Pentecostals, who had experienced the "baptism in the Holy Spirit" and practiced such divine gifts as speaking in tongues and miraculous healing by prayer. These Pentecostals, or *charismatics* as some preferred, included everything from Episcopalians and nearly a million Roman Catholics, to faith healers and assorted tent preachers. Most Evangelicals, though, were basically conventional Protestants who held staunchly to the authority of the Bible and to orthodox Christian doctrines. They believed in making a conscious personal commitment to Christ: a spiritual encounter, gradual or instantaneous, known as the born-again experience.

Who Are the Charismatics?

The term *charismatic* is used with great variety. There are charismatic denominations such as Assemblies of God, but charismatics also make up significant percentages of other denominations, such as the Episcopalians.

As a simple way to begin, people typically are described as charismatic if the exercise of the more dramatic spiritual gifts, such as tongue speaking, healing, and acts of prophecy, is an important and routine part of the church's worship and an individual believer's personal devotion.

In spite of the growth of the evangelical movement and its sudden visibility in the media it gave little evidence of reshaping the ideas and ideals of American culture. It had little impact in the government or the universities or the communication centers of the nation. The reasons for estrangement from politics, education, and the media lie in the early years of the twentieth century.

Historian George M. Marsden of Notre Dame compares Evangelicals in twentieth-century America to rootless immigrants in a new land. Only in this case Evangelicals never crossed the ocean to experience the shock of a new land. They simply held their ground while the rest of the country changed.

As we have seen, after the Civil War Southern Evangelicalism was battered by defeat and a sense of hopelessness. Much of the northern wing turned to premillennialism, the belief that Christ's return was imminent and that society would inevitably get worse before it occurred. By the late 1800s the great evangelist Dwight L. Moody literally preached a lifeboat ethic: "I look on the world as a wrecked vessel. God has given me a lifeboat and said, 'Save all you can.'" Thus many conservatives withdrew from the social arena. Evangelical historian Timothy Smith describes this as the Great Reversal.

The roots of fundamentalism lie in this surrender of social concern. In the 1880s and 1890s Bible study and personal holiness seemed more rewarding than the reform of American life.

Beginning with a small meeting at Swampscott, Massachusetts, in July 1876, Evangelicals from many denominations gathered in summer Bible conferences to discuss the second coming of Christ. The Baptist minister A. J. Gordon of Boston played a leading role in organizing two large prophecy conferences in New York (1878) and Chicago (1886) at which the essentials of premillennialism were hammered out: The world will continue to decline into sin until the Antichrist is loosed for one last orgy of destruction, at the end of which time Christ will return with his saints to establish an earthly reign of one thousand years. A peculiar form of premillennialism was articulated with growing clarity in such conferences. Its name, dispensationalism, is not very suggestive, but the last three dispensations (ages) before eternity are crucial to its classical version. Jesus offered himself as a literal king for the nation of Israel to rule from Jerusalem; the Hebrew people rejected his offer. This rejection marked the end (or the postponement) of the first of these three ages. The next age was the age of the church; being rejected as Israel's king, Jesus turned his attention to the non-Hebrews. To these Gentiles he offered another covenant of grace and forgiveness that followed the covenant of law and obedience. Eventually, this age runs its course, ending in failure, as does every covenant. Jesus' second return marks the beginning of the last of the three ages: he returns as king and rules through Israel over the entire world for one thousand years. This version of premillennial thinking was a serious departure from historic premillennialism; it demanded that God had two different peoples, Israel and the church. These two peoples stem from two completely unrelated covenants, which operated by completely different economies: grace versus obedience to the law. In its original form, it breaks several longstanding beliefs: that Jesus and his church fulfilled the Old Testament promises, the unity of the Bible, grace in the Old Testament, and Jesus' call for obedience in the New Testament. Additionally, there was much in the New Testament that was for Israel and not for the church, most remarkably the Sermon on the Mount. Many amendments to this theory have made it more acceptable to more orthodox-minded believers (such as Presbyterians). Today it is widely held among the conservative Protestants. Ironically, it shares some convictions with modern thinkers: with liberals, it holds that Jesus was initially to be understood in earthy, political terms; it also explains (in concert with other ideas, such as the cessation of gifts) why the current church life seemed so different from the experience reflected in the Bible.

Three Crucial Ages of Dispensationalism

	...Jewish age	Church age	1,000 year rule
People	Israel	Church	Israel/ World
Predominant Race	Hebrews	Gentiles	Hebrews/ World
Jesus' role	Jesus comes to be king over Israel.	After rejection, Jesus turns to Gentiles and mercifully dies to pay for sin.	Jesus returns to rule for 1,000 years.

During the same years other Evangelicals turned to holiness conferences. Concern for a second blessing, entire sanctification, or Christian perfection had always been a main tenet of Methodist revivalism. In the late nineteenth century members of other religious communions came to share this concern. Holiness groups, such as the Church of the Nazarene, as well as deeper life conferences, urged believers to yield themselves to reliance on the Holy Spirit as a way to find the victorious Christian life.

While increased attention both to the end times and to personal Christian living had firm biblical roots, it also gave traditional Evangelicals a way of maintaining their faith in a culture over which they were steadily losing control. If they could not shape the affairs of men, they could find comfort in the world of the Spirit.

THE APPEARANCE OF FUNDAMENTALISM

Fundamentalism is usually dated from a series of twelve small books published from 1910 to 1915 containing articles and essays designed to defend fundamental Christian truths. Three million copies of the books were sent free to theological students, Christian ministers, and missionaries all over the world.

The project arose in the thinking of Lyman Stewart, a wealthy oilman in Southern California, who was convinced that something was needed to reaffirm Christian truths in the face of biblical criticism and liberal theology. After listening to the Reverend Amzi C. Dixon preach in August 1909, Stewart secured Dixon's help in publishing *The Fundamentals*.

Stewart then enlisted the financial support of his brother, Milton, and Dixon, pastor of the Moody Church in Chicago, chose a committee, which included the evangelist R. A. Torrey, to assist in the editorial work.

Sixty-four authors were eventually chosen to appear in *The Fundamentals*. The American premillennial movement and the English Keswick Conference were well-represented. Other conservatives, however, were also among the contributors, including E. Y. Mullins of Southern Baptist Seminary and Benjamin B. Warfield of Princeton Seminary.

World War I delayed the outbreak of the "modernist-fundamentalist" controversy in the Protestant denominations. But shortly after the doughboys came home from Europe, Baptists, Presbyterians, Methodists, and the Disciples of Christ launched their own war of words over the values and the dangers of liberal theology in the churches.

In 1920, Curtis Lee Laws, Baptist editor of the *Watchman-Examiner*, called "fundamentalists" within the Northern Baptist Convention to a conference in Buffalo, New York. This group of conservatives, popularly called The Fundamentalist Fellowship, were moderate conservatives. They believed that the modernists were surrendering the fundamentals of the gospel: the sinful nature of man, his inability to be saved apart from God's grace, the centrality of Jesus' death for the regeneration of the individual and the renewal of society, and the authoritative revelation of the Bible. This group was the first to apply the name *fundamentalist* to itself. They were unable to gain the adoption of a confession of faith among Northern Baptists, but Laws and his associates did not consider their cause a lost one. In 1924 Laws wrote that certain schools of his denomination had checked the inroads of liberalism and that the investigation of the mission societies, advocated by the fundamentalists, resulted in changes that made the creation of a new mission unnecessary. More militant Baptists disagreed with Laws and formed the fundamentalist General Association of Regular Baptists for fundamentalists.

The Presbyterian champion of orthodoxy was Professor J. Gresham Machen of Princeton Theological Seminary. In 1929 the General Assembly of the Presbyterian Church authorized a reorganization of the seminary. Machen and a small retinue of distinguished professors at the school felt that a merger of boards strengthened the liberal influence in the school. They withdrew from Princeton in protest and founded Westminster Theological Seminary in Philadelphia.

When Machen refused to break his ties with the Independent Board of Presbyterian Foreign Missions, he was brought to trial in his church's courts and found guilty of rebellion against superiors. As a result conservatives in the denomination founded the Orthodox Presbyterian and the Bible Presbyterian churches.

At the heart of these modernist-fundamentalist differences were conflicting views of the Bible. While a variety of positions could be found in each camp, Shailer Mathews and Machen may be taken as representatives of the two parties that emerged.

Mathews was professor of historical theology and Dean of the Divinity School at the University of Chicago. In 1924 his book *The Faith of Modernism* set forth his case for a view of the Bible based upon "scientific investigations." Confessional theology, he said, considers Scripture supernaturally given.

> The modernist uses Scripture as the trustworthy record and product of a developing religion . . . . In discovering this experience of God

and accepting it as his own religious ancestry the modernist affirms the trustworthiness of the Scripture . . . . Christianity becomes not the acceptance of a literature but a reproduction of attitudes and faith, a fellowship with those ancient men of imperfect morals whose hearts found God.

All the hallmarks of liberal theology are here: (1) the evolutionary philosophy applied to religion; (2) the optimistic view of man centering in his religious experience; and (3) the moralistic conception of God, who can so readily be "found" by man.

In 1915, in *The Princeton Theological Review*, Professor Machen, probably the most articulate defender of orthodoxy, answered the modernist's appeal to historical and literary methods. "The student of the New Testament," he said, "should be primarily an historian. . . . The Bible contains a record of something that has happened, something that puts a new face upon life . . . It is the life and death and resurrection of Jesus Christ. The authority of the Bible should be tested here at the central point. Is the Bible right about Jesus? . . . A teacher and example, or a Savior?"

Here, too, are the marks of early fundamentalism: (1) a supernatural Jesus attested by his resurrection from the dead; (2) a trustworthy Bible, the fountain of the Christian faith; and (3) the need of men to have "a new face upon life."

WILLIAM JENNINGS BRYAN, SYMBOL OF CHANGE

Squalls in the denominations, however, were indicators of wider winds of change in America. If we looked for one man whose life illustrates the shift in American views, few would serve as admirably as William Jennings Bryan.

Thanks to television, Broadway, and the movie *Inherit the Wind*, the mere mention of Bryan's name recalls that packed courtroom in Dayton, Tennessee, where, on a hot July day in 1925, Bryan and Clarence Darrow nearly came to blows over the Genesis account of man's origin.

The setting was the trial of John Scopes, who had been arraigned for violating Tennessee's law against the teaching of evolution in the public schools.

Darrow, at the height of his powers as a courtroom artist, confused and embarrassed the aging Bryan's attempts to defend the biblical record. A press corps overwhelmingly hostile to Bryan's point of view disgorged millions of words of coverage to a watching nation. The image of a sweat-streaked Bryan wilting before the searing rational assault from Darrow maintains its overrated and largely undeserved place as a symbol of the stupidity of Bible-believing American Christians. Ironically, it was Bryan who was the true political progressive. *Inherit the Wind* leaves a conspicuously deceptive impression. One would gather that Bryan was a hyper-conservative naysayer and Darrow was the progressively minded forward-thinker. Writers invented a story line that Bryan had bullied Mr. Scopes's fiancée to legitimize the trial strategy of demonizing Bryan.

The irony of Bryan's image as a bigoted fanatic arises from the fact that all of his life he stood for the common man. No one fought harder for "the average American." It was Bryan who was against social Darwinism and championed women's right to vote. These two ideas are linked: if emotionally oriented women had not evolved enough to be sufficiently rational then they should not be allowed to vote. As leader of the Progressive cause in the Democratic party, Bryan was a three-time candidate for president of the United States, and secretary of state in the cabinet of President Woodrow Wilson. As Wilson's secretary of state Bryan expressed his devotion to peace by negotiating arbitration treaties with thirty countries. When the crisis of 1914 broke, however, his treaties proved ineffective after the Germans sank the *Lusitania* on May 7, 1915. President Wilson and the cabinet opposed the use of the treaties. This conflict of policy led to Bryan's resignation.

This near end of his political career, however, only meant new opportunities in Bryan's reforming and religious career. He soon threw himself into the Prohibition cause and played no small role in securing passage of the Eighteenth Amendment outlawing alcoholic beverages across the country after January 1920. This was probably the last successful evangelical crusade for a moral America.

Later, Americans tended to view Prohibition as the austere weapon of a pack of bluenosed Puritans who found life a joyless thing and were determined that no one else should be allowed to distill a drop of pleasure from it. That attitude is itself an example of the shift in American culture.

Bryan saw Prohibition as another struggle against those selfish interests that put private profit above human welfare and feed upon the helplessness of the masses. Those who labor for Prohibition, he wrote, "are helping to create conditions which will bring the highest good to the greatest number, . . . for it is not injustice to any man to refuse him permission to enrich himself by injuring his fellowmen."

Bryan's last great crusade was the one that drew him directly into the fundamentalist movement, the effort to outlaw the teaching of evolution in the public schools of America.

Prior to the 1920s Bryan frequently revealed his awareness of the teachings of Darwin and the dangers they posed for public morality. As early as 1905, after reading Darwin's *Descent of Man*, he said that the biologist's conception of man's origin would weaken the cause of democracy.

In the spring of 1921 Bryan issued a series of attacks on evolution that instantly placed him in the forefront of fundamentalist forces. Whether evolution was right or wrong was not his concern. He never intended to refute evolution on scientific grounds. "The objection to evolution," he said, "is not, primarily, that it is not true. The principle objection is that it is highly harmful to those who accept it."

His lecture, "The Menace of Darwinism," was printed in pamphlet form and widely distributed. Morality and virtue, he wrote, are dependent upon religion and a belief in God, and therefore anything that weakens belief in God weakens man and makes him unable to do good. By putting man on the level of a brute and ignoring all spiritual values, evolutionary theory applied to social theory robbed man of his major stimulus to moral living. Without a moral compass it seemed reasonable that the strong should flourish and not be inhibited by concern for the weak.

Legal opposition to evolution took the form of thirty-seven anti-evolution bills introduced into twenty state legislatures between 1921 and 1929. They were drawn up by a generation that ratified the Eighteenth Amendment, products of an American belief that legislative action can assist public morality.

The Scopes Trial was the consequence of the law adopted in Tennessee, which made it unlawful for a public school teacher "to teach the theory which denies the story of divine creation of man as taught in the Bible, and to teach instead that man has descended from a lower order of animals."

The immediate issue before the Dayton court was whether John Scopes, the young high school biology teacher, had violated the Tennessee law. But the legal question was strictly secondary. Businessmen and reporters turned the trial into a circus. The star performers were Bryan, who served as a prosecuting attorney, and Clarence Darrow, Chicago's brilliant, well-known lawyer, who defended Scopes. Both men saw the larger dimensions of the trial.

"My only purpose in coming to Dayton," said Bryan with a glance at Darrow, was "to protect the Word of God against the greatest atheist or agnostic in the United States!" The courtroom broke into applause. Darrow argued that nothing less than intellectual freedom was on trial and proceeded to make Scopes the real plaintiff and Bryan the real defendant. He used Bryan's own testimony as evidence of fundamentalist stupidity.

When all was over, Scopes was found guilty and fined a token sum. Bryan, thus, won in Dayton, Darrow in the rest of the country. Five days after the trial Bryan passed away quietly in his sleep, leaving all of his reform causes behind. In a very real sense the evangelical crusade for a Christian America died with him.

A short time later the Great Depression hit America hard and evangelical Christianity struggled with the rest of the country. It survived in assorted voluntary societies and radio broadcasts, but the public often stereotyped fundamentalists as closed-minded, ignorant, belligerent, and separatistic.

THE RENEWAL OF EVANGELICAL CHRISTIANITY

After World War II, however, evangelical Christianity returned to public prominence in America. Its best known voice had a soft North Carolina accent. Billy Graham became a household name by preaching to thousands in every major stadium in the United States, by a regularly scheduled radio broadcast, and by telecasts on national networks. *Decision* magazine, published by his evangelistic association, went to multiplied millions of homes.

Graham had grown up in the Southern Baptist and Southern Presbyterian tradition. He had trained at Bob Jones University, Florida Bible Institute, and Wheaton College. After a pastorate in Western Springs, Illinois, a suburb of Chicago, he entered full-time evangelistic work with a youth organization called Youth for Christ. After a highly successful and widely publicized evangelistic campaign in Los Angeles (1949) Graham's fame spread rapidly. He was soon conducting city-wide crusades around the world.

Billy Graham, however, was only the most prominent name in a new style evangelicalism. Many conservative Christians expressed dissatisfaction with the drift of fundamentalism between the two world wars. Most had no criticism of the doctrines of the movement, but they felt it had stumbled into the mire of some unfortunate emphases.

As early as 1947 Carl F. H. Henry in his *Uneasy Conscience of Modern Fundamentalism* expressed distress over fundamentalism's failure to apply basic Christian truths to crucial problems confronting modern man.

In 1956 Billy Graham led a group of Evangelicals in launching a new periodical called *Christianity Today*. Carl Henry left his teaching post at Fuller Theological Seminary to serve as editor. In the beginning the magazine was sent without charge to theological students and clergymen of various doctrinal persuasions, assuring it of a wide circulation.

In the first issue Henry said the magazine aimed to express historical Christianity to the present generation. The founders felt that theological liberals had failed to meet the moral and spiritual needs of people. The editors accepted unreservedly the "complete reliability of the written Word of God." But they intended to present the implications of the gospel for every area of life.

The evangelical awakening gained unexpected reinforcement in 1960 from another source of personal Christianity, Pentecostalism. The Pentecostal experience—"the baptism of the Holy Spirit with the evidence of speaking in tongues"—was not new. The spark of twentieth-century Pentecostalism was a three-year-long revival, beginning in 1906, at the Azusa Street Mission in Los Angeles. There were personal experiences of tongue speaking earlier, but Azusa Street ignited worldwide Pentecostalism. Christians from all over North America, Europe, and the Third World visited Azusa Street and carried the fire back home.

Pentecostal denominations followed. The largest in the United States were the Assemblies of God, the Church of God in Christ, the Church of God, and the Pentecostal Holiness Church. These were usually filled with socially and economically depressed people. That is the reason the secular press took note in 1960 when the Pentecostal experience broke out in middle-class Lutheran and Episcopal congregations. That made hot copy.

This new explosion of Pentecostal passion was dubbed neo-Pentecostalism. Its fallout drifted in all directions. Soon America was dotted with charismatic prayer groups, composed mostly of members of mainline Protestant churches. They claimed to have found a new dimension in their Christian lives through the Pentecostal baptism.

Among the Lutherans, the American Lutheran Church saw most of the action in the early 1960s. Controversy that erupted in 1963 was only subdued when authorities issued guidelines for practicing Pentecostals. Then in 1967 the experience touched Missouri Synod Lutheran circles. Several of its ministers were defrocked because of public statements on the issue.

The extent of Pentecostal penetration of Lutheran churches was suggested in 1972 by the more than ten thousand who attended the First International Lutheran Conference on the Holy Spirit in Minneapolis, Minnesota.

In 1970 the General Assembly of the United Presbyterian Church in the U.S.A. issued a report on "The Work of the Holy Spirit." Reflecting two years of careful study, it was hailed as one of the best official statements on the charismatic renewal and brought about considerable growth in the movement. By 1975 some spokesmen estimated that between ten thousand and fifteen thousand members of the United Presbyterian Church and the Presbyterian Church in the U.S.A. had received the Pentecostal baptism.

These two denominations—Lutherans and Presbyterians—are only representative of the growth in other mainline Protestant denominations and in Roman Catholicism.

As the 1970s closed in the United States, Evangelicals of all varieties were troubled by the question, does faith matter? For decades they had assumed that significant numbers of born-again Christians would make a difference in the moral climate of America. The 1970s, however, brought that assumption to a severe test. Evangelicals had their numbers, but American society was plagued by crime, divorce, racism, violence, sexual perversion, alcoholism, and drugs. Some observers wondered if Arthur Schlesinger Jr. could have been speaking not only of Jimmy Carter but of all Evangelicals: "If you feel that, bully for you, but it is totally irrelevant."

Suggestions for Further Reading

Levine, Lawrence W. *Defender of the Faith.* New York: Oxford, 1965.

Marsden, George M. *Fundamentalism and American Culture.* New York: Oxford, 1980.

Noll, Mark, David W. Bebbington, and George A. Rawlyk, eds. *Evangelicalism.* New York: Oxford, 1994.

Quebedeaux, Richard. *The New Charismatics.* Garden City, NY: Doubleday, 1976.

Sandeen, Ernest R. *The Roots of Fundamentalism.* Chicago: University of Chicago Press, 1970.

*Synan, Vinson. *The Century of the Holy Spirit: 100 years of Pentecostal and Charismatic Renewal, 1901–2001.* Nashville: Thomas Nelson, 2001.

Woodbridge, John, Mark A. Noll, and Nathan O. Hatch. *The Gospel in America.* Grand Rapids: Zondervan, 1979.

CHAPTER 44

NEW CREEDS
FOR BREAKFAST

The Ecumenical Movement

SOMETIME BEFORE THE ASSEMBLY of the World Council of Churches in
1961 at New Delhi, India, Willem Adolph Visser't Hooft was having
breakfast in a Leningrad hotel with a delegation of Russian Orthodox
leaders. At the time the constitutional definition of the World Council was, "A fellowship of churches which accept our Lord Jesus Christ
as God and Saviour." The Russians complained that this definition
overlooked the Trinitarian basis of Christianity prized by Orthodox
churches.

Visser't Hooft recalled that Protestants had often voiced another
complaint: the absence of any mention of Scripture. And he saw that
he had a chance, by the right words, to stress the unifying elements
of Christianity while diplomatically playing down differences. "So," he
later recalled, "I took the breakfast menu and wrote out a new formula."

A few months later at New Delhi the Council adopted Visser't Hooft's
breakfast-menu definition as the Council's new credo. It reads, "The
World Council of Churches is a fellowship of churches which confess
the Lord Jesus Christ as God and Saviour according to the Holy Scriptures and therefore seek to fulfill together their common calling to the
glory of one God, Father, Son and Holy Spirit."

That breakfast maneuver was one of the most brilliant moves of
Visser't Hooft's long career as General Secretary of the World Coun-
cil. It brought thirty million Russian Orthodox Christians within the
Council and changed the face of the ecumenical movement.

In the sixteenth century only four major divisions separated the churches of the Reformation: Lutheran, Reformed, Anabaptist, and Anglican. Soon, however, a number of denominations appeared on the scene, most of them established by believers convinced of the importance of some particular teaching of Scripture. By the twentieth century more than two hundred denominations crowded the landscape in the United States alone. The force within Christianity was centrifugal—away from centralization—often independent, and sometimes divisive.

In the twentieth century, however, another force, this one centripetal, drew Christians toward cooperation, merger and united action. We call this force *ecumenism*.

MOVEMENTS TOWARD CHRISTIAN UNITY

Ecumenical means worldwide or universal. Applied to Christian churches, it implies the oneness of Christians in the faith, wherever they may be found. This unity can be either a spiritual reality apart from organizations of men, as Evangelicals are inclined to argue, or an effort to create some federation of churches or some merger of denominations. We call the spirit of unity *ecumenicity* and the organizational effort the *ecumenical movement*. The creation of national and worldwide councils of churches we label *conciliar ecumenism*.

On very few subjects do all men think alike. Certainly Christians do not think alike about their faith. They have their differences about doctrine, morality, worship, and organization. And they hold their views not as mere opinions but as religious convictions.

As a result Christians disagree over the divisions in Christianity. Some defend their denominational distinctives; others call them a sin and a scandal. In either case, ecumenicity was one of the hallmarks of twentieth-century Christianity.

How, then, have Christians expressed this spirit of unity?

The first significant effort in modern times to encourage cooperation among Protestants was the Evangelical Alliance. Organized in London in 1846, the Alliance brought together Christian believers from fifty evangelical bodies in England and America. In time branches were established in nine European countries. The Alliance promoted religious liberty and encouraged cooperative activities, but toward the end of the nineteenth century its enthusiasm cooled.

As the Alliance, composed of individuals, showed signs of apathy, a new expression of unity appeared: a federation of churches (or denominations). In 1908 thirty-one American denominations joined in the

Federal Council of Churches. While the Council was active in issuing pronouncements on social, economic, and political questions, many conservative churchmen criticized its liberal theology. In 1950 the Federal Council was absorbed by a larger body, the National Council of Churches of Christ.

However, the most ambitious expression of ecclesiastical ecumenism is the World Council of Churches, formed in 1948 at Amsterdam. It is helpful to think of the World Council as a major river, a religious Mississippi, flowing from three tributaries. These three streams are The International Missionary Council, The Conference on Life and Work, and The Conference on Faith and Order. All three trace their sources to that peak of modern ecumenical history, The International Missionary Conference at Edinburgh in 1910. The Edinburgh conference drew together over one thousand delegates from all over the world to consider the problems of world missions in the non-Roman Catholic world. In discussing missions the delegates discovered a great sense of unity.

The early decades of the ecumenical movement were overshadowed by four towering leaders: an American, John R. Mott; a Canadian, Charles H. Brent; a Swede, Nathan Söderblom; and a Dutchman, Willem A. Visser't Hooft.

John R. Mott (1865–1955), a Methodist layman, combined a deep religious faith, evangelistic zeal, power over public assemblies, and compelling, convincing speech. At the age of twenty-three he became student secretary of the International Committee of the Young Men's Christian Association (YMCA). Sensing the need for greater coordination of student work, he founded in Sweden the World's Student Christian Federation, bringing together student ministries in America, Great Britain, the Scandinavian countries, and Germany. The work of the Student Federation gave Mott hundreds of personal contacts in Christian ministries and made him a natural choice for chairmanship of the Edinburgh Missionary Conference.

After the epoch-making Edinburgh Conference, Mott served as chairman of the Continuation Committee. When the International Missionary Council was created in 1921, he served for twenty years as its first chairman. No leader of the world council of churches contributed more to the spread of Christianity. Charles Brent (1862–1929) was a Canadian Anglican who served as a missionary to the Philippine Islands. Unlike Mott, who had a passionate zeal for unity based on the love of Christ, Brent was more conscious of the doctrinal differences that separated the churches. He saw Anglicanism as the bridge that might span these differences. When the Edinburgh Conference voted to explore ways of overcoming the conflicts among mission-sending societies, Brent carried the recommendation to his fellow Anglicans at their triennial convention in Chicago. On his urging the convention appointed a committee to invite "all Churches which accept Jesus Christ as God and Saviour to join in conferences following the general method of the World's Missionary Conference, for the consideration of all questions pertaining to Faith and Order of the Church of Christ."

Due to World War I and its sequel, the first World Conference on Faith and Order was unable to meet until 1927. That year at Lausanne, Switzerland, 150 representatives from 69 denominations met in August and passed a series of resolutions that laid the foundations for the future World Council.

Brent believed that cooperation among churches was possible only on the basis of agreement on essentials of the faith. Disunity, he said, is fundamentally creedal. Until these differences are resolved, Christians will find no authentic unity. Faith and Order became synonymous with belief and worship.

THE LIFE AND WORK MOVEMENT

Nathan Söderblom (1866–1931), Lutheran Archbishop of Uppsala in Sweden, was the founder and chief promoter of the Life and Work Movement. When the King of Sweden unexpectedly appointed him archbishop in 1914, conservatives within the church questioned his orthodoxy. Not without reason.

Söderblom rejected faith in the divine and human nature of Christ because he considered it unacceptable to modern man. He stressed revelation as an ongoing process, not limited to the apostolic age. True religion, he said, rests not in our conception of God but in our moral character. Religion is what a man is or what he does, not what he believes.

Söderblom, therefore, did not expect to find Christian unity by doctrinal agreement, as Brent hoped, but by history. Each Christian group, he said, should respect the others and share with the others their doctrinal differences and gradually the one revelation to the human race would unfold through the successive ages of man.

Söderblom's great work, however, was not in theology but in bringing Christians together in common concern. He was the mastermind behind the First Conference on Life and Work held at Stockholm. In August 1925, five hundred delegates from thirty-nine countries and ninety-one denominations decided that the problems of social morality were too great to be solved by individual effort. The Christian community must accept responsibility for the common good.

Strange as it may seem, by 1937 both the Conference on Faith and Order and the Conference on Life and Work recognized that the quest for Christian unity demanded a new, more inclusive organization. While meeting in Britain that year the two conferences joined in issuing a call for the formation of the World Council of Churches.

Adolf Hitler and World War II delayed the creation of the World Council, but in 1948 the first assembly convened in Amsterdam, bringing together 351 delegates representing 147 denominations from 44 countries. The principal nonparticipants were the Roman Catholics, many conservative Evangelicals, and the Russian Orthodox.

During these significant early years of the World Council, the General Secretary was Willem Adolph Visser't Hooft (1900–1985). Following in the footsteps of John R. Mott, Visser't Hooft had served as secretary of the World's Committee of the Y.M.C.A. and then in the same office in the World's Student Christian Federation. In 1938 he seemed the natural choice to lead the Provisional Committee that shaped the World Council of Churches at Amsterdam.

Swiss Theologian Karl Barth had a vast influence on Visser't Hooft. "Barth felt that the church had almost lost its soul in making adjustments to historical trends," Visser't Hooft once said. "He called the church again to be itself." He recalled that the unofficial slogan of the men who launched the ecumenical movement was "Let the Church be the Church." And this, said the Dutch leader, "did not mean that the church should run away from the world. It did mean that the church was not merely an echo of trends in the world."

One of Visser't Hooft's pet projects after World War II was the creation of an Ecumenical Institute in Switzerland for the training of leaders in the church unity movement. In the United States one evening at dinner with financiers Thomas W. Lamont and John D. Rockefeller Jr., he described the plan to Rockefeller, who replied, "You must ask for more money." Rockefeller later contributed about $1 million to set up the Ecumenical Institute at Boissy, Switzerland.

Thanks to Visser't Hooft's diplomacy an assembly of the World Council of Churches became a colorful mosaic of cultures, continents, and concerns. Every gathering had theological conservatives from Eastern Orthodox countries of Eastern Europe and the Middle East, secular theologians from Europe and North America, Evangelicals from Europe and the Third World, confessional Lutherans from Scandinavia, and liberation spokesmen from Latin America.

The World Council did not claim to be a super-church. According to its constitution it could not legislate for its member churches. Its aim was understanding and cooperation among its members and

Christian unity wherever possible. Statements of the assemblies inevitably reflected a compromise of competing views, as Visser't Hooft's breakfast in Leningrad so well illustrates.

Later assemblies were held at Evanston, Illinois (1954); New Delhi, India (1961); Uppsala, Sweden (1968); and Nairobi, Kenya (1975). At New Delhi the Russian Orthodox Church joined the Council and the International Missionary Council was brought under World Council administration.

With the passing of the years, the doctrinal emphasis of the Faith and Order Conferences declined and the social concerns of Life and Work increased. The assemblies at Uppsala and Nairobi reflected the inroads of secularism in the churches. Concern for social questions like racism, war and peace, poverty and unemployment, alcoholism and drug addiction, and the women's liberation movement became so integral to the councils of churches in various countries that the specific aim of fostering reunion among the dismembered church bodies was left increasingly to other agencies and institutions.

DENOMINATIONAL MERGERS

The World Council of Churches, however, was only the most conspicuous expression of the ecumenical movement. Zeal for unity also created denominational mergers and international alliances.

In the United States, where denominationalism has been so pronounced, over thirty mergers of denominations were completed from 1900 to 1970, including such major creations as The United Methodists and United Presbyterians. In some cases they were reunions of church bodies that had split over such issues as the race question in the nineteenth century (Methodists) or of groups in the same tradition that had immigrated to America from different countries (Lutherans).

Outside the United States the most significant merger was the Church of South India, formed in 1947 through the union of three religious bodies: the Anglican Church of India, Burma and Ceylon; the South India Province of the Methodist Church; and the South India United Church, itself the result of a movement that brought Presbyterian, Congregational, and Dutch Reformed bodies into union.

A proposed merger of similar dimensions would create a new church of nineteen million members in the United States. The idea was originally advanced in 1960 by Eugene Carson Blake, chief executive officer of the United Presbyterian Church in the U.S.A. (Northern Presbyterians) and later General Secretary of the World Council of Churches. Blake proposed that the Protestant Episcopal Church and Northern Presbyterians jointly invite the Methodists and the United Church of

Christ to form a new Christian Church. Dismayed at the hundreds of divisions within Protestantism, Blake said, "I don't believe it is God's will to have so many churches in the United States."

The proposal was welcomed by Protestant Episcopal Bishop James A. Pike, who said, "The Holy Ghost is on our side whenever we break through the barriers between Christian bodies. He will increasingly provide guidance to show the ways in which we can defeat the complacent obstinacy of our national church bodies in this regard."

At the General Convention of the Protestant Episcopal Church at Detroit in September 1961, the House of Bishops considered the proposal to accept the invitation of the United Presbyterian Assembly. A whole day had been reserved for debate on the issue, and a huge crowd jammed the side aisles of the room in Cobo Hall to witness the fireworks. Within thirty seconds or so the motion was passed unanimously.

"I'm quite speechless!" gasped presiding Bishop Arthur C. Lichtenberger. Echoing apparently in the minds of all the delegates were the words of the prayer uttered by Bishop Lichtenberger just before the first vote was taken: "Look mercifully, O Lord, on the broken body of Thy Church."

The convention closed with a stirring appeal from the House of Bishops for the reunion of world Christianity. Declaring that the challenge is one that "in faithfulness to God we cannot evade," the bishops urged Christians "to work and pray without ceasing until by God's grace and in His time the divisions by which we dishonor our one Lord are done away."

With the support of the other participating denominations the Consultation of Church Union (COCU) launched its search for a plan of merger. Later the Consultation changed its name to the Church of Christ Uniting in order to allow other denominations to join in the merger. The passing of time, however, dampened the early enthusiasm. After twenty years the participating denominations continued to search for the right formula for union.

Besides these mergers the twentieth century brought together world confessional alliances. Churches throughout the world with similar confessions of faith and church organizations have met periodically for discussion and fellowship. Among these alliances are:

The International Congregational Council,
The Mennonite World Conference,
The World Methodist Conference,
The Baptist World Alliance,
The Lutheran World Federation, and
The World Alliance of Reformed and Presbyterian Churches.

Through all these years the most persistent critics of conciliar ecumenism were the conservative Evangelicals. Holding staunchly to the authority of the Bible, Evangelicals know that Jesus prayed that his disciples would be one, but they question the federation form of Christian unity.

They challenge the inadequate doctrinal basis of the World Council and its commitment to evangelism. They are especially troubled by the increasing involvement of the World Council in political activities in developing nations.

Since the Uppsala Assembly (1968) the World Council appears to consider the unity of the church as a sign of the unity of mankind. Conservative Evangelicals contend that this can easily lead to support for humanistic goals for society rather than a distinctively Christian witness. The difference in church and world becomes less a matter of faith and unbelief and more a difference in oppressed and oppressor. Salvation becomes liberation.

EVANGELICAL EXPRESSIONS OF UNITY

Deeply rooted in revivalism, Evangelicals have always stressed the necessity of a personal religious experience. They have little interest in the proper form of the church; their primary concern is the mission of the church. George Whitefield spoke for Evangelicals of every generation when, preaching from the courthouse balcony in Philadelphia, he raised his eyes to the heavens and cried out,

> Father Abraham, whom have you in heaven? Any Episcopalians? No! Any Presbyterians? No! Any Independents or Methodists? No, no, no! Whom have you there? We don't know those names here. All who are here are Christians . . . . Oh, is this the case? Then God help us to forget party names and to become Christians in deed and truth.

In the early 1940s American Evangelicals created two organizations: the National Association of Evangelicals and the American Council of Christian Churches. Both were loyal to orthodox Christianity but differed in their structure and in their attitude toward conciliar ecumenism. The American Council was especially critical not only of the National Council and World Council of Churches but of all who were in any way associated with them.

On the international level Evangelicals turned to a series of congresses to encourage united effort in evangelism. Inspired by the massive crusades of evangelist Billy Graham, The World Congress on Evangelism in Berlin (1966) drew participants from more than one hundred countries and stimulated regional and national conferences on most continents.

The 1974 International Congress on World Evangelization, meeting in Lausanne, Switzerland, gave clear evidence of a new maturity in evangelical views of Christian unity. An international group of 142 evangelical leaders under the honorary chairmanship of Billy Graham invited 2,700 participants to the Swiss city to stimulate regional groups for evangelization and to forge the Lausanne Covenant, signed by the vast majority of the participants.

The Covenant affirms "that the church's visible unity in truth is God's purpose." Two reasons support this evangelical stress on oneness: the first is theological, the second pragmatic.

The unity of the church, says the Covenant, is a gift of God through the Spirit, made possible by the cross of Christ: "He is our peace" (Eph. 2:14). The Covenant recognizes that this unity may take many forms, but "organic unions" do not always maintain unity "in truth" (Eph. 4:13).

The pragmatic reason for "visible unity in the truth" is that "evangelism . . . summons us to unity." How can we preach a gospel of reconciliation and remain unreconciled?

As a result of the Lausanne Congress, a forty-eight-member Continuation Committee for World Evangelization was created. The Committee selected an African leader, the Reverend Gottfried Osei-Mensah, as executive secretary and set about "to encourage and assist where necessary in the formation of regional and national committees to advance world evangelization in every area."

Thus, as the 1970s closed, the ecumenical spirit in the World Council of Churches apparently had turned to social concerns—at times employing overt political instruments—as the primary expression of Christian unity. Among conservative Evangelicals the aim was the restoration of evangelism to its central place in the mission of the church with the hope that unity would follow.

Suggestions for Further Reading

Brown, Robert McAfee. *The Ecumenical Revolution*. Garden City, NY: Doubleday, 1969.

Douglas, J. D., ed. *Let the Earth Hear His Voice*. Minneapolis: World Wide Publications, 1975.

Goodall, Norman. *The Ecumenical Movement*. London: Oxford University Press, 1961.

Hardon, John A. *Christianity in the Twentieth Century*. Garden City, NY: Doubleday, 1971.

Neill, Stephen. *Twentieth Century Christianity*. Garden City, NY: Doubleday, 1963.

CHAPTER 45

THE MEDICINE
OF MERCY

Roman Catholicism: Vatican II

VATICAN COUNCIL II WAS a spectacle. The four-hour opening ceremony gave every appearance of the inauguration of "a new era for
the Church." The white miters of the bishops rippled through crowded
St. Peter's Square; the portable throne of the Pope bobbed above the
stream of white like a royal barge, flanked by two rustling ostrich-
feather fans; and the choir sang *Ubi caritas et amor Deus ibi est*: "Where
charity and love are found God is present."

But Vatican II was more than a show—much more. It revealed to the
world the deep-seated presence in Roman Catholicism of a new spirit
crying out for change in the Age of Ideologies, it shattered the Protestant view of the Catholic Church as a monolithic and absolutist system,
and it marked the tacit recognition by the Catholic church, for the first
time, that those who left it in the past may have had good cause.

The traditional image of the Church of Rome, created largely by
the Council of Trent, was an impregnable fortress under attack from
the forces of secularism, modernism, and individualism. Within the
walls men could gain security and salvation because there they could
find the changeless truths of God, the true Sacrifice of the Mass, and
papal infallibility. In 1950 Pope Pius XII (1939–1958) reflected this
image when, in his encyclical *Humani Generis*, he decried the attempts
of some theologians to update Church teachings and "to weaken the
significance of the dogmas . . . by seeking to free them from concepts

and formulations long held by the Church and to return instead to the language of the Bible and the Fathers . . . ."

Vatican II (1962–1965) introduced another image. It spoke of the Church as a "Pilgrim People." It saw the Church, under God, moving through the world, along with other pilgrims, caring for the weak and weary. The Council made few claims of success or certainties, for pilgrims have not arrived. They are on the way.

How can we explain this revolution in Rome? What events conspired to challenge the besieged mentality in Roman Catholicism?

THE GOOD SHEPHERD, POPE JOHN

The prince singularly responsible for throwing open the windows of change in the Catholic castle was Angelo Roncalli. We know him as John XXIII.

Pope John often said the idea of the council came to him like a sudden inspiration of the Holy Spirit. Indeed, after his election on October 28, 1958, he ruled barely ninety days before proclaiming to the world, on January 25, 1959, his plan to convoke a council.

In many ways, however, Angelo Roncalli was uniquely prepared for his moment in history. He was almost an intuitive judge of human hopes and needs. As a young priest he spent a year teaching the life and thought of the early church fathers at the Pontifical Lateran Seminary in Rome before his superiors concluded that he was not quite safe. He dared to propose such unthinkable ideas as that mixed marriages might be allowed in certain circumstances. He languished as a letter copier in the Oriental Congregation of the Vatican until officials discovered they needed an apostolic visitor to remote Bulgaria (1925–34). From there Roncalli went for ten years to Muslim Turkey and was transferred from exile to troubled France near the end of World War II only because the Holy See did not want to spare a top man for that messy post. But Roncalli's humility and abilities charmed the French. In 1953 Pope Pius XII gave him a cardinal's red hat and appointed him spiritual leader of Venice.

Everywhere, John made a point of meeting and befriending non-Catholics. While in Turkey he helped rescue and provide for Jews escaping from Nazi Germany, and in France after the war he recoiled in horror when he saw films of Jewish bodies piled high at Buchenwald and Auschwitz: "How could this be? The mystical body of Christ!" When a group of Jews visited him after he became Pope, he walked up to them and simply repeated the biblical greeting: "I am Joseph, your brother."

In the papacy John asked to be known not as a political or learned pope but as "the good shepherd defending truth and goodness." He often sallied out of the Vatican to orphanages, jails, schools, and churches. On one occasion he even granted a papal audience to a traveling circus and fondly patted a lion cub named Dolly. He dispensed with such customs as that of barring visitors from St. Peter's dome while the pope was walking in the garden below. Said John, "Why shouldn't they look? I'm not doing anything scandalous."

After Pope John announced his intention to convene a general council, he said its purpose would be *aggiornamento*, an Italian term for "bringing up to date." It suggests not only adaptation to the outward life of contemporary society but also a complete inward change of thought. John apparently planned for the council to turn from the rigid legal patterns of the past and devote itself to the pastoral concerns of the present. Many expected *aggiornamento* to lead to a revolutionary change in the Church equal in magnitude to Constantine's conversion or the Reformation. Such a transformation called for the overthrow of the close connection of religion and politics that Constantine had introduced and a renunciation of the narrow spirit engendered by the Counter Reformation. Certainly John's aim was a Church in tune with the contemporary world. *Aggiornamento*, by anyone's definition, was an ambitious program.

From the beginning of that brisk October, when 2,540 out of 2,908 eligible cardinals, patriarchs, bishops, and abbots arrived in Rome, it was apparent Vatican II would be a council unlike any other. The sheer weight of numbers showed that. There had been only 600 to 700 fathers at the First Vatican Council, which proclaimed the infallibility of the pope in 1869–70. At the eighteen-year-long Council of Trent, which condemned the Protestant Reformation, only about 200 members voted on the decrees. This time there were 230 fathers from a country that had been mission territory until 1908: the United States. The American group was second only to the Italian, which had 430 members. There were 230 Africans and more than 300 from Asia.

Vatican II was the first council not called to combat heresy, pronounce new dogmas, or marshal the Church against hostile forces. The Council of Trent (1545–63), for example, reaffirmed the validity of indulgences, questioned by Luther, and built a doctrinal fortress against the Protestant Reformation. Pope John showed that Vatican II was called not against but for something. The Pope's opening speech was a mandate for a predominantly pastoral council rather than a doctrinal one. The days of the state church, he recognized, were over. In the age coming to birth, he said, the Church must not seek to maintain its authority by weapons of repression. It must "rule with the medicine of mercy rather than with severity." The purpose of the Council, therefore, was to enable the Church "to bring herself up to date." The modernization would bring nearer the time of the reunion of Christendom, when Christ's prayer "that they may be one" should be fulfilled.

These were brave words. When the bishops and abbots took their green upholstered folding chairs two days later for the initial working session they were soon tested. The fathers' first task was to elect members to ten permanent commissions. On their desks, for "guidance," they found lists of the members of the preparatory commissions. These commissions had been directed by cardinals of the Curia, the Vatican-based, Italian-controlled church civil service. The "guidance" lists suggested to the fathers that everything would go more smoothly if they elected the Curia-favored experts who had done the preparatory work. The issue was, who would run the council—the Curia or the fathers themselves? And implicit in that question was the even more fundamental question of how open the Vatican would be to influences from the outside world.

It did not come to a vote that day. A slightly stooped, white-haired, hawk-nosed figure rose from the presidency table of ten cardinals. Facing the two long rows of council fathers, he said, "We will not accept the lists of candidates prepared for us before the Council opened. On the other hand, we have not had time to pick our own candidates and we request a delay to make our own dispositions."

The request was seconded and approved, and the assembly broke up after meeting less than half an hour. The man who made the motion was Achille Cardinal Lienart, seventy-eight-year-old Archbishop of Lille in northern France. Cardinal Lienart had spent six months preparing for the Council. What many fathers interpreted as a harmless method of speeding up the elections he recognized as a maneuver to give the Council a special orientation. But the bishops showed they would not simply approve the decision of Curia specialists. When they elected the ten commissions two days later the final list was balanced and international.

CONSERVATIVES AND PROGRESSIVES

That bit of strategy in the opening days of the Council drew the lines between the two main groups of bishops, who became known as "conservatives" and "progressives." On the conservative side, said Father Francis J. McCool, a Jesuit Bible scholar from Maryland, were "those who see in the future a threat to the past." On the progressive side were "those who see in the future the promise of the future." The two conceptions collided on almost every issue.

The men chiefly responsible for the conservative position belonged to the Roman Curia, the central administrative body in Rome. Mostly aging Italians quite insulated from the modern world, they exerted vast influence and control not only on worldwide Catholicism but on the pope himself. They had usually been satisfied with the Church the way it was and had looked upon any efforts to change it with deep hostility.

If there was one man who represented the conservative view it was the erudite seventy-two-year-old Alfredo Cardinal Ottaviani. Born in his father's bakery in the Trastevere section of Rome, Ottaviani had spent most of his life inside the one square mile of the Vatican. He was in a sense the prisoner of his function, which was to keep watch over the purity of doctrine and to condemn heresy. In the pontifical yearbook his name appeared twenty-three times, and he was a member of seven congregations, two commissions, and one tribunal, and was protector of twenty-two religious orders. His critics said that he felt everything new is wrong. But he actually said everything new is not necessarily right.

Many conservative officials had not wanted the Council at all and referred to it privately as "the Pope's folly." They tried to sabotage and delay the preparatory work, for they thought the Council would harm the Church by revealing its internal differences. They were determined to keep intact the decision-making powers of the Curia under the control of Italian churchmen proud of their parochialism.

The progressive clerics had no single leader but gathered around an able group of cardinals from Germany, France, Austria, and the Low Countries. Typical of them was Jan Cardinal Alfrink, the tall and athletic leader of the Church in Holland. Alfrink had so many contacts with the Protestant "separated brethren" in Holland that one Italian newspaper branded him "anti-Roman."

The Council pursued its work through four distinct meetings. The first session lasted from October 11 to December 8, 1962. For the next three years, during the autumn months, three additional sessions met.

The conflicting views of the conservatives and progressives were apparent from the start. During the first session the progressives wanted to change the liturgy of the church to allow for modern languages instead of the traditional Latin and to encourage the participation of laymen in the mass. The conservatives objected, predictably.

More fundamental issues arose over the proposed document (schema) on divine revelation. Prepared by the theological commission under Cardinal Ottaviani, the statement uncompromisingly emphasized the two sources of revelation, Scripture and tradition, recognized by Roman Catholicism since the Council of Trent. The progressives, seeing no point in stressing Catholic-Protestant differences, wanted to present Scripture and tradition as two channels of a single stream. The central question was, were some truths of the faith found only in tradition or were all truths of the faith found in Scripture?

The debate raged for nearly two weeks. Finally 1,368 council fathers voted to shelve the Ottaviani document, but the vote was still short of the needed two-thirds majority. Pope John, watching the proceedings in his apartment over closed-circuit TV, intervened and had the proposal rewritten by a new committee co-chaired by Cardinal Ottaviani and Augustin Cardinal Bea, Jesuit head of the newly created Secretariat for Promoting Christian Unity and a leader of the Council progressives. Said Canadian Father Gregory Baum, a Council theologian, "This day will go down in history as the end of the Counter Reformation."

On June 3, 1963, in the midst of preparations for the next session, Pope John XXIII died. The whole religious world paused to mourn. On June 21 Cardinal Montini, Archbishop of Milan, succeeded to the papacy as Pope Paul VI. The new pope immediately announced his intention to continue the Council.

During the second session, in the fall of 1963, the new progressive understanding of the Church clashed with the traditional notions of the conservatives. Vatican I had proclaimed the infallibility and the primacy of the pope. Vatican II tried to explain how the whole company (college) of bishops related to the pope in the government of the Church. Conservatives defended papal sovereignty; progressives urged greater power for the bishops (collegiality).

Among several critical debates during the third session (September 14 to November 21, 1964) was the one over religious liberty. Would a declaration of freedom of religion make the truth of God relative? Would it feed a spirit of indifferentism? "It doesn't matter what you believe so long as you are sincere."

The third session also wrestled with guidelines for the life and ministry of priests, the mission of laymen in the world, and missionary work in non-Christian areas.

The last session from September 14 to December 8, 1965, renewed the debate on freedom of religion. The declaration of the Council on the right to freedom of conscience proclaimed that no state had the right to prevent through external pressure the preaching and acceptance of the gospel. At the same time the Church turned away from the assumption held since the age of Constantine that wherever it possessed the means (as in Spain and Italy) it had the right to exercise public power to enforce its religious demands and to further its work of salvation. By accepting the decree, Roman Catholicism solemnly renounced in principle any use of external force against the voice of conscience. Its proclamation on December 7 marked a radical break with a fifteen-hundred-year-old practice.

An impressive celebration on St. Peter's Square ended the work of the Council on December 8, 1965. *Revolutionary* is probably too strong a term for Vatican II. The traditional theology and the papal government of the Church remained intact. The sixteen decrees of the Council, with few exceptions, reflected some compromise worked out between the progressives and the conservatives.

A TIDAL WAVE OF CHANGE

Yet the Council did represent a significant break with the angry spirit of the Council of Trent and the defensive mood of Vatican I. Vatican II turned the face of Roman Catholicism toward the world, not in anger but in concern.

The work of the Council was sufficiently earthshaking to launch a tidal wave of change in the Church. The decade after the close of the Council proved to be the most tumultuous in the modern history of the Church. So many spiritual and religious landmarks were suddenly swept away that the average Catholic was left in a state of complete bewilderment.

The first wave of the deluge struck when the new liturgy was introduced shortly after the Council. Having been taught to think of the mass as a mysterious, unchangeable set of ceremonies originating with Christ himself, the average Catholic was not intellectually, spiritually, or emotionally prepared for what happened. He saw the altar brought forward and the priest face the congregation; instead of whispering the prayers in Latin, he now read them aloud in the language of the people. Many of the old ceremonies were discarded. Previously worshipers kept a prayerful attitude, hardly noticing other worshippers, but now they were asked to greet one another with a "sign of peace."

The most fundamental issue, however, focused on church authority. Until the arrival of Pope John and the Second Vatican Council, the typical Catholic took the authoritarian structure of the Church as a dictate of divine revelation. They thought of the pope as a kind of superhuman ruler whose every word possessed a supernatural authority; even the bishop they regarded with awe. In this state of affairs, few Catholics questioned the autocratic procedures customary in the

Church, though to outsiders they often appeared medieval. No one dared to challenge the bishop in the rule of his diocese as a personal fief, or the pastor in running his parish.

Vatican II raised the hopes of the progressives but they soon found that in spite of all the fine words of the Council little changed in practice. The basic structure of the Church of Rome remained pyramidal, with power flowing downward from the pope, its infallible head. The Second Vatican Council took pains to safeguard his absolute authority and merely gave the bishops a consulting position, leaving the pope free to use them or not in his governing of the Church.

In light of the new understanding of the Church projected by the Council, many Catholics found these authoritarian structures intolerable and began to agitate for democratic reforms. They dissented, demonstrated, engaged in church sit-ins, and made use of the press.

The Church of Rome reached a state of extreme tension in 1968 when Pope Paul issued his encyclical *Humanae Vitae*, condemning the use of artificial methods of contraception. He put his authority on the line, making his decision against the overwhelming majority of his birth control commission. The whole affair precipitated one of the most serious crises for papal authority since Luther.

Gradually a strong body of opinion emerged critical of the pope for not acting in cooperation with the bishops in issuing his encyclical. The outstanding spokesman for this point of view was Cardinal Suenens, archbishop of Malines, Belgium, and one of the architects of Vatican II. In speeches, press conferences, and writings, Suenens called for an end to the medieval papacy and never tired of reiterating his theme: The pope should no longer act as though he were outside the Church or above the Church.

Almost as serious as the birth control crisis was the Church's prohibition of divorce. According to this law, no truly sacramental marriage between baptized Catholics can be dissolved, even by the pope. In cases where the partners no longer can live peaceably together, they might be granted the Church's permission to separate but without the right to remarry as long as either partner remains alive. In spite of the tremendous hardships this policy created for those involved in broken marriages, few dared to challenge the law until Vatican II.

But once the facade of immutability and infallibility began to crack under the pressure of post-conciliar events, a number of priests and theologians began to question the wisdom and scriptural validity of the rigid divorce law. They wanted the Church to continue preaching the sacredness of marriage as a sacrament and as a lifelong commitment, but they called for a more flexible pastoral approach in dealing with couples whose marriage had failed.

THE CRISIS OF IDENTITY

Amid all the upheaval the Church experienced a major exodus of priests, brothers, and nuns. From 1962 to 1974 the total number of seminarians in the United States alone decreased by 31 percent; and between 1966 and 1972 nearly eight thousand American priests left the public ministry.

The root cause of this crisis appeared to be the question of the priest's identity. What does being a priest really mean? The sacredness that once surrounded the priesthood seemed odd when compared with the New Testament descriptions of a minister. Moreover, the democratic trend in the Church made the old caste system of priesthood seem medieval. As church membership became a matter for the personally committed in a secular society rather than the born-Catholic type, the need for the priest to bear the whole burden of the Church's mission diminished.

According to Cardinal Suenens, the conflict over authority in the Church traced to two contrasting theologies: One sees the Church as, above all, a fellowship of spiritual communities held together in essentials by their recognition of papal primacy; the other, the traditional one, sees the Church as a medieval superstate governed by an absolute monarch whose aim is to impose its will upon its members and upon society.

Cardinal Suenens found hope for the future of the Church in a new movement stressing personal Christianity, the Catholic Charismatic Renewal. Leaders traced its beginnings to the spring of 1966 when two laymen on the faculty of Duquesne University, Pittsburgh, Pennsylvania, realized they lacked the power of the early Christians to proclaim the gospel. They gave themselves to prayer. They shared their concern with others on the faculty. Then in August 1966 two young men in attendance at the National Cursillo Convention (a Catholic renewal movement born in Europe in the late 1940s) introduced into this circle a book that had intrigued them: Protestant David Wilkerson's *The Cross and the Switchblade*. After personal contacts with Protestant charismatics in the Pittsburgh area, several Duquesne faculty members received the Pentecostal baptism, marked by speaking in tongues. By the middle of February 1967, at what historians of the movement call "the Duquesne weekend," the experience had come to a group of students and faculty on a wider scale.

News of the Pittsburgh experiences soon reached the University of Notre Dame, Notre Dame, Indiana. Home prayer meetings, encouraged and assisted by members of the Protestant Full Gospel Business Men's Fellowship, saw a number of Catholics receive the baptism. Shortly after Easter the "First National Catholic Pentecostal Conference" was held on the Notre Dame campus. About one hundred students, priests, and faculty members, chiefly from Notre Dame and Michigan State, were in attendance. The gathering drew considerable publicity and became an annual event. Growth was phenomenal. The 100 of 1967 became 11,500 (including 7 bishops and 400 priests) at the Sixth Conference in June 1972. By that time Catholic Pentecostalism was a vigorous, international movement called Catholic Charismatic Renewal.

As the 1970s closed the Church of Rome had in many ways ventured some distance from the secure walls of her medieval fortress. Like her Protestant "separated brethren" she found her journey through the Age of Ideologies a perilous and often uncertain pilgrimage.

Suggestions for Further Reading

Abbott, Walter M., ed. *The Documents of Vatican II.* New York: Guild Press, 1966.

Berkouwer, G. C. *The Second Vatican Council and the New Catholicism.* Grand Rapids: Eerdmans, 1965.

Dolan, John P. *Catholicism: An Historical Survey.* Woodbury, NY: Baron's Educational Series, 1968.

Gillis, Chester. *Roman Catholicism.* New York: Columbia University Press, 1999.

McCarthy, Timothy. *The Catholic Tradition: Before and After Vatican II, 1878–1993.* Chicago: Loyola University Press, 1994.

Ranaghan, Kevin and Dorothy. *Catholic Pentecostals.* New York: Paulist Press Deus Books, 1969.

THE AGE OF GLOBAL EXPANSION AND RELOCATION

1900–

More people have become Christians in the last one hundred years than at any other time. When focusing upon the evangelistic embrace of faith, it is arguable that more has happened in the last one hundred years than has happened in all of the church's previous history. The great missionary push of the late 1800s and early 1900s has contributed to this explosive growth largely south of the Equator. Yet the new growth seems to have its own distinctive character and Spirit-given initiative. Ironically one time strongholds of Christian mission in Europe and North America are seeing dormancy and decline. History will record if the new centers of Christianity in the Global South and beyond can maintain a faithful Christian character and give witness to this unprecedented work of the Spirit. Also time will tell if signs of Spiritual stirring will revive a faithful witness in the West. Without the Spirit's stirring the label "post-Christian" will become more fitting with time.

The Age of Global Expansion and Relocation

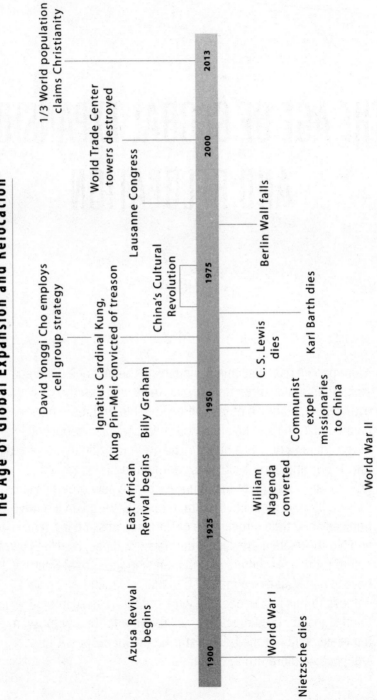

CHAPTER 46

CHRISTIANITY IN THE WEST

Decline and Reconstruction

T HE STATE OF RELIGION in the West is very uncertain. Opinions abound. Some believe that Christianity's influence upon culture is a thing of the past. Many describe the West as "post-Christian." Still others seem to think that the Evangelical church has won, in the sense in that people today would identify Evangelical beliefs as "Christian," as distinguished from liberalism. Others, fully informed about declining numbers, sense that North America is poised for another great work of the Spirit. In terms of the book of Revelation, many in the church are unsure whether they are the new Israel or the old Babylon. Both directions need to be explored. First, however, we must attempt to grasp some features of the twentieth century and its story.

As the twentieth century began, conservative Christians struggled with emerging progressive or liberal Christians who appeared to be capturing the culture. Liberals tapped into a sense of moral and spiritual progress that awaited flourishing Western civilization. These liberals claimed to grasp the moral cause and vision of Jesus without being distracted by the distorting doctrine and liturgy of traditionally minded believers. Other liberals generously recognized the sincere and genuine religious capacity of every individual person; they reasoned that, while the outward expression may be different for Buddhists and Baptists, the inner religious experience was the same at root. These progressive ideas seemed to capture much of the culture of Northern and Western Europe and North America. Many influential institutions in the

West, such as universities, were characterized by these dispositions or were given to a materialism that rejected spiritual beings. Conservatives answered the challenge with revival fervor and intellectual muscle. The fundamentalist movement countered liberal teaching as best they could (though they ironically shared many pivotal notions of modernity).

The most effective answer seemed to rest in preaching. Some estimate that a million people responded to the evangelistic call of Billy Sunday. The most effective evangelist, Billy Graham, would share the gospel internationally. The most effective apologetic voice, C. S. Lewis, came from the university classroom to articulate a rendering of traditional Christian beliefs. The most influential theologian was Karl Barth. While not a conservative evangelical, he served their cause effectively by calling the church and academy back to revelation in light of the inhumanity of manmade religion witnessed in the two World Wars.

By the time of C. S. Lewis and Billy Graham, the landscape had changed. Two World Wars displayed a pernicious evil that weighed heavily against the optimism of the progressives. For a time, Evangelicals seemed to eclipse their liberal challengers with some sense of confidence that the conservative message had prevailed. After the wars, it became apparent that Evangelicals were facing other enemies, contributing to a great fading or passing of vibrant Christian faith. Theorists attribute a variety of contributing factors to this sense of decline. Some say that an endless preoccupation with self-indulgent individual prerogative and fulfillment has eroded a sense of community and moral values. Affluence has given an ever-increasing standard to be chased. Many have noted that "haves" and "have-nots" alike embrace this endless quest to acquire goods, a failure of virtue called *consumerism*. With some exceptions, churches bless this economic quest and avoid the teaching of Jesus concerning money.

Technology plays a part in the daily lives of Westerners that would be hard to imagine just a few years ago; the twentieth century saw the emergence of television and the amazing network of material accessible via the computer. The iPhone was introduced in 2007 and has already become standard equipment for most college students. Smart phones provide individual, private, portable access to entertainment, information, and instant social feedback or connection with other viewers.

Technology is part of a globalizing tendency that is changing business and creating a common culture, especially for young people. Where technology will go next is unknown, and its consequences are also mysterious. Some see it as democratizing knowledge: it makes information available to more persons, just as the alphabet printing press did. Evidence leads others to conclude that modern communications technology causes people to suffer from weakened capacity to concentrate and diminished creativity. With capacity for good or bad, it may just epitomize and aggravate the self-centered culture we have already noted. Others say the church is to blame. It seems often only a reflection of its culture and not an agent of change. Secularism is one of the numerous names and descriptions of this fading of faith.

SECULARIZATION

The modern understanding of secularization has a complicated history. A central notion for today's understanding is that one can clearly distinguish what is religious from what is non-religious. This may seem odd to readers who are acclimated to this idea, but at one time pursuing the knowledge of God was thought to be an undertaking that required an entire life venture, drawing upon any field of knowledge. Knowing God required a distinctive lifestyle, sacred practices, and a new community. Today the knowledge of God is thought to be an intellectual or academic venture that requires neither conversion nor even belief in God! Some would even claim that religious commitments disqualify or hinder the intellectual pursuit of the idea of God. Scholars blame various movements for this change: Medieval Scholasticism or its collapse (picturing God as merely one influence among the many), Protestant Scholasticism (relying upon arid intellectual gymnastics), and the emergence of the nation-state (truncating the idea of God and the arena where he may be served), to name a few suspects. But perhaps each of these contributes to today's circumstances where we see religion as a distinct body of knowledge to go along with biology or physics, and belonging to a distinctly private or personal realm.

In today's world, *secularism* refers to movements that wish to eliminate or restrict the influence of religion. The secular and religious are inversely proportioned; when religion is gaining ground, secularization is losing ground, and vice versa. In this climate, secularly minded critics paint a scenario rooted in the Enlightenment; as more of the world is accounted for by natural explanations, people will eventually realize that they do not need a category for the supernatural. Hostile voices against religion see faith as not merely unnecessary but evil; these angry voices claim that religion is the root cause for most of the problems the world has faced. To be sure, the church has faced smarter atheists; but the hostility of today's atheists and secularists calls for the removal of religion and even the removal of Christianity from the public record. The description of western culture as "christophobic" is not a serious exaggeration.

Smarter Atheists

David Bentley Hart, in *Atheist Delusions: The Christian Revolution and its Fashionable Enemies*, observes that recent harsh critics offer an unfitting reading of the past. They blame religion in general and Christianity in particular for virtually every evil known to man. Nietzsche (1844–1900) was wiser and better trained. What was mad about Nietzsche's "madman" was not that he denied that there was a God. Nietzsche thought that most educated people had ceased to believe in God. Culture judged the "God-denier" because it was unable to come to grips with the consequence of doing without God.

Nietzsche knew that Western civilization's entire moral vision was rooted in a particular notion of God and that the morality of the West would need to be entirely reworked. Because Nietzsche knew the history of the West, his conclusion points in the opposite direction from today's critics. Belief in God is not simply the problem with the great Western vision of morality. God is the foundation without which Western values are unsustainable.

Alister McGrath thinks the hostile rhetoric comes from panic: Christianity is growing, and an unprecedented number of world-class scientists are coming to affirm God. These facts counter the prevailing secular mythos, that education will lead people away from God.

Perhaps as disturbing as the hostility to faith is an indifference to Christianity. The culture at large seems not to notice or care; the language of the Bible that once shaped discourse of all educated citizens seems missing from everyday life. Numerous studies show that believers have less knowledge and commitment to key Christian teachings than ever before. Those who still defend the doctrines or teachings of Christianity ironically offer secular explanations, and co-opt Christianity into a God-sponsored version of self-help therapy. One tangible expression of secularization is the decline in church attendance and affiliation. Europe typically reports church attendance under 10 percent, and in some places under 5 percent. This decline is more remarkable given that the largest churches in many European capitals are led and attended by immigrants from the Global South.

SHIFT IN WESTERN CHRISTIANS AND CHURCHES

The consequences of secularism's rise held dramatic changes for the church in the West. Among the privileged Protestant mainline churches—the Episcopalians, Methodists, Presbyterians, United Church of Christ, major Lutheran bodies, and Christian Church

(Disciples of Christ)—the impact was largely negative. They were perceived as symbols of the old established but irrelevant past. As a result, the mainline bodies saw their membership figures and their finances decline from the mid-1960s onward, suggesting that these churches were moving from the mainline to the sideline.

In sharp contrast, conservative Protestants were generally flourishing, including Evangelical, fundamentalist, charismatic, and Pentecostal church groups. To take one striking example during this age, the Pentecostal Assemblies of God multiplied from a half million to more than four million. By 1990, figures on Roman Catholicism in the United States had also jumped, in their case to fifty-five million. Large numbers of these new Catholics could be traced to the explosive growth of the U.S. Latino population. The Roman Catholic Church in America would grow beyond one-third Hispanic. Conservative churches explained that their stable and growing numbers were due to their fidelity to faith and Scripture; others included the notion that conservative churches gave solid answers and were efficiently organized.

EVANGELICAL RESPONSES: RESCUE, RECLAIMING, AND RELEVANCE

Collectively, conservative churches exhibited three responses to the encroaching secularism. One response was rooted in a speculative anticipation of the end of time, or at least the beginning of the end times. In this popular system, the contemporary world was seen as increasingly lost and having little to do with God's plan for the church. Because of the increasing evil and moral failure, they believed that the removal of the church, or Rapture, would happen very soon. Hal Lindsey published a string of runaway best sellers, including *The Late, Great Planet Earth* and *Satan is Alive and Well On Planet Earth.* These books created a devout expectation that Jesus must be coming anytime; this heightened awareness showed that redeeming the fallen world was futile.

Ministry and mission alike must be given to preparing souls before the end comes. Even some Christian critics thought this evangelical fervor took on Gnostic shades, in that it depreciated God's creation and his intention to redeem it; the body as well as the soul was to be redeemed. After several decades of missed deadlines for Jesus' return, the movement lost steam, though any number of headlines involving the Middle East or the European Union could awaken this mindset and give opportunity for another book to update the situation. Evangelicals did not abandon this approach to the future, but they generally came to sense that they had at least applied it in a dubious fashion. Perhaps inconsistently, some of the same personalities participated in the next approach, seeking to contest Christian claims upon the world and nation. The approaches blend together in practice.

The next approach was to battle secular forces on political and cultural turfs. Jerry Falwell was pastor of the Thomas Road Baptist Church in Lynchburg, Virginia, but after creating a political action group called the Moral Majority in 1979, he became the first prominent spokesman for the so-called Religious Right. The label stood for a coalition of fundamentalist, Pentecostal, Evangelical, and Catholic Christians, driven by concern for the decline in American morality, who had become extremely active in the political arena. The core of the movement was a loose alliance of groups led by the Moral Majority. Clustered around an agenda defending traditional moral values and conservative political goals were The Christian Voice, led by Robert Grant; Concerned Women for America, under the leadership of Beverly LaHaye; and the Freedom Council, formed by Pat Robertson, a televangelist who became an unsuccessful candidate for the Republican presidential nomination in 1988.

The passion of the Religious Right lay in their perception that the United States was falling under the influence of secular humanism and that traditional family values were under attack in the media and the public schools. Several explosive national issues seemed to ignite this new conservative reaction. First, in 1973 the U.S. Supreme Court's decision in the *Roe v. Wade* case agreed with Jane Roe, a young single Texas woman, that her right to privacy included her right to terminate her pregnancy by abortion. Many Catholics and Protestants, who held that human life begins at conception, were shocked and dismayed by the decision. Second, in 1978 a ballot proposition in California tried to expand legal protection of homosexuals. When a group of conservative pastors organized to defeat the measure, the Internal Revenue Service warned them that the tax-exempt status of their churches was endangered by their political activity. The pastors thought this was reason enough to form The Christian Voice. They were unwilling to give up their fight. Finally came the battle over the Equal Rights Amendment, the movement to grant women the legal protection of an amendment to the Constitution. Like many conservative Christians, Jerry Falwell was opposed to the wording of the amendment adopted by Congress. He felt that it would allow homosexual marriages and adoptions and would allow women to be drafted into the armed services. So in Virginia he fought successfully against the ratification of the amendment.

These three issues—abortion, homosexual rights, and feminism—served to mobilize conservative Christians for battles in the political arena, soon to expand to include other moral and political issues. To achieve their goals, the Religious Right relied heavily on the ministries of televangelists. Falwell's *Old Time Gospel Hour* and Robertson's Christian Broadcasting Network (CBN) and *700 Club* led a host of Christian-sponsored radio and television outlets in promoting the conservative moral and political agenda. On radio, a child psychologist-turned-broadcaster, Dr. James Dobson, enlarged his radio ministry called *Focus on the Family* into a powerful voice for traditional family values. Perhaps most significant politically, these groups succeeded in educating and mobilizing fundamentalists and Pentecostals, a segment of the American population that had once been politically inactive.

A third approach involves another change of course or strategy. Numerous Evangelicals sought to be less confrontational and would attempt to engage the new changing culture on its own terms. These churchmen observed that they ministered within the age of individual self-expression. They created user-friendly churches that made religion almost totally a matter of personal choice. Desiring to evangelize, practitioners performed market analysis in an effort to offer an experience that would meet with the approval of the target audience. Some fashioned an experience that would be comfortable to a religious seeker. A great variety of churches adopted a practical self-help approach; a special version of allegory was embraced to extract techniques from the Bible, which suddenly became a manual for success in life.

The megachurch phenomenon illustrates the third approach of seeking relevance. With the decline of denominations in American public life and the increasing privatization of religion, large churches gained an increasing share of churchgoing America, or, as some crassly called it, "the religious market." These large churches grew at least in part because they shed the negative image of denominational Christianity and appealed to popular religious tastes. Like the seventy-six million members of the post-World War II generation, megachurches liked to think of themselves as independent and highly individualized.

With attenders in the thousands, Sunday morning services in these churches were usually well attended. But their buildings were filled the rest of the week, too, with Bible classes, support groups, field trips for seniors, weight loss classes, and children's activities. The appeal to popular taste was revealed in several common characteristics: First, these congregations seldom carried a denominational label. They much preferred "chapel," "center," or "community" on the sign out front. The name was a symbol of their openness to people with diverse backgrounds and problems: divorce, addictions, and depression. Second, the worship in these large congregations was marked by fast paced and enthusiastic popular religious music. The choice of music has been increasingly influenced by a Christian commercial music industry. Third, they were built around the attractive ministry of a magnetic preacher who possessed a winsome personality. The sermons stressed the Bible's application to day-to-day life. Fourth, these large churches give an image of efficiency and affluence. Buildings were often new; the staff of ministers was well trained and effective; services were available for every imaginable need.

Historians tend to view this development as another example of Americans' privatization of faith. Even in the excitement of a large crowd, attenders of a megachurch were looking for faith that served the private life: help on child rearing, family unity, and personal emotions. Experienced churchgoers found these churches uncomplicated, by comparison with the small neighborhood churches where they had formerly attended. Americans sought a private house, a private means of transportation, a private garden, a private laundry, and self-service stores. Even within families, Americans had come to expect that each member of the family should have a separate room and even a separate television, phone, and car, at least when economically possible.

Many megachurches continue to flourish, but many others have plateaued. A new generation may well seek community to compensate for individualism and isolation; some seek a new approach that will appeal to the emerging generation. Hundreds of new churches also appeared throughout the United Kingdom and the United States, all attempting to reach out to the postmodern generation. "Those who fail to change their ministry ways," said the new voices, "risk hiding the gospel behind forms of thought and modes of expression that no longer communicate with the new emerging generation." Emerging churches were intent upon emphasizing feelings and affections rather than rationality and linear thought, on personal experience over propositional truths, on inclusion rather than exclusion, and on participation in corporate worship in contrast to lost-in-the-crowd, megachurch individualism.

TROUBLING SIGNS

Sobering signs show that conservative evangelical efforts (to prepare for spiritual rescue from a dying world or to reclaim a Christian character for the nation by political victory or to connect with the lost culture) have not stemmed the tide of secularization. Taken together, numerous signs indicate that "old-time religion" may be moving swiftly toward a minority status within the culture. Conservatives could no longer look at church decline as a mainline or liberal church problem. When many conservative denominations began to decline, haunting questions emerged: Will conservative denominations follow liberal church declines? Will the North American Christian landscape soon resemble that of Europe? Conservatives could no longer take solace in slowing declines in the early 1990s. Recent Pew Research Center numbers measure religious affiliation at its lowest since their earliest records in 1930. Now one in five Americans claims to have no religious affiliation; for adults under age thirty, the number jumps to one in three. Also conservative Christians have lost ground on the three initiatives targeted by the Religious Right: abortion, homosexual rights, and feminism. Legal limitations upon same-sex marriage received serious damage in June, 2013. California's Proposition Eight and the Defense of Marriage Act were both set aside in Supreme Court action. Additionally, conservative believers in the West feel threatened by several ongoing issues.

ONGOING STRUGGLES

The institutions of the family and marriage have suffered. Traditional notions of couples being married before they live together and the enduring nature of marriage are not recognized by the larger culture or Christian church members in a consistent fashion. The general culture abandoned the traditional idea of marriage long before it came under siege by same-sex interests. Single-parent families (which have reached one in five) and working women (at least forty percent of the work force) add to the destabilized nature of the home.

On the morning of September 11, 2001, Americans were dramatically confronted with radical terrorism. They discovered that religion, even religious zealots, would shape the political landscape for the foreseeable future. Two airliners filled with jet fuel crashed into the two towers of New York City World Trade Center. Having failed to bring down the buildings in 1993, this time they succeeded. A third plane flew into the Pentagon, and passengers struggled with hijackers before a fourth plane, intended for the White House, crashed in southwest Pennsylvania. Almost every American can see the Trade Center buildings collapse in their mind's eye.

Within days of 9/11, President George W. Bush declared war on the terrorists and, after rallying a coalition of largely Western nations, the president—less than a year in office—sent troops to Afghanistan, where the terrorists called the Taliban had found a haven and a training ground. With the cooperation of key Afghan warlords, the American-led coalition was able to topple the Taliban and drive it from power within a matter of months. Osama bin Laden, leader of the most feared jihadists, was later found and shot, but only after he had inspired and directed new attacks upon the "infidels."

Within months, a new government was in place in Kabul, the Afghan capital. The invasion of Iraq, the reported haven of other jihadists, and the toppling of Saddam Hussein from power soon followed in the American-led coalition's war against terror. The war in Iraq, however, a much larger and stronger country, proved to be far more complex and difficult than the Afghan conflict.

Modernity and Islam

One of the common explanations for the term *modernity* is religious and political in nature. In this approach, a nation-state is modern if it tolerates differing religious expressions under its larger national umbrella. The state is to some degree neutral or generic in a religious sense and allows differing voices, such as Islam and Christianity to live in the same state. This concept is helpful in understanding Islam. After World War I, almost the entire Arab world was placed under a state (some very contrived, placing antagonistic groups together under one flag) that was overseen by a European nation (and in the eyes of most Arabs, these are also Christian States). This arrangement is part of a larger picture called imperialism.

While Christians had altered their practice to agree to a modern state not long after the Reformation (the Thirty Years' War), Islam is by nature almost necessarily social and political; Islam's voices typically think that Islam must be translated into government-sanctioned laws to be faithful. For a time, the Muslim world lived in modern states sponsored by European countries at gunpoint. Rulers such as Sadat in Egypt and the Shah of Iran brutally suppressed radical voices to make these modern states possible. Egypt and Iran were thought to be westernized. Once the Arab peoples began to exercise political independence, radical voices within Islam proved effective in seizing control. Iran's revolution brought a sudden change from a westernized nation to one governed by strict Islamists. Time will tell which countries among the Arab people will select strict Islamic states or embrace some sort of modern solution.

At present, the voices of radical Shiite Muslims seem to shape much of the political landscape and the culture. Modern Muslims, which most students view as the majority, seem quite stifled. The rise of radical Islam has changed the religious landscape across the globe, and many Arab countries are now radicalized. It should be observed that Islamic rulers have historically tolerated Christian citizens as long as they submitted to being second class citizens within Muslim nations.

Today, Christians in the Arab world are suffering. In 1900, the Middle East and North Africa were 15 percent Christian; one hundred years later, estimates were 5 percent. The once-significant numbers of Arab Christians have declined as they have been persecuted into submission, exiled, or murdered. Perhaps as significant is the presence of Muslim peoples living in the West with missionary and even militant purpose. Christians are wise to be alert to the risk and danger that radical Islam holds for them in the Arab or Western worlds. Christians will face a still greater danger of infidelity to Christ if Muslims do not encounter the love of Christ in tangible witness and care.

Persistent testimony of Muslim conversion and openness to the gospel is difficult to measure; reports of Muslims encountering Jesus in their dreams, the curiously positive reception some that evangelical Christians receive in the Arab world, the persistence of underground churches, and Christians willing to serve and live among Muslims give some encouragement for a continued Christian presence in the region. These Christians who are called to live in the Arab world are some of the champions of the missionary venture.

Added to the awareness and danger of Muslim radicals, the church was also called to face a new wave of immigration to the country. The Hart-Cellar Act was a part of the Civil Rights legislation. The Act stimulated immigration from Asia, the Middle East, and Africa. Illegal immigration from South and Central America also accelerated racial diversity. Though voices from the church led the way to progress in the matter of race, the evangelical church has largely maintained racial segregation as well as segregation by economic standing. Race and economic class go hand in hand; for example, a black family will be more readily accepted in a largely Anglo church if they share a similar lifestyle.

Also as missions were exploding around the globe, Western Christians were beginning to struggle with the practice. Evangelical denominations and mission-sending organizations were facing budget cuts. Evangelicals wondered if missionaries should address more humanitarian concerns over concerns about salvation; they also struggled as to what degree missionaries imposed their cultural bias upon the nationals; they also were humbled by more extensive encounters with world religions. Racial and geographical diversity, the awareness of Islam, and globalizing technology all bring these issues home. Missionary zeal seemed easier overseas; it seemed more complicated when the world had come near geographically and grown smaller technologically.

DEFEATED OR RECONSTITUTING?

News of Christianity's demise in the West may be premature. Minimally, it will be influential because of its money and educational institutions. Western degrees are often still privileged in the Global South. More complete assessment is difficult, though several observations may help. The cultural environment is increasingly secular and hostile to faith. Christians looking for Christendom (a Christian domain marked by an organic and cooperative partnership between the state and church) will be disappointed. Christians and their convictions can expect to be more marginalized and persecuted. Pastors being prosecuted for hate speech and Christian schools losing federal dollars seem almost unavoidable. The mainline denominations will experience general decline, although they will vary regarding their acclimation to cultural norms; some may return instinctively to the great tradition of the church and rediscover the gospel (this approach is called post-liberalism).

Certain churches in the Pentecostal tradition, nondenominational circles, and conservative denominations will continue to grow. The real progress will rest in new church starts, which are grossly underreported. These churches are pliable and portable; they can meet in store fronts and in cell groups. They are almost impossible to track or count.

A personal parable may help illustrate. I (R. L. Hatchett) was raised in a neighborhood Baptist church. Our church, the Methodists, and Church of Christ churches were the norm in our humble circumstance. Our church buildings looked like churches and were nicer than our own homes. When a charismatic nondenominational church began to meet in an old grocery store space, the contrast was unmistakable. They had a long sign with too many words. They were even poorer than we were. They were unconnected to larger bodies and institutions (like mission programs and seminaries). Most of all, they were the periphery or exception, whereas we were the norm. Now almost fifty years later, these upstart churches are not the periphery but the numerical norm. The immediate future belongs to groups like this that are independent and entrepreneurial.

The new norm is composed of the Pentecostals and nondenominationals; their emergence signals a change in the understanding of Christianity for the future in the West. We are engaged in a reconstruction period that follows this sociological revolution; the evangelical population will now be found predominantly in this mobile, minority-rich matrix. They display a certain Anabaptist-like character. They are not all pacifists (though some forget that many Pentecostals were conscientious objectors in World War I) and some may nostalgically look for the good days of a Christian America, but they see themselves as countercultural; they focus on discipleship and community; they will partner to meet needs but do not have the political disposition and orientation of older Evangelicals.

Other signs of life are found in a variety of places. The rigorously academic and spiritually devout young Catholics in America seem strong in mind and heart and number. One is encouraged as well by youth gatherings such as Passion. In 2013, sixty-four thousand college age students met in Atlanta during their Christmas break. Each Passion conference, whether in the states or overseas, fills to capacity. Numerous initiatives call for renewal and revival. An ecumenical group, Renovaré, crosses denominational lines to learn about spiritual formation. We pray for the Spirit to move.

Suggestions for Further Reading

Bellah, Robert N. et al. *Habits of the Heart: Individualism and Community in American Life*. New York: Harper & Row, 1985.

Bennett, William J. *The Index of Leading Cultural Indicators*. New York: Simon and Schuster, 1994.

Collins, Kenneth J. *The Evangelical Moment: A Promise of an American Religion*. Grand Rapids: Baker Academic, 2005.

George, Timothy, ed. *Pilgrims on the Sawdust Trail: Evangelical Ecumenism and the Quest for Christian Identity*. Grand Rapids: Baker, 2004.

*Noll, Mark. *The Old Religion in a New World: the History of North American Christianity*. Grand Rapids: Eerdmans, 2002.

Shelley, Bruce, and Marshall Shelley. *The Consumer Church*. Downers Grove, IL: InterVarsity Press, 1992.

*Weigel, Georg. *The Cube and the Cathedral: Europe, America, and Politics Without God*. New York: Basic Books, 2005.

Wuthnow, Robert. *The Struggle for America's Soul, Evangelicals, Liberals, and Secularism*. Grand Rapids: Eerdmans, 1989.

CHAPTER 47

SHIFT TO THE GLOBAL SOUTH

What is the "New Christianity"?

A T THE START OF the twentieth century, the map of global Christianity that D. L. Moody or Vladimir Lenin might have known had been completely reshaped. In 1900, only 10 percent of the world's Christians lived in the continents of the south and east, but a century later at least 70 percent of the world's Christians lived there. More Christians worshiped in Anglican churches in Nigeria each week than in all the Episcopal and Anglican churches of Britain, Europe, and North America combined. There were ten times more Assembly of God members in Latin America than in the United States. There were more Baptists in Congo than in Great Britain. And there were more people in church every Sunday in communist China than in all of Western Europe or in North America.

Philip Jenkins, Distinguished Professor of History at Baylor University, said at the time that religion in the new century even showed signs of replacing ideology as the prime animating force in human affairs. "If we look beyond the liberal West," he wrote in *The Atlantic Monthly*,

we see that another Christian revolution . . . is already in progress. Worldwide, Christianity is actually moving toward supernaturalism and [what he called] neo-orthodoxy, and in many ways toward the ancient world view expressed in the New Testament: a vision of Jesus as the embodiment of divine power, who overcomes the evil forces that inflict calamity and sickness upon the human race.

494

Jenkins spoke especially of "the Global South" or those areas of the earth that Westerners once thought of as the Third World, and he argued that contemporary Christianity had shifted south and the earth's preponderant weight appeared to be "pear-shaped." In this south or Third World, Jenkins wrote, we find huge and growing Christian populations: at the dawning of the twenty-first century, 480 million in Latin America, 360 million in Africa, and 313 million in Asia, compared with 260 million in North America.

The shift, he said, portended trouble for the traditional cultural empire of the North Atlantic, the liberal religious establishment. Perhaps the broadest public hint, Jenkins wrote, was provided by the 1998 Lambeth Conference, where southern Christians used their numerical clout to promote opinions thoroughly unfashionable in the North Atlantic (or the West). "Queen Victoria's ex-empire," said Jenkins, "from southern Africa to Singapore struck back."

The growth of Christianity in post-colonial Africa had been especially relentless. In 1900, Africa had just 10 million Christians out of a continental population of 107 million, about 9 percent. At the turn of the twenty-first century, the Christian total stood at 360 million out of 784 million souls, or 46 percent. And that percentage, scholars predicted, was likely to continue rising, because Christian African countries had some of the world's most dramatic rates of population growth. Within the first twenty-five years of the twenty-first century, scholars expected the population of the world's Christians to grow to 2.6 billion, making Christianity by far the world's largest faith. We must seek to describe this new Christianity even if we resort to western ways of seeing.

GLOBAL CHRISTIANITY AS A PENTECOSTAL OR CHARISMATIC

The unmistakable first observation about the churches below the equator is that they are charismatic. "The gifts" play a prominent role in public worship and private devotion. Grasping the history of this movement will prepare the reader for encountering the Global South. Several movements prepare and anticipate the emergence of contemporary Pentecostalism. The Methodist and Holiness movements were perfectly suited for the North American frontier with an egalitarian character that could cross economic, racial, and gender barriers. Culminating 150 years of Holiness theology, by 1900 Pentecostals embraced and amended a Holiness tradition incorporating several emphases.

The "third blessing" approach acknowledged the first blessing of conversion and a second blessing whereby the believers were stirred and moved to sanctification or holiness (the emphasis that evolved from Wesley). Additionally, they acknowledged a third blessing, which was Spirit baptism. Spirit baptism included a special empowerment for service (empowerment being an emphasis of the Keswick Movement). Pentecostals also affirmed that the Spirit baptism was accompanied by speaking in tongues. The Spirit's outpouring was tied to the last days, in the imagination of many. Prophecy conferences and the reemergence of pre-millennialism (that Christ would return to establish a thousand-year reign) added to the sense of expectation. Numerous healing ministries also contributed to the picture of God's preparing his people for ministry.

Also, internationally noted revivals in India, Wales, and Korea gave encouragement to the Pentecostal movement. The Welsh revival witnessed a presence and power of the Holy Spirit. Its spokesman, Evan Roberts, taught that such an experience of the Holy Spirit was a necessary condition to revival. The "Korean Pentecost" set the stage for many enduring practices of the Korean church to this day, such as early morning prayer meetings and the practice of simultaneous prayer.

Pentecostal and Charismatic

These terms are sometimes used interchangeably. Pentecostal often refers to the events and denominations that follow from the Azusa revival in the early 1900s. Pentecostal denominations, such as Assemblies of God and Church of God, frequently believe the gift of the Spirit is marked by speaking in tongues.

Typically, people are described as charismatic if the exercise of the more dramatic spiritual gifts, such as tongue speaking, healing, and acts of prophecy, are an important and routine part of the church's worship and an individual believer's personal devotion. The term *charismatic* more routinely refers to Pentecost-inspired teaching, practices, and worship that are now embraced in the church far beyond the Pentecostal denominations.

Two men stand at the center of Pentecostal origins as typically told. An ex-Methodist minister, Charles Parham, drew inspiration from several sources before he eventually laid hands upon Agnes Ozman. She spoke in tongues, and Parham believed that she spoke the Chinese language. Others received the Spirit and also spoke in tongues. Parham's language was thought to be Swedish. Parham believed that these actual languages were miraculously spoken (xenolalia) and would to lead to international missionary ventures. William Seymour, though segregated from the white learners, listened to a three-month Bible school that Parham led in Houston, Texas. Soon after, Seymour became pastor at an African American Holiness Church in Los Angeles. They rejected his teaching concerning tongues, but some witnessed Seymour lay hands on his host, Edward Lee. Lee experienced an almost unconscious state that was followed by tongue speaking. At the same meeting, seven more received the baptism of the Spirit accompanied by tongues, including Seymour himself.

Soon Lee's home could not hold the racially mixed group that came to see and receive Pentecost. The Azusa Revivals follow. The story of the emergence and mission of the pentecostal and charismatic movements that follow is arguably the most important story of the twentieth century for understanding Christianity today. Measuring the expansion and growth of the Pentecostal denominations is only a fraction of the story because charismatic and Pentecostal influences are the primary contributors to non-denominationalism. Even more impressively, charismatic theology and practice now characterize many believers in the mainline denominations and Catholic life.

American students of the movement observe three recent movements of the Spirit. The first wave refers to the outpouring of the Spirit at Azusa and the emergence of the major Pentecostal denominations that followed. The second wave denotes a sweeping encounter and embrace of charismatic life spilling over into mainline Protestant denominations and Catholicism in the 1960s and early 1970s. The third wave saw the embrace of signs and wonders by conservatives; it began in the 1980s at Fuller Seminary in California around the teaching and ministry of John Wimber. The Vineyard network of churches is a lasting sign of this movement that saw many evangelicals swept into charismatic experience.

Some historians place the commonly told story of the rise of Pentecostalism within larger frameworks. Azusa may be part of an international and multicultural outpouring of the Spirit; Azusa might be the Jerusalem of the new Pentecost or one of many Pentecosts occurring around the globe at about the same time. It may be the predominant expression of a more encompassing age of Spirit-centered renewal that includes the contemplative streams, as expressed in Henri Nouwen and Richard Foster. It may also be seen as part of a larger scenario, the steady decline of liberalism that was being replaced by more conservative or evangelical upsurges. While each of these has merit and interest, the scope of this movement seems to eclipse most other factors.

This blending of categories with various denominations makes the Pentecostal/charismatic movement almost impossible to enumerate. Modest assessments claim they account for just more than one in four Christians today, though the number and influences may be much greater. The remarkable gain in percentage is even more breathtaking because of Christianity's unprecedented growth in the century during the same period.

The Numerical growth of Pentecostals and Charismatics is also staggering.

Regions as Designated by David Barrett	Number of Charismatic/ Pentecostal Christians in Millions in 1900	Number of Charismatic/ Pentecostal Christians in Millions in 2000
Africa	.9	126
Asia	0	135
Europe	0	37.6
Latin America	0	141.4
North America	0	79.6
Oceania	0	4.3

It is easy to understand scholars slightly overemphasizing when they claim that the global expansion is actually the Pentecostal expansion.

ROOTS IN WESTERN MISSIONARY VENTURES

Missionaries are frequently criticized as serving both Christ and commerce. They are pictured as agents of colonial expansion and unable to distinguish between the gospel message and their own cultural preferences. Kenyan Jomo Kenyatta famously captures this critical perspective: "When the missionaries came to Africa they had the Bible and we had the land. They said 'Let us pray.' We closed our eyes. When we opened them we had the Bible and they had the land." Recent students of missionary endeavors give missionaries a better name, noting that they often advocate justice and independence.

Missionary influence is inevitable. Mark Noll distinguishes between the missionaries' direct influence and the more lasting model they leave behind. In one sense, the East African Revival could not have been more Western or American. Revivalist Charles Finney was consciously adopted as a model by Joseph Church and others. Finney's revival materials were even read aloud. Church employed Keswick theology and a Scofield Study Bible. He spoke of Western politics and practiced Western medicine.

But Noll warns that a conclusion that Westerners have manipulated the East Africans may not tell the whole story. In reality, there are numerous influences that coalesce. Also, a deeper understanding of why these missionary voices were influential instead of others may teach us more about the African culture. Many studied persons measure these cultural interactions and conclude that the East African Revival was genuinely African in character. The larger significance of Noll's book, *The New Shape of World Christianity: How American Experience Reflects Global Faith*, is that it looks beyond the question of the precise direct influence that Western missionaries had upon the Southern nations. Noll looks beyond this important question to a broader understanding of America's influence upon the expansion of Christianity in the Global South. He shifts our focus from the question of what missionaries did and addresses what version of Christianity they modeled before the Global South believers.

Christianity was brought to America by European Christians; it is the product of missions itself. But Christianity has taken a distinctive shape in North America. Understanding this distinctive form is the key to seeing the missionary's greatest influence. Several ideas will help us delineate the character of North American Christianity. Generally speaking, American Christianity is a voluntary Christianity and less an expression of Christendom.

Christendom

Most simply, Christendom refers to a Christian domain: lands that are occupied by Christians, as opposed to adherents to other religions. Typically today, the term is used with cultural and political considerations: a culture may embrace Christian values and adopt them as law (for example, blue laws, which restrict some merchandise being sold on Sunday). Some think the term assumes the idea that Western civilization is the product of Christianity. Generally, a religious arm (the church) and a secular arm (the civil government) serve different purposes but also serve to accomplish a united reality. In the most extreme expression of Christendom, a state church, all Christians in the domain would be counted as citizens, and citizens would be counted as Christians.

The most thoroughgoing rejection of Christendom is found in the Anabaptists. They did not envision the church as organically or organizationally tied to the state; they viewed the church as independent from any government and a corresponding geographical region. Instead, the church was composed of people who voluntarily embraced covenant membership. While this approach seems simple enough to Americans today, the Anabaptists were hunted and cruelly murdered by both Protestants and Roman Catholics. Challenging Christendom was dangerous business.

Anabaptists argue that an informal Christendom exists in America. Even though no particular brand of Christianity or Church is named by the government of the United States (disestablishment), Christians still see their nation as Christian in some sense and see the church as obligated to serve the state, much like a chaplain. American Christians see themselves between the extreme of Anabaptist independence and full-blown Christendom as modeled in Europe. The shift away from the Christendom model, however subtle, is crucial to understanding American Christianity.

The Christianity that grew most rapidly in North America, and that has been most widely embraced in the Global South, was voluntary. In North America it also emphasized personal, individual conversion. Americans embraced Bunyan, whose *Pilgrim's Progress* (1678) both illustrates and proliferates a Christianity that focuses upon the Christian life of the individual. Bunyan does not abandon Puritanism, yet his story has the effect of communicating that Christianity was the matter of an individual conversion and pilgrimage. In the revivals and awakenings that shaped American religion, the emphasis again fell upon conversion of the individual. Sometimes this emphasis is received in the global churches despite their more communal and collective orientation.

American churches also received leaders more readily upon the basis of gifting and initiative rather than institutional or hierarchical status. Wesley's influence may be a case in point: his innovative organizational skills contribute to his legacy, not his efforts to maintain ties to the Church of England. In the end, it is the voluntary, independent, and innovative disposition of Western missionaries that left the lasting mark upon the churches of the Global South.

ENACTING THE BIBLE

Today the Bible has a special resonance with the Global South. Thankfully, the missionary vision has often included a vigorous effort to translate the Bible into the language of the nationals. We may rightly observe that the act of translation holds ample opportunity for Western missionaries to import their own cultural bias. Yet the effect of translation was not more cultural manipulation, but a boost for cultural independence. Several scholars have noted the centrality of biblical translation to the emergence of independent thinking. An empowerment results from receiving the Bible in one's own language. It promotes an embrace of their local customs for the nationals. Bible readers are happy to find that some customs or practices find parallels in the Bible once its pages are opened and explored.

Some contrast the globalizing effect of Islam's preference of a single language for the Koran with the endorsement of local customs and culture when the Bible is translated. Additionally, nationals could assess what the missionaries had taught by examining Scripture for themselves. A common illustration is found among Africans who discovered that the great patriarchs were polygamists and wondered why the missionaries were so adamant about monogamy.

The real work of indigenization began when the translations were encountered; then readers could appropriate the language, imagery, and culture of the Bible for themselves. Mark Noll has catalogued a variety of cultural approaches to the Bible. The West typically reads the didactic and missionary letters of Paul as a key to reading the remainder of the Bible. Some Africans take Leviticus to be central. They identify with a sense of holiness and ritual. In Leviticus, they discover that categories such as clean and unclean are rooted in the Bible and not products of merely pagan superstition. Some Asian Christians concentrate upon Proverbs, where they find that God has interest in wisdom that they once sought in Confucian sources.

Christians in the Global south seem to appropriate the Bible in a direct manner; they read with a sense of immediacy as though the Bible was written directly to them. Western readers, by contrast, observe a historical distance between the world as they see it and the world of the Bible. What stands out to these readers is how different their experience is from the New Testament experience. It is frequently noted that, for Pentecostals, the New Testament, with its tongue speaking, healings, demonic encounters, and spiritual warfare, is not strange but the blueprint for how the Christian life is to be lived. By contrast, Western interpreters commonly translate the occurrences of the New Testament into more familiar categories; for example, they routinely conclude that exorcism would be understood as a form of mental illness today. Even the evangelical and fundamentalist believers in the West develop strategies for explaining the distance between the text and their contemporary experience. Classical dispensationalism, for example, sought to distinguish the teaching in the Bible that belonged to the church and the directions and guidance that were addressed to the other people of God, Israel. By stipulating that these two peoples were absolutely unrelated, it forbade mixing or confusing messages; it lamented Christians appropriating the Sermon on the Mount when it was addressed to Israel.

Perhaps more drastic still is an approach called cessationism, which argued that the time for miracles and charismatic gifts had ceased. One of the intellectual anchors of the fundamentalist movement (and no friend to the dispensationalists), B. B. Warfield, argued that Christians today are not to expect miracles. He held that miracles were concentrated in three clusters to give credence to a new revelation. Miracles abounded when Moses delivered the law, when Elijah and Elisha proclaimed prophecy, and when Jesus announced the kingdom. These theories illustrate how very conservative Christians in the West, like their liberal counterparts, sought to ease the discomfort of readers who sensed that their church experience was very different from that of the Bible.

Worldview and metaphysics (a term you can functionally replace with the question, "What is real?") are crucial. General observations about philosophical issues are dangerous, but it is fair to observe that Christians in the Global South see the world around them as manifesting a vivid interaction between what we may call a spiritual (non-material) realm and a material (concretely physical) realm. Westerners typically hold that a mastery over the material realm (perhaps through science) alters or even negates the need for the spiritual realm.

A crude thought experiment may be helpful. A shaman or prophet tells his tribe that they are sick and dying because the gods are punishing them for betraying their allies. This spiritual interpretation of the events holds until a Western researcher tests the water and discovers that the well water is corrupted. The researcher's verdict is that the gods had nothing to do with it; microscopic bugs in the water were making people ill. This simplistic dilemma rules for many Westerners: a thing has either a natural or a supernatural cause, which makes no more sense than to ask whether you wish to ride the bus or take your lunch to school.

Such an illustration helps us picture an encroaching materialism. Believers in the West often acclimate to the dominant view. They fear that knowledge may make God unnecessary. They abandon Christian teaching, such as God sustaining the world or God not being merely another acting agent. Some reject the idea of God altogether or accept a provisional deism. In such a muted theism, God is offstage and barely makes appearances; demons, spirits, and angels are downplayed. For most Western believers, only a modest vista exists for the spiritual. For the Global South, the physical and spiritual worlds interact. In such a world, demons or spirits may influence a person's mood or well-being. Both the spiritual and material realms are firmly in mind. They enter the text of Scripture with less hindrance.

THE GOSPEL AND SOCIAL JUSTICE

The church of the Global South is routinely situated in poverty. The designation *Third World* communicates this observation. It is fair to note that not all people in the Global South are poor, but struggle with social injustice is the unavoidable context and circumstance of much of the Global South. Believers there have a greater disposition to believe that the gospel addresses the issue of poverty. Liberation theologians claim that Jesus sought liberty from oppressive economic systems. These theologians read the Bible as addressing social injustice and call for Christians to practice justice rather than merely proclaiming it. Conservative Evangelicals in the Global South are influenced by voices of liberation to a greater degree than their North American counterparts. Still they maintain an emphasis upon the good news of a redemptive act of Jesus. Yet even in understanding Christ's redemptive work, their circumstance shapes them.

This sensitivity to social injustice influences even the most basic of doctrines. The church articulates three major approaches to understand what Jesus did for the human family to accomplish salvation: (1) Evangelicals typically rely upon an approach that sees Christ as our representative or substitute who died on the cross to accomplish salvation. (2) Other believers, especially in modern liberal camps, see the cross as a dramatic demonstration of God's love. When understood, this drama overwhelms our reluctance to believe that God loves us and awakens us to love God in response. These two theories are dominant among the Western church. In one, Jesus bears our individual penalty or debt as sinners. In the second approach, Jesus addresses our incapacity to receive and share love. (3) A third theory has persisted in the Eastern Church and was its most typical approach to the atonement for one thousand years. In this approach, Jesus addresses the bondage we experience. The human family inescapably faces oppressive evil and a personal spiritual enemy (Satan and his demons). Additionally, we face sin that we are unable to defeat in our own strength. Finally, we face death. Everyone is subject to death. These enemies will have victory over us and inevitably write the final chapter to our life story. But Jesus, in his very coming into the world, his death, and his resurrection, broke the grip of death and defeat. His victory over death is the sign that he is the champion victory-giver. Anyone who has solidarity with Jesus will share in his victory.

The Global South is often rooted in this victory motif called "Christus Victor." Their personal prayer, liturgy, and practice are shaped by its vision of victory over enemies. People living in the Global South do not need an act of the imagination to picture these enemies. Political turmoil, corruption, violence, and seemingly inescapable economic oppression are understood as manifestations of the brokenness of creation. The Jesus of the Gospels combats evil with power as a sign of the coming kingdom. Paul claims that creation itself groans for redemption. The hope and experience of its liberation is overpowering. This understanding of Jesus and his mission, though long neglected in the West, lies at the root of the theology and worship of the church in the Global South.

OTHER CHARACTERISTICS: WHOLE-BODIED WORSHIP FOR THE WHOLE WORLD

Churches outside the West have a sense of solidarity that is hard for Westerners to grasp. We come from the most radically individualistic culture in history. When you talk to students from the West about who they are, they will concede they belong to groups, but they don't think they have communicated who they are until they have distinguished an individual identity. Westerners think the real you is captured in the individual data that sets you apart from your family and community (distinguishing individual information over group information). For most people in the world, the opposite is true: they believe their genuine identity is conveyed when they tell you the groups to which they belong. One could argue that both a group identity and an individual identity are necessary, but if Americans are extreme individualists we may have trouble grasping the practices of the church elsewhere. In numerous cultures an entire group will convert. Also there exists a sense of being united or joined as a church body that seems metaphorical or incredible to one from the West.

Solidarity is visible at the gathered worship of the church. Vibrant singing is a whole-body exercise for many believers in the Global South. This is boisterous compared to many Western churches, but it can be joined with sacramental worship. Intercessory prayer composes a major element in worship; separate seasons of prayer can last for hours. Many believers think that God continues to speak as he did to prophets long ago. The Bible is not displaced by this ongoing gift of prophecy. New prophetic words very often begin in the study of Scripture when a certain phrase becomes the root of the new prophetic word.

David Yonggi Cho is pastor of the world's largest church in South Korea. When asked why the church incorporates women into its leadership in a strongly male-oriented culture, he answers simply, "God told me." Believers in the Global South, especially Charismatics, live with a sense of expectation that God speaks and grants believers gifting as prophets. A more vivid sense of encounter with evil also describes believers beyond the West. These believers engage the spiritual warfare specified by Paul in Ephesians 6. Engaging the manifestations of these spiritual enemies in corporate worship is one of the central features of global Christianity in general and Pentecostalism in particular. Allan Anderson, a leader in Pentecostal studies, recognizes that the conviction that God has restored healing to the church is central to its character and growth. He writes, "in many cases, the ability of the preacher to heal is the primary cause of church growth." Renouncing and denouncing the demonic and prayers for healing find their place in worship.

Finally, Christians in the Global South embrace missions from their earliest days. As with Pentecostalism, many believe they are a part of a great eschatological moment. In this moment, God is creating a people called out from every race to complete his work. An illustration is seen in China when the Chinese house church movement first began. Their groups faced intense opposition as they walked from village to village preaching the gospel. Whole villages would come out and throw rocks and rotten fruit and vegetables at "the scum" of society—the cripples, beggars, and blind who believed in Christ. But they endured. For decades they went underground, but when they grew dramatically under Communist authority, they were often known as the "Back to Jerusalem" movement, back to the Near East and the Islamic world. The designation is often misunderstood in the West, for it is not suggesting the evangelization of Jerusalem or Israel. When the Chinese say "Back to Jerusalem," they have in mind the geographical advance of the gospel throughout history. The gospel started in Jerusalem and then spread in a generally westward direction into North Africa and Europe. So, with a Chinese mindset, the Back to Jerusalem movement sees that to fulfill the Great Commission it must encircle the whole globe with the gospel until it gets back to where it began.

The Back to Jerusalem movement, then, in the closing years of the twentieth century, treasured hopes of sending 100,000 missionaries to 51 nations. Their aim was not Jerusalem or Israel but all the countries and unreached people groups between China and Jerusalem. They had in mind the old Silk Road, which once brought trade from the Middle East to China, and along this road were to be found approximately 5,200 unreached people groups and tribes, including many Muslims. Many believed that they had been called to spread their faith to these Muslims. Some even talked of sending as many as 100,000 missionaries to the Middle East.

Suggestions for Further Reading

Aikman, David. *Jesus in Beijing.* Washington, DC: Regnery, 2003.

*Anderson, Allen. *To the Ends of the Earth: Pentecostalism and the Transformation of World Christianity.* New York: Oxford University Press, 2013.

*Jacobsen, Douglas. *The World's Christians: Who they Are, Where They Are, and How They Got There.* Oxford, UK: Wiley-Blackwell, 2011.

*Jenkins, Philip. *The Next Christendom: The Coming of Global Christianity.* 3rd ed. Oxford, UK: Oxford University Press, 2013.

Lambert, Tony. *China's Christian Millions.* London: Monarch, 1999.

*Latourette, Kenneth Scott. *Christianity in a Revolutionary Age.* Vols. 4–5. New York: Harper and Row, 1961–62.

Marshall, Paul, ed. *Radical Islam's Rules: The Worldwide Spread of Extreme Shari'a Law.* Lanham, MD: Rowman & Littlefield, 2005.

*Noll, Mark, *The New Shape of World Christianity: How American Experience reflects Global Faith.* Downers Grove, IL: InterVarsity Press, 2009.

CHAPTER 48

WINDOWS TO THE CHRISTIAN WORLD

Places and Persons of Faith

W E ARE HUMBLED TO remember that we describe the Global Church
in Western terms. As Randy Richards has written, "generaliza-
tions are always wrong and usually helpful." Perhaps some texture can
be added to our description and exposition of the Global South by
encountering the stories, however briefly, of a few places and the people who together comprise the great people of God.

CHINA

We will consider first and at greatest length the amazing story of faith
in China. China had known great hostility over religious turmoil. One
religious uprising led to twenty-five million deaths! Christian missionary efforts had been received with suspicion and resulted in an expulsion of missionaries in the ninth and thirteenth centuries. The Jesuits
had more enduring but modest success in the 1600s. Still other Christians complained that the Jesuits had compromised Christian teachings in order to make them accessible to the Chinese.

Western nations made China the focus of their missionary work in
the late 1800s and early 1900s. After World War II, a civil war broke
out between the Nationalist Party led by Chiang Kai-shek and the
Communist Party led by Mao Zedong. Eventually the Nationalist Party
was pushed off the mainland, settling in Taiwan. The Communists
formed The People's Republic of China and expelled the Christian

missionaries in 1949, despite their long tenure in the country. Many wondered whether Christians would survive, given China's past violence over religion, the suspicion that Christianity was a tool of Western imperialism, the weak, nominal state of some converts, and the Communists' hostility to religion.

At first there was an effort to control Christianity and other religions. Mao Zedong believed that the faith would die a natural death when the oppression and manipulation of religion was restrained. Governing bodies were created to ensure patriotic compliance in matters of religion. The Protestant Three-Self Patriotic movement (1955) and the Catholic Patriotic Association (1957) became powerful bodies that censured and coerced compliance in the name of loyalty to the nation. Chinese Christians were badly divided. Some joined and endured difficulties to ensure that a Christian voice would survive in China. Others protested that such cooperation was a compromise of the faith.

The Protestant organization took its name from an old missionary strategy that called for churches to be more self-reliant: "self-governing; self-supporting, and self-propagating." The co-opted terms had additional meaning for Communists, who saw Western influence as necessarily oppressive. The Protestants who cooperated were viewed as traitors. They were called the "3 self-church," but more commonly now "the registered Church." The others risked life and limb to maintain independence. They were called "the underground church," "the house church," and more commonly today, "the unregistered church." The Chinese government's policy included brutal persecution, but it also believed that isolating Chinese Christianity from Western influence would lead to its collapse. A later Chinese policy attempted to bring religion to a brutal end. Chairman Mao himself instigated the Great Proletarian Cultural Revolution (1966–1976). Massive brutality, re-education, and cult-like veneration of Mao Zedong were the norm. Church property was confiscated, and even those Christians who had cooperated with the registered churches were persecuted.

After Mao Zedong's death, more moderate voices gained influence in China. Deng Xiaoping embodied this more open approach. President Jimmy Carter normalized relations with China in January of 1979. Visiting the United States, Deng Xiaoping thanked Carter for benefiting the people of China, and asked if he could extend a kindness toward Carter. Carter told him that as a young boy he had given five cents a week to build hospitals and schools in China and had viewed missionaries as heroes of his faith. Carter observed that China forbade missionaries, Bibles, and freedom of worship, and requested that all three be allowed. Deng Xiaoping asked for time to think over the requests. He answered Carter the next morning. He said that China would not allow missionaries but would authorize the distribution of Bibles and would pass a law allowing free worship. Permitting the printing and distribution of Bibles came more quickly, and in 1982 a law began the process of allowing Christians greater freedom to worship. The actual freedom to worship varies greatly from region to region, but more and more the unregistered (underground) churches are holding open meetings and the registered churches are enjoying greater liberty.

The lines of hostility are diminishing, with cooperation between the legal registered church and the unregistered churches becoming more typical. Another important voice and influence has emerged in addition to the registered and unregistered churches. China's economic success has brought entrepreneurs from around the globe. Internationals with passports are given the legal right to free worship and assembly. These churches composed of Christians from across the world form an important spiritual influence and liaison to the other churches in China.

The number of converts in China is mind-bending. A conservative estimate for 2000 is 89 million believers, a full 7.1 percent of the Chinese population.

CARDINAL KUNG: FAITHFUL RESOLVE

Ignatius Cardinal Kung, Kung Pin-Mei (also Gung Pin Mei) was ordained in 1930 and in 1950 became the first native-born Chinese bishop of the important port city of Shanghai. He was imprisoned in 1955 for his unwillingness to renounce the pope and recognize the legitimacy of Chinese efforts to control the Catholic Church. The authorities paraded the bishop before a huge audience at the Dog Racing Stadium to denounce the pope. Instead, he defiantly shouted, "Long live Christ the King, long live the pope." He was imprisoned for the next five years before being convicted of treason in 1960. For the next twenty-five, years he was isolated and kept alone except for times of physical labor. He was not given a Bible or a rosary. He was not allowed correspondence or contact with his family.

After the death of Chairman Mao, China was moving slowly toward a more open economy and, to a lesser and slower extent, a more open culture. Deng Xiaoping arranged a banquet for the cardinal and bishop of Manila, Jaime Sin, in 1984. This Filipino churchman had been instrumental in the popular uprising that unseated Ferdinand Marcos. As a gesture to this openness, the old bishop, who had been in prison for almost thirty years, was invited to the banquet. The carefully marshaled circumstances did not permit the two churchmen to share a personal or private moment. Still, the old bishop seized the opportunity to share a song. Defiantly he sang a song in Latin based on Matthew 16:18: "Upon the rock I will build my church." His resolve had survived thirty years of labor and isolation. The next year, the Chinese would release Kung for "health reasons." Not even Cardinal Sin knew that evening that Pope John Paul II had already named Kung as a cardinal but had done so *in pectore* (literally *in the heart*, a secret designation when publicity might be inappropriate or even dangerous). Kung's life runs a remarkable course. He attempted to work with Chinese authorities but later defied them. Thirty years of isolation and labor did not silence the resolve of this believer. Many worried that the Jesuits had compromised Christianity; others wondered why any genuine believer would ever work with the registered church. Yet time has given evidence of the Spirit's soul-building to fashion strong faith from humble beginnings.

KOREA

Korea's encounter with Christianity is atypical. With some qualification, Koreans actually brought Christianity to Korea. In 1784, Yi Singhun was baptized while on a diplomatic mission to China. He returned with literature by the famous Jesuit missionary Mateo Ricci. Despite not having a priest, the Korean Christians baptized each other and held mass. In 1794, a priest from China, James Chou, was secretly sent to Korea where he took up ministering to almost four thousand practicing Christians. Persecution followed these Catholics who were feared to have alliances with foreign power; waves of martyrdom, including Chou himself, continued for nearly half a century.

In 1873, King Ko-jong displayed a greater openness toward western influence. In this new era, Catholics grew in number. A Scottish Presbyterian missionary, John Ross, translated the New Testament for the Koreans while serving in China. By the 1880s, numerous Protestant missionaries began work in Korea.

The Protestant work reached a young man named Sun Chu Kil. His family moved to Pyongyang in 1885. That same year, several American Presbyterian missionaries arrived. These missionaries supported Bible translation and employed the strategy of John Nevius, an American missionary to China. Nevius supported strong, self-reliant churches. The missionaries' arrival corresponded with the Korean's disillusionment over its political circumstance. Korea was forced to exist in the shadow of China, Russia, and Japan. Kil had struggled with his Taoism and begun to explore Christianity. One of the American missionaries, Samuel Moffett, invited Kil to read *Pilgrim's Progress*. During a season of spiritual struggle, Kil spent a night weeping and praying and was converted.

Kil took an active part in church leadership and evangelism among the working class. In 1903, he entered Pyongyang Presbyterian Seminary (supported by Moffett). Reports of the Welsh revival provoked Kil to hold morning prayer meetings where they petitioned for a Korean revival. Near the end of a ten-day training series for new converts, a missionary publically confessed "stubbornness and pride." Soon many others began to publically confess. Kil himself acknowledged his inappropriately handling a will. The meeting lasted from eight in the evening until two in the morning. The Koreans prayed simultaneously; each believer prayed aloud at the same time. Some say the many spoken voices make a symphony pleasing to God. Numerous Westerners have observed this as a distinctive experience of the Korean spirituality (though it is done elsewhere).

In 1910, the Japanese annexed Korea and ruled over it until the end of World War II. They were brutal toward the churches. Many Christians led in advocating independence from Japan. Kil was a powerful voice in the movement, though he maintained his embrace of Christian nonviolence. For once, Christians earned a reputation for standing against the forces of colonization. In time, Kil was appointed to an influential pastorate: Central Presbyterian Church. His leadership in independence eventually cost him his life and the life of his son. He turned himself in to authorities after his peers in the independence movement were arrested; after his release, he died of complications resulting from his mistreatment. Mark Noll reports that Kil preached over seventeen thousand sermons and shared in starting sixty different churches

After World War II, Korea was divided between the Soviet-supported North and the South, supported by the United States. The fighting ceased in 1953, but the brutality towards Christians remained in place. The Communists struck out against the church. At that time, two-thirds of Korean Christians were in the North. It is very difficult to assess the state of Christianity in North Korea because of the extremely secretive posture of the government. In South Korea, several Christian groups have flourished. Presbyterianism, Pentecostalism, and, more recently, Catholicism have all grown remarkably. Consequences of the Korean Revival were a catalyst to explosive growth. In 1914, one in one hundred Koreans was Protestant. By 2010, one in three Koreans was Christian.

Korea is home to the world's largest churches. The Yoido Full Gospel Church has well over a million members. Its cell structure serves as model and perhaps inspiration to churches around the world. South Korea follows only the United States in the formation of seminaries and sending missionaries around the globe. These missionaries take with them the policy of building self-reliant churches, but also share a Korean spirituality that is different in form and character. This distinctive spirituality is rooted in prayer. Visitors report that Korean simultaneous prayer stands out. The centrality of prayer is seen in the Prayer Mountain. Koreans book time at retreat centers for the purpose of prayer and fasting. Pastor David Yonggi Cho of the Yoido church credits the growth of the church, not to its cell structure or its amazing efficiency, but to its prayer.

EAST AFRICAN REVIVAL

The stories of two men and the friendship they forged is one piece of the great revival to sweep across East Africa. Both of these men suffered discouragement. Simeon Nsibambi was born in 1897. He was converted in 1922. Numerous opportunities helped create the hope and expectation that he would be selected to study abroad, but it was not to be. God addressed Simeon's severe disappointment in a vision. In the vision, God asked him to compare the value of the scholarship with the value of the gospel message and the forgiveness that had been granted him.

Dr. Joseph Church was converted as a student at Cambridge in August, 1920. Cambridge had known evangelical stirrings. American evangelist D. L. Moody had preached at Cambridge almost four decades before Church's experience of conversion. In the wake of Moody's meeting, numerous Cambridge students were called to serve in missions, including the Cambridge Seven who targeted China. One such student, George Lawrence Pilkington, went to Uganda where he witnessed a revival in 1893, a precursor to the revival to follow. Dr. Church applied his skills as a doctor in Africa where he also distinguished himself as an able missionary.

By 1929, Church was undergoing a serious physical and spiritual discouragement. He longed for companionship to address his emptiness when he encountered Simeon Nsibambi. The two shared their longings for revival for themselves and Africa. They prayed and studied the Bible together for two days. The experience and unity of purpose was life changing. Noll cites Church's reflections upon the meeting "as the time that God in his sovereign grace met with me and brought me to the end of myself and thought fit to give me a share in the power of Pentecost."

The fellowship that included these two would grow to be extended again and again. In September, 1935, another group met for spiritual renewal; their thinking was shaped by the Keswick theme that complete surrender to Christ preceded Spiritual breakthroughs. They planned and initiated a series of meetings that may be identified as the revival's starting point. The group included Joseph Church (the only Anglo) and Simeon Nsibambi. William Nagenda soon joined the circle and would become more influential than any other group member in the revival's spread. Two important words reveal the revivalist nature of this outpouring: *abaka* means *on fire*; *balokole* means *the saved*.

Some credit this core leadership not only for preaching but for the organizational wisdom to send groups out in teams that involved lay persons. The revival's geographic sweep moved from North Uganda to include Kenya, Rwanda, Burundi, and Tanzania (then Tanganyika). It touched many internationally beyond the region. The numbers defy all imagination. The percentages of Christian adherents near the century's end are as follows: Uganda 89 percent, Kenya 79 percent, Rwanda 81 percent, Burundi 90 percent, and Tanzania 51 percent.

William Nagenda and Joe Church made perhaps the most effective team. Nagenda's strong family was a vindication to his powerful preaching. Nagenda also was involved in one of the important tests faced during the revival. In 1941 twenty-nine students were expelled from Bishop Tucker Theological College. The school's leadership were alarmed at the revival zeal of these *balokole*, or saved ones. Thankfully the (all Anglo) school authorities were able to restore almost every student, including William Nagenda. Students were able to express their revival fervor and remain loyal to the denomination; this flexibility proved very important for the revival movement. The movement, however, crossed denominational lines at numerous points. Brethren, Seventh Day Adventists, Mennonites, Baptists, and Methodists all report participation in the revival.

Another celebrated voice of the movement is Festo Kivengere. Kivengere was born to a ruling family and worked as a shepherd as a young boy. The young shepherd read children's stories about Jesus as he worked. He was converted during an evangelistic meeting. He studied theology, pastored a church, and was eventually ordained as bishop in the Anglican Church. He befriended Billy Graham and served as his translator as well as appearing at Graham's crusades. Kivengere's courage encountering Idi Amin was widely admired. Amin murdered his archbishop, Janani Luwum, and Kivengere remained in exile until

Amin's ouster. During this time, he became an internationally recognized voice for social justice and for all of Africa. His theology was firmly rooted in the cross. Kivengere believed that Christ called him to love Amin despite his atrocities.

In China, Korea, and East Africa we observe several common elements. Each has an array of its own rich Christian cultures while having indebtedness to missionary efforts. Each has seen remarkable numerical growth. Each has produced believers who give to Christ in their bearing suffering and extending grace.

Suggestions for Further Reading

*Anderson, Allen. *To the Ends of the Earth: Pentecostalism and the Transformation of World Christianity.* New York: Oxford University Press, 2013.

*Hill, Jonathan. *Zondervan Handbook to the History of Christianity.* Grand Rapids: Zondervan, 2006.

*Jacobsen, Douglas. *The World's Christians: Who they Are, Where They Are, and How They Got There.* Oxford, UK: Wiley-Blackwell, 2011.

*Osborn, H. H. *Pioneers in the East African Revival.* Winchester, UK: Apologia, 2000.

*Noll, Mark A. and Carolyn Nystrom. *Clouds of Witnesses: Christian Voices from Africa and Asia.* Downer Grove, IL: InterVarsity Press, 2011.

*Spickard, Paul R. and Kevin M. Cragg, *A Global History of Christians: How Everyday Believers Experience Their World.* Grand Rapids: Baker, 2004.

EPILOGUE

R.L. Hatchett

In sum: "to be saved" in the Pauline view means to become part of the *people* of God, who by the Spirit are born into God's *family* and therefore joined to one another as one *body*, whose gatherings in the Spirit form them into God's *temple*. God is not simply saving individuals and preparing them for heaven; rather he is creating a *people* for his name, among whom God can dwell and who in their life together will reproduce God's life and character in all its unity and diversity.

Gordon Fee

PAUL, THE SPIRIT, AND THE PEOPLE OF GOD

This book has left a trail of stories that explain who we are. We have read the story of the right-believing early Christians who kept the church on track by capturing some of the mystery of who Jesus is. We have read the story of the Protestant Reformers who tried to capture the heart of the gospel by exploring the Scripture. We have read the story of believers who held to faith instead of yielding to liberal leanings. We have read stories about awakenings that have influenced our prosperous culture. These stories explain who we are: we are orthodox (right-believing), Protestant, conservatives or Evangelicals in North America. This is the profile of many of Dr. Shelley's students and readers through the years.

It is right to tell our own stories and find our place in God's grand story. Many today, however, sense that a preoccupation with the success of our story may be costly. A fascination with our own story may make it appear as a zenith or conclusion. We are then prone not to see and appreciate others and rightly measure ourselves; with our story wrongly appraised we face discouragement and the risk of losing track of where God's grand story is heading. The unprecedented growth of Christianity in the last one hundred years requires reassessment. At present, both ends of Christian history profoundly speak in unison. Gordon Fee reminds us that the first Christians understood that God was fashioning a people to be taken from of all peoples of the world. These were often taken from low status or rank to be granted the privilege to belonging to God's people. Today God is gathering a people for Himself from almost every conceivable place and people.

The transition and hardships in the Western church may be understood in part in this light; the Western experience may be a microcosm of what is happening in the world at large; Western Christians are losing status and even facing persecution, yet they also are witnessing an ingathering of this diverse people.

Problems and dangers abound; it is not irreverent to wonder about numerous matters. Are these new believers superstitious or naïve? Is their faith nominal, paper thin? Can they break with their culture? How could the Rwanda genocide happen on the turf of the East African Revival? We rightly should also ask similar questions of ourselves: Is our practice of Christianity shaped or misshaped by our affluent culture? Have we not seen Christian brother bear arms against Christian brother in our own Civil War? We should also ask if we have things to learn from the Christians of the Global South: Do we understand solidarity? Is our metaphysics stifling to the Spirit? Appraising our stories again may lead us to value belonging to the people of God above all else.

This circle persists. Reading church history rightly helps us read the Bible rightly; reading the Bible rightly helps us read church history rightly. We may read with new appreciation if we can discern the theological significance of the church as God' people gathered from the nations.

Come to him, a living stone, though rejected by mortals yet chosen and precious in God's sight, and ⁻†like living stones, let yourselves be built into a spiritual house, to be a holy priesthood, to offer spiritual sacrifices acceptable to God through Jesus Christ.⁻†For it stands in scripture:

> "See, I am laying in Zion a stone,
>   a cornerstone chosen and precious;
> and whoever believes in him will not be put to shame."

To you then who believe, he is precious;
     but for those who do not believe,
"The stone that the builders rejected
     has become the very head of the corner,"

and

"A stone that makes them stumble,
     and a rock that makes them fall."

They stumble because they disobey the word, as they were destined
to do.

But you are a chosen race, a royal priesthood, a holy nation, God's
own people, in order that you may proclaim the mighty acts of him who
called you out of darkness into his marvelous light.

Once you were not a people,
     but now you are God's people;
once you had not received mercy,
     but now you have received mercy.
(1 Peter 2:4–10 NRSV).

Bruce Shelley

TODAY, AFTER TWO THOUSAND years, Christianity is the faith, at least
nominally, of one-third of the earth's population. From a handful
of fishermen, tax collectors, and youthful troublemakers in an obscure
province of Judea, the faith has spread over the globe to claim the loyalty of nearly a thousand million inhabitants of our planet.

Surely one of the more remarkable aspects of Christianity today is
how few of these professed believers have ever seriously studied the history of their religion. In an earlier age adherents of one faith seldom
encountered adherents of another. Few were required to defend their
religion against the criticisms of a rival faith. In our day, however, when
mass media make the world our neighborhood, the ignorance of Christians is hard to justify.

The movement toward separation of church and state has all but
removed religion from public education. That is true. But even Christian education in many denominations has done little to give members

any sort of adult understanding of the faith. Should we really be surprised, then, when today's Christian so frequently blends gross errors with orthodox confession or defends some pagan practice as Christian conduct?

Informed Christians might be tempted to ask, "If the righteous man is scarcely saved, where will the impious and sinner appear?" (1 Peter 4:18). But they know that human failure is always only half the story. They realize how often the church has been its own worst enemy and how frequently renewal has come from some totally unexpected source. Time and again the church has discovered some unseen Power turning aside a threat to its existence or transforming a crisis into an opportunity for growth. Torrid persecutions served to purge the household of faith. Heresy's spread clarified the church's basic beliefs. And the sudden appearance of barbarian hordes opened doors for further expansion. This ability to face new challenges and to tap the sources of renewal is one of the secrets of Christianity's growth.

The way forward usually meant a studied look backward, back to the image of God revealed in the story of Jesus. Christians have always considered the age of Jesus and his apostles a kind of model for all the other ages. It gave to the church its faith in Jesus, the resurrected Messiah, and the hope of forgiveness of sins through him. And the age demonstrated, in the life of Paul, that the gospel of grace recognizes no boundaries of nation, race, sex, or culture.

The catholic Christianity that accepted this truth spread rapidly throughout the Mediterranean world. It confronted the alien ideas of Gnosticism, Marcionism, and Montanism and called a lie, a lie by appealing to the apostolic writings and to the orthodox bishops who guarded them. At the same time, Christians faced the persecuting power of Rome and dared to die heroically as martyrs, witnesses to other believers to follow in their train.

This seed of martyr's blood, as Tertullian called it, eventually bore abundant fruit in the conversion of the empire. The Imperial Age began in 312 when Constantine caught a vision of Christ. Before the fourth century closed Christianity became the official religion of the sprawling Roman state. A church in the catacombs was one thing, but what does Christianity have to do with palaces?

Under the emperor's tutelage the church learned to serve the seats of power by formulating the faith for the masses. Hence the age of great councils. Those Christians who had no yen for palaces headed for the wilderness in search of another way to grace. Revered hermits soon found themselves in the vanguard of a movement: monasticism, the wave of the future.

Most Christians, however, saw the hand of God in the happy wedding of Christian church and Roman state. In the East the marriage continued for a millennium. A mystical piety flourished under the protection of orthodox emperors until 1453, when invading Muslim Turks brought the Byzantine empire to its final ruin. The fall of Constantinople, however, meant the rise of Moscow, the new capital of Eastern Orthodoxy.

In the West it was a different story. After the fifth century, when barbarian Germans and Huns shattered the empire's defenses and swept into the eternal city itself, men turned to Augustine's *City of God* for explanations. They found a vision for a new age. We call these centuries medieval. People who lived in them considered them Christian.

Their reasons lie in the role of the pope who stepped into the ruins of the fallen empire in the West and proceeded to build the medieval church upon Rome's bygone glory. As the only surviving link with the Roman past, the Church of Rome mobilized Benedictine monks and deployed them as missionary ambassadors to the German people. It took centuries, but the popes, aided by Christian princes, slowly pacified and baptized a continent and called it Christendom, Christian Europe.

Baptized masses, however, meant baptized pagans. By the tenth century spiritual renewal was an obvious necessity. It started in a monastery in central France called Cluny and spread until it reached the papacy itself. The greatest of the reforming popes was Gregory VII. His zealous successors carried the papal office to the zenith of earthly power. No longer the cement of a Roman empire, the church of the twelfth century was itself a kind of empire, a spiritual and earthly kingdom stretching from Ireland to Palestine, from earth to heaven. The crusades and Scholastic philosophy were witnesses to this papal sovereignty.

Power, however, corrupts. The church gained the world but lost its soul. That, at any rate, is what a steady stream of reformers preached: Waldensees, Franciscans, Albigensees. Amid the strife for earthly power and the evidences of barren religion in the fourteenth and fifteenth centuries, many Christians turned to the Bible for fresh vision and renewal.

Reform came with a fury. Martin Luther sounded the trumpet, but hosts of others rallied to the cause. The period we call the Reformation marks the mobilization of Protestantism: Lutheran, Reformed, Anglican, and Anabaptist. By the mid-sixteenth century the Reformation had shattered the traditional unity of western Europe and had bequeathed to modern times religious pluralism.

The Church of Rome resisted this attack upon tradition. She mustered new troops, especially the Society of Jesus. She sent out fresh waves of missionaries to Asia, Africa, and Latin America. She waged war in France, the Netherlands, and Germany. But in the end, Christendom slipped into yesteryear. In its place arose the denominational concept of the church, which allowed modern nations to treat the churches as voluntary societies separated from the state.

Novel schools of thought filled the seventeenth century. None was more powerful than Reason itself. It asked, who needs God? Man can make it on his own. Christians screamed their objections, but the idea spread until secularism filled the public life of Western societies. God remained, but only as a matter of personal choice.

Christians could no longer appeal to the arm of power to suppress such heresies. So, many of them turned instead to the way of the apostles, prayer and preaching. The result was a series of evangelical revivals: chiefly Pietism, Methodism, and the Great Awakening. By preaching and personal conversions, Evangelicals tried to restore God to public life.

The Age of Progress saw Christians of all sorts wage a valiant struggle against the advance of secularism. Out of the evangelical awakenings came new efforts to carry the gospel of Christ to distant lands and a host of social service ministries in industrialized Europe and North America. From the ramparts of Rome a defensive papacy fired a barrage of missiles aimed at the modern enemies of the Catholic faith. In spite of Christians' best efforts, however, Christianity was slowly driven from public life in the Western World. Believers were left with the problem we recognize in our own time: How can Christians exert moral influence in pluralistic and totalitarian societies where Christian assumptions about reality no longer prevail?

The depth of the problem was apparent in the Age of Ideologies, when new gods arose to claim the loyalties of secular men. Nazism exalted the state, Communism worshiped the party, and American Democracy revered the individual and his rights. Supposed enlightened modern nations waged two global wars in an attempt to establish the supremacy of these new deities. When no single ideology prevailed, a cold war of coexistence settled upon the once Christian nations. Through these troubled times the denominations struggled over orthodox and liberal theologies, sought fresh ways to recover a lost unity, and reflected a new hunger for apostolic experiences.

After World War II vigorous new Christian leadership emerged in the Third World, offering fresh hope for a new day for the old faith. Had missionaries from the neo-pagan nations of Europe and North

America succeeded in giving Christianity a stake in the future by carrying the gospel to Asia, Africa, and Latin America?

Only time will tell. But Christians can hope because faith always reaches beyond earthly circumstances. Its confidence is in a person. And no other person in recorded history has influenced more people in as many conditions over so long a time as Jesus Christ. The shades and tones of his image seem to shift with the needs of men: the Jewish Messiah of the believing remnant, the Wisdom of the Greek apologist, the Cosmic King of the Imperial Church, the Heavenly Logos of the orthodox councils, the World Ruler of the papal courts, the monastic Model of apostolic poverty, the personal Savior of evangelical revivalists.

Truly, he is a man for all time. In a day when many regard him as irrelevant, a relic of a quickly discarded past, church history provides a quiet testimony that Jesus Christ will not disappear from the scene. His title may change, but his truth endures for all generations.

NOTES

Chapter 1

The opening description of crucifixion reflects Bamber Gascoigne, *The Christians* (New York: Morrow, 1977), 17.

The quotations in this chapter, as well as many vivid details, are from the descriptions of Jesus' times in *Great People of the Bible and How They Lived* (Pleasantville: Reader's Digest Association. 1968), 308, 338, 370, 379–81.

Chapter 2

The description of Antioch as well as the quotation about Jerusalem and its fall are from *Great People of the Bible*, 406, 407, and 390.

Chapter 3

For the text box see Rodney Stark, *The Rise of Christianity: A Sociologist Reconsiders History*. (Princeton: Princeton University Press, 1996).

The story about King Abgar is found in Eusebius's *Ecclesiastical History*, book I, section XIII.

Professor Ward Gasque's introduction to Irenaeus and Tertullian is found in Eerdman's *Handbook to the History of Christianity* (Grand Rapids: Eerdmans, 1977), 75–77. This volume, edited by Tim Dowley, is one of the best introductions to church history available.

Celsus' criticism of Christians comes from Origen's *Against Celsus*, book III, section 44.

Julian's views of Christian behavior are in a letter to Arsacius, high priest of Galatia, recorded in Sozomen's *Ecclesiastical History* V. 16.

Chapter 4

The Martyrdom of Polycarp is one of the better known stories from the early church. It can be found in *Early Christian Fathers*, edited by Cyril C. Richardson (Philadelphia: Westminster, 1953), 141–58.

The contrast between Jewish and Christian proselyting I have drawn from Paul Hutchinson and Winfred E. Garrison, *20 Centuries of Christianity* (New York: Harcourt, Brace and Co., 1959), 30–31.

Pliny's letter to Trajan is recorded in *A New Eusebius,* edited by J. Stevenson (London: S.P.C.K., 1960), 13–14.

I found *The Early Church* by Henry Chadwick (Middlesex: Penguin, 1967), 54–60, helpful in "Reasons for the Gospel's Spread."

Chapter 5

The Mahatma Gandhi quotation is echoed in Robert Johnson, *The Meaning of Christ* (Philadelphia: Westminster, 1958), 63.

The discussion on "Faith and Theology" reflects the insights of J. W. C. Wand, *The Four Great Heresies* (London: A. R. Mowbray, 1955), chapter 1.

The Charles Bigg quote can be found in Charles Williams, *Descent of the Dove* (New York: Meridian Books, 1956), 23.

The Old Roman Creed appears in *Documents of the Christian Church*, edited by Henry Bettenson (London: Oxford University Press, 1963), 23–24.

The C. S. Lewis quotation is from his *Mere Christianity* (New York: Macmillan, 1952), book 2, chapter 5.

The description of orthodoxy under "Faith and History" and the comparison of *virgin* and *born* are from William Hordern, *A Layman's Guide to Protestant Theology* (New York: Macmillan, 1974), 1, 13.

The text box "What Gnostics Believe" is adapted from J.N.D. Kelley, *Early Christian Doctrines*, 26.

The text box "The Gospel of Thomas," is adapted from Craig Evans, *Fabricating Jesus* (Downers Grove, IL: InterVarsity Press, 2006), 71.

The imagery found in text box "Understanding Gnosticism Today" arose out of a lecture titled "Did We Get Jesus Right? Jesus in the Canonized and Apocryphal Gospels," by Simon Gathercole and response by David Chapman at Lanier Theological Library on September 8, 2012.

Chapter 6

The account of the believer in Sicily comes from Herbert B. Workman, *Persecution in the Early Church* (London: Charles H. Kelly, 1906), 275–76.

Origen's views about the meanings of Scripture come from his work *On First Principles*, Book IV, sections 7–8.

"The Question of the Apocrypha" reflects the clear discussion of Floyd Filson, *Which Books Belong in the Bible?* (Philadelphia: Westminster, 1957).

Chapter 7

The quotations from "One Early Christian" and from Athenagoras can be found in Adolph Harnack, *Mission and Expansion of Early Christianity* (New York: Harper, 1962), 207–9.

This chapter draws upon the discussion "Forgiveness of Sins" in Roland H. Bainton, *Christendom*, vol. 1 (New York: Harper & Row, 1964, 1966). I have reshaped Bainton's helpful explanation of Cyprian's attitude.

Adapted from Everett Ferguson, *Church History, Volume One: From Christ to the Pre-Reformation* (Grand Rapids: Zondervan Press, 2005), 114–119.

Chapter 8

Tertullian's tirade against philosophy is from his work *Prescriptions Against the Heretics*, section 7. The quotation by Origen about the purpose of creation is from his work *On First Principles*, book II, section II, 4.

The quotation from Clement about wisdom comes from *A History of the Church* by August Franzen (New York: Herder and Herder, 1969), 37.

Chapter 9

The description of Diocletian and Galerius is a reshaped account from Hutchinson and Garrison, *20 Centuries of Christianity*, 44–48. The quotations are from this work.

Ambrose's letter to Theodosius, letter 51, is quoted in Robert Payne, *Fathers of the Western Church* (New York: Viking Press, 1951), 78–79.

The quotation by Bamber Gascoigne is from his *The Christians*, 44–45.

Chapter 10

The quotation from the bishop is from Gregory of Nyssa and is quoted in W. H. C. Frend, *The Early Church* (Philadelphia: Lippincott, 1966), 186–87.

The Nicene Creed appears, among many other places, in Philip Schaff, *Creeds of Christendom*, vol. 2 (New York: Harper, 1919), 58–59.

Eusebius of Caesarea's enthusiastic remarks are from his *Life of Constantine*, III, 15.

William Hordern's anecdote is in his book *A Layman's Guide to Protestant Theology*,15–16.

In the discussion of the Trinity, I found help in Fisher Humphrey, *The Almighty* (Elgin, IL: David C. Cook, 1976), esp. 102–7; Compare Roger Olson, *The Story of Christian Theology: Twenty Centuries of Tradition & Reform* (Downers Grove, IL: InterVarsity Press, 1999); also see also Justo Gonzalez, *A Concise History of Christian Doctrine* (Nashville, TN: Abingdon, 2006).

Chapter 11

J. S. Whale's observation at Cambridge is from his book *Christian Doctrine* (London: Fontana Books, 1957), 102.

David F. Wright's discussion of the Christology debate is in Eerdmans' *Handbook to the History of Christianity*, 156ff. The quotation is on page 171.

The Chalcedonian definition may be found in Henry Bettenson, *Documents of the Christian Church*, 51–52.

The chart is drawn from numerous handbooks on doctrine. One can see elements and influence adapted from Strong, Gonzalez, and Coppedge. Allen Coppedge, *The God Who is Triune: Revisioning the Christian Doctrine of God*, (Downers Grove, IL: InterVarsity, 2007); Justo Gonzalez, *A Concise History of Christian Doctrine* (Nashville, TN: Abingdon, 2006); and A. H. Strong's, *Systematic Theology*. For the summary quotation see Tony Lane, *A Concise History of Christian Thought*. Revised. (Grand Rapids: Baker, 2006), 61.

Chapter 12

St. Anthony's experience in the desert may be found in Anne Fremantle, *Treasury of Early Christianity* (New York: Mentor, 1960), 400.

The quotation describing Jerome is Roland Bainton's from his *Christendom*, vol. 1, 135.

The section "The Genius of the West" draws freely from Williston Walker's sketch of Benedict in his *Great Men of the Christian Church* (Chicago: Chicago University Press, 1908), 103–14. The quotations in this section are from this work.

Chapter 13

Augustine's quotations about his early life are from his *Confessions*.

The contrasts between Pelagius's and Augustine's views of sin and grace echo Williston Walker's clear statement in *Great Men of the Christian Church*, 76–79.

Augustine's observation about the worldly city is from his *City of God*, especially book XIV, 28 and book V, 19.

On the Church's reception of Augustine see Justo Gonzalez, *The Story of Christianity: Volume One: The Early Church to the Dawn of the Reformation*, revised and updated. (New York: HarperCollins, 2010), 250.

Chapter 14

Valentinian's decree and Leo's quotation may both be found in Friedrich Gontard, *The Chair of Peter* (New York: Holt, Rinehart, and Winston, 1964), 138; 142–43.

Chapter 15

The opening scene is from Kallistos Timothy Ware's *The Orthodox Church* (Middlesex, Eng.: Penguin, 1964), 51.

Harlie Kay Gallatin's helpful description of icons is from Eerdman's *Handbook*, 247–48.

The words of the Russian envoys appear in Stephen Neill, *Christian Missions* (Middlesex: Penguin, 1964), 89.

Chapter 16

Clovis's prayer and baptism story appear in Roland Bainton, *Christendom*, vol. 1, 145–46.

Chapter 17

Gregory the Great's quotations in this chapter can be found in Philip Schaff, *History of the Christian Church*, vol. 4 (Grand Rapids: Eerdmans, 1950), 212–15, 228.

Some biographical details in this chapter were taken from Robert Payne, *The Fathers of the Western Church* (New York: Viking, 1951).

The story of the monk Copiosus is recorded in Odo J. Zimmerman, *Saint Gregory: the Great Dialogues* (New York: Fathers of the Church, 1959), 266–70.

Chapter 18

The opening episode is reshaped from the account in Friedrich Gontard, *The Chair of Peter*, 180–81.

The politics of the Holy Roman Empire can be confusing to the layman. I have leaned heavily upon the treatment of a standard history text. In the sections "Ideas Die Slowly" and "Architect of an Empire" I have abridged Charlemagne's rise to power from T. Walter Wallbank, Alastair M. Taylor, and Nels M. Bailkey, *Civilization Past and Present* (Glenview, IL: Scott, Foresman, 1975), 190–93. The explanation of feudalism is a condensation of pages 197–98, and the paragraphs dealing with the Germanic Kingdoms conflicts are an abbreviated version of pages 243–45.

David Bentley Hart, *The Story of Christianity* (London, Quercus: 2007), pp. 116–117.

Chapter 19

Suger's remark about the Gothic style appears in Anne Fremantle, *Age of Faith* (New York: Time-Life, 1965), 124.

Pope Urban's call to the crusade and the crusader quotation are both found in *Civilization: Past and Present*, 209–210.

See Robert Wilken, *The First One Thousand Years*, (New Haven, CT: Yale, 2012), 288 and following for Christians under Muslim rule.

Chapter 20

The scholar Olbert's behavior is described in *Civilization: Past and Present*, 250. The description of "The Magnetism of an Able Teacher" comes from *Age of Faith*, 94–96. The quotations in this section are from this well-written work.

Chapter 21

See the note on Albigensian Crusade by David Bentley Hart, *The Story of Christianity* (London: Quercus, 2007), 141.

Chapter 23

John Hus's prayer is quoted in Herbert B. Workman, *Dawn of the Reformation*, vol. 2 (London: Epworth, 1953), 325.

For the inquisition note see Glenn Sunshine, *The Reformation for Armchair Theologians* (Louisville: Westminster John Knox Press, 2005), 96–99.

Chapter 24

The best biography of Martin Luther is Roland Bainton, *Here I Stand* (Nashville: Abingdon, 1950). It contains the quotations in this chapter, including the hymn describing Luther's spiritual journey (66–67). In order to introduce these quotations, I have used the colorful summary of Luther's life found in *Time*, March 24, 1967, 70–74, without attempting to identify quotations within quotation.

For the theology and text boxes see Alister E. McGrath, *Historical Theology: An Introduction to the History of Christian Thought*, 2nd ed. (Malden, MA: Wiley-Blackwell, 2013).

Chapter 25

The quotation from the martyred mother is found in Thielman J. Van Braght, *Martyr's Mirror* (Scottdale, PA: Mennonite Publishing House, 1951), 984–87.
I am indebted to John H. Yoder and Alan Kreider for their helpful summary of Anabaptist beliefs found in Eerdman's *Handbook*, 399–403.

Chapter 28

A brief summary of Loyola's life and the Jesuit order appeared in *Time*, April 23, 1973, 40–48. We have drawn some descriptions from this article.
The quotations on the horrors of hell is from the *Spiritual Exercises*, 58.

Chapter 32

The response to Ezra Stiles from Benjamin Franklin is quoted in Winthrop S. Hudson, *American Protestantism* (Chicago: University of Chicago Press, 1961), 13.
The quotation from Baron von Holbach can be found in *Civilization*, 393–94.
The Diderot quotation is found in Frank E. Manuel, *The Age of Reason* (Ithaca, NY: Cornell University Press, 1951), 30.
For Renaissance Humanism see Alister E. McGrath. *Historical Theology: An Introduction to the History of Christian Thought*, 115–16.
For the ancient wisdom of Revelation, see Robert Wilken, *The Spirit of Early Christian Thought: Seeking the Face of God* (New Haven, CT: Yale, 2003).

Chapter 33

The quotations from the *Pensées* appear in many editions. Among them is the Modern Library edition, Blaise Pascal, *Pensées* (New York: Random House, 1941).
The quote about August Herman Francke is as quoted by Tom Streeter in *The Church and Western Culture: An Introduction to Church History* (Bloomington, IN: AuthorHouse, 2006), 319.
The sketch of Zinzendorf reflects Williston Walker's treatment in *Great Men of the Christian Church*, 308–16.

Chapter 36

The conditions and events of the French Revolution are condensed from *Civilization*, 451–61, and from Peter Gay, *Age of Enlightenment* (New York: Time-Life, 1966), 167–68.
The account of the loss of the papal states and Vatican Council II is a summary of August Franzen's treatments in *A History of the Church*, 384–94.

Chapter 37

The quotation from G. M. Trevelyan can be found in Ernest Marshall Howse, *Saints in Politics* (London: George Allen, 1953), 178. I have found this book most helpful for this chapter.

For the supplement to Bebbington's description of Evangelicalism see Thomas Kidd, *The Great Awakening; The Roots of Evangelical Christianity in Colonial America* (New Haven, CT: Yale, 2007).

Chapter 38

The attitude of the British East India Company is an echo of Hutchinson and Garrison, *20 Centuries of Christianity*, 279.

The summary of Carey's translation work is from Stephen Neill, *The Christian Society* (New York: Harper, 1952), 202.

For a good treatment of Fuller see James Leo Garrett, *Baptist Theology: a Four-Century Study.* (Macon, GA: Mercer, 2007).

I have tried to give voice to this immediacy in reading Scripture; see R. L. Hatchett. "The Hermeneutics of Conversion," in *The Ties That Bind: Life Together in the Baptist Vision*, eds. Gary Furr and Curtis Freeman (Macon GA: Symth and Helwys, 1994).

Chapter 39

The Timothy Flint portrait of the western preacher is quoted in Edwin Scott Gaustad, *Historical Atlas of Religion in America* (New York: Harper & Row, 1962), 41.

The Willard Sperry explanation of black religion was to an English audience: *Religion in America* (Boston: Beacon Press, 1963), 193.

The quotations by President Woolsey and by H. L. Mencken come from George Marsden's chapter in *The Evangelicals*, eds. David F. Wells and John D. Woodbridge (Nashville: Abingdon, 1975), 122–23.

Chapter 40

The summary of the "Spokesmen for Liberalism" draws upon Hordern, *A Layman's Guide*, 44–49. The quotations are from these pages.

Chapter 41

The Dickens quotations from *Hard Times* appears in *Civilization: Past and Present*, 487–88. The brief discussions of Marx and Engels are also drawn from this volume.

The information on Bishop Ketteler and Cardinal Manning comes from Thomas Bokenkotter, *A Concise History of the Catholic Church* (Garden City, NY: Doubleday, 1977), 314–16.

The Rauschenbusch explanation of the Social Gospel is from *A Theology of the Social Gospel* (New York: Macmillan, 1917), 5.

Chapter 42

The discussion "Christians Under Hitler" draws upon Richard Pierard's fine article, "An Age of Ideology," found in the *Eerdman's Handbook*, 576–78. The final quotation is from 587–88.

Chapter 43

The quotations from Shailer Mathews and from J. Gresham Machen can be found in Robert L. Ferm, *Issues in American Protestantism* (Garden City, NY: Doubleday, 1969), 262–87.

For the Scopes trial see Gary Wills, *Under God: Religion and American Politics* (New York: Simon and Schuster, 1900).

Chapter 44

The George Whitefield quotation appears in William Warren Sweet, *The Story of Religion in America* (New York: Harper, 1950), 141–42.

Chapter 46

See the article on "secularization" in *The Blackwell Encyclopedia of Modern Christian Thought* (Malden, MA: Blackwell, 1993).

George Weigel, *The Cube and the Cathedral: Europe, America, and Politics Without God* (New York: Basic Books, 2005), 12.

For smarter atheism see David Bentley Hart, *Atheist Delusions: The Christian Revolution and its Fashionable Enemies* (New Haven, CT: Yale, 2009) and Alister McGrath, *The Twilight of Atheism: The Rise and Fall of Disbelief in the Modern World* (WaterBrook Press, 2006).

For stirrings among Muslims see Tom Doyle with Greg Webster, *Dreams and Visions: Is Jesus Awakening the Muslim World?* (Nashville, TN: Thomas Nelson, 2012).

Chapter 47

Philip Jenkins's "The Next Christianity" is found in *The Atlantic*, October, 2002, 53–68.

Pentecostals stood in the vanguard of the Southern Counter-Reformation. Though Pentecostalism emerged as a movement only at the start of the twentieth century, chiefly in North America, Pentecostals a century later were at least 400 million strong and heavily concentrated in the global South. By 2040 or so there could be as many as a billion, at which point Pentecostal Christians alone would far outnumber the world's Buddhists and would enjoy rough numerical parity with the world's Hindus.

For the roots and early history of Pentecostalism see Allan Anderson, *An Introduction to Pentecostalism: Global Charismatic Christianity* (New York: Cambridge, 2004), chapters 2 and 3.

See Jenkins, *The Next Christendom*, 40 for the Kenyatta quote.

For the ratio (1 in 4) of Charismatics to the total number of Christians see Pew Forum on Religion

and Public Life (December 19, 2011), "Global Christianity: A Report on the Size *and Distribution of*
the *World's* Christian Population."

The chart on Pentecostal numbers is adapted from Mark Noll, *The New Shape of World Christianity: How American Experience reflects Global Faith* (Downers Grove, IL: InterVarsity Press, 2009), 22. Noll depends upon the numbers of David B. Barrett's *World Christian Encyclopedia*, 2nd ed. (New York: Oxford University Press, 2001).

See Noll, *The New Shape of World Christianity,*185 for East Africa.

See A. Greg Carter, *Rethinking Christ and Culture: A Post Christendom Perspective* (Grand Rapids: Brazos Press, 2006) 14–15 for descriptions of Christendom.

For Bunyan see Linda Woodhead, *Introduction to Christianity* (New York: Cambridge, 2004), 204–5.

See Mark Noll on the Bible and translation (relying upon Senneh), *The Shape of World Christianity,* 22–24, 36.

For liberation theology see Paul R. Spickard and Kevin M. Cragg, *A Global History of Christians: How Everyday Believers Experience Their World* (Grand Rapids: Baker, 2004), 429.

The "mass-produced affection" quotation is from Carol Flake, *Redemptorama: Culture, Politics, and the New Evangelicalism* (New York: Penguin Books, 1984), 17.

In his *Becoming Conversant with the Emerging Church* (Grand Rapids: Zondervan, 2005), D. A. Carson writes, "At the heart of the Emergent Church movement—or as some of its leaders prefer to call it, the 'conversation'—lies the conviction that changes in the culture signal that a new church is 'emerging.' Christian leaders must therefore adapt to this emerging church. Those who fail to do so are blind to the cultural accretions that hide the gospel behind forms of thought and modes of expression that no longer communicate with the new generation, the emerging generation" (p. 12). Many observers have associated the emerging church with postmodernity.

Professor David E. Wells has written, "This postmodern outlook comes in all kinds of shapes and expressions, which is what probably explains the multiplicity of definitions which have been advanced. Its own ethos almost guarantees that there will be no such thing as a postmodern outlook but rather there will be many different postmodern perspectives. Yet what they have in common is that they all believe that meaning has died. This has to be qualified immediately by the assertion that what has most obviously died is the kind of rational meaning which the Enlightenment provided—but postmoderns find no grounds for any other kind." From *Above All Earthly Pow'rs* (Grand Rapids: Eerdmans, 2005), 67.

Chapter 48

The description of the underground church scene is from "China's Christian Underground," by Fang Bay, *U.S. News & World Report,* April 30, 2001. And the striking shift in the global map is found in Christopher J. H. Wright's "An Upside Down World" in *Christianity Today*, January 2007, 42.

David Aikman's story and report from China can be found in his *Jesus in Beijing*. The Su Wenxing story is on pages 258–60.

In the early years of the twenty-first century, the Christian population of South Korea also continued at a rapid pace of nearly 6 percent annually, bolstered by vigorous evangelistic efforts and also by the favor of the government, which viewed Christianity as an ideological means of resisting the encroachment of communism.

For the stories I depend upon Mark Noll and Carolyn Nystrom, *Clouds of Witnesses: Christian Voices from Africa and Asia* (Downer Grove, IL: InterVarsity Press, 2011); Jonathan Hill, *Zondervan Handbook to the History of Christianity* (Oxford: Zondervan, 2006); Allen Anderson, *To the Ends of the Earth: Pentecostalism and the Transformation of World Christianity* (New York: Oxford University Press, 2013); Paul R. Spickard and Kevin M. Cragg, *A Global History of Christians: How Everyday Believers Experience Their World* (Grand Rapids: Baker, 2004); and Douglas Jacobsen, *The World's Christians: Who they Are, Where They Are, and How They Got There* (Oxford, UK: Wiley-Blackwell, 2011).

The Carter story is related by Daniel Vestal; cf. also http://www.washingtonpost.com/wp-srv/newsweek/religion.htm

For the conservative numbers I depended upon the Pew Forum on Religion and Public Life (December 19, 2011), "Global Christianity: A Report on the Size and Distribution of the World's Christian Population," 67.

For the East African revival I follow Mark Noll, *The New Shape of World Christianity*, 169–183.

On line, *The Dictionary of African Christian Biography* provides well-informed articles; numerous other sources are helpful including Wesley L. Handy's missionforum.wordpress.com.

For Further Study

In addition to the books mentioned at the end of each chapter and in these notes, other reference books offer leads to material to satisfy the curiosity of the most eager student. *The Oxford Dictionary of the Christian Church*, 3rd ed., revised, edited by F. L. Cross and Elizabeth A. Livingstone (New York: Oxford University Press, 2005) and *The New International Dictionary of the Christian Church*, edited by J. D. Douglas (Grand Rapids: Zondervan, 1978) have articles and additional suggestions for reading on the issues within the chapters of this volume.

To pursue some interest stimulated by the chapters in this volume dealing with American Christianity, the student can also find articles and book suggestions in *Dictionary of Christianity in America*, edited by Daniel C. Reid (Downers Grove, IL: InterVarsity, 1990). A whole range of maps for the study of Christian history appear in *The Macmillan Atlas History of Christianity* by Franklin H. Littell (New York: Macmillan, 1976).

LIST OF POPES FROM LEO I TO THE PRESENT

The Roman Catholic Church lists forty-eight popes before Leo I.

440–461	Leo I
461–468	Hilary
468–483	Simplicius
483–492	Felix III
492–496	Gelasius I
496–498	Anastasius II
498–514	Symmachus
498	Laurentius*
514–523	Hormisdas
523–526	John I
526–530	Felix IV
530–532	Boniface II
530	Dioscorus*
533–535	John II
535–536	Agapetus I
536–537	Silverius
537–555	Vigilius
556–561	Pelagius I
561–574	John III
575–579	Benedict I
579–590	Pelagius II
590–604	Gregory I†
604–606	Sabinianus
607	Boniface III
608–615	Boniface IV
615–618	Deusdedit
619–625	Boniface V
625–638	Honorius I
640	Severinus
640–642	John IV
642–649	Theodorus I
649–655	St. Martin I
654–657	Eugenius I
657–672	Vitalianus
672–676	Adeodatus
676–678	Domnus I
678–681	Agatho
682–683	Leo II
684–685	Benedict II
685–686	John V
686–687	Conon
687–692	Paschal*
687	Theodorus*
687–701	Sergius I
701–705	John VI
705–707	John VII
708	Sisinnius
708–715	Constantine I
715–731	Gregory II
731–741	Gregory III
741–752	Zacharias
752	Stephen II
752–757	Stephen III
757–767	Paul I
767–768	Constantine II
768–772	Stephen IV
772–795	Adrian I
795–816	Leo III
816–817	Stephen V
817–824	Paschal I
824–827	Eugenius II
827	Valentinus
827–844	Gregory IV
844–847	Sergius II
847–855	Leo IV
855–858	Benedict III

855	Anastasius
858–867	Nicholas I
867–872	Adrian II
872–882	John VIII
882–884	Marinus
884–885	Adrian III
885–891	Stephen VI
891–896	Formosus
896	Boniface VI
896–897	Stephen VII
897	Romanus
897	Theodorus II
898–900	John IX
900–903	Benedict IV
903	Leo V
903–904	Christopher
904–911	Sergius III
911–913	Anastasius III
913	Lando
914–928	John X
928–929	Leo VI
929–931	Stephen VIII
931–936	John XI
936–939	Leo VII
939–942	Stephen IX
942–946	Marinus II
946–955	Agapetus
955–964	John XII
963–965	Leo VIII
964–965	Benedict V
965–972	John XIII
973–974	Benedict VI
974–983	Benedict VII
983–984	John XIV
984–985	Boniface VII
985–996	John XV
996–999	Gregory V
997–998	John XVI*
999–1003	Sylvester II‡
1003	John XVII
1003–1009	John XVIII
1009–1012	Sergius IV
1012–1024	Benedict VIII
1012	Gregory VI*
1024–1033	John XIX
1033–1045	Benedict IX
1045	Sylvester III
1045–1046	Gregory VI
1046–1047	Clement II
1048	Damasus II
1049–1054	Leo IX
1055–1057	Victor II
1057–1058	Stephen X
1059–1061	Nicholas II
1061–1073	Alexander II
1061	Honorius II*
1073–1085	Gregory VII§
1086–1087	Victor III
1088–1099	Urban II
1099–1118	Paschal II
1100	Theodoricus*
1102	Albertus*
1105–1111	Sylvester IV*
1118–1119	Gelasius II
1118–1121	Gregory VIII*
1119–1124	Calixtus II
1124	Celestine*
1124–1130	Honorius II
1130–1143	Innocent II
1130–1138	Anacletus II
1138	Victor IV*
1143–1144	Celestine II
1144–1145	Lucius II
1145–1153	Eugenius III
1153–1154	Anastasius IV
1154–1159	Adrian IV
1159–1181	Alexander III
1159–1164	Victor IV*
1164–1168	Paschal III*
1168–1178	Calixtus III*
1178–1180	Innocent III*
1181–1185	Lucius III
1185–1187	Urban III
1187	Gregory VIII
1187–1191	Clement III
1191–1198	Celestine III
1198–1216	Innocent III
1216–1227	Honorius III
1227–1241	Gregory IX
1241	Celestine IV
1243–1254	Innocent IV
1254–1261	Alexander IV
1261–1264	Urban IV
1265–1268	Clement IV
1271–1276	Gregory X
1276	Innocent V

1276	Adrian V		1566–1572	Pius V
1276–1277	John XXI		1572–1585	Gregory XIII
1277–1280	Nicholas III		1585–1590	Sixtus V
1281–1285	Martin IV		1590	Urban VII
1285–1287	Honorius IV		1590–1591	Gregory XIV
1288–1292	Nicholas IV		1591	Innocent IX
1294	Celestine V		1592–1605	Clement VIII
1294–1303	Boniface VIII		1605	Leo XI
1303–1304	Benedict XI		1605–1621	Paul V
1305–1314	Clement V		1621–1623	Gregory XV
1316–1334	John XXII		1623–1644	Urban VIII
1334–1342	Benedict XII		1644–1655	Innocent X
1342–1352	Clement VI		1655–1667	Alexander VII
1352–1362	Innocent VI		1667–1669	Clement IX
1362–1370	Urban V		1670–1676	Clement X
1370–1378	Gregory XI		1676–1689	Innocent XI
1378–1389	Urban VI		1689–1691	Alexander VIII
1389–1404	Boniface IX		1691–1700	Innocent XII
1394–1423	Benedict XIII		1700–1721	Clement XI
1404–1406	Innocent VII		1721–1724	Innocent XIII
1406–1415	Gregory XII		1724–1730	Benedict XIII
1409–1410	Alexander V*		1730–1740	Clement XII
1410–1415	John XXIII*		1740–1758	Benedict XIV
1417–1431	Martin V		1758–1769	Clement XIII
1431–1447	Eugene IV		1769–1774	Clement XIV
1439–1449	Felix V*		1775–1799	Pius VI
1447–1455	Nicholas V		1800–1823	Pius VII
1455–1458	Calixtus III		1823–1829	Leo XII
1458–1464	Pius II		1829–1830	Pius VIII
1464–1471	Paul II		1831–1846	Gregory XVI
1471–1484	Sixtus IV		1846–1878	Pius IX
1484–1492	Innocent VIII		1878–1903	Leo XIII
1492–1503	Alexander VI		1903–1914	Pius X
1503	Pius III		1914–1922	Benedict XV
1503–1513	Julius II		1922–1939	Pius XI
1513–1521	Leo X		1939–1958	Pius XII
1522–1523	Adrian VI		1958–1963	John XXIII
1523–1534	Clement VII		1963–1978	Paul VI
1534–1549	Paul III		1978	John Paul I
1550–1555	Julius III		1978–2005	John Paul II
1555	Marcellus II		2005–2013	Benedict XVI
1555–1559	Paul IV		2013–	Francis I
1559–1565	Pius IV			

* indicates Antipope
† Gregory I is called Gregory the Great
§ Gregory VII is known as Hildebrand
‡ Sylvester II is known as Gerbert

PEOPLE

MOVEMENTS

EVENTS